W9-ABI-420

An Introduction to SOCIOLOGY

An Introduction
R. Serge Denisoff / Ralph Wahrman
BOWLING GREEN STATE UNIVERSITY

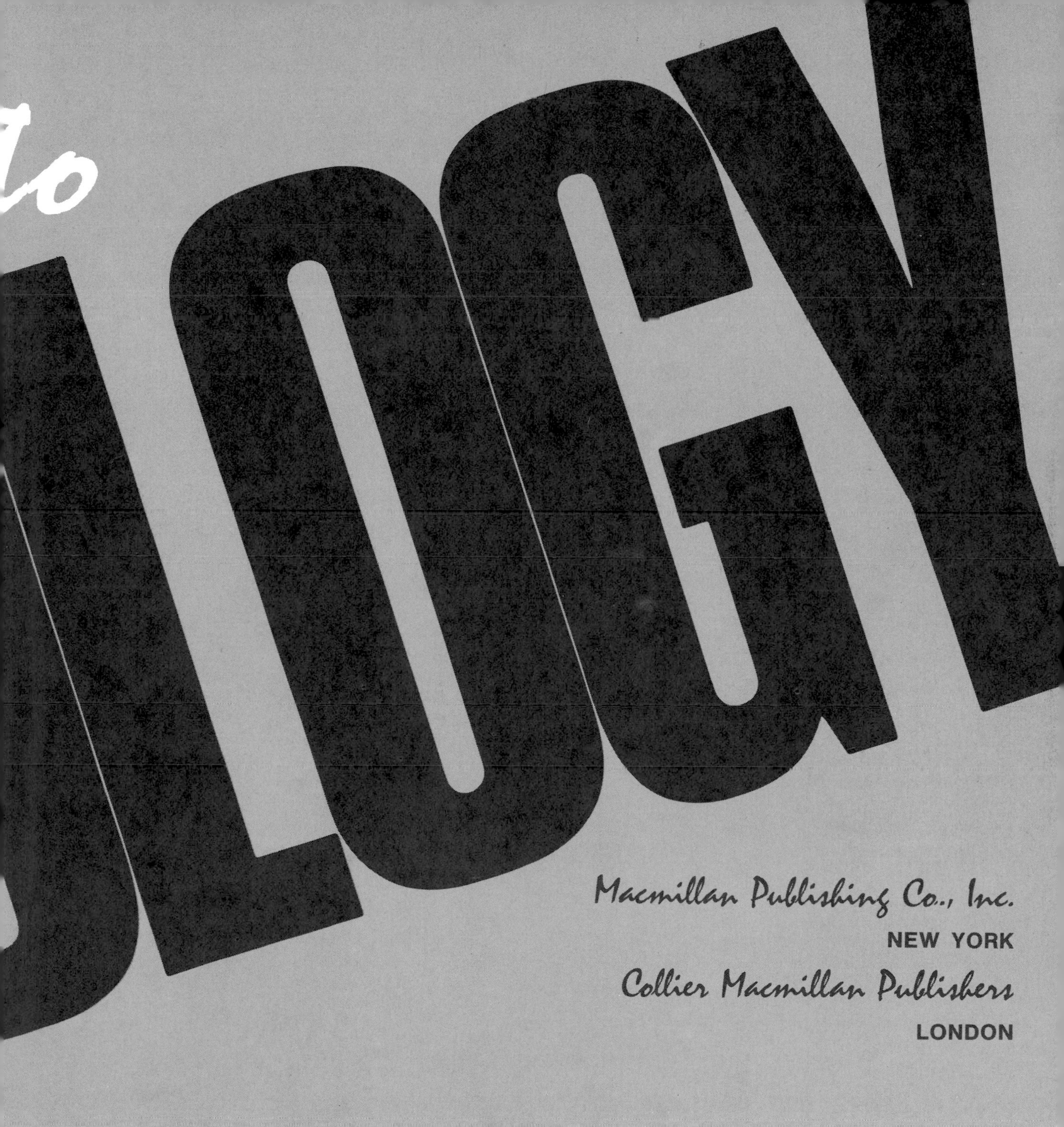

Macmillan Publishing Co., Inc.
NEW YORK
Collier Macmillan Publishers
LONDON

To: Jessie and Sam Wahrman—My first teachers. R. W.

To: Grelun Landon R. S. D.

Macmillan Publishing Co., Inc.
866 Third Avenue, New York, New York 10022

Collier-Macmillan Canada, Ltd.

All photos courtesy of Magnum Photos, Inc., New York.

Library of Congress Cataloging in Publication Data

Denisoff, R Serge.
An introduction to sociology.

Includes bibliographies and index.
1. Sociology. I. Wahrman, Ralph, joint author.
II. Title.
HM51.D45 301 74-2869
ISBN 0-02-328320-3

Printing: 12345678 Year: 567890

A SOCIOLOGIST who teaches in Los Angeles once quipped, "The impossible dream is a good intro book." He was referring to the universal problem in teaching "Introductory Sociology" of finding a solid text that also turns students on. The usual introductory text is either sociologically sound but dull as dishwater and written in incredibly complicated language or as clear as Mickey Mouse and equally profound. Balancing soundness and clarity is no minor or easy task. As James M. Henslin suggested in a recent issue of *Contemporary Sociology:*

> As most instructors know so well, selecting a text for the introductory course in sociology can be an excruciating task. Where is the one which presents the excitement of the sociological perspective, key ideas about life in contemporary society, an analysis of the way society hangs together, substantive areas of sociology, good cultural comparative data, is well written, and is one which students don't find a chore to read? The search for such a text is frustrating, for it does not appear to exist.
>
> Perhaps some of the elements in this arbitrary list of desirable characteristics are mutually incompatible and such a text can never be written.

Ever since Robert Park and Ernest Burgess published the first introductory book in 1921, every text has had to cover certain core topics. Any major deviation from this pattern (no matter how interesting) has met with commercial failure. On the other hand, the rigidity of many standard texts has totally alienated generations of students. Folksinger Pete Seeger dropped out of Harvard as a freshman because he couldn't stand the "scholargok" of his sociology professor. Somewhere between these two extremes we felt there might be an answer.

This book is an attempt to provide a lucid and interesting introduction to the field without losing the elementary nuts and bolts of sociology. This is an ambitious undertaking. We hope that the goal has been at least partially achieved. The reader, of course, will have to be the final judge. In the writing of this book a large number of people helped with suggestions, criticisms, encouragement, and clerical assistance. Our erstwhile "boss" Ken Scott promised, cajoled, and did everything an editor is supposed to do to produce a book. Working with Ken was a pleasure. We also wish to thank T. Neal Garland, Margaret M. Poloma, William Feigelman, Reginald F. Touchton, and Jack Schwartz for their individual comments and criticisms. Joe Kivlin was most helpful in providing us the time to meet our publishing deadlines. As always, Phyllis Eaton and Lauretta Lahman did a splendid job in typing and preparing the manuscript for publication. Juliette Golant's photo research was invaluable. A special debt is owed to Dr. Edward G. Stockwell, who authored the chapter on demography.

R. SERGE DENISOFF
RALPH WAHRMAN

Contents

ONE
Stranger in a Familiar Land 1

TWO
Origins of Sociology 13

THREE
Research Methods 35

FOUR
Culture 49

FIVE
Have You Ever Seen a Society? 79

TEN
Intergroup Relations 279

ELEVEN
Deviance 319

TWELVE
Demography 363

THIRTEEN
Collective Behavior 399

FOURTEEN
Popular Culture 431

FIFTEEN
Social Movements 453

SIXTEEN

Social Change 489

ONE

Stranger in a Familiar Land

Why Study Sociology?

A SONG popularized by Creedence Clearwater Revival reported that an unidentifiable flying object had fallen "out of the sky just a little bit south of Moline." It crashed into a cornfield. Presumably this thing was a craft from outer space. A spaceship with thinking creatures aboard. Let's imagine we're there. After securing their ship they deplane and switch on their hyperfragilistic invisibility shield. They enter the city of Moline unnoticed. They see large structures of plastic, brick, and wood standing in long rows. Long strips of gray concrete and cement run between these structures. White lines extend down the middle of these strips.[1]

On these strips are the inhabitants of Moline. They have different sizes, shapes, and colors. Commonly the residents of this small town walk on four round black rubber objects—two in front, two in back—with two yellow eyes that open only in darkness. They sleep with their eyes closed. Some sleep outdoors, others have wooden or plastic caves in which to rest. During the hours they travel—no doubt searching for food—flashing yellow, green, and red lights salute them. These steel objects, called cars by their two-legged slaves, live in buildings next to quarters housing their underlings. These flashy creatures feed only upon liquid substances that the slaves call gasoline. Food is available from restaurants with strange colored markings that are placed by the side of the cement strips. At the restaurants waiters in white or gray costumes pour the food into the steel monsters of Moline.

This is how a Vulcan might report the inhabitants of Moline to his home planet out in the Celestial Universe. It's possible, as in science fiction, to construct an entire society on the basic premise that the controlling creature on the planet Earth is the automobile. Our extraterrestrial visitors, without knowing what the citizens of Moline take for granted in their everyday lives, could easily come to these apparently farfetched conclusions. The absurdity of this interpretation is found in the statement, "Cars are the people of Moline, Illinois." Earthlings know this is not true. Cars are the *servants* of people. The Vulcans did not know this. Because Vulcans reproduce by using assembly lines and produce automobiles the same way we produce babies, they took for granted that two-eyed, four-wheeled metal objects must be the inhabitants of Earth. Their assumptions influenced what they saw. These assumptions were wrong. But what about the citizens of Moline? Is their understanding of the workings of that small Illinois community better than that of the Vulcans? "Certainly!" the residents would shout in one loud voice, and they would be correct. Why?

They understand that the flashing lights on street corners are there to tell them to stop, or to slow down, or to continue. They also realize that a red light that's not on a busy city street may have other meanings. It could identify a fire station. It also used to mean that a house of ill-repute was in operation. As a resident, rather than a stranger in a strange land, each of us knows the meanings of these symbols. However, as magicians prove daily, things are not always what they seem; the hand is quicker than the eye. The actual workings of the world in which we live may also be hidden from the eye.

The Inhabitants of Moline.

In some respects our observations may be as inaccurate as those of the Vulcans. Consider the bus or streetcar that always appears to be going the wrong way.[2] Standing on a street corner in the pouring rain waiting for a bus going west, you find that buses seem to pass you at five-minute intervals, all heading in an easterly direction. Finally, a westbound bus arrives and you get on, loudly complaining that the bus company's scheduling is all fouled up. The driver contradicts you: "The schedule is the same in both directions." Who is right? You, the waterlogged student, or the transit authority? Is your observation correct? Find out for yourself. Don't board the bus. Stand in the wet at the bus stop in the early morning hours and stay until the later hours of the night counting each passing bus going both east and west. *Then* you will know who's right. But few people would be willing to settle an argument about "what is real" by investing this much time and effort.

A traffic cop stops a driver for running a poorly placed stop sign. He immediately protests. "But *nobody* stops there!" The officer replies, "You're the only one *I've* seen run that sign." With a twenty-dollar fine and a stern judge's lecture facing the driver he may return to the scene of the crime to put the officer's statement to a test. In the comfort of his car, motion-picture camera rolling, he finds that in fact the patrolman was wrong. Of one thousand cars he observes, only two stop for that sign. With this evidence in hand he will face the judge in the morning.

The leap from the assumption that what we see is all there is to see into a more critical stance usually requires some motivation. Faced with losing a bet or paying a fine a person may begin to question a fact he took for granted. "Elton John records for United Artists," contends a student. "No," answers his friend. The solution is found in the record store catalog. Television character Archie Bunker, at his favorite bar, challenges a fellow customer about who was the vice-presidential candidate on the Republican ticket in 1964. "It was Cabot Lodge," says Archie. "The hell," says the patron. "It was some guy named Miller. From New York, I think." Archie Bunker, as usual, is wrong. He finds this out by calling or visiting the public library or consulting some other *neutral* source like the *New York Times Almanac* or the *Information Please Almanac*. We have little reason or incentive to check out bus schedules or to find out who was the 1964 Republican vice-presidential hopeful. To do so involves reexamining something we take for granted in our daily lives and a bit of effort.

Going to the public library for Archie Bunker means leaving his usual haunts, his easy chair, or his favorite television program. The outraged citizen observing the corner with the poorly placed traffic sign also stepped out of his normal patterns of behavior to find out whether or not he was right. The study of society requires this kind of effort, this kind of willingness to put our beliefs to a test, to risk learning that what we have always known to be true is, in fact, false.

Why do we ask questions about society? Sometimes we ask because we see things we don't like, and we want to know what causes them and whether or not they are inevitable, so that, hopefully, we can remove the causes and change the world. Sometimes we ask questions just because we suddenly find that things we took for granted, things we assumed were true of everyone, turn out to be untrue for other people, other societies, and other times. What we took to be "human nature" turns out to be twentieth-century, midwestern, white, Protestant, American behavior.

Sometimes what sets us thinking about the world is something trivial. For example, in the United States we tend to stand eighteen to twenty-four inches from people while we chat. In Latin America people tend to stand twelve inches apart.[3] Now honestly, when was the last time you noticed how far you stand from people when you talk to them? If a Latin should insist on moving closer until he feels comfortable, you would discover yourself backing away, being chased across the room. *And* you would become aware of something you always took for granted.

We often take for granted that greed and war and competition are universal, part of human nature. But there are societies that do not have such things. Either *they* are not "human," or "human nature" is not what we thought it was.

To learn about society, anyone else's or our own, we must learn to take nothing for granted, to ask questions about things that everyone "knows" to be "true." Much of the time we will discover that these things are *not* what they seem. Or that what is true under some circumstances is not true under others.

Whether our study of society is based on a desire to change it or on a desire simply to understand it, we must make an extra effort to go beyond our usual assumptions. We must try to become voyagers in the inner space of the world in which we live. We must step back and take an *objective* look at the world. Obviously this is more easily said than done. Max Weber, the pioneer German sociologist, cautioned social scientists that they must not allow their political ideas to bias their lectures.[4] From Weber came the notion of the value-free approach to social science, that is, eliminating nonscientific beliefs from scientific work in the social sciences. The practical problems of living in society, however, make the total separation of the *sociologist as citizen* from the *sociologist as sociologist* impossible.

The chemist or physicist enters his laboratory, puts on his white lab coat, and begins his day's experiments. He can put aside his political, moral, and religious views in doing his work. Although these may have some bearing on what he feels should be done with his findings, these views do not influence what he finds.

Students of society can't make this distinction between their professional and personal lives as easily as the student of chemistry or physics. The things sociologists study are, after all, often quite relevant to political, moral, and religious philosophies, philosophies held not only by nonsociologists but also by the sociologist.

Man is not totally value-free as he has reasons for studying certain questions rather than others.[5] For example, the student of race relations may study the cause of inner-city riots because he wants to stop them. Why he wants to stop them becomes a valuative question. Does he desire racial harmony or merely the lack of disruption? Is he interested in suppressing minorities or in eliminating the precipitating causes of the riots? These valuative biases should not affect the study of social events but sometimes they do.

It is hard to be completely objective on issues we feel strongly about. We are rarely as knowledgeable and aware of our own faults as are other people.[6] Although not able to withdraw totally, the social scientist does try to be as honest with himself and his peers as is humanly possible in dealing with social events. To ensure this honesty, the sociologist attempts to use those tools that seem most reliable and objective.

As we have mentioned, a library is a neutral source because it has no stake in who wins a bet or an argument. For social scientists the neutral source is not a person or a book with all the answers but a set of techniques and ideas that we call the *scientific method.* We will say more about this in Chapter Three, but for the moment let us simply mention that the scientific method involves a set of rules, procedures, and techniques that are generally successful at (1) enabling the social scientist to arrange his observations in such a way that if his ideas about the world are wrong he is likely to find out that he is wrong; (2) where bias does slip into his research, making it possible for other people to spot the way his biases guided his study; and (3) enabling other people who are skeptical about his findings to reproduce his studies and therefore to find out for themselves whether his findings were correct.

By following these rules anyone else should end up with the same findings that he ends up with (although if they do not share his biases they may still draw somewhat different *conclusions*). To put it another way, if my competent study finds that 75 percent of American women believe that women are smarter than men, any other competent research—be the researcher male or female, black or white, Democrat or Republican, gay or straight—that makes use of the same techniques should show the same results, regardless of whether the researcher personally agrees or disagrees, approves or disapproves.

What we have said so far is that to understand human behavior one must attempt to stand back, be detached, and see the world through new eyes. But what is it that makes sociologists different from other students of human behavior?

How Does Sociology Differ?

Economists, political scientists, historians, psychologists, and anthropologists are all students of human behavior, as are sociologists. Although all of the social sciences would agree on the importance of detachment and scientific method, they would debate what sorts of things we ought to know about in order to understand human behavior. Let's illustrate this by asking, "How do you study prostitution?" Prostitution has been of interest to many social scientists and nonscientific observers, but each has studied it from a different perspective.

For the *economist* the issues are relatively simple. Some people want such a service and are willing to pay for it. A more sophisticated way of saying the same thing is found in Edwin Lemert's review of interpretations of this profession: "Our laissez-faire economy and its integration through a price system allows the relatively free operation of supply and demand whether it be commerce in grain futures or sex services."[7] Some people find they can sell sex and make more money from this activity than from other activities. This approach cannot explain, nor does it try, why a society that puts a price on so many things condemns the renting or sale of one's body rather than inviting the seller to join the Chamber of Commerce. Nor can it explain, if money is the only consideration, why *more* young ladies don't choose this profession in preference to other activities that pay much less. These are questions that involve noneconomic considerations.

The *psychologist* wants to know how the girl who becomes a prostitute differs psychologically from the one who does not. Did she love her father or did she hate him? Is she oversexed? Undersexed? Did she come from a broken home? Does she secretly want to be humiliated? To humiliate her family? Is she searching subconsciously for affection? Psychoanalyst Harold Greenwald in a study of call girls believes this last explanation is the best. He wrote:

I found not one example of a permanent, well-adjusted marital relationship between the parents. Not one of these girls reported growing up in a happy home where her parents got along well together. In fifteen, or three-fourths of the cases, the girls' homes were broken before they reached adolescence. This contrasts with about one-fourth of the general population which comes from broken homes. . . . The girls never saw any evidence of sympathy or affection between the parents. This absence of warmth and permanence between the parents made it difficult for these girls to form any kind of attachment to the family. When a girl cannot form an attachment to her family, does not feel close to them, there is no way in which she can absorb the values of our society, which most of us generally absorb from parents to whom we feel close.[8]

There are yet other psychological interpretations of the streetwalker or call girl. Lemert wrote:

A girl with a strong case of inferiority may have a compulsive need to be sexually promiscuous, and some such girls may eventually find an adjustment as prostitutes. Urgent need to rebel against authority may be expressed by a woman through flagrant violations of the community's sexual taboos.[9]

The emphases here are on motives and personality.

The *sociologist* asks questions like these: Is prostitution the result of the society's desire to hook sex to marriage and the family? Does the existence of a special class of women who supply not only sex but also intellectual stimulation and companionship (the case in ancient Greece and many other nations) result from keeping "respectable" women uneducated, isolated, and boring? Does letting women have sexual freedom reduce the need for professional prostitutes? Why do we condemn the prostitute and not her customer? Would we lose more than we would gain by arresting the customer?

Consider Kingsley Davis's analysis:

> Since the basic causes of prostitution—the institutional control of sex, the unequal scale of attractiveness, and the presence of economic and social inequality between classes and between male and female—are not likely to disappear, prostitution is not likely to disappear either. However, the particular form and scope of the institution may change. One such alteration follows from the appearance of sexual freedom among the women of the middle and upper classes. The greater the proportion of free, mutually pleasurable intercourse, the lesser is the demand for paid prostitution. This, it seems, is the true explanation of the diminution of prostitution in contemporary Western industrial countries.[10]

Did you notice that nowhere is there any mention of needs, motives, personality characteristics, or any other individual or personal characteristics? You might say that sociologists are not interested in *prostitutes* but in *prostitution* and the way that characteristics of the society support or discourage its existence.

In a sociological analysis it is important to understand *how* prostitution is linked to other patterns of behavior in society. Let's borrow some more from Kingsley Davis. His treatment of prostitution is a model for sociological reasoning. He says prostitution is condemned in industrial societies because it is *seen* as disruptive and promiscuous and without any recognizable societal value. "The prostitute's affront," he wrote," is that she trades promiscuously. She takes money or other valuables for each act of intercourse. She is indifferent not only to sexual pleasure but also to the partner. Her 'selling' and her indifference therefore reflect a pure commercialization of the sexual relation."[11] The most objectionable aspect of prostitution, he contended, is not either indifference or economic gain, as both are found in the normal marital relationship. Wives occasionally respond indifferently to their husbands, and the marriage contract is an economic one. Promiscuity, then, is the offending characteristic of the streetwalker and the call girl. The sociological question becomes "Why?" The reason given is that promiscuity is a threat to a stable industrial society:

> "Unless there is some kind of social order in the distribution of sexual favors, a war of all against all will tend to result. The objection to promiscuity tends to arise and persist because the societies that have this sentiment are, in this respect at least, more capable of surviving than those that do not have it. In the eyes of the members of a society, a woman's sexual favors should ideally be given only in a situation that is an operating part of the social structure.[12]

The reason is simply that sexual promiscuity, Davis suggested, could lead to the downfall of the family. If people can get sexual satisfaction anywhere, anytime, why bother with all of the unpleasant aspects of marriage and the child-raising process? Sex is an important and exciting part of marriage. But what happens when this attraction is available everywhere?

By looking at the subject of prostitution, we begin to see that different students of human behavior see the same thing in different ways. What does a car mean? The psychologist may describe it as an "extension of personality." The economist sees it as an object that can be bought and sold. The sociologist may identify the car as symbolic or as a badge of social standing. So it is with students of prostitution. Each asks questions that reflect his interests. Economists want to look at the economic aspects of prostitution just as psychologists try to find psychological reasons for this sexual activity. Sociologists look at people as being parts of groups that are interrelated with one another. One group has an impact upon another. Prostitution may affect the stability of the family and the entire society.

What Is Sociology?

What is sociology, then? *Sociology is the study of those aspects of man that result from his being a member of society.* In other words, sociologists are interested in the consequences of the fact that people live and die among other people, that they exist in groups.

Despite their common biological characteristics people vary enormously. Society transforms a tiny, howling, redfaced animal into a person. In all societies, people must eat, sleep, and mate. What is eaten, when, and where are the result of social arrangements and not of biology. Where, when, and with whom he sleeps are the result of social arrangements and not man's biology. Why he mates, when, how, whether, and with whom are responses to his social environment and not his biology. Sociologists examine these social arrangements, their causes, and their consequences.

As you learn more sociology you'll start becoming aware of the enormous number of things that the idea of "social arrangments" covers. Émile Durkheim, writing in nineteenth-century France, argued in a slightly different vocabulary that the sociologist's job is to isolate the properties of human association. He called these properties or characteristics *social facts.*[13] *Social facts are those events, processes, and actions that result from human association.*

It is important to remember while studying social facts that sociologists do look at areas that are the predominant domain of the sister social sciences. They are interested, for example, in the effects of social phenomena on personality. Are there differences, they may ask, by social class, race, or religion in the frequency of mental illness? Does the kind of treatment you get (if any) for mental illness depend on these differences? (The answer to both questions is yes.) Sociologists share many interests with political science. For example, they may ask: How does social standing affect one's politics? Under what circumstances do minority groups use violence to overcome political powerlessness? Sociologists share with anthropology an interest in the way various aspects of the society support or weaken other aspects of the society: How does the religious system support the economic system? How do changes in the family affect the religious system? How do changes in the educational system affect parent-child relationships? Sociologists share with economists an interest in the social costs and determinants of economic activities.

Sociologists often use techniques borrowed from anthropology, psychology, history, political science, and economics to study properties of social relationships. In recent years the differences between these disciplines have become increasingly blurred, with social scientists joining hands to study the problems of minority groups, political protest, population growth, and economic development. Nonetheless, each discipline continues to have its own perspective and major spheres of influence.

Summary

Sociologists are strangers in a familiar land by their own choice. They attempt to step back and look at the world in which they live. By temporarily withdrawing they try to understand society. To do this they must take the trouble to look beyond their everyday experiences and cherished beliefs. Sociologists present their research in such a way that ideas that seem to be "facts" can be either proved or refuted. By standing on the rainy corner the disgruntled passenger may establish the routing schedules of the bus company. Sociologists do the same thing, but under more comfortable conditions. Both are trying to discover what is real in the everyday world.

Sociologists look at aspects of life *beyond* the biological and psychological. In doing this they use tools and ideas from other social sciences. However, they lack the central focus of their sister disciplines. Each discipline stresses a particular process in the social world. Indeed, there are within sociology several important schools with differing points of departure in their attempts to understand the products of human association.

Notes

1. This description is elaborated in a film from the National Film Board of Canada.
2. Example from J. Toby, "Undermining the Students' Faith in the Validity of Personal Experience," *American Sociological Review,* **20** (1955), 717–718.
3. E. T. Hall and W. F. Whyte, "Intercultural Communication: A Guide to Men of Action," *Human Organization,* **19** (1960), 5–12.
4. H. H. Gerth and C. W. Mills, eds., *From Max Weber: Essays in Sociology* (New York: Oxford University Press, 1946), p. 150.
5. See A. Gouldner, "Anti-Minotaur: The Myth of a Value-Free Sociology," *Social Problems,* **9** (1962), 199–213.

6. G. Myrdal, "How Scientific Are the Social Sciences?" *The Journal of Social Issues,* **28**:4 (1972), pp. 151–170.

7. E. Lemert, *Social Pathology* (New York: McGraw-Hill Book Company, 1951), p. 246.

8. H. Greenwald, *The Call Girl: A Social and Psychoanalytic Study* (New York: Ballantine Books, 1958), pp. 108–109.

9. Lemert, op. cit., p. 245. Also see C. Winick and P. M. Kinsie, *The Lively Commerce: Prostitution in the United States* (Chicago: Quadrangle Books, 1971).

10. K. Davis, "Sexual Behavior," in R. Merton and R. Nisbet, eds., *Contemporary Social Problems* (New York: Harcourt Brace Jovanovich, Inc., 1966), p. 371.

11. Ibid., p. 265

12. Ibid., p. 165. For an extension see S. Kaalaf, *Prostitution in a Changing Society: A Sociological Study of Legal Prostitution in Beirut* (Beirut: Khayats, 1965).

13. E. Durkheim, *The Rules of Sociological Method,* 8th ed. (S. A. Solovay and J. H. Mueller New York: The Free Press, 1964), pp. 1–13.

TWO

Origins of Sociology

Sociology and Philosophy

SOCIOLOGY is the child of philosophy. Nearly all of the original ideas about the nature of man and society came from the pens of Greek and European philosophers who spent centuries wrestling with the question, "What is reality?" Their search had two parts. They wished to know "What *is*" and then "what *ought* to be." This last concern divorced them from contemporary sociologists, who are concerned with "what is." However, the separation of "is" and "ought to be" did not take place until long after the mid-nineteenth-century.[1]

Philosophers were the first sociologists. Plato, the ancient Greek philosopher, was convinced that through knowledge he could make the world that "is" into the world that "ought to be." His starting point was that the world that "is" is unnatural. Why? Because it is imperfect: if it were in accord with the laws of nature, it would also be perfect. What are these laws? What is perfection? It is the job of the philosophers to find out. Plato's quest for natural laws began what in time became the sociological search for social facts and patterns of human behavior.

Plato (427?–347 B.C.). Philosophers were the first sociologists.

Philosophers deal primarily with ideas and abstractions. Many of their arguments about the nature of man and society are not provable, and they do not agree on ways to test whether one model of society is better than another.

The Industrial Revolution (roughly 1750–1900) transformed many of the ideas of men. Some of them in the eighteenth century began to think that political systems and even entire societies could be transformed by ideas. The American Revolution of 1776 was such an attempt. More important for sociology was another attempt of men to remake society in the name of an idea: the French Revolution of 1789.

The Influence of the French Revolution

Rousseau and the French philosophers of the eighteenth century looked at a Europe dominated by kings and the Church. Comparing what they saw with their models of man in the "state of nature," they condemned the world they saw as "unnatural." The French Revolution was a result of this criticism and an attempt to recreate a "natural" world.

Meanwhile, the Industrial Revolution was also in full swing. Families were leaving their farms and moving into the cities. Farmers were becoming factory workers. Society was becoming more complex, more technical. Science and

Jean-Jacques Rousseau (1712–1778) argued in his **Origins of Inequality Among Men** ***(1753), that the society as the source of much evil should be replaced by a "state of nature."***

technology gained a popularity and a respectability previously unknown. European writers celebrated the progresss of man through *reason* and condemned tradition, superstition, and religion as barriers to progress to a new, "natural" world.

As some saw it, the French Revolution was an accomplishment that had grown out of man's imposition of reason upon society. "Liberty, fraternity, and equality" had replaced the monarchy and the Church. Nobles no longer had places of special privilege and some of them even had their heads chopped off. According to social philosopher Herbert Marcuse:

> The French Revolution enunciated reason's ultimate power over reality. . . . The principle of the French Revolution asserted that *thought* ought to govern reality [and that] what men think to be true, right, and good ought to be realized in the actual organization of their societal and individual life.[2]

Some scholars were critical of the French Revolution and the changes resulting from the Industrial Revolution. To the critics, the French Revolution was hardly a triumph of reason. The imposition of "reason" in France spawned the excesses of the Reign of Terror, which so horrified Europe. The indiscriminate executions of those believed to oppose the First Republic moved many to claims that the French Revolution was *against* nature, whereas others argued, despite the abuses, that it was a step toward the ideal society.

The central issues generated by the French Revolution involved the nature of man, society, and social change. From the social and philosophical debates that followed there emerged two dominant orientations or schools of thought in sociology, those of "order" and "conflict."

Order and Man's Role

The desire of social critics to restore order is a theme that permeates early sociological writings.[3]

Beginning with the British statesman Edmund Burke and the French Catholic conservative Louis de Bonald, some critics condemned the French Revolution as being *against natural law;* rather than a return to nature, it was a violation of nature's law. Burke saw the state and the entire society as an organism that had evolved over a long period of time, an organism that should not be tampered with by man. Society, he urged, was "a partnership not only between those who are living, but between those who are dead and those who are to be born."[4] De Bonald, a French noble, echoed this sentiment, contending that man is born into society and becomes part of it. The society as is becomes the natural order of God. The French Revolution, he argued, was open rebellion against divine order.

Society, critics of the French Revolution insisted, was greater than the sum of its parts. "Man," wrote De Bonald, "exists in and for society." Conformity and agreement upon social rules were sacred. Misbehavior would disrupt the natural order of things. Conformity was the price of living in society. Social health was stability and lack of disorder. The human body has mechanisms that return from a state of need to a state of fulfillment. Biologists call this process *homeostasis.*

Early sociologists treated society as a large human body. Society, therefore, also goes through the process of homeostasis. It goes from a state of imbalance to one of balance or equilibrium, social equilibrium being the ideal state. British sociologist Herbert Spencer, writing in the nineteenth century, even gave each part of society a job to do in restoring equilibrium. Courts and legislative branches, for example, were to overcome inequalities between groups.

It was at this point in history, in the opening decades of the nineteenth century, that ideas about the nature of society were wedded to what scholars believed to be science. The study of society was to be based on the same principles as any other science. It was no longer to be mere philosophical speculation. The stress upon the scientific technique is what separates sociology from philosophy. As we said in the last chapter, sociology must be more than mere opinion, no matter how sophisticated or learned the persons who express the opinions. Sociologists put their opinions to empirical tests that can prove them right or wrong. This is not always true with philosophical models.

Count Henri de Saint Simon (1760-1825) and his followers were early advocates of a planned society.

Auguste Comte (1798–1857) is often called the father of sociology.

Count Henri de Saint-Simon, looking at the France of the 1820s, hoped to create social harmony through science. He called for a *science politique,* or science of production, that would bring the aspirations of the workers into line with those of their employers. Saint-Simon, in fact, was the first major advocate of employee-management relations as an area of serious study. Today he would be placed in the category of a spokesman for the local labor relations board. But in his day, the idea of workers sitting down at the same table as their employers was considered radical.

Saint-Simon's student and secretary, Auguste Comte, introduced sociology as the science that would find the natural laws of social change. Having done this, sociologists would announce them to the appropriate governmental authorities. Sociologists would be the new "priesthood of humanity," the social

Émile Durkheim (1858–1917) investigated the sources of social organization and stressed the importance of shared values and collective institutions.

engineers of the train of history. But sociologists would not *create* the historical tracks; they would guide change, not cause it.

Frenchman Émile Durkheim, one of the founders of sociology, said that equilibrium was merely the state in which all people agreed upon rules and morals. This he called *social integration,* or consensus. As he saw it, integration was essential for the existence of society.

At one time the Catholic Church had supplied the rules and ideas for the consensus that held the society together. Given the Church's loss of power after the French Revolution, another agency had to be found to resolve the differences in society, to produce the consensus without which the society would dissolve. Durkheim felt that sociologists should provide rules upon which a new consensus could be based.

As you can see, behind the critical reactions to the French Revolution was an overriding concern with balance, stability, authority, cohesion, solidarity, and gradual evolutionary growth in some *orderly* fashion. The idea was that as long as change seems to be inevitable, we should be able to develop a positive science of humanity that will let us find the equilibrium or balance between human needs and social opportunities.

Many of the basic beliefs of the order school have been inherited by the school that contemporary sociologists call *structural functionalists.* At the turn of the century, the structural functionalists such as Émile Durkheim and Herbert Spencer portrayed society as a single unit with contributing parts. Everything any one part of the society did had consequences for all of the other parts of the society and for the whole society.

The basic premise of this structural-functional school is that every "structure" or set of social arrangements that exists over time must be making some sort of contribution to the continuation of the society (fulfilling some kind of "function"). Some forty years later, Robert K. Merton suggested that not all parts of the society actually contribute to its operation. He identified some activities as being *dysfunctional;* dysfunctions harm the adjustment of the society.[5] He thought the job of sociologists was to figure out what part a social practice plays and how it fits into the whole system.

In the 1940s American sociologists like Robert Merton and Kingsley Davis, although accepting the idea that everything is *connected* to everything else in society, chose to study the interconnections between one aspect of society and another, one interconnection at a time, rather than the entire social order all at once. Davis, for example, examined the relationship of prostitution to family stability. Merton examined the old urban political machines and their contribution to bringing the newly arrived immigrants into the political system. Only Talcott Parsons among current American sociologists has steadfastly continued to try to study the total organic system suggested by Durkheim and his intellectual ancestors.

These are the basic assumptions of the order school generated in reaction to the French Revolution.

Order-Equilibrium Functional Model

1. Rules are basic elements of social life.
2. People must be committed to the society in which they live.
3. Social life depends on group unity.
4. Social life is based on cooperation.
5. Social systems rest on agreement on the rules.
6. Society recognizes the correctness of authority.
7. Societies tend to continue over time.[6]

Conflict: Evolution or Revolution?

As the crowd storming the Bastille ignited the imaginations of those committed to social order and harmony, it also gave rise to the "conflict" perspective in sociology.

The German philosophers watched the French Revolution with mixed feelings. They deplored the disorder and the mindless Reign of Terror that followed the deposing of the old order. But several aspects of the Revolution greatly influenced German philosophy for over a century and created the underpinnings of Karl Marx's writings and the basis of what has come to be called the *conflict perspective.*

The nineteenth-century German "idealists," especially Georg W. F. Hegel, wanted to continue the work of the French Revolution without its failures. As Hegel saw it, man is an actor in the drama of history. Just as in a play, the actor brings the script to life—*but the script has already been written.* The actor can ad-lib his lines, but even if he makes some small changes, the plot and the end of the play are fixed and the play is going to come out essentially as it was intended by the script writer to come out.

Actors in the play that most interested Hegel express opposing ideals and values. One exclaims, "I'm right!" The other dissents, "No, I'm right!" They argue. In the course of the discussion and debate, the level of knowledge of both actors increases. Argument or competition is the way wisdom grows. Finally, after the exchange they compromise and through competition progress takes place.

Hegel took this argument and expanded it from the level of two people arguing to another level, that of opposing models of "what ought to be," for example, the forces of change versus forces for the preservation of what exists. The process of competing idea systems (such as change versus preservation) he called the *dialectical process.* Idea systems were historical forces for Hegel. Ideologies and political and religious beliefs all fit his definition of a historical force. The dialectical process simply refers to the competition of two opposing

Georg W. F. Hegel (1770–1831) was a German Philosopher who attempted to explain social change by use of the "dialectic."

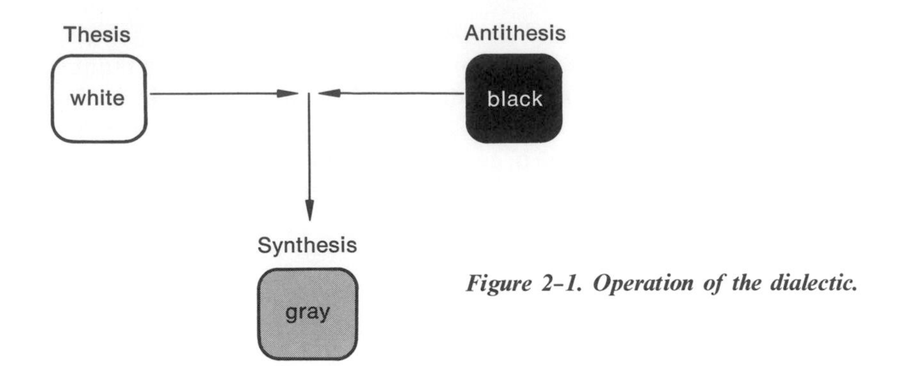

Figure 2–1. Operation of the dialectic.

forces and the emergence of a new force from this clash. The dialectic starts with one force (called a *thesis*). It is challenged by a new force (called the *antithesis*), an opposing force. The result of the battle between the thesis and the antithesis is a third force, a *synthesis* that incorporates both. Consider the example of the idea of racial segregation encountering the opposing notion of integration. The two conflict, as happened in the 1960s, and an outcome different from both emerges, not quite integration but not quite segregation either.

Each time a new synthesis is reached, said Hegel, a better form of knowledge and truth is born. As each synthesis is challenged by an opposing set of ideas, a new synthesis comes into being. Ultimately, through the continuing clash of ideas and the replacement of old ideas with newer, better, higher ideas, man will become aware of the "mind of God."

In contrast to the thinkers we've been discussing, Hegel welcomed conflict. He thought struggle against the old was good; it led to social betterment. Only through struggle would progress come. As Hegel saw it, there is a natural law, and the history of man is moving toward discovering this law and taking the form described in that law. The job of the philosopher was to discover what the law is and describe it. What "is" then should be brought in line with what "ought to be." In this sense the French Revolution became very important. The crowds in the streets searching for "liberty," Hegel thought, were trying to bring the "is" in line with the "ought to be." The problem, for Hegel, was that the mobs of France lost sight of the script. The French sociologists added to the development of bringing the "is" together with the "ought to be." Their idea was to use the tools of science to accomplish this task. Some, like the early "order" theorists, said that the "is" is identical to the "ought to be" (if it "is" that's probably the way it *ought* to be). Others said the "is" needed to be transformed.

"Philosophers have described the world," wrote the Hegelian Karl Marx, "our task is to change it." The rules of philosophy were inadequate for this job. The German idealists were totally convinced of the power and reality of reason and ideas. Marx, however, was more taken with the power of technology and the economic groups it had created. He believed reality was in the world of matter, not ideas. The techniques of science, thought Marx, fit nicely with his stress on economic conditions. The tools of biology, chemistry, and physics could be used to understand opposing *economic* units or groups throughout history.[7] Opposing economic groups (let's call them classes) are what is important, not ideas. This process of conflict he called *dialectical materialism.* Dialectical materialism involves a clash between groups having different economic interests. One class is on top and owns the majority of the material resources. They are the ruling class. The have-nots are the exploited class. The ruling class robs those on the bottom of the economic scale. The only way the exploited class can improve its condition is to displace the group on top. History, for Marx, was a battle between these units. The French Revolution appeared to support Marx's contention. He believed he could foresee the final

Karl Marx (1818–1883) added materialism to Hegel's dialectic.

historical outcome with the victory of the workers over their rulers and the establishment of a new kind of world (see Chapters Nine and Sixteen for a discussion of Marx's ideas).

The writings of Karl Marx were the takeoff point for conflict theory in European sociology and, indeed, many other social sciences. Many social observers developed their own theories of society either to support or to refute Marx's view of history.[8]

In the United States, conflict-oriented theory was ignored by sociologists for nearly half a century, being revived only after World War II. In his influential book, *Functions of Social Conflict,* Lewis Coser reintroduced social conflict. He wrote that social conflict when limited in its goals is a way of creating *harmony* in the society. He contended that group unity or cohesion could result when individuals compete for common goals or when a society or family becomes closer through a fight with outsiders.[9]

Ralf Dahrendorf, a German sociologist, reintroduced conflict as essentially political rather than economic or historical. He said that conflict occurs in the political arena and that groups, be they associations, labor unions, corporations, political parties, or protest movements, compete for positions of authority on the basis of their interests.[10] They argue about who is going to choose the goals and set the direction of the group's future. Conflict was no longer a grand historical perspective in either the Hegelian or Marxist tradition but just another process by which society made adjustments in order to survive.[11]

The major idea stemming from the conflict perspective is found in its radical and even revolutionary beginnings. Man, according to Karl Marx and his followers, is essentially good. Only social conditions make him evil. Crime, contended the anarchists and the communists, is a product of poverty and disease caused by the condition of society. Moreover, man, being good, can and should undertake the job of re-creating society into a natural state for mankind. People should become the engineers of history. This theory is quite compatible with the arguments of Saint-Simon and even Auguste Comte, although the latter two would suggest that violence was *not* the midwife of history. Rather, reasoning together was the best route to social development.

The Marxists contended that the source of conflict is man's basic need to survive under conditions of scarcity. People are not receiving the proper amount of food, clothing, shelter, and all of the things they need and want. Scarcity is created by the uneven economic placement of groups. One group is always seen as having a monopoly upon power, wealth, and prestige. The have-nots are pictured as trying to overcome this imbalance.

In order to achieve social health, the Marxists thought, man must be given the opportunity to realize his needs, wants, and potential in society. However, the coercive nature of authority and economic wealth make this difficult unless those on the bottom of the social ladder use similar tools, that is, force, violence, and disobedience. This violent blueprint for social betterment, freedom, and self-actualization made conflict theory suspect in the minds of many early sociologists.

A more significant objection to the conflict perspective was its bias toward change. Marx and his followers urged that society must change. The "ought to be" must become the "is." This notion violates the canon of science that calls for objectivity. (Recall Max Weber's appeal for value-free sociology.) In the turbulent 1960s, a small but important number of sociologists embraced the conflict school. Even Karl Marx was rehabilitated. Sociologists began to look for the testable aspects of Marx's theory rather than at his more political statements. Students of crime and delinquency previously wedded to the order school began to look upon these disruptive events as indicators of social conflict rather than mere pathological behavior. "Riots" were described as "rebellions." Men in prison were not "criminals" but "political prisoners." Although not the dominant perspective, in the 1970s the conflict perspective has become increasingly popular with sociologists. The conflict theorist's outlook can be summarized as containing the following propositions:

Conflict-Coercion-Power Model

1. Interests are basic elements of social life.
2. Social life involves coercion.
3. Social life involves groups with different interests.
4. Social life generates opposition, exclusion, and hostility.
5. Social life generates conflict.
6. Social differences involve power.
7. Social systems are not united or harmonious.
8. Social systems tend to change.

In order to understand these rather complex models of society and man, it may be useful to apply them to several common aspects of everyday life.

Order and Religion

Religion is a topic widely treated by both the order and the conflict schools. In the order perspective religious ceremony is presented as making four contributions to keeping society together, according to Émile Durkheim. Man needs rules in order to live in society. The first contribution of religion is to create *self-discipline* in the individual. This prepares the individual for social existence because he will be able to accept rules and regulations. The second function is the creation of unity or *social cohesion.* "Ceremony," wrote Harry Alpert, "brings people together and thus serves to reaffirm their common bonds and to enhance and reinforce social solidarity."[12] A third contribution is the *continuation of tradition* and the social heritage of a society. Faith is renewed at religious rites with phrases and songs or hymns such as "Faith of Our Fathers" and "The Old Rugged Cross" (or "The Star-Spangled Banner" at

High God	Type of Society: Simple	Type of Society: Complex
Present	2 (refute theory)	17 (support theory)
Absent	17 (support theory)	3 (refute theory)

Table 2–1. Complexity of Society and Worship of High God

Source: R. P. Cuzzort, *Humanity and Modern Sociological Thought* (New York: Holt, Rinehard & Winston, Inc., 1969), p. 33.

public events). Society is then, as Edmund Burke suggested, "a partnership not only between those who are living, but between those who are dead and those who are to be born." Finally, the religious ceremony creates a sense of euphoria or a pleasant sensation of *well-being.* The individual is made to feel good while singing and participating with the group assembled in a church, a synagogue, or a temple. In these four ways religion helps to keep the society together.

Guy Swanson carried Durkheim's argument even further. Swanson felt that if there is a link between religion and society then there should be some connection between the kind of god that is worshiped and the nature of the society.[13] He presented the argument that a powerful single person, god ("high god"), would be worshiped in societies with conflicting groups. This type of god is necessary if the society is to resolve its differences. On the other hand, Swanson continued, small societies with little conflict have no need for such a god.

Swanson put this idea to the test. He examined some thirty-nine primitive societies, comparing their social relations with the type of god they worshiped. Swanson and his aides classified societies on the basis of simple/complex social relations and the type of god they worshiped. According to the order model a strong, powerful god should only appear in those societies with complex social relations. Simple societies should not have such a god. In the study they found nineteen simple societies and twenty with complex characteristics. In seventeen cases, Swanson found that high gods appeared in complex societies. In seventeen cases simple societies did not have a high god. Only five cases went against Swanson's arguments. Thirty-four cases out of thirty-nine is very good statistical evidence that there is some connection between the type of society and the kind of god worshiped.

Conflict and Religion

For those using the conflict perspective, religion may take on other meanings. Some sociologists have suggested that strong religious feeling in a society with many different religions can generate conflict. Lewis Coser noted, "Nor did Durkheim's theory take cognizance of the historical evidence that indicates that religion, although it may draw men together, may also separate them and set them against each other."[14] The belief that one religion is superior to another has to generate conflict, hostility, and persecution. History is full of

Organized Religion: social glue or a source of conflict?

examples in which a dominant state religion suppresses and discriminates against those holding opposing theological views. In the United States, as Will Herberg noted, officially we believe in the plurality of religious groups, and we argue that people ought to go to church, *any* church or other place of worship, on Sunday.[15] At the same time, various religious bodies have attempted to force their views on others by having them incorporated into law. Prohibition was a product of Fundamentalist Protestant political activity. Laws prohibiting the use of birth control pills and abortion found the Catholic Church as their main champions, although these laws had been instituted by Protestants. Movements like the Black Muslims use religion as the foundation of their beliefs. By engaging in political activity, religious organizations become engaged in (what Coser and Dahrendorf label) conflict. Even at the level of international conflict, religion plays a significant role. For example, some political conservatives feel that the relationship between the United States, the Republic of China, and the Soviet Union is a struggle between the religious values of the West and the godless materialism of Communism and is a justification for crusades.[16] Although contributing to social solidarity, therefore, religion can also be seen as a source of conflict.

A more ambitious example of the conflict school is Karl Marx's interpretation of religion. Marx believed religion is "the opiate of the massess." He argued that religion blinded men to the nature of the real world. It obscured the "ought to be" of society. Religion did all of the things that the order school said it did: it truly reflected the "is" of society—but he was concerned with the "ought to be." Religion allows men to accept the world in which they live rather than aspiring to the one Marx wished to create. Religion, argued Marx, obscures the fundamental fact of life: the economic nature of man. Man must survive economically. Man by looking toward heaven accepts the exploitation of capitalist society. The Industrial Workers of the World had a song titled "Preacher and the Slave." They sang the following verse:

> You will eat, bye and bye,
> In that glorious land above the sky.
> Work and pray, live on hay,
> You'll get pie in the sky when you die.

The "bosses" justify their existence through the use of religion. The millionaire founder of Standard Oil, John D. Rockefeller, defended the excesses of the early robber barons in American industry saying, "This is not an evil tendency in business. It is merely the working out of nature and a law of God."[17] Anticapitalists replied that by glossing over economic problems, religion only *postponed* the inevitable dialectical outcome of a Communist "heaven on earth." Whether Marx and his supporters were right or wrong is hard to say because there is no way of testing a belief system about the future.

For another illustration of the difference between the order and conflict perspectives, let us look at the role of popular music in America.

Order and Popular Music

Popular music is an entertainment medium. People listen to it because "it makes them feel good" or "you can dance to it." Both the schools we have been discussing would add some new views to what we usually think about the music heard in the Top Forty. Popular music's contribution to an orderly society might be described as occurring in four areas: (1) it teaches adolescents the rules of courtship; (2) it brings young people together; (3) it maintains and upholds institutions and social action; and (4) it makes people feel good.

1. *Popular music teaches adolescents the rules of courtship.* The songs teenage girls are initially exposed to are innocent statements of puppy love by idols such as Bobby Sherman, David Cassidy, or Donny Osmond. The songs are harmless. The Beatles' original hit was "I Want to Hold Your Hand." The Monkees' "Day Dream Believer;" David Cassidy's "I Think I Love You" and Donny Osmond's "Go Away, Little Girl" are all innocent statements of romance. The idol is the nine-to-twelve-year-old's fantasy love object before she begins to date. When she does begin "going out" the idol is dropped and music becomes background noise for everyday activities. A teen-ager told the *New York Times,* "When you are 13 and have a real date, you don't go for crushes anymore."[18]

An analysis of song lyrics in 1966 reported that popular songs began to discuss the courtship process with the beginning of an active search for a love relationship. Many songs, such as "Somebody Groovy," "Love Is Like an Itching in My Heart," or "You Don't Have to Say You Love Me," talk about falling in love.[19]

All of these songs describe the quest for a love relationship. Having found it, the couple enjoys a state of joy and sharing. Consider Shades of Blue in their hit song "Oh, How Happy You Have Made Me" or Donna Fargo's "Happiest Girl in the Whole USA." A song sung by Petula Clark underlines the importance of need: "I couldn't live without your love . . . . gotta have you all the time."

As in real-life romances, the emotional high is replaced by the third stage: breaking up. Literally hundreds of songs deal with this unhappy experience with titles like "You've Lost That Lovin' Feeling," "Breaking Up Is So Hard to Do," "Don't Bring Me Down," or "Baby, Please Don't Go." The relationship, having been wrecked on the sea of love, finds the rejected member going into isolation to discover the Meaning of Life. Neil Diamond's "Solitary Man" and Paul Simon's "I Am a Rock" stress the need to withdraw and repair one's wounds. Popular songs explain to their young listeners the supposed mysteries of life and love in the most general terms.

2. *Popular music brings young people together.* A sixteen-year-old girl attending a concert expressed a common sentiment; "I come here because all my friends are here." Pop music brings people together at dances, concerts, or rock music festivals. Popular music at these gatherings instills a distinct *generational identity* as performers address their fans as "brothers and sisters." Woodstock and other such gatherings echoed Frank Zappa's comment about the influential film *Blackboard Jungle;* "They have made a movie about us,

therefore we exist."[20] At the Woodstock festival on the second day the announcement was made, "There are a lot of us here. If we are going to make it, you had better remember that the guy next to you is your brother."

Many concerts and festivals have been billed as "celebrations of life," stressing the cohesive aspects of popular music. Sociologists Johnston and Katz have also reported that friendship groups and cliques have been formed around interest in popular music and specific idols. "Elfans," members of the international Elvis Presley fan clubs, are just one example. Pop music in some ways does bring people together.

3. *Popular music maintains and upholds the institution of marriage.* As a majority of the songs found in the *Billboard* "Hot One Hundred" show, the theme of "simple, sexy, and sad" is predominantly wrapped in "June, spoon, moon." Romantic love is the subject of a vast proportion of songs, thus furthering the institution of a family unit regardless of its organization (see Chapter Eight).

Love songs, as we have seen, are still very much a part of the courtship process. Most people are buyers of pop records during the courtship ages of nine through twenty-four. Once people are married they tend to lose interest in pop music.

4. *Popular music makes people feel good.* Music is an emotional art. It evokes feeling states. It may make one feel good and happy. It can depress one, as in the case of "my baby just left me" songs. Broadcast popular music is certainly not designed to depress listeners. People listen to the radio and buy records to enjoy them. Songs with an unhappy ending must be in the context of love, a supposedly happy state. Even the teen-age coffin songs of the early 1960s, like "Teen Angel," "Tell Laura I Love Her," and "Patches," all promised full reunion some day in heaven. When asked why they liked the group several Beatles' fans told a psychologist, "They make me feel wonderful" or "The beat and their personalities moved me so much that I had to scream my appreciation I was so excited."[21]

In these four ways popular music contributes to the existence of society and its institutions. Conflict theorists can take the same music and come to different conclusions.

Conflict and Popular Music

Current popular music can be seen as being a symbolic cause for several competing groups. It is nearly the exclusive domain of young people under the age of twenty-five. Individuals who condemn popular music are usually of another generation or an older age group. The opposite forces in the combat over this medium are *generational units.*[22] "Turn down that noise!" command parents. The younger generation, as German sociologist Karl Mannheim noted, are in opposition but this is a temporary state, as adolescents, too, will pass into adulthood and then ask their children, "How can you call that music?" The younger generation in industrial societies appear to be at odds with their parents and the society.

Although this may be a passing phase, many observers have called the music of the 1960s and 1970s songs of rebellion and dissent. During this time pop music, or at least part of it, became a tool for protest. It was transformed into a vehicle to bring the "ought to be" into the "is." In 1969 social psychologist Herbert Goldberg called the popular music of the time

> a revealing and fascinating reflection of the psyche of contemporary youth. Through it we can see the perceptiveness, the openness, the sensitivity, the intellectuality, as well as the anger, the ambivalence, the emotional alienation and isolation, the chaos, the destructive and the paradoxical aspects of today's young generation.[23]

Charles Reich in his popular book *The Greening of America* told millions of believing readers, "Rock music has been able to give critiques of society at a profound level and at the same time express the longings and aspirations of the new generation. The music has achieved a relevance, an ability to penetrate to the essence of what is wrong with society, a power to speak to man 'in his condition,' that is perhaps the deepest source of its power."[24]

Popular music, then, is a field of generational conflict just as the strike is a sign of labor-management disagreement. Two views of the generational antagonism are open to both scholarly and valuative interpretations. On the one hand, the sociologist may examine the lyrics of popular songs and determine if the conflict is strictly symbolic or if it has real meaning for its listeners. One sociologist, James Carey, concluded that pop music was a "preparation of individuals for collective action of one sort or another. . . . One implication for concerted action that can be drawn from the lyrics is a physical separation from the parent society and the construction of some kind of utopian world."[25] Lyrics were viewed as reflecting and *leading* generational conflict.

A more radical view of pop music as revolutionary in nature embraces the idea that there is an independent force in the sound. When rock 'n' roll erupted into the consciousness of American youth in the 1950s, John Sinclair, a political writer, saw its infectious driving beat as an irresistible force of energy. This force was to fix "All That Was Wrong With Amerika." Rock music, in his words, was "holy and pure" and a vehicle for bringing "beauty, love, and freedom" to America. The sheer driving force of the music would capture the minds of its listeners and move them to reject what Sinclair called "death culture" and to create a better world.[26] These two interpretations underline the differences found in the conflict perspective. Carey's argues that the lyrics of popular music advocate change. The other belief is that the music has within it an unseeable power to reach the same goal (presumably by hypnosis).

Summary

In comparing the order and conflict perspectives, it is important to remember that one (the order school) is concerned with how society sticks together. The other (the conflict school) concentrates on how separate groups attempt to achieve different goals. Regarding religion and popular music, the order school is concerned with how these two aspects of life bring people together and teach them to live together in an orderly society. The conflict people looking at the same things stress the ways in which religion and music drive people apart into opposing groups. Religion, they argue, divides people of different beliefs and countries, for example, Catholics and Protestants in Northern Ireland. However, the conflict itself creates unity within these religious groups. "I am a Catholic" or "I am a Protestant" is a statement of group identification and belonging.

So it is in popular music. Popular music separates people on the basis of age groups and generations. Young adults and their younger sisters and brothers like popular music, whereas their parents may see it as noise or even as part of a sinister conspiracy. Again, younger people can say, "it's our music" and identify with it. The liking of a particular kind of music can become important within groups.

Both schools are looking at the same events and coming to somewhat different conclusions. Why? The answer is found in the assumptions we discussed in the first part of the chapter. A sociologist interested in describing religion or popular music tells what "is." If he believes that the world is essentially harmonious and orderly, he will focus on that aspect. On the other hand, a sociologist may say that conflict and competition are the natural order of things. He would then talk about how opposing religious bodies and age groups fight it out. Both are stressing the "is" of society as they see it, depending on their theoretical value judgments. However, some writers, like Karl Marx and John Sinclair, are concerned with how things "ought to be." Their writings are about changing the world. They, then, place what "is" in the framework of what "ought to be." Religion is *false* consciousness, Marx wrote, because it postpones the revolution he saw as the natural course of history. John Sinclair also wants a change. Popular music should bring about a change that destroys what he termed the "death culture of Amerika." Both Marx and Sinclair read into everyday life meanings that sociologists cannot accept: because of the "ought to be" in the critics' arguments it is impossible to refute them or to prove that they are right about what "inevitably" must happen until it happens someday in the future. Consequently, the sociologist will treat the "ought to be" as idle speculation. The "is" part of the order and conflict schools, like Archie Bunker's bet, can be tested by a neutral source. This source is the scientific method, which should help us decide which view is the most promising for understanding the world in which we live.

Notes

1. See W. Durant, *The Story of Philosophy: The Lives and Opinions of the Great Philosophers* (New York: Simon & Schuster, Inc., 1953).

2. H. Marcuse, *Reason and Revolution: Hegel and the Use of Social Theory* (Boston: Beacon Press, 1960), pp. 6–7.

3. See R. A. Nisbet, "Conservatism and Sociology," *American Journal of Sociology,* **57** (1952), 167–175; J. Horton, "Order and Conflict Theories of Social Problems as Competing Ideologies," *American Journal of Sociology,* **71** (1966), 701–713; and G. E. Lenski, *Power and Privilege: A Theory of Social Stratification* (New York: McGraw-Hill Book Company, 1966), pp. 14–17, pp. 441–443.

4. E. Burke, *Reflections on the Revolution in France* (New York: E. P. Dutton & Co., Inc., 1960), p. 117.

5. R. Merton, *Social Theory and Social Structure,* 1968 Enlarged Edition (New York: The Free Press, 1968), pp. 100–109.

6. Points paraphrased from P. Cohen, *Modern Social Theory* (New York: Basic Books, 1968), p. 167.

7. See T. Bottomore and M. Rubel, eds., *Karl Marx: Selected Writings in Sociology and Social Philosophy* (New York: McGraw-Hill Book Company, 1956), pp. 12–14.

8. See H. S. Hughes, *Consciousness and Society* (New York: Vintage Books, 1957).

9. L. Coser, *Functions of Social Conflict* (New York: The Free Press, 1956).

10. R. Dahrendorf, *Class and Class Conflict in Industrial Society* (Stanford, Calif.: Stanford University Press, 1959).

11. For a review see C. Fink, "Some Conceptual Difficulties in the Theory of Social Conflict," *Journal of Conflict Resolution,* **12** (1968), 412–460; and S. D. Nelson, *The Concept of Social Conflict* (Ann Arbor: University of Michigan Press, 1971).

12. See H. Alpert, "Durkheim's Functional Theory of Ritual," *Sociology and Social Research,* **23** (1938), 103–108.

13. G. E. Swanson, *The Birth of the Gods: Origin of Primitive Beliefs* (Ann Arbor: University of Michigan Press, 1960).

14. L. Coser, *Continuities in the Study of Social Conflict* (New York: The Free Press, 1967), p. 174. Also see J. S. Coleman, "Social Cleavage and Religious Conflict," *The Journal of Social Issues,* **12** (1956), 44–56.

15. W. Herberg, *Protestant, Catholic, Jew: An Essay in American Religious Sociology* (Garden City, N. Y.: Doubleday & Company, Inc., 1955).

16. See D. Bell, ed., *The Radical Right* (Garden City, N. Y.: Doubleday & Company, Inc., 1963); R. A. Rosenstone, ed., *Protest from the Right* (Beverly Hills: Glencoe Press, 1968); and for an original source, B. J. Hargis, *Communist America. . . Must It Be?* (Tulsa: Christian Crusade, 1960).

17. Quoted in R. Hofstadter, *Social Darwinism in American Thought* (Boston: Beacon Press, 1955), p. 45.

18. A. Taylor, "'David' They Yelled, and Parents Quietly Paid," *New York Times* (March 13, 1973), p. 44.

19. See J. T. Carey "Changing Courtship Patterns in the Popular Song," *American Journal of Sociology,* **74** (1969), 720–731.

20. The quote is a paraphrase of A. Camus' famous statement, "I rebel—therefore we exist." F. Zappa, "The Oracle Has It All Psyched Out," *Life* (June 28, 1968), p. 85.

21. A. J. W. Taylor, "Beatlemania—A Study of Adolescent Enthusiasm," *British Journal of Social Clinical Psychology,* **5** (1966), 83.

22. R. S. Denisoff and M. H. Levine, "Generations and Counterculture: A Study in the Ideology of Music," *Youth and Society,* **2** (1970), 33–58.

23. H. Goldberg, "Feeling Rock Music: The Message in the Medium," *Voices: The Art and Science of Psychotherapy,* **5** (1969), 47–48.

24. C. A. Reich, *The Greening of America* (New York: Random House, Inc., 1970), pp. 267–268.

25. J. Carey, "The Ideology of Autonomy in Popular Lyrics: A Content Analysis," *Psychiatry* (May, 1969), p. 163.

26. J. Sinclair, *The Guitar Army* (New York: World Publishing Company, 1972).

THREE

Research Methods

Collecting Evidence

SOCIOLOGISTS spend a lot of time gathering information about divorce rates, murder rates, population figures, and many other things that the rest of us simply explain and argue about without ever thinking of checking into the actual facts. Read the editorial page of your newspaper and the columnists and you will see. People argue about why so many able-bodied men are receiving welfare payments without any concern for the fact that every careful study indicates that very few men who are able to work are on relief.[1] People debate the effects different social policies will have instead of running small tests and finding out the consequences.

Sociologists are interested in finding out *what* the situation is and *then* in explaining *why* it is so. We spoke earlier about the scientific method. The scientific method is merely a set of rules for collecting evidence about what is and why it is *in such a way that if we are wrong we will find out that we are wrong.* If we are right, also, we want other people to agree with our findings. This means that they must be able to examine our evidence and to agree with our conclusions.

The first rule for collecting evidence is that other people should be able to observe and reproduce your findings. If you say that you know something because your "intuition" says it is so, no one else has or can see your intuition and they will refuse to believe you. If you argue that something is true because your mother or your god told you so, other people will argue that their mother or their god told them the opposite and that your kind of evidence is not acceptable.

When sociologists say that your evidence must be "observable," they mean that other people must be able to examine your evidence and agree that it does support your claims. There are many issues that cannot be studied by means of the methods we are talking about because there is nothing tangible you can bring to a neutral person to ask him to examine. What is Beauty? What is Truth? What is the Ideal? What is God's Will? These are things that can't be studied by any method known to science. They have to be evaluated by a different set of standards than the ones we are talking about.

A second rule for collecting evidence, closely related to the first, is that you must do it in such a way that your ideas of what *is* can be *falsified.* In other words, you have to be able to find out if you are wrong. In our daily lives, we're pretty careless about testing the things we believe in. We insist that washing the car brings rain but we ignore all the times our clean car did not get wet. We believe women are bad drivers and then we see that the "idiot" driving in front of us is a man. That just proves that he was *taught* by a woman. If a woman drives well that proves nothing; obviously we just haven't watched her long enough. We seem often to be like the man who kept insisting that he was dead despite his neighbor's attempts to convince him that he wasn't. "Do dead men bleed?" "No." The neighbor jabbed him with a pin and drew blood. The response? "I guess dead men *do* bleed!"

A competent researcher specifies in advance the kind of findings he would consider evidence for his arguments and the kind that would suggest he is wrong. When someone, social scientist or layman, makes an assertion about the world, you ought to ask him, "What would it take to convince you that you are wrong? What evidence would you need?" If he answers that there is *nothing* (even hypothetically) you could show him that would convince him he is wrong, you are wasting your time talking to him. Walk on by.

Operational Definitions

One of the first things a sociologist will ask when you say you have discovered something is, "What did you mean by each of the terms you used?" Let's imagine you claim to have found that "Catholics" are "happier" than "Protestants." How did you decide who was "Catholic"? You may have defined as Catholic anyone born Catholic, anyone who says he is Catholic and who has been to mass at least twice this month, or anyone who says he has had an audience with the Pope. How did you decide who is "happy"? Anyone who is married? Anyone who is single? Anyone who says, "Yes, I'm happy"? Who was a "Protestant" in your study? Did you study only male "Protestants"? Whites only? Baptists only? You can see how the way terms are defined can make a great difference in the kinds of results you get. We are not arguing that one way of defining a term is better than another but simply that unless other people know what you meant by a term, they can't duplicate your study nor can they even know what you are talking about.

An *operational definition* describes the research operations that are necessary if one is to observe the idea or concept being defined. It's very much like a recipe. Instead of asking, "What steps do I go through to produce tomato soup?" we're asking, "What steps do I go through to decide who is Catholic and who is Protestant?" An operational definition answers the question: How do I know one when I see one?

Causal Logic

Variables and Constants

Let's say you have defined your terms so that other people know what you mean when you use each one. The reason for doing your study in the first place is that you want to account for something. You want to know why some people are happy and others are unhappy, why some people are poor and others are not, why some people smoke marihuana and others don't, why one society has a high suicide rate and another has a low suicide rate. There are any number of things you might want to explain, things that sometimes occur and sometimes do not, that sometimes increase and sometimes decrease. Let's call these *variables,* or things that vary.

Let's call the variables you want to explain *dependent variables,* variables that depend on the existence of other variables. Let's call those other variables *independent variables.* What you are trying to do is argue that your dependent variable is "caused" by your independent variable. If I were to argue that Catholics are happier than Protestants, religion (Catholic or Protestant) would be my independent variable and happiness/unhappiness would be my dependent variable.

A *constant* is a characteristic of a person, a group, or a society that does not vary. You can explain a variable only with other variables. *You can't use a constant to explain a variable.* To put it another way, if two things or groups have something in common (a constant), you cannot use this common characteristic to explain a difference between these groups. For example, if you want to explain *why* "alienation" has increased over the last fifty years, first you have to demonstrate that in fact "alienation" *has* increased over the last fifty years. Unless you can show that there is more (or less) "alienation" now than fifty years ago, you have not shown it is a "variable," that there is anything to explain. If you can show that it has varied, that it is a variable, you still have to demonstrate that what you are attributing this change to is also a variable and has also changed over the last fifty years. You hear that the cause of student unrest, female dissent, and black protest in the 1960s and 1970s is oppression. You disagree with the statement. You are not trying to argue that these groups are not often mistreated but simply that because they have apparently not undergone an increase or a change in the extent to which they are oppressed, you cannot attribute the existence of protest (a variable) to oppression (a constant).

A marked growth in the use of narcotics by adolescents over the last thirty years cannot be attributed to the "fact" that "Parents don't treat their children with understanding and the children resent it" unless it can also be demonstrated that there has been some noticeable change in the way parents treat their children, an increase in the extent to which they mistreat or misunderstand them. In other words, you can explain a variable only with another variable and not with a constant. This, of course, is why sociologists reject most biological explanations of social phenomena. As far as we can tell, our species has undergone no major biological change over the last few million years, and man is biologically the same species all over the world. Because the biology of our species is a constant, we can't explain differences between societies or historical periods by using this constant.

Explaining a Variable with Another Variable

Let's imagine you want to show that listening to rock music gives people pimples. That is, you are going to try to demonstrate that people between twelve and twenty who listen to "a lot of" "rock music" have "more pimples" than people of the same age who listen to "very little" "rock music." After you operationally define "rock music," "a lot of," "very little," and "more pimples," what do you have to do next? There are four things that you have to do to make your case that rock music (your alleged independent variable) causes pimples (your dependent variable).

You must demonstrate (1) that listening and pimples covary*; (2) that listening precedes pimples in time; (3) that no third variable causes both listening and pimples; and (4) that your explanation of why listening to rock music causes pimples is better than any other interpretation of why rock music should cause pimples. The first of these is the easiest and the last is the hardest to do and the point on which there is most bickering.

To demonstrate that two things covary you must show that significantly more of the people who listen to "a lot of" rock have pimples than do those who listen to "very little." Next, you have to make clear that listening to the music came *first* and then the pimples broke out. Is it possible that people who have a lot of pimples become self-conscious and therefore afterward spend more time at home alone listening to rock records? Third, you have to demonstrate—even if you can show that the music did, in fact, come first, before the pimples appeared—that there isn't some third factor responsible for both. Is it possible that people who have money have more pimples and listen to more rock music, that prosperity is the cause of both? That is, does money make it possible to buy more records and to buy more chocolate and other foods that cause pimples? Let's imagine that older teen-agers listen to more music than younger ones and that they also have more pimples. Is it possible that maturity causes both appreciation of rock music and pimples? Your study has to demonstrate that even when you compare people of the same age (twelve-years-olds with twelve-year-olds, thirteen-year-olds with thirteen-year-olds, and so on) or the same income, the relationship between listening and pimples is just as strong and does not disappear. If a third variable causes both of your supposed variables we call the relationship between your supposed variables a false or *spurious* relationship.

Your last step is to argue that your explanation of the relationship is correct, and this step is the hardest one to demonstrate. But it is also the most important. We can agree that one variable seems to cause the other and still disagree about whether one explanation is better than the other. *The details of the relationship are as important as the demonstration of the relationship.* A researcher once trained a caterpillar to jump over a pencil whenever he yelled, "Jump." He then systematically removed the caterpillar's legs, right front, then left front, right rear, then left rear, and observed the effects of removing the legs. When he had removed all of the poor insect's legs, he commanded it to jump, and of course it could not. He then wrote in his notes, "If you remove all of a caterpillar's legs, it becomes *deaf*!"

*Two variables covary if an increase or decrease in one is accompanied by an increase or decrease in the other.

The key question to ask is "Is that the *only* way to explain these findings?" We find that the average of black children's scores on standard IQ tests is lower than the average of white scores on the same tests, and this finding appears again and again. The critical question is not "Is there a relationship between race and scores on IQ tests?" The critical questions are "How do we account for the relationship?" and "How do we show that one explanation is better than another? It has been argued that blacks are simply less intelligent than whites,[2] that the tests are "culture bound" and are really testing the child's home environment rather than his actual potential,[3] that blacks are nervous when a white tester administers the test,[4] that blacks aren't as highly motivated to do well on tests as white middle-class children are,[5] that poor blacks are more likely to suffer from bad prenatal and perinatal care and that this produces brain damage,[6] and that because the social environments of blacks and whites are so different there is no way to show that the differences in test scores are attributable to biological differences rather than to environment.[7]

Note that the issue is not *whether* there is currently a relationship between race and tested IQ but *which explanation is the correct one.* The answer to that question has important consequences. Which alternative explanation we accept makes a difference, an important one, for the society.

The Coleman Report[8] found that the more white children in a school the better the performance of black children, although there was no change in the performance of the whites. Why? How many reasons can you offer for this? Is it something about the way teachers behave? What might they do differently than when blacks are in the majority? Is it something about the parents' pressure on the school? How would you prove you are right? As you can see, explaining why and demonstrating that your explanation is better than other explanations is a tricky business that can have consequences not only for the scientific value of your findings but also for people's lives.

Let's stop and restate what we have said so far. To be scientifically acceptable your evidence must be reproducible by other people. You can explain variables only by means of other variables. If you want to claim that one variable "causes" another, you must show (1) that it covaries with the other (when you see changes in one, you see changes in the other); (2) that it precedes the other in time; and (3) that no third variable causes both. You also have to demonstrate that your explanation makes better sense than some other explanation.

Research Designs

There are three basic designs or research plans sociologists use to collect their information or data: *experiments, sample surveys,* and *case studies.*

Experiments

In an experiment the researcher manipulates one variable and examines the effect of this manipulation on some other variable. This is the most elegant

Table 3–1. Results of Experimental and Control Groups the Same

	Experimental group (given stimulus)	*Control group (not given stimulus)*
Before	100 people with colds	100 people with colds
After	5 people with colds	5 people with colds
Difference (After/Before)	95 people	95 people

design and provides the standard against which other designs are judged. Sociologists don't use it very often because many of the things that interest us can't be manipulated. If we want to know about the effects of a flood on community solidarity we cannot go out and create a flood. If we want to know if children who are beaten become delinquent more often than those who are not, we'd have a very hard time finding parents who will *volunteer* to beat their children so we can study what happens. How would we study the spread of Communism in Asia with an experiment? Nevertheless, sociologists do sometimes make studies by means of experiments. We could experiment with new types of prison systems, with the effects of guaranteed incomes, with many things we simply argue about now.[9]

Before the researcher does his manipulating, he does two things. He gathers together the people who are going to be experimented on and assigns them *randomly** to two or more groups, and he measures them on the dependent variable to make sure that the groups start out equally—equally sick, poor, bigoted, neurotic, ignorant in Spanish, delinquent, or equally anything that he is going to try to change. If he does not measure before he starts he will not be able to tell how much change, if any, there has been.

In what we call the *classic experiment* the researcher has two groups, one of which he is going to do something to and one of which he leaves alone. The first we call the *experimental group,* and the second is the *control group.* If the researcher finds that the experimental group has changed and the control group has not, he can argue that whatever he has done caused the change. If both groups change equally, even though he didn't do anything to the control group, he would be hard pressed to prove that his experiment had any impact. We use the control group because we don't want to assume that our stimulus was effective when it wasn't. Consider the example in Table 3–1. The example shows the effects of a new cold medicine. Each group originally had one hundred people with bad colds who were randomly assigned to try a new medicine or to do nothing. A week later, having given the experimental group the medicine and the control group nothing, we find that only five people in the experimental group still have colds; but on the other hand, only five people

*Random assignment means that we use some scheme worked out in advance so that the decision about who goes into which group is out of our hands. Usually we use a random numbers table worked out by a computer. We assign each subject a number, then assign him to his groups according to the order specified by the list in advance.

Table 3-2. Results of Experimental and Control Groups Different

	Experimental group	Control group
Before	100 people with colds	100 people with colds
After	5 people with colds	95 people with colds
Difference (After/Before)	95 people	5 people

who did *not* have the medicine still have colds. It looks as if people get better with or without the tonic. Would you go out of your way to get such a cold medicine? Had there been no control group that medicine could have looked pretty potent.

Consider some more everyday examples. The Democrats come into office and the economy moves up. Shall we say that the Democrats "caused" increases in the gross national product? If you say yes you are also saying that had the Republicans come into office, the economy would *not* have improved. Note that things that didn't happen can't be used to demonstrate much. Could it be that no matter who came into office the economy was due for an upturn? Let's look at another example, as shown in Table 3-2. The medicine used in this example seems to be a lot more effective than the one used in Table 3-1.

This design is valuable for demonstrating covariation. Before this medicine was used there were many colds. Afterwards, there weren't. No medicine, little improvement. This design also handles the question of which came first: *first* the medicine, *then* the cure. This experiment also handles many of the problems of spuriousness because random assignment to groups will in most cases work out so that the groups are matched on all the characteristics one might consider relevant to the question (in this case, getting better). In other words, by letting some objective randomizing procedure determine who goes into which group, you are minimizing the chances, for example, that one group will have all the younger, stronger people and the other all the older, weaker people and that this is the real reason why the first group gets better faster. If you randomly assign people to your groups you will find almost always that you end up with equal numbers of old, young, male, female, blond, brunette, black, brown, yellow, red, white, nice, and nasty people in each group. That's hard to believe, but it's true. (Of course, you can always check on this before you start administering your treatment just to make sure.) If your two groups are matched on every variable you can think of that might have a bearing on your results and if the *only* way your two groups differ is that one had your treatment and the other did not, the results must have come from something in your treatment. (You may have to do some more experimenting to find out what it was about your treatment that did the trick.)

As we have mentioned, however, sociologists don't experiment as often as they do surveys and case studies, for practical and ethical reasons.*

*Surveys and case studies raise ethical questions, too, of course.[10]

Sample Surveys

How would you find out what proportion of the American public favors the current welfare system? Right! You'd go out and ask. How would you find out how many people read a daily newspaper? The same way. If you want to know about something current like the number of people favoring gun control, which may change every time another public figure is shot, there is no way you can design an experiment to study it. You have to go out and ask. That is what the term *survey* refers to, asking people about something that interests you, be it gun control, attitudes toward Armenians, pornographic movies, beliefs about mobility in America, or evidence of a relationship between rock music and pimples.

When we speak about a *sample* survey, we are speaking about a study that does not ask questions of everybody, which, of course, would be quite difficult, but rather of a sample of people carefully selected to be *representative* of whatever group interests us: a sample of doctors, or a sample of blacks, or whites, or registered voters, or men, or women, or teen-agers.

It seems hard to believe that a sample of two or three thousand voters or television watchers or mothers could really be representative of a nation of two hundred million people, but it is true. It is as true as the fact that if your doctor needs a sample of your blood, he can take some from your arm rather than having to drain all of your blood to find out if you have mono or not. In this case, "carefully" selecting a sample again means selecting a sample *randomly*. Random sampling again means not *haphazard* sampling but sampling according to a plan made up in advance and designed to give every subject or respondent an equal chance of being included in the study. If we don't select randomly then we won't have a very useful sample, and even if we were to ask fifteen million voters about their preferences we would get less accurate results than we would by carefully selecting three thousand voters. In other words, if we want to study voter choice we can't ask only rich people or poor people or younger people; we must select our sample so that it represents all of the groups of people who will be voting.

There's no need here for a technical discussion of how we might select a random sample of voters or students or parents or whatever, but the basic principle involves setting up a procedure that specifies which people to ask—every seventh or tenth or seventeenth person, or the head of every ninety-seventh household, and so on—and that will take the decision about who to ask out of our hands once the study gets going.

Sociologists aren't often interested merely in the answers in what we usually think of as a "poll." They are generally interested in going beyond the specific answers to the larger issue of which kind of people give what answers in a survey. They want to know, for example, not only how many families want one, two, three, or five children but also what the differences are between people who answer differently. Is education related to their answers? Sex? Religion? Income? Race?

We might want to know something about divorce and we might ask married and divorced people questions like "How old were you when you got married?" "What is your religion?" "Are you religious?" "Do you both have the same religion?" "How high is your income?" "Did your family approve of the marriage?" "Were you still in school when you got married?" Now we are getting beyond mere polling and trying to answer more or less causal questions. What's the relationship between parental politics and children's politics? Between church attendance and delinquency? Between size of home town and the probability of dropping out of college?

Sociologists do most of their research with surveys. It is harder to demonstrate causal relationships with surveys than with experiments, but covariation is pretty easy to show. For example, it's not hard to show that people who watch TV a lot tend to read much less than people who watch TV only when the news is on. However, it is usually harder to show which variable came first: Does TV distract one from reading or are TV watchers people who would not read even if all televisions sets vanished tomorrow, who were nonreaders even before TV existed?

It is harder with a survey to show that there is not some third factor involved that produces both variables. Less well-educated people, for example, may find watching television easier than reading books and less expensive than going to the movies. A survey researcher has to take special pains to show that even if he controls, or holds constant, other variables that might be relevant, the relationship still appears. In this case, if he holds education "constant" by looking only at high school graduates or only at college graduates, the relationship between reading and TV watching should still appear and can't be attributed to education.

It is also harder to show with a survey that before some event happened two different groups were matched on every variable but the one the researcher considers important. If we wanted to show that the younger the couple, the greater the chances their marriage will end in divorce, we might start by getting a sample of one hundred divorced men and a sample of one hundred married men of the same age, let's say forty. We would ask, among other things, "How old were you when you got married?" Let us say we get results that look like those in Table 3–3. It looks as though very few of the people who married at twenty or below stayed married and as though few people who waited until they were at least twenty-one got divorced. We may agree that age at marriage seems to predict divorce chances pretty well. Shall we call

Table 3–3. Relation of Divorce to Age at Marriage

Age at Marriage	*Divorced*	*Married*
20 or older	27%	73%
20 or below	73%	27%
	(fictitious figures)	

it the "cause"? Is it possible that marrying early and divorcing are both signs of impulsiveness? Might not religion have something to do with the results, or prosperity, or education? We can break down our figures and compare, say, college-educated, rich, Protestants and all other combinations of the variables of religion, economic level, and education. And we might discover that no matter what subgroups we compare, age at marriage is related to likelihood of divorce. We have to take special pains to collect all of this information on the possible other factors that might cause the relationship we found. If we had been permitted to do an experiment, we would have matched our groups in advance and randomly commanded some couples to marry early and others later and then studied age and likelihood of divorce. There would be much less question at the end of the study about whether the married and divorced couples differed in some respects other than age at marriage, because in the experiment we would have seen to it that age was the only variable in our two groups. It isn't impossible to handle in a survey the three other causal problems, but it's much harder to prove our point.

Finding which explanation for the relationship accounts best for the results is also harder with a survey than with an experiment. We have the apparent independent variable and our dependent variable, but we are not in a position to demonstrate easily with a survey *how* the two are related, even when there is no question that they *are* related. Does early marriage lead to regrets and arguments about what people might have accomplished if they had waited? Does early marriage mean that people had less time to choose a partner than people who waited? Does early marriage lead to earlier childbirth, so that forty-year-old unhappy people who married early have grown children and feel freer to divorce than people who married later and whose children are young? As we pointed out earlier, we have to show not only that our predicted relationship exists but also that *our explanation of why it exists* is correct. It is harder to do these things with surveys than with experiments, but they can be done.

Case Studies

Despite the fact that we use a *sample* of the group that interests us in a survey rather than asking everyone in the country, we end up with a good deal of information from a large number of people. Three thousand questionnaires make a large pile. What kind of depth does a survey produce? We've asked an hour's worth of questions of each of these many people, but how much can we really learn about anyone in an hour? Some sociologists argue that they would prefer to study fewer people and spend more time to "really" get to know each of these people. Sometimes sociologists will study a whole community for five years, or a boys' gang for a year, or a Mafia family for a year. There's no question that a person who studies a single "case" or a few cases, be they communities, gangs, or families, gets to know them a good deal better than a survey researcher knows any one respondent.

The person who does a case study can get insights that any other type of researcher would never get in years of surveying or experimenting. In fact, case studies are a wonderful place for a survey researcher or experimenter to find ideas to test, but they do not themselves produce very good *evidence* for two reasons. Case studies rely on a very few units, often one unit. The question that is hardest for the researcher to answer is, "How typical is this unit of anything?" Someone offers to sell you three warehouses full of film about a family from Santa Barbara, California. Before you spend your money, consider this. What will it tell you about any family other than that one? They must be a sample of some kind of family but just *what* kind of family? California families? White families? American families? Twentieth-century families?

Case studies also give the researcher and the reader all kinds of interesting ideas about causes of things, especially if the study traces something about the case over time. We might study the effects of having a dog on family solidarity, or we might follow one labor-management dispute over time, or one social movement over time, or study the effects of a flood on one community, but given a sample of one unit we can't call our case study a *test* of anything. Let's say we study one small town and find that the mayor is a Republican and a thief. We can't seriously argue that because *one* mayor was both a Republican and a thief that these two things *always* covary, can we? A sample of one is not very good evidence, especially when we don't know what it's typical of. In our everyday lives we would never say something as silly as, "I once owned a Ford and it was a 'lemon'; Fords are terrible cars;" or "I knew three Armenians and they were lazy and didn't have any sense of rhythm; *all* Armenians are lazy and unrhythmic." Nevertheless, despite their defects as evidence, if you read through some of sociology's case studies, you will find some fascinating things and get some fascinating insights into the world around you.

Theory and Research Methods

We have discussed some of the ways sociologists go about collecting data. The examples we used were intended to show you something about the logic of explanations. But they were not necessarily good illustrations of *what* sociologists study and why. Sociologists don't generally pull hypotheses out of the air and say, "Why don't I study rock music and pimples today?" They try to study things that have relevance to sociological theories. They assume that there is no sense in developing theories unless they help us explain the world, and they do research to make sure that their theories do have some support in the world beyond the armchair.

In other words, current sociological theories tell sociologists *what to look for* and their research tells them *whether or not it's there.* The sort of theory discussed in Chapter Two is rarely produced by sociologists these days. The terms and concepts are almost impossible to do satisfactory research on, and the theories were stated in such a way that it is almost impossible to falsify them.

Most sociologists prefer theories less sweeping, about narrower themes and questions than those of the grand theorists. On the other hand, sociologists must avoid becoming collectors of carefully researched but useless information. They try to stay away from saying either, "I don't know if what I say is true, but it's important" or "What I say is clearly true even though it may not be worth knowing."

No Universal, Timeless Laws

One of the things beginning sociology students have trouble understanding is why things sociologists say about them don't square with their own experiences and observations. Sociologists say, "Minority groups members tend to . . ." and as a member of a particular group you say, "Well, I don't and neither does anybody else in *my* minority group." Are you blind? Are sociologists liars?

Let's start from the other direction. You're right but the sociologists are right, too. Since the days of the grand theorists sociologists have learned that it is very unlikely that they are going to come up with statements that are true under all circumstances, for all time. Their findings depend for their truth on certain *other* things' being true. The theorists and the researcher share the responsibility for specifying *under what conditions* a statement is true and when it is not. Notice sociologists do *not* say that a finding that disagrees with theirs is wrong but simply that if both are discovered by competent people, each must have been studying the issue under different circumstances and the task is to learn *how* those circumstances differed.

Would you agree that "If you strike a wooden match on a stone, it will light up"? That one of the unspoken assumptions in this proposition is "as long as you're not underwater," and another is "also assuming it is not a defective match"? In the same way, the statement that "Women in a society that looks down on women will share that scorn and look down on themselves" may hide an assumption like "unless their consciousnesses are raised," or "unless they are well educated," or "unless they have had a domineering mother."

Sociologists are interested in making statements and generalizations that account for the behavior of large numbers of people who share certain characteristics (age, race, religion, social class, and so on), and they are not disturbed by the existence of apparent exceptions to a rule: they are also very much interested in the apparent exceptions. In fact, they often learn more about the majority from studying the minority than they do from studying the majority.

A final word about what sociologists do. As you may have noticed, the variables that interest sociologists are not the kinds of things most of us would think about examining offhand. Our key variables are characteristics of groups—societies, communities, families—and of relationships between people, not personal characteristics.

Summary

Sociologists are interested in finding out what appears to be true and then why it is true. To claim a causal relationship the researcher must demonstrate *covariation, precedence in time,* and *absence of third factors,* and he must demonstrate that his *explanation of the details of the relationship is sound.* Where they are appropriate, experiments have logical advantages. Surveys are the only way of examining current, changeable states of affairs. Case studies give us depth at the cost of generality. Theories are guides to what is worth *studying.* Research tells theorists what is worth *saying.*

Notes

1. U.S. Department of Health, Education and Welfare, "Welfare Myths vs. Facts" (pamphlet) (Washington, D.C.: U.S. Government Printing Office, 1972).

2. A. R. Jensen, "How Much Can We Boost I.Q. and Scholastic Achievement?" *Harvard Educational Review,* **39:**1 (1969), 1–123. See also A. M. Shuey, *The Testing of Negro Intelligence* (Lynchburg, Virginia: J. P. Bell, 1958).

3. See the "Chitling Test" on p. 73. V. John and L. S. Goldstein, "The Social Context of Language Acquisition," *Merrill-Palmer Quarterly,* **10** (1964), pp. 265–275. See also L. E. Tyler, *The Psychology of Human Differences,* 3rd Ed. (New York: Appleton-Century-Crofts, 1965).

4. B. A. Pasamanick and H. Knoblock, "Early Language Behavior in Negro Children and the Testing of Intelligence," *Journal of Abnormal and Social Psychology,* **50** (1955), 401–402. See also B. J. Forrester and R. A. Klaus, "The Effect of Race of the Examiner on Intelligence Test Scores of Negro Kindergarten Children," *Peabody Papers in Human Development,* **1**:7 (1964), 1–7.

5. P. Mussen, "Differences Between the TAT Responses of Negro and White Boys," *Journal of Consulting Psychology,* **17** (1953), 373–376.

6. R. F. Harrell, E. R. Woodyard, and A. I. Gates, "Influence of Vitamin Supplementation of Diets of Pregnant and Lactating Women on Intelligence of Their Offspring," *Metabolism,* **5** (1956), 555–562. See also B. A. Pasamanick and H. Knobloch, "Brain Damage and Reproductive Causality," *American Journal of Orthospychiatry,* **30** (1960), 298–305.

7. O. Klineberg, "Negro-White Differences in Intelligence Test Performance: A New Look at an Old Problem," *American Psychologist,* **18** (1963), 198–203.

8. J. S. Coleman et al., *Equality of Educational Opportunity* (Washington, D.C.: U.S. Government Printing Office, 1966).

9. D. Elesh, "Sociological and Economic Results of the New Jersey-Pennsylvania Negative Income Tax Experiment," paper presented at the annual meeting of the American Sociological Association, New York, August 1973.

10. G. Sjoberg, ed., *Ethics, Politics and Social Research* (Cambridge, Mass.: Schenkman Publishing Co., 1967).

FOUR

Culture

MAN IS DIFFERENT from the other animals. He has a highly developed brain. It's a good thing he has this brain because physically he's a pretty wretched creature. He lacks the strength of the elephant, the speed of the antelope, the fur of the weasel, the fangs of the wolf, the dog's sense of smell, the digestion of the goat, and the musk of the skunk. Nonetheless, he survives and manages somehow to live all over the world, in all climates, and usually avoids being eaten by the other beasts.

Because man has the ability to create *culture,* he overcomes the fact that he is born helpless and useless and dependent on others for his survival. He is unlike other animals in that most of them are running around shortly after they're born. Some species of antelope, for example, can walk thirty minutes after they are born and can run fast enough to keep up with a slowly moving herd by the time they are three or four hours old. Most humans do not begin to walk until well after their first birthday.

What Is Culture?

Culture is probably the loosest, least precise term you'll be exposed to in this text. It does *not* refer to what some people would call "couth," or sophistication. Even the most uncouth people you know possess "culture."

It's a loose concept because it covers many, many things. Culture refers to *all* of the things learned and shared by members of a society, all of the things that the squalling infant who spits from all ends will have to learn to be able to function in his society. The infant must learn how to speak the language of his society, what to eat, when to eat, whom to worship, when to worship. He learns that the world is round (or flat), that 2 and 2 are 4, that he will select a mate for love (or money), marry, raise children, and die, and then, perhaps, have an afterlife.

He learns that certain colors are nice and others are ugly, that some goals are worth seeking and others are not, that certain kinds of people are good and others are not, that some behavior is "natural" and good and other behavior "unnatural" and bad. He learns how to use tools, what sitting positions are comfortable, what to do to his hair, what to wear or not to wear, and so on. The "and so on" includes thousands upon thousands of other things that the infant will *learn* as a member of his society.

Humans become humans or *social beings* by learning the values, beliefs, and behavior patterns of their society. These are what we describe with that deceptively simple term *culture.* As we've indicated, the things the culture of our society teaches us are things that we start out knowing nothing about. Initially, they are things that our society believes in but that we don't know about and don't care to know about. For example, as long as we are fed, we don't care what we're fed. But at some point, we start insisting that the foods preferred by our society are the *only* foods we care to eat. Other foods favored by members of other societies turn our stomachs. Our digestive systems reject what

Culture refers to all of the things learned and shared by members of a society.

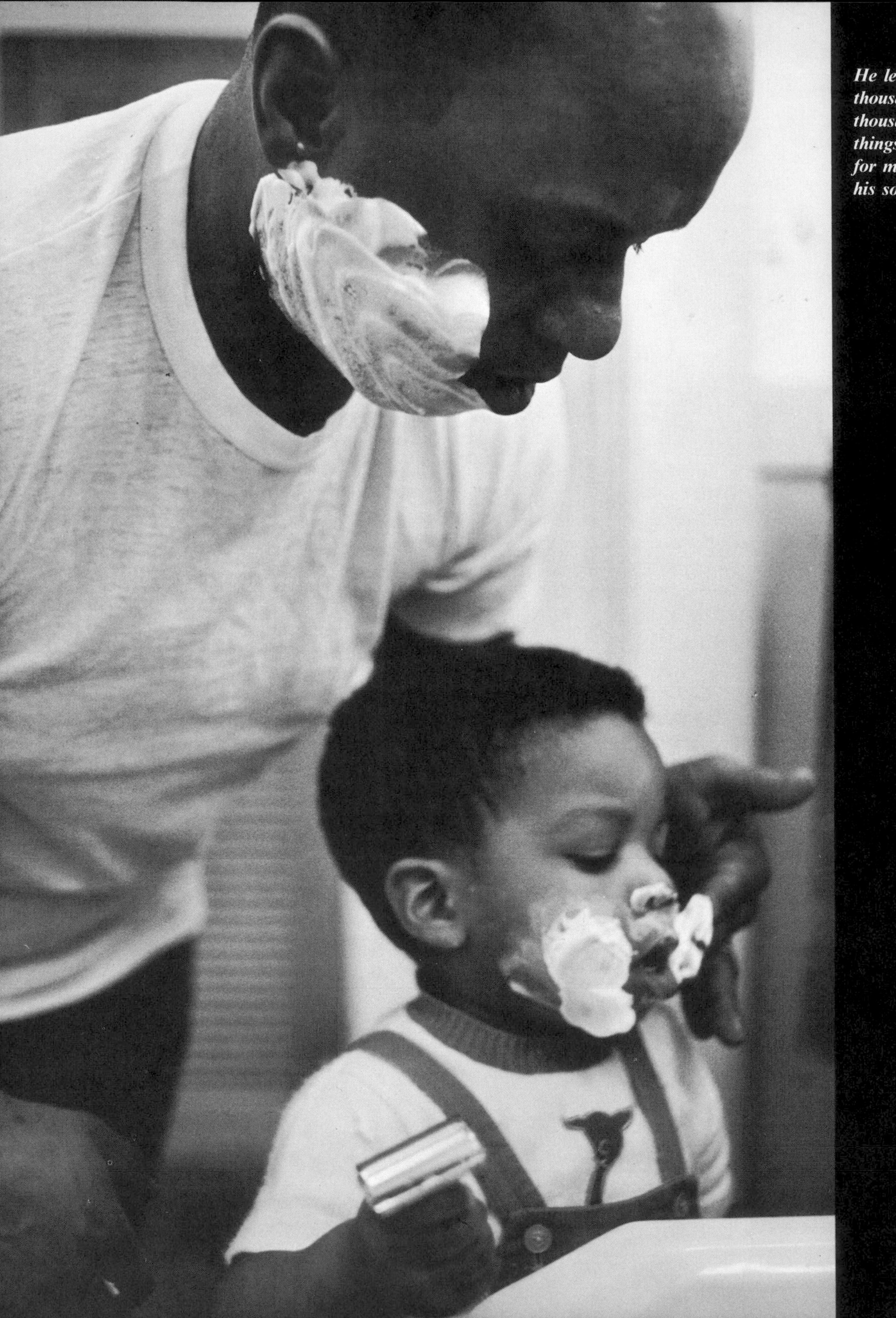

He learns the thousands upon thousands of things necessary for members of his society.

Humans become social beings by learning the values, beliefs, and behavior patterns of their society.

our minds say is not fit to eat. What was initially outside us—our culture's ideas of proper food, in this case—becomes a *part of us.* Our bodies reject what our culture says is not appropriate food. An American can tell himself that rotten venison or blubber are nutritious, but his body says no. He may accept intellectually the idea that tree grubs may be more nutritious than a Twinkie, but he's not likely to stop off at the neighborhood rotten log for a worm on his way home from school.

No child is naturally modest. Every society has certain ideas about what areas of the body should be covered in the presence of strangers or members of the opposite sex. In the Middle East it is the woman's face, in Tierra del Fuego the back, in the United States the genitals. If the forbidden area is seen by a stranger, say, while one is skinny-dipping, the body reacts, people blush, faces get red. There is, in other words, a *physical* response. The rules become a *part* of us, as do the conditions under which the rules don't apply. The girl who is embarrassed and flustered at having a strange male see her in ankle-to-neck flannel pajamas can go to the beach wearing two band-aids and a cork and, because her culture defines this as proper, be not the least bit embarrassed.

Language and Symbols

The first important thing about culture is that man has the ability to use language. Events don't simply register on our minds in the same way as an image registers on a photograph. Instead, we *process* and *interpret* what we see. We make sense of our observations in terms of what we already know and believe, the ways in which our culture has taught us.

One of the things that makes man different from other animals is the fact that he is able to use *symbols.* A symbol is something that stands for something else. A word, a picture, a gesture may stand for some tangible object, but more important, it may stand for something intangible. Consider sign language. If you are playing charades, or are speaking to someone who doesn't speak your native language, you can pretty easily indicate things like "sun," "eat," or "sleep" with your hands. What would you do to indicate "necessary," "tomorrow," "virtue," "never", "outer space"? The easy symbols are low-level symbols (or signs), the harder ones are higher-level, abstract symbols: there are very few tangible things you can point to if you want to indicate them, but we do have the ability to express in words whatever it is that we want to indicate.

Let's go a step further. Because man has language, he can talk about things that aren't physically present; he can even talk about things that don't exist—ghosts, witches, demons, unicorns, Santa Claus—and other people in his society will know what he's talking about. This ability to use abstract symbols makes it possible to learn from other people's experiences: this kind of berry is poisonous, that swamp has quicksand in it, that farming technique is the most efficient if there hasn't been much rain this season.

One of the things that make man different from other animals is the fact that he is able to use symbols.

Because man has this ability to use language, he *interprets* his world. He gives events *meaning*. He imposes order on the world. And he does this as a member of a society. Learning one's culture entails learning the meanings that his society attaches to events. We see these physical features and we say "beauty." Observing that behavior we say "good." We see this skin tone and we say, "he's a black" or "he's a white," and we place some kind of value on that category, black or white. We associate the skin tone we observe with other information and we respond to that person on the basis of what we believe about blacks and whites.

We belch and in our society others are insulted. In many other societies a belch is a compliment to the host or hostess: it's bad taste *not* to belch. A belch has no meaning until we impose a meaning on it, until we interpret it. Events, gestures, behavior are good, bad, or indifferent depending on the significance our society places on them. We have the ability through language to assign meanings—"good," "bad," "proper," "improper," "insulting," "decent," "noble," "beautiful," to all kinds of events. Societies differ in what they attach these kinds of labels to. *But these events have no meaning by themselves.* Each culture *applies* meaning to events, and although these meanings sometimes seem arbitrary, members of the society who share the culture do not consider them optional. They insist that all decent people should do things as the rest of the "decent" people do them.

Bring your lunch to school in a greasy paper bag. Wear white socks with a business suit to an interview. Wear a paper party hat to the movies or a hat with earlaps. What kind of response do you think you'd get? Are there "meanings" in the socks, bag, hats, or earlaps, or are the "meanings" imposed by those who watch you and decide that you're some sort of unsophisticated ass?

Culture and Patterns

What we're saying so far is that each society has a set of ideas about the nature of the universe, about good, bad, or indifferent behavior, and about the appropriate techniques for getting various things accomplished. We call this variety of things people born into a society must learn *culture*.

You were certainly aware even before you opened this book that there are all sorts of customs and values that one society accepts and another may consider silly, useless, immoral, or insane. Reading about these differences in newspapers or magazines gives us a very misleading idea of what culture is all about because we get the impression that a culture is made up of stray bits and pieces, a custom here, a belief there. As we learn more about any given society we realize that culture is *patterned*. Customs tend to fit together, to support one another. Change in one custom often requires changes in all sorts of other customs. Sociologists call this patterning *cultural integration*. By this they mean that all parts of the culture are tied together in one way or another. For example, we often read about the unwillingness of Indians to kill and eat cattle despite the fact that the country has perpetual oversupplies of people and perpetual undersupplies of food. We are puzzled by the fact that Hindus refuse to slaughter their cattle. They consider cattle sacred. Cattle seem to wander around freely, defecating all over the place. Marvin Harris[1] pointed out that there are a lot of sound economic reasons for *not* slaughtering them. Indian agriculture requires oxen to pull plows. The cows produce oxen as well as other sources that couldn't be easily provided without themselves putting a strain on the food-producing economy. Fewer cows would still produce oxen, but the Indians would have to divert resources from food production to feed the fewer, better cows. Letting the cattle eat whatever junk they can scrounge up costs nothing: they eat stubble from the fields and grass in ditches, between railroad tracks, on steep hills, and in other places that couldn't be farmed anyway. Now cattle produce dung, which is vital as cooking fuel and fertilizer. Dung equivalent to 45 million tons of coal is burned annually, costs nothing, and is "delivered" to the door daily. Some 340 million tons of dung are used annually as fertilizer in a country that is forced to squeeze three harvests a year from the land.

Though Hindus don't eat beef, the cattle that die naturally or are slaughtered by non-Hindus are eaten by the poor lower castes who would never get any protein if everyone else did eat beef.

The hides and horns of the cattle when they die are used in the enormous leather industry.

So we end up with a situation in which sacred cows that don't consume any resources needed by people, produce fuel, fertilizer, and oxen to pull plows, all of which could not be supplied as cheaply in any other way. Rather than being harmful, the religious ban on slaughtering cattle helps India survive.

As we look at customs in the context of their culture, they often make a great deal of sense to us even in terms of Western thinking. There are other customs that perhaps will never make sense to us in terms of *our* culture, but in the context of the culture of which they are a part they are sensible and significant to the people who perform them.

By and large very few people are self-conscious about what they do. They are taught that certain things are proper and that there is an approved way of doing things, a way in which things have always been done. If someone were to ask us how we can write, "*Dear* Mr. Smith, you are a bastard. *Sincerely* yours . . ." how would we explain our use of *dear* except by saying, "That's the proper way of writing a letter"? We know that the *k* in *knife* is as useless as the *b* in *lamb.* Why can't we persuade other people to take us seriously when we propose dumping the useless letters?

Ethnocentrism

Every culture encourages *ethnocentrism.* The term refers to the judging of other people's culture in terms of one's own. The basic premise of ethnocentrism is that *your* culture is valuable only insofar as it does what *mine* does. What

I speak is language. What you speak is babbling. My currency is "real money." Yours is "worthless." My country's values are God's values. My political system is the model yours should follow (We once fought a war to "Make the World Safe for Democracy." In fact, we fought that war several times without asking if the world wanted to be made safe for democracy!) I practice a religion, but you have pagan superstitions. My sex practices are virtuous, whereas yours are obscene and indecent. Boxing and football are "sporting events," but bullfighting is "brutality" to Americans; the reverse is true for Spaniards. Americans think sex on television is obscene, but violence is not. Swedes on the other hand print information in the newspaper TV section on how many incidents of violence and what kind of violence are on the day's programs so that parents can decide whether or not they want to let their children watch TV.

Enthnocentrism, as you can imagine, does not encourage mutual understanding and tolerance. Nor does it help scientific understanding. As you will recall from earlier chapters, the social scientist's concern is with answering questions on the order of "Under what conditions will societies do *X*?" and in that sort of question there really isn't much room for making value judgments.

Consider this fictional dialogue between an Eskimo and a white man:

"You said the fellow you killed provoked you?"

"So it was."

"He insulted Asiak?" [an Eskimo wife]

"Terribly."

"Presumably he was killed as you tried to defend her from his advances?"

Ernenek [her husband] and Asiak looked at each other and burst out laughing.

"It wasn't so at all," Asiak said at last.

"Here's how it was," said Ernenek. "He kept snubbing all our offers although he was our guest. He scorned even the oldest meat we had."

"You see, Ernenek, many of us white men are not fond of old meat."

"But the worms were fresh!" said Asiak.

"It happens, Asiak, that we are used to foods of a quite different kind."

"We noticed," Ernenek went on, "and that's why, hoping to offer him at last a thing he might relish, sombody proposed him Asiak to laugh [have sexual intercourse) with."

"Let a woman explain," Asiak broke in. "A woman washed her hair to make it smooth, rubbed tallow into it, greased her face with blubber, and scraped herself clean with a knife, to be polite."

"Yes," cried Ernenek, rising. "She had purposely groomed herself! And what did the white man do? He turned his back to her! That was too much! Should a man let his wife be so insulted? So somebody grabbed the scoundrel by his miserable little shoulders and beat him a few times against the wall—not in order to kill him, just wanting to crack his head a little. It was unfortunate it cracked a lot!"

"Ernenek has done the same to other men," Asiak put in helpfully, "but it was always the wall that went to pieces first."

The boundaries of "us" and "them" are established.

The white man winced. "Our judges would show no understanding for such an explanation. Offering your wife to other men!"

"Why not? The men like it and Asiak says it's good for her. It makes her eyes sparkle and her cheeks glow."

"Don't you people borrow other men's wives?" Asiak inquired.

"Never mind that! It isn't fitting, that's all!"

"Refusing isn't fitting for a man!" Ernenek said indignantly. "Anybody would much rather lend out his wife than something else. Lend out your sled and you'll get it back cracked, lend out your saw and some teeth will be missing, lend out your dogs and they'll come home crawling tired—but no matter how often you lend out your wife she'll always stay like new."[2]

Note that each man is *interpreting* this custom in terms of the meanings it has in his own culture—and that because of this ethnocentrism each is insulted by the other's behavior where no offense was intended.

Gerald Suttles, describing a low-income neighborhood in Chicago in which members of four ethnic groups live uneasily together, points out that words, gestures, and clothing are interpreted differently by the four groups. These interpretations add to the discomfort and uneasiness the members of each group feel in the presence of the other groups and do nothing to minimize their suspicions of one another. Clothes are not only ways of covering one's nakedness. They are also "techniques of boundary maintenance." By use of clothing styles, gestures, street rap, people are able to determine who belongs to their group and who is an outsider. This is how the boundaries of "in" and "out," "us" and "them" are established. (The changes in clothing styles since Suttle's study make no difference.)

Language differences between each ethnic group are often exacerbated by nonverbal acts which accompany or supplant speech. First-generation Italians, for example, have an entire repertory of gestures that are not even fully understood by their own children. Negro boys, in turn, have a "cool" way of walking ("pimp's walk") in which the upper trunk and pelvis rock fore and aft while the head remains stable with the eyes looking straight ahead. The "pimp's walk" is quite slow, and the Negroes take it as a way of "strutting" or "showing off." The whites usually interpret it as a pointed lack of concern for those adjacent to the walker. Negro girls provide a parallel in a slow "sashay" that white males sometimes take as an unqualified invitation to their attentions. . . .

The other ethnic groups think it odd that a group of Mexican men should strike a pose of obliviousness to other people and even to their nearby wives and children. Puerto Ricans, on the other hand, are disparaged because they stand painfully close during a conversation and talk in such a voluble manner as to "jabber." Whites say that Negroes will not look them in the eye. The Negroes counter by saying the whites are impolite and try to "cow" people by staring at them. . . .

The males show much greater differentiation [than females] in their apparel. They seem the primary bearers of those emblems of clothing that express ethnic differences and it is among them that examples of this differentiation are most apparent. Examples of this differentiation are easily observed. Italians often gather on the sidewalks in sleeveless undershirts and standard (unpegged) pants. Young Italians wear the same "old-fashioned" undershirts but sometimes deviate by wearing none at all. Older Negro men are inconspicuous in their work clothes and standard suits. Younger Negroes, however, stand out with their dress shirts, blazers, pointed shoes ("points"), tight pants ("hiphuggers"), and expensive hats ("lids"). Mature Puerto Ricans unbutton their flowered shirts to display a decorative St. Christopher's medal. Felt collars, ruffled shirts, and cummerbunds are formal dress for some of the Mexican males. The Negroes crop their hair and shave their forelocks to achieve a higher brow. Italian barbers "shape" hair with a straight razor, and adult Mexican males let their sideburns grow and allow their forelocks to land directly over a portion of their forehead.

The most pronounced and consistent differences between male adolescents in the Addams area are summarized in [Table 4–1]. The widest differentiation is between the Negro and the Italian boys; the Mexican and Puerto Rican boys fall somewhere in the middle.

In general, these observations on clothing seem to warrant two separate conclusions. First, insofar as these differences are not understood by all ethnic groups, they constitute another occasion for wariness and avoidance between ethnic groups. Second, each style of clothing tends to reiterate local ethnic differences that have been observed elsewhere. The Negro boys do not have

Table 4–1. Distinctive Types of Clothing Worn by Boys in Each Ethnic Group

Type	*Negro*	*Italian*	*Mexican*	*Puerto Rican*
"SAC" Sweater	Does not occur	Very rare	Common	Only if boy in Mexican group
Gauster (half coat belted in back and wide trousers)	Common	Does not occur	Very rare	Very rare
Ivy (thin lapels, tight sleeves and trousers)	Common	Does not occur	Does not occur	Does not occur
Heavy workshoes	Very rare	Common	Common	Rare
Black pants	Rare	Common	Common	Common
Black leather jacket	Rare	Common	Common	Common
Blazer	Common	Does not occur	Rare	Rare
Ruffled shirt	Does not occur	Does not occur	Common	Common
Vests	Rare	Does not occur	Common	Common
Hat	Common	Does not occur	Rare	Rare
Casual sweater	Common	Does not occur	Does not occur	Does not occur
Spanish shoes (with high heels)	Does not occur	Rare	Common	Common
Sleeveless undershirt	Rare	Common	Rare	Rare

Source: Gerald D. Suttles, The Social Order of the Slum. Chicago: University of Chicago Press, 1968, p. 69.

a distinctive costume for purely local situations but address themselves to a wider audience. The style of dress associated with the Italians can be worn only locally and governs a self-presentation that can be appreciated only within their own ethnic section. The Puerto Ricans and Mexicans lie between the other two ethnic groups. A few items in their wardrobe seem to be a part of their traditional culture and might appeal to other Mexicans and Puerto Ricans all over Chicago. Otherwise, the Mexicans and Puerto Ricans selectively share various items that are provided by the Italians or Negroes. Differences in clothing, then, reflect the degree of provincialism prevalent in each ethnic group.[3]

Cultural Relativism

What is being suggested is that for scientific purposes customs have to be understood in terms of the culture of which they are a part. Whether we approve or disapprove of them, we can *understand* other people's customs only in terms of their culture. Once we learn to suspend judgment we may find that we see a good deal of sense in other people's behavior, that we understand things that never made sense before. Or we may decide that now that we understand, we still don't approve of Nazism, or any number of other -isms.

When it comes to the details of universal practices, the range is mind-boggling.

The *cultural relativist* position (that customs can be understood only in terms of the culture of which they are a part) does not commit us to approving or disapproving anyone else's culture, but adopting it will enable us to be a bit less smug and self-righteous and a bit wiser. It may also make it possible for us to avoid destroying other societies because they haven't "seen the light."

The Study of Culture

What do we learn when we study "culture"? Man is an amazingly flexible creature. He can learn to live with a fantastic variety of customs and beliefs and still survive. One important implication of this idea is that the kinds of things we like to think of as "human nature" are not fixed. In our ethnocentrism we tend to explain our worst behavior by assuming that "that's human nature." As we study the ways of other humans, we discover that there is no *single, specific* set of behaviors that are universal to mankind. On the other hand, there are certain broad categories of things we find universally. Man everywhere marries and procreates (family). Man everywhere develops arrangements for producing, distributing, and consuming goods (economy). Man everywhere develops some sort of system for distributing power (government). Man everywhere develops explanations for his place in the universe (religion). Man everywhere develops procedures for teaching children what they will need to know to function in their society (education). These standard practices sociologists call *social institutions.* There are other things that we find universally: music, art, medicine, body ornaments, personal names, food, taboos, funeral rites, incest rules, and many more. When it comes to the details of these universal practices, the range is mind-boggling.

Our concern in this book is not with *all* of culture but with certain aspects of culture: values, norms, and subcultures. Anthropology, our sister social science, has historically studied small, unindustrialized societies, societies small enough so that an observer can attempt to understand how almost all of the different aspects of the culture fit together. In small, traditional societies there is reason to believe that the various aspects of the culture are *integrated.* That is, the smaller patterns we referred to earlier support one another *closely* and changes in one aspect of the culture affect the entire culture.

When we switch to studying the industrialized, complex societies that sociologists have traditionally studied, we find that the extent to which various aspects of the society are consistent with and support one another becomes *problematic* (something to be *asked about* rather than assumed). We don't know how loosely related different aspects of a society can be before the society disintegrates.

Norms

Every society has rules, standards, and ideas about what is proper and improper, right and wrong. People in every society take for granted that other

One culture's appropriate behavior may violate another's norm.

people know these rules and will abide by them. A *norm* is a rule. Sometimes sociologists make a distinction between two types of norms: *folkways* and *mores.* The distinction is basically between rules that deal with "proper" behavior (folkways) and "moral" behaviors (mores).

A person who violates folkways is considered odd, peculiar—but not wicked or immoral. What are some American folkways? Don't wear white socks with a tuxedo. Don't pick your nose in public. Don't put your elbows on the table. Cover your head in a synagogue. Uncover your head in a church. Serve your company dinner on your good china. Drink coffee from your cup and not your saucer. This is a very brief list of folkways. What they all have in common is that if you violate them people give you funny looks. They gossip about you. If you're poor, they think you're lazy or ignorant; if you're prosperous, they think you're eccentric. But people don't threaten to punch you in the mouth. Nor do they feel angry and consider you *immoral* if you violate folkways.

Mores, on the other hand, are norms that we attach a moral connotation to. A man walking down the street wearing high heels and make-up arouses an urge in many people to stomp him into the ground. Wiping your nose on an American flag, seducing a child, living "in sin," using profanity in front of a nun, murder, rape. These are violations of rules that people take much more seriously.

Every society has thousands of rules that may strike *us* as peculiar. To the members of that society they are a serious matter. As we indicated a few pages back, we interpret and evaluate behavior. We don't merely register what we see. We give it meaning and we respond in terms of the meaning it has for us. Whether the person violating the norms does so through indifference or ignorance, we're distressed. We try to teach our children to do what's right by our society's standards, and for the most part they accept these standards ultimately as their own.

Values

Every society has norms. Ask people, "Why do you follow this rule? What's the reason for it?" The answer (assuming you get one other than "That's the way we do things") is likely to reflect the *values* of the people answering your question. In other words, "Why should I work hard?" gets you an answer like "You'll be able to make *money* and gain *status* in the eyes of the people in your community" or "It's healthier" or "God wants it that way." "What's wrong with living together without marriage?" "It threatens the family system."

In other words, in the eyes of the members of a society, abiding by norms makes it possible to achieve or support certain values. Values are abstract ideas about what is good. Order, justice, equality, individual liberty, freedom—these are some of the values in whose name we are prepared to see others die (and sometimes to die ourselves).

Consider attempts at persuasion such as advertisements, editorials, or political speeches. The persuader is trying to convince us to buy something or to accept some social policy. Generally his argument follows the pattern of "If you vote this way (or buy this product), you will be able to achieve this value." To what values are persuaders in American society trying to hook their products? Sex appeal? Status? Sophistication? Speed? Being the first on the block to own one? Having the biggest, the newest, the latest? To what values do we try to hook social policies? Equality? Liberty? Justice? Economic growth? Clean environment? Did you ever notice that completely opposed programs may be justified in terms of the same set of values? For example, wars are nearly always fought in the name of liberty, freedom, and a lasting peace in the world.

Subcultures

When we study complex, large, industrial societies, we find that there are sizable numbers of people who share certain values and customs and beliefs with the larger culture. However, they have other characteristics that they share with one another but not with the rest of society. We call these *subcultures.*

As we examine the United States, for example, we see regional subcultures, occupational subcultures, ethnic subcultures. It has been suggested that there is a "youth" subculture, a "counterculture," a "culture of poverty," a "subculture of violence," and a "delinquent subculture."

Is There a Culture of Poverty?

There has been a good deal of discussion and argument about whether there is a "culture of poverty." The term comes to us from the late Harvard anthropologist Oscar Lewis, who suggested that in capitalist societies there is a subclass of poor people (not all poor people, but about 20 percent of the poor) who have developed—in response to deprivation and misery—a set of traits and values that enable them to cope with the world and that they pass on from one generation to the next. Lewis described the situation thus:

> Once it comes into existence it tends to perpetuate itself from generation to generation because of its effect on children. By the time slum children are age six or seven, they have usually absorbed the basic values and attitudes of their subculture and are not psychologically geared to take full advantage of changing conditions or increased opportunities which may occur in their lifetime.[4]

Among the seventy-odd characteristics that Lewis saw as making up this culture of poverty were these: little ability to put off immediate gratification and plan for the future; a sense of resignation and fatalism; feelings of powerlessness, inferiority, and personal unworthiness; free unions, consensual marriage; a trend toward the mother-centered family; frequent resorts to violence in settling quarrels; and a relatively high incidence of abandonment by the male of mothers and children.

Lewis's idea was picked up and popularized by Michael Harrington, whose book *The Other America: Poverty in the United States* had a strong influence on President Kennedy and was the chief intellectual stimulus for the legislative War on Poverty.[5] These legislative programs were "designed very explicitly to correct the social, occupational, and psychological deficits of people born and raised to a life of poverty."[6] In other words, the programs assumed that the best way to eliminate poverty was to change the poor, particularly the values and attitudes of the children of the poor; the parents were presumably too far gone to change. Emphasis was placed on such things as Head Start and the Job Corps rather than raising minimum wages or finding jobs for parents.

Within sociology and anthropology there was a great deal of debate and discussion on this approach. The general public seems to have accepted the idea that poverty may produce a vicious cycle in which poverty leads to even more poverty. Lewis's critics insist that although there is some evidence suggesting that certain behaviors occur more *frequently* among the poor than among the prosperous, there is more than one way of accounting for them.[7] What Lewis saw as evidence of a culture—values and beliefs accepted, shared, and consciously transmitted from one generation to the next—the critics argue are really stray traits that are *situational* responses to poverty, which the poor would cheerfully dump if they could get decent jobs. Where supporters of Lewis[8] argue that it is ethnocentric to ask the poor to accept "middle-class values," his critics argue that the poor do not value their misery or their responses to misery. When one generation ends up behaving like the parent generation, the critics contend, it is not through cultural transmission. Rather, it is a result of their going out into the world and *independently* experiencing the same failures as their parents—failure to get a job that pays a living wage, failure to succeed at holding a family together, failure at making long-range plans that show any prospect of working out.

Although those who have argued against the existence of a culture of poverty have been persuasive, there is a risk in accepting an oversimplified version of the "situational response" theory. Poverty, deprivation, and discrimination leave scars. Children don't have to be consciously taught to expect little from the world; they can pick up doubts about their own chances of success when they can see in living color on any street corner evidence of failure to beat the system by those who believed they could make it.[9]

Ethnic Subcultures

Once we believed that the immigrants to America would lose their distinctive heritages. America was to be a "melting pot." Over time we've discovered that the melting-pot process never occurred and that many of the descendants of our immigrants have no great desire to be melted down. Although the members of these diverse groups may dress like "Americans," work at the same jobs, watch the same TV programs, and eat the same frozen TV dinners, they feel most comfortable associating with people like themselves, have distinctive customs and values, and take pride in their identities as members of these groups *as well as* in being "Americans."

There is a bit more to ethnicity than a simple failure or reluctance to dump old customs. To a large extent, "ethnic" identities have been created *in America* rather than brought over on the cattle boats. People who came to America thinking of themselves as people from *this* province or *that* village ended up discovering that they had many things in common with people from all over their parent country. In other words, the children of someone who thought of himself as a Neapolitan or a Sicilian or a Calabrian ended up thinking of themselves as Italian-Americans (or Polish-Americans, Japanese-Americans, Irish-Americans, or German-Americans). They had in common, aside from values, customs, and beliefs, both the experience of facing the common problems of adapting to a new country that classified them all the same way and the recognition that organizing to protect their common interests was more profitable than trying to protect them alone. In recent years, younger members of many ethnic groups have become *more* conscious of their ethnic identities than their parents had been.[10]

Andrew Greeley suggests that ethnic groups have typically gone through a six-stage process in adapting to American society: (1) culture shock; (2) organization and emergent self-consciousness; (3) assimilation of the elite; (4) militancy; (5) self-hatred and antimilitancy; and (6) emerging adjustment.[11]

Culture shock. In the first stage, the immigrants have just arrived. Patterns of behavior established in the "old country" are jolted and jarred. The old culture is thought to be under savage attack. The old ties no longer apply. What are they to do? Where are they to go when something is needed? What manner of dress, behavior, and the like are appropriate? Cultural shock creates a stranger in a strange land.

Organization and self-consciousness. One man confronted with a new world cannot cope with it. He may not understand the language. The traffic lights, the signs, the ads are all foreign to him. In organization the immigrant finds security. Social clubs are formed. Clergymen, precinct captains, leaders of fraternal organizations—all become important in the community. Children are entering the public school system, adults are learning the language. Immigrants are becoming semiskilled or skilled workers. The leaders of the community become concerned about whether the distinctive features of the community will be lost as the group becomes "Americanized." They want to preserve their culture and yet they also want to become Americans.

Assimilation of the elite. The group moves into what sociologists sometimes call the lower middle class. Members become storekeepers, skilled workers, policemen, firemen, trade unionists. Parents scrimp and save to send their children to college. Group pride increases. Some of the talented children move into the larger society as they become writers, professors, artists. They are not really a part of the old group but they're not fully accepted by the larger society either. Their background embarrasses them.

Militancy. Militancy is the fourth phase. The immigrant group has more middle-class members. It has political power. It feels uncomfortable with the larger society. The group's members are suspicious. They warn each other of the dangers of associating with the larger society and at the same time feel compelled to become better at everything the society does than the natives.

Meanwhile, organizations have been developing that duplicate everything in the larger society. Greeley points out that American Catholicism has produced a Catholic lawyer's guild, a Catholic physician's guild, Catholic historical, sociological, and psychological societies, schools, and hospitals, and Catholic versions of everything that the larger society has. This is also the time when the group is very conscious of its Americanism. It becomes superpatriotic. The immigrant group is out to prove they're as American as any other group and maybe a little bit more. The group is conscious of past rejection by the society and it bothers them. The ethnic group is busily demonstrating not only to the world outside, but also (especially) to itself, that it is not inferior, and it is demonstrating this noisily, aggressively, and uncompromisingly. Suspicion and distrust of the larger society and noisy, highly selective pride in the accomplishments of one's fellow ethnics are the order of the day. It is at this stage, one must note, that the ethnic group is most difficult to deal with and most likely to engage in conflict with other ethnic groups.[12]

Self-hatred and antimilitancy. In the fifth phase, the ethnic group produces a substantial upper-middle-class and professional group. During the stage of self-hatred and antimilitancy, this college-educated group does try to leave the immigrant group, but as members of the larger society they are embarrassed by the militancy of the old-timers—they think the old-timers are provincial and narrow. The younger members of the group criticize every aspect of their own tradition and almost every institution that tries to keep the culture alive. Greeley suggests that the critics can live neither with their ethnic backgrounds nor without them.

Emerging adjustment. The final stage, emerging adjustment, appears with a new generation, secure in their upper-middle-class experience, confident that they can be part of even an upper class. They find it hard to understand the militancy of the fourth phase or the militant self-hatred of the fifth. They can't understand why they can't be a part of the larger society and still be loyal to their own traditions.

Young people are interested in the cultural and artistic background of their ethnic tradition. People travel to the old country to see how their grandparents and great-grandparents lived. The differences are a matter of fun, interest, and curiosity to the youngest members of the group: "It is about this time that the members of an ethnic group that has reached the top begin to wonder why other groups, which have not moved so far along, are so noisy, raucous, and militant."[13]

This is not the place to pursue the question of whether these particular stages are inevitable or reversible.

In what follows we will point to some differences among ethnic groups in values and behavior. Please be warned. It is awfully easy to observe or read about *tendencies* like those that follow and to assume that you now know *all* the important things about an ethnic group, and it is easy to change statistical tendencies into stereotypes and caricatures. With these warnings in mind, look at some ethnic group differences in responses to pain.

Mark Zborowski studied responses to pain on the part of three groups: Italians, Jews, and "old Americans" (white Protestants) at a hospital in New York.[14] All suffered from the same illnesses, illnesses that are quite painful, like ruptured vertebral disks and spinal lesions. Although no one in his right mind *enjoys* pain, members of the three groups handled it differently. The Italians and the Jews talked about their pain a good deal, moaned, and groaned, crying unashamedly when the pain was severe. In pain they wanted to be in the company of others, to hear expressions of sympathy. Old Americans tended to avoid any public display of moaning and groaning. They made a conscious attempt to minimize their pain, to avoid complaining and provoking pity.

The Jews and the Italians were both quite emotional when they suffered, but Zborowski reports that the Italians were concerned with the immediate fact of pain. The Jews were concerned about what it signified for their own health and welfare and the future of their families. Once they were given a pain killer the Italian patients forgot their suffering and relaxed. The Jews were often reluctant to accept these drugs. They worried about whether they might be habit forming. They pointed out that the relief from pain would be only temporary and that the cause wouldn't be removed. They feared that the drug might mask some symptom the doctor should know about.

Zborowski suggested that when one deals with a Jewish and an Italian patient in pain, for the former it is more important to relieve the anxieties with regard to the sources of pain, whereas for the latter it is more important to relieve the actual pain.

The Italians tended to have confidence in their doctors, particularly after the doctors had relieved their pain. The Jews were skeptical (because the fact that the doctor can relieve pain doesn't mean that he can cure the illness that caused it). The Jews checked the diagnoses and treatments of one doctor against the opinions of other specialists in the field.

The "old Americans" were concerned with the significance of the pain, as were the Jews, but the Jews' anxieties and pessimism about the future contrasted with the optimism about the future of the "old Americans." The "old Americans" approached illness differently from the other two groups. They thought of the body as a machine: if something breaks down, take it to a pro, an expert who will find the defect. The doctor has the know-how so you let him have your confidence. If he doesn't have the cure now, eventually it's bound to be discovered. The security and confidence of the "old Americans" increased, according to Zborowski, in direct proportion to the number of tests, X-rays, examinations, injections, and so on they received. These gave them the feeling that something useful was being done. The "old Americans" preferred being treated at the hospital to being treated at home. The Jews and the Italians disliked the impersonality of the hospital and wished they could be treated at home.

The patterns observed for each group don't represent the behavior of each member of each group. There were individual differences within each group, some resulting from social or economic class, some from personality differences, some from the disease the patient suffered. The first-generation Jews and Italians behaved more like the people described than did second- or third-generation Jews and Italians. But Zborowski noted that though the third-generation Jew or Italian *behaved* unemotionally, like the "old Americans," his *attitudes* were like those of the first generation: anxiety about the meaning of the pain if he was Jewish and lack of concern about the significance of the pain for his future if he was Italian.

Where do these attitudes come from? What supports them? Zborowski suggested that these attitudes toward pain and these ideas about what kinds of reactions one is entitled to expect from others are learned from the family from earliest childhood along with the rest of one's culture. The Jewish and Italian patients reported that their parents, particularly their mothers, were overprotective and overconcerned about their health and worried when they participated in sports, games and fights. They got constant reminders about avoiding colds, injuries, and fights. The childrens' crying brought sympathy, concern, and help. From these kinds of experiences a child learns to pay attention to each painful experience and to look for and expect help and sympathy. In the Jewish families it wasn't necessary to be in pain: any deviation from the child's normal behavior was thought of as a possible sign of illness. The Italian parents were less concerned about what a child's aches and pains signified, but they were very sympathetic about the actual discomfort. In both kinds of families the children were praised for avoiding physical injuries and scolded for not avoiding drafts and bad weather and for taking part in rough games and fights. The parents often interpreted an injury to the child as punishment for the wrong behavior.

"Old American" parents handled things differently. The child was told "not to run to mother with every little thing," to take pain "like a man," to stop being a "sissy," not to cry. The parents approved of participation in physical sports and encouraged it. The child was taught to expect to be hurt in sports and games and to fight back if others picked on him. But the parents were conscious of threats to a child's health and taught him to take immediate care of any injury. If the child was hurt, the thing to do was to keep calm and not get emotional or cry but to avoid unnecessary pain and other unpleasant consequences by applying proper first aid and getting to a doctor.

Zborowski suggested that there is a relationship between responses to pain transmitted to children and the role of the father and the culture's concept of masculinity. In the "old American" family, the mother tries to teach the child to resist pain. In the Italian family, the mother inspires the child's emotionality. In the Jewish family, *both* parents express worry and concern about the child's health. Traditionally stoicism is not equated with masculinity, nor are verbal complaints equated with weakness among Jews, as is the case for Italians and "old Americans."

Zborowski's study goes back some twenty years. Nonetheless, even in the 1970s we find differences among ethnic groups in all kinds of behavior. As we noted earlier, ethnicity is alive and well in America. We find ethnic group differences in attitudes toward race relations and toward political issues (on both the ethnics tend to be *more* liberal than native American Protestants, contrary to stereotypes),[15] in attitudes toward education, in choice of occupation, in income levels, in reading habits, in frequency of visits to relatives and

Table 4–2. Aptitude Test Scores of Four Ethnic Groups by Social Class—Table of Means[a]

Group	N[b]	Class	Verbal	Reasoning	Numerical	Spatial
Jewish	40	Middle class	62.6	56.7	59.2	56.5
	40	Lower class	54.7	48.5	50.2	47.0
Chinese	40	Middle class	51.2	55.9	56.0	56.7
	40	Lower class	45.2	51.8	51.8	52.0
Negro	40	Middle class	55.8	53.9	51.2	52.9
	40	Lower class	44.0	41.5	39.6	40.1
Puerto Rican	40	Middle class	47.3	48.7	49.2	49.4
	40	Lower class	39.3	42.5	42.9	45.3

[a]Normalized standard scores on total groups for each test. $\bar{X}$ (mean or average) = 50, *SD* (standard deviation) = 10.
[b]N = number of subjects.
Source: Adapted from D. H. Clark, G. S. Lesser, and G. Fifer, "Mental Abilities of Young Children from Different Cultural and Social Class Backgrounds." Paper presented at American Psychological Association, 1964.

psychiatrists—in nearly any area sociologists ask questions about. One illustration of ethnic differences is the way that members of different groups respond to IQ tests. We find that the groups described in Table 4–2 differ in the particular skills they possess. The majority of sociologists and psychologists believe that IQ does not reflect something inherited but rather a response to the child's social environment and the stimulation it provides. Although it is by no means clear *why* members of each ethnic group are stronger in certain intellectual skills than in other intellectual skills, the table indicates that despite social class differences within each group, the scores suggest that each group emphasizes and encourages certain kinds of skills and deemphasizes others.[16]

There have been complaints by and on behalf of members of groups that have traditionally not done well on the standard IQ tests that they are "culture bound."[17] What this means is that, as members of these groups and other critics see the situation, the questions traditionally asked are not objective tests of "native" intelligence but are tests of the kinds of experiences a child has been exposed to by his parents and community.

Although many sociologists, anthropologists, and psychologists believe that this is a valid complaint, they find it easier to point to "biased" questions on existing tests than to invent "pure" questions that are not loaded unfairly in favor of middle-class whites.

Adrian Dove has constructed a test that illustrates the point the critics of current IQ tests are trying to make. On Dove's "Chitling Test" (Table 4–3), black slum youngsters will probably do quite well, whereas children who have not been exposed to these same experiences are likely to appear ignorant. Take the test and see how you do.

Contracultures

Ethnic subcultures share many customs and values with the larger society's culture, and they differ on others, but generally the differences are a matter

Table 4–3. The Chitling Test

1. WHO DID "STAGGER LEE" KILL?
   (A) His mother, (B) Frankie, (C) Johnny, (D) His girlfriend, (E) Billy.
2. A "GAS HEAD" IS A PERSON WHO HAS A . . .
   (A) Fast-moving car, (B) Stable of "lace," (C) "Process," (D) Habit of stealing cars, (E) Long jail record for arson.
3. IF A MAN IS CALLED A "BLOOD," THEN HE IS A . . .
   (A) Fighter, (B) Mexican-American, (C) Negro, (D) Hungry hemophile, (E) Redman or Indian.
4. IF YOU THROW THE DICE AND 7 IS SHOWING ON THE TOP, WHAT IS FACING DOWN?
   (A) Seven, (B) Snake Eyes, (C) Boxcars, (D) Little Joes, (E) 11.
5. CHEAP CHITLINGS (NOT THE KIND YOU PURCHASE AT A FROZEN-FOOD COUNTER) WILL TASTE RUBBERY UNLESS THEY ARE COOKED LONG ENOUGH. HOW SOON CAN YOU QUIT COOKING THEM TO EAT AND ENJOY THEM?
   (A) 45 minutes, (B) 2 hours, (C) 24 hours, (D) 1 week (on a low flame), (E) 1 hour.
6. "DOWN HOME" (THE SOUTH) TODAY, FOR THE AVERAGE "SOUL BROTHER" WHO IS PICKING COTTON (IN SEASON) FROM SUNUP UNTIL SUNDOWN, WHAT IS THE AVERAGE EARNING (TAKE HOME) FOR ONE FULL DAY?
   (A) $.75, (B) $1.65, (C) $3.50, (D) $5, (E) $12.
7. A "HANDKERCHIEF HEAD" IS . . .
   (A) A cool cat, (B) A porter, (C) An Uncle Tom, (D) A hoddi, (E) A preacher.
8. "JET" IS . . .
   (A) An East Oakland motorcycle club, (B) One of the gangs in "West Side Story," (C) A news and gossip magazine, (D) A way of life for the very rich.
9. "AND JESUS SAID, 'WALK TOGETHER, CHILDREN . . .'"
   (A) "Don't get weary. There's a great camp meeting," (B) "For we shall overcome," (C) "For the family that walks together talks together," (D) "By your patience you will win your souls" (Luke 21:19), (E) "Mind the things that are above, not the things that are on earth" (Col. 3:3).
10. IF A PIMP IS UP TIGHT WITH A WOMAN WHO GETS STATE AID, WHAT DOES HE MEAN WHEN HE TALKS ABOUT "MOTHER'S DAY"?
    (A) Second Sunday in May, (B) Third Sunday in June, (C) First of every month, (D) None of these, (E) First and fifteenth of every month.
11. JAZZ PIANIST AHMAD JAMAL TOOK AN ARABIC NAME AFTER BECOMING REALLY FAMOUS. PREVIOUSLY HE HAD SOME FAME WITH WHAT HE CALLED HIS "SLAVE NAME." WHAT WAS HIS PREVIOUS NAME?
    (A) Willie Lee Jackson, (B) LeRoi Jones, (C) Wilbur McDougal, (D) Fritz Jones, (E) Andy Johnson.
12. WHAT IS WILLIE MAE'S LAST NAME?
    (A) Schwartz, (B) Matsuda, (C) Gomez, (D) Turner, (E) O'Flaherty.
13. WHAT ARE THE "DIXIE HUMMINGBIRDS?"
    (A) A part of the KKK, (B) a swamp disease, (C) A modern gospel group, (D) A Mississippi paramilitary group, (E) Deacons.
14. "BO DIDDLEY" IS A . . .
    (A) Game for children, (B) Down home cheap wine, (C) Down home singer, (D) New dance, (E) Mojo call.
15. "HULLY GULLY" CAME FROM . . .
    (A) East Oakland, (B) Fillmore, (C) Watts, (D) Harlem, (E) Motor City.
16. WHICH WORD IS MOST OUT OF PLACE HERE?
    (A) Slib, (B) Blood, (C) Gray, (D) Spook, (E) Black.

the answers:

1. (E) 3. (C) 5. (C) 7. (C) 9. (A) 11. (D) 13. (C) 15. (C)
2. (C) 4. (A) 6. (D) 8. (C) 10. (E) 12. (D) 14. (C) 16. (C)

of history, accident, or coincidence rather than a result of a conscious desire to be different. A *contraculture* is another kind of subculture, one in which conflict with the larger culture is by no means accidental. The members are well aware of the conflict and take pride in the fact that they *don't* do things the way the larger society does.

J. Milton Yinger defined a *contraculture* as containing a "theme of conflict with the values of the total society."[18] It is this conflict that makes a contraculture distinct from a subculture. The contraculture *is at odds with* one or more values of the society, whereas subcultures may go about their daily business oblivious to dominant cultural values. The Amish communities, for example, care little for the trappings of technological society, and they deliberately keep themselves isolated from it as much as possible.

Various people have theorized on youth as a contraculture. Theodore Roszak's *The Making of the Counter-Culture* presented youth and their style of life as being a "counter-culture.[19] The notion of *counterculture* stresses two ideas. The first is that the counterculture is a rejection of the existing culture.[20] The second is that the counterculture is an emergence of a new, competing culture. Charles Reich called this new culture *Consciousness III.*[21] The counterculture and Consciousness III have been presented as possessing these general characteristics: 1) they are antitechnological; 2) they are the product of affluence; and 3) they are supported by the young.[22]

As Reich sees it, technology is the highest form of organization. Sophisticated technology requires a great deal of planning that involves individual cooperation. The more sophisticated the technology, the less individual freedom there is. It is here that a major paradox or contradiction takes place, according to Reich. The affluence produced by technology should make possible greater individual freedom, but instead it keeps down human potential. Man becomes an affluent *extension* of the machine and the giant corporation. This imbalance makes possible the emergence of a counterculture, an alternative to the existent technological society. Reich observed, "Men become aware of their alienative posture through consumerism. The Corporate State creates dissatisfaction in order to stimulate consumerism. Herein lay the 'seeds of its own destruction.' The State *must* keep on creating dissatisfaction, it has no choice."[23] The reaction to this dissatisfaction is the rise of the counterculture, which is made possible by the very wealth created by technology. In other words, the technology that threatens man's freedom also creates the affluence that makes it possible to withdraw from the "system." The counterculture, therefore, is made up of those well-to-do persons who can, in fact, withdraw from the system and establish their own new way of life.[24] Nearly all observers agreed that white middle-class youth made up the bulk of those participating in the counterculture of the late 1960s and early 1970s. They were able, according to Reich, to *escape* the Corporate State. Young people could drop out. They could do many things forbidden to their elders, who are tied to the Corporate State. "There are a few years," wrote Reich, "when they pulse to music, know beaches and the sea, value what is raunchy, wear clothes that express their bodies, flare against authority, seek new experience, know how to play, laugh, and feel, and cherish one another."[25] Theodore Roszak and Charles Reich developed a list of common characteristics that they believed described the counterculture and Consciousness III (see Table 4–4). These characteristics stressed antiorganizational themes as well as the importance of "feeling states."

This view of the counterculture, although popular in the 1960s, has been widely criticized.[26] One of the basic problems is the broadness of the term. For example, many characteristics attributed to the counterculture are widespread throughout this generation of young people and even among older people.[27]

Despite the vagueness in the popular use of the term *counterculture,* Yinger's original idea of the contraculture is a useful one. It allows us to look at another dimension of social change, a *cultural* dimension as opposed to the traditional view that economics and politics are the major sources of social change (see Chapter Sixteen).

Table 4–4. Roszak and Reich's Characterizations of the Counterculture

Roszak's Counter Culture	*Reich's Consciousness III*
"I am a human being; do not mutilate, spindle, or tear."	"Acceptance of self."
"We do not need theories so much as experience."	"Deep skepticism of both linear and analytic thought."
"A revolution that expects you to sacrifice yourself is one of daddy's revolutions."	"It is a crime to allow oneself to become an instrument, a projectile designed to accomplish some extrinsic end, part of an organization or a machine."
Rejection of technostructure.	"Does not believe in the antagonistic or competitive doctrine of life."
Conviction that the poets have known better than the ideologists, that visions mean more than research.	Refusal to classify people or analyze them.
". . . unprecedented penchant for the occult, for magic, and for exotic ritual."	Openness to any and all experience.
Rejection of the corporate state.	New line of work.
Pop and rock groups seen as the real prophets of the rising generation.	Music all-important.
Antitechnological.	Antitechnological.
WASP (white Anglo-Saxon Protestant) middle-class youth.	WASP middle-class youth.

Summary

Each of us is born into an ongoing society. What makes societies possible is the fact that man has the capacity to create and use *symbols.* With these symbols man creates *culture,* a term that refers basically to the ideas and techniques shared in a society. These ideas and techniques enable man to learn from other men and from experience and to adapt to and survive in an amazing number of physical environments.

Notes

1. M. Harris. "The Cultural Ecology of India's Sacred Cattle," *Cultural Anthropology,* **7** (1966), 51–66.
2. H. Ruesch, *Top of the World,* (New York: Harper and Row, 1950; Pocket Books, 1951), pp. 87–88.
3. G. Suttles, *The Moral Order of a Slum* (Chicago: University of Chicago Press, 1968), pp. 68–71.
4. O. Lewis, *La Vida: A Puerto Rican Family in the Culture of Poverty—San Juan and New York* (New York: Random House, Inc., 1966), p. xiv.
5. M. Harrington, *The Other America: Poverty in the United States* (New York: Macmillan Publishing Co., Inc., 1962).
6. T. Gladwin, *Poverty U.S.A.* (Boston: Little, Brown and Company, 1967).
7. The volume edited by Eleanor Burke Leacock contains, for example, articles by sixteen sociologists and anthropologists critical of Lewis. E. B. Leacock, ed, *The Culture of Poverty: A Critique* (New York: Simon & Schuster, Inc., 1971).
8. Perhaps Lewis's most articulate supporter is Walter Miller. See, for example, "The Elimination of the American Lower Class as a National Policy: A Critique of the Ideology of the Poverty Movement of the 1960s," in D. Moynihan, ed., *On Understanding Poverty* (New York: Basic Books, 1968), pp. 360–316.
9. A balanced discussion of the reasons it is so difficult to demonstrate the relative merits of the "cultural," "situational," and "psychological maiming" explanations for the behavior of the poor can be found in S. Spilerman and D. Elesh, "Alternative Conceptions of Poverty and Their Implications for Income Maintenance," *Social Problems,* **18** (1971), 358–373.
10. See, for example, J. M. Goering, "The Emergence of Ethnic Interests: A Case of Serendipity," *Social Forces,* **49** (1971), 379–384.
11. The following section draws heavily on A. Greeley, *Why Can't They Be Like Us: Facts and Fallacies About Ethnic Differences and Group Conflicts in America* (New York: Institute of Human Relations Press, 1969).
12. Ibid., p. 34
13. Ibid., p. 35
14. M. Zborowski "Cultural Components in Response to Pain," *Journal of Social Issues,* **8** (1952), 16–30.
15. A. M. Greeley, "Political Attitudes Among American White Ethnics," *Public Opinion Quarterly,* **36** (1972), 213–220.
16. D. H. Clark, G. S. Lesser, and G. Fifer, "Mental Abilities of Young Children from Different Cultural and Social Class Backgrounds." Paper read at meetings of American Psychological Association, 1964. An interesting study on the college level is D. W. Sue and B. A. Kirk, "Differential Characteristics of Japanese-American and Chinese-American College Students," *Journal of Counseling Psychology,* **20** (1973), 142–148.
17. See, for example, W. Labov, "The Logic of Nonstandard English," in D. P. Giglioli, ed., *Language and Social Context* (Middlesex, England: Penguin Books, 1972), pp. 174–215.
18. J. M. Yinger, "Subculture and Contraculture," *American Sociological Review,* **25** (1960), p. 630.

19. T. Roszak, *The Making of the Counter-Culture* (Garden City, N.Y.: Doubleday & Company, Inc., 1969). Also see D. Horowitz, M. Lerner, and C. Pyes, eds., *Counterculture and Revolution* (New York: Random House, Inc., 1972).

20. K. Westhues, *Society's Shadow: Studies in the Sociology of Countercultures* (Toronto: McGraw-Hill-Ryerson, 1972), pp. 10–11.

21. C. Reich, *The Greening of America* (New York: Random House, Inc., 1970).

22. See R. S. Denisoff and M. Pugh, "Roszak and Reich Return to the Garden: A Note," in R. S. Denisoff, O. Callahan, M. H. Levine, eds., *Theories and Paradigms in Sociology* (Itasca, Illinois: F. E. Peacock Press, 1974), pp. 426–430.

23. Reich, op cit., p. 216.

24. Brigitte Berger, "'People Work'—The Youth Culture and the Labor Market," *The Public Interest,* **35** (1974), 55–66; also see P. Berger and B. Berger, "Blueing of America," *New Republic* (April 13, 1971), 20–23.

25. Reich, op cit., pp. 169–170.

26. P. Nobile, ed., *The Consciousness III Controversy* (New York: Pocket Books, 1971).

27. See T. A. Lambert, "Generations and Change: Toward a Theory of Generations as a Force in Historical Process," *Youth and Society,* **4** (1972), 21–45.

FIVE

Have You Ever Seen a Society?

What Is Society?

SOCIETY IS ONE of those words that we use freely in our daily conversation but that seems to defy definition. What and whom do we mean by "society" in such phrases as "Society encourages . . ." or "Society forces us to . . ." or "Society disapproves of . . ."? Clearly, *society* is sometimes a shorthand way of referring to *something* about the rules and customs and relationships within a particular large group. Is there any more to the concept of society than this? Does it refer to anything "real"? Could an astronaut see a society from Skylab? No. All he can see is the planet Earth with its water and land masses. Could the pilot and passengers of a jet see a society as they pass over a given chunk of land? Again, no. They see people and buildings and trees and automobiles but not American society or French society or German society.

Are there such things as societies? *Society* is a word sociologists use to describe relationships that we can observe the results of but that we can't see or touch as we could, say, a rock or a chicken or a football. Again, *society* is a word sociologists use to refer to customs, rules, and sets of political and economic relationships among a particular group of people. We can see the people, but we can't touch or see the relationships or rules or customs. Does this mean that the term *society* does not refer to anything real, that the football *team* is not as *real* as the football? No, it means that we don't have to be able to see or touch or smell something for it to be real. Consider, for example, a mosaic. It is made up of rocks and pebbles. They are real. So is the mosaic. But they are not identical. What distinguishes a mosaic from a sack full of pebbles is that the pebbles that make up the mosaic are in a certain distinctive physical relationship to one another, light ones here, dark ones, skinny ones, dull ones, there.

It would be incorrect to say that the mosaic is only a bunch of pebbles: it is a number of pebbles *in a certain relationship to one another.* Dump the pebbles that make up the mosaic back into a sack and you no longer have a mosaic, just a bunch of pebbles. It there a difference between an ocean wave and ten gallons of water? Between a triangle and three straight lines? Between a *person* and 120 assorted pounds of bone, blood, and hair? Between a television and 60 pounds of wire, plastic, and glass? In each case there *is* a difference, of course, and the source of the difference is the *relationship* between the parts when those parts are put into a certain kind of relationship rather than into another kind of relationship.

When we speak about mosaics or triangles or ocean waves, or television sets, we are basically talking about *physical* relationships between parts: one part is next to or under or on top of another. When we speak of relationships between people we are talking not only about physical relationships, like who lives near or far from whom, but about legal, economic, emotional, and intellectual ties and relationships between people that are as real as physical relationships.

A football team is not only eleven people in funny clothes; it is also eleven people who share certain ideas, who follow certain rules, whose behavior is

It would be incorrect to say that a mosaic is only a bunch of pebbles.

coordinated in such a way that they don't all try to run with the ball and they don't trip over each other. Again, what you can see, touch, and smell is only a part of what makes up a team. You can see the *results* of the relationships but not the actual relationships. Without the relationships you'd simply see eleven guys in funny outfits stumbling over each other. Take eleven strangers, refuse to tell them what position each is to play, and refuse to let them discuss any kind of strategy. Just hand one of them a football and tell them that you want them to start playing against a *team*; then you blow the whistle, watch the strangers get creamed. There *is* a difference between eleven stray bodies and a team, despite the fact that if both the team and the strangers were just sitting on their respective benches you couldn't tell them apart.

Consider the College All-Stars, who almost yearly lose to the winners of the Super Bowl. Are the Super Bowl champions all that much better? Man for man the answer is probably no. Why then do the All-Stars get beaten nearly every year? Simple. The championship team has played together for some time. There is a set of relationships between them. The quarterback knows which way his end will turn in a given "down and out" situation. The All-Stars are together for only a few weeks. They have all of the skills but lack the relationships. A star quarterback from LSU or Stanford is not going to know the habits of the All-American tight end from USC or the wide receiver from Texas.

The point we are trying to make is that there is a difference between groups and individuals even though individual members form the groups, that a group is more than a haphazard collection of individuals, and that groups are "real" entities.

A society is a certain kind of group. What is it that makes any group a "real" entity, be it a society or a community or an organization or a family? The *relationships,* the *rules* by which those relationships function, and the *consequences* of those relationships.

Consider a master and a slave. They are both human beings. To the sociologist, both are not only people but, more important, they are people who are in a certain *relationship* to each other. One owns the other. The master has the power to kill or sell or whip the slave; the slave has virtually no power over his owner. That relationship is as real as the water each displaces when he gets into the bathtub.

Many sociologists call such a relationship a *social structure:* slavery is a social structure made up of masters and slaves. This is a very real structure to the people in it. They act on the fact that they are either masters or slaves. The master has a great deal of freedom, whereas the slave does not. If the slave decides to move to the next town, he places himself open to various forms of punishment. Yet the master can do the same with impunity.

Because we rely so much on our senses to tell us about the world, it is sometimes hard to accept the idea that something (like a society) can be real even though we can't touch it or see it or smell it. A large part of the sociologist's job is pointing out things that can't be seen or touched or smelled but that we can see the *results* of and that affect our lives every day.

As Peter Berger eloquently describes it:

> Society is external to ourselves. It surrounds us, encompasses our life on all sides. We are *in* society, located in specific sectors of the social system. This location predetermines and predefines almost everything we do, from language to etiquette, from the religious beliefs we hold to the probability that we will commit suicide. Our wishes are not taken into consideration in this matter of social location, and our intellectual resistance to what society prescribes or proscribes avails very little at best, and frequently nothing. Society, as objective and external fact, confronts us especially in the form of coercion. Its institutions pattern our actions and even shape our expectations. They reward us to the extent that we stay within our assigned performances. If we step out of these assignments, society has at its disposal an almost infinite variety of controlling and coercing agencies. The sanctions of society are able, at each moment of existence, to isolate us among our fellow men, to subject us to ridicule, to deprive us of life itself. The law and the morality of society can produce elaborate justifications for each one of these sanctions, and most of our fellow men will approve if they are used against us in punishment for our deviance. Finally, we are located in society not only in space but in time. Our society is a historical entity that extends temporally beyond any individual biography. Society antedates us and it will survive us. It was there before we were born and it will be there after we are dead. Our lives are but episodes in its majestic march through time. In sum, society is the walls of our imprisonment in history.[1]

When we talk about societies, we are talking about a number of people in a set of real relationships. The people involved in these relationships we can see. The relationships we cannot see or smell or taste, but they are the reality encompassed in the concept of "society." *The reality is in the relationships.*

The Characteristics of Groups

We have been suggesting that a society is a certain kind of group and that groups are real. What is a group? How do you tell a group from a stray collection of strangers? A group, be it a family, a gang, a business organization, a political party, or a society has at least these four characteristics:

1. The members interact with each other over some period of time. They communicate through words, gestures, writing, or music and in doing so affect and influence each other's behavior.
2. Each member of a group identifies himself as part of the group and is recognized as part of the group by the other members. There is in the minds of the members the idea that they are somehow distinct from other groups and that some people belong ("we") and others do not ("they"). Sit in a restaurant with a date and tell your date a funny story. The waiter joins in the laughter. You glare at him and mutter to yourself, "Who made him a partner?" He doesn't belong to the little group composed of you and your date.
3. Each member of the group is expected by the others to accept certain responsibilities and duties and to abide by certain norms, and he is also entitled to certain privileges as a result of membership.
4. There is a division of labor in the activities carried out by the members of the group. Some lead, others follow. Some cook, others provide food. Some teach, others learn. Whatever the nature and the activities of the group, some sort of arrangement is made that results in different people doing different things and making different contributions to the goals of the group. This is so whether it's a group of friends or a family or a business organization or a society.

A society is a group. It is different from other groups—like families, gangs, political parties, business organizations, or communities—in a number of important respects: (1) a society is larger than other groups and contains other groups. It's not a subgroup of any other group. Perhaps the only thing members of the subgroups have in common is the fact that they all are part of the same society. (2) A society has a distinctive culture shared by most or all of its members. (3) The addition of new members and the replacement of old members of a society almost always occurs through biological reproduction and the socialization of the newborn members. A society doesn't have membership drives or a personnel office. (4) A society lasts longer than the lifetimes of the individual members. (5) A society is self-sufficient and independent of any outside group. It possesses (or controls its citizens' access to other societies that possess) the resources, power, rules, and technology required for the society to continue in its existing form over time. As Alex Inkeles observes:

According to this definition, the ordinary township in the United States, despite its high material culture and complex organization, would not be considered a society. It does not have the power to organize its own defense, and as a rule to deal with a murder it is obliged to rely on county or state police, courts, jails, and the like. A monastery would not qualify, even if its rules covered murder, because it makes no provision for sexual recruitment of new members. But these are essentially technical reservations. A simpler, although somewhat macabre, way to think about whether a group qualifies as a society would be to imagine that all other communities in the world except this one were suddenly to disappear. If there were a good chance that the surviving community would go forward in substantially its present form through subsequent generations, then it qualifies as a society. Most primitive tribes, however small, and virtually all nation states clearly meet this requirement. If a community could not survive under such a severe test, or could do so only by developing or elaborating many new institutional arrangements, such as a system of law and justice for which it formerly depended on a larger social system, then it does not qualify as a true society.[2]

We have insisted in various ways over the last few pages that terms like *society* and *group* describe relationships between people and that the relationships are as real as the people engaged in them. The rest of this book deals with the consequences and effects upon us of the relationships in which all of us are involved.

Look, Jane! See Society Sing and Dance!—A Problem with Language

Let us add a warning about an important point. We've argued that a relationship between people is as real as the individual people are. Nevertheless, the language used to describe *individuals* is not necessarily the proper language for describing *relationships.* Sociologists have not yet developed a language that is completely appropriate for describing relationships, so they sometimes fall back on the vocabulary of individuals or use it as a way of summarizing briefly what would otherwise take many pages or many books to describe. Although they are quite aware that societies do not have heads, arms, legs, brains, gall bladders, kidneys, and so on, sociologists (and laymen) often speak as though society *were* a person.

We say, "The society distributes wealth unequally" when we mean something like, "The nature of political and economic relationships in this society is such that members of certain groups tend consistently to receive much larger shares of the society's wealth than members of other groups." We say that society "approves of," "encourages," "discourages," "creates," "lives," "dies," or does other things that a set of relationships simply cannot do. Relationships don't really die, get sick or well. Relationships do not hop, skip, or jump, become hungry or thirsty or angry or happy. As you can see in the quote from Berger several pages earlier, the sort of phraseology appropriate for individuals lends itself to quite eloquent and dramatic statements, but it is important that we not take it too literally.

You will notice this language problem particularly in the writings of some sociologists who speak of societies having needs or problems that seem to be fulfilled or resolved magically and automatically. They intend to say something like, "*It is as though* the society knew that this or that situation was causing problems and *as though* some guiding force was changing things to eliminate these problems." The "as though" sometimes gets left out of sociologists' writings; so you, the reader, will have to remember to put it back in as you read their work.

We have argued that "society" is both real and abstract. We are not normally aware of the impact society has on us because it's so hard to visualize. Sociologists who discuss society seem to be sitting on Mount Olympus, the legendary home of the Greek gods, and from this detached position trying to cover what we might call the Big Picture. In our daily lives we are aware of only bits and pieces of this Big Picture. We are aware of the people and groups with which we interact daily—our families, our friends, our classmates, our coworkers, our neighbors—rather than the patterns and connections that the sociologist sees when he tries to understand and describe how all of these small-scale relationships fit together. The remainder of this chapter will follow this "natural sociological" order and discuss families and friendship groups, formal and informal relationships and groups, and finally the Big Picture: cities and types of societies.

How Do Groups Differ?

We deal with many groups in the course of a lifetime, and on any given day we interact in several different kinds of relationships. What characteristics of these groups should we pay attention to? Three of the dimensions sociologists have found to be significant in understanding differences in groups and their functioning are *size, complexity,* and *emotional intensity.*

The *size* of a group is all-important as it determines the kind of relationships that can take place within it. The smaller the unit, the more intimate and intense the relationship can become. The family is a compact, tightly knit group held together by blood, economics, and high emotional intensity. We may not hold the people we work with or attend lectures with in such close regard. Our emotional commitment to our college or home town certainly is not as great,[3] partly because these involve many thousands of people.

Complexity refers to what a group does. A group of girls who form a fan club to praise their favorite television or recording star is relatively simple. They come together to listen to records, admire their hero, and write fan letters. A business organization with a multitude of tasks is a much more complex and diversified group. Each department has a different assignment. In a recording company the A&R (artists and repertoire) people are concerned with the kind of sound on the record whereas the accounting department cares only about how the record sells; neither department has more than the vaguest idea of the nature of the other's work or problems.

Emotional intensity varies from group to group. Generally, the smaller and the less complex the group, the more emotional it becomes. The members also feel less concern about the welfare of those *outside* the group and they are more likely to be upset if the relationship should come to an end.

The German sociologist Ferdinand Toënnies, writing in the nineteenth century, distinguished between two types of relationships and two kinds of societies based on such relationships. The three properties—size, complexity, and emotional intensity—were at the heart of his distinctions. He argued that society had traditionally been based on one kind of relationship but that as a result of industrialization the industrialized nations were rapidly being based on the other. He was not particularly enthusiastic about the change.

According to Toënnies, traditional society was based on a *Gemeinschaft* ("community") or highly personal relationships in which people were bound to each other by emotional ties—like love, affection, and mutual respect—by kinship ties, and by tradition. The agricultural society he was describing was a simple one and a small one, a society in which people were aware of their great similarities. Other people were valued for their personal qualities and not what they could do for one. People cared about one another. They felt responsible for one another's welfare. *Gemeinschaft* relations were based upon *intimacy* and *tradition.* Although the relationships were simple ones, tradition imposed some form of social regulation upon these relationships. For example, the courtship process—when people began courting, whom one married—was influenced by tradition. Frequently marriages were arranged by the parents or the elders of the group.

Table 5-1. *Gemeinschaft* and *Gesellschaft* Societies

	Societal Type	
Social Characteristic	*Gemeinschaft*	*Gesellschaft*
Dominant social relationship	Fellowship Kinship Neighborliness	Exchange Rational calculation
Central institutions	Family law Extended kin group	State Capitalistic economy
The individual in the social order	Self	Person
Characteristic form of wealth	Land	Money
Type of law	Family law	Law of contracts
Ordering of institutions	Family life City life Rural village life Town life	 Rational life Cosmopolitan life
Type of social control	Consensus Folkways and mores Religion	Convention Legislation Public opinion

*See Chapter Sixteen, "Social Change," on the evolutionary aspects of these forms.

Source: Don Martindale, *The Nature and Types of Sociological Theory* (Boston: Houghton Mifflin Company, 1960), p. 84.

In Toënnies's view, the *Gesellschaft* ("society") or seemingly impersonal relationship (what the United States is today) finds people dealing with each other at an impersonal level. People are faces in a crowd. Other people are means to an end. They perform services for us and once we have paid them their fees we owe them nothing. They owe us nothing. Our responsibilities for one another begin and end with whatever is written in a formal contract. If the bus driver, the waitress, the professor, the boss have personal lives outside our formal relationship it is a matter of indifference to us. Results count. People don't.

The *Gesellschaft* relationship is simply one of economic use or utility. The economic system of a social group, of course, is dictated by that group. In the *Gesellschaft* relationship, the economic system is impersonal and complex, stressing rationality. People engage in economic activity in large organizations governed by rules and regulations. Occupations are predefined by special educational requirements. People frequently must submit to tests in order to become firemen, policemen, physicians, lawyers, university professors, and even garbage men. The duties of each role are painfully detailed in manuals and other work guides. Over time, because of the specialization of occupations, jobs increasingly come under the umbrella of large corporations, where people are separated by divisions, departments, and floors. In universities, biology professors rarely know teachers of sociology, although they belong to the same faculty.

Put quite simply, the *Gemeinschaft* relationship stresses the individual; the *Gesellschaft* focuses upon the object (see Table 5–1). In the first case, people are ends in themselves. In the latter, people are means to some end. These relationships provide sociologists with a means to categorize groups.

Primary Groups

Charles Horton Cooley, one of the first American sociologists, introduced the notion of *primary* groups in 1909.[4] The primary group was presented as having a "face-to-face" relationship marked by a high amount of cooperation, permanence, and intimacy. The group possesses a "we" feeling of belonging. The face-to-face aspect suggests that the group is small. Cooley identified only a few groups that fit his definition: "the family, the play-group of children, and the neighborhood or community group of elders."[5] In such a group individuals enjoy a warm and *seemingly* unstructured existence. It is a group in which we can relax, just hang out, do what we want to. It is *apparently* a world of nonwork, as play activity or chores undertaken in the family do not seem to demand participation or have reward systems (mothers, fathers, and children don't get promotions, raises, or medals for good performance). Within these primary groups people *learn* the whys and wherefores of social living. Cooley called primary groups "the nursery of human nature" (see the next chapter, "Socialization"). Groups that appear to be without membership requirements, or specialized roles that people must play, nevertheless do make demands upon the individual.

The family is perhaps the purest example of a primary relationship.

The peer group,* one of social equals, is a case in point. It is a group in which a child participates. The peer group, or "play-group," as Cooley called it, has some social structure and has membership requirements. Frederick Elkin and Gerald Handel have provided us with at least three characteristics.[6] The peer group, they claimed, has *age requirements.* All members must be about the same age. Just look at any group of children playing in a schoolyard or on the street and this fact becomes obvious. Even groups of little toddlers, two to three years of age, have membership barriers. The ability to speak at least the most simple sentences is a necessity for membership.

Within peer groups members generally have different amounts of power and prestige: there are leaders and followers. Activities are organized around what *some* members want to do. Others just go along. The biggest or toughest kid

* *Peer group* is a term generally applied to preadult groups. However, a group of adults who are social equals is also technically a peer group.

Peer groups.

on the block may be a leader. Leaders may also be chosen on the basis of some other quality, such as athletic ability or physical attractiveness.

The peer group is centered around some focus or interest. As the members get older their common interests become the glue that holds the group together. Preteen girls may band together to write and speak the praises of a teen-age idol. All the while the child in the peer group is informally learning to participate in society, to share, to get along with others.

It is hard to find an example of a pure primary group (or a pure secondary group). This notion of "primaryness" is basically a matter of degree. A family, in principle, is about the purest example we can find of a primary relationship. A primary relationship is a relationship in which we know each person as a complete individual rather than, say, just as a merchant or a mailman or a teacher. It is a relationship in which we're prepared to excuse and forgive people if they do something wrong. It is a relationship in which we take off the masks we sometimes wear when we're away from it. It is a relationship that we value for its own sake rather than because we can profit from it in some way. "I enjoy the relationship" is sufficient justification for continuing a primary relationship. A primary relationship is also one in which there's no specific set of obligations that, if fulfilled, let us say we've done our job: a mother or brother can't say, "My office is closed. Come back tomorrow after nine." Nor does a mother say, "My contract doesn't require me to dust or vacuum; I just cook and sew," or "I will put on bandaids but for enemas you've got to see the specialist down the hall." Finally, some sort of emotional investment is necessary for a primary relationship to be successful, whereas you can get a shoeshine or a mail delivery or a six-pack of beer quite easily without having any kind of emotional ties to the other people in the transaction.

Secondary Groups

Cooley never used the term *secondary group,* but it seems to be the natural term to use to discuss the opposite of a primary group. When sociologists use this term they mean all groups that are not primary. A secondary group is generally large, cold, anonymous, and, most important, *impersonal.*[7] Secondary groups can be any unit, from a class of students enrolled in introductory sociology to either of America's two major political parties. There are many types of secondary groups.

Organizations are large secondary groups. Sociologists think of an organization as a group of human beings deliberately formed to pursue or seek some goals or combination of goals.[8] Some examples of organizations are record companies, schools, churches, prisons, and the armed services. Etzioni notes three important characteristics of organizations:[9]

1. Organizations are structured in such a way as to help the unit to achieve its goals. Parts of each organization are assigned jobs, tasks, and responsibilities and are provided the power to perform certain acts that will allow them to

achieve their goal. Record companies have publicity departments to advertise their latest releases. The U.S. Army has a particular unit that is in charge of feeding the troops in the field, and yet another is concerned with providing ammunition for its guns. Universities have many departments that serve students interested in studying many different subjects.

2. Organizations are constantly engaged in the process of self-correction and redirection. Leaders of an organization must constantly direct and reinforce the commitment of its members and the departments they belong to. However, as we will see, organizations can easily be distracted from their original goals. For example, parts of the unit may find it convenient to do their own thing regardless of whether or not it is of any help to the goals of the organization. Union leaders may find it to their advantage to maintain cordial relations with corporation executives rather than getting the best contract for their rank and file.[10]

3. Organization leaders attempt to use people in the most efficient way possible. People with the proper qualifications and good organizational performance are rewarded and promoted, and people who do not appear to meet the standards of the organizations are dismissed or let go. This process applies to the drummer who cannot count to four in a rock band as well as to the corporation president who bankrupts the company.[11]

Organizations can be further subdivided in terms of the *formality* of the organization. Organizations vary in the extent to which they are *formal* or *informal.*

Formal Organizations

The formal organization is a structure *determined by management,* which provides a blueprint for its operation. This blueprint includes job specifications, lines of communication, rules and regulations for conduct, wages, standards of quality, and so on. A police department is such an organization: every rank and responsibility is clearly stated in a manual. At a university, student standing and standards of performance and quality are also formally defined. A student passes or fails a class according to a standard that is expressed by the letter grades of A, B, C, D, and F.

One interesting and dramatic illustration of a formal organization is the Mafia or Cosa Nostra. The formal organization stems from the "family," which is headed by a "don" or "*capo.*" The *capo* heads an almost military line of command. He commands a counselor (*consigliere*) and a series of lieutenants (*caporegima*), who in turn have "soldiers." The *caporegima* and their soldiers are given special tasks to pursue, such as numbers, loan sharking, and prostitution.

Formal organizations have rules and regulations. Robert Anderson presents four basic regulations of the Cosa Nostra:

Table 5-2. A Formal Organization (the Cosa Nostra)

Source: The Challenge of Crime in a Free Society, A Report of the President's Commission on Law Enforcement and Administration of Justice (Washington, D.C.: U.S. Government Printing Office, 1967), p. 194.

BOSS

Consigliere (Counselor)

Underboss

Caporegima (Lieutenant) | Caporegima (Lieutenant) | Caporegima (Lieutenant) | Caporegima (Lieutenant) | Caporegima (Lieutenant)

Soldiers

(Members grouped under Lieutenants)

Corruption: Police and Public Officials

Through threats, assault, and murder, enforce discipline over members, non-members and fronts on orders from leader.

With and through non-member associates and fronts—participate in, control or influence

Exercising Control in Multi-State Area

Legitimate Industry	*Illegal Activities*
Food products	Gambling (numbers, policy, dice, bookmaking)
Realty	Narcotics
Restaurants	Loansharking
Garbage disposal	Labor racketeering
Produce	Extortion
Garment manufacturing	Alcohol
Bars and taverns	Others
Waterfront	
Securities	
Labor unions	
Vending machines	
Others	

1. Members of the Mafia help one another and avenge every injury of a fellow member.
2. Members help and defend any other member who is under arrest or being prosecuted by the law.
3. Members divide all profits along lines suggested by the capo.
4. Members maintain silence about the organization upon pain of death.[12]

Bureaucracy: The Ultimate Formal Organization

A bureaucracy, according to German sociologist Max Weber, is a group organized in such a rational way as to set rules and regulations and to have people obey them through the use of rewards and punishment, all in the effort to achieve some goal.[13] These rules and regulations, rewards and penalties are all designed to generate *efficiency* in five ways:

1. Each bureaucracy has a high degree of specialization. Each part has special tasks. Every bureau, every job assignment has very clearly defined contributions to be made to the organization.

2. Positions are ranked on the basis of "high or "low," or in an *hierarchical* fashion. The higher up the bureaucratic ladder, the more the authority and responsibility. President Harry S Truman had a famous motto on his desk in the Oval Office: "The buck stops here." From positions of authority individuals issue commands and give orders to those below them.

3. Rules define what people do. These rules limit what a person is allowed to undertake. For example, a carrier is to deliver the mail, not sell stamps or issue money orders. This eliminates any informal overlap because the bureaucracy assumes that each individual has one specific skill and no more.

4. Individuals are hired, promoted, and rewarded on the basis of ability, education, and technical knowledge. A sociologist is hired by a university or a government agency on the basis of the number of courses he has taken and degrees he has. The *personality* of the candidate is not supposed to have any bearing on the hiring, just his *qualifications.* Knowledge is the main criterion for employment in a bureaucracy.

5. Each position in the organization has different rewards of money, power, and prestige (see Chapter Nine, "Stratification"). The possibility of advancement is the individual's incentive for doing his job. An employee is rewarded for improving his skills and for the length of time he remains in the organization. This system promotes both efficiency and loyalty.

By combining these five characteristics a bureaucracy should be technically efficient, "with a premium placed on precision, speed, expert control, continuity, discretion, and optimal returns on input. The structure is one which approaches the complete elimination of personalized relationships and non-rational considerations (hostility, anxiety . . .)."[14]

Of course, anyone who has dealt with a bureaucracy, such as the U.S. Army, the campus registrar, or the welfare office, is painfully aware that bureaucracies do not work the way Weber described them. There are many criticisms of bureaucracies. Two of the more persuasive criticisms come from Thorstein Veblen and Robert Michels and Karl Mannheim.

Thorstein Veblen described bureaucracies as causing "trained incapacity," a state in which an agency can respond in only one way, regardless of what the conditions may be. Recall the famous Army dictum, "There is a right way of doing things, a wrong way of doing things, and the Army way of doing things." As many new soldiers quickly discover, the Army "way of doing things" is frequently not appropriate to the situation.

Robert Merton broke this criticism down into four propositions:

1. Bureaucracy demands the same response to situations and strict devotion to the rules.
2. Bureaucracy leads to an absolute devotion to the rules, thus losing track of the purpose of the rules.
3. Situations arise which are not covered by the rules.
4. The very elements which make for efficiency and rationality in some situations may produce just the opposite results under different conditions.[15]

The other major criticism comes from Robert Michels and Karl Mannheim: both men criticized the bureaucracy for not considering the human or individual factor in bureaucracies.

In his influential book *Political Parties,* Robert Michels said that "democracy is inconceivable without organization." Michels was saying that people could band together and form an organization that would be a "weapon of the weak in their struggling with the strong."[16] By uniting in groups, people could rationally and efficiently pool their efforts to improve their conditions, *or so it seemed.*

By examining the socialist and trade union movements of Western Europe, Michels found that "organization means oligarchy." An oligarchy is a ruling group of people in an organization or a collection of organizations that rule a society. In the process of describing how oligarchies appear, Michels gave birth to what has come to be called the *iron law of oligarchy.*

The "iron law" posits that each organization has certain internal tasks that must be performed if the group is to survive. However, not all of the members have either the skills or the desire to perform these tasks. Those people who have both qualities, skill and desire, rapidly assume positions of responsibility and gain authority within the organization. As time goes on, these leaders become primarily concerned with their own positions and power. Michels wrote:

> The consciousness of power always produces vanity, an undue belief in personal greatness. The desire to dominate, for good or for evil, is universal. . . . In the leader, the consciousness of his personal worth, and of the need which the mass feels for guidance, combine to induce in his mind a recognition of his own superiority (real or supposed), and awake, in addition, that spirit of command which exists in the germ in every man born of woman.[17]

At this point the leaders become almost totally concerned with preserving their own positions rather than actively pursuing the goals of the organization.

Union and political leaders, Michels contended, become more concerned with being reelected to their power positions than with the needs and desires of the membership. In this way, he argued, the human quest for personal power interferes with the purposes of the organization. Michels argued that no matter how democratic the goals of an organization, *inevitably* the leaders will take over the organization and convince themselves that their personal interest in their positions is really a sign of their concern for the welfare of the membership.

Karl Mannheim, in *Man and Society in an Age of Reconstruction,* also pointed to the difference between the organization and its members. The organization has two basic perspectives or ways of thinking. The *substantial* perspective involves seeing the total or Big Picture. In the *functional* perspective each task is compartmentalized. The functional perspective is illustrated by the proverbial "Blind men and the elephant": each man knows only the part of the elephant he has touched.[18] What seems rational to the leaders of the organization may not seem rational to the rank and file. The organization, then, in order to continue operating, must force the compliance of its members. Individuals lose track of the organization's goals and become "bureaucrats." Mannheim feels that bureaucrats "cannot see the forest for the trees." They do not see the total picture. Note that *bureaucrat* and *bureaucracy* can be used formally in describing a type of organization, or they can be used as an insult. (Sociologists usually use the terms in a formal sense.)

Informal Organization

The informal organization is defined as *those relationships between members and parts of the organization that go beyond the formal requirements.* Ways of communicating not spelled out in the management blueprint and friendships among coworkers are a part of the informal organization. The concept of informal organization "is a very convenient tool," writes sociologist Nicos P. Mouzelis, "as it draws the attention of the student of bureaucracy to the inherent and continuous tension between rational coordination of activities and the spontaneous pattern formation of interpersonal relations and unofficial values and beliefs."[19]

The informal organization of any group is defined both by its members and by the tradition of the organization. The informal relations both *complement* and *work against* the formal structure of the organization.

Gresham Sykes, in *The Society of Captives,* provides an example of how informal relations allow an organization to achieve at least part of its goals. Prisons, according to Sykes, have three tasks to perform. They must (1) control the inmates; (2) reform them; and (3) also take care of their daily needs. However, once the prisoner is behind the cold gray walls the power of the custodians to motivate him is limited. The number of incentives that can be given the captive is quite small. Force can be used only when justified. The situation is unique in that prison officials "find themselves in the uncomfortable position of needing the labor of their captives far more than do the captives themselves: and at the same time the officials prohibit (and are prohibited from) the use of effective rewards and punishments, to secure conscientious performance."[20]

The task of the captors, then, is to motivate the prisoners to adhere to the formal goals of the prison: (1) control of the inmates is maintained by the use of rewards (earlier release, parole, job assignments) and punishment; (2) punishment and rewards, in turn, influence the inmates' attitudes toward reform; (3) the goals of control and rehabilitation, however, must give way to the everyday problems of feeding, housing, and clothing the residents of the prison. The formal organization of the prison is not enough. Therefore informal relations in the prison become very important.

Consider the role of the correctional officer or guard who must perform certain tasks. He cannot accomplish these tasks without the help of the prisoners in his charge. Therefore, he must resort to informal means to accomplish the formal goals. Sykes suggests:

> To a large extent the guard is dependent on inmates for the satisfactory performance of his duties; and like many individuals in positions of power, the guard is evaluated in terms of the conduct of the men he controls. A troublesome, noisy, dirty cellblock reflects on the guard's ability to "handle" prisoners and this ability forms an important component of the merit rating which is used as the basis for pay raises and promotions. . . . A guard cannot rely on the direct application of force to achieve compliance nor can he easily depend on threats of punishment. And if the guard does insist on constantly using the last few negative sanctions available to the institution—if the guard turns in Charge Slip after Charge Slip for every violation of the rules which he encounters—he becomes burdensome to the top officials of the prison bureaucratic staff who realize only too well that their apparent dominance rests on some degree of cooperation. A system of power which can enforce its rules only by bringing its formal machinery of accusation, trial, and punishment into play at every turn will soon be lost in a haze of pettifogging detail.[21]

In order to gain cooperation the guard resorts to numerous informal methods to motivate his charges, including special favors for his crew. These favors may be passed on to other inmates in return for other favors. What results is a bartering system of favors. Immate workers gain power over their fellows by being close to the custodians. It is to their advantage to maintain the status quo. The guard, in turn, is happy to have a clean cellblock and an apparently well-run unit.

In the instance of the correctional institutions, informal relations between administrator and inmate allow the organization partially to accomplish its goals.[22]

Dean Harper and Frederick Emmert found a similar routine in the U.S. Postal Service. In order to accomplish the *formal* requirements of the organization, *informal* practices became all-important.[23]

According to the U.S. Postal Service, the postman was to follow certain rules and regulations. He was *required:*

1. To deliver mail in the *order* indicated by his route book.
2. Not to use a private car or truck for delivering or carrying mail.
3. To place mail in a mailbox or give it to the person living at the address.
4. To deliver the material on the day he received it unless told otherwise by a supervisor.
5. Not to delay the mail in any way.
6. Not to walk on grass or take any other shortcut from house to house.

However, the mail carrier systematically violated these rules, thus *helping* the Post Office Department to accomplish its goals:

1. The carrier arranged his route so as to finish as quickly as possible. He would use countless routes until he found the most convenient, which was hardly ever in keeping with the order book. In the process the mail was delivered with greater haste and efficiency. On heavy days, if the prescribed route had been followed the postman would not have finished in time.

2. The use of a private car was common despite the regulation against it. The auto provided two major advantages: one could get to the route quickly and could also use its trunk as a relay box, thus cutting down the number of times the carrier had to return to a box. All of this saved time.

3. Postmen deposited mail where it was convenient for both the patron and themselves. The convenience factor was often at odds with the department regulations.

4–5. Mail, especially third- and fourth-class mail, was frequently saved until a light day, such as Saturday. This allowed the postman to get important mail delivered the day it arrived, on time, and also minimized the time required to put up or "case" the morning mail. This was, of course, a delay of *some* mail.

6. Mailmen *always* walked on lawns unless specifically requested not to do so. Some cut through back yards and even hopped rooftops in some areas with large apartment houses.

All of these violations allowed for the swift and more efficient operation of the Postal Service. When being timed by supervisors, however, postmen conformed exactly to work rules. When the supervisor came along to time him, the carrier painstakingly waited for a bus, never crossed a lawn, thus adding minutes if not hours to the route. As many strikers have discovered, the ideal method of stopping or curtailing production is simply to obey all the rules as outlined by the supervisor. Informal relationships can become *innovative* as they create ways of goal achievement that go beyond the formal rules and regulations (see Merton on innovation in Chapter Eleven, "Deviance").

The best way for a record company to get a hit record is to have your local Top Forty radio station play it. "Airplay" is the name of the game for record companies. Get three or four AM stations in major cities such as New York, Chicago, Detroit, and Los Angeles to air the record and it is a hit. The reason for this curious situation is that Top Forty charts or hit lists are based on what is played in twenty-five major cities. Three or four stations "get behind the record" and it looks like a monster hit. Other stations in other major cities then play it. As simple as this sounds, only 2 percent of the 130 singles released each week get on the charts. Of those, nearly 95 percent are by established singers. Consequently, it is easier to be struck by lightning than to have a "hit" record.[24]

The key to success is to persuade the program director of a radio station to play your "brand-new sensational" record. Now the problem is that there are some 50 companies producing a total of 130 records a week, all competing for three or four open slots on the playlist (a list of records to be played on the radio). *Formally,* record companies have their field people—promotion men—deliver the record to the radio station. It will then be reviewed and on occasion added to the "hit-bound" list. *Informally,* some promotion people use every device possible to get next to the program director. In *rare* cases promotion people have supplied cash, color television sets, airline tickets, and prostitutes to program directors. Generally promotion men try to "gain the trust and friendship" of the program director. This is done in a million small ways. If the promotion person is successful and the program director accepts his opinions as valid then the chances for that salesman's record company are greatly improved.

Informal relations can in some cases support only a portion of the formal goals of an organization while violating others. For example, most major colleges and universities have athletic programs. The winning of championships and the gaining of national recognition are very important for alumni associations and for school administrators because winning brings the school national recognition. On the other hand, the traditional role of the university, believe it or not, is to educate the students. What happens then when one of the star athletes is not capable of dealing with classroom material? Peter J. Lutz, a former UCLA wrestler, illustrated one answer to this question. It was not necessary for him to attend any classes in order to graduate because he could make other arrangements to pass the classes. Lutz was found out when skepticism was expressed over his ability to work a forty-hour week and take classes and maintain a 3.36 (B) grade-point average.[25]

Under questioning, Lutz said that class attendance was "not required" for one science class and that the grade was determined entirely by a paper.

"I had a music class, Music of Brazil," he added. "The teaching assistant in that class is a manager on the football team. . . . I explained my situation to the teaching assistant and he gives me the grade because I am an athlete and I have to work—so he gave a C."

Katz said Lutz had neither attended class nor had he written a paper.

In a science class with a required examination, Lutz said a teaching assistant allowed him to take the exam with him during the evening.

In History 106C, he recounted in testimony, "I went into the teaching assistant's office. He had a review session and said, 'Write down everything I say.' He gave me the test and the blue book. He said: 'You may use your notes.' In my notes were the answers to the exam. I got a B."

In his Development of Jazz class, Lutz said, "If a professor refused or did not want to cooperate with me in taking the exam at a different hour—the class is very large and split into two sections—it would be possible to have someone take the exam for me."[26]

The ultimate in innovative informal relationships is found in the sub rosa or under-the-table activities of bribery, payola, and other illegal acts.

In some situations informal relations may work completely against the formal organization and its goals. One example comes from the sphere of law enforcement. The following quote is from a correctional officer in the California Department of Corrections who felt that the informal relations at San Quentin prison interfered with the formal goals of the prison:

The staff is composed of three types of categories: 1) college students, 2) retired military personnel, and 3) persons who have been with the Department many years. The college student, who works for the CDC, does not take much interest in the Department and its programs because he considers the position as a means to an end. Secondly, assuming the student disagrees with Department policy interpretations, he does not protest so as not to incur the wrath of the administrators of the institution. The retired military person in the CDC takes the line of least resistence in the various institutions since he only works to supplement his government pension. "Old Timers" or persons who have been with the Department resent the new policies of the Department since much of their authority has been taken away from them by the policies. The "Old Timer" resents the two previously mentioned groups because of their indifference to the Department. This attitude, among others, only tends to deepen the gulf between the three general groups. In conclusion the CDC staff can be characterized as operating in a factional and disorganized manner with little regard for the CDC or its inmates.[27]

A similar phenomenon can be spotted in many urban police departments, where informal indoctrination actually interferes with the formal goals of the law enforcement organization. Arthur Niederhoffer describes how informal groups work in the New York City Police Department.[28] In these groups the rookie patrolman quickly learns the major informal ethic of "You gotta be tough, kid, or you'll never last." The ethic of being "tough" frequently goes against the actual purpose of the police department. Paul Chevigny states, "The man who asserts his constitutional rights is just as likely to be treated as a 'wise guy' as the man who openly insults a policeman. To a policeman it is his authority that counts, not the *legality* of his authority."[29]

Yet the role of the police is to enforce the law and protect the rights of the citizen.

Ellwyn R. Stoddard found an informal code operating in a mid-city police department. The acceptance of the code determined the status of a patrolman.

Stoddard reported that if the recruit accepts the code "he is welcomed into the group and given the rights and privileges commensurate with his new status. If he does not, he is classified as a 'goof' and avoided by the rest."[30] The code, according to Stoddard, included the following practices:

Mooching—the act of receiving free coffee, cigarettes, meals, liquor, groceries, or other items either as a consequence of being in an underpaid, undercompensated profession *or* for the possible future acts of favoritism which might be received by the donor.

Chiseling—an activity involving police demands for free admission to entertainment whether connected to police duty or not, price discounts, etc.

Favoritism—the practice of using license tabs, window stickers, or courtesy cards to gain immunity from traffic arrest or citation (sometimes extended to wives, families, and friends of recipient).

Prejudice—situations in which minority groups receive less than impartial, neutral, objective attention, especially those who are less likely to have "influence" in City Hall to cause the arresting officer trouble.

Shopping—the practice of picking up small items such as candy bars, gum, or cigarettes at a store where the door has been accidentally unlocked after business hours.

Extortion—the demands made for advertisements in police magazines or purchase of tickets to police functions, or the "street courts" where minor traffic tickets can be avoided by the payment of cash bail to the arresting officer with no receipt required.[31]

This code in some extreme cases may even condone criminal acts, such as bribery, shakedowns, perjury, and premeditated theft. Police officers who are aware of the code and who merely engage in some minor actions like accepting "free cups of coffee" and free meals choose not to inform upon their brother officers' bluntly illegal acts.[32]

Informal relations, then, can both complement and work against formal aspects of an organization. Ideally, the informal and the formal organization should be pulling in the same direction; however, as we have seen, this is not always the case.

Voluntary Associations

Voluntary associations are the groups people join even when they don't have to do so to make a living. They usually participate in these groups during their spare time and are not paid for their participation. Voluntary associations are usually directed toward one specific goal, but they may also provide pleasure for their members.

A more formal definition is provided by Arnold and Caroline Rose: "A voluntary association develops when a small group of people, finding they have a certain interest (or purpose) in common, agree to act together in order to try to satisfy that interest or achieve that purpose."[33] In this way, voluntary organizations differ from the more formalized bureaucratic structures. Voluntary associations range from the loosely knit American political parties, which charge no dues, have no membership cards, and make few demands upon the membership, to the more structured fraternal organizations like the Masons, which have elaborate rituals and requirements for membership. These include service groups such as the Lions, Rotary, and Kiwanis clubs, political interest groups such as the National Rifle Association, the Air Force Association, or Americans for Democratic Action, and numerous other groups like the Little League, the Red Cross, the League of Women Voters, the Boy Scouts, and parent-teacher groups.

Expressive Voluntary Associations

Expressive groups are those voluntary associations that exist to satisfy the needs of the members within the organization. Sports clubs, hobby clubs, and social clubs are primary examples. Singles clubs, "lonely hearts clubs," and computer-dating services are expressive groups.

Lonely hearts clubs numbered at least 500 in 1961. At one time membership estimates ranged from 100,000 to 4 million.[34]

Following World War II, when people flocked to the large urban centers, they found themselves alone in a strange new environment. In search of friends and companions the new arrivals went to neighborhood bars and dance halls, visited resorts, and joined all sorts of social clubs. Failing in these social situations, some people turned to lonely hearts clubs.[35] The operators of these voluntary associations advertised themselves as "marriage brokers." They arranged for people to meet in the "cold, impersonal city." The operator of one club said, "Many will have to remain lonely, or muster their courage and come to someone like me."[36] Ads in club publications such as *The Western Heart* read:

> *The saddest words of tongue or pen*—"It Might Have Been" . . . just because you have not as yet found your ideal is no reason for you to give up and go on your lonely, desolate and thoroughly miserable way. There are plenty, yes hundreds, of persons just waiting to hear from you—handsome, beautiful, wealthy, home-bodies, sports lovers—they are of assorted descriptions and from every walk of life—perhaps just down the street or in some adjoining city or nearby state. But the first move is up to you—*Are You Up To It?* I am sure you are!
>
> *The First Move?* Why naturally, it is to fill out the application below and mail it in.[37]

In more recent years the number of lonely hearts clubs has been diminished by the origin of computer-dating services, singles clubs, and singles-only apartment complexes. Mechanical dating services had people filling out long forms

Organization Title	No. of Members
American National Red Cross	36,000,000
American Automobile Association	15,000,000
AFL–CIO	13,500,000
YMCA	7,000,000
Boy Scouts of America	5,000,000
American Association of Retired Persons	5,000,000
4-H Foundation	5,000,000
Girl Scouts of America	3,700,000
Order of the Eastern Star	3,000,000
American Legion	2,700,000
Veterans of Foreign Wars of the U.S.	1,700,000
Benevolent and Protective Order of Elks	1,500,000
Independent Order of Odd Fellows	1,200,000
Loyal Order of Moose	1,200,000
Knights of Columbus	1,180,000
Young Democratic Clubs of America	1,000,000
Lions International	1,000,000
Fraternal Order of Eagles	850,000
National Rifle Association of America	825,000
National Grange	600,000
Camp Fire Girls	600,000
Young Republican National Federation	600,000
B'nai B'rith	500,000
National Association for the Advancement of Colored People	420,000
Audubon Society	260,000
Common Cause	200,000
Young Americans for Freedom	70,000
Zero Population Growth	25,000
American Sociological Association	14,140
American Federation of Astrologers	3,000
Auto License Plate Collectors Association	1,462
Dutch Settlers Society of Albany	269
Horatio Alger Society	195

Table 5–3. Representative Associations and Societies in the United States

Source: Compiled from figures given in *The World Almanac, 1974.*

that were supposedly fed into a computer in order to find the ideal date or marriage partner.

One club advertised:

WHEN YOU MEET YOUR IDEAL DATE . . .

You'll both discover what you've been missing! Suddenly life becomes a thrilling adventure the moment you meet someone who enjoys you simply because you're you.

Together, you walk hand in hand through days filled with fun. See the sparkle in your eyes when you look upon each other. Share smiles that show what life's all about.

That happens whenever two personalities blend beautifully together. Whenever two people share similar values. Whenever they love doing the same things.

To accomplish this feat the ad went on to explain the mechanics of computer dating:

But for most people, finding someone this compatible is only a dream, not a reality. They settle for less and choose someone based upon physical attraction, for security, out of loneliness, or for some other psychological reason. In fact, it's been shown that for every 100 people you're attracted to, only three or four are really right for you!

With such odds, it would take you years and years of diligent searching to find just one date who's compatible with you. But with the aid of a computer, you can be matched in seconds with more ideal dates than you'd normally meet in your lifetime. . . . .

Our computer can introduce you to them, but first it must learn who you are.

Computer-dating services denied they were lonely hearts clubs, as "our members don't join because they need to meet just someone . . . they join because they know that computer dating is the way to meet the *right* someone." However, they were expressive organizations that operated to find pleasure for members within the association.

Singles bars began in New York when a perfume salesman purchased a bar and called it TGIF (Thank God It's Friday), now called "Friday's." The bar was a gathering place for single people under thirty-five. This concept has mushroomed into a vast industry servicing single young adults. *Newsweek* described the singles bars:

The *modus operandi* at a singles bar is as structured as the mating rituals of an aboriginal tribe. Wednesdays and Fridays are the most popular nights for comparison shopping, and it is essential to build exactly the right eye contact before rendezvous and docking. "If you get the uninterested look," confides Detroit bachelor Doug Bryant, "that means she's not playing your show and you just have to sit back and see what happens." As for openers, "Do you come here often?" is considered a no-no (*everyone* at a singles bar is there for the first time), but "Didn't I see you at Fire Island?" will at least establish a certain status.

It helps to know the regional jargon. In Chicago, to "deal" or "put the gaff" means a straight cut proposition, while in New York, "G.U." (Geographically Undesirable) connotes anyone who lives in Brooklyn or Queens with mother. The cardinal *faux pas* is to strain for a laugh. Comedian Jackie Vernon, a "professional bachelor" (who is now married), confesses that he achieved absolutely no success with this opener: "Excuse me, but I think I dropped my Congressional Medal of Honor under your seat."

Understandably, the more discriminating singles are quickly turned off by the blatant "body shop" atmosphere of the typical singles bar. A pretty Detroiter compares the scene to "a cattle auction," while Don Spark, proprietor of New York's Goose & Gherkin Ale House, wearily dismisses his own enterprise as "a place where predatory men prey on neurotic women and where impotent men are preyed upon by castrating females." Even so, the prey seem to keep returning to the hunting grounds. Michael O'Keefe, whose two Manhattan singles bars gross over $1 million a year, suggests the main reason: "For city dwellers, the bar scene fills an immense social vacuum. Let's face it, people don't meet at church any more."[38]

"Swinging" or mate swapping is another variation of an expressive voluntary association. Again, contacts are established through a club or an established group of people.[39] All of these groups addressed to sex and companionship—lonely hearts clubs, computer-dating services, and singles and swingers clubs—are expressive voluntary associations.

Instrumental Voluntary Associations

The *social influence* or *instrumental* form of voluntary association finds people coming together for the purpose of influencing or changing some segment of society. Lobbies, political clubs, interest groups, cults, social movements, and political parties are social influence or instrumental groups. (Instrumental groups are further discussed in Chapter Fifteen, "Social Movements.").

It is important to mention that social influence groups sometimes operate as both expressive and instrumental organizations, depending on the *motives of the participant.* People participate actively in political parties for many reasons, ranging from a sense of patriotism to basic self-interest and even greed or meeting members of the opposite sex. Certain categories of people are found in the two major American political parties. The Gallup Poll asked a nationwide sample how they envisioned a typical Democratic Party member, and a Republican response was that Democrats were "middle-class . . . common people . . . a friend . . . an ordinary person . . . works for his wages . . . average person . . . someone who's thinking of everybody."[40] Furthermore, Democrats were seen as more apt to be blue-collar, urban, Southern, or professional, especially academics and intellectuals.[41]

Republicans, on the other hand, were described by Democrats as "better class . . . well-to-do . . . big businessman . . . money voter . . . well-off financially . . . wealthy . . . higher class."[42] Republicans, according to the poll, were most likely to live in suburbs, have higher salaries, and be self-employed or in the corporate sector of society.

Participation in the activities of political parties is tied to a number of factors, like social position, opportunity, and desire.

Participation in party politics has long been believed to be tied to one's *social position.*[43] For example, a self-employed person is more likely to be involved in politics than one tied to a time clock. Imagine an assembly-line worker telling his foreman, "I'm taking the afternoon off to help Congressman X." Doctors and lawyers and, indeed, students can organize their time in such a way as to take an afternoon off. In a word, occupation, a form of social position (see Chapter Nine, "Social Stratification"), creates *opportunity* for participation.

However, as political scientist Robert Lane suggests, other variables also contribute to political participation.[44]

People in the lower social and economic positions in society have less leisure time available to them. Consequently, they do not often participate in political party activities. However, Lane and others add another dimension. People at the bottom of the social ladder have less reason to become involved.[45] Lane contends that the following factors are influential:

1. Lower-status people feel little control over political affairs.
2. Public policy is clearly geared to upper-status people more than lower.
3. Lower status people do not benefit individually from political decisions.
4. Lower status people lack political experience and influence and, therefore, feel uncomfortable in political situations.
5. Lower-status norms tend not to stress "social responsibility."
6. Lower-status persons have less capacity to deal with abstract issues and less awareness of their larger social environment.[46]
7. "Lower-status persons are less satisfied with their lives and communities, leading in a minimally class-conscious society to withdrawal from civic activities, or, alternatively, to participation in deviant politics."[47]

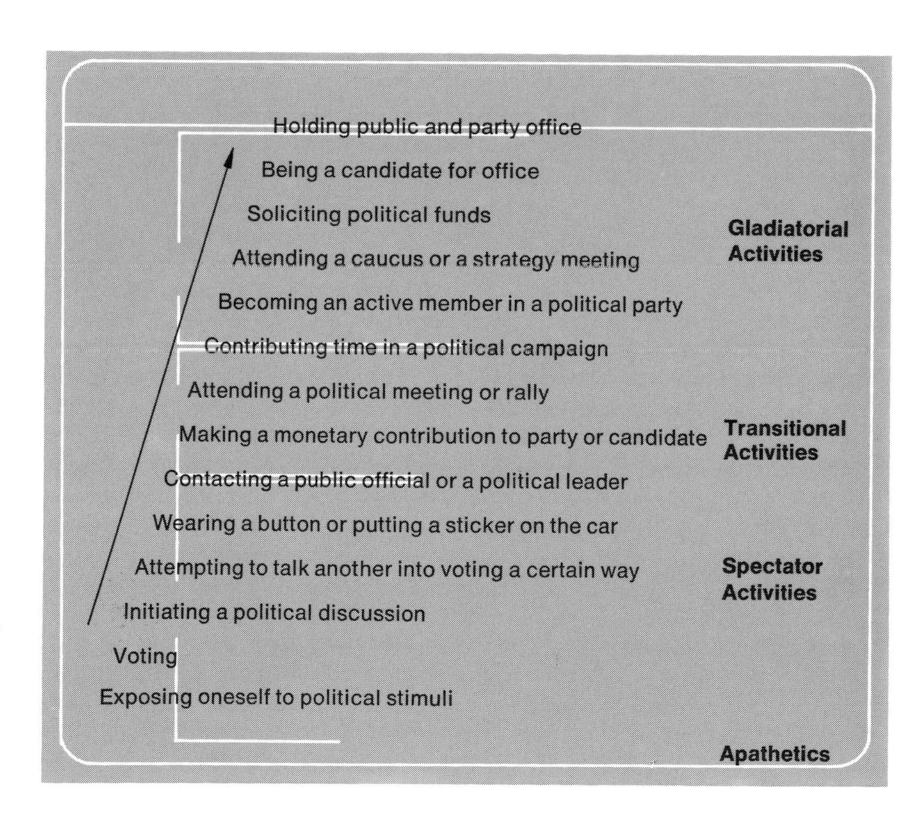

Figure 5-1. Levels of Political Involvement. (*Source:* Lester Milbrath, *Political Participation.* [Chicago: Rand McNally & Co., 1965], p. 18.)

Subsequent studies tend to confirm these propositions about the relationship of social position and *desire.*[48] One's occupation, education, and income do influence whether one decides to act, to vote, or to work in a political party.

Lester Milbrath, a political scientist, suggested a scale of political involvement.[49] He broke down participants into three groups. One group is passive and does not engage in any political activity. These people are termed *apathetics.* A second, larger group is involved in "seeking information, voting, discussing, proselyting, and displaying preference." These are the average voters, whom Milbrath called the *spectators.* The final group Milbrath called *gladiators,* who "battle fiercely to please the spectators, who have the power to decide their fate. The spectators in the stands cheer, transmit messages of advice and encouragement, and, at given periods, vote to decide who has won a particular election battle."[50] (See Figure 5-1.)

Political parties, then, are a form of *instrumental* voluntary association. People come together in order to bring about changes in the political system either by voting for the candidate of their choice or by implementing some policy or program.

Involuntary Associations

There is such a thing as an *involuntary association.* As the name implies, these are groups that people become a part of against their will. Prisons, mental hospitals, and other correctional institutions with bars and walls contain people who would rather be elsewhere.[51] For the draftee, the U.S. Army is an involuntary organization. Involuntary units generally are formal and bureaucratic, thus making their operation as simple as possible. Still, as the discussion of prison inmates showed, informal relations do have an impact on the most regimented of organizations.[52]

Where We Stand

From the shelter of the home we move to peer groups, finally graduating into the world of secondary groups. We move progressively through different, larger, and more impersonal and complex groups. There are many different types and even subclassifications of secondary groups. We have discussed in this chapter formal-informal associations and voluntary-involuntary organizations. All of these units make up that entity we call *society.*

The critical question for the sociologist is, "How do all these parts stay together to make up a society? What is the social glue of society?"

Remember that a group is held together by a set of social relations that identify its members as being separate and distinct from nonmembers. Boundaries are created.

Groups may develop a strong feeling of unity based on homogeneity.

Boundaries are very important because they constitute walls or barriers between social units. Groups may develop a strong feeling of unity ("us") based on similarity or *homogeneity* (sameness of age, occupation, sex, marital status) and may be strongly emotional and antagonistic toward outsiders ("them"). Boundaries hold members together in a group, but they can also keep entire groups apart and can result in conflict.[53]

Lewis Coser presents three points that outline the functions of what he calls "boundary maintenance":[54]

1. Boundaries create and continue the identity of social groups.

2. Boundaries establish the identity of the group while separating the unit from other groups.
3. Boundaries structure the way society is put together on the basis of "in-out," "high-low," and other statements of "them" and "us."

Richard Hoggart describes the working-class English view of the world of "them" and "us" this way:

> 'Them' is a composite dramatic figure, the chief character in modern urban forms of the rural peasant-big house relationships. The world of 'Them'; . . is the world of the bosses, whether those bosses are private individuals or, as is increasingly the case today, public officials. 'Them' may be, as occasion requires, anyone from the classes outside other than the few individuals. A general practitioner, if he wins his way by his devotion to his patients, is not, as a general practitioner, one of 'Them'; he and his wife, as social beings, are. A parson may or may not be regarded as one of 'Them', according to his behavior. 'Them' includes the policemen and those civil servants or local-authority employees whom the working-classes meet—teachers, the school attendance man, 'the Corporation', the local bench. Once the Means Test Official, the man from 'the Guardians' and the Employment Exchange officer were notable figures here. To the very poor, especially, they compose a shadowy but numerous and powerful group affecting their lives at almost every point: the world is divided into 'Them' and 'Us.'
>
> 'They' are 'the people at the top', 'the higher-ups', the people who give you your dole, call you up, tell you to go to war, fine you, made you split the family in the 'thirties to avoid a reduction in the Means Test allowance,'get yer in the end', 'aren't really to be trusted', 'talk posh', 'are all twisters really', 'never tell yer owt' (e.g., about a relative in hospital), 'clap yer in clink', 'will do ya' down if they can', 'summons yer', 'are all in a click (clique) together', 'treat y' like muck.'[55]

If this is the case, if we find it so easy to divide the world into "us" and "them," we may ask, "Why then is society not a war of 'each against all'?" The answer to this question lies in *social integration.*

Integration: The Glue of Society

Émile Durkheim, the French sociologist, in *The Division of Labor in Society* presented society as being the sum total of all of the ways that men interact with one another in a specific place and time. Society, he reasoned, was more than just the sum total of its groups and its people; it also included the *invisible but very real* relationships of people to each other. When we relate to one another there are common understandings that are communicated through language, gestures, glances, and a variety of other types of shared symbols. These understandings Durkheim termed *social facts.* These understandings are the result of human association and color all of the relationships that develop between people. Courtship is a social fact. People have developed relationships that lead to marriage. Dating, proposing, and so on are parts of the courtship process. It is a process that is already laid out for the participants. Society is made up of people, groups and shared ideas.[56]

Society, being the result of human cooperation, cannot be a war of each against all. It must have a certain amount of unity, shared understanding, or integration. According to Durkheim, *social integration* means the binding of the group into a single unit with "beliefs and sentiments held in common."[57] These common beliefs are what hold society together. Consequently, Durkheim's vision of a society is that of a body with interrelated parts all interacting with one another. Every action has its reaction. Consequently, limits or constraints must be placed on each part.

Durkheim elaborated his view of social integration by describing what he felt were two distinct types of solidarity (or ways of being tied together): *mechanical* and *organic.*

Mechanical solidarity is based upon a "common consciousness or a sense of likeness with one's fellows."[58] This type of solidarity binds people to their society by means of common outlooks and attitudes. Tradition is a source of mechanical solidarity. It is handed down generation after generation and is accepted without question. Belief in God, in one's country, in one's mother are all sources of mechanical solidarity.

Durkheim argued that mechanical solidarity is upheld and reinforced by punitive law. Dissenters are repressed in one way or another. Heretics were burned at the stake. Teen-age girls believed to be breaking the rules in Puritan Salem were burned or drowned. With the growth of technologically sophisticated societies, mechanical solidarity began to give way as the only form of unity.

Technology introduced task specialization or the division of labor. Contemporary society, which includes a large number of occupations and groups, is organized on the basis of the division of labor. The division of labor is the basis of *organic solidarity.* People are united by mutual need and dependence. In a world of many occupations, different experiences and problems make it hard to communicate with or understand people who don't share one's occupation or one's social world. However, these different groups *all* contribute to the maintenance of society and therefore *need one another,* even if they don't have much else in common. The links between the groups are *complementary.* The gas station attendant needs the farmer for his food. The farmer needs equipment made by a firm whose workers require the attendant to fuel their cars. Quite simply, each unit is tied up with the other. An interesting illustration of this chain of needs occurred because of the energy crisis in 1973 and 1974. A major part of the energy crisis was the shortage of petroleum. This shortage had an impact on nearly every aspect of human activity. Not only was gasoline hard to get but many other sectors of the economy were affected. Electric power stations cut back wattage because they could not obtain enough oil to run their plants. Users of electricity, in turn, were touched. Many products not commonly associated with petroleum were affected. Phonograph records, plastic toys, auto upholstery, tires, rubber products, electrical appliance parts, and many other items were hard to get. The mobile-home and house-trailer industry was almost wiped out. All of this because of a scarcity of oil. These links aptly demonstrate how diverse elements of society are hooked together.

Another example comes from the popularity of the Beatles. Certainly the Beatles had an impact upon record sales, but they also touched other sectors of the society that had nothing to do with music. A *Los Angeles Times* headline read, "Long Hair Fad: Barbers Face Empty Chairs." The article reported:

> Hair—despite man's evolution as history's "naked ape"—is something that grows on you. Everybody knows that. But few think much about it.
>
> Except barbers.
>
> For years, barbers knew that—regardless of war or peace, depression or affluence—some 30 million males would, about every two weeks, pass through their padded swivel chairs for a trim.
>
> Then, in 1964, the every-two-weeks haircut began to disappear. Lawyers, bankers, salesmen and truck drivers were slowly stretching the time between clippings—some to as long as 3½ to 4 weeks.
>
> The result, for the average barber, was a serious, and immediate, financial pinch. For many, the "pinch" was enough to force them out of barbering. Some hired on as mail sorters or grocery store stockmen.
>
> The mechanism was simple: A customer who began coming in every 3½ weeks instead of every two was buying 14 haircuts a year instead of his normal 26—an instant, individual revenue drop of almost 50 percent.
>
> Multiply that by many customers and, as one Los Angeles barber who was forced to close said, "You got the quick end of a small business. That simple."
>
> As shop owners soon noted, it wasn't simply the generally longer hair that was killing business. It was the growing tendency to permit the hair on the back of the neck to lengthen.
>
> For the first time since most barbers could remember, the well-groomed American male no longer required a neck shave and ear outline every 10 days or so to be presentable.
>
> On the contrary, hair that touched the shirt collar or lapped at the ear lobes was very much "in"—even in the most natty or button-down circles.
>
> Today, the barber business is believed to be down between 35 percent and 40 percent nationally, with no immediate end to the crisis in sight.[59]

As this illustration indicates, people and groups are linked together. These interrelations can result in conflict. If in 1969 the barbers as a group decided that they would continue to cut hair as they had in the past they would have found themselves in direct conflict with the prevailing trend. But instead they became "hair stylists" and "shapers" to accommodate the new trend. They needed customers to continue to operate. Customers required barbers to cope adequately with the new hair lengths. A common understanding was reached.

All technological societies have both mechanical (complementary) and organic (different) interrelationships. Ralph Turner suggests the importance of having a consensus underneath the technological differences.

First, an individual while performing his special job must feel that others are performing theirs. He must believe that those around him have a sense of common duty and responsibility. The average citizen believes that the fire department will come in case of smoke billowing from a house and that the corner grocery store will have an adequate supply of food and drink.

Second, group consensus sustains the value of work. "Your job is important" or "You're doing a fine job" gives the individual a feeling of well-being and importance. His self-esteem rises and he is encouraged to further good deeds. Remember how you felt when your parents praised and rewarded a good report card?

Finally, a belief in a common goal keeps the different groups together and pulling in the same direction. During a time of national crisis, for example, people are more willing to sacrifice their own gain to the common cause. Unions suspend their interests; profits are controlled; everyone rallies around the flag with slogans like "My country, right or wrong."[60]

In these three ways, Durkheim answered the question, "Why is society *not* 'a war of each against all'?" Common needs are translated through values and norms into the glue that holds society together (see Chapter Two on the assumptions behind this view of society).

Following Durkheim's lead, American sociologists like Talcott Parsons and Kingsley Davis developed elaborate models of man in society.[61] Within their models the central ingredient is the glue or tie between the individual, the group to which he belongs, and the society in which he lives.

Durkheim, in a follow-up work to *The Division of Labor in Society,* demonstrated the tie between man and society in an examination of suicide.[62] Suicide, Durkheim wrote, was connected to social integration. He identified three types of suicide (see Table 5–4).

Altruistic suicide occurs when a person's tie to the group is so strong as to create a sense of total moral obligation. A person takes his own life because of a sense of duty. "If he fails," wrote Durkheim, "in this obligation, he is dishonored and also punished, usually by religious sanctions."[63] The individual identifies his interests entirely with those of the group. Nathan Hale's famous gallows statement, "I regret I have but one life to give for my country," reflects his sense of duty. Captured spies who swallow poison rather than revealing government secrets assume a total moral obligation. Francis Gary Powers, a U-2 pilot shot down on a spy mission over the Soviet Union in 1960, was widely condemned for not taking this fatal course of action. The now outlawed practice of suttee in India, in which a wife was thrown upon the funeral pyre of her deceased husband, is also a case in point. The Japanese airmen called *kamikazes* ("divine wind"), who loaded their planes with bombs and crashed them into American naval vessels during World War II, perished in these missions.

These cases of total integration are rare in complex societies except in those

Belief in a common good keeps groups together and pulling in the same direction.

Table 5-4. Suicide and Social Integration

Types of Suicide	Level of Social Integration
I Altruistic	High
II Egoistic	Low
III Anomic	Conflicting demands (low integration)

groups that stress duty, tradition, and esprit de corps, such as the military, the Cosa Nostra, or secret societies.[64] In time of national crisis, altruism increases and individual sacrifice is stressed by the government. President John F. Kennedy, in a famous statement, said, "Ask not what your country can do for you; ask what you can do for your country."

Egoistic suicide, wrote Durkheim, is caused by "excessive individualism" or a weak link between the individual and society: "The more weakened the groups to which he belongs, the less he depends on them, the more he consequently depends only on himself and recognizes no other rules of conduct than what are found in his private interests."[65] An individual needs to identify with groups that provide him with a feeling of belonging and impose restraints upon his actions. Apart from the group, the individual becomes an island with no sense of community or group pride.[66] The fewer the social ties, the greater the chance of suicide. For example, the single person living in a cold, impersonal city is believed more likely to commit suicide than a married person who resides in a small town.

"Hot lines" are designed to combat feelings of loneliness and isolation. Troubled people are invited to call "crisis centers" and talk through their feelings with a friendly voice. The purpose of this program is to make the caller feel wanted and socially significant. Hot-line volunteers convey the message that society does care about the individual.

Many writers have felt that egoistic suicide is a direct result of the *Gesellschaft* (impersonal) form of society characterized by loss of community. This loss of community greatly concerned Durkheim because the breakdown could lead to yet a third form of suicide. This form of suicide is the result of organic solidarity. *Anomic* suicide is caused by a lack of clear-cut norms (rules). The many groups in society make conflicting demands upon the individual. He is left in a situation in which no clear guidelines exist. This leads to a low degree of social integration. This type of suicide occurs when times are rapidly changing or when individuals are plunged into foreign environments. Culture shock—a response to a new environment—may lead to suicide. In a new situation many persons are not able to cope with new social conditions and laws they do not understand.[67]

Durkheim's three categories of suicide were designed to illustrate the importance of social integration for both the individual and society. This concern has been taken up by sociologists in one of the most popular concepts in sociology, *alienation.*

Alienation: Apart from What?

Alienation is a state of separateness. John Calvin, the French theologian, introduced the idea that man was alienated. Man was alienated from God because of his "fall from grace." The German philosopher George W. F. Hegel further popularized the concept of alienation, suggesting that man existed apart from the *Geist* (the spirit of history or total knowledge of the universe).[68] Karl Marx made alienation more worldly by saying that capitalism was the cause of this state because it robbed man of his basic human nature.[69]

Sociologists use the term *alienation* much more broadly. Alienation rapidly became associated with the rise of the technological society and the place of the individual in it.[70] Many groups have been identified as being alienated. Eric and Mary Josephson provided a partial list:

> women, industrial workers, white-collar workers, migrant workers, artists, suicides, the mentally disturbed, addicts, the aged, the younger generation as a whole, juvenile delinquents in particular, voters, non-voters, consumers, the audiences of mass media, sex deviants, victims of prejudice and discrimination, the prejudiced, bureaucrats, political radicals, the physically handicapped, immigrants, exiles, vagabonds, and recluses.[71]

This list is not exhaustive. However, as the Josephsons have remarked, nearly all groups in advanced society have been identified as being alienated.

One of the most widely used descriptions of alienation was developed by the social psychologist Melvin Seeman. Men feel alienation, he claimed, in five fundamental ways:

1. *Powerlessness* places the individual in a large, austere environment where his feelings and desires are not taken into account by those in charge. The usual example is the assembly-line worker in the automobile plant.[72]

As Arthur Haley expressed it:

> But neither pay nor good fringe benefits could change the grim, dispiriting nature of the work. Much of it was physically hard, but the greatest toll was mental—hour after hour, day after day of deadening monotony. And the nature of their jobs robbed individuals of pride. A man on a production line lacked a sense of achievement; he never made a car; he merely made, or put together, pieces—adding a washer to a bolt, fastening a metal strip, inserting screws. And always it was the identical washer or strip or screws, over and over and over and over and over and over and over again, while working conditions—including an overlay of noise—made communication difficult, friendly association between individuals impossible. As years went by, many, while hating, endured. Some had mental breakdowns. Almost no one liked his work.
>
> Thus, a production line worker's ambition, like that of a prisoner, was centered on escape. Absenteeism was a way of partial escape; so was a strike. Both brought excitement, a break in monotony—for the time being the dominating drive.[73]

The line is the controlling factor in the assembly plant. The worker must adjust his wants to the demands of the conveyer belt. Even going to the toilet is determined by the availability of a "relief" man.

Powerlessness is also found in the realm of politics. People feel they have no influence over events or conditions as they are decided in the halls and cloakrooms of Congress and in the Oval Office of the White House.[74] Voters in the millions appear to have stayed home during the 1972 presidential election, feeling they had little to say in either the nominating or the electing of the nation's leader.[75] Powerlessness, as might be expected, is generally more prevalent among people who genuinely lack any power over their conditions of life. The poorly educated, the poor, the aged, the handicapped, all who are dependent upon others, fit into this area.

2. *Meaninglessness* describes the apparent chaos of everyday life. People need meaning in life, but complex societies are difficult to comprehend. We frequently ask, "Why are things done *that way* rather than in a more sensible manner?" Why are income tax forms so complicated or college enrollment sheets so difficult?[76] Meaninglessness is demonstrated in many ways, daily.

Alienation has become associated with the use of technological society and the place of the individual wthin it.

Consider the college curriculum. Why are some courses required? It is frequently difficult to defend some of these courses. Originally, Ph.D. candidates were forced to meet language requirements because many important books and articles were available only in German and French. Some hundred years later, most of these important documents have been translated, yet in many graduate schools the requirement continues.

3. *Normlessness* is the cause of Durkheim's anomic suicide. That is, people are confused about the norms or rules of a given situation. How does one act in a certain setting? Which of the two forks is to be used with the salad? What happens when a freshman from a small, conservative town is confronted for the first time by a party at which marihuana is being smoked? Should he conform to the norms of the party or to those of his parents?

The farmer experiences great amounts of normlessness. He has little if any control over climate, prices, and, indeed, consumer taste. Segments of the entertainment and the fashion industries experience a similar condition. What fads are going to be "in" this season or year? Are consumers ready for a new singing sensation or an original style of clothing, writing, or television series? These are all conditions of normlessness.

4. *Isolation* is perhaps the central condition of alienation. The isolated person is one removed either physically or emotionally from his society. An extreme case is the schizophrenic, who lives in a psychic world of his own making. However, there are other forms of isolation. The genius is isolated by his own brilliance. The artist, musician, or writer lives in a world of visions, sounds, and images. The American intellectual is an isolate arguing unpopular positions and receiving little or no acceptance.[77] Colin Wilson says the isolated person, or outsider, "stands for Truth." He has a sense of strangeness, of unreality: "The outsider is a man who cannot live in the comfortable, insulated world of the bourgeois [the middle class] accepting what he sees and touches as reality."[78]

5. *Self-estrangement* is the least explicit of the five forms of alienation. It is a psychological concept that refers to "the person experiencing himself as an alien. He has become, one might say, estranged from himself."[79] We can simplify this rather complicated definition by saying that a person is *totally unhappy with his present circumstances.* The real situation contradicts the person's feeling of what "ought to be." Sitting through a dull two-hour lecture may elicit such unhappiness. After the period is over the student returns to the "is" of college life. Charles Walker and Robert Guest presented an example of self-estrangement:

The job gets sickening—day in and day out plugging in ignition wires. I get through with one motor, turn and there's another motor staring me in the face. It's sickening. The assembly line is no place to work, I can tell you. There is nothing more discouraging than having a barrel beside you with 10,000 bolts in it using them all up. Then you get a barrel with another 10,000 bolts, and you know every one of the 10,000 bolts has to be picked up and put in exactly the same place as the last 10,000 bolts.[80]

Sociologist Ely Chinoy added many statements uttered daily on the job that are reflective of self-estrangement. Alienation shows itself in many ways, he wrote:

In the sad comment, "The only reason a man works is to make a living;" in the occasional overview of resentment, "Sometimes you feel like jamming things up in the machine and saying goodbye to it;" in the cynical observation, "The things I like best about my job are quitting time, pay day, days off, and vacations;" in the complaint, "There is no interest in a job in the shop;" and in the resigned answer to questions about their work, "A job's a job."[81]

The five traits of alienation presented by Seeman are reactions to the development of technological society. The move from Toënnies's *Gemeinschaft* to *Gesellschaft* or from Durkheim's mechanical to organic social relations is believed to be the reason for the breakdown of social integration leading to suicide and the feeling of alienation.

The change from the intimacy of a small village or town to the impersonality of a large city is frequently cited as the cause of many social ills, ranging from the breakdown of the family to many types of crime, and, of course, anomie and alienation (see Chapter Eleven, "Deviance"). Man in the big city or the big organization is presented as a small boat in a huge ocean tossed about with no rhyme or reason by social forces beyond his control.

Some sociologists have taken issue with this characterization of the essence of complex social systems.[82] Some have suggested that the simple "good old days" were not quite as simple or free of stress as Durkheim, Marx, and many others seem to suggest. The West, as movies and television continually show, was not free of crime or violence. The streets of Tombstone during the days of the Earps, Clantons, Ringos, and Hollidays were hardly safe or tranquil. Life in small towns, although perhaps intimate, was also stifling and repressive for many people. The low divorce rate in the pre-World War II days did not necessarily mean most marriages were happy ones "made in heaven." Some were created in the pits of hell. Leo Hershkowitz, discussing crime in New York City, said, "The people who complain about life today, they wouldn't have lasted a week then." The *New York Times* reported, "The old records [from the coroner's office] of such things as infanticide and suicide make contemporary New York seem almost idyllic by comparison."[83] Some sociologists have noted, as did Durkheim, that although complex social relationships may create some problems and exact a cost, these are merely the price of living in a technological, sophisticated world with all of its material and creature comforts. This is a highly controversial subject, as the relationship of the individual's freedom to the good of all society is one loaded with different assumptions

Isolation is found in various forms and degrees.

about individual and social responsibility. One famous case centered around the freedom "to cry 'Fire' in a crowded theater." Does a man exercising his freedom of speech possess the right to endanger the lives and safety of other people? In a famous opinion by Oliver Wendell Holmes, the Supreme Court thought not. As society becomes more complicated, it is difficult to deny the erosion of individual choice.[84] Many emotional and convincing arguments have been presented by politicians, philosophers, and, indeed, social scientists on this constriction of freedom. Sociologists term the restraint of individual action *social control.*[85] Social control may range from the mere voluntary obeying of accepted rules to totalitarian repression (see Chapter Six, "Socialization"). The form of social control that has attracted the most attention during the 1960s and 1970s has been allied with technology. The belief that "Technology will save us" has been changed to the belief that "Technology will enslave and destroy us."[86]

This warning cry has come in many different forms and from many diverse places, but the basic thesis is, by now, quite familiar. Technology has become so complex that individual human desires are being replaced by the needs of the complex society. Two responses to this dilemma appeared. The first involved the rejection of the machine and a return to the simpler life. Writers such as Theodore Roszak and Charles Reich urged that young people, especially, would transform society to a freer state of self-realization.[87]

The second reaction came from psychologist B. F. Skinner, who urged that technology could be used to teach people the *proper way* to live in society, thus relieving the feelings of despair, boredom, and alienation. In the process some individual choice would have to be surrendered. Not surprisingly, Skinner's ideas have been widely criticized.[88] However, the points raised in *Walden II* and *Beyond Freedom and Dignity* cannot simply be put aside. Should the organization of society be based upon a plan devised by social and behavioral scientists? This question has no simple answer.

Types of Societies

In historic discussions of the nature of society a number of models have arisen. Some are utopian and attractive. Other models of society are less attractive, are even dark and sinister.

In our everyday language we place labels on societies. We use such terms as *underdeveloped, developed, progressive, repressive, freedom loving, dictatorial, open, closed, folk, urban, primitive, advanced,* and so on. Sociologists have also been fascinated with terms such as *folk, feudal, urban, technological, mass* and *totalitarian.* Most of these classifications have not been terribly helpful, as societies rarely fit *totally* into any one category.

Consider Montesquieu, the eighteenth-century social philosopher who judged social orders by their size. The smaller the society, he claimed, the freer and more democratic it was. The larger ones, he reasoned, were rigid and dictatorial.

Montesquieu, of course, was making his judgments based on the world as it existed in his time.[89] When we look at the world in which we live, this stress on size is not terribly useful. Societies like those of Haiti, Albania, and Uganda are small in size and very dictatorial. Larger social units like India are politically democratic and free of a strong dictator. There seems to be no simple relationship between size and democracy.

Some anthropologists and economists have tied size to economic development. The usual picture is that small societies are primitive and larger ones are more technologically developed. In order to be technologically developed, a society must have enough people so that it can spare some from hunting and food gathering. Obviously, if all of the human energy is being spent daily on the business of survival, there is time for little else. However, after the basic needs are taken care of, then growth should take place. Once a society is past this "takeoff" point, size appears to be less and less important to the amount of development (see Chapter Sixteen, "Social Change").

Many large societies are economically underdeveloped. On the other hand, many small societies enjoy all of the bounties (and troubles) of technological sophistication. As we can see, size really does not tell us much about different societies except in the most generalized and often misleading way. This confusion is not limited to the variable of size. Other measures are equally unclear. Despite these difficulties sociologists do appear to agree on some of the characteristics found in certain kinds of societies.

Perhaps the most useful and simplest way of identifying societies comes from the late anthropologist Robert Redfield. Redfield divided society into two models: *folk* and *urban*. Redfield characterized the folk society as "small, isolated, nonliterate, and homogeneous with a strong sense of group solidarity."[90] He went on to say that all of the opposite traits are to be identified with urbanism. Therefore, urbanism, for Redfield, was "large, open, literate, heterogeneous, without much group solidarity."[91] Let's look at some of the qualities of a folk society.

A folk society is *small*. Primitive tribes contain only a few thousand people. Hamlets in the Appalachian Mountains have populations in the hundreds. Urban areas, on the other hand, range into the millions, with Los Angeles and New York City pushing close to 10 million.

The folk society is *isolated*. Folk societies have little contact with outsiders. There are countless movies, mainly westerns, that graphically show the little town stuck in the "middle of nowhere" that fears the "stranger." James Hilton's Shangri-La, a mythical Tibetan mountain kingdom, was presented in novel and film as a society happy in its isolation from the complex world below. Urban areas, on the other hand, are linked by bridges and freeways with other urban areas. Airports, train stations, bus terminals, the family car all link the city dweller with far-off places.

The folk society is *nonliterate*. Redfield suggested, "The folk communicate only by word of mouth; therefore, the communication upon which understanding is built is only that which occurs within the little society itself.[92] There are no written records or books. People communicate through oral tradition by means of folksongs, myths, and stories that are handed down from generation to generation. Many of our familiar children's stories and songs, for example, were transmitted from grandmother to mother to daughter and so on for many centuries. Folklorist Alan Dundes says, "The amazing thing is that folklore, in the vast majority of cases, is saved for posterity without the aid of writing or print."[93]

In the urban society, newspapers, television, books, and records keep track of everyday life. Literacy is essential to functioning in the complex city. History, science, and all forms of information on skills and resources are stored in libraries and universities. A person is forbidden to drive a car without a license, yet to obtain a license one must pass a *written* examination.

Folk society is *homogeneous.* People in the society are very much alike. This is a recurrent theme. Some tribes are believed to have a "consciousness of kind." That is, they believe the same things, share similar beliefs, and rarely if ever deviate from the group's rules. Disobedience is generally met by some type of removal from the group. Removal could mean anything from exile to imprisonment or even death.

The urban society, on the other hand, is heterogeneous. People come from many different walks of life—different ethnic groups, income groups, races, and so on. Cities are a rainbow of different groups.

The folk society has a strong sense of *group solidarity* or integration. Following Toënnies and Durkheim, Redfield saw the folk society as having a strong feeling of belonging. There is an ethos of "them" and "us." There are the "insiders" and the "outsiders."

The urban society is loosely organized. There is little sense of community—although many New Yorkers and San Franciscans might not agree. City dwellers have been presented as transients with no sense of community. Their sense of alienation and anomie are high.[94]

By now you no doubt have spotted some problems with these classifications. A Brooklynite may scoff, "What, no community?" Or someone else may say, "Why can't folk societies be literate; what about some American Indian tribes with a written alphabet?" All these questions are valid ones. However, we must remember that Redfield's model was one of generalizations basically addressed to what a folk society *usually* is.

For a better picture of the urban society, the work of sociologist Louis Wirth is important. Wirth suggested that urbanism was a special form of social organization. This form of organization was characterized by "a relatively large, dense, and permanent settlement of socially heterogeneous individuals.[95] Herbert Gans summarizes Wirth's view of the city:

Number, density, and heterogeneity created a social structure in which primary group relationships were inevitably replaced by secondary contacts that were impersonal, segmental, superficial, transitory, and often predatory in nature. As a result, the city dweller became anonymous, isolated, secular, relativistic, rational, and sophisticated. In order to function in the urban society, he was forced to combine with others or organize corporations, voluntary associations, representative forms of government, and the impersonal mass media of communications.[96]

In simpler form, urbanism involves very large groups of different people in one place. The urban society is one in which most of the citizens live and work in cities. According to Wirth, the urban way of life had certain unique properties. The urban society featured impersonal relations as secondary groups replaced primary ones. It seems that the bonds of kinship were weakened; the family was less important; the traditional neighborhood was disappearing; in sum; "the traditional basis of social solidarity" was on the decline. Wirth's view of urbanism reflected the way many sociologists looked at American life in the 1920s and 1930s. The rural, folk, pastoral ways of life had faded into history, and now men were thrown into the cold, concrete world of urbanism, which seemed to lack the warmth of a small-town past. Sociologists who came after Wirth began to elaborate and refine his picture of the urban society.[97]

Richard Dewey expanded on some of Wirth's ideas. Dewey argued that there was no difference between urbanism and industrialism.[98] The urban and the technological societies were, in fact, the same.[99] Furthermore, Dewey thought that urbanism was characterized by only five properties:

1. *Anonymity.* It is impossible for large numbers of people to know one another. In the urban society we are all strangers except to those we know.

2. *Division of labor.* Because of their complexity urban societies require that many different tasks be accomplished. The food must be delivered, garbage collected, electricity and gas provided. Thousands of jobs are involved in the maintenance of the urban technological society.

3. *Heterogeneity.* Because of size, the division of labor, and migration patterns, urban societies are made up of many varied people, groups, values, and customs. The urban society is a pluralistic one, a melting pot of people.

4. *Impersonality and formality.* The notions of alienation and anomie are but two products of the impersonal character of the urban complex. People become objects to serve, to order, or to ignore. One is "a face in the crowd."

5. *Status symbols.* Status symbols are signs of social position. How do we tell who is important on a crowded street or in the elevator of an office building? Symbols identify people for us. How do we respond to the man driving the Rolls Royce? What does wearing a mink coat mean? Wearing a gold shield with a number suggests something as well. In the urban society, with its size and anonymity, symbols allow people to get along with one another, at least when the symbols are recognized and reacted to.

Herbert Gans, Scott Greer, and other sociologists have also found traits of urbanism in the suburbs.[100] This reminds us that urbanism is not tied merely to big cities or metropolitan areas. Rather, entire societies, even with pockets of rural and underdeveloped areas, can be termed urban when they display these five characteristics.

Mass Society

The conditions of urban society have caused some sociologists to call it *mass society.* Mass society mirrors urban society, as it is populated by people who are "not directly related to one another in a variety of groups."[101] Another way of saying the same thing is that mass society is the *loss of community* or the decline of the folk society.

The concept of mass society has been a popular one. Sociologists and laymen alike have used it in a number of ways to describe the urban society. Many characteristics of the urban society and the mass society are the same. In fact, the causes of both are similar.[102]

Mass society in America is a product of the Industrial Revolution. The growth of the factory, the plant, and the city brought men together from all parts of the countryside and from the small towns and villages of America. The division of labor made them dependent upon each other. The baker needs the television repair man, who in turn requires the services of someone else. These ties, however, are economic and not personal ones. In this impersonal world the role of the family and the local community have changed. The ways of the past have been lost. Few new values have arisen to take their place. The standards of the old, upheld by "cultured" people, have also declined. The leadership of educators, politicians, and the "old" families have been brought into question. Values, morals, and norms have been in a constant state of change. Insecurity is an all-pervasive state of life. In this state of insecurity men have begun to search for social anchors, in a sense "a quest for community." Mass society, according to Nisbet, is characterized by: "Enlarging masses of individuals detached from any sense of community, status, or function, turning with a kind of organized desperation to exotic escapes, to every sort of spokesman for salvation on earth, and to ready-made techniques of relief from nervous exhaustion. . . . increasingly individuals seek escape from the freedom of impersonality, secularism, and individualism."[103] Religious revivals and nostalgia crazes, argues Nisbet, are symptoms of the mass society. Other sociologists have attributed more dire consequences to mass society. Some see mass society as the forerunner of a dictatorial totalitarian state like those in Nazi Germany and China.[104] Mass society has also been closely tied to many social ills such as crime, delinquency, insanity, drug addiction, and many others.[105]

Some sociologists, although agreeing that urban-mass society does exact a toll of human despair and misery, also see it as providing diversity and new social opportunities. Edward Shils is one who sees mass society as also having a positive side. He writes, "Larger elements of the population have consciously learned to value the pleasures of eye, ear, taste, touch, and conviviality. People make choices more freely in many spheres of life, and these choices are not necessarily made for them by tradition, authority, or scarcity. The value of the experience of personal relations is more widely appreciated."[106] The very conditions that give rise to mass society also provide a freedom for the individual to experience new people, ideas, tastes, and the like that are not available in the folk society with its stress on sameness and tradition. The small traditional community is often intolerant of new and different ideas, of nonconformity. Because of the traditional closeness and emotional ties, your family and neighbors in the name of "love" crush you if you don't fit the mold *they* fit, if you don't conform. It is the diversity of jobs, restaurants, life styles, and all of the other good things in urban society that make it attractive and interesting.

Sociologists who take the mass society approach to urban society are generally harshly critical of it. They decry the breakdown of some of the traditional features of society. The urban society is presented as one full of social ills and problems.

Other writers, like Shils, acknowledge that the urban society as mass society has its problems but also suggest that along with the problems come many opportunities. They also accuse the critics of comparing the worst features of a *real* society with the best features of a society that they know only through their imaginations and the idealized versions of history presented by movies, television, and the *Reader's Digest.*

A variation upon the mass society is the *totalitarian society.* In the totalitarian society one group, usually the government, has total and absolute power. The totalitarian society has been described as the next stage *after* mass society: The breakdown of traditional groups in mass society will leave the individual alone and unprotected. All of the groups we belong to give us some power. The labor union, the fraternal organization, and countless voluntary associations protect the individual and provide a sense of belonging. Take these away and man is powerless and alienated. This powerlessness and alienation allows any one power group to act without legal limits, as occurred in Russia in the 1930s and also in Nazi Germany. Hitler's Germany and Stalin's Russia are used as classic examples of a totalitarian society. There the individual has no influence with the state and its enforcement arm, the secret police. The trial without jury, the midnight arrest, the jail sentence without charges or defense are all symptoms of a totalitarian society.[107]

The concept of totalitarianism is a *political* one. Totalitarianism is not necessarily a consequence in an industrial or urban society. However, as George Orwell illustrated in his frightening book *1984,* technology can very much aid a "Big Brother" type of social system in keeping track of its citizens.

Summary

A society is a collection of relationships. These relationships are ordered in a vast number of ways. Some are rigid and highly structured; others are loose and informal. We have groups that are large. Others are small. Some are friendly whereas others are impersonal. The sum total of these groups add up to a society.

Notes

1. P. Berger, *Invitation to Sociology* (Garden City, N.Y.: Anchor Books, 1963), pp. 91–92.
2. A. Inkeles, *What Is Sociology?* (Englewood Cliffs, N.J.: Prentice-Hall, Inc., 1966), p. 70.
3. R. Dubin, *The World of Work* (Englewood Cliffs, N.J.: Prentice-Hall, Inc., 1958); and D. Jenkins, *Job Power: Blue and White Collar Democracy* (New York: Random House, Inc., 1973).
4. C. H. Cooley, *Social Organization* (New York: Schocken Books, Inc., 1962).
5. Ibid., p. 24.
6. F. Elkin and G. Handel, *The Child and Society: The Process of Socialization,* 2nd Ed. (New York: Random House, Inc., 1972), pp. 123–124.
7. R. Bierstedt, *The Social Order,* 3rd Ed. (New York: McGraw-Hill Book Company, 1970), p. 289.
8. T. Parsons, *Structure and Process in Modern Societies* (New York: The Free Press, 1960), p. 17. A. Etzioni, in *Modern Organizations* (Englewood Cliffs, N.J.: Prentice-Hall, Inc., 1964), p. 3, uses a similar definition.
9. Ibid., p. 3.
10. See C. W. Mills, *New Men of Power* (Boston: Beacon Press, 1958); Philip Zelznick, *TVA and the Grass Roots* (Berkeley: University of California Press, 1949); and S. M. Lipset, M. Trow, and J. Coleman, *Union Democracy: The Inside Politics of the International Typographical Union* (New York: The Free Press, 1956).
11. L. J. Peter suggests that this characteristic doesn't always appear. He observes, "Every employee tends to rise to his level of incompetence." This means the last promotion is always *one too many.* A good first baseman could make a terrible manager of a baseball team. A man who's been a good salesman gets promoted to sales manager. A good teacher is promoted to principal. See *The Peter Principle* (New York: William Morrow & Co., Inc., 1969). For a variation, see L. Tracy, "Why Don't More Things Go Wrong," *Intellectual Digest* (1972), 41–42.
12. R. T. Anderson, "From Mafia to Cosa Nostra," *American Journal of Sociology,* **71** (1965), 308.
13. H. H. Gerth and C. W. Mills, *From Max Weber: Essays in Sociology* (New York: Oxford University Press, 1946), pp. 196–208.
14. R. K. Merton, *Social Theory and Social Structure,* Rev. Ed. (New York: The Free Press, 1968), p. 250.
15. Ibid., p. 254.
16. R. Michels, *Political Parties: A Sociological Study of the Oligarchical Tendencies of Modern Democracy* (New York: The Free Press, 1962), p. 61.
17. Ibid., p. 206.
18. K. Mannheim, *Man and Society in an Age of Reconstruction* (New York: Harcout Brace Jovanovich, Inc., 1940), p. 53.
19. N. P. Mouzelis, *Organization and Bureaucracy: An Analysis of Modern Theories* (Chicago: Aldine Publishing Company, 1968), p. 70.
20. G. Sykes, *The Society of Captives* (Princeton, N.J.: Princeton University Press, 1958), p. 30.
21. Ibid., p. 56.
22. See B. R. Berk, "Organizational Goals and Inmate Organization," *American Journal of Sociology,* **71** (1966), 522–534; and D. Street, "Inmates in Custodial and Treatment Settings,"

American Sociological Review, **30** (1965), 40–56. In an industrial setting similar findings have appeared. See especially F. J. Roethlisberger and W. J. Dickson, *Management and the Worker* (Cambridge, Mass.: Harvard University Press, 1939).

23. D. Harper and F. Emmert, "Work Behavior in a Service Industry," *Social Forces,* **41** (1963), 216–225.

24. See R. S. Denisoff, *Solid Gold: The Pop Record Industry* (New Brunswick: TransAction, 1974).

25. "They Shall Pass—If They're Athletes," *New York Times* (July 9, 1973), 45, 49. Also see G. Eskenazi, "For the Superstar, a First Class Ticket," *New York Times* (March 14, 1974), 46.

26. Ibid., p. 49.

27. An interview with a San Quentin correctional officer, San Francisco, California, 1962, conducted by R. S. Denisoff.

28. A. Niederhoffer, *Behind the Shield: The Police in Urban Society* (Garden City, N.Y.. Doubleday & Company, Inc., 1967).

29. P. Chevigny, *Police Power: Police Abuses in New York City* (New York: Vintage Books, 1969), p. 81.

30. E. Stoddard, "The Informal 'Code' of Police Deviance: A Group Approach to 'Blue-Coat Crime,'" *Journal of Criminal Law, Criminology, and Police Science,* **59,** (1968), 208.

31. Ibid., p. 208

32. See W. A. Westley, "Secrecy and the Police," *Social Forces,* **34** (1956), 254–257. A graphic illustration is found in Peter Maas, *Serpico* (New York: Bantam Books, 1974).

33. A. Rose and C. Rose, *Sociology: The Study of Human Relations,* 3rd Ed. (New York: Alfred A. Knopf, Inc., 1969), p. 295.

34. See H. Toch, *The Social Psychology of Social Movements* (Indianapolis: The Bobbs-Merrill Co., Inc., 1965), pp. 94–98.

35. See M. G. Riege, "The Call Girl and the Dance Teacher: A Comparative Analysis," *Cornell Journal of Social Relations,* **4** (1969), 58–71.

36. C. Lane, "Cupid Is My Business," *American Magazine* (February, 1949), p. 31.

37. Quoted in Toch, op cit., from *The Western Heart* (May–June 1961), 9.

38. "Games Singles Play," *Newsweek* (July 16, 1973), 53–54.

39. See C. Palson and R. Palson, "Swinging in Wedlock," *Society,* **9** (Feb. 1972), 28–37; also M. L. Walshok, "The Emergence of Middle Class Deviance: The Case of Swingers," *Social Problems,* **18** (1971), 488–495.

40. Quoted in S. M. Lipset, *Political Man,* Rev. Ed. (Garden City, N.Y.: Anchor Books, 1961), p. 305.

41. See R. M. Scammon and B. J. Wattenberg, *The Real Majority: An Extraordinary Examination of the American Electorate* (New York: Coward, McCann and Geohagen, Inc., 1970).

42. Lipset, op cit., p. 305. Also see N. D. Glenn, "Class and Party Support in the United States: Recent and Emerging Trends," *Public Opinion Quarterly,* **37** (1973), 1–20.

43. See S. M. Lipset, P. F. Lazarsfeld, A. H. Barton, and J. Linz, "The Psychology of Voting: An Analysis of Political Behavior," in G. Lindzey, ed., *Handbook of Social Psychology* (Reading, Mass.: Addison-Wesley Publishing Co., Inc., 1954), pp. 1124–1175.

44. R. E. Lane, *Political Life* (New York: The Free Press, 1959), pp. 220–234.

45. See M. B. Levin, *The Alienated Voter: Politics in Boston* (New York: Holt, Rinehart, & Winston, Inc., 1960); and more recently, S. M. Lipset and E. Raab, *The Politics of Unreason: Right-Wing Extremism in America, 1790–1970* (New York: Harper and Row, Publishers, 1970).

46. Lane, op cit., p. 234.

47. Ibid., p. 234.

48. See R. A. Dahl, *Pluralist Democracy in the United States: Conflict and Consent* (Chicago: Rand-McNally & Co., 1967).

49. L. W. Milbrath, *Political Participation* (Chicago: Rand-McNally & Co., 1965).

50. Ibid., p. 15.

51. See the discussion of prisons in the next chapter; also see E. Goffman, *Asylums: Essays*

on the Social Situation of Mental Patients and Other Inmates* (Garden City, N.Y.: Anchor Books, 1961).

52. See A. Solzhenitsyn, *A Day in the Life of Ivan Denisovich* (New York: E. P. Dutton & Co., Inc., 1963).

53. See G. Simmel, *Conflict*, trans. K. H. Wolff (New York: The Free Press, 1955) and L. Coser, *The Functions of Social Conflict* (New York: The Free Press, 1956).

54. Coser, op cit., p. 38.

55. Richard Hoggart, *The Uses of Literacy* (Boston: Beacon Press, 1961), p. 62.

56. E. Durkheim, *The Division Of Labor in Society* (New York: The Free Press, 1964).

57. See R. Nisbet, *The Sociological Tradition* (New York: Basic Books, 1966), pp. 83–97.

58. R. H. Turner, "Types of Solidarity in the Reconstituting of Groups," *Pacific Sociological Review,* **10** (1967), 61.

59. R. Kistler, "Long Hair Fad: Barbers Face Empty Chairs," *Los Angeles Times* (December 21, 1969), 1.

60. Turner, op cit., p. 63.

61. See M. Black, ed., *The Social Theories of Talcott Parsons: A Critical Examination* (Englewood Cliffs, N.J.: Prentice-Hall, Inc., 1963); and K. Davis, *Human Society* (New York: Macmillan Publishing Co., Inc., 1949).

62. E. Durkheim, *Suicide: A Case Study in Sociology,* trans. J. A. Spaulding and G. Simpson (New York: The Free Press, 1951).

63. Durkheim, *Suicide,* p. 219.

64. See M. Janowitz, *The Professional Soldier* (New York: The Free Press, 1964); also see N. MacKenzie, ed., *Secret Societies* (New York: Holt, Rinehart & Winston, Inc., 1967), and D. Rogers, *"Since You Went Away": From Rosie the Riveter to Bond Drives: World War II at Home* (New Rochelle, N.Y.: Arlington House, 1973), p. 209.

65. Durkheim, *Suicide,* p. 209.

66. See R. Nisbet, *The Quest for Community* (New York: Oxford University Press, 1953).

67. See K. C. Cirtautas, *The Refugee* (New York: The Citadel Press, 1963); also W. I. Thomas and F. Znaniecki, *The Polish Peasant in Europe and America,* (Chicago: University of Chicago Press, 1918–1920).

68. See H. Marcuse, *Reason and Revolution: Hegel and the Rise of Social Theory* (Boston: Beacon Press, 1960).

69. See E. Fromm, *Marx's Concept of Man* (New York: Frederick Ungar Publishing Co., Inc., 1963); compare with John Horton, "The Dehumanization of Anomie and Alienation: A Problem in the Ideology of Sociology," *British Journal of Sociology,* **15** (1964), 283–300.

70. See M. H. Lystad, "Social Alienation: A Review of Current Literature," *The Sociological Quarterly,* **13** (1972), 90–113.

71. E. Josephson and M. Josephson, eds., *Man Alone: Alienation in Modern Society* (New York: Dell Publishing Co., 1972), p. 13.

72. For excellent fictional accounts, see A. Haley, *Wheels* (New York: Bantam Books, 1973); and H. Swados, *On the Line* (Boston: Little, Brown and Company, 1957).

73. Arther Haley, *Wheels* (New York: Doubleday & Company, 1971), pp. 28–29.

74. See Levin, op cit., pp. 64–66; also J. Horton, "Powerlessness and Political Negativism: A Study of Defeated Local Referendums," *American Journal of Sociology,* **67** (1962), 485–493.

75. See T. White, *The Making of the President, 1972* (New York: Atheneum Publishers, 1973).

76. See M. Seeman, "Powerlessness and Knowledge: A Comparative Study of Alienation and Learning," *Sociometry,* **30** (1967), 105–123; and J. Holian, Jr., "Alienation and Social Awareness Among College Students," *Sociological Quarterly,* **13** (1971), 114–125.

77. See Lipset, op cit., pp. 332–371; F. Znaniecki, *The Social Role of the Man of Knowledge* (New York: Harper Torchbooks, 1968); and P. Rieff, *On Intellectuals: Theoretical Case Studies* (Garden City, N.Y.: Doubleday & Company, Inc., 1970).

78. C. Wilson, *The Outsider: The Seminal Book on the Alienation of Modern Man* (New York: Delta Books, 1956).

79. E. Fromm, *The Sane Society* (New York: Holt, Rinehart & Winston, Inc., 1955), p. 120.

80. C. R. Walker and R. Guest, *Man on the Assembly Line* (Cambridge, Mass.: Harvard University Press, 1952), pp. 54–55.

81. E. Chinoy, *Automobile Workers and the American Dream* (New York: Doubleday & Company, Inc., 1955), p. 85. This discussion is based on R. Blauner, *Alienation and Freedom: The Factory Worker and His Industry* (Chicago: University of Chicago Press, 1964), pp. 115–123.

82. D. Wrong, "The Oversocialization Concept of Man in Modern Sociology," *American Sociological Review,* **26** (1961), 183–193.

83. R. Blumenthal, "Early Files Depict a Grim but Familiar City," *New York Times* (March 29, 1974), p. 31.

84. See B. F. Skinner, *Beyond Freedom and Dignity* (New York: Doubleday & Company, Inc., 1972); compare with N. Chomsky, *Problems of Knowledge and Freedom* (New York: Pantheon Books, Inc., 1971).

85. See E. F. Borgatta and H. J. Myers, eds., *Social Control and the Foundations of Sociology: Pioneer Contributions of E. A. Ross to the Study of Society* (Boston: Beacon Press, 1959).

86. See J. Ellul, *The Technological Society* (New York: Alfred A. Knopf, Inc., 1964); V. C. Ferkiss, *Technological Man: The Myth and the Reality* (New York: George Braziller, Inc., 1969); H. Marcuse, *One-Dimensional Man: Studies in the Ideology of Advanced Industrial Society* (Boston: Beacon Press, 1967); and D. Callahan, *The Tyranny of Survival* (New York: Macmillan Publising Co., Inc., 1974).

87. C. Reich, *The Greening of America* (New York: Random House, Inc., 1970); T. Roszak, *The Making of a Counterculture: Reflections on the Technocratic Society and Its Youthful Opposition* (Garden City, N.Y.: Doubleday & Company, Inc., 1969).

88. For a summary see A. F. Freedman, *The Planned Society: An Analysis of Skinner's Proposals* (Kalamazoo, Mich.: Behaviordelia, Inc., 1972).

89. W. Stark, *Montesquieu: Pioneer of the Sociology of Knowledge* (London: Routledge and Kegan Paul, Ltd., 1960).

90. R. Redfield, "The Folk Society," *The American Journal of Sociology,* **52** (1947), 295.

91. See H. Miner, "The Folk-Urban Continuum," *American Sociological Review,* **17** (1952), 529–537.

92. Ibid.

93. A. Dundes, *The Study of Folklore* (Englewood Cliffs, N.J.: Prentice-Hall, Inc., 1956), p. 219.

94. See L. Srole, "Urbanization and Mental Health: Some Reformulations," *American Scientist,* **60** (1970), 576–583.

95. L. Wirth, "Urbanism as a Way of Life," *American Journal of Sociology,* **44** (1938), 1–24.

96. H. Gans, "Urbanism and Suburbanism as Ways of Life: A Re-evaluation of Definitions," in A. Rose, ed., *Human Behavior and Social Processes* (Boston: Houghton Mifflin Company, 1962), p. 626.

97. For a review, see C. S. Fischer, "Urbanism as a Way of Life: A Review and an Agenda," *Sociological Methods and Research,* **1** (1972), 187–242.

98. R. Dewey, "The Rural-Urban Continuum: Real but Relatively Unimportant," *American Journal of Sociology,* **66** (1966), 60–66.

99. Some sociologists have strongly disagreed, saying that many large cities, especially in the Middle East and Africa, have little if any industry. See G. Brandmeyer and T. Blackwell, "The Rural-Urban Continuum—Is It Culture-Free?" in R. S. Denisoff, ed., *Sociology: Theories in Conflict* (Belmont, Calif.: Wadsworth Publishing Co., Inc., 1972), pp. 168–179.

100. Gans, op cit.; and S. Greer, "Urbanism Reconsidered: A Comparative Study of Local Areas in a Metropolis," *American Sociological Review,* **21** (1956), pp. 19–25.

101. W. Kornhauser, *The Politics of Mass Society* (New York: The Free Press, 1959).

102. An excellent review of the mass society argument is found in Daniel Bell, "America as a Mass Society: A Critique," in *End of Ideology,* Rev. Ed. (New York: Collier Books, 1962), pp. 21–28; L. Bramson, *The Political Context of Sociology* (Princeton, N.J.: Princeton University Press), pp. 27–43; also Kornhauser, op cit., pp. 21–38.

103. R. Nisbet, op cit., pp. 30–31.

104. See C. J. Friedrich, ed., *Totalitarianism* (Cambridge, Mass.: Harvard University Press, 1954); H. Arendt, *The Origins of Totalitarianism* (New York: Harcourt Brace Jovanovich, Inc., 1951); and E. Fromm, *Escape from Freedom* (New York: Farrar, Strauss & Giroux, Inc., 1941).

105. See B. Rosenberg, I. Gerver, and F. W. Howton, eds., *Mass Society in Crisis: Social Problems and Social Pathology* (New York: Macmillan Publishing Co., Inc., 1971).

106. E. Shils, "Mass Society and Its Culture," in N. Jacobs, ed., *Culture for the Millions? Mass Media in Modern Society* (Boston: Beacon Press, 1959), p. 3.

107. See A. Solzhenitsyn, *Gulag Archipelago* (New York: Harper & Row, Publishers, 1974).

SIX

Socialization

What is Socialization?

INFANTS are adorable, helpless, and useless. They're not fit to associate with humans. They can't contribute anything sensible to a conversation. They have no table manners. They can't control their tempers or their bowels. They require a good deal of attention and time, and in return, if the parents are lucky, they may get a smile and the smile is more likely to be the result of gas rather than of appreciation.

Somehow we do manage to transform these little beasts into people who work, worship, and raise families, who carry out the many tasks that keep society going. The process by which these "useless" animals are transformed into humans capable of carrying out the responsibilities groups and societies require of their members we call *socialization.* Socialization is the process by which other people make infants fit to live among humans (as *human* is defined by each society and by each group within the society). Who socializes the child? His parents, his neighbors, his friends, his school teachers, the mass media, his co-workers. All tell the child in one way or another, "If you want us to accept you, you had better learn this skill, these values, these habits, these bits of information, these beliefs, these attitudes."

Infants have a lot to learn. Almost everything a human does is learned. We have, unlike many insects and animals, no instincts, patterns of behavior "wired in" before we are born. Not everything we learn as humans is what our teachers (parents, friends, teachers, clergymen, and so on) *intended* to teach us, but nonetheless, just about everything about us is the result of a learning process. Nor do our teachers always agree on what we should learn. Our friends may want us to be rough and tough; our parents may want us to be sweet and gentle. Our teachers may want us to be studious; our buddies may want us to take school less seriously. Our clergymen may encourage us to turn the other cheek; our TV programs may encourage us to punch anyone who annoys us. Despite these occasional situations in which behavior that makes one group proud of us distresses another group, we generally manage to do enough of the "right" things to be members in good standing of those groups that matter to us.

A good deal of the socialization process involves our learning to perform certain *roles* properly. What are "roles"?

Roles

Remember the Vulcans from Chapter One? Imagine that they prolong their visit and finally realize that it is not the automobile but the human who inhabits Earth. They sit in their spaceship and try to figure out what makes humans tick. At first they see a large number of activities taking place: people are sitting in the park, people are sitting in schoolrooms, people are working in offices, sweeping streets, cooking meals, painting pictures, walking down the street together, holding hands, skipping, having fist fights, chewing bubble gum, and performing a million other activities. Is there any pattern to all of these behaviors? After a while the Vulcans notice something, a pattern. They notice that some activities are mainly performed by men, others by women, some only by youngsters, some by older people. Some jobs seem to be limited to black, brown, yellow, and red men, others to white men or white women. Some activities are performed only by people in certain occupations. The Vulcans are obviously using crude categories: age, sex, race, occupation; but they keep looking. They look at other societies and discover that one society seems to have activities that don't seem to occur in others: one society has many computer programmers and few buffalo hunters, another the reverse. In one society the men do most of the agricultural work and the women make the pottery; in another the women do the farming and the men do the pottery making. Nevertheless, activity in each society varies with sex, age, and race. These are

Almost everything the human does is learned.

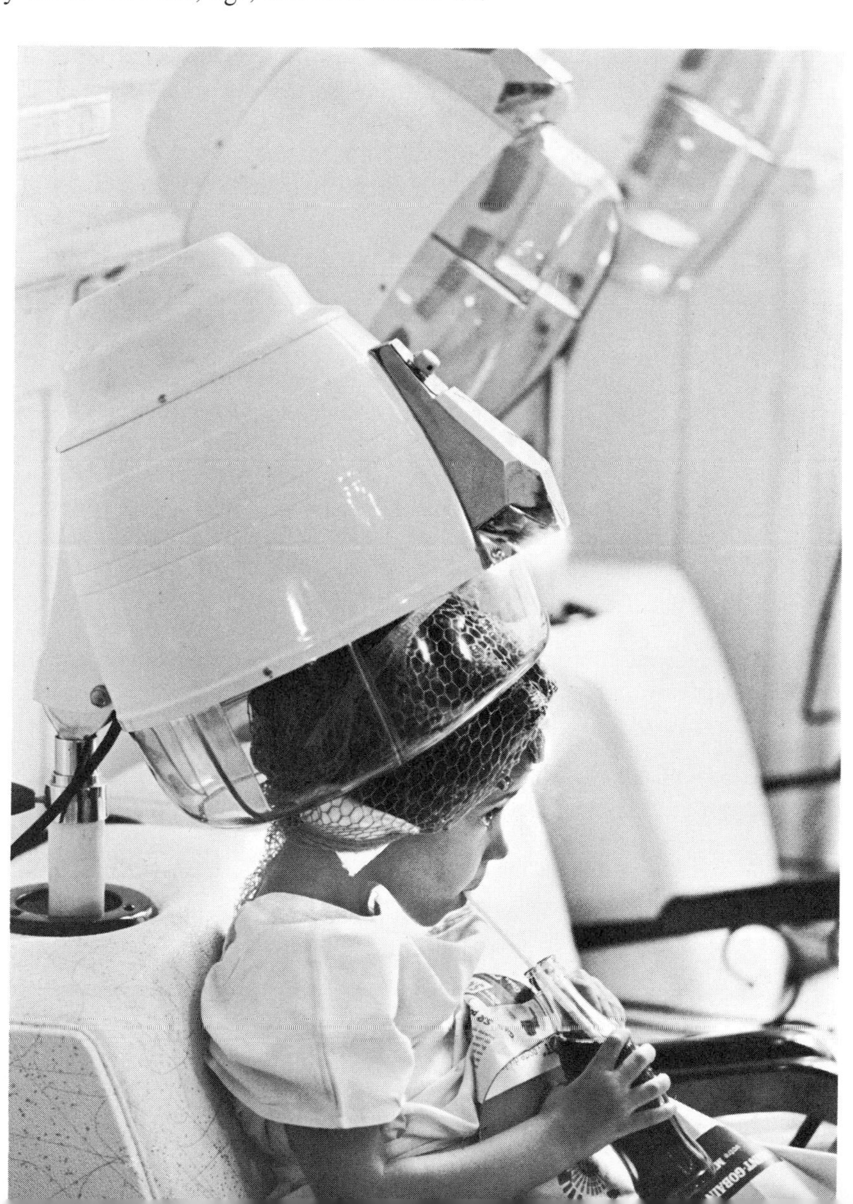

crude categories, but they help our friends understand and predict the behavior of the people they are observing.

Let us ask our Vulcan friends to go back home, come back in twenty-five years, and observe again. They discover that the same activities are taking place: children skipping, teachers lecturing, students sleeping, farmers farming, women taking responsibility for child rearing and housework, minority group members working at certain jobs, majority group members working at other jobs. There have been changes over the twenty-five years in some of the details of what our friends observe, but compared to the similarities, the changes are quite small. There are some new words in the vocabularies but the languages are recognizable as English, French, Russian, and so on. There are a few more women in one occupation and a few less in another, but the outlines of each society are pretty much the same. Now, over the course of these twenty-five years there have been some personnel changes. The children of the last visit are now workers and parents. Some of the parents have died, others have retired; the people who are now children had not been born twenty-five years earlier. The categories and patterns continue but the personnel change. There's a new crop of teachers but they still put their students to sleep. A new crop of mothers remind children to wear clean underwear (in case they are run over by a car and have to be undressed at the hospital).

The observers notice that each society seems to assign different activities on the basis of sex, age, race, and occupation. They see that these activities are pretty much the same whether we look at the society over a period of time or whether we observe the different people in the same category at any point in time. Teachers lecture; students take notes; bus drivers collect fares and drive buses; policemen guide traffic, referee family fights, and arrest law violators; doctors examine people and prescribe medicine.

Our intergalactic visitors also notice that by and large the relationships among people are quite predictable and smooth. Students come into a new course. If nothing else, they know that they will take notes, and that the prof will determine the course content and will give them exams. Students will raise their hands when they want to speak. Patients come into a new doctor's office and successfully predict that the doctor will ask them to remove their clothing, ask where it hurts, tell them what medicines to take. The doctor predicts that when he says, "Remove your clothes," the patient will not say, "You first!" Nor will the patient respond to "Where does it hurt?" with "You're the doctor, you tell me." Nor will the patient say, "I've got a pain in my arm. The doctor down the street wants ten dollars to fix me up. What do you bid?"

We have been leading you into the concept of "roles." Earthlings, like the Vulcans, have figured out (1) that each society possesses many social categories or *roles:* mother, father, child, student, teacher, doctor, patient, driver, passenger, and so on; (2) that if you know something about another person's category, the role he is performing, you can pretty well predict what a person in that category will do and say, and you know what that person expects you to do;

and (3) that you need not know any more about that person than the name of the role he is performing to interact with him smoothly. We can look at society as made up of roles and relationships rather than as a collection of people. You can have a successful visit to the doctor without knowing whether he is married or single, a good parent or a bad one, whether he is Jewish or Catholic. These are all irrelevant to your relationship. If he is a competent doctor, none of these characteristics have any bearing on what happens in his office.

You watch a ball game. You can predict the behavior on the field of a pitcher by reading the rule book that describes his roles. You cannot predict his behavior on the field by knowing about his personality structure or whether he is a wife swapper in his private life.

No matter what the family problems or life history of your bus driver, he will collect your fare and stop to let you off at one of the bus stops on his route. You can predict successfully that he won't suddenly decide to drive the bus from the Bronx to Miami because he's bored with the Bronx. Nor will he be likely to listen to your personal problems or offer you advice on income tax loopholes.

The Vulcans have discovered something that you were aware of but not *fully* aware of. If you were asked to make up a list of the things that you expect of a date and that a date has a right to expect of you, you'd have a hard time putting together a *complete* list. The reason you'd have a hard time is that most of the expectations we have when we enter into a social situation aren't conscious. We realize that we expected certain things *only* when the other party *doesn't* do what we expect.

Consider dating. You can have a date with almost anyone of the appropriate age and sex in the United States and usually predict quite well what kinds of things will happen and what things won't happen. There are many things you expect of a date but wouldn't put down on a list. If your date *doesn't* do what you expect, you will become quite aware of the fact that you had these expectations. For example, consider two young people on their first date with each other. How would she react if he asked the waiter to give *her* the check? How would he react if *she* called *him* and asked him for a date and if she offered to collect him at his dorm? How would he react if when he asked for a goodnight kiss she kicked him in the shins and screamed? If she picked the most expensive item on the menu instead of watching carefully to see how expensive his order is, what would he think? If she ate that expensive meal and then told him she couldn't date him next week because her husband had asked for next Saturday first, would he feel that she should have told him that she was already married before she accepted the date with him? In each case one party to the date took for granted that the other understood how a date is supposed to behave.

We expect certain behavior as a result of knowing the role of a "date" in our society. Unless our expectations are violated we may not ever be aware of how much we predict, usually quite accurately, about the way others will behave when we know nothing more about them than their social category, like "date," "male," "female," "teacher," "parent," "waitress," and so on.

As we go through our daily routines we meet many people. We know how to respond to these people because we know what roles they perform. We are responding to the roles rather than to the people. They respond to our roles rather than to us as individuals. One person asks us to undress. Another person asks us for information about our income. A third asks us about our sex life. Do we get angry and tell them what to do with their requests? Not if the first is a doctor, the second a representative of the Internal Revenue Service, and the third a psychiatrist. We would probably go along with their requests, not because they are nice people or because they'll punch us in the nose if we don't comply, but because their roles as doctor, IRS agent, or psychiatrist require them to make these requests and because our roles as patients or citizens require us to cooperate.

Outside working hours if these people were to make such requests (how dare they!) we would justifiably refuse to listen. Same person, but not the same role. We're responding to the role and not the person.

The Vulcans observe that if we know the name and nature of the role, we know what to expect of the person performing the role.

We started this chapter by talking about the human infant, an adorable, ignorant creature. The infant becomes human by learning to perform the roles appropriate in his or her society: male, female, student, parent, worker, customer, and so on. One way of looking at a society, the way our Vulcans and many sociologists look at societies, is to consider a society a network of roles. Socialization, then, involves learning to perform roles. People can get along with other people, strangers or not, relatively smoothly because each knows what is expected of him and what he has a right to expect of the other person.

As we've also observed, over a period of time the roles stay pretty much the same although the people in them may come and go. This is so partly because we come to accept the way we perform our roles as the only way to perform them and therefore don't care to change them, and partly because other people take our roles for granted and base *their* behavior on what they expect *us* to do. We have to have other people's permission to change our roles because a change in *our* roles requires *them* to change, too. If your professor decides he doesn't want to lecture and wants you and your classmates to do all the work of preparing lectures and picking topics for discussion, you're likely to complain: "That's your job, not mine," or "I counted on this course's taking up just so much of my time before I signed up. Even if I wanted to go along with these changes, I can't. I don't have the time."

Let's go into a bit more detail about roles. We've suggested that we can look at a society as a network of roles or that we can think of smaller segments of a society as collections of roles: educational roles, political roles, economic roles, family roles, religious roles.

Roles or People?

We can view a *society as a network of roles* rather than a collection of people. Doing this helps us understand how we can transact most of our daily business quite smoothly, with people we have never met before, knowing only the names and nature of their roles. It also helps us understand how a society can continue over time to be much the same though particular people come and go. The roles remain and new generations learn to perform them in much the same way as the older generations.

The concept of role also helps us understand the fact that the same person observed at different times of day seems to be several different people, that he changes his character as he changes his roles. Think of someone you believe you know quite well, someone you've known for a while. Most of us tend to describe people in terms of traits, characteristics that we believe a person possesses all the time, in any situation, over long periods of time. We say that a person is "warm," "friendly," "moral," "generous," and we assume that other people who know him agree that these traits describe him. It's frustrating to meet someone who has known a person you have known for an equally long time who insists that those traits don't describe this person at all, that he's quite the opposite. The traits that you think of as being as unchangeable as a leopard's spots you're told you've got all wrong. You say Charlie's generous, the other person says he's stingy; you say Charlie's very square, he says Charlie's wild, drinks like a fish, chases women. You finally say, "Darn it! I've been his clergyman for five years. I've seen a hundred demonstrations that I've got this guy pegged right." The other person says, "Well, I've been his co-worker for five years. I've seen him behave the way I told you at a dozen conventions, at a hundred sales conferences. I've watched him fire a half-dozen guys without blinking an eye." Each of you is assuming that the traits you attribute to Charlie describe stable characteristics that he takes from one situation to another. Instead, you are finding that Charlie has many roles, that he plays each role a different way and really *is* a different person in each role. Charlie as church member, Charlie as businessman, Charlie as father, Charlie as Army Reserve member: they're different roles and Charlie seems to become a different person as he changes roles. Which one is *really* Charlie? All of them! You'll have a hard time convincing people who've observed him in only one of these roles that they don't have the one-and-only, real Charlie. This is so in large part because he behaves the same way over time *in a given role.* Year in, year out he's a generous father and a stingy boss, a cautious businessman and a reckless poker player. He's the same man as long as he is playing the same role. Individuals perform *multiple roles.* That is, daily we play a number of roles.

Is there, then, nothing that we carry from role to role? Are we really that changeable? There's no agreement among sociologists or, in recent years, psychologists.[1] Sociologists have tended to emphasize *situational* factors in understanding behavior. They emphasize pressures on, and experiences of, people *in* a particular role. Psychologists have tended to stress *personal* factors, internal factors, such as traits, that the person brings to the role.

We often respond to roles rather than people.

Neither approach alone will give a complete explanation of a given person's behavior, and in recent years each discipline has moved toward the recognition that behavior involves both internal and external factors. Sociologists, nevertheless, continue to be impressed by the similarities in the way people handle roles despite differences in personality, temperament, and life history.

Consider these two quite dramatic experimental illustrations of the power of roles to produce behavior that almost all of us would vigorously deny *we* are capable of. The first experiment was conducted by psychologist Stanley Milgram, the second by Phillip Zimbardo.

The Milgram Experiment[2]

In 1963 Stanley Milgram advertised in local newspapers for people to serve as subjects in an experiment, offering them four dollars for their participation in a one-hour memory and learning project at Yale University. By doing this he managed to get a cross section of the community rather than the usual college sophomores as research subjects. (His subjects were skilled and unskilled workers, 40 percent; white-collar, sales, and business people, 40 percent; and professionals, 20 percent. Ages: 20 percent in their twenties, 40 percent in their thirties, and 40 percent in their forties.)

Imagine that you are a volunteer subject. You, the volunteer, show up at Milgram's laboratory and meet another subject and the experimenter who pays you both the four dollars and fifty-cent carfare for having showed up: ". . . the money is yours simply for coming to the laboratory. From this point on, no matter what happens, the money is yours." You and the other person are told that the experimenter is interested in understanding more about memory and learning, particularly the effects of punishment on learning. One of you is to be the teacher, one of you the pupil. You're to draw lots to decide who is to be the teacher and who the pupil. You draw the slip of paper that says "teacher."

The learner is taken into another room. You follow and watch him being strapped to a chair ("to avoid any excessive movement"). A metal bracelet is attached to his bare arm and wires are attached to it. He asks, "Is there any danger?" The experimenter says, "Although the shocks can be extremely painful, they cause no permanent tissue damage." Now you and the experimenter go back into the other room and he shows you his electric-shock generator. It has thirty lever-type switches on it. Under each is a little red light and when the researcher flips the main power switch, a big purple light on the generator goes on. Under the switches are labels: 15 volts, 30 volts, 45 volts, 60 volts; every switch is 15 volts higher than the last up to the thirtieth, 450 volts. Under the numbers appear the words "Slight Shock," "Moderate Shock," "Strong Shock," "Very Strong Shock," "Extreme Intensity Shock," "Danger: Severe Shock." As the numbers go up above 400 volts the words are replaced by red *X*'s.

The experimenter then explains to you what you're supposed to do. You're to read a list of word pairs over your microphone to the other person (the learner). After you've read him the complete list, you go back to the beginning of the list and you recite the first word of the pair and four alternatives for the second word, one of which is correct. The pupil is to tell you the second word by pulling one of four switches in front of him. If he is wrong and pulls the wrong switch, you will pull one of the levers. On the first mistake, you pull the first lever (15 volts), on the second mistake, the second (30 volts), and so on. On the thirtieth mistake you pull the thirtieth lever (450 volts).

The experimenter gives you a little shock (45 volts) to give you an idea of what the machine can do.

As the experiment proceeds the learner makes more and more mistakes. With each mistake, you, the teacher, move up one lever. The pupil or "victim" is not one to suffer in silence. While you're pulling those switches, he is yelling and banging the wall and moaning and groaning. At 150 volts, he yells, "Experimenter, get me out of here! I won't be in the experiment anymore! I refuse to go on!" The experimenter asks you to ignore that: "Please continue. Whether the learner likes it or not, you must go on until he has learned all the pairs correctly. So please go on." He continues to scream. You start worrying about the effects of shock on this poor guy. The experimenter says, "The experiment requires that you continue." You continue. He screams, louder, louder. Around 360 volts . . . no scream. No sounds. Silence. You look at the experimenter. His response? "If he doesn't answer within five or ten seconds, count it as a wrong answer!" You are frightened. Maybe he's dead. (In one version of the experiment the learner, a man of fifty or so, claimed to have a heart condition.) "Please go on!" You continue until you've given him 450 volts and stay at 450 volts until the experimenter says you can stop. Finally the experimenter tells you it's all right to stop and he goes in to the other room to release the learner.

Perhaps you are saying to yourself, "Not me. I would have quit way earlier. I couldn't do that." Perhaps. We doubt it, though. The experiment we described briefly here was carried out in several variations using more than a thousand adult volunteers in the early 1960s. Before we tell you about the variations, let us make clear that the "learner" was actually a confederate of the experimenter, an amateur actor who never received any of those electric shocks. The subject who became the "teacher" and got 45 volts was the only one who got any kind of shock. Milgram had described his experiment to a panel of forty psychiatrists and asked them to predict what subjects would do. They predicted that most subjects would quit at 150 volts, that fewer than 5 percent would go as high as 300 volts, and that about one volunteer in a thousand would go all the way to 450 volts.

The variation we just described Milgram called "Voice Feedback;" the teacher could hear the learner's voice but couldn't see him. In another variation the "learner" was in another room and couldn't be seen *or* heard. His answers were given by means of the electric switches, which he did not pull after 300 volts. This variation was called "Remote Feedback." In the "Proximity" variation the victim was seated in the room with the teacher, who could see and hear him screaming, twitching, and jerking. In the fourth, or "Touch Proximity" condition, the victim sat near the teacher. But instead of having an electrode attacked to his arm, he had to touch a metal plate to get a shock. The teacher had physically to force the victim's hand down onto the shock plate if the learner refused to do it voluntarily. (Of course, each subject was randomly assigned to serve in only one of these variations.)

In the Remote Feedback condition, in which the learner couldn't be seen or heard, twenty-six of the forty volunteers obeyed the experimenter completely, even giving the 450-volt shock three times as they'd been ordered. All forty went to at least 300 volts. In the Voice Feedback condition, in which the victim could be heard but not seen, twenty-five of forty subjects went up to 450 volts. In the Proximity condition sixteen of forty volunteers went all the way to 450 volts. In Touch Proximity, in which the subjects had to arm-wrestle with the victim, twelve volunteers wrestled him all the way to the end. The proportion of subjects who defied the experimenter and who refused to continue shocking the victim varied from 70 percent in the Touch Proximity situation to 34 percent in the Remote Feedback situation. How do we account for the fact that these citizens were so obedient that had there been a real victim with a real heart condition they could have killed him? It wasn't the money, which the subjects could keep whatever happened and, of course, being working people, didn't need. It wasn't that the subjects caught on to the fact that this was all a rigged experiment—they didn't.

More important, it wasn't that Milgram had somehow rounded up a group of sadists. His subjects were given a number of personality tests. By and large, these tests didn't produce anything particularly notable or useful in the way of information about the characteristics of his volunteers. Nor did they show much difference in the personalities of those who obeyed instructions and those who defied the experimenter. Not everyone obeyed the experimenter, as we have indicated, but the variable that made the most difference in the *rate* of defiance was closeness to the victim, not the personality of the subject. Why did the subjects obey the experimenter? They had volunteered for the *role of "subject"* in a scientific experiment. The role of "good subject" committed them to follow the instructions of the Scientist conducting the research project. The Scientist's role entitled him to give the subject orders in the name of Science. In the eyes of the subjects, Science gave the researcher the Authority to ask the subject to do whatever was necessary to contribute new knowledge to Science.

As Milgram notes, his authority as a scientist is a good deal weaker than the authority of a government that calls up people to be soldiers. His authority is backed by no power. A subject who quits the experiment can't be arrested or shot or fired from his job for his defiance. Nevertheless, "normal" people can be made, in a laboratory, to do horrifying things to other people when they take on the role of "subject." It's harder to get subjects to carry out the role of "good subject" when they can see and hear the consequences of their obedience than when the victim is out of sight. Nevertheless, it is the situation rather than the personality traits of the subjects that we must explore to understand what happened in Milgram's laboratory.

We should mention here that Milgram is not interested in trying to find ways to make people more obedient. He is interested in trying to understand what must be done to make subjects more defiant. He has found that if the experimenter leaves the room, the subject will not shock the victim. If the experimenter supplies the subject with a confederate who appears to be a fellow subject and the confederate defies the experimenter, the subject will also defy the experimenter and refuse to shock his victim. Again, these are variations in the situation, variations in social support. The subjects are still "average," "decent" people like us, not simply "good guys" and "bad guys." We haven't the space to discuss the ethics of doing such research or to discuss other studies that have been built on the Milgram study or to discuss the obvious parallels to such occurrences as My Lai, but we believe we have given you the beginnings of an understanding of the importance of the "role" and the "situation" in influencing our behavior. A final note on the Milgram experiment: a recent study reproduced the Milgram experiment in Germany[3] (where we like to think the phrase "I was only following orders" was invented) and showed that German subjects are no more obedient than Americans—or to put it another way, Americans are no less obedient to authority than Germans.

The Zimbardo Experiment[4]

The second experiment was carried out by psychologist Phillip Zimbardo and his associates at Stanford University, Craig Haney, Curtis Banks, and David Jaffe. Zimbardo created a prison in the basement of the psychology building of Stanford for a two-week experiment. The experiment lasted only six days, at which point Zimbardo decided he did not dare continue it. Zimbardo had advertised in the newspaper for male students who would be given fifteen dollars a day to participate in a psychological study. He administered a battery of psychological tests and interviews to the seventy applicants to eliminate men who had any kind of psychological problem, medical disability, or history of criminal activity or drug abuse. He was left with twenty-four subjects. He flipped a coin to decide *randomly* who was to become a "prisoner" and who was to become a "guard." *There were no differences between the two groups before the experiment was started. The toss of a coin decided who would take which role, prisoner or guard.*

The basement prison was set up after consultation with prison experts, including one who had spent seventeen years as a prisoner in such places as

San Quentin, Soledad, and Folsom. "Cells" for the prisoners were built out of laboratory rooms. The corridor was made into the "yard," the only place outside his cell where a prisoner could walk. A small closet became the "hole," or solitary confinement. There were no windows and no clocks. The prisoners were routed from their beds in the middle of the night by the real Palo Alto police, handcuffed and hauled down to the police station, accused of having committed a felony, booked, fingerprinted, and left blindfolded in a cell for a while. The Stanford experimenters then collected them, put them in a car and drove them down to the "Stanford County Jail," where the rest of the experiment took place.

The prisoners were searched, stripped naked, deloused, and then given their uniforms, a dress worn with no underclothes. Each uniform had the prisoner's number on it. To each prisoner's ankle a heavy chain was bolted and it was worn at all times. On their feet the prisoners wore loosely fitting rubber sandals and on their heads nylon stocking caps, which were to be worn day and night (a substitute for shaving the prisoner's hair off). All of these things—the dresses, chains, caps—were intended to disorient, deindividualize, and humiliate the prisoners. The procedure wasn't intended to be an exact reproduction of a prison situation but rather to be a reproduction of the important psychological features of a prison.

The guards wore identical khaki uniforms and silver reflector eyeglasses, to make eye contact impossible. They carried billy clubs, whistles, and handcuffs. The guards were given no formal training and were given a good deal of freedom to decide how to handle prisoners as long as they maintained "law and order" in the prison.

The prisoners were required to get permission from the guards for such things as writing letters, smoking, or going to the toilet. The prisoners were addressed by number and required to address one another by prison number. The guards were addressed as "Mr. Correctional Officer."

The first night the prisoners were routed from their beds for the first "count":

The ostensible purpose of the count was to provide a public test of the prisoners' knowledge of the rules and of their ID numbers. But more important, the count, which occurred at least once on each of the three different guard shifts, provided a regular occasion for the guards to relate to the prisoners. Over the course of the study, the duration of the counts was spontaneously increased by the guards from their initial perfunctory 10 minutes to a seemingly interminable several hours. During these confrontations, guards who were bored could find ways to amuse themselves, ridiculing recalcitrant prisoners, enforcing arbitrary rules, and openly exaggerating any dissension among the prisoners.

The second morning found the prisoners in rebellion. They took off their stocking caps, yanked off their numbers, and barricading themselves in their cells, taunted and cursed the guards. The night-shift guards volunteered to stay on duty without pay to help the morning-shift guards.

The guards met and decided to treat force with force. They got a fire extinguisher that shot a stream of skin-chilling carbon dioxide and forced the prisoners away from the doors; they broke into each cell, stripped the prisoners naked, took the beds out, forced the prisoners who were the ringleaders into solitary confinement, and generally began to harass and intimidate the prisoners.

After crushing the riot, the guards decided to head off further unrest by creating a privileged cell for those who were "good prisoners" and then, without explanation, switching some of the troublemakers into it and some of the good prisoners out into the other cells. The prisoner ringleaders could not trust these new cell mates because they had not joined in the riot and might even be "snitches." The prisoners never again acted in unity against the system.

The breakup of the prisoner rebellion appeared not only to have crushed prisoner morale but also to have encouraged the guards to indulge themselves in the exercise of arbitrary power:

It was after this episode that the guards really began to demonstrate their inventiveness in the application of arbitrary power. They made the prisoners obey petty, meaningless and often inconsistent rules, forced them to engage in tedious, useless work, such as moving cartons back and forth between closets and picking thorns out of their blankets for hours on end. (The guards had previously dragged the blankets through thorny bushes to create this disagreeable task.) Not only did the prisoners have to sing songs or laugh or refrain from smiling on command; they were also encouraged to curse and vilify each other publicly during some of their counts. They sounded off their numbers endlessly and were repeatedly made to do pushups, on occasion with a guard stepping on them or a prisoner sitting on them.

The first prisoner was released after thirty-six hours of prison life because of "extreme depression, disorganized thinking, uncontrollable crying, and fits of rage." The experimenters released him reluctantly because they were sure he was trying to "con" them. They couldn't believe that a volunteer in a mock prison could really be suffering and disturbed to that extent. On each of the next three days another prisoner developed similar symptoms and had to be released. A fifth prisoner, after the mock parole board had rejected his parole appeal, had to be released because he developed a "psychosomatic rash" over his entire body.

From the first to the last day, Zimbardo and his associates report a significant increase in the use of "abusive tactics," such as insults to the prisoners, threats to them, the use of nightsticks and fire extinguishers to keep the prisoners in line, references to the prisoners in "impersonal, anonymous, depreciating ways: 'Hey, you," or 'You (obscenity) 5401, come here.'"

Everyone and everything in the prison was defined by power. To be a guard who did not take advantage of this institutionally sanctioned use of power was to appear "weak," "out of it," "wired up by the prisoners," or simply a deviant from the established norms of "appropriate guard behavior."

Not all guards behaved cruelly. Some did little favors for the prisoners, avoided situations in which prisoners were being harassed, and were reluctant to punish prisoners. But Zimbardo notes that

> . . . the behavior of these good guards seemed more motivated by a desire to be liked by everyone in the system than by a concern for the inmates' welfare. No guard ever intervened in any direct way on behalf of the prisoners, ever interfered with the orders of the cruelest guards or ever openly complained about the subhuman quality of life that characterized this prison.

Although the cruel guards were in a minority, Zimbardo notes that the prison could not have functioned without the cooperation of the "good" guards. The harsher guards set the tone of the prison and created a capricious, arbitrary environment:

> Over time the prisoners began to react passively. When our mock prisoners asked questions, they got answers about half the time, but the rest of the time they were insulted and punished—and it was not possible for them to predict the outcome. As they began to "toe the line" they stopped resisting, questioning, and, indeed, almost ceased responding altogether. . . . [They] learned the safest strategy to use in an unpredictable, threatening environment from which there is no physical escape—do nothing, except what is required. Act not, want not, feel not and you will not get into trouble in prison-like situations.

This prison, remember, was not a real prison, but for these subjects—guards and prisoners—it became quite real:

> Prisoner 819, who had gone into a rage followed by an uncontrollable crying fit, was about to be prematurely released from the prison when a guard lined up the prisoners and had them chant in unison, "819 is a bad prisoner. Because of what 819 did to prison property we must all suffer. 819 is a bad prisoner." Over and over again. When we realized 819 might be overhearing this, we rushed into the room where 819 was supposed to be resting, only to find him in tears, prepared to go back to prison because he could not leave as long as the others thought he was a "bad prisoner." Sick as he felt, he had to prove to them that he was not a "bad" prisoner. He had to be persuaded that he was not a prisoner at all, that the others were also just students, that this was just an experiment and not a prison and the prison staff was only research psychologists.

Observe the changes in the thinking and behavior of Guard A as recorded in his diary:

> *Prior to the start of experiment:* "As I am a pacifist and nonaggressive individual I cannot see a time when I might guard and/or maltreat other living things."
>
> *After an orientation meeting:* "I doubt whether many of us share the expectations of 'seriousness' that the experimenters seem to have."
>
> *First Day:* "Feel sure that the prisoners will make fun of my appearance and

I evolve my first basic strategy—mainly not to smile at anything they say or do which would be admitting it's all only a game. . . . At cell 3 I stop and setting my voice hard and low say to 5486, 'What are you smiling at?' 'Nothing, Mr. Correction Officer,' 'Well, see that you don't.' (As I walk off I feel stupid.)"

Second Day: "5704 asked me for a cigarette and I ignored him—because I am a non-smoker and could not empathize. . . . Meanwhile since I was feeling empathetic towards 1037, I determined not to talk with him. . . . after we had count and lights out (Guard D) and I held a loud conversation about going home to our girlfriends and what we were going to do to them."

Fourth Day: ". . . The psychologist rebukes me for handcuffing and blindfolding a prisoner before leaving the [counseling] office, and I resentfully reply that it is both necessary security and my business anyway."

Fifth Day: "I harass 'Sarge' who continues to stubbornly overrespond to all commands. I have singled him out for special abuse both because he begs for it and because I simply don't like him. The real trouble starts at dinner. The new prisoner (416) refuses to eat his sausage. . . . we throw him into the Hole ordering him to hold sausages in each hand. We have a crisis of authority—this rebellious conduct potentially undermines the complete control we have over the others. We decide to play upon prisoner solidarity and tell the new one that all the others will be deprived of visitors if he does not eat his dinner. . . . I walk by and slam my stick into the Hole door. . . . I am very angry at this prisoner for causing discomfort and trouble for the others, I decided to force-feed him, but he wouldn't eat. I let the food slide down his face. I didn't believe it was me doing it. I hated myself for making him eat but I hated him more for not eating."

Sixth Day: "The experiment is over. I feel elated but am shocked to find some other guards disappointed somewhat because of the loss of money and some because they are enjoying themselves."

The subjects and the guards were middle-class, "normal" college students. The setting was not a real prison but a simulation of *some* of the features of a real prison. Despite the apparent artificiality of the situation, the roles the "guards" and the "prisoners" took on became horrifyingly real and the experimenters decided to call it quits after only six days. (Ironically, they aborted the experiment the day before the Attica prison uprising.)

Zimbardo sums up his idea of what all of this demonstrates:

The pathology observed in this study cannot be attributed reasonably to preexisting personality differences of the subjects, that option being eliminated by our selection procedure and random assignment. Rather, the subjects' abnormal social and personal reactions are best seen as a product of their transaction with an environment that supported the behavior that would be pathological in other settings, but was "appropriate" in this prison. Had we observed comparable reactions in a real prison, the psychiatrist undoubtedly would have been able to attribute any prisoners' behavior to character defects or personality maladjustment, while critics of the prison system would have been quick to label the guards as "psychopathic." This tendency to locate the source of behavior disorders inside a particular person or group underestimates the power of situational forces.

The Milgram and Zimbardo studies are quite dramatic in their demonstrations of the effects of the "situation" and the "role" on their subjects' behavior. In our everyday lives we do essentially the same things as these subjects did. *We become our roles.* They aren't merely parts of an abstract script, to be performed casually and indifferently, but become integral parts of us while we are performing our roles. As we switch roles we become different people, but all of those people are real.

The Development of the "Self"

Chapter Four suggested that we *interpret* events and *impose meaning* on the world rather than simply responding to the world automatically. John slaps Joe. What does it mean? How should Joe respond? John commands Joe to do something. How should Joe respond? Obviously those questions are unanswerable unless we first decide who Joe and John are. John slaps Joe. Is John a baby and Joe his father? Is John a student who has been insulted by Joe, a fellow student? Is John Joe's father, punishing Joe for setting fire to the family's dog? How Joe responds depends on his answer to the question, "Who am I?" An adult, a student, a child? The appropriate response depends on the *role* each plays. If a baby slaps an adult, that's cute. If a fellow student belts you, that's an invitation to a fight. If a parent swats a child, that's his choice as a parent and disciplinarian. The slap itself *has no meaning* except in terms of the roles of the "slapper" and the "slappee."

John gives Joe a command. Perhaps John's a doctor commanding Joe to take his medicine regularly and to give up smoking. Perhaps John is an employee telling his boss, Joe, that Joe must start coming to work on time. Joe fires John because he doesn't believe in taking orders from his own employee. "Who the hell does he think he is? Who does he think I am?" asks Joe. Before either party can act or make sense of the other's behavior, in these two situations or in any other social situations, he has to identify his own role and the other person's role.

This ability to ask "Who am I?" and "What is expected of me?" and the ability to answer those questions accurately result ultimately from our ability to make a distinction between ourselves and everything that is *not* ourselves and our ability to see ourselves through other people's eyes. For George Herbert Mead, a philosopher who had enormous influence on many sociologists, the ability to talk to ourselves, to look at our own behavior as objectively as we look at other people's behavior, and to tell ourselves what we ought to be doing, given our roles, is what makes us human.[5]

Mead and his followers suggest that at birth we don't make any distinction between ourselves and the world around us. As infants we bite our pacifiers, our blankets, anything we can get hold of. A baby may even bite his own foot. If he's got, say, a tooth or a tooth-and-a-half, biting his foot is a first lesson in making distinctions between "self" and "not self."

No one cares if babies bite their feet or not, but as the baby gets a bit older, people do start responding to the baby's behavior. They're pleased with his behavior or they're displeased with it. They hug him and kiss him, or they yell at him, even administer a spanking occasionally. The child starts to develop a conception of "me" and "them," "them" being mostly the child's mother. Mother sometimes likes what the child does and hugs him, sometimes doesn't like it and swats his bottom.

What's this child's response? Perhaps he says to himself something like this: "I am consistent in my behavior. I follow a simple rule: I do whatever I feel like doing. This giant called Mama is not consistent. Sometimes Mama likes what I do and she hugs me. Sometimes she gets angry and paddles me. Unless I learn to psych out this inconsistent nut, one of these days she's going to kill me. Let me see if I can put myself in her shoes, learn to think the way she does, so I can anticipate how she's going to react to whatever I do. If I get her psyched out properly, I can avoid doing whatever it is that annoys her and do the things that she'll like." This construction of a little child's dialogue with himself is obviously imaginary, but we suspect that this is a pretty good description of the beginnings of children's learning to take on someone else's role, to see themselves through someone else's eyes, and to guide their own behavior accordingly.

Watch a two-year-old on his way to stick his finger in the electric outlet if you want to see the beginnings of this process. He says, "No. No. Mustn't do that," and as he is telling himself that he *mustn't,* he *does.* The "no" is the child's reconstruction of what his mother would be saying. The dialogue is between the part of his mind that we can say represents his impulses (Mead called this the *I*) and the part of his mind that we can say represents the planting of his society's perspectives and rules inside his mind (Mead called this the *Me*).

The two-year-old in our example is telling himself what not to do, just as his mother would tell him or he would tell another two-year-old. Mead called this ability to talk to yourself as if you were talking to someone else the ability to "become an object" to yourself. He argued that becoming human, developing a "mind," is the result of this kind of internal communication process and is possible because we have the ability to use language to communicate both with other people and with ourselves.

The ability to communicate with ourselves, to have the sort of internal dialogue we invented for our two-year-old, makes it possible to anticipate other people's behavior and other people's responses to our behavior. Furthermore, this ability to have an internal dialogue makes it possible to answer the questions "Who am I in this situation?" and "Who does he think *he* is?" and "Who does he think *I* am?" Unless we can answer these questions we don't know how to behave appropriately, nor can we make sense of the other person's behavior. (We may know what others expect of us and refuse to do it, but that's another matter.)

A two-year-old is beginning to develop this ability to anticipate other people's reactions to his behavior. And as he gets older, he will get to be as good at it as we adults are: it's not an easy thing to do.

Seven-year-olds are better at doing this than two-year-olds, but they're still not very good at it. Jean Piaget performed an experiment about fifty years ago[6] in which he explained to one seven-year-old how a water faucet works. Once he was sure the child understood, Piaget asked the seven-year-old to explain it to another seven-year-old who had been waiting outside. The explanation of the "teacher" to the "student" ran something like this: "You turn that thingamabob there and it opens the door and the water comes out of that widget there." (The child doing the explaining pointed in the general direction of a diagram of a faucet as he did this.) Meanwhile, the child receiving the explanation was wondering, "What's a 'thingamabob'? Where's the 'door'? What's a 'widget'?" and the first child couldn't understand why the second one didn't understand his explanation.

We can recognize what was happening. The first child was just not yet capable of saying to himself, "What would I have to have pointed out to me if I didn't understand how faucets work?" Because he couldn't put himself into the other fellow's shoes, he couldn't explain what he wanted to explain, nor could he understand why the other child was so thick. Meanwhile, the other child hadn't the foggiest idea of what the first one was talking about. We adults may not always be terribly sensitive observers, but even the slowest normal adult can do the kind of role taking that Piaget's seven-year-olds could not.

Not only do we develop the ability to see ourselves through other people's eyes, but *what we see of ourselves in other people's eyes has an effect on what we think of ourselves.* Charles Horton Cooley (the sociologist who developed the concept of the "primary group") introduced the concept of the "looking-glass self."[7] By this he meant that we not only have an idea of what we look like to others but that we also have feelings about whatever it is that we think they see. We believe people are admiring us and we feel proud. We believe that people are sneering at us and we feel humiliated. Other people are the "looking glass" in which we see ourselves. We know what other people think of us (or we believe we do) and the knowledge that we draw from their words, their expressions, their behavior toward us tends to become a part of how we know ourselves and what we believe about and feel about ourselves.

Walk over to the nearest four-year-old and ask, "Are you an introvert or an extrovert?" Most likely he'll give you a puzzled look and say, "I don't know. My mommy never told me." On the other hand, the child knows that he is a "good little boy," a Christian, a Moslem, a Jew, a Buddhist, an American, a Mexican, a Chinese, or whatever, because Mommy said so or Daddy said so. In growing up the child will become many other roles as well: mother, father, doctor, lawyer, "good athlete," "good student," "responsible citizen," "nice girl," "drunkard," "thief," "slut," "healthy person," "sick person," and so on. All will be parts of the person's "self" and guides to how to act and how to expect others to react.

Earlier in the chapter we raised the question of why someone we know as one person can be known to other people as what appears to be a completely different person and why over long periods of time the "different" person each group seems to know behaves so consistently. We can offer part of an explanation by means of what we have just said about the "self." That is, each of us has an idea of himself as *X*-role (*X*-role might be "myself as parent," "myself as wife," "myself as husband," "myself as student," "myself as citizen," and so on). The details of "myself as *X*-role" result from our treatment by other people while we're in that role, our lessons from other people about what that role involves and how it should be performed, the amount of flexibility the role permits, and our own skills, abilities, and personal preferences as they apply to that role. Once we have somehow made our agreement with ourselves and others about what we are going to do in *X*-role, we become comfortable in that role and committed to playing it a certain way. And other people come to expect that we'll continue to play it that way. Unless something quite dramatic occurs, we will continue to perform the role the same way indefinitely and let outside observers (like sociologists and psychologists) worry about whether or not we're "consistent" from one role to the next.

Another Perspective on Roles

We started this chapter with a particular way of looking at socialization and role learning. In oversimplified form it might be described this way: the society is a network of roles and the socialization process somehow indoctrinates each child into the one-and-only way of performing each role. Many sociologists suggest that this "structural" model of a passive lump of a child being completely molded by his society is an overly simplified version of a very complicated process. They argue that this version doesn't make provision for changes in roles or discontent with roles or resistance to being completely socialized. It's not that the approach is wrong, they observe, it just doesn't go far enough. We don't always identify ourselves with our roles, we sometimes perform the roles and go through the motions without believing in them or making them a part of ourselves. Critics suggest that the structural approach to roles is quite useful for understanding differences among societies—the most dependent American wife may be more independent, say, than the most independent wife in some other society. But when we look more closely at the way people in the "same" role perform within the same society, we notice a much wider range of ways of behaving (although the society does place outer limits on what can be done within a given role) than the structural model makes provision for.

The school of sociological thought that has been derived from the work of Mead (the approach is sometimes called *symbolic interaction*) has been most prominent in denying a model of roles as parts of a play in which all the parts *must* be played the same way except for trivial personal variations. They prefer a model that also uses the analogy of a play with a script, but a script that gives the players only the barest outlines of what their roles should be. It's a script that forces us to improvise, to ad-lib, to create the details of our roles, to negotiate with one another about who does what to whom. They see the results of these negotiations as being always open to renegotiations.[8]

At this point in the development of sociology as a scientific discipline it is hard to say which approach will ultimately be the most useful. The truth probably lies between the extremes of exaggerating or minimizing the extent to which our roles determine our behavior. We can think of many examples that support one approach or the other, but having examples is not as useful as having evidence. We have learned a good deal from both approaches, but we still need to know a good deal more before we can dare reject either approach.

Related to the question of how much flexibility roles permit are some other controversies: Dennis Wrong,[9] in a classic article on the "oversocialized conception of man," complained that our existing sociological models don't pay sufficient attention to such things as selfishness and lust for power and various biological drives that he argues are too deeply imbedded in man's nature to ever be completely "socialized."

Wrong complains that sociologists tend to assume that man is basically a neutral creature, badly in need of approval from others and shaped by his society: if man is wicked it is because his society makes him wicked; if man is good he owes his goodness to his society, too.

Wrong and other critics maintain that man is *not* neutral clay to be molded by society but rather has a certain basic nature. Wrong argues that man is basically an unsociable, selfish creature who is always fighting and resisting attempts to socialize him completely. On the other hand, many critics (we might call these romantics) argue that man is by nature a good creature who would develop his talents, his skills, and his goodness if only society would get out of the way and stop corrupting him.

Overlapping the question of whether man is basically and naturally good, bad, or indifferent is the question of whether man is a passive creature that society does things to or an active creature who sometimes fights society and sometimes cooperates in his own socialization but who is always an active participant in the socialization process.[10]

These are not questions that can be answered in twenty-five words or less. Nor are they questions that one study or a dozen studies will resolve. They are not trivial questions. Whether or not sociology can demonstrate that one answer has more scientific support than another, in our daily lives and our public policies we *assume* that one or another answer *is* true. Our social welfare policies, for example, assume that man is basically a lazy, greedy creature and that if we make it easy to get welfare payments or to live in dignity on a welfare budget, people will quit their jobs and "chisel" forever. As another example, if we should permit sex (according to many conservatives) or violence (according to many liberals) to appear on TV, the thin veneer of civilization and socialization will be ripped off and our children will become, in the first case, rapists and in the second case mass murderers.

Whether or not we discipline our children by beating them or by reasoning with them, we have in the backs of our minds some idea of what kind of creature we're working with, a perverse creature whose wicked impulses are to be controlled and crushed or a delicate flower whose good impulses must be encouraged and brought to full bloom.

We cannot give you *The Truth.* Man is too complicated a creature to be described by simple slogans and formulas. We hope to offer you *insight.* Zigler and Child express the scientific (rather than ideological) approach quite well:

> [T]he essential question is not whether man is basically an active or passive agent or inherently good or bad, but rather whether all possibilities must be considered in arriving at a comprehensive view of socialization. We advocate the broad approach. We need not choose between the active and passive views of man; we need to use them both. The active, mediational cognitive characteristics of the child are important in the socialization process at every stage of development; on the other hand, they do not determine every aspect of the socialized behavior which emerges. What constitutes achievement in one culture, for example, probably has little to do with the active mediational structures of the child and much to do with the particular character and nature of the society. . . .
> That we need not choose between the positive and negative should also be evident. A child possesses biological appetites and behavioral propensities, continued expression of which would make any social order impossible. There is an aspect of man that is primitive and gluttonous. This fact directs the student of socialization to a concern with the problem of impulse control and to the particular practices employed by the society in blocking or rechanneling individual characteristics which pose a threat for the social order. On the other hand, to say that socialization is nothing more than this is also an error. Observations of the child's desire to become an increasingly effective social being do not seem to be illusory. There appear to be inherent forces in the child which align themselves on the side of socializing agents, thus making the child an active and cooperative figure in his own socialization.[11]

Role Strains and Conflicts

We observed earlier in this chapter that because we know other people's social categories or roles, we expect certain things of them and we know what things they expect of us. Most of the time we are correct. We get what we expect. What we are prepared to give others is what they expect us to give them. We should also point out that we often expect, and demand, behavior from others that they are unable, or unwilling, to produce. Furthermore, we are often unsure of what *we* ought to be doing. (Your first day at a new job or at a new school should bring back memories about this kind of confusion.)

We can call these situations in which we disagree with others about what they or we ought to be doing, given our respective roles, situations of *role strain.*

Some of these role strains stem from personal characteristics. For example, the role of door-to-door salesman demands that we be willing to knock on many people's doors and to be friendly and outgoing hour after hour. Not all of us can bring ourselves to do this. The role of "boss" may require us to fire people or bawl them out. We may find that our temperaments don't permit this. The problem lies in us and not the demands of the role. There's no other way to be a door-to-door salesman or a boss. If we want the role, we'll have to change. On the other hand we may not have the physical characteristics necessary for the roles we would like to perform. We're simply too small to be professional football fullbacks, too slow to be Olympic runners, or too clumsy to be brain surgeons. Again, the problem lies within us and not in the nature of the role.

The discussion that follows emphasizes some strains that are a result of the nature of our roles rather than of temperamental or physical limitations. These are problems that even the most flexible, well-balanced or skillful of us are likely to encounter and with which we have to grapple. These role strains result from the structure of the roles, not from us or our personal limitations, although we may personally feel guilt, inadequacy, embarrassment, anger, or frustration.

Unclear Roles

The more clear the requirements of a role, the more confidently we can behave and the less likelihood there is that someone else will disagree with our ideas of what to do.

Newly developed roles, for example, are generally unclear. Schwartz describes some of the problems that women trained as traditional nurses had when they entered the new role of psychiatric nurse. The nurses were asked to treat each patient as an individual, to recognize each patient's needs, and to try to satisfy them. Patients (in this case, chronic schizophrenics) were to have extreme freedom limited only by considerations of the patient's health and safety and the nurse's physical and psychological comfort. Traditional nurses' training and the personal preferences of some of the nurses conflicted with these new ideas, and the general outlines of the new role also left a great deal of room for disagreement and personal interpretation:

> The emphasis upon responding to patients in individualized ways and the consequent reduction in shared patterns of action resulted in nurses handling the same patient behavior in different ways. Nurses who wanted privacy in the nursing office while making out reports found that other nurses permitted patients free access to the office, sometimes to their great annoyance. Some nurses wanted to remove the food cart after nourishments had been served; others preferred to leave the cart on the ward for the entire evening, even though a patient usually played with the food and threw it around the ward.[13]

Wardwell describes the relatively new role of chiropractor:

In addition to the ambiguity in the definition of the role of any doctor, the chiropractor's role is ambiguous for several other reasons. There is vast ignorance on the part of the patients and potential patients as to what chiropractors do, and, more important, chiropractors themselves disagree on the question of what chiropractic treatment should be. The "straights" limit themselves to spinal manipulation alone, sometimes "adjusting" only upper cervical vertebrae, while the "mixers" also use heat, light, air, water, exercise, diet regulation, and electric modalities in their treatment. State laws differ as widely in the scope of practice they permit. In most states chiropractors are limited to spinal manipulation and simple hygienic measures, while in others they may perform minor surgery, practice obstetrics, and sign death certificates.[14]

Not only are new roles unclear, so are roles in the process of change, like the role of wife.

Back in the 1930s Clifford Kirkpatrick observed that there were at least three distinct roles of wife, differing greatly in rights and obligations: the "traditional wife and mother," "the companion," and "the partner." He described the different roles this way:

Traditional Wife and Mother: Privileges—support, alimony in case of divorce, a certain amount of domestic authority and respect, and sentimental gratitude from husband and children. Obligations—bearing and rearing children, making a home, acceptance of a dependent social and economic status and a loyal subordination to the husband's interests.

The Companion Role: Privileges—leisure, sharing pleasures with the husband, a romantic emotional response, funds for expensive clothes and entertainment, chivalrous attention. Obligations—preservation of beauty under penalty of marital insecurity, rendering efficient ego and sexual satisfaction, and the cultivation of social contacts advantageous to the husband's career.

The Partner: Privileges—equal social and moral liberty, economic independence, equal control of family finances, exemption from one-sided domestic service. Obligations—renunciation of alimony in case of divorce except in case of children, sharing of legal responsibilities, willingness to forego appeals to chivalry, and willingness to seek employment when family need arises.[15]

Kirkpatrick found, as he asked students how they viewed their expectations for the role of wife, that two kinds of problems or conflicts appeared. In the first, the female liked one role and the male preferred that she take on a different one. The second kind of problem came from the tendency of many males to demand that the female fulfill a large number of obligations selected from each of the three roles but to be willing to accord her only a small range of privileges. Many females, likewise, tended to demand many privileges from each role but to accept a minimum of obligations. Since that time the roles available to wives have continued to change, offering more alternatives but also offering more opportunity for disagreement and strain.

Other Role Partners

The problems of deciding how to come to grips with a changing role are hard to resolve when only two people, like a married couple, are involved. They become much harder to resolve if the nature of your role is such that many people have a legitimate right to demand that you play it a certain way (especially if they each have different ideas of what that certain way should be).

Gross, Mason, and McEachern's[16] study of the role of school superintendent provides a number of illustrations of this problem of satisfying many role partners. School superintendents deal with school boards, with principals, with community leaders, with teachers, and with parents. Gross and his associates found that on some issues superintendents agreed with other superintendents and that school board members agreed with other board members about the superintendent's role, but that superintendents and school boards couldn't agree with each other.

On other issues, the boards agreed but the superintendents were divided. On still other issues, the boards and the superintendents agreed. They agreed, for example, that the superintendent should pay the teachers as little as possible. The teachers, on the other hand, disagreed and insisted that the superintendent's obligation was to get them as much money as possible.

The more other roles your role touches upon, the greater the potential for disagreement and the greater the likelihood that someone will be angry at your not fulfilling your role obligations "properly." The important point is that this kind of problem is built into the role: regardless of his personal qualities or limitations *anyone* who takes on the role of superintendent takes on these kinds of strains as well.

Multiple-Role Occupancy

Just as having an unclear role or a role on which others cannot agree carries with it problems attributable to the role and not the person, *multiple-role occupancy* is a source of potential strain.

We play many roles in the course of our daily lives and usually we perform one role at a time. We can be one person at work and another at home, one person with our friends and another with our parents. What happens when we are hit by two of our roles at the same time? As a mother or father who never misses work, we may discover that today a child is sick and someone has to stay home and care for the child rather than going to an important business meeting. Do we act like a good parent or a good employee? If one of us must stay home, which one? Why? The source of the problem now is not the question of how to be a good employee or how to be a good parent. Normally we perform each role at different times and places and we perform it smoothly. The problem here is that both hit us at once and we can carry out only one. Which one? If we choose to be a parent we'll miss something important at the meeting. If we go to the meeting, we're not being a very responsible parent and we'll feel guilty throughout the meeting.[17]

Here's an illustration from Gilbert and Sullivan's comic operetta *The Mikado* of some of the problems multiple-role occupancy can produce. (Ko-Ko is the Lord High Executioner. Pooh-Bah is the Lord High Everything-else.)

Ko-Ko: Pooh-Bah, it seems that the festivities in connection with my approaching marriage must last a week. I should like to do it handsomely, and I want to consult you as to the amount I ought to spend upon them.

Pooh-Bah: Certainly. In which of my capacities? As First Lord of the Treasury, Lord Chamberlain, Attorney-General, Chancellor of the Exchequer, Privy Purse, or Private Secretary?

Ko-Ko: Suppose we say as Private Secretary.

Pooh-Bah: Speaking as your Private Secretary, I should say that, as the city will have to pay for it, don't stint yourself, do it well.

Ko-Ko: Exactly—as the city will have to pay for it. That is your advice.

Pooh-Bah: As Private Secretary. Of course, you will understand that, as Chancellor of the Exchequer, I am bound to see that due economy is observed.

Ko-Ko: Oh! But you said just now "Don't stint yourself, do it well."

Pooh-Bah: As Private Secretary.

Ko-Ko: And now you say that due economy must be observed.

Pooh-Bah: As Chancellor of the Exchequer.

Ko-Ko: I see. Come over here, where the Chancellor can't hear us. (*They cross the stage.*) Now, as my Solicitor, how do you advise me to deal with this difficulty?

Pooh-Bah: Oh, as your Solicitor, I should have no hesitation in saying, "Chance it—"

Ko-Ko: Thank you. (*Shaking his hand.*) I will.

Pooh-Bah: If it were not that, as Lord Chief Justice, I am bound to see that the law isn't violated.

Ko-Ko: I see. Come over here where the Chief Justice can't hear us. (*They cross the stage.*) Now, then, as First Lord of the Treasury?

Pooh-Bah: Of course, as First Lord of the Treasury, I could propose a special vote that would cover all expenses, if it were not that, as Leader of the Opposition, it would be my duty to resist it, tooth and nail. Or, as Paymaster-General, I could so cook the accounts that, as Lord High Auditor, I should never discover the fraud. But then, as Archbishop of Titipu, it would be my duty to denounce my dishonesty and give myself into my own custody as First Commissioner of Police.

Ko-Ko: That's extremely awkward.[18]

In some respects we are all Pooh-Bahs, and although Pooh-Bah's problems are amusing, our own multiple-role problems generally are not. It's no fun deciding between having a career and being a "good" parent. As an employer would you fire an incompetent employee? Even if he's your brother or your son? Would you find it easy to be a white policeman in a black neighborhood? Would it be harder if you were black? Why? Could you drop bombs on another nation in wartime? What difference would it make if your grandmother still lived there (as did the grandparents of many German-American, Japanese-American, and Italian-American soldiers during World War II)?

Lewis Killian's[19] study of relief workers in disasters illustrates the problems that can occur when the usual, taken-for-granted, time-and-space differences in where and when we perform our roles break down. Killian studied disasters such as tornadoes and explosions in which police, firemen, and public utilities workers found themselves torn between their roles as family members and their roles as troubleshooters. On the one hand, they were anxious to get home to find out how their families were—in fact, whether their families were still alive. On the other hand, their professional roles were vital to the health and safety of the community, and leaving their posts was not something they could take lightly. Again, the problem is one not of knowing how to carry out either role but rather of knowing which role should be carried out at a particular time.

Role Discontinuities

We play many roles in the course of a lifetime. Many of the roles come in sequences. First, one is a child, then an adolescent, then an adult, then an older adult, for example. The concept of discontinuities was developed by Ruth Benedict.[20] She observed that it is easier to take on a new role if the previous role has given a person some kind of preparation for it in terms of such things as skills, behavior patterns, and the motivation to take on the new role.

Discontinuities occur between two roles to the extent that the first role either does not prepare a person for the next role, or that the first role requires behaviors and expectations that are the opposite of whatever the new role requires. Benedict observes that we expect our children to be sexless, non-responsible, and submissive. Adults are expected to be sexual creatures who are responsible and independent. Not only must the adult learn *new* behaviors but he must *un*learn *old* behaviors. In the next step the adult, whose self-image is that of a productive worker and a taxpayer, a protector and adviser to the young, retires. Then he must get used to being nonproductive, to being a person whose advice is not appreciated, and is probably resented, by the young.

In an "ideal" society (or any other system of roles), what one learns in one role is usable in the next. Schooling in many primitive societies involves teaching children skills (hunting, fishing, farming) that the child will use as an adult. This teaching minimizes discontinuity. Most societies train girls to cook and sew, to care for children, and to do other household tasks that they will use as wives and mothers. Generally these are societies that assume that girls will become wives and mothers: there are no alternative roles.

Our society, on the other hand, sends women to college to learn skills and attitudes that may well have to be unlearned, buried in a closet, or ignored if the woman is to take on the role of wife and mother to the exclusion of having a career. The worker promoted to foreman and the enlisted man promoted to officer are others in new roles that demand that old roles be unlearned. It is possible to arrange roles that follow in some sort of sequence so that what one learns in one role does not have to be unlearned. It is easier to do this if the new role is in some way considered more valuable than the old one, if there is some incentive for taking on the new role, and if the price of change is made to seem reasonable compared to the costs.

Aging in our society is *not,* by and large, something that is valued. Unfortunately we don't get a choice. We must grow older whether we choose to surrender our youth or not. But when was the last time you saw an advertisement for a skin lotion or potion that said, "Now *you* can look ten years older," or "We have discovered the secret of perpetual middle age"? Would you like to be five or ten years older? Would you lose more than you'd gain? Again, the source of the role strain lies not in the peculiarities of the individual but in the way roles are organized or structured in his group or society.

Minimizing Role Strains

Given the wide range of social factors that can produce role strain, why isn't there more of it? Just as the structure of roles can produce strain, roles can be structured to minimize or eliminate certain kinds of strain.

If a role is *unclear* we may demand a worker's or a student's orientation manual or a labor union contract or a marriage contract that spells out just what is or is not to be expected of us in a given role. Note that a marriage contract differs from the other two examples. To the extent that marriage involves a primary relationship, it also involves obligations and privileges that can't be simply ignored on the grounds that they're not in the contract. Nevertheless, the intention of those who write such contracts is obviously to get certain things clarified early in the course of the relationship rather than to assume that there's agreement where there is not.

Problems that are the result of having *multiple role-partners* can sometimes be minimized if certain role partners are given more power than others. This makes it possible for the one who is harassed to tell the weaker partners that he agrees with them but has no choice but to listen to the more powerful partner (whether or not that's really true). For example, a professor who is expected to spend *all* his time publishing professional articles *and* to spend *all* his time teaching and consulting with students may sacrifice his students for the sake of keeping his job. To the extent that people know that others are also leaning on you, they may find it easier to forgive you for not doing what they expect. Sometimes roles are set up so that we can easily hide from one group the fact that we're doing another group's bidding. This insulation also makes it easier to decide whom to listen to without having to worry that someone who has different ideas will find you out.

We can sometimes avoid *multiple-role* conflicts by the simple procedure of not letting them get started. Many organizations have rules that prohibit members of the same family from working in the same department of that organization. The problem of deciding what to do with the Italian-American, Japanese-American, and German-American pilots was a simple one: each bombed the others' grandmothers. Judges do not try their relatives; doctors do not generally treat members of their own families. Our laws forbid a wife to testify against her husband, a priest to testify against someone who has confessed a crime, a doctor or psychiatrist to testify against a patient. In each case the legal system tells the wife, the priest, or the doctor, "Don't worry about your role as 'citizen'; ignore it. We won't ask you to jeopardize the valuable contributions your role enables you to make by destroying the trust people have in the confidentiality of their relationship with you." On the other hand, newspaper reporters found in the early 1970s that our legal system did not offer them this privileged relationship; and therefore, although they may be professionally dead if they betray their confidential sources, they are in legal trouble if they don't.

Another way of handling multiple-role strains is to separate roles by time and place so that you can be one person here and another somewhere else, one person before 5 P.M., another after 5 P.M.

Discontinuities can sometimes be anticipated, and we can attempt either to change the earlier roles or to bring them in line with what the later roles will demand. Many business organizations warn people that they are due to be promoted and allow them to take on the duties of the new roles slowly under some old-timer's supervision, making the change a bit easier when it finally occurs officially. We don't know of any successful procedure for getting people used to the changes that will come with aging and retirement. *In principle,* slowly giving up job responsibilities and working fewer hours should ease the transition to retirement. Getting children off to school or to marriage or to their own apartments ought to help parents start to get used to the changes that will occur with retirement. In practice, though, the role of "senior citizen" is generally thought to be so unrewarding that we find few people anxious to think about it until it is absolutely necessary.[21]

Male and Female, Here and There

We have many roles that we play throughout the day. We also have many "selves," or ways of viewing ourselves in particular roles (some sociologists call these views *identities*). But not all of our roles are equally important and not all of the ways we view ourselves have the same impact on us. We take some roles and some "selves" (or identities) very much to heart. Not only do *we* take them seriously, *others* take them seriously. Most of what we know about ourselves is the result of the way other people respond to us. Other people respond to us on the basis of the social categories we fill. We have also observed that as we watch other people's behavior we find it easy to assume that the behaviors they exhibit are signs of personality traits rather than behavior their roles demand or permit them to display.

For many thousands of years we have observed that men and women are different and we have assumed that this must be a sign of inborn psychological differences between men and women. It is only in this century that we have become aware of the extent to which the different behaviors are learned rather than the unfolding of biologically based characteristics.

Our ideas of "proper" and "natural" behavior for males and females include the idea that men will be active, aggressive, rational manipulators of the world and that women will be passive, gentle, emotional guardians of the home and the family.

As we have learned more about other societies we've come to realize that those behaviors we consider "natural" are not "natural" elsewhere. This discovery suggests either the silly idea that these other people are *not* "human" or that our ideas about what is "natural," "human" behavior are in need of modification.

Margaret Mead's investigation of three tribes in New Guinea is an interesting illustration of how "male" and "female" behavior can vary.[22] Mead studied three tribes: the Arapesh, the Mundugumor, and the Tchambuli. The Arapesh and the Mundugumor assume that the two sexes are essentially the same. The Tchambuli assume that the two sexes are different but that the differences are the opposite of the differences that we see in our society. In the Arapesh culture both men and women are responsive and sensitive to the needs of others and avoid competition and aggressiveness. Both sexes, in other words, exhibit behavior that we in the West consider feminine. Men and women are alike in Mundugumor society, too. Both sexes are characterized by hostility, aggressiveness, violence, and lack of consideration for the rights and feelings of others. Both sexes exhibit behavior we would consider masculine.

Among the Tchambuli Mead found a reversal of our Western sex roles. Tchambuli men are sensitive, carefully groomed, artistic, emotionally unstable, and given to bickering. Tchambuli women, on the other hand, are stable, practical, dominant, and aggressive in matters of sex. This study suggests that we humans are a quite malleable species, that sex-role behavior is something more than a simple unfolding of biologically programmed tendencies.

Mead's three tribes are not the only groups that exhibit behaviors that don't match our sex-role stereotypes. Ethel M. Albert,[23] an anthropologist who has studied a number of Central African tribes, reports that although Western societies assume that men, because of their skeletal and muscular build, are suited for heavy labor, most Africans believe the opposite. When Albert told some African women that men did the heavy work in her country, they

We must learn our ideas of "proper" and "natural" behavior for males and females.

expressed disapproval. They felt that Americans were making a mistake because "everyone" knows that men drink too much and don't eat enough to keep up their strength. They're too tense and too inclined to wander about to develop the kinds of muscles and habits necessary for sustained agricultural labor. Men, they argued, are not suited by nature for this kind of work.

Albert observes, too, that whereas we expect men to be sexually aggressive and women to be passive or evasive in sexual matters, some African and American Indian societies believe that women are more driven by sex than men. Among Zuñi Indians it's the groom and not the bride who looks forward to the wedding night with fear and apprehension.

In Iran, according to Edward T. Hall,[24] emotional and intellectual sex roles are roughly the reverse of those in Western cultures. Men are not expected to be strong and silent. They're expected to show their emotions and even have tantrums. If they don't, other Iranians are likely to think that they lack vital human traits and are probably not dependable. Iranian men like poetry and are supposed to be sensitive, intuitive, and not very logical. In Iran, it is the women who are supposed to be logical and practical.

We should point out that in these societies, as in ours, there is a range of temperaments. Not all Arapesh are equally gentle. Not all Mundugumor are equally aggressive. Not all Tchambuli men are equally passive or Tchambuli women equally aggressive. In our own society, even in infants, we can notice differences in what we might call temperament. Some babies are quiet and sweet, some are active and cranky. We are *not* denying that there may be some differences of metabolism and of hormones that make it easier or harder for people of one biological sex to learn the role their society considers appropriate for males or females. We *are* attempting to point out that there is a wide range of temperaments and potentialities among both biological sexes that our conceptions of male and female and those of other societies do not take into account.[25] No one has any "pure" data that would let us say, for example, that *X* percent of men are "naturally" suited for our "official" male role and *Y* percent don't fit the "mold," or that *X* percent of women are "naturally" suited for the "official" female role and *Y* percent don't fit the mold.

We can speculate and estimate, but we can't really give precise figures because the attempt to socialize children into male and female roles begins at birth (with the proverbial blue and pink blankets). If we observe mothers with three-week-old infants, we can see differences in the way they're held, the speed with which parents respond to their crying, and so on. Some of this difference is due to minor sex differences, some to the infant's own unique temperament, some to the mother's ideas of how to treat male and female babies, some to the combination of the three.[26]

It is clear that *most* of what we observe and label *male* or *female* behavior results from our having encouraged and demanded certain behaviors and having discouraged and stifled other behaviors. The behaviors we produce in males and females are ultimately the result of our ideas of sex-role appropriateness rather than a simple, automatic unfolding of the limitations and potentialities of the creatures born as males and females.

Ascribed and Achieved Roles

We learn many of our roles as adolescents or as adults—occupational roles, for example. One important reason that we choose occupational roles rather than having them assigned from birth is our awareness that most occupational roles require a certain amount of talent and interest. We can't point to an infant and say, "You will become a concert pianist" or "You will become a brain surgeon." We *do* say, "You will become a male (or female)." You *are* a Hindu or a Buddhist or a Christian, Moslem, or Jew. You *are* white or black, American or Italian. Again, these are social categories or roles that *anyone* is apparently capable of taking on successfully. They don't require any special talent.

Sociologists describe roles that are assigned to us on the basis of biological characteristics, like sex or race or age, or on the basis of some characteristic of the parents we're born to (caste, class, religion) as *ascribed* roles. Roles that require choice or talent on our part before we take them on sociologists call *achieved* roles. Student, parent, doctor, president are "achieved."

In principle, these are distinct and different kinds of roles, but in practice our "ascribed" roles often have a bearing on whether or not we try to take on (or others permit us to take on) certain "achieved" roles. We observed earlier that the way we see ourselves is a reflection of our roles and social categories. Our ascribed roles become a deeper, more central part of the way we see ourselves than the roles we achieve later in our lives. A number of studies suggest that to the extent that these ascribed roles and cateogries are considered "superior" by others, we come to see ourselves as superior. To the extent that our ascribed roles and categories are considered "inferior" by others, we think of ourselves as inferior. We don't know precisely how this occurs, nor do we know what it takes to reverse or minimize these feelings of inferiority. We have reason to believe that such feelings of inferiority prevent us from accomplishing or attempting to accomplish things for which we do have the capacities and abilities.

Here are some examples of what we mean by "feelings of inferiority." Philip Goldberg[27] conducted an experiment in which he asked women to read some articles on a variety of topics. Some were attributed to John T. McKay, some to Joan T. McKay. They were the same articles but the sex of the alleged authors was varied. If the author was "male," the women thought the articles were clearer, were more persuasive, and indicated greater competence than if the articles' author was "female." *But it was the same article.*

W. E. Lambert and some associates[28] asked French-Canadian and English-Canadian students to listen to some recordings. Half were in French, half in English. The subjects were asked to listen to the voices and to *ignore* the content ("Mary had a little lamb" recited either in French or in English) and to judge *only from the voice* the kind of person who was doing the reciting. Unknown to the subjects, the speakers were five bilingual students who spoke perfect French and perfect English. The English-Canadian students could "hear" that the English speakers were taller, better looking, more intelligent, more dependable, kinder, more ambitious, and of better character than the French. (Remember, they were actually judging the same people twice without being aware of it.)

The French-Canadians *also* judged the English speakers more favorably than they judged their fellow French-Canadians on "good looks, height, intelligence, self-confidence, dependability, ambition, sociability, character and likeableness." In other words, they agreed with the English that the French were inferior.

J. T. Shuval[29] found that immigrants to Israel from Europe and the Middle East had negative attitudes toward North African immigrants. They believed that the North Africans were aggressive, dirty, and uncultured and had a variety of undesirable personal traits. Sixty percent of the Europeans applying for a housing development said they would prefer European neighbors. Sixty percent of the *North Africans* said they would prefer Europeans as neighbors. They felt their fellow North Africans were aggressive, dirty, and uncultured and had a variety of undesirable personal traits.

Similar findings have been reported for American blacks. What it takes to reverse these negative self-conceptions is a matter of debate, although there's not much debate over the idea that minority status can do damage to the way we see ourselves and that this damage is not an easy thing to reverse.

Summary

The human becomes human through a process of socialization. Most of socialization involves learning roles: sex roles, family roles, occupational roles, and so on. Our roles become a part of us. Acquiring the ability to perform our roles requires that we be able to see ourselves as "objects." In this way we develop what is called a self, which allows us to function as social beings.

Notes

1. See, for example, W. Mischel, "Continuity and Change in Personality," *American Psychologist,* **24** (1969), 1012–1018; and W. Mischel, *Personality and Assessment* (New York: John Wiley & Sons, Inc., 1968); and D. W. Fiske, *Measuring the Concepts of Personality* (Chicago: Aldine Publishing Company, 1971). See also O. Brim, "Personality Development as Role Learning," in J. Iscoe and H. W. Stephenson, eds. *Personality Development in Children* (Austin: University of Texas Press, 1960), pp. 127–159.

2. See S. Milgram, "Behavioral Study of Obedience," *Journal of Abnormal Social Psychology,* **67** (1963), 371–378; S. Milgram, "Issues in the Study of Obedience: A Reply to Baumrind," *American Psychologist,* **19** (1964), 848–852; and S. Milgram, "Liberating Effect of Group Pressure," *Journal of Personality and Social Psychology,* **1** (1965), 127–134. See also D. Baumrind, "Some Thoughts on Ethics of Research: After Reading Milgram's 'Behavioral Study of Obedience,'"

American Psychologist, **19** (1964), 421–423. The quotes used here come from A. C. Elms's description of the experiment as he experienced it as Milgram's assistant; see A. C. Elms, *Social Psychology and Social Relevance* (Boston: Little, Brown and Company, 1972). For an analysis of this research see S. Milgram, *Obedience to Authority* (New York: Harper & Row, Publishers, 1974).
3. D. M. Mantell, "The Potential for Violence in Germany," *Journal of Social Issues,* **27** (1971), 101–112.
4. See P. Zimbardo et al., "A Pirandellian Prison," *Sunday New York Times Magazine* (April 8, 1973); and C. Haney, C. Banks, and P. Zimbardo, "Interpersonal Dynamics in a Simulated Prison," *International Journal of Criminology and Penology,* **1** (1973), 69–97.
5. See G. H. Mead, *Mind, Self and Society* (Chicago: University of Chicago Press, 1934); and A. Strauss, *George Herbert Mead on Social Psychology* (Chicago: University of Chicago Press, 1964). A recent history of the development of Mead's thought on the self is J. W. Petras, "George Herbert Mead's Theory of Self: A Study in the Origin and Convergence of Ideas," *Canadian Review of Sociology and Anthropology,* **10** (1973), 148–159.
6. J. Piaget, *The Language and Thought of the Child* (1st Ed. 1924; New York: Humanities Press, 1959).
7. C. H. Cooley, *Human Nature and the Social Order* (New York: Charles Scribner's Sons, 1902).
8. See S. Stryker, "Fundamental Principles of Social Interaction," in N. Smelser, ed., *Sociology: An Introduction,* 2nd Ed. (New York: John Wiley & Sons, Inc., 1973), pp. 495–547, for a lucid discussion of the differences and similarities between these two approaches.
9. D. Wrong, "The Oversocialized Conception of Man in Modern Sociology," *American Sociological Review,* **26** (1961), 183–193. See also an expanded version of this article in *Psychoanalysis and the Psychoanalytic Review,* **49** (1962), 53–69. This article is followed by a rebuttal by T. Parsons, "Individual Autonomy and Social Pressure: An Answer to Dennis Wrong," 70–79. See also R. S. Broadhead, "Notes on the Sociology of the Absurd: An Undersocialized Conception of Man," *Pacific Sociological Review,* **17** (1974), 35–45.
10. There is a good discussion of these issues in E. F. Zigler and I. L. Child, eds, *Socialization and Personality Development* (Reading, Mass.: Addison-Wesley Publishing Co., Inc., 1973), particularly pp. 28–36.
11. Ibid., pp. 35–36.
12. See P. F. Secord and C. W. Backman, *Social Psychology* (New York: McGraw-Hill Book Company, 1964), Chapters 14–16.
13. C. G. Schwartz, "Problems for Psychiatric Nurses in Playing a New Role on a Mental Hospital Ward," in M. Greenblatt, C. J. Levinson, and R. H. Williams, eds., *The Patient and the Mental Hospital* (New York: The Free Press, 1957), 402–426.
14. W. A. Wardwell, "The Reduction of Strain in a Marginal Social Role," *American Journal of Sociology,* **61** (1952), 16–24.
15. C. Kirkpatrick, "Inconsistencies in Marriage Roles and Marriage Conflict," *International Journal of Ethics,* (1936), 444.
16. N. Gross, W. S. Mason, and A. W. McEachern, *Explorations in Role Analysis* (New York: John Wiley, & Sons, Inc., 1968).
17. For interesting discussions of the strains felt by wives and husbands, respectively, in two-career families, see M. M. Poloma, "Role Conflict and the Married Professional Woman," in C. Safilios-Rothschild, ed., *Toward a Sociology of Women* (Lexington, Mass: Xerox Publishing Co., 1972), pp. 187–198; and T. N. Garland, "The Better Half? The Male in the Dual Professional Family," in the same book, pp. 199–215.
18. W. S. Gilbert, *The Mikado* (New York: Bondee and Liveright, Inc., 1917).
19. L. M. Killian, "The Significance of Multiple-Group Membership in Disaster," *American Journal of Sociology,* **57** (1952), 309–313.
20. R. Benedict, "Continuities and Discontinuities in Cultural Conditioning," *Psychiatry,* **1** (1938), 161–167.

21. See F. M. Carp, ed., *The Retirement Process* (Washington, D.C.: U.S. Government Printing Office, Public Health Service), 1968.

22. M. Mead, *Sex and Temperament in Three Primitive Societies* (New York: William Morrow & Co., Inc., 1935).

23. E. M. Albert, "The Roles of Women: A Question of Values," in S. M. Farber and R. H. L. Wilson, eds., *The Potential of Women* (New York: McGraw-Hill Book Company, 1963).

24. E. T. Hall, *The Silent Language* (New York: Doubleday & Company, Inc., 1959).

25. See J. Money and A. A. Ehrhardt, *Man and Woman, Boy and Girl* (Baltimore: The Johns Hopkins Press, 1972), for a thorough technical treatment of the biological evidence. For a readable popular treatment see M. Scarf, "He and She: Sex Hormones and Behavior," *New York Times Magazine* (May 7, 1972), 30–31, 101–104.

26. See H. A. Moss, "Sex, Age and State as Determinants of Mother-Infant Interaction," *Merrill-Palmer Quarterly,* **13** (1967), 19–36; and also S. Goldberg and M. Lewis, "Play Behavior in the Year-Old Infant; Early Sex Differences," *Child Development,* **40** (1969), 21–23.

27. P. Goldberg, "Are Women Prejudiced Against Women?" *Transaction,* **5** (1968), 28–30.

28. W. E. Lambert, R. C. Hodgson, R. C. Gardner, and S. Fillenbaum, "Evaluational Reactions to Spoken Language," *Journal of Abnormal and Social Psychology,* **60** (1966), 44–51. W. M. Cheyne reports similar results with Scottish and English voices, the Scottish ascribing "superiority" to the English: W. M. Cheyne, "Stereotyped Reactions to Speakers with Scottish and English Regional Accents," *British Journal of Social and Clinical Psychology,* **9** (1970), 77–79. See also H. Tajfel, G. Jahoda, C. Nemeth, Y. Rim, and N. B. Johnson, "The Devaluation of Children of Their Own National and Ethnic Group: Two Case Studies," *British Journal of Social and Clinical Psychology,* **11** (1972), 235–243.

29. J. T. Shuval, "Self-Rejection Among North African Immigrants to Israel," *Israel Annals of Psychiatry and Related Disciplines,* **4** (1966), 101–110.

SEVEN

Who Socializes Us?

WE start out as helpless, ignorant infants and then become helpless, ignorant children. Our families are just about the only people we know as children and we take their statements, behavior, rewards, and punishments very seriously. As we get older we are exposed to other people, particularly the school and the peer group, who also teach us to behave along the lines our society considers proper.

The Family

The child is socialized into a *segment* of his society by his family. They represent a particular slice of the society. They are of a particular social class, a particular ethnic group, a particular religion, region, and race. The view of the world a child gets is a result of the family's social "locations." As Frederick Elkin and Gerald Handel observe:

> A child is born into a family, and his family gives him his location in society. From the moment of his birth, before he has had the opportunity to take any actions on his own, the child is located in society—as middle class or working class, child of a teacher or truck driver, Christian or Jew, member of a dominant or a subordinate ethnic group, member of a family respected or scorned by neighbors. His family's—and therefore his—location in these social groupings affects the experiences he will have as he matures. It will determine, to a significant degree, not only what form his socialization opportunities will take, but also at what ages, in what order, and with whom.[2]

The family is also the place where the child has his or her first intimate relationships. The child learns to trust others, to cooperate with others. He learns jealousy perhaps. He learns which feelings can be expressed and which ones should be buried. The child learns something about what ambitions he should cultivate and what habits are important to cultivate. The child learns also how a father and mother ought to treat each other and learns appropriate behavior for males and females by watching and learning from both parents. In short, children learn how a family operates by watching their own families.

Herbert Gans suggests that in North America there are three basic kinds of families in terms of the relationship between parent and child: the *adult-centered* family, the *child-centered* family, and the *adult-directed* family.[3] Each of these he sees as most characteristic of a particular social class. The adult-centered family Gans sees as typical of the working class. Children are not planned. They come naturally and regularly and are *not* at the center of family life:

> Rather, they are raised in a household that is run to satisfy adult wishes first. As soon as they are weaned and toilet-trained, they are expected to behave themselves in ways pleasing to adults. When they are with adults, they must act as the adults want them to act; to play quietly in a corner, or to show themselves

The family is the place where the child has his or her first intimate relationship.

off to other adults to demonstrate the physical and psychological virtues of their parents. Parents talk to them in an adult tone as soon as possible, and, once they have passed the stage of babyhood, will cease to play with them. When girls reach the age of seven or eight, they start assisting the mother, and become miniature mothers. Boys are given more freedom to roam. . . .

But while children are expected to behave like adults at home, they are able to act their age when they are with their peers. Thus, once children have moved into their own peer group, they have considerable freedom to act as they wish, as long as they do not get into trouble. The children's world is their own, and only within it can they really behave like children. Parents are not expected to supervise, guide, or take part in it. . . . The child will report on his peer group activities at home, but they are of relatively little interest to parents in an adult-centered family. If the child performs well at school or at play, parents will praise him for it. But they are unlikely to attend his performance in a school program or a baseball game in person. This is his life, not theirs.[4]

The *child-centered family,* Gans suggests, is typical of the lower middle class.

The most easily shared interest is the children, and the parents communicate best with each other through joint child-rearing. As a result, this family is child-centered. Parents play with their children—which is rare in the working class—rear them with some degree of self-consciousness, and give up some of their adult pleasures for them. Family size is strongly influenced by educational aspirations. If the parents are satisfied with their own occupational and social status, and feel no great urgency to send their children to college, they may have as many children as possible. For each child adds to their shared enjoyment and to family unity—at least while the children are young. Sometimes, the child will dominate his parents unmercifully, although child-centered parents are not necessarily permissive in their child-rearing. Rather, they want the child to have a happier childhood than they experienced, and will give him what they believe is necessary for making it so. One of their child-centered acts is the move to the suburb, made not only for the child's benefit, but also to make their child-rearing easier for themselves, and to reduce some of the burdens of child-centeredness. They give the child freely over to the care of the school, and to organizations like the Scouts or Little League, because these are all child-centered institutions.[5]

The *adult-directed family,* Gans suggests, is typical of the upper-middle-class family.

Among college-educated parents, education and educational aspirations shape family life. College education adds immeasurably to the number of common interests between husband and wife, including activities other than child-rearing. Consequently, these parents know what they want for their children much more clearly than does the child-centered family, and their relationship to the children is adult-directed. Child-rearing is based on a model of an upper-middle-class adulthood characterized by individual achievement and social service for which parents want the child to aim. As a result, the child's wants are of less importance.

Such parents devote much time and effort to assuring the child receives the education which will help him to become a proper adult. For this purpose, they may limit the size of their families; they will choose their place of residence by the quality of the school system; they will ride herd on the school authorities to meet their standards; and, of course, they will exert considerable pressure on the children to do well in school.[6]

Gans's observations on what is "typical" for different classes tells only part of the story. We know relatively little about differences and variations *within* each class, but the class differences he observed obviously launch children into quite different worlds.[7]

The School

The school puts the child under the supervision of nonrelatives for the first time. It is also the child's first move from a primary, personal set of relationships to a secondary, impersonal world. Elkin and Handel note that the school (and the church) are the first agencies to encourage the child to develop loyalties and ties to the world beyond the family, to the social and political order in particular.

The school also prepares the child to read, write, and do arithmetic, to develop skills that will be useful in adult life. The school is generally less useful in preparing children from certain kinds of families than those from others. This appears to be the case in other nations as well as the United States. Part of the difficulty lies in the nature of the skills, habits, and attitudes brought from home by the children. Some of the difficulty lies in the generally more limited supplies of money and other resources allotted to schools in predominantly poor neighborhoods. Also part of the difficulty lies in the expectations that schools have about how little lower-class children are likely to learn even if the school *were* to give such children a maximum of effort and resources (which they don't do).

Regardless of where we choose to place the responsibility, the fact remains that as currently constituted, "The effectiveness of the school as a socializing agency depends to a major degree upon the kind of family its children come from."[8]

Elkin and Handel suggest that the child's classroom performance contributes to his own ideas about himself and to the ideas others in the school system have about him, ideas that have a bearing on the child's future:

The classroom environment is one in which a child is being evaluated in a variety of ways—by teacher comments, self-judgments, classmate judgments, report cards, marks, and comments (and perhaps gold stars, red stars, or blue stars) on exercises and papers, classroom displays of the "best" papers, requests that he stay after school or bring his parents in for a conference. . . .

This ongoing and multifaceted process of evaluation contributes to socialization in two main ways. The first is that *the evaluations become processed into the child's developing self.* He learns certain of society's values and norms, and in this way his self is transformed: He learns to be neat, prompt, able to follow instructions, and so forth—or he learns that he is not very good at being neat or prompt or at following instructions. He learns to think of himself as being good in math or not so good in math, good or not so good in reading, and so on. These evaluations of his achievements in skills, subject matters, and social performances thus gradually accrue to his emerging self. The child thus comes to know himself as a particular kind of social being, one who may aspire to certain kinds of future opportunities but not to others.

While his self is thus evolving, the child is also acquiring a certain kind of reputation among teachers and a "cumulative record" which is semipublic. The quality of this record (and reputation) serves as a ticket of admission (or refusal) for later opportunities, and this is the second main way in which evaluation affects socialization. At any given point during the formation of his reputation and record, their quality at that point affects the child's progression to the next step—for example, whether he will be put into a fast, slow, or average section, whether he is doing well enough in classwork to be allowed participation in school team

The school is the child's first move from a primary, personal set of relationships to a secondary, impersonal world.

sports, whether he has done well enough in lower grades to be admitted to college-preparatory curricula in high school, whether he has done well enough in high school to be admitted to a college (and, if so, to what kind of college, with how much encouragement in the way of scholarships, and the like). In short, the school classroom functions as a system of selection for sequences of interlocking opportunities leading to particular kinds of adult roles.[9]

Peers

Peers (children of the same age) contribute to our socialization in three respects.

First, peer groups give us our first experiences with *equals,* as opposed to adults like teachers and parents. Peers offer a kind of companionship, attention, and goodwill that parents can't supply, in return for behavior like skill at games, which parents are indifferent to.

Second, to the extent that peer groups include children of slightly different ages and skill levels, children can find models for what they will be in the near future. Adults are models for the very *distant* future.

A third contribution of the peer group is that it gives children a chance to develop close relationships of their *own* choice.

Peer groups, in other words, are the place where we begin to become independent of our parents and a place where we develop standards for judging ourselves quite separate from those of the adult world.

Resocialization

Although we do not stop learning new roles as adolescents and adults, the adult's learning process is, in most respects, easier than is the socialization process for children. The child knows nothing until he is taught. The adult knows how to read and write and has a variety of skills and habits and personal characteristics upon which later socialization can build. There are agencies that attempt to make major modifications in people, to *reconstruct* or *resocialize* people, rather than to make minor changes in their behavior.

Certain techniques seem to be necessary if major changes are to be made in adults (or adolescents). Basically these techniques involve taking people apart and putting them back together again a different way. If the thought of taking people apart and putting them back together again makes you think of brainwashing, you are on the right track. The procedures and practices used by the Chinese Communists, which came to be known as "brainwashing" in the early 1950s, actually involve procedures used in only slightly different and milder forms in other places. These include military academies and military training camps, convents, monasteries, religious revival meetings, Alcoholics Anonymous, Synanon, sensitivity groups, and group psychotherapy sessions. What these agencies do is to recreate the helplessness, powerlessness, and confusion of childhood to break their "pupils" down, while offering the pupil a new, more acceptable, approved way to put the pieces together. Having introduced the term *brainwashing,* let us point out that the various agencies we listed would be horrified and insulted if they were accused of brainwashing anyone. They might accept the terms *reeducation* or *resocialization* more easily, but the principles are essentially the same, regardless of what name we give the process.

Peer groups give us our first experience with equals.

Brainwashing

Strictly speaking the term *brainwashing*[10] refers to procedures developed and refined by both the Soviet Communists during the reign of Joseph Stalin and the Chinese Communists to attain either or both of these goals: (1) to compel an innocent person to admit publicly, in all sincerity, that he has committed serious crimes against the "people" and the state, and (2) to reshape an individual's political views coercively so that he abandons his previous beliefs and becomes an advocate of Communism. Both ends are attempts to make someone accept as true what he previously considered false and to see as false what he previously considered true.

The Soviet Communists have been mainly concerned with the confessional side; the Chinese have been mainly concerned with developing ideological conformity, or "thought reform." Both use essentially the same procedures. Our concern here will be with the Chinese version largely because it is intended to be more thorough, to go far beyond a simple confession. The Soviets were content to bring people rapidly to the point where they could be used to "confess" in a public "show" trial and then be shot or sent off to Siberia.

Let us note one other important difference. The Soviets tended to work on one prisoner at a time, whereas the Chinese tend to work on small groups of prisoners simultaneously.

These are the basic tactics used by both to effect "thought reform":

(1) *Total control.* The prisoner's entire existence, down to the most intimate needs, is governed by strictly enforced rules that cover both waking and sleeping hours. *The objectives are to keep the subject under constant psychological harassment and to drive home the lesson that his jailers are omnipotent and he is powerless.*

(2) *Uncertainty.* In the weeks immediately following his arrest, the prisoner will not be informed of the specific charges against him, and his pleas for a bill of particulars are met by angry declarations that he is fully aware of the nature of his crimes and by a demand for immediate and full confession. The accused thus finds himself in an appalling dilemma: *he can hardly conduct an effective defense, given his ignorance of the charges, and he cannot satisfy the demand for a confession, since he does not know what it is that he is alleged to have done.*

(3) *Isolation.* Once arrested, the accused is completely *cut off from the outside world* and *receives only such information about his family and friends as his custodians see fit to give him.* Where the isolated unit is the group rather than the individual, the program design *minimizes the possibility of relationships going beyond the group.*

(4) *Torture.* The accused is also subjected to a variety of *other mental and physical torments.* He may be told that his wife has divorced him or that his closest friends have signed statements testifying to his guilt. Relays of questioners will work on him for 12 or 16 hours at a stretch, during much of which he will be kept in acute or chronic pain. The prisoner will be sent back to his cell, allowed

to fall asleep, and promptly recalled for another session. This process will be continued until the prisoner finally reaches the desired degree of mental malleability.

(5) *Physical debilitation and exhaustion.* Prison diet is planned to ensure rapid loss of weight, strength, and stamina. *Eventually the subject is so weakened that prolonged mental effort becomes increasingly difficult, if not impossible.* The disruption of sleep, particularly under conditions of constant interrogation, tension, and terror, greatly accelerates this process of debilitation and exhaustion.

(6) *Personal humiliation.* From the moment of his arrest, the prisoner is made to realize that his "criminal" behavior has *deprived him of any previous claim to personal dignity or status.* His degradation will be almost in proportion to his previous eminence and importance.

(7) *Certainty of guilt.* Perhaps one of the most insidious devices employed is the complete and *unyielding assumption of the prisoner's guilt* manifested by his interrogators. This certitude partially justifies, even in the prisoner's mind, the stringency of the measures applied to elicit a confession.[11]

The sequence of events, as Albert Somit describes them, is roughly as follows:

After an initial period of disbelief and shock, the prisoner begins painfully to reflect upon his past behavior, hoping to recall some chance act or remark that, grossly misconstrued, could account for the apparent certainty of his guilt. With the passage of time he becomes increasingly incapable of coping intellectually with his jailer's arguments. Eventually, he concedes that any past deed which might even remotely have had "objective" subversive consequences, intended or not, may reasonably be viewed as criminal by the regime.

One aim of brainwashing is to destroy the distinction between guilt and innocence, the other to obliterate the borderline between fact and fancy. . . . The prisoner will fight desperately to maintain his faith in his innocence and in his previous values, but his strength is steadily sapped by physical debilitation, fatigue, pain, deprivation, humiliation, and degradation.

Concurrently he begins to sense, if only subconsciously, that life becomes slightly less unbearable during those periods when he shows progress in conceding the possibility of his guilt, or when he evidences a greater receptivity to Marxist doctrine. Living conditions improve and there is a lessening of physical pain; even his interrogators become more friendly and less impersonal. Contrariwise, intervals in which little progress is made or in which the prisoner "regresses" are promptly followed by a return to the old mode of existence now all the more intolerable. . . . Compliance is rewarded, resistance punished. Inevitably, he reaches that stage of hope and despair where, in Orwell's classic example, he most desperately *wants* to believe that "two and two make five."

In all probability, acceptance of the concept of "objective" guilt makes the point of no return. What follows . . . is really a slow piecing together of detail into a confession. Confessional verisimilitude may necessitate the incrimination or denunciation of others, but by this time the prisoner is as confused about the guilt or innocence of others as he is about his own.[12]

The critical steps are these:

1. Isolation from friends and relatives also isolates the individual from social support for the ways he likes to see himself, the ways he is used to seeing himself. His captors will try to convince him that he is a scoundrel, a wretch, or a criminal or anything else they choose to call him, and there's no one available to help him maintain any other view of himself.

2. The prisoner is made helpless and dependent on his captors, much as a child is dependent, for even the slightest thing. He does not eat, sleep, go to the toilet, smoke a cigarette, or leave his room without permission.

3. The prisoner's old identity is destroyed. The way he normally sees himself is challenged. The prisoner is not a "mistreated person" or a "misunderstood patriot," or an "upstanding citizen," as he would like to claim. He is instead an "imperialist," an "enemy of the people," a "traitor." All of these are someone else's definitions of what the prisoner is and challenge the way he normally looks at himself.

4. Intensive examination of the prisoner's behavior and beliefs is tied to required personal confessions. This has the effect of pointing out to him what a miserable creature he is and *always has been.* The prisoner's work habits, his beliefs, his every movement are used as evidence that his whole life history indicates his wretchedness. In essence, his whole life history is relived but with new explanations in a new vocabulary from a different perspective to show the significance of the "real" meaning of everything he's ever done. And he is forced to supply material for this analysis through confession, to collaborate in his own reconstruction of his identity. The first three steps are basically concerned with telling the prisoner that he is worthless and morally defective. Step four not only contributes to taking the victim apart but is, in part, also concerned with putting him back together again along *new* lines.

5. The prisoner is offered a new, acceptable identity. The prisoner is offered a vision of what he can become if he is willing and able. He is wretched, but there *is* hope if he is willing to change. Each step he takes toward this new, valuable identity is rewarded and encouraged and supported by the captors.

6. Other members of the group, particularly those further along in their "thought reform," in their own change toward the new identity, exert pressure on the prisoner to see the light and help him to redefine himself. He, in turn, will have to do the same to others to prove his sincerity and involvement. This is a very important step *for those doing the pressuring,* perhaps more important for them than for the person being pressured.[13] It requires them to commit themselves to the new identity. A much milder, more benign version of this occurs in certain teaching situations. There's evidence that if we take children who don't read well and put them in charge of other children who barely read at all, both the child doing the "learning" and the one doing the "teaching" learn a great deal. The "teacher" often benefits even more from his taking on this new role than does the pupil.[14]

All of this sounds quite abstract. Let us therefore proceed to some concrete illustrations of what we're discussing. Dr. Vincent went through the full treatment at the hands of the Chinese Communists. Let us start with his experiences.

THE CASE OF DR. VINCENT[15]

Dr. Charles Vincent, a French doctor, had practiced medicine in China for twenty years. One day in the early 1950s he was grabbed by five police on the streets of Shanghai. They produced a warrant for his arrest and they took him to a "reeducation center" or house of detention, where he spent the next three and a half years. After a few preliminaries he was placed in an eight-foot by twelve-foot cell with eight other prisoners, all Chinese. These were specially selected. Each was "advanced" in his personal "reform" and anxious to apply himself to the reform of others as a way of gaining "merits" toward his own release. The "cell chief" identified himself and addressed Vincent by his new prison number. The prisoners formed a circle around him, denouncing him as an "imperialist" and a "spy," demanding that he "recognize" his "crimes" and "confess everything." He denied being a spy. The more he denied it the more his cellmates insisted that he was lying, that the "government never makes a mistake." This procedure was known as a "struggle." Vincent underwent many of these.

After several hours Vincent was taken for his first interrogation to a small room that held an interrogator or "judge," an interpreter, and a secretary. The judge insisted that Vincent confess his "crimes against the people." Vincent denied having committed any. For several hours he was asked questions about his activities, his professional associations, his friends and acquaintances, and his connections with his own embassy and agencies of the United States, Japan and Nationalist China.

During ten hours of interrogation Vincent produced what information he could, while the judge insisted that: "The government knows all about your crimes. That is why we arrested you. It is now up to you to confess everything to us, and in this way your case can be quickly solved and you will soon be released." Finally, when Vincent again denied that he was a spy, the judge got angry. Vincent was sent from the room with handcuffs on, his arms behind his back. Ten minutes later he was returned to the judge. He denied that he had committed any crimes and found himself on his way back to the cell with chains on his ankles. That was about 6 A.M.:

"When you get back with your chains, your cellmates receive you as an enemy. They start 'struggling' to 'help' you. The 'struggle' goes on all day to 8 P.M. that night. You are obliged to stand with chains on your ankles and holding your hands behind your back. They don't assist you because you are too reactionary. . . . You eat as a dog does, with your mouth and teeth. You arrange the cup and bowl with your nose to try to absorb broth twice a day. If you have to make water they open your trousers and you make water in a little tin in the corner. . . . In the W.C. someone opens your trousers and after you are finished they clean you. You are never out of the chains. Nobody pays any attention to your hygiene. Nobody washes you. In the room they say you are in chains only because you are a reactionary. They continuously tell you that if you confess all, you will be treated better."

Toward the end of the second day he was called for another interrogation. He invented an American spy ring that he had "belonged" to. Pressed for details, he couldn't substantiate his story and went back to his cell for more "struggle." On the third night he realized that the officials were very interested in his activities and contacts. He began to reconstruct and confess every conversation with friends and associates he could remember, because "I thought they were trying to prove I gave intelligence to friends."

Interrogations, ever more demanding, took up the greater part of each night; these were interrupted every two or three hours for a rapid and painful promenade (in chains) which served to keep the prisoner awake, to increase his physical discomfort, and to give him a sense of movement ("in order to convince you to speed up your confession"). During the day, he was required to dictate to another prisoner everything he had confessed the night before, and anything additional he could think of. When he was not dictating the confessions or making new ones, he was being struggled. Every activity in the cell seemed to be centered around him and his confession. . . . Every word, movement, or expression was noted and written down by other prisoners, then conveyed to the prison authorities.

For eight days and nights, Vincent experienced this program of alternating struggle and interrogation, and was permitted no sleep at all. Moreover, he was constantly told by his cellmates that he was completely responsible for his own plight. ("You want the chains! You want to be shot! . . . Otherwise, you would be more 'sincere' and the chains would not be necessary.") He found himself in a Kafka-like maze of vague and yet damning accusations: he could neither understand exactly what he was guilty of ("recognize his crimes") nor could he in any way establish his innocence. Overwhelmed by fatigue, confusion, and helplessness, he ceased all resistance.

"You are annihilated . . . exhausted . . . you can't control yourself, or remember what you said two minutes before. You feel that all is lost. . . . From that moment, the judge is the real master of you. You accept anything he says. When he asks how many 'intelligences' you gave to that person, you just put out a number in order to satisfy him. If he says, 'Only those?,' you say, 'No, there are more.' If he says, 'One hundred,' you say, 'One hundred' . . . you do whatever they want. You don't pay any more attention to your life or to your handcuffed arms. You can't distinguish right from left. You just wonder when you will be shot—and begin to hope for the end of all this."

A confession began to emerge, one full of exaggerations, distortions, and lies, but one also closely related to real people and events in Vincent's life. Each night he would sign a written version of the day's confession, signing with his thumbprint because his hands still weren't free.

After three weeks of this he was forced to make exhaustive lists of everyone he had known in China and anything he knew about their activities. He gave his interrogators "truths, half truths and untruths." The descriptions became exposés and denunciations.

Still the clamor from the judge, officials, and cellmates was the same as it had been since the moment of imprisonment: "Confess . . . Confess all . . . You must be frank! . . . You must show your faith in the government! . . . Come clean! . . . Be sincere! . . . Recognize your crimes! . . ."

At this point—about two months from the date of his arrest—Vincent was considered to be ready for a beginning "recognition" of his "crimes." This required that he learn to look at himself from the "people's standpoint"—to accept the prevailing Communist definition of criminal behavior, including the principle that "the people's standpoint makes no distinction between news, information, and intelligence." . . .

"For instance, I was the family physician and friend of an American correspondent. We talked about many things, including the political situation. . . . The judge questioned me again and again about my relationship with this man. He asked me for details about everything we had talked about. . . . I admitted that at the time of the 'liberation,' when I saw the horsedrawn artillery of the Communist army, I told this to my American friend. . . . The judge shouted that this American was a spy who was collecting espionage material for his spy organization, and that I was guilty of supplying him with military intelligence. . . . At first I did not accept this, but soon I had to add it to my confession. . . . This is adopting the people's standpoint. . . .

"I knew a man wno was friendly with an American military attaché. I told him the price of shoes and that I couldn't buy gasoline tor my car. I had already agreed that this was economic intelligence. So I wrote that I gave economic intelligence to this man. But they made it clear that I must say that I received an espionage mission from the American military attaché through the other person, to collect economic intelligence. . . . This was the people's standpoint."

Just as Vincent was getting the hang of looking at things from the "people's standpoint," he was surprised by an improvement in his status:

The handcuffs and chains were removed, he was permitted to be comfortably seated when talking to the judge, and he was in turn addressed in friendly tones. He was told that the government regretted that he had been having such a difficult time, that it really wanted only to help him, and that in accordance with its "lenient policy" it would certainly treat him kindly, and soon release him—if only he would make an absolutely complete confession, and then work hard to "reform" himself. And to help things along, pressures were diminished, and he was permitted more rest. This abrupt reversal in attitude had a profound effect upon Vincent; for the first time he had been treated with human consideration, the chains were gone, he could see a possible solution ahead, there was hope for the future.

He was given more friendly guidance in rewriting his entire confession over and over and over. (Three times he balked and denied certain things suggested for his confession and found the chains back on for two or three days at a clip.)

Meanwhile, he was initiated into the regular cell routine: carefully regimented arrangements for sleeping and awakening, for eating and for relieving oneself. Freed of the chains, he could join the others on the two daily excursions to the toilet (everyone running head down, to an area with two open toilets, each permitted about forty-five seconds to attend to his needs with sharp criticism directed at anyone who took longer than this), and to the use of the urine bucket in the cell. He was still addressed only by prison number, and continued to receive food adequate for survival but poor in quality. And the sores and infections caused by his chains and handcuffs were given more attention, including local applications and penicillin injections.

Then, three weeks after the beginning of "leniency," he began to take part in the cell's organized "re-education" procedures. This meant active involvement in the group study program—the *hsüeh hsi*—whose sessions took up almost the entire waking existence of the prisoners, ten to sixteen hours a day. Led by the cell chief, its procedure was simple enough: one prisoner read material from a Communist newspaper, book, or pamphlet; and then each in turn was expected to express his own opinion and to criticize the views of others. Everyone was required to participate actively, and anyone who did not was severely criticized. Each had to learn to express himself from the "correct" or "people's viewpoint"—applied not only to personal actions, but to political, social, and ethical issues. With each of the prisoners feeling that his freedom or even his life might be at stake, the zeal of the participants was overwhelming. . . .

Discussions starting at an intellectual level would quickly become concerned with personal analysis and criticism. When Dr. Vincent was found wanting in his adoption of the "people's standpoint" or when his views were considered "erroneous," it became necessary for him to "examine himself," and look into the causes of these "reactionary" tendencies. He had to search out the harmful "bourgeois" and "imperialistic" influences from his past for further evaluation and self-criticism. Every "question" or "problem" had to be "solved," according to the "facts," in order to get to the "truth," viewing everything, of course, from the "people's standpoint" . . . .

"In the cell, you work in order to recognize your crimes. . . . They make you understand your crimes are very heavy. You did harm to the Chinese people. You are really a spy, and all the punishment you received was your own fault. . . . In the cell, twelve hours a day, you talk and talk—you have to take part—you must discuss yourself, criticize, inspect yourself, denounce your thought. Little by little you start to admit something, and look to yourself only using the 'people's judgment.' "

There were daily discussions of Marxist theory, of Russian and Chinese history, and of current events. All discussions sooner or later got back to the "thought problems" each prisoner was having that prevented him from making progress. Each had to express his reactions and "wrong thoughts":

"You have to get rid of and denounce all your imperialist thoughts, and you must criticize all of your own thoughts, guided by the official. If not, they will have someone else solve your problem and criticize you more profoundly. . . . You have a problem—you have to denounce it—a schoolmate has to help you—his help has to have 'proper standpoint.' . . . I am quiet—they say, 'You have a problem.' They have schoolmates to solve my problem, to demonstrate I am on the wrong side because the Chinese Communists have to proceed in another way. Their way is reform rather than compulsion. He demonstrates that the Soviet revolution was different from the Chinese revolution—that the Chinese capitalist suffered through the imperialists because we imperialists never gave them the opportunity to develop their industries. . . . They have to explain the facts until I am convinced. If I am not convinced I must say I don't understand, and they bring new facts. If I am still not satisfied, I have the right to call an inspector—but I wouldn't, I would just accept, otherwise there might be a struggle. . . . You are all day under the compulsion of denouncing your thoughts and solving your problems. . . . If you continually denounce your thoughts, you can be happy denouncing yourself. You are not resisting. But they keep a record, and after one week if you are not saying anything, they tell you you are resisting your re-education. . . . If you think out five or six problems it is a good manifestation; you are progressing because you like to discuss your imperialist thoughts. This is necessary, because if you don't get rid of these thoughts, you can't put in new ones."

If Vincent did not produce enough "wrong thoughts" he was criticized for not being "sincere," for not taking an active enough part in his thought reform. When others felt he was not wholeheartedly involved in his own reform but just going through the motions, he was accused of "spreading a smokescreen," "window dressing," "finding a loophole," or "failing to combine theory with practice."

Part of each day's study time was devoted to "daily life criticisms." Any aspect of one's working, eating, or sleeping habits could be material for discussion, evidence of one's lack of sincerity, and occasion for a model lesson:

Where Vincent was found wanting in any of these, this was attributed to "imperialist" or "bourgeois" greed and exploitation, in contrast to the "people's attitude" of sharing and cooperation. When considered lax in his work, he was criticized for lacking the "correct labor point of view"; when he dropped a plate, this was wasting the people's money; if he drank too much water, this was "draining the blood of the people"; if he took up too much room while sleeping, this was "imperialistic expansion."

While all of this was going on Vincent would still hear talk of the release of men who had "accepted their reeducation" and of men who were shot because they resisted.

After more than a year of this continuous "reeducation," he underwent another series of interrogations, aimed at reconstructing, refining, and polishing his confession. He had a better grasp of the "people's standpoint" and the confession seemed more real to him:

"You have the feeling that you look to yourself on the people's side, and that you are a criminal. Not all of the time—but moments—you think they are right. "I did this, I am a criminal." If you doubt, you keep it to yourself. Because if you admit the doubt you will be "struggled" and lose the progress you have made. . . . In this way they built up a spy mentality. . . . They built up a criminal. . . . Then your invention becomes a reality. . . . You feel guilty, because all of the time you have to look at yourself from the people's standpoint, and the more deeply you go into the people's standpoint, the more you recognize your crimes."

He went through another fourteen months of full-time reeducation, applying Communist theory to his personal situation, demonstrating his increasing "recognition" of his crimes:

"After two years, in order to show that you are more on the people's side, you increase your crimes. . . . I said I wasn't frank before, there were really more intelligences. . . . This is a good point. It means that you are analyzing your crimes. . . . It means that you realize your crimes are very big, and that you are not afraid to denounce yourself . . . that you trust the people, trust your reeducation, and that you like to be reformed."

By now he was becoming more active and skillful at helping and criticizing others. He even came to believe a good deal of what he was saying.

"You begin to believe all this, but it is a special kind of belief. You are not absolutely convinced, but you accept it—in order to avoid trouble—because everytime you don't agree, trouble starts again."

During his third year, he was called in for a new revision of his confession. It became briefer, more concrete and persuasive. He still had not been sentenced for his crimes and he began to think about his sentence:

"You have the feeling that your sentence is coming and that you will be sent somewhere else . . . and you are waiting. . . . You think, 'How long—maybe twenty–twenty-five years.' . . . You will be sent to reform through labor . . . to a factory or to a field. . . . They are very generous about this. . . . The government is very generous. The people are very generous. . . . Now you know that you cannot be shot. . . . But you are thinking that your crimes are very heavy."

He was then told his "attitude" had improved, and he was transferred to a different wing of the prison and given treasured privileges like an hour of outdoor exercise a day and permission to give French lessons to new prisoners and to give medical classes. He was grateful. He took this all as an indication that

". . . they weren't against my work or my profession but were only against my reactionary mind. To show that my work was well accepted, that they accepted my theories. . . . To show what it means to live among people, if I become one of the people. . . . To put in my mind that life among the people is good."

Soon after this he was called in for a formal signing of his confession—in French in his own handwriting, and in Chinese translation. This session was filmed, recorded, and widely distributed inside and outside of China.

A short time later he was called before the judge, and after three years of "solving" his case, he was read both the charges and the sentence: for "espionage" and other "crimes" against the people, three years of imprisonment—this considered to be already served. He was expelled immediately from China, and within two days, he was on a British ship heading for Hong Kong.

Other Examples of Resocialization

The procedures used to brainwash Dr. Vincent are the same basic procedures used by many other resocialization agencies, in somewhat milder form. The quotations you are about to read describe military training, delinquent rehabilitation, and drug addict rehabilitation, but these are just a small sample of agencies and activities that use similar principles and procedures to take people apart and put them back together again a new way. (Prisons and mental institutions generally have more resources available to "take people apart" and make them adjust to the orderly routines of the institution than resources and staff to "put them back together again.")

Essexfields (Delinquents)[16]

Early in his Essexfields career, the boy "tells his story" in a group meeting. The boy's story is a detailed and intimate account of every deviant act he can recall having committed and his reason for committing it. During the boy's telling of his story, other group members attempt to break down his rationalizations of his prior behavior. They cross-examine him and probe for his opinions and feelings; they force him to state his reasons for his behavior in explicit terms and to explain why his behavior was wrong. After the formal telling of his story, the boy is assigned problems by the group which they feel are the cause of his trouble. There is virtually an endless list of problems, ranging from "light-fingered," "drinking," and "duking" (fighting) problems through "family," "going along with the boys," and "easily discouraged" problems to "loud mouthing," "easily aggravated," and "inconsiderate of others" problems. . . . the group may "go deep into a boy's problem"; that is, focus on one of the problems and probe deeply and at great length. . . . Thereafter, group members constantly remind the boy of the "real" reasons for his delinquency and expect him to work on overcoming these problems.

Cross-examining a boy in or out of the group tends to inhibit his playing a false reformed role (known to the boys as "playing a role"). It also prevents a boy's engaging in passive and ritualistic behavior until his time is up. . . . It seems to induce introspective anxiety and tension which forces the boy to question his attitudes and rationalizations as well as his behavior. . . . "Confessing" on one's self is viewed by the group as the supreme test of a boy's sincerity. . . .

The boy who does conform and accept conventional behavior patterns is rewarded by the group. He may move through a series of status positions based upon whether or not he has been "helped," that is, whether or not he conforms. Being known as a "helped boy" is quite meaningful to the Essexfields boy because it is a distinction shared by only a few members of the group at any one time. . . .

The delinquent usually conceives of himself in a negative and self-defeating way. Such a self-image permits the boy to engage in delinquent behavior without questioning his own actions. . . .

As a result of his Essexfields experience, the typical boy no longer sees himself as a delinquent but as a boy with problems. . . . The concept that "problems" lie at the root of law-violating behavior is inculcated to the extent that all of a boy's activity is seen in the context of his understanding and overcoming his "problems." In this sense, a boy is no longer defined by significant others as delinquent.

Integrity House (Drug Addicts)[17]

The pre-interview of a prospective inmate begins the image-breaking process, first by stripping away any sense of identity the applicant may have, and second, by providing him with a new identity as a "sick" person. The staff stresses that the applicant will be required to demonstrate his need for help; if he is admitted to the program, the relationship will be that of the server and the served. The successful applicant must begin to demonstrate his willingness to believe that he not only has a problem but that he *is* the problem at the very first interview. He must begin to think of himself as an "emotional infant," the definition given him by Integrity. . . .

Integrity can exist only in a situation where prisons also exist, for Integrity is a viable choice only when jail is the only alternative. . . .

Applicants, accustomed to the more custodial concept of "doing your own time," or "playing it cool," are unprepared for the reception given them at Integrity. The staff often has the problem of a resident being too passive to elicit much of anything that can be used as "signs" of psychological problems; in this case, the passivity itself becomes the object and "symptom" of "sickness," in true pseudopsychological fashion.

"Haircuts," night probes and other tactics are used to provoke the inmate who, once angry, is over his "passivity" and will raise his new-found "feelings" in the weekly encounter group for the entire community. The staff members then have "data" from which they can work on the inmate. Even though they have elicited this data artificially, they never consider their role in generating the conflict but always focus back on the inmate. This is largely possible because of the structure of the encounter group itself: often, more than one staff member is present and any inmate can say anything he desires about the inmate who is the center of attention. In this manner, any encounter session has the appearance of pitting the entire community against the individual; those who "contribute in this positive manner" are in reality contributing to their own release and advancement and privilege. . . . The therapeutic activity makes it more and more difficult to avoid one's "sickness." The staff constantly refers to incidents from an inmate's life history as evidence of his disorder, and all segments of the community pressure him to accept this "evidence" and to confess his past misdeeds to others. . . .

Marine Basic Training[18]
[The Marine drill instructor] works sixteen hours a day and one is always on duty, seven days a week. His tools are physical prowess, for he must be able to demonstrate everything better than the best man in his platoon, brutality, fierceness, pride, and total determination. Add a dash of sadism and the uncanny ability to seek out and exploit a man's weakest points. He begins with an absolute belief in the Marine Corps and ends with the conviction that his training mission is akin to a religious call.

The way he fulfills his job is first by pounding his charges to helpless, hopeless blobs. So terrified are the recruits of the seemingly insane paranoid who has power of life and death over them that their only conceivable salvation is to try to please this man, somehow to reduce his rage. It is a frightening thing, even to one who has been through it, to see a platoon in the first days of the "shock stage," that period of about a week when the D.I. deliberately sets about to disperse the civilian attitude and reduce each man to recruit level. The boot [recruit] is frantic, physically and mentally. Nothing makes sense to him; he lives in absolute terror, because there is neither reason nor logic to what is happening to him. The D.I. will deliberately indulge in wild inconsistencies only to confuse his charges more. And when they are completely confused, then and only then is it time to take the first step in teaching. Boot training is pure anarchy in action, real military Dada. Destroy totally, then rebuild anew. . . .

[A D.I. says] . . . "I think what motivates a man most of all is the feeling that he's part of a unit, and it has to be a small unit where he knows everybody and knows them well. In our case it's the platoon. You know damn well that the thing we emphasize more than anything is to get them to pull together as a unit. How many times do we tell them that every man is completely dependent on every other man? Why do we have mass punishment? Not because it's fair, and not because it's the meanest thing we can do, but because they have to learn that if one man fouls up then *everybody* suffers. One man doping off can cost the lives of twenty. *Nobody* is an individual when he's here, and so nobody can make an individual decision. Whatever a man does affects everybody else, and that's what they have to learn. You get a man who'd rather die than let his platoon down and you have a motivated damn Marine."

Resocialization, to be effective even in the short run, requires an enormous amount of time and effort and staff. We don't have any rigorous research that would tell us how effective these drug and delinquency programs actually are (and for what kinds of people) or how one can effectively resist the pressures for change.[19] What little evidence we have indicates that most of these programs

The D.I. deliberately sets about to disperse the civilian attitude and reduce each man to recruit level.

are effective mainly while one is in the program and can find no social support for his forbidden behaviors or his old identity. (Even the extremely rigorous Chinese brainwashing procedures lose their potency once the victim leaves the country and his captors.)

Summary

A number of groups and agencies in society teach us their values and norms. Beginning with the family, each group we have contact with socializes us. There are also institutions which attempt to *re*socialize us and which share quite similar techniques. These techniques can be remarkably effective, at least in the short run.

Notes

1. F. Elkin and G. Handel, *The Child and Society: The Process of Socialization,* 2nd Ed. (New York: Random House, Inc., 1972).
2. Ibid., p. 103.
3. H. Gans, *The Urban Villagers: Group and Class in the Life of Italian Americans* (New York: The Free Press, 1962), pp. 54–57.
4. Ibid., pp. 55–57.
5. Ibid., p. 55.
6. Ibid., pp. 55–56.
7. For a thorough review of the literature on social class and socialization, see A. C. Kerckhoff, *Socialization and Social Class* (Englewood Cliffs, N.J.: Prentice-Hall, Inc., 1972), particularly the overview in Chapter 7.
8. Elkin and Handel, op. cit., p. 113.
9. Ibid., pp. 118–119.
10. See A. Somit, "Brainwashing," in D. Sells, ed., *International Encyclopedia of the Social Sciences* (New York: Macmillan Publishing, Co., Inc., 1968), Vol. 2, pp. 138–142.
11. Ibid., pp. 139–140.
12. Ibid., p. 140.
13. See D. R. Cressey, "Changing Criminals: The Application of the Theory of Differential Association," *American Journal of Sociology,* **62** (1955), 116–120; and D. R. Cressey, "Social Psychological Foundations for Using Criminals in the Rehabilitation of Criminals," *Journal of Research in Crime and Delinquency,* **2** (1965), 49–59.
14. See P. Lippitt, R. Lippitt, and J. Eisenman, *Cross-Age Helping Package* (Ann Arbor, Mich.: Institute for Social Research, 1969). Also V. L. Allen and R. S. Feldman, "Learning Through Tutoring: Low Achieving Children as Tutors," *Journal of Experimental Education,* **42** (1973), 1–5.
15. The section on Vincent is drawn from R. J. Lifton, *Thought Reform and the Psychology of Totalism* (New York: W. W. Norton & Company, Inc., 1961), pp. 19–32. See also J. T. Richardson, M. Harder, and R. B. Simmonds, "Thought Reform and the Jesus Movement," *Youth and Society,* **4** (1972), 185–202.
16. F. Scarpitti and R. M. Stephenson, "The Use of the Small Group in the Rehabilitation of Delinquents," *Federal Probation,* (1967), 45–50. See also L. T. Empey and J. Rabow, "The Provo Experiment in Delinquency Rehabilitation," *American Sociological Review,* **26** (1961), 679–696; W. H. Gordon, "Communist Rectification Programs and Delinquency Rehabilitation Programs: A Parallel," and L. T. Empey and J. Rabow, "A Reply to Whitney H. Gordon," *American Sociological Review,* **27** (1962), 256–258; and L. T. Empey's discussion of the origins

and results of the Provo Experiment, pp. 371–374 and 395–404 in H. Gold and F. R. Scarpitti, eds., *Combatting Social Problems* (New York: Holt, Rinehart, & Winston, Inc., 1967).

17. D. Colburn and K. Colburn, "Integrity House," *Society,* **10** (1973), 39–45. Integrity House is modeled closely after Synanon. On Synanon see D. Casriel, Inc., *So Fair a House: The Story of Synanon* (Englewood Cliffs, N.J.: Prentice-Hall, Inc., 1963); and A. Yablonsky, *The Tunnel Back: Synanon* (New York: Macmillan Publishing Co., Inc., 1965). See also E. Sagarin, *Odd Man In* (Chicago: Quadrangle Books, 1969); and D. Scott and H. L. Goldberg, "The Phenomenon of Self-Perpetuation in Synanon-Type Drug Treatment Programs," *Hospital and Community Psychiatry,* **24** (1973), 231–233, for somewhat skeptical views of Synanon.

18. R. A. Aurthur, "Going Back to Boot Camp, Parris Island, S. C.," *Esquire* (September, 1965), pp. 127ff. See also L. Zurcher, "The Naval Recruit Training Center," *Sociological Inquiry,* **37** (1967), 85–98; and S. Dornbusch, "The Military Academy as an Assimilating Institution," *Social Forces,* **33** (1955), 316–321.

19. M. K. Whyte observes that the Chinese have had mixed success in using "thought reform" on criminals in the corrective labor camps. Few are "reformed," but the procedures seem to keep the inmates too busy to develop the inmate codes and inmate subcultures we find in Western prisons. See M. K. Whyte, "Corrective Labor Camps in China," *Asian Survey,* **13** (1973), 253–269.

EIGHT

The Family

THE HUMAN INFANT is a helpless creature who requires a great deal of care and attention if it is to survive and ultimately become a functioning member of its society. Every society, if it is to survive, must replace those who die with new members. The family is the group that is given the responsibility for producing and protecting these new members of society.

The family is a universal institution. Every known society has a family system. Although all societies have some sort of arrangement we can call a "family" system, the nature of family systems is so varied that it is almost impossible to come up with a single, precise definition of what a family is. (No matter how we define *family,* some historian or anthropologist seems to be able to find some obscure society or segment of a society somewhere that is an exception.)

Functions of the Nuclear Family

In a classic survey of the anthropological literature, George Murdock suggested that everywhere the nuclear family, consisting of male, female, and their unmarried children, performs four basic functions necessary to the continuation of any human society. These four functions are control of sexual relations, economic cooperation, reproduction, and socialization.[1]

Sexual Relations

Sex is a powerful drive that has the potential for disrupting the cooperative relationships necessary for maintaining a society. All known societies place restrictions of various kinds on sexual expression. Through a socially approved marital relationship the nuclear family gives sexual privileges to the husband and wife and thereby channels and controls this basic drive. There's more to marriage than sex, of course, and in many respects sex is the *least* important factor in accounting for the existence of marriage. Murdock's examination of 250 societies showed that there was a great deal of sexual freedom permitted the unmarried in most societies, yet most of the people in these societies eventually married. In many of these societies extramarital sexual affairs were permitted. In other words, the existence of marriage can't be attributed *solely* to the need to control sex, though physical pleasure is certainly an important aspect of marriage.

Economic Cooperation

Every known human society has developed economic specialization and cooperation between the sexes, partly as the result of biological differences between men and women and partly as a result of culturally learned ideas of what constitutes a proper division of labor. Because men are usually considered physically more powerful, they *usually* take on the heavier and more strenuous tasks. Women, tied to the demands of childbearing, generally are assigned household tasks and child-rearing activities. The economic services provided by the husband and the wife complement one another and make them dependent on one another.

Every society segregates economic activities by *age* as well as sex. In some societies young children contribute very little; in other societies they're quite useful. As children get older they contribute more. When parents get older they often become dependent on their children for care and economic assistance. This exchange of services and economic assistance helps account for the universality of the family.

Reproduction

All societies place heavy emphasis on the reproduction function of the nuclear family. A married couple is expected to produce children and take care of them. In some societies children are so highly valued that the husband isn't permitted sexual access to his wife until she has first established (with someone else) her ability to produce children. In many societies the husband is allowed (or forced) to dissolve the marriage when the wife proves to be barren (the husbands are assumed to be capable of fathering children; if none are born, it's presumed to be her "fault").

Socialization

In almost all societies the family is expected to take on the basic responsibility for socializing children so that they will someday be able to function adequately as adults. Generally the father is responsible for training the sons for adult male roles, the mother for preparing the daughters for adult female roles.

Even in modern industrial societies where outside agencies like the school have a significant part in giving the child skills, the family plays a significant role in socializing children (see Chapter Seven, "Who Socializes Us?").

Murdock's argument that the nuclear family (1) is universal and (2) *everywhere* carries out these four functions has been challenged by other scholars—remember that a claim that something is *universal* requires only *one* exception to be considered false. The two most frequently cited exceptions to Murdock's claim for the universality of the nuclear family are the Nayar, a Hindu caste group in southern India,[2] and the Israeli kibbutz. We will discuss the kibbutz later.

The Nayars, up until the late eighteenth century, had a *matrilineal* system. That is, people traced their descent through the female line. Inheritance also occurred through the female line. A typical household contained a woman and her children, her married daughters and their children, her brothers, her sisters' children, and some of her other relatives—aunts and uncles—on her mother's side. Her brothers and uncles lived in these households and visited their "wives" for a few hours or overnight after the evening meal, when they weren't off fighting wars somewhere. (Nayar men were part of the militia and spent a good deal of their time away from home at war.) Each Nayar girl, before she reached adolescence, went through a symbolic marriage ceremony with a man (any man) of the proper caste. He tied a gold ornament (called a *tali*) around her neck during the ceremony, spent four days with her, and then took off on his own and might never see her again. She wore the *tali* around her neck for the rest of her life, and when her *tali*-husband died she mourned him. The *tali*-tying ceremony was apparently a way of legitimating the woman's right to bear children.

After this ceremony the woman was free to take on a second type of husband (a *sambandham*). The *tali*-tying husband was what we would call her legal husband and the *sambandham* husbands what we would call her lovers. A Nayar woman might have seven or eight regular lovers. (Each of them might have a number of Nayar mistresses, too.) The lovers came either from her own Nayar caste or from a higher caste, the Nambudiri Brahman caste. These lovers did not live with her. They dropped by after dinner, planted a spear outside her hut, and spent the evening. If another lover came by and saw a spear in front of her hut, he went away and came back some other time. Because the men might also have more than one "wife," if one was booked the man might visit a different one.

The children were a part of the *mother's* family rather than the father's. Who the biological father was *did not matter* as long as *one* of the mother's lovers was willing to take public responsibility for being the biological father. *Responsibility* is not quite the proper term because actually the biological father had only the obligation to pay for the delivery costs of the child, after which he had *no other* rights or responsibilities related to the child. The mother's eldest brother took on the support and socialization responsibilities we usually think of as the father's. Although the man who publicly claimed to be the biological father had little to gain or lose by doing so, it was important that *someone* take on this role. If no one wanted to admit to being the biological father, the mother and child might be expelled or even killed.

Let's put the Nayar system in context. The Nambudiri Brahman caste was a very wealthy one. The wealth was in the form of land. They had a rule that estates could not be divided. In each family the eldest son could marry and he could marry only a Nambudiri girl. The other brothers could *not* marry or have children (this would apparently bring pressure to divide up the estates). The unmarried Nambudiri men could, by taking Nayar "wives," take care of their sex drives without this having any consequences for the land ownership system. The Nayar profited from this arrangement because it enabled them to control their children completely without interference from any outsiders. Because the mother's eldest brother took the responsibility for the child, the mother's family kept the children under family control. The only losers in this system were the Nambudiri women who weren't married to eldest sons. They weren't permitted to marry outside their own group and lived in a state of strict seclusion. They could go out only if they were completely enveloped in clothes and kept their faces hidden by an umbrella. (In fact, those who *did* get married to an eldest son did not make a public appearance at their weddings or at any other event. A Nayar girl stood in for them.)

The Nayar system challenges the idea that the nuclear family is a universal institution for carrying out the four functions Murdock described because the ties between "husband" and "wife" were weak. The *tali*-tying husband might never be seen again. The *sambandham* husbands were also generally tied to the women only very loosely. Even where the husband-wife relationship was stable, the husband had virtually nothing to do with the rearing of the children. Nor did he make any *economic* contribution to his wife's support. Nor was sex tied to the husband-wife relationship. A woman could have many lovers and as long as she had gone through the *tali*-tying ceremony this was legitimate. The reason a "father" had to come forward to claim the child was apparently to demonstrate that the child's father was from the proper caste and that the *family* had not been "polluted" by contact with a lower caste.

There's some controversy over whether the Nayar were actually a *society* or just a *segment* of Indian society and whether they therefore challenged Murdock's assumption that the nuclear family universally (in every *society*) has the four functions he described. In two senses this is an academic question. First, if these functions aren't universal they are almost universal, and any pattern to which there are less than a handful of exceptions out of several thousand known societies is obviously a significant one and a pattern that has demonstrated it can serve society effectively.

The second sense in which it is an academic question is that the Nayar system has changed over the last century toward a system in which the nuclear family *does* tend to have the four functions that Murdock described. The pattern of visiting husbands has practically disappeared. We are discussing a system that has changed toward the nuclear family system in response to the commercialization and industrialization of India.

On the other hand, because some of these four functions can apparently be carried out successfully by some unit other than the nuclear family without the society's falling apart, the nuclear family may not be indispensable. We don't know for sure whether or not there are certain functions that a *family* system, nuclear or otherwise, *must* take care of and other functions that other social arrangements can take away from or share with the family without threatening the survival of a society.

Reiss suggests,[3] for example, that the only activity that is universal (found in *all* family systems we know of) is the responsibility of giving emotional support and emotional response to the child. He argues that this is universal and necessary and that without such emotional support the child will be unable to enter into emotionally healthy relationships with others in the society when it grows up.

The Extended Family

Although almost everywhere we can find the nuclear family, the nuclear family is not always an important unit within the society. Frequently it is a minor subdivision of a large, *extended* family, and the larger family may be the more important unit. An extended family is composed of brothers (or sisters), their spouses and children, and/or their parents and their married children. They all live in the same household or near the house of the head of the family, who is generally the oldest male. Traditionally, especially before industrialization, the extended family was so much more significant than the nuclear family that a strong tie between husband and wife could be considered a threat to the survival of the more important family unit, the extended family. In fact, the family might (successfully) command the offending couple to divorce because their relationship had become too close and threatened the ties of the husband (or wife) to the extended family.

In Japan and China, for example, the wife was subordinate to her mother-in-law. If the mother-in-law felt that her son's bride was incompetent in her work around the house or if in some other way the bride displeased her, she could demand that her son divorce the offending woman. He was obligated to do so. The more he loved the wife, the more admirable divorcing her was because it proved that he was truly a devoted son. The bond between blood relatives was more significant than the bond of matrimony between husband and wife.

Marriage Forms

In most societies people are permitted to have more than one spouse. The marriage system in which a man is permitted only one wife and the woman only one husband is called a *monogamous* system. If the man may have more than one wife or the wife may have more than one husband, the marriage system is *polygamous.* There are two basic forms of polygamy. If the man may have more than one wife, we call this *polygyny.* If the woman may have two or more husbands, we call this practice *polyandry.*

The system of wives having multiple husbands is rare. Still more rare is a system in which several men and several women are married to each other (group marriage). Although there are some societies in which group marriage has been known to take place, we don't know of any societies in which it is the dominant form. In those few instances in which group marriage has occurred, it seems to have developed out of polyandrous arrangements and to have coexisted along with polyandry.

In 1957 Murdock compiled data on some 565 societies.[4] In none was group marriage the dominant form. In only four societies, polyandry (multiple husbands, one wife) was the dominant form. Roughly a quarter of the 565 societies practiced "strict monogamy." Roughly 70 percent of the societies had systems in which polygyny was practiced; but although the men were permitted more than one wife, most of them did not, in fact, take more than one wife. In many countries it takes a great deal of wealth to support several wives and only the wealthy and powerful can afford them. As Raphael Patai[5] observed in regard to North Africa and the Middle East:

To have more than one wife was (and remained in traditional circles) a mark of high status, of prestige, and of wealth. . . . Polygyny continued to be practiced in Israel throughout the Biblical period, but it seems to have been restricted to men who occupied leading positions, who were rich, or had some other claim to distinction. . . . This is the general rule in the Middle East to this day, while the simple people, both in Biblical times and today, had (and have) to be satisfied with one wife, or at least with one at a time.

On the other hand, in other countries in which wives are important contributors to the economy, having more than one wife contributes to one's wealth. For example, among the Siwai in the Solomon Islands one gains wealth by giving feasts. Pork is the main dish at these feasts, and pig raising is linked to prestige. Furthermore, pigs are beloved pets for the Siwai; they aren't only pig *raisers,* they are pig *lovers:*

When Siwai natives call their pigs by name, grin with pleasure as the beasts troop in squealing, carefully set out food for them in baskets and discuss their merit with noticeable pride, it becomes apparent to an observer that these people look upon their pigs as pets. . . . Even granted that a man must occasionally butcher a pig to celebrate an event, he rarely ever uses a pig which he, himself, has raised. After years of looking after a beast, a native becomes fond of it. For example, Sinu of Jeku village invited a number of friends to help him build a house and promised them a pork banquet as a reward. When time came for killing his pig, he said he couldn't bring himself to do it. Then someone suggested that he do what was ordinarily done; exchange his pig for that of someone else; he again demurred. Finally, he bought another pig and butchered it.[6]

Given their interest in *pigs,* the Siwai are also interested in *wives,* because the women in this society grow the food needed to raise the pigs. The more wives, the more pigs one can support:

It is by no mere accident that polygynous households average more pigs than monogamous ones. Informants stated explicitly that some men married second and third wives in order to enlarge their gardens and increase their herds. They laughed at the writer's suggestion that a man might become polygynous in order to increase his sexual enjoyment. ("Why pay bride price when for a handful of tobacco you can copulate with other women as often as you like!") Opisa of Turunom did not even trouble to move his second wife from her village to his own. She, a woman twenty years his senior, simply remained at her own home and tended two of his pigs.

Some of the wealthiest, most influential men had several wives; but when it was suggested to informants that polygyny was a sign of renown, they vigorously denied it; stating that the main reason for the custom is to increase herds.[7]

Aren't the wives jealous of one another? Although in many societies there appears to be no jealousy among co-wives, in many others there appears to be a great deal of jealousy.

In other words, jealousy is *not inevitable* when women share husbands. But on the other hand, it wouldn't be accurate to say that it is easy to socialize jealousy out of people, as we can see in this description by Sinu, the Siwai:

There is never peace for long in a polygynous family. If the husband sleeps in the house of one wife the other one sulks all the next day. If the man is so stupid as to sleep two consecutive nights in the house of one wife, the other one will refuse to cook for him, saying, "So-and-so is your wife; go to her for food. Since I am not good enough for you to sleep with, then my food is not good enough for you to eat." Frequently the co-wives will quarrel and fight. Kanku (Sinu's maternal uncle) formerly had five wives at one time and the youngest one was always raging and fighting the others. Once she knocked an older wife senseless and then ran away and had to be forcibly returned. Since then all but one of those wives had died, and there is peace in Jeku—not a single polygynous family. Formerly there was no sleeping at night; the co-wives were continually shouting and throwing things at one another. Kanku had absolutely no control over them.

Some husbands who intervene in their wives' quarrels, or persist in showing favoritism, do so at the risk of poisoning or sorcery. Wives have ample opportunity to murder or frighten their husbands by feeding them poison or by collecting some of their exuviae [sweat, hair, body wastes] for dirt sorcery. A few such women were pointed out to me as having actually killed their husbands. Nor were they censured generally for their deeds; other natives agreed that the murdered husbands bring upon themselves such trouble by having more than one wife.[8]

There are some practices that appear to minimize the occurrence of jealousy and that tend to occur in polygynous societies:

1. *Marriage to sisters.* Apparently co-wives who are sisters get along better than co-wives who are not. Generally co-wives who are sisters tend to live in the same living quarters. Co-wives who aren't sisters tend to have separate living quarters. (In societies that practice polyandry a woman tends to marry several brothers. This also seems to minimize jealousy.)

2. *Equal rights of co-wives.* Co-wives tend to have *clearly defined equal rights in certain matters,* in sex especially and in regard to economics and personal

possessions. For example, the Tanala of Madagascar require the husband to spend a day with each co-wife in succession. Not doing so constitutes adultery and entitles the offended wife to sue for divorce and alimony of up to one third of the husband's property:

> For purposes of cultivation, the husband's land is divided among the wives as equally as possible. Each wife works her section and can claim the husband's assistance on her day. This economic claim over the husband goes as far as that if he hunts or fishes on that day the wife has a right to half his take or to half the money received from the sale of any surplus. From the produce of her section of land each woman feeds herself and her children, also the husband on the day he is with her. If there is a surplus to be sold, one-half of the proceeds go to the husband as ground rent. The other half is the property of the wife, and she usually banks it with her own family. In a well-organized conjugal group the women usually take turns working on the land while one of them remains at home to cook and tend the children. The whole family will eat first at one house and then at another, so that, if there are three wives, cooking and dish-washing will fall to the portion of any one of them only on every third day. . . . Wives will not infrequently carry on love affairs with the full knowledge of their fellow-wives without fear of betrayal. The female half of the family is thus able to control family policies to a considerable degree, and henpecked husbands are by no means unknown. If the husband tries to coerce one wife, the rest will resent it and make his life miserable by those unofficial methods with which all women are familiar. The wives receive added power from the fact that the husband is theoretically in complete control and cannot appeal for outside help without making himself ridiculous.[9]

3. *Special privileges for senior wives.* Senior wives have special privileges. For example, among the Tonga of Polynesia, the first wife has the status of "chief wife." Her house is to the right of her husband's and is called "The House of the Father." The other wives are called "small wives" and live to the left. The chief wife has the right to be consulted first, and it is expected that her husband will sleep under her roof before and after a journey. These privileges could make the secondary wives jealous, but apparently they are balanced by a slight favoritism toward the newer, younger, perhaps more attractive wives. The first wife, then, is compensated (more or less) for her loss of physical attractiveness with increased prestige.

In closing our discussion of polygyny, let us observe three points: (1) it is quite widespread; (2) it is not clearly correlated with any sort of economic need; and (3) a woman's status is not necessarily lower than it is in monogamous societies. As Ralph Linton observed in relation to these three points:

> Polygyny, that is, plurality of wives, is considered the most desirable form of marriage in a very large part of the world's societies. It does not seem to be directly correlated with any particular set of economic conditions or even with the primary dependence of the society on the labor of either men or women.

It exists alike in societies in which women do most of the work and every wife is an added asset to the conjugal group and in those in which men carry the economic burden and each wife is an added liability. Although such factors do not seem to influence the ideal pattern, they naturally limit its exercise. Where wives are an asset, even a poor man can be polygynous unless the bride-price is prohibitive, and actual plurality of wives tends to be common. Where wives are a liability, few men can afford the luxury of an extra wife.

. . . Polygyny does not necessarily imply a high degree of male dominance in the marriage relationship or even a low position of women in the society. Polygynous societies are as variable in this respect as are monogamous ones. While there are a few cases in which the wives are completely dependent upon the husband, in most instances their rights are well guarded. When the plural wives are congenial, the women of a polygynous household may form a block, presenting a solid front against the husband and even dominating him.

. . . There are few polygynous systems in which the position of the male is really better than it is under monogamy. If the plural wives are not congenial, the family will be torn by feuds in which the husband must take the thankless role of umpire, while if they are congenial he is likely to be confronted by an organized female opposition. Among the subhuman primates the male can dominate a group of females because these females are unable to organize among themselves. He can deal with them in detail. The human male cannot dominate his wives in the same degree, since they can and do organize for both defense and offense. If all a man's wives want a particular thing, they can work on him in shifts and are fairly certain to get what they want.[10]

Societies, as we have seen, show enormous variety in their arrangements for marriage systems. There are even societies (like Dahomey) in which a married *woman* may take another woman for a wife and have children. (The female "husband" selects the males who are to father these children biologically, but *she* is in charge of this family, not her male husband. *She* is the head of the household formed by the wife and children.)

"Them" and "Us"

Can people be *happy* under the marriage systems we have been discussing? The question is an ethnocentric one. It assumes that people marry so that they can be happy. If we were to mention this assumption to the people of these societies, they would be puzzled. Of all the possible reasons they might have for marriage, "love" and "happiness" would be at the bottom of the list.

When we think of the "family" we Americans think of the *nuclear* family, independent of other relatives, as the basic family unit. We consider personal happiness as the main reason for entering a marriage and its absence as the main reason for dissolving a marriage. As we've observed before, we Americans value the marital tie and consider blood ties as something nice to maintain (if we get along well with our relatives) but much less important.

In societies in which the extended family is significant (that is, in most societies), the extended family is a unit on which people depend for *economic* survival (it may own all the land and tools) and for carrying out *religious* activities (family religious shrines and ancestor worship). It is the agency that protects its members from enemies. The extended family also has *social welfare* functions and takes care of a member if he is sick or old, takes care of his children if he should die, feeds him if his crop has failed. It may also be a *political* unit: in the absence of a formal legal system, the elders decide who is right or wrong and who is to be punished and how. For example, the head of the family in ancient Rome could put any member of his own family to death if he chose to and no one outside the family had any business butting in on this family affair.

The personal relationships we have with our spouses, with whom we share our triumphs and failures, our fears and hopes, in many societies are replaced by the sharing of these emotional experiences with *relatives* of one's own sex and age. (To some extent this is still true of blue-collar families in contemporary industrial societies.)

Societies and Families

In our society, as in other complex, urbanized, industrialized societies, we do not rely on the extended family for many things. Our basic family unit is the nuclear family. We can *also* find the nuclear family as the basic unit in extremely *simple* societies. The extended family is found mainly in societies with sedentary, agricultural economies. In societies that live by hunting and by gathering food from trees and bushes, and that therefore keep moving around in search of food, we tend *not* to find the extended family. The nuclear family is found in societies with very *simple* economies and in very *complex,* industrial economies. In agricultural societies, in which the ownership and control of land is more or less permanently the basis of a family's prosperity, we find the *extended* family as the key family unit.[11]

In hunting and gathering societies, in which there is no economic sense in owning land and passing it on from generation to generation, and in industrial societies, in which money rather than land is the basic form of wealth, we find the *nuclear* family as the significant unit. It also seems to be the case that societies that emphasize geographic mobility—chasing game for the hunter or chasing after jobs for the adult in the industrial society—are also conducive to the breaking or weakening of extended family ties.

Industrialization and the Family

As we've indicated, industrial societies tend to be societies in which the extended family is relatively insignificant. The relationship between industrialization and the decline of the extended family isn't as simple and direct as it appears to be. We can't say that industrialization *causes* the decline of the extended family or that *unless* the extended family declines industrialization cannot occur. It is probably more accurate to say that the nuclear family and industrialization support each other, although they may originally have developed independently of one another.[12]

It nevertheless does seem to be true that all over the industrializing world there are changes taking place in family systems, which may or may not be directly the result of industrialization and the effect of these changes is *fewer* kinship ties with distant relatives and greater emphasis on the nuclear family. William Goode[13] has pointed out that this trend does not necessarily mean that all industrialized societies are moving toward the kind of nuclear family system that we have in the United States. We are not the last ultimate step

There is a general worldwide trend toward some variant of the nuclear family.

on the evolutionary scale of societal and family systems. Other societies may develop nuclear family systems very different from ours.

Morris Zelditch has also observed that the extended family may decline in significance even where industrialization does not occur. He has suggested that "apparently, any kind of nonsubsistence expanding economy or even political changes can destroy the authority structure on which the descent group and extended family depend."[14]

He pointed to four basic conditions that can produce such a decline:

1. Kinship and occupational structures become differentiated so that one's occupation may be very different from those of other members of his family

2. Income and status come to depend on factors that aren't controlled by the extended family; for example, one doesn't have to inherit his family's land (or union membership) or business to be able to make his own living.
3. Sons begin to contribute more status and income to their families than do their fathers.
4. The self-interests of family members are not identified with the continuity of the family.

None of these conditions require industrialization. Goode[15] also suggested that *ideological* changes or changes in values are helping to transform non-Western family systems and that these changes may precede or develop simultaneously with the coming of industrialization. He suggested that in all family systems there are some points of strain and that these points of strain make them vulnerable to change. Women and the young are, in the traditional extended family, subordinate to males and their elders, and therefore among women and the young (as well as among intellectuals) "radical" new ideologies find especially fertile ground.

One such ideology is that of *economic progress,* the idea that technological development and producing wealth is more important than preserving traditional customs. A second ideology is that of *individualism,* the idea that personal welfare and happiness are more important than family continuity. A third ideology is the ideology of *equalitarianism,* the idea that women should have equal rights with men. These values may have as much impact on family change as does industrialization.

Some General Trends

Some of the elements that are bringing about the general *worldwide* trend toward some variant of the nuclear family as the significant unit are these: (1) free choice of spouse; (2) more equal status for women; (3) equal rights of divorce; and (4) the equality of individuals against class or caste barriers. Let's look at these briefly, one at a time.

Free Choice of Spouse

Where extended family systems are strong and significant, there's a family interest in making sure that young people marry other people who will not threaten the extended family's strength. Parents and other family members arrange marriages for young people. Love as a basis for marriage is discouraged because ties between the couple may conflict with obligations to the larger family. Generally, one partner moves to the home or neighborhood of the other's family and is more or less cut off from the support of his or her family (usually it is the wife who must move). In urbanizing societies young married couples often set up their own households, and the ability of one's spouse to get along with one's family is no longer as important. The relationship between husband and wife takes on great importance. We should point out that young people can and sometimes do fall in love in many societies, but in societies based on the extended family love is *not* considered a basis for selecting a mate. In these societies marriage arrangements of various kinds are developed to keep this potential for love from *interfering* with marriage.[16] Goode pointed to four arrangements that minimize the interference of love in the marriage system.[17]

1. *Arranged marriages between children.* Among the Hindus, for example, the average age of females at marriage in 1891 was twelve to fifteen years. By 1941 the figure had risen slowly to fourteen to seventeen years. This practice of child marriage, of course, gives the children little opportunity to fall in love and no way to do much about it if they did.

2. *Preferential marriage systems.* A second way of controlling love's effect on marriage is the preferential marriage system. What this means is that the society has rigid rules about whom one ought to marry. For example, among the Bedouin Arabs, the traditionally approved marriage is between a young man and his father's brother's daughter. In other societies the mother's brother's daughter might be seen as the appropriate mate. In other words, in a preferential marriage system, the range of legitimate marriage partners is restricted in such a way as to make it more or less impossible to marry anyone *but* one's cousin (or some other relative), regardless of one's own choice and regardless of whom one does or doesn't love.

3. *Seclusion of women.* Seclusion of women is a third practice that has the effect of keeping women from *meeting* anyone with whom they could fall in love. Such a system also tends to keep potential marriage partners from meeting each other before marriage. Family representatives or matchmakers make the contacts between families, and the two major considerations in the selecting of a match for one's son or daughter are the size of the bride-price or of the dowry and the reputation of the potential spouse's parents and/or kin group.

In such systems families that have little wealth or reputation have less to lose by having their children marry into lower-status groups, and they tend to permit their children to have a greater say in whom they marry. Very prosperous families have more invested and more to lose by a bad alliance and tend to be more involved in and more stubborn in such choices. Again we point out that a marriage is *not only* an alliance between two people but may also be a political, social, and economic alliance between two extended family groups. Let us also point out that the bride-price given the girl's family or the dowry given the groom's family may be a large sum of money or a list of services that it may take one family (including relatives) *years* to pay off.

4. *Chaperonage.* A fourth arrangement that has the effect of keeping love from interfering with marriage is chaperonage. Instead of keeping young people apart physically as in the practice of seclusion, chaperonage permits young

people to meet with other *carefully selected* marriageable young people, but they are almost never alone together. A parent or some other chaperone is always watching, keeping them out of mischief. The young people may sometimes be alone but only *after* they're engaged. In other words, *first* one gets engaged and *then* one can get to know the other person and perhaps fall in love.

More Equal Status of Women

As women gain the right to choose their own husbands, they also gain the power to name their own terms, which usually include greater influence within the marriage and refusal to be a second or third wife. Today education for women, particularly higher education, is spreading rapidly. As women become more active participants in the economy and are able to earn independent incomes, they also develop a greater measure of equality. We are not claiming that women have full equality but simply that worldwide equality is increasing. As Goode observed, *no* family system now grants *full* equality to women, and none is likely to do so as long as much of the daily work involving house and children is considered women's responsibility. This lack of equality is also observable in the dissolving of a marriage.

Equal Rights of Divorce

When we speak of "divorce" we are speaking of a modern legal idea that certain grounds entitle marriage partners to have the marriage dissolved by some official body, such as a court, that decides on the merits of the case. In many non-Western (and ancient) societies what dissolves a marriage is the *repudiation* of a wife by her husband or his family, with the husband or his family the sole judge of whether this should take place.

In many countries women are demanding that they have protection against unjust repudiation by their husband or his family. They're also demanding equal rights in such things as grounds for divorce, and they're asking that the same or comparable grounds for divorcing a *wife* should also be grounds for divorcing a husband. Again, this is a *trend.* In most countries husbands still have greater divorce rights than women, as well as other legal prerogatives.

As an indication of some of the legal differences between the sexes which are under worldwide challenge, we offer this news item:

BEIRUT, Lebanon, March 3, 1973—A man who choked his 15-year-old daughter to death because he said she "flirted with boys" has just been released from prison on a presidential pardon after serving nine months of a seven-year sentence.

The father, Abdallah Wawhar Sharid, a well-to-do Saudi Arabian, benefited from a custom here, established in the penal code, that permits a man to kill a female member of his family who "dishonors the family" through sexual misconduct.

In cases that may involve simply a gesture of affection by an unmarried woman toward a male acquaintance, a father or brother who kills must be given a lenient sentence, often as little as two years at hard labor.

The Lebanese Constitution declares that "all Lebanese are equal before the law," but legal codes make clear distinction between men and women in many areas.

For instance, a woman can be charged with adultery on the basis of a love letter or suspicion based on hearsay evidence, but a man can be so charged only when he is caught with another woman in his home or if he appears repeatedly in public with a woman who is not his wife. In any case, the sentence for a man is only half that for a woman.

In 118 "crime of honor" cases studied . . . 65 percent of the killings were carried out by a brother of the victim using a knife.

Abdallah Lahoud, a judge, said that a brother who kills is often proud of having acted in defense of "honor." He said, "This reflects a tribal mentality which considers a man to be chief of the tribe and a woman nothing."[18]

Equality of Individuals Against Caste or Class Barriers

As Gerald Leslie observed:

To some degree, the trends toward free mate choice, equality for women, and equal divorce rights are part of a larger ideological change. A pervasive philosophy of individualism appears to be spreading over much of the world—a philosophy which militantly asserts the importance of the welfare of the person over any considerations of the continuity of the group. This is a radical philosophy, at least as radical as the movement for redistribution of large land holdings which has attracted so much Western attention. The worth of the individual comes to be more important than inherited wealth or ethnic group. The individual's status comes to be evaluated not so much by the lineage into which he was born as by his own accomplishments. The status of the family, then, must be determined for each generation anew.[19]

He further observed that these trends are simply *trends:*

It would be a serious mistake to conclude that extended family systems the world over have broken down. Most societies in the world today have unilineal descent systems, extended families, and male domination. The trends toward conjugal family systems, widespread as they are, generally are confined to the more urbanized, industrialized regions. The great masses of population in the hinterlands of countries like China and India, to say nothing of preliterate societies, are relatively unaffected. Moreover, these changes, where they appear, often are viewed as social problems, as symptoms of the breakdown of time-honored ways. Men and women, young and old are pitted against one another. One should not construct a stereotype of societies emerging from the darkness of autocratic extended family systems into the light of conjugal systems held together by ties of affection. It has yet to be shown that the sum total of human happiness is greater under one system than under another.[20]

As Goode suggested, there are advantages *and* disadvantages to the extended family system and also to the conjugal (based on the marriage bond) family system:

For the evaluation of [current] changes the individual reader must rely on his own philosophy. Some will see them as the advent of a new and fruitful era, a period in which men and women will find a richer personal life, in which they will have a greater range of choices in their own emotional fulfillment. They will rejoice to learn that young Chinese brides do not have to bring tea to their mother-in-law in the morning or wash their feet, that young Chinese grooms and brides may openly express their love for one another. They will be pleased that the Indian husband who has tired of his wife may not take an additional secondary mate into his household, or that the Arab husband finds divorce a much more tedious, awkward, and expensive affair than it once was. They will be glad that it is only the rare young European woman who now has to acquire a dowry in order to make a desirable marriage, and they will be pleased that increasingly in the major family systems, when either a husband or wife finds no happiness in marriage, either can break it and perhaps find happiness with someone else.

But still others will view all of these processes with suspicion, skepticism, or dismay. They may see them as the breakdown of major civilizations. They will see the Western pattern of the conjugal family spreading like a fungus over other societies, leading inevitably to a decline in their quality and the ultimate destruction of the achievements of our time. They will know that although under a system of arranged marriages some people did not find love, almost everyone had a chance at marriage; and more pain and trauma can come from the disruption and dissolution of love under the conjugal system. They will insist, moreover, that although the older systems weighed heavily upon the young and upon women, the elders did, in fact, have more wisdom, and the young in time grew older and took their place in the community, while both men and women in their turn, and according to their positions, received the honor, respect, and power to which they once had to submit.[21]

The American Family

As we have noted, industrialization and the nuclear family as the basic family unit seem to have appeared at roughly the same time. The fact that they covary, or exist side by side, does not necessarily mean that one caused the other. They may well have developed independently of one another. Nevertheless, they can and do affect one another—even if the effects are not direct and simple ones—once the movement toward industrialization and the trends toward the decline of the extended family system are under way.

Talcott Parsons[22] and others have argued that the nuclear family system is well adapted to the occupational demands of an urban, industrial society. The argument presented by Parsons more or less runs along these lines: in an industrial society the most significant factor in a family's social-class position is the occupation of the male breadwinner. (The first question we normally ask of a man we've just met is, "What do you do for a living?") Our economic system encourages men to try to move up on the occupational ladder to better paying, more prestigious jobs. The male's self-esteem and public reputation and the family's public standing rest on his occupational position. A man who does not work is considered a moral defective. This is true of both the person on welfare and the "playboy" who is independently wealthy and who does not have to work.

Occupational and financial success are the major goals for American males. We encourage men to move away from their families if this will mean job opportunities. We encourage the idea of hiring people on the basis of skill and competence rather than family connections or family obligations. In many traditional societies, anyone who would hire someone who is not a relative just because he is *competent* or reject a relative for a job just because he is *incompetent* would be considered an antisocial scoundrel. So would anyone who moved away from his family just because he could get a better job somewhere else. This emphasis on achievement rather than ascription and on social and geographic mobility is not conducive to maintaining strong extended family ties, or any ties that interfere with occupational success.

The role of the woman in this picture is basically to "keep the home fires burning." Her job is to give the husband moral and emotional support in his occupational endeavors and to be a housewife and mother. If she were to go out and try to make a living on a full-time, serious basis rather than, say, as a part-time supplementer of the husband's salary, this would create "destructive" competition within the family. If she had a full-time job that she vigorously pursued, she would be reluctant to move wherever new opportunities for her husband beckoned. Her role is to be in charge of emotional activities within the family. She is the manager of tensions, the maker of a stable home, a rest-and-relaxation-center, an emotional-battery-recharging station for the man, who faces the dog-eat-dog competition and aggravation of the outside occupational world; she is also the key socializer of children. The husband's family role is primarily to cope with the outside world, to be the disciplinarian and the rational decision-maker, and to carry out the garbage.

The family has certain specialized functions in our industrial society: (1) meeting the adult's psychological needs for warmth and affection and (2) socializing the children. In traditional societies families have many more functions than these two. Parsons observed that in the industrialized society these other functions have been turned over to other specialized agencies, enabling the nuclear family itself to become a specialized agency focusing solely on affection and socialization. Education, religion, social welfare, and economic activity have been transferred to other agencies—schools, churches and Sunday schools, hospitals, old-age homes, and factories—that can handle these activities more "efficiently."

This description sounds a bit like a caricature of American society. It wasn't intended that way by Parsons. In the early 1950s, when Parsons formulated these ideas, many people felt that if it wasn't quite an accurate description of the "typical" American family it soon would be and should be. In certain respects it is an accurate description of the relationship of the family and the industrial system. For example, compared to the family system in other societies, we don't have a very complicated kinship system. The nuclear family does not have as many functions as it once had. Nor does the extended family. We *do* judge the family on the basis of its success in providing psychological satisfactions for members. We *do* rely on parents for the early socialization of their children. The family is *not* the single work unit it once was in an earlier day—back on the farm.

On the other hand, many critics of Parsons' formulation point out that married couples aren't the isolated unit cut off from all family ties that this view seems to imply.[23] A large number of studies indicate that Americans do maintain family ties, despite social and geographic mobility. This is particularly true for those who are *not* upper middle class (the class that Parsons was apparently talking about), and for ethnic groups. Remember Parsons was attempting to give an overview of the family system from a quite abstract perspective. Therefore, he did not qualify his statements to take into account many factors like racial and ethnic differences in family ties. He believed that the other classes were moving in the direction of the model he proposed.

Table 8-1 indicates that a good many Americans live near their parents and siblings (brothers and sisters) and see them regularly. There is also evidence that a good deal of assistance, advice, and money passes between family members—particularly between parents and their married children, as indicated in Table 8-2. There is also substantial evidence that despite geographic mobility, family members can and do maintain close emotional ties through letters, phone calls, and visits.

Table 8-1. Family Relationships of Religious and Ethnic Groups

	Live in Same Neighborhood with			See Weekly		
	Parents	*Siblings*	*In-laws*	*Parents*	*Siblings*	*In-laws*
Catholics						
Italians	40%	33%	24%	79%	61%	62%
Irish	17	16	16	49	48	48
Germans	10	13	10	48	31	41
Poles	29	25	24	65	46	53
French	15	23	24	61	41	62
Protestants						
English	19	13	12	39	26	35
Germans	12	13	14	44	32	39
Scandinavians	14	11	17	39	26	31
Jews	14	12	14	58	33	58

Source: National Opinion Research Center Study as cited in A. M. Greeley, *Why Can't They Be Like Us?* (New York: Institute of Human Relations Press, 1969), p. 52.

Table 8–2. Direction of Assistance Between Kin by Major Forms of Help

	Direction of Service Network				
Major Forms of Help and Service	*Between Respondent's Family and Related Kin*	*From Respondents to Parents*	*From Respondents to Siblings*	*From Parents to Respondents*	*From Siblings to Respondents*
Any form of help	93.3%[a]	56.3%	47.6%	79.6%	44.8%
Help during illness	76.0	47.0	42.0	46.4	39.0
Financial aid	83.0	14.6	10.3	46.8	6.4
Care of children	46.8	4.0	29.5	20.5	10.8
Advice (personal and business)	31.8	2.0	3.0	26.5	4.5
Valuable gifts	22.0	3.4	2.3	17.6	3.4

[a]Totals do not add up to 100 percent because many families received more than one form of help.
Source: Marvin B. Sussman, "The Isolated Nuclear Family: Fact or Fiction," *Social Problems,* **6** (Spring 1959), 338.

Many sociologists have argued that we do not have the "classic" extended family system, with its strong control over every aspect of the family members' lives and its incompatibility with a modern industrial system. *But,* they argue, we don't have the "isolated" nuclear family that Parsons suggested either. Rather, we have a "modified extended family" system that supports emotional ties between family members, does not interfere with occupational mobility, and does not interfere with the day-to-day functioning of the nuclear family, which is in most respects independent of the larger family unit.[24]

Parsons suggested that our kinship system and nuclear family system are well adapted to the requirements of an industrial society for achievement and mobility.

In recent years observers of the family have asked whether the *reverse* is true as well. If the contemporary family is well adapted to the needs of an industrial society, is technological society well adapted to the needs of the contemporary family? Many critics of contemporary society and the so-called modern family suggest it is not. A number of criticisms have been leveled at the sort of family system that Parsons described, suggesting that it is not an ideal family system and that an urbanized, highly industrialized society is not the ideal society. Most of the critics seem to assume that unless the occupational system changes the family system cannot be changed.[25]

Women in the American Family System

If the woman is limited to being a homemaker, a mother, and an emotional "battery charger" for her husband and children, critics complain, an unfair burden is put on her. Her own talents and abilities must remain undeveloped. She must live her life and fulfill her ambitions through the lives of her husband and children. It is only in the past few decades that we have considered housekeeping and child rearing a full-time job for women. Critics argue that in the past women also were *providers* for their families.

Jessie Bernard suggests that every marriage is, in fact, *two* marriages—*his* marriage and *her* marriage. She observes that a considerable body of research literature going back more than a generation shows that

> more wives than husbands report marital frustration and dissatisfaction; more report negative feelings; more wives than husbands report marital problems; more wives than husbands consider their marriages unhappy, have considered separation or divorce, have regretted their marriages; and fewer report positive companionship. Only about half as many wives (25 percent) as husbands (45 percent) say that there is nothing about their marriage that is not as nice as they would like. And twice as many wives (about a fourth) as husbands (about 12 percent) in a Canadian sample say that they would not remarry the same partner or have doubts about it. Understandably, therefore, more wives than husbands seek marriage counselling; and more wives than husbands initiate divorce proceedings. . . .
>
> . . . Even among happily married couples, fewer wives than husbands report agreement on such family problems as finances, recreation, religion, affection, friends, sex, in-laws, time together, and life aims and goals; and more report serious marital difficulties. The proportions were not great in most cases, but the proportion of those happily married wives who reported no difficulties at all was considerably lower than the proportion of happily married men who reported none. The wives reported problems in more than twice as many areas as did husbands.[26]

The role of housewife as provided for in contemporary industrial society is not necessarily a satisfying one.

Symptom	Married Men	Never-Married Men
Nervous breakdown	− .76	+1.00
Felt impending nervous breakdown	− .51	− .07
Nervousness	+ .31	−1.05
Inertia	− .76	+ .29
Insomnia	−1.17	+1.92
Trembling hands	− .23	− .52
Nightmares	− .75	+1.28
Perspiring hands	+ .55	−1.18
Fainting	− .11	+ .81
Headaches	+ .80	−1.96
Dizziness	+ .24	− .79
Heart palpitations	+ .02	−3.87

Table 8–3. Selected Symptoms of Psychological Distress Among Married and Never-Married White Men

Source: National Center for Health Statistics, *Selected Symptoms of Psychological Distress* (U.S. Department of Health, Education, and Welfare, 1970), Table 17, pp. 30–31.

Symptom	Married Men	Married Women
Nervous breakdown	− .76	+ .57
Felt impending nervous breakdown	− .51	− .18
Nervousness	+ .31	+1.05
Inertia	− .76	+1.00
Insomnia	−1.17	+ .60
Trembling hands	− .23	− .54
Nightmares	− .75	0.00
Perspiring hands	+ .55	+ .38
Fainting	− .11	+ .26
Headaches	+ .80	+ .97
Dizziness	+ .24	− .10
Heart palpitations	+ .02	+ .46

Table 8–4. Selected Symptoms of Psychological Distress Among Married White Men and Women

Source: National Center for Health Statistics, *Selected Symptoms of Psychological Distress* (U.S. Department of Health, Education, and Welfare, 1970), Table 17, pp. 30–31.

Aside from these hints that the role of wife, as provided for in contemporary industrial society, is not necessarily a satisfying one for the wife, Bernard suggests that the role of housewife/mother may be positively *harmful* to the wife's mental health. She cites evidence from a variety of studies that indicate that white married women suffer from a wider variety of symptoms of psychological distress* than do single white women and white married or single men.

As you can see from Table 8–3, white married men are mentally "healthier" than white single men are. Table 8–4 indicates that white married *men* are generally "healthier" mentally than white married *women.* Table 8–5 indicates that white single women are "healthier" than white married women. Bernard implies that the two columns "Single" and "Married" in Table 8–5 could be labeled "Before" and "After." Table 8–6 indicates that white unmarried men

*In the tables that follow, "−" indicates a lower than expected incidence of the characteristic; "+" indicates a higher than expected incidence of the characteristic. The numbers indicate how *much* higher or lower than expected the incidence of the characteristic is. For the details of how these expectations were worked out, see page 41 of the report from which the tables were drawn.

Symptom	Single Women	Married Women
Nervous Breakdown	− .86	+ .57
Felt impending nervous breakdown	−4.48	− .18
Nervousness	−3.04	+1.05
Inertia	−6.34	+1.00
Insomnia	−1.68	+ .60
Trembling hands	− .76	− .54
Nightmares	−2.35	0.00
Perspiring hands	−1.18	+ .38
Fainting	+ .09	+ .26
Headaches	−1.63	+ .97
Dizziness	−2.97	− .10
Heart palpitations	−3.43	+ .46

Table 8-5. Selected Symptoms of Psychological Distress Among White Women by Marital Status

Source: National Center for Health Statistics, *Selected Symptoms of Psychological Distress* (U.S. Department of Health, Education and Welfare, 1970), Table 17, pp. 30–31.

Symptom	Never-Married Men	Never-Married Women
Nervous breakdown	+1.00	− .86
Felt impending nervous breakdown	− .07	−4.48
Nervousness	−1.05	−3.04
Inertia	+ .29	−6.34
Insomnia	+1.92	−1.68
Trembling hands	− .52	− .76
Nightmares	+1.28	−2.35
Perspiring hands	−1.18	−1.18
Fainting	+ .81	+ .09
Headaches	−1.96	−1.63
Dizziness	− .79	−2.97
Heart palpitations	−3.87	−3.43

Table 8-6. Selected Symptoms of Psychological Distress Among Never-Married White Men and Women

Source: National Center for Health Statistics, *Selected Symptoms of Psychological Distress* (U.S. Department of Health, Education, and Welfare, 1970), Table 17, pp. 30–31.

are not in as good shape psychologically as white unmarried women. The essence of what the tables indicate is that *marriage is psychologically good for white men, but not good for white women.*

Table 8-7 indicates that if we divide the married women's group into those who work and those who are housewives, there's a remarkable drop in the incidence of almost all of the symptoms on the list in those who work. In short, the idea that wives ought to stay home and "hold down the fort" may fit the needs of the occupational system and the husband, as outlined by Parsons, but it is not especially healthy for the wives.

Gove[27] notes that the mortality (death) rates from a variety of causes* for married men and married women compared to those for single men and single women indicate that marriage diminishes death rates for *both* sexes, but the differences between married and single *men* are large, whereas the differences between married and single *women* are much smaller. He accounts for these

*Suicide, homicide, accidents, alcoholism, tuberculosis, and diabetes.

Symptom	Housewives	Working Women
Nervous breakdown	+1.16	−2.02
Felt impending nervous breakdown	− .12	+ .81
Nervousness	+1.74	−2.29
Inertia	+2.35	−3.15
Insomnia	+1.27	−2.00
Trembling hands	+ .74	−1.25
Nightmares	+ .68	−1.18
Perspiring hands	+1.28	−2.55
Fainting	+ .82	−2.69
Headaches	+ .84	− .87
Dizziness	+1.41	−1.85
Heart palpitations	+1.38	−1.56

Table 8–7. Selected Symptoms of Psychological Distress Among White Housewives and Working Women

Source: National Center for Health Statistics, *Selected Symptoms of Psychological Distress* (U.S. Department of Health, Education, and Welfare, 1970), Table 17, pp. 30–31.

mortality differences and mental health differences between the sexes (which are not as great in small, traditional, culturally isolated communities) in terms of the stresses built into women's roles in modern industrial societies:

First, most women are restricted to a single societal role—housewife, whereas most men occupy two such roles, household head and worker. . . . If a male finds one of his roles unsatisfactory, he can frequently focus his interest and concern on the other role. In contrast, if a woman finds her family role unsatisfactory, she typically has no major alternative source of gratification.

Second, it seems reasonable to assume that a large number of women find their major instrumental activities—raising children and keeping house—frustrating. . . . The occupancy of such a static, technically undemanding position is not consonant with the educational and intellectual attainment of a large number of women in our society. . . .

Third, the role of housewife is relatively unstructured and invisible. It is possible for the housewife to put things off, to let things slide . . . to brood over her troubles. In contrast the job holder must meet demands that constantly force him to be involved with his environment. Having to meet these structured demands should draw his attention from his troubles, and help prevent him from becoming obsessed with his worries.

Fourth, even when a married woman works, she is typically in a less satisfactory position than the married man. There has been a persistent decline in the relative status of women since 1940 as measured by occupation, income, and even education. . . .

Fifth, several observers have noted that the expectations confronting women are unclear and diffuse.[28]

The evidence on mortality and mental illness already cited suggests that George Bernard Shaw, who once claimed, "All women should marry. But no men," may have had things backwards.

The question of whether wives' working is good for the *husband's* mental health is not answered in the study from which Tables 8–3 through 8–7 are

Table 8–8. Marital Status of Women Workers: March 1972

Source: U.S. Department of Labor, June 1973.

Marital Status	All Women		Women of Minority Races	
	Number	Percentage Distribution	Number	Percentage Distribution
TOTAL	32,939,000	100.0	4,176,000	100.0
Single	7,477,000	22.7	920,000	22.0
Married (husband present)	19,249,000	58.5	1,991,000	47.4
Husband's 1971 income:				
Below $3,000	1,925,000	5.8	281,000	6.7
$3,000–$4,999	2,194,000	6.7	394,000	9.4
$5,000–$6,999	2,926,000	8.9	406,000	9.7
$7,000 and over	12,204,000	37.1	910,000	21.8
Other marital status	6,213,000	18.9	1,265,000	30.0
Married (husband absent)	1,500,000	4.6	538,000	12.9
Widowed	2,570,000	7.8	412,000	9.9
Divorced	2,143,000	6.5	315.000	7.5

drawn. We have some evidence from other studies that whether the wife works through choice or necessity has some bearing on the husband's attitude as well as on other aspects of family interaction.

Orden and Bradburn[29] find evidence that where the wife works by choice this produces more tensions and disagreements, but *also* more satisfaction for *both* husband and wife than if she stays home. If she works because she *must,* this increases tension and *diminishes* the satisfaction and happiness of *both* husband and wife, more than if she had stayed at home.

As we've observed, there's evidence that the family system that Parsons described is not necessarily an ideal one from the point of view of the housewife. Many women seem to have figured this out for themselves. An increasingly larger proportion of women is moving into the labor market. As Table 8–8 indicates, roughly two thirds of the women currently working—the single, the divorced, the widowed, and the wives of men making less than $7,000 a year—*need* the money. And the money is paramount regardless of whether they also want an opportunity to get out of the house or whether they believe that there is more prospect of intellectual or emotional fulfillment in the labor market than in the home.

Children in the American Family System

There's also been a good deal of criticism of the usefulness of the family system as outlined by Parsons for raising children properly. Some of the criticism is based on the idea that contemporary occupational roles take the father out of the home and break up the family as a work unit. We have few family businesses and few family farms compared to an older, "simpler" time. Children, male children in particular, can't learn the male role by observing their fathers in action. The family loses whatever strength comes from having common work goals and common interests and activities.

The second line of criticism suggests that where making money and achieving professional success is a cultural goal, fathers give their children too little attention and affection because their time and energy is too wrapped up in their own careers.

A third form of criticism suggests that contemporary children suffer not so much from not having parents whose jobs they can observe and take part in, or from the emphasis on material success for fathers, as from an absence of physically and emotionally close relatives.

The first criticism seems to suggest that if we could go back to an economy based on small family businesses and family farms, certain family problems would be minimized. The second criticism suggests that if we could lose our admiration of occupational and financial success, children would get more attention and affection. The third criticism seems to be focused on the nature of our household system rather than on the way parents make a living or on the time and emotional involvement parents invest in making a living.

Although, as noted, Americans are not completely cut off from relatives, the nuclear family is nonetheless a distinct, independent unit. Our households rarely contain grandparents or other relatives. For the most part how we raise our children is our own business, unless we *ask* for advice and assistance from our relatives. If one parent dies or leaves, the nuclear family is shattered. To appreciate the point of the third criticism, we have to look to *non*-Western family systems rather than to the recent or distant past of Western European and American families.

In Asian and African systems particularly, the larger family is *the* significant social unit. More important, the child "belongs" to the mother's branch of the family or to the father's branch of the family. If a parent harms a child or neglects a child, it is the *family's* child and the *family's* interest that is threatened. Likewise if a parent is absent, there are many aunts and/or uncles who will take care of the child. In our own family system, the emotional relationship between parent and child is much more intense, adult relatives are not co-parents, and a defective or brutal or missing parent can't be easily substituted for.

Arlene Skolnick has observed:

Once the point has been made it seems rather obvious that the all-your-eggs-in-one-basket system of the isolated family imposes strains on both mother and child. . . . Mother's feelings become very important because she is the only mother you have. If she gets angry with you, there's no place else to go; nor is there any place for her to go to rest or to get out of an angry mood. This sets the stage for emotional outbursts, which at the extreme may result in child abuse, but more frequently result in scoldings and complaints, perhaps spankings, sometimes accidents. It's not a matter of villains, or bad parents, but rather an ecological one: great demands being placed on limited parental resources of time, energy, and money.[30]

She goes on to say that our family system gives parents a good deal more power over the child than does the extended family system, but the community doesn't back the parent up in the use of this power as does a traditional system:

In the tribal family or traditional kin group, the child not only does not belong to parents in the same way as he does to isolated nuclear parents, but also the parent deals with his child according to a script written by the larger culture. The culture's traditional beliefs and superstitions strengthen the parents' position in dealing with a child and, again paradoxically, can make the parent more relaxed, warm, and affectionate. In the old system, the parent resembles an administrator in a large bureaucracy, carrying out policies made by higher authorities. The child may disobey or fail to carry out an assigned task, but he is unlikely to argue with very many of the rules themselves. Even if he does, however, the parent can argue back that it's beyond his power to change the rules. What the parent loses in personal power he more than makes up for in institutional backing for his position. By contrast, the American parent is often uncertain about rules because no community tradition exists, and advice from experts may be contradictory and difficult to apply. Whether or not the parent is unsure, the child recognizes the parent as the source of the rules—the parent is the legislator as well as the executive and the judiciary. Thus the stage is set for submission or resentment or rebellion.[31]

By now it must be obvious that any family system is going to have certain sources of strain built into it. Traditional family systems offer more psychological security to all family members, but the young and the women have less power and freedom.

Contemporary family systems offer more independence and less security than traditional systems. The old have little power, the young and the women have increasingly greater equality, but a price is paid for this freedom in loneliness, isolation, tensions, and insecurity.

Divorce

The high demands we place on marriage are reflected in our divorce statistics. We have a much higher divorce rate than fifty years ago, as you can see in Table 8–9. The table also indicates that roughly the same proportion of marriages are as likely to dissolve in a given year now as a hundred years ago, except that now they are more likely to be dissolved by divorce than by death. Much of the high divorce rate can be attributed to our belief that people are entitled to a happy marriage and our unwillingness to stick with an unhappy one.

Table 8-9. Annual Marital Dissolutions by Death and Divorce, and Rates Per 1,000 Existing Marriages, 1890–1970

Year	Dissolutions per year		Per 1,000 existing marriages			Divorces as Percent of Total Dissolutions
	Deaths[a]	*Divorces*[b]	*Deaths*	*Divorces*	*Total*	
1860–64	197,200	7,170	32.1	1.2	33.2	3.5
1865–69	207,000	10,529	31.1	1.6	32.7	4.8
1870–74	226,400	12,417	30.3	1.7	32.0	5.2
1875–79	238,600	15,574	28.7	1.9	30.6	6.1
1880–84	285,400	21,746	30.6	2.3	33.0	7.1
1885–89	290,400	27,466	27.6	2.6	30.2	8.6
1890–94	331,800	36,123	28.3	3.1	31.3	9.7
1895–99	328,800	45,462	24.9	3.4	28.4	12.1
1900–04	390,800	61,868	26.5	4.2	30.6	13.7
1905–09	427,400	74,626	25.4	4.4	29.8	14.9
1910–14	453,600	91,695	23.7	4.8	28.5	16.8
1915–19	551,000	119,529	26.0	5.6	31.6	17.8
1920–24	504,200	164,917	21.9	7.2	29.0	24.6
1925–29	573,200	193,218	22.6	7.6	30.3	25.2
1930–34	590,800	183,441	21.9	6.8	28.7	23.7
1935–39	634,600	239,600	21.9	8.3	30.2	27.4
1940–44	656,400	330,557	20.4	10.3	30.7	33.5
1945–49	681,200	485,641	19.2	13.7	32.8	41.6
1950–54	692,400	385,429	18.2	10.0	28.3	35.9
1955–59	733,600[c]	385,385	18.3	9.2	27.8	34.2
1960–64	n.a.	419,600	n.a.	9.6	n.a.	n.a.
1965–69	n.a.	544,800	n.a.	11.7	n.a.	n.a.
1960	790,400	393,000	18.9	9.4	28.3	33.2
1961	789,200	414,000	18.7	9.8	28.6	34.4
1965	820,800	479,000	18.5	10.8	29.4	36.9
1970	908,200	715,000	19.3	15.2	34.5	44.0

[a]Includes deaths of Armed Forces overseas during 1917–1919 and 1940–1955.

[b]Includes annulments.

[c]Average for 1955 and 1959 only.

Source: 1860–1955, adapted with permission of the author from Paul H. Jacobson, *American Marriage and Divorce,* Copyright ©, 1959 (Rinehart & Co., Inc.) Xerox Corp. Book Publications, OP 31,415, Ann Arbor, Tables 42 and A-6,7,22,26,27, and 28; 1956–1970, from Kingsley Davis, "The American Family in Relation to Demographic Change," Commission on Population Growth and the American Future, Vol. 1, p. 256, Table 8.

C. F. and C. B. Thwing accounted for the increases in divorce this way:

The last fifty years have apparently changed the marriage relation from a permanent and lifelong state to a union existing during the pleasure of the parties. The change thus swiftly wrought is so revolutionary, involving the very foundations of human society, that we must believe it to be the result not of any temporary conditions, but of causes which have been long and silently at work. . . . The belief is prevalent, and seems to be growing, that marriage is a civil contract, and a civil contract only. Like other contracts, it is entered into for the pleasure and convenience of the parties, and, like other contracts, may be terminated when pleasure and convenience are no longer served.[32]

Of course, the idea that marriage is a breakable contract is not the only cause of the increasing divorce rate. The availability of alternatives to an unhappy marriage also contributes something to divorce rates. As the Thwings suggested:

In nearly every business, trade, and profession, women now appear as the competitors of men. Fifty years ago, the household and the school house marked the boundaries of the sphere of woman's work. The industries in which she now engages are numbered by the hundreds. Such a radical change made in so short a time cannot fail to exercise a disturbing effect on the family. If she fails to find happiness, justice, and recognition of her personality in her position as wife and mother, a woman is now independent of this position, so far as the supply of her needs is concerned. Means of a decent livelihood for a competent woman open on every side.[33]

As it happens, the Thwings were making these observations in *1887,* almost ninety years ago. They were describing, as they saw it, the breakdown of the family system, and they would certainly be horrified to see current divorce figures. Nevertheless, marriage has not died in the United States. Although divorce rates are high, so are remarriage rates and marriage rates.

The divorce rate does not necessarily mean that we don't like the *idea* of marriage. As Kingsley Davis pointed out:

In 1968 and 1969, a fourth of all women remarrying after divorce were under 25 years of age! The median age at remarriage after divorce (for those remarrying in 1968) was 30.7 for women and 35.1 for men. . . . Age for age, the remarriage rate is higher among the divorced than it is among the single population. In other words, a young woman age 24 has a higher probability of marrying if she has been divorced than if she is still single. In 1969, the remarriage rate for divorced women aged 14 to 24 was 478 per 1,000, and for divorced men 495 per 1,000. At such rates, of course, the divorced population would soon be consumed if it were not constantly fed by newly divorced recruits. In the Marriage Registration Area* only 73.3 percent of the marriages occurring in 1968 (in which the previous marital status of both parties was given) were to couples in which neither party had been married before. The percent of marriages in which one or both parties had been divorced was 22.9 percent, as compared to 8.4 percent in which one or both had been widowed.[34]

Davis stressed that marriage is not dying in America:

The significance of the brisk rate of remarriage is plain: It means that the American people do not have a high and rising rate of legal divorce and annulment because they are losing interest in marriage and the family. Rather, they have such a high rate because they desire a compatible marriage and a satisfactory family. Thus, despite a high legal divorce rate, a high proportion is married—higher than any other industrial society. Americans expect a great deal out of

*There are twenty six states that request information on previous marriages and certain other useful information when people apply for marriage licenses and for divorce.

the state of wedlock, and when a particular marriage proves unsatisfactory, they seek to dissolve it and try again. They would rather risk a poor first marriage than to postpone marriage, and they would rather get a divorce early than to continue a bad marriage.[35]

Experiments in Changing the Family

The rise (and fall) of the thousands of communes in the United States in the 1960s and 1970s reflected discontent on the part of large numbers of young people with the materialism and competitiveness of American society and unhappiness with various aspects of American family life.[36] Experiments in communal living are not a new phenomenon. In nineteenth century America there were more than a hundred similar attempts to create small utopian communities all across the country. Almost all lasted only a few years before they fell apart because of internal weaknesses, were destroyed by hostile neighbors, or were dissolved because of a combination of the two.

Observers of the contemporary commune scene observe that today's communes tend to be unstable, too. Much of the failure can be attributed to conflict between an ideology of extreme individualism and the necessity of discipline and commitment and surrender of individuality if a commune is to survive.

Bennett Berger and his associates observed:

Like any other value system, moreover, the hip-communal one is replete with logical contradictions and discontinuities between theory and practice. Freedom and communal solidarity can and do cause conflicts, and the balance between privacy and communal sharing is a recurrently thorny problem in several of the communes we have observed. Despite the emphasis on spontaneity and impulse, the apples have to be picked when ripe, the goats have to be milked regularly, the meals have to be cooked and the dishes washed. Despite the benignity of nature, something's got to be done about the flies in the kitchen and the mice in the cupboard. Despite egalitarianism, some communards are deferred to more than others; despite the emphasis on the present and the immediate, wood has to be laid in for the winter, and crops put in for the growing season, and money set aside for the rent or the mortgage and the taxes; despite transcendent ecstasy, the communards have to be discreet about acid or peyote freak-outs in town. And they'll wear clothes when alien eyes will be offended by their nudity.[37]

In many respects the ideals of contemporary communal movements are reminiscent of those of earlier communal movements, particularly in the desire to create what is in essence an extended family based on fellowship rather than kinship. In some respects the goals of contemporary communes are less radical than those of some of the communes of a hundred years ago.

The Israeli kibbutz movement[38] has been a highly successful communal system, surviving while maintaining and attaining most of its original ideals. One of the intentions of the founders was to abolish the nuclear family.

Whether they have done so successfully is a matter of controversy that depends to a large extent on the way one defines *family.* Some sociologists have argued that, along with the Nayar society we discussed earlier in the chapter, the kibbutz is an exception to Murdock's contention that the nuclear family is universal.[39]

Before we get into that, let's go into some facts and figures.[40] A kibbutz is a collective settlement, basically agricultural, in which all property is owned by the community except for some small personal items. Workers do not get salaries for their labor; the profits go to the community treasury, from which they can draw if they need anything, be it food, clothing, medical care, college tuition, or anything else. The first kibbutz was established in 1909 by emigrants from Eastern European countries to Israel. Currently there are 240 of these settlements, ranging in size from one hundred members to two thousand members. Almost all of the kibbutzim (plural of *kibbutz*) are now organized into federations that cooperate and pool their resources for certain purposes. Each of the major federations is affiliated with a political party. The Ichud federation is the largest (83 settlements) and is the least ideological. The Artzi federation is the next largest, with 75 settlements, and is the most militantly collectivist. The Meuchad federation (58 settlements) is somewhere in the ideological middle. (Of the remaining 24, 16 are affiliated with a small religious kibbutz movement, 6 with another small federation, and 2 are unaffiliated.)

The kibbutzim have some ninety-five thousand members, roughly 3 percent of Israel's population. The kibbutzim account for some 30 percent of the country's agricultural production, and the 232 kibbutz factories account for about 7 percent of the nation's total manufacturing output. The kibbutzim also supply about 40 percent of the officers in the army's elite combat units and about the same high percentage of combat air force pilots.

The kibbutzim were founded by young Jewish emigrants from Eastern European countries, particularly Russia. They came to Israel to develop a homeland for Jews that would avoid many of the forms of exploitation they had experienced in the lands they had escaped. The founders of the kibbutzim were strongly influenced by Marxist ideas about labor and the family. They were also influenced by the ideas of the Russian writer Lev Nikolaevich Tolstoi, who presented them with a somewhat romantic view of the virtues of working the soil and communing with nature. The natural environment they found in Israel was largely barren desert and malarial swamp. In most of the countries they came from, Jews had been forbidden to own land, and the founders of the kibbutzim felt that there was something "unnatural" about being merchants and intellectuals, as their parents had been. They wanted to create a new breed of intellectual workers who were close to nature and the soil. Their settlements were to be thoroughly democratic, with all major decisions made by worker committees, with all jobs rotated regularly so that all would share the pleasant and the unpleasant jobs. All income was to belong to the community, and there was to be no hierarchy of income or power because all would be equal partners in work and authority. Salaried labor would not be hired by the kibbutzim because this would be a form of exploitation.

The family was seen as a unit that could draw people's energy and emotions away from the larger community and that was therefore a threat. The patriarchal family system they'd left behind was also seen as a system that made women and children economically dependent on the male, and therefore it had to be eliminated if men and women were ever to be equals.

The founders of the kibbutz system tended to be young and unmarried and, initially, children were not much of a problem. As children came, it was decided that they would be put into communal nurseries and raised by special children's nurses. Any ties they had to their parents and any ties between the parents themselves were voluntary and based only on affection, because the woman and the child had no economic ties to the father: both men and women worked and the community supplied food, medical care, and shelter for all.

The kibbutzim did not require a marriage ceremony until very recently. All that was necessary for a couple to become a couple in the eyes of the community was their request to the housing committee for a room together. In the early days couples were discouraged from spending their leisure time together and kept friendships, work schedules, vacations separate.

Children, as we've said, do not live with their parents. Instead, they live in a children's house along with other children their own age under the supervision of special nurses. The nurses are in charge of discipline, toilet training, and almost every other training activity that has traditionally been assigned the family (and the mother, in particular).

The parents' only real "family" task is to give children affection and the individual attention that the nurse/caretaker can not give the half-dozen children assigned her. Children visit their parents several hours a day after work and on weekends and holidays. The parents put the children to bed back at the children's house and then go about their business. The child's clothes, food and shelter, education, and discipline are not the direct responsibility of the parents but of the community as a whole. The role of the biological parent, male or female, is to give children affection and to talk and play with them. It's more like the role of a grandparent or an uncle or aunt in our society, and there's not much difference between the roles of mother and father in this respect: they pamper their children equally and leave the bulk of the discipline to the nurses.

Taking the responsibility for children out of the hands of the mother frees her, in principle, from a large part of her traditional role. Another major part of the traditional woman's role is that of housekeeper. Women on a kibbutz are more or less freed from this role by community kitchens and communal laundries. Private apartments are small with little in the way of furniture. There is little need for fancy clothing, and sewing and mending can also be turned over to full-time specialists. In the old days, when shirts or dungarees were dirty, they were taken to the community laundry and in their place one took a clean set of clothes from the top of the pile. These days a certain amount of money is set aside for members to buy personal clothing with,[41] and people have insisted that size labels be put into the communal clothes so they can more easily find clothes that fit them.

This kibbutz system has worked out according to plan in most respects. In the realm of family life, it broke the power of the father over women, children, and the household, and it eliminated the legal, economic, and personal dependency of the wife on the husband. The child-rearing system has apparently been quite effective in producing happy, physically and emotionally healthy children who are imbued with the community's ideals and are on good terms with their parents, with little evidence of a "generation gap."[42]

In the *economic* realm the kibbutz has also kept to most of its ideals.[43] Workers rotate jobs, elect their "bosses," and participate heavily in all decision making in factory and farm. Some kibbutzim have in recent years taken to hiring outside labor for their factories, whereas others, to eliminate the need for outside labor, have become highly automated.

The kibbutz system has *not* been completely successful in two areas. First, it has not been able to abolish the family completely. The nuclear family is still a distinct unit, although it has lost its economic functions. And second, the kibbutz has not equalized the sexes as intended.

The failure to abolish the family as a distinct emotional unit does seem to have caused much regret. The original founders had feared that any such personal relationship would divert people's physical and emotional energies from the community's needs, and they felt that the creation of *any* group, especially a family group, intermediate between the individual and the whole community would diminish the strength of public opinion as a form of social control.[44]

Apparently the commitment of the members to the ideals and goals of the community has been sufficiently great so that the existence of the family as a separate and distinct psychological unit has not interfered with or competed with loyalty to the community. Particularly in established (rather than beginning) kibbutzim, the family seems to have reinforced the solidarity of the community.

It is not absolutely clear why the *complete* equality between the sexes desired by the founders did not occur, but we do have some clues.[45] When we say there is not complete equality between the sexes, we are referring to the failure of the kibbutz to alter the division of labor by sex. In terms of legal and sexual and economic equality, the sexes *are* equals. In the early days of the kibbutzim a very strong effort was made to deny that there were any differences between the sexes except for the obvious physical differences. Women were discouraged from wearing makeup and from dressing differently from men; chivalry was scorned as "bourgeois." Single people of both sexes shared dormitory rooms. Women worked in the fields and served in the military. In the early days there were no children and no old people and no possessions to speak of. A couple shared a bare room and ate only in the community dining room, and both did "productive" work in the fields.

As children came, heavy agricultural work became harder for mothers to perform. They took leave of the work in the fields for several months after the birth of a baby to nurse and care for it. There was also a need for people to take care of the children and to be teachers. Washing and mending clothes, administering finances, and cooking became full-time jobs as the communities grew, and somehow the women ended up in these jobs. Although *all* work is considered "noble," economically productive *physical* labor is considered more noble than clerical, administrative, or service work on the kibbutz. Men who were capable of physical labor apparently were reluctant to take on the service jobs, and women and older men were stuck with them. Once women left the fields and other "productive" areas of the kibbutz economy to have children, they also lost touch with the work in the fields and became more familiar with the service side of the community. They also became reluctant to join committees that dealt with things they had lost touch with, and they concentrated in committees dealing with education, consumption, health, and welfare, activities in which they had greater expertise. Men predominate in committees dealing with overall planning, the management of economic production, and security issues, areas more closely related to their own job experience. However, there are very few committees that are *exclusively* male or female. In most committees both sexes are represented.

The failures of the founders' intentions in the two areas of family life and sexual equality in work assignments are apparently related to each other. Many women found themselves assigned full time to activities not very different from those they would have done part time in a home—cooking, mending, washing clothes, child care—and felt these tasks were not "fulfilling." As a result many sought fulfillment in family roles, particularly in motherhood (which is a part-time activity). Consequently many of the women were less willing to join any committees that demanded great quantities of time after work hours and were also less willing to take on any jobs that took them far from home and their children. As time went by, then, sex-linked job differences led to greater interest in the family, and, in turn, family roles led to less interest on the part of women in certain kinds of jobs. Underlying the not-quite-equal roles of the sexes is the nature of the original kibbutz concept of equality. It was essentially a concept of a "masculine" role for both sexes based on physical labor. The women weren't capable of filling that kind of role. They generally didn't have the strength to be men's equals in that area. Men were not anxious to perform the service jobs that the community's value system ranked lower than productive physical labor. We might say that if equality for women means being masculine, women are doomed to being second-rate men. Given that kibbutz women, particularly once they started bearing children, found themselves unable to compete on men's terms, and given that childbearing was an activity that men could not perform, it was, perhaps, inevitable that women would move away from denying their "femininity." The kibbutz women today take a more active interest in family matters, in children's education, in preserving their complexions, in clothing than did the women in the early days of the kibbutz system. Apparently the second- and third-generation women have been a bit of a disappointment to their militant mothers and grandmothers in this respect.[46]

In short, the distinction between male and female roles is very slight within the home, a bit stronger in committee work, and relatively strong in the world of work. The failure to convince men to take on service jobs and the reluctance to honor these jobs as highly as nonservice jobs have led the women to focus more energy on their family roles and to reinstate the nuclear family to a position of importance, rather than abolishing it as originally intended.

There are still significant differences between family roles on the kibbutz and in our society. The role of the male as a worker outside the home has not been changed but his role as a father has changed radically. As Suzanne Keller[47] observed:

> The child views his father as special, and sees him as the husband of his mother, as a worker in the kibbutz, and as playmate and giver of gifts. Unlike the father in a typical Western family, however, the kibbutz father can be an even more permissive and nurturant figure than the mother, for in the household shared by the couple, even in a kibbutz, it is still the woman who must keep things in order and make demands for cleanliness and comportment. Since living quarters are small such demands are unavoidable, but they do fall to the mother. The father is not considered responsible for household activities. "His occupational role makes him a hero in the eyes of the growing child. Most of the occupations are known even by small children, and among the first words a child learns are the names of his parents' occupational roles. . . . According to the existing pattern of the division of labor, his father will be the one who is recognized as responsible for the farm . . . in the eyes of the child, the wider world."[48]

In all fairness to the kibbutz, we should note that the *ideal* of equality between the sexes has not been surrendered even if it has not been completely attained.[49] There's been a strong effort to mechanize and organize service jobs efficiently to make them easier and to free women for other occupations. There has also been a strong effort to professionalize service occupations like nursing, housekeeping, and child care, to turn them into semiprofessions by means of courses and seminars and other specialized training. Kibbutzim have also branched into new occupations that are not sex-typed—social work, psychological therapy, and counseling—and into new industries and crafts that offer women a larger range of occupational choices.

Talmon has reported that kibbutzim try to have proportional representation on all committees and put pressure on women to participate in as many committees as possible. She observed that

The nomination committee will often prefer a female candidate to a male one of equal or even better qualifications. This balancing mechanism serves as an antidote to the limiting effects of occupational sex-role differentiation and overcomes to some extent women's reluctance to accept office. Apprenticeship in a committee enables women to gain experience and to develop new interests and new skills. Quite a number of women who were at first very insecure in their new roles have gradually become active and competent participants in the deliberations of their committee.[50]

Talmon also reported that there are also *symbolic* attempts to neutralize or deny the differences in sex roles by insisting that men take part in certain occupations for short periods of time:

The most important example is participation of men in work in the kitchen and the dining hall. They are drafted by a system of rotation in which each man serves a two- to three-month period. Most of the men serve in the dining hall where everyone can see them every day. Similar mechanisms operate in the family, too, particularly in the participation of fathers in taking their children out for their daily walk and in putting them to bed in the children's houses. Their participation in what is regarded as a typically feminine task serves as a highly visible symbolic denial of segregation.

Participation of men in feminine tasks has a practical value, but its main significance lies in its symbolic meaning as "atonement" for differentiation. Essentially, it is a token interchangeability. Women participate in masculine tasks much more and for much longer stretches than men in feminine tasks. Girls and young women are assigned to work in masculine occupations for a number of years. When they grow older and have children they leave these occupations and settle down in services and child care. Work in productive labour is regarded as an indispensable *rite de passage* for most women.[51]

The kibbutz has gone a long way in changing family roles, community relationships, and occupational roles in the directions some critics of the American family and occupational system have been advocating, but it seems to be easier to produce radical changes in the family on paper—in blueprints for a model society—than to attain them *completely* in real life.

Summary

The family is the institution that reproduces and socializes new members of a society. The form that the family takes varies from society to society as does the form of marriage. In all societies the nuclear family is an identifiable, distinct psychological unit, but in most traditional nonindustrial societies the basic *economic* unit is the extended family. In industrial societies the nuclear family tends to be economically independent of the extended family and to specialize increasingly in and to be judged by its success at producing emotional satisfactions for its members.

Notes

1. G. P. Murdock, *Social Structure* (New York: Macmillan Publishing Co., Inc., 1939).

2. See K. E. Gough, "Is the Family Universal: The Nayar Case," in N. Bell and E. Vogel, eds., *A Modern Introduction to the Family* (New York: The Free Press, 1960), pp. 76–92; and J. P. Mencher, "The Nayar of South Malabar," in M. F. Nimkoff, ed., *Comparative Family Systems* (Boston: Houghton Mifflin Company, 1965), pp. 163–191.

3. I. L. Reiss, "The Universality of the Family: A Conceptual Analysis," *Journal of Marriage and the Family,* **27** (1965), 443–453.

4. G. P. Murdock, "World Ethnographic Sample," *American Anthropologist,* **59** (1957), 686.

5. R. Patai, *Sex and Family in the Bible and the Middle East* (New York: Doubleday & Company, Inc., 1959), pp. 29–40, quoted in W. N. Stephens, *The Family in Cross-Cultural Perspective* (New York: Holt, Rienhart & Winston, Inc., 1963), p. 54.

6. D. Oliver, *A Solomon Island Society* (Cambridge, Mass.: Harvard University Press, 1955), pp. 352–353, as quoted in Stephens, op. cit., p. 54.

7. Ibid., p. 55.

8. Ibid., p. 58.

9. R. Linton, *The Study of Man* (New York: Appleton-Century Crofts, 1936), pp. 183–187, as quoted in Stephens, op. cit., pp. 50–51.

10. Ibid.

11. M. F. Nimkoff and R. Middleton, "Types of Family and Types of Economy," *American Journal of Sociology,* **66** (1960), 215–225; and R. Blumberg and R. F. Winch, "Societal Complexity and Familial Complexity: Evidence for the Curvilinear Hypothesis," *American Journal of Sociology,* **77** (1972), 898–920.

12. See S. M. Greenfield, "Industrialization and the Family in Sociological Theory," *American Journal of Sociology,* **65** (1961), 312–322. Also see F. F. Furstenberg, "Industrialization and the American Family: A Look Backward," *American Sociological Review,* **31** (1966), 326–337; and E. A. Wrigley, "The Process of Modernization and the Industrial Revolution in England," *Journal of Interdisciplinary History,* **3** (1972), 225–260.

13. W. Goode, *World Revolution and Family Patterns* (New York: The Free Press, 1963).

14. M. Zelditch, "Cross-cultural Analysis of Family Structure," in H. T. Christensen, ed., *Handbook of Marriage and the Family* (Chicago: Rand McNally & Co., 1964), p. 469.

15. See W. Goode, op. cit., Chapter 1, and G. Leslie, *The Family in Social Context,* 2nd Ed. (New York: Oxford University Press, 1973), Chapter 3.

16. "Survey Shows 62.8 Percent in Japan Wed for Love," *New York Times* (January 6, 1974), p. 8.

17. W. Goode, *The Family* (Englewood Cliffs, N.J.: Prentice-Hall, Inc., 1964), pp. 40–41.

18. J. de Onis, "'Honor' Killing Fought in Beirut," *New York Times* (March 5, 1973), p. 8.

19. Leslie, op. cit., p. 70.

20. Ibid.

21. Goode, *World Revolution,* op. cit., pp. 379–380.

22. See particularly T. Parsons, "The American Family: Its Relations to Personality and the Social Structure," in T. Parsons and R. F. Bales, *Family, Socialization and Interaction Process* (New York: The Free Press, 1955), pp. 3–21; and T. Parsons, "The Normal American Family," in S. M. Farber, P. Mustachi, and R. H. L. Wilson, eds., *Man and Civilization: The Family's Search for Survival* (New York: McGraw-Hill Book Company, 1965), pp. 31–50.

23. See particularly M. B. Sussman and L. Burchinal, "Kin Family Network: Unheralded Structure in Current Conceptualizations of Family Functioning," *Marriage and Family Living,* **24** (1962), 231–240; E. Litwak, "Occupational Mobility and Extended Family Cohesion," *American Sociological Review,* **25** (1960), 9–21; and E. Litwak, "Geographical Mobility and Extended Family Cohesion," *American Sociological Review,* **25** (1960), 385–394. But see also G. Gibson, "Kin Family Network: Overheralded Structure in Past Conceptualizations of Family Functioning," *Journal of Marriage and the Family,* **34** (1972), 13–23.

24. Litwak, "Occupational Mobility and Extended Family Cohesion," op. cit.

25. For a discussion of this see R. L. Coser and G. Rokoff, "Women in the Occupational World: Social Disruption and Conflict," *Social Problems,* **18** (1971), 535–554.

26. J. Bernard, *The Future of Marriage* (New York: World Publishing Company, 1972), pp. 26–27.

27. W. R. Gove, "Sex, Marital Status and Mortality," *American Journal of Sociology,* **79** (1973), 44–67.

28. W. R. Gove and J. F. Tudor, "Adult Sex Roles and Mental Illness," *American Journal of Sociology,* **78** (1973), 812–835.

29. S. R. Orden and N. Bradburn, "Working Wives and Marital Happiness," *American Journal of Sociology,* **74** (1969), 392–407.

30. A. Skolnick, *The Intimate Environment: Exploring Marriage and the Family* (Boston: Little, Brown and Company, 1973), p. 299.

31. Ibid.

32. C. F. Thwing and C. B. Thwing, *The Family: An Historical and Social Study* (Boston: Lee and Shepard Publishers, 1887), as quoted in I. L. Reiss, *The Family System in America* (New York: Holt, Rinehart & Winston, Inc., 1972), p. 317.

33. Ibid.

34. K. Davis, "The American Family in Relation to Demographic Change," in C. F. Westoff and R. Parke, eds., Commission on Population Growth and the American Future, *Research Reports, Volume 1, Demographic and Social Aspects of Population Growth* (Washington, D.C.: U.S. Government Printing Office, 1972), pp. 235–265.

35. Ibid. For an interesting discussion of and comparison of the various ways we measure divorce rates, e.g., divorce rate per 1,000 population (3.7 in 1971; 4.3 in 1946); per 1,000 married women fourteen years old and over (14.6 in 1971; 17.9 in 1946); per 1,000 married women fourteen to fifty-four years old (20.5 in 1971; 21.3 in 1946); and per 1,000 married women fourteen to forty-four years old (28.0 in 1971; 27.3 in 1946) see P. C. Glick, "Dissolution of Marriage by Divorce and Its Demographic Consequences," paper read at International Population Conference, Liège, Belgium. September, 1973.

36. Some good sources are R. Houriet, *Getting Back Together* (New York: Coward, McCann and Geohegan, Inc., 1971); R. M. Kanter, *Commitment and Community: Communes and Utopias in Sociological Perspective* (Cambridge, Mass.: Harvard University Press, 1972); and B. Zablocki, *The Joyful Community* (Baltimore: Penguin Books, 1971).

37. B. M. Berger, B. M. Hackett, and R. M. Miller, "Child Rearing Practices in the Communal Family," in H. P. Dreitzel, ed., *Recent Sociology, No. 4: Family, Marriage and the Struggle of the Sexes* (New York: Macmillan Publishing Co., Inc., 1972), p. 276.

38. There is a good bibliography of studies of the kibbutz in B. Schlesinger, "Family Life in the Kibbutz of Israel: Utopia Gained or Paradise Lost?" in Dreitzel, op. cit., pp. 301–331.

39. See M. E. Spiro, "Is the Family Universal? The Israeli Case," *American Anthropologist,* **56** (1954), 839–846, in which he argues it is not; and M. E. Spiro, "Is the Family Universal? The Israeli Case," in N. V. Bell and E. F. Vogel, eds., *A Modern Introduction to the Family* (New York: The Free Press, 1960), pp. 64–75, in which he argues that perhaps it is.

40. The source of the figures is S. Stern, "The Kibbutz: Not by Ideology Alone," *New York Times Magazine* (May 6, 1973), pp. 36ff.

41. On these small personal budgets, see F. J. M. Selier, "Some Functional and Structural Aspects of Family Life in a Communal Society: The Financial Sector of the Kibbutz Family," mimeographed (Amsterdam: Free University, 1972).

42. See L. Y. Rabkin and K. Rabkin, "Children of the Kibbutz," *Psychology Today,* (September 1969), 40–46.

43. On this point, see M. Rosner, "Worker Participation in Decision-Making in Kibbutz Industry," in M. Curtis and M. S. Chertoff, eds., *Israel: Social Structure and Change* (New Brunswick, N.J.: Transaction Books, 1973), pp. 145–158; U. Leviatan, "The Industrial Process in Israeli Kibbutzim: Problems and Their Solutions," in Curtis and Chertoff, op. cit. pp. 159–172; and Stern, op. cit.

44. On this point see Y. Talmon, "The Family in Revolutionary Movement: The Case of the Kibbutz in Israel," in M. F. Nimkoff, ed., *Comparative Family Systems* (Boston: Houghton Mifflin Company, 1965), pp. 259–287; and Y. Talmon, "The Case of Israel," in R. L. Coser, ed., *The*

Functions of the Family (New York: St. Martin's Press, Inc., 1964), pp. 582–617.

45. See on this point, A. I. Rabin, "The Sexes: Ideology and Reality in the Israeli Kibbutz," in G. H. Seward and R. C. Williamson, eds., *Sex Roles in Changing Society* (New York: Random House, Inc., 1970), pp. 285–307; Y. Talmon, "Sex-Role Differentiation in an Equalitarian Society," in T. E. Lasswell, J. H. Burma, and S. H. Aronson, eds., *Life in Society* (Chicago: Scott, Foresman and Company, 1965), pp. 144–155; and S. Keller, "The Family in the Kibbutz: What Lessons for Us?" in Curtis and Chertoff, op. cit., pp. 115–144.

46. See R. Bondy, "Granddaughter Wants Conservative Femininity," *Hadassah Magazine* (May 1972), pp. 9, 38; and J. Kahanoff, "Grandmother Was a Militant Feminist," *Hadassah Magazine* (May 1972), pp. 8–9, 30–31.

47. Keller, op. cit., p. 132.

48. R. Bar-Yoseph, "Assisting Kibbutz Parents in the Tasks of Childrearing," in H. K. Geiger, *Comparative Perspectives on Marriage and the Family* (New York: Little, Brown and Company, 1968), p. 166, as quoted in Keller, op. cit., p. 132.

49. Talmon, "Sex-Role Differentiation in an Equalitarian Society," op. cit.

50. Ibid., p. 154.

51. Ibid., p. 155.

NINE
Social Stratification

Stratification Systems

IN EVERY SOCIETY we find *inequality* in the distribution of power, prestige, and property. Some people have a good deal of each, some have almost none, and some are in between. In fancier language, every society is *stratified,* which means that there is some kind of *hierarchy* of groups of people, some higher (having more power, property, and prestige) and some lower (having less power, property, and prestige).

The sociologist who studies stratification systems is interested in a variety of things. He tries to answer questions like: How do such systems come to be? Are they inevitable? How do such systems differ from each other and why? How come in some societies one can't move out of the place in the system that he's born into and in others he can? Why is it that in one society or one type of society good things are distributed more (or less) unequally than in another? In the United States roughly 20 percent of the national income (before taxes) goes to the most prosperous 5 percent of families, as it also does in Sweden. Here are the percentages of income before taxes going to the top 5 percent of families in some other countries: Great Britain, 21 percent; West Germany, 24 percent; Ceylon, 31 percent; Colombia, 42 percent; Kenya, 51 percent; Southern Rhodesia, 65 percent.[1] Sociologists are also interested in the explanations offered in each society for why some people are rich (or respected or powerful) and others are not.

Sociologists have found that position in the stratification system has an impact on just about every aspect of life and death. Some of the things they have found related to position in the stratification system in the United States and elsewhere are chances of surviving birth; amount of schooling; voting patterns; reading and television-watching habits; chances of getting into and out of trouble with the law; tastes in art, music, perfumes, candy, furniture; sexual behavior; obesity; child-rearing behavior; number of close friends; attitudes toward foreign aid and civil liberties; chances that one's marriage will survive; likelihood of mental illness and of treatment for mental illness; and so on. These are just a *brief* sampling of some of the thousands of differences sociologists have found to be related to position in the stratification system.

Sociologists speak about "social classes" more often than they speak about "locations in the stratification system." A "class" system is only one type of stratification system. It is found in industrial societies, and most sociological studies have been done in industrial societies. There are three other kinds of stratification systems: *slave* systems,[2] *caste* systems, and *estate* systems.[3] Slave and caste systems tend to be *closed* systems, meaning that one's position at birth determines his location for life. Estate and class systems tend to be *open,* that is, there's an opportunity to move up or down.

Slave Systems

Slaves are people more or less forcibly tied to some stronger group and classified by the society as property. The defining characteristic of slavery is that the slave is subject to an owner who is answerable to no one for anything he does to a slave. The owner has the right of life and death over the slave. Slave marriages are rarely considered legally binding. The owner can dissolve a slave family any time he chooses to. Members of the slave group are without the privileges of citizens and most civil rights. Historically the economic foundations of Athenian Greece, Imperial Rome, and the South in the pre-Civil War United States rested on slavery.

There are about *2 million slaves* in Asia, Africa, and South America *today,* according to the U.N. Human Rights Commission.[4]

Caste Systems

A caste system is a "hierarchy of *endogamous** divisions in which membership is hereditary and permanent."[5] When we speak of "caste" the Indian Hindu system comes most easily to mind. Although this is the most elaborate and complicated example of a caste system, it is hardly the only one. Being born a black in South Africa, an Eta in Japan, or a black in the United States determines one's occupation, his style of life, and with whom he may eat, sleep, and drink.

In every society certain positions are acquired by *ascription* and others by *achievement.* An ascribed position is given to you (or forced on you) on the basis of something "biological," like whom you're born to (you get to be the king of England by being the eldest son in the royal family), or the color of your skin (you are born black, white, yellow, and so on), or your sex (you're born male or female). Other positions are *achieved* by you. You do (or don't do) something to get into these positions: you say "I do" to get married, you go to school, you win an election, you take an oath, and so on. For example, female is an *ascribed* status; wife is an *achieved* status.

In a caste system, you are ascribed or born into your most important position, your caste group, and you live in that caste. There's nothing you can do personally to break out of your caste. The Indian caste system is a system with four basic subdivisions. The highest are the Brahmans, who supply the priests, the intellectual leaders, and the teachers. Below them are the Kshatriya caste, which supplies kings, princes, nobles, and warriors. Below them are the Vaisya caste: the merchants, shopkeepers, industrialists, craftsmen, and farmers. Further below them are the Sudra caste: the laborers and unskilled workers. A fifth group, not considered part of the caste system but somewhere below and outside it, are the outcasts or "untouchables," who do the dirtiest work—remove corpses, wash clothes, and so on.

Priests are higher than kings in this society because it is a religious system, supported by supernatural justifications. In principle, if one does whatever

*An *endogamous* group is one in which people are required to choose marriage partners from the same group. In the case of caste, the legal system backs this up. In the case of religious or ethnic groups, endogamy may be enforced only by religious rules or social pressure.

things are appropriate to whichever caste he is in, in the next life he will be reborn into a higher caste.

The Indian caste system is enormously complicated. Within the four main castes there are several *thousand* subcastes, each assigned a certain range of occupations and a set of elaborate ceremonial rules and taboos. The whole system of ceremonial rules is based on the idea of the purity of the Brahmans and the complete impurity of the untouchables. Most fantastic is the belief that the breath, or even the shadow, of an untouchable will pollute another person. In some places untouchables are required to wear cloths over their mouths in order that their breath might not pollute. In Poona they are not permitted within the city walls between 3 P.M. and 9 A.M. because during the early morning and late afternoon sun their bodies cast long shadows. In at least one region there are not only untouchables but unseeables, a caste of washerwomen who have to do their work between midnight and daybreak and not show themselves except during the hours of darkness.

All castes other than the Brahmans are graded in terms of their purity by the extent to which there are provisions to safeguard them against pollution by the untouchables. In some regions, for instance, the untouchable may not come closer than 124 feet to a Brahman, although he may come within half that distance to an intermediate caste person and as near as 7 feet to some lower-caste person. In another region the specified distances are from 96 feet down to 36 feet, the distance from Brahmans always being the greatest. Wells are polluted if a Sudra man draws water from them. The water of a stream is polluted if a Sudra walks across a bridge over it. A Sudra can pollute an idol in a temple if he comes closer than 7 feet and if he does not cover his mouth and nostrils with his hands. Even the glance of a Sudra falling on a cooking pot necessitates throwing away the contents of the pot. Public roads near temples cannot be traveled by untouchables. There are places where untouchables are required to carry sticks or brooms to designate their status.[6] The caste system lays out one's occupation, what foods he can eat and with whom, whom he can marry, which temple he can worship at, how he must address those above him. A man can fool around with women from lower castes, but no man from a lower caste can fool with women from a higher caste.

Though there is no way an *individual* can move up in the world, his caste might move up *as a group* either because it changes its occupation or because of changes in the way its occupation is evaluated.[7]

There are religious justifications offered for the existence of the caste system, but it is obviously an economic and political system too, with political and economic power and education the exclusive privilege of the top three groups.

In recent years India has instituted laws to guarantee the untouchables equal rights with the other castes. In the cities, to some extent, these laws are honored. In the villages the old customs still hold and an untouchable still risks his life if he "contaminates" a higher caste by going near their well or wearing shoes on their streets.

A recent news article indicates that in response to the continued discrimination against them, some 2 million untouchables have converted to Buddhism.[8]

The Indian system is the most elaborate and thorough example of a caste system; however, there are other systems that have many of the same characteristics.

South Africa, for example, has quite an elaborate system for ensuring white supremacy over blacks and other nonwhites. The major groups are the 4 million white Afrikaners, 2 million coloreds (persons of mixed racial origins), half a million Asians, and 15 million native blacks or Bantus. As in India, interaction between these groups is limited to master servant relationships,[9] and every aspect of the society is oriented toward keeping the 4 million whites in power. The privileges of the nonwhites are totally at the command of the ruling white minority. Where it is economically necessary to permit blacks to enter occupations previously reserved for whites, the salaries are lower for the nonwhites, who may form unions but are legally forbidden to strike. For example, Indian and mixed-blood doctors are paid 52.3 percent and black doctors 47.8 percent of white doctors' salaries. David Mechanic reported that black miners get 50 to 60 cents for an eight-hour shift, roughly one seventeenth of what white miners earn. Mechanic also cited a survey by South Africa's Productivity and Wages Association that indicates that 80 percent of African workers earned less in 1972 than the $93 a month that constitutes the poverty line.[10]

Early studies of the position of American blacks utilized the caste model. Gunnar Myrdal's classic work *An American Dilemma* identified the antebellum South as being structured in a caste system. The post-Reconstruction rural regions also adhered to this framework. Writing in 1944, Myrdal observed, "The caste system is upheld by its own inertia and by the superior caste's interests in upholding it. The beliefs and sentiments among the whites centering around the idea of the Negroes' inferiority have been analyzed and their 'functional' role as rationalizations of the superior caste's interests has been stressed."[11] Raymond Mack, following this suggestion, compared blacks to India's untouchables saying, "A Negro in the United States can no more change to white than an outcast can change to Brahmin."[12] Arnold Rose saw a series of similarities between caste systems in colonial and emerging nations and the United States.[13] He noted that in both (1) segregation of races in every area existed; (2) interracial sexual relations were discouraged; (3) white-black relations were mostly economic; (4) economic relations were unequal; and (5) blacks did not enjoy equal legal-political rights. And, of course, remnants of social rules about "contamination" and deference, similar to those described for the untouchables, continue today. For example, consider whites' reluctance to try on the same clothes as blacks in clothing stores, to eat or drink from the same utensils, to use the same razors, scissors, and combs in a barbershop. And compare this information about the American South with what we said about India and South Africa:

A large body of law grew up concerned with the segregation of employees and their working conditions. The South Carolina Code of 1915, with subsequent elaborations, prohibited textile factories from permitting laborers of different races from working together in the same room, or using the same entrances, pay windows, exits, doorways, stairways, or windows at the same time, or the same "lavatories, toilets, drinking water buckets, pails, cups, dippers, or glasses" at any time. Exceptions were made of foremen, floor scrubbers, and repair men, who were permitted association with the white proletarian elite on an emergency basis.[14]

Some sociologists have argued that American race relations can be better understood by the use of a *class* or *colonial* model rather than a caste model, though they recognize the reasons that some see parallels with a caste system, particularly for the period before the Supreme Court abolished legal supports for segregation. (It wasn't until 1967 that the Supreme Court abolished Virginia's laws against interracial marriage.)

Robert Blauner has noted that

Colonialism traditionally refers to the establishment of domination over a geographically external political unit, most often inhabited by people of a different race and culture, where this domination is political and economic, and the colony exists subordinated to and dependent upon the mother country. Typically the colonizers exploit the land, the raw materials, the labor, and other resources of the colonized nation; in addition a formal recognition is given to the difference in power, autonomy, and political status, and various agencies are set up to maintain this subordination. Seemingly the analogy must be stretched beyond usefulness if the American version is to be forced into this model. For here we are talking about group relations within a society; the mother country–colony separation in geography is absent.[15]

While acknowledging some differences, Blauner does feel that American blacks do fit a colonial model. In support of his contention that black communities are "colonies," Blauner quotes Kenneth Clark's description of Harlem, which can be applied to any black ghetto:

Ghettoes are the consequence of the imposition of external power and the institutionalization of powerlessness. In this respect, they are in fact social, political, educational, and above all, economic colonies. Those confined within the ghetto walls are subject peoples. They are victims of the greed, cruelty, insensitivity, guilt, and fear of their masters. . . .

The community can best be described in terms of the analogy of a powerless colony. Its political leadership is divided, and all but one or two of its political leaders are shortsighted and dependent upon the larger political power structure. Its social agencies are financially precarious and dependent upon sources of support outside the community. Its churches are isolated or dependent. Its economy is dominated by small businesses which are largely owned by absentee owners, and its tenements and other real property are also owned by absentee landlords.

Under a system of centralization, Harlem's schools are controlled by forces outside of the community. Programs and policies are supervised and determined by individuals who do not live in the community.[16]

Although there is undoubtedly some validity in the idea of the black community as a "colony," most sociologists believe that social class and ethnicity are more useful concepts for understanding the recent past and the future prospects of blacks.[17]

Estate Systems

Class and estate systems, as we noted earlier, are more open than caste and slave systems of stratification. The estate system emerged in feudal times in Europe and we still see signs of it in Arab and South American countries that have a hereditary aristocracy. The Indian caste system is divided by function, that is, each caste takes care of certain functions: religion, military activity, economic activity, and agriculture, ranked in this hierarchical progression.

The feudal estate system had functional classifications, or orders, too, but each function was of roughly equal importance. The four major functions were politics, the military, religion, and commerce, each with its own separate hierarchy as indicated in Figure 9–1.

There were religious and legal supports for the feudal system as there are for the caste system, but the feudal system did make provision for movement from one order to another as well as up or down in any order. You may recall

Figure 9–1. The Feudal System.

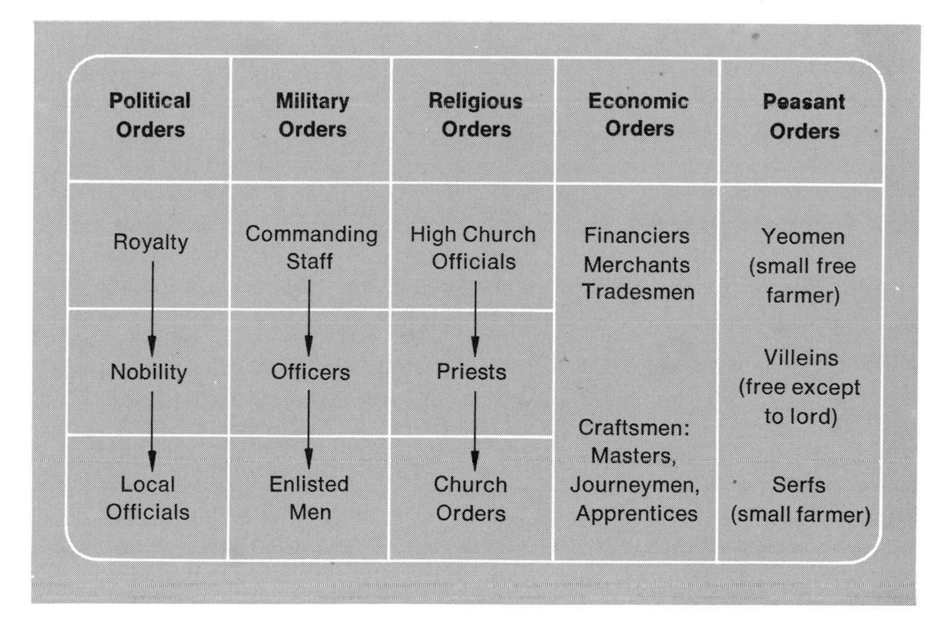

that the religious orders practiced celibacy (abstention from sex) and *had* to draw replacements from other orders. There were no legal barriers to mobility but in practice there wasn't very much movement, particularly where peasants were concerned.

The estate system ran something like this: in return for military assistance, royalty made grants of land to the nobility, who gave land to knights and other soldiers. All the way up the chain, the grants of land were exchanged for oaths of loyalty and military protection by those under one's control. Down at the bottom of the system were the peasants, who were attached to the land and sold or transferred with the land. Some of these were serfs, who were not free, and some were yeomen and villeins, who were technically free but depended on the land for a living.

The merchants and craftsmen lived in towns and were not tied to the land itself, but in the beginning the towns were set up near the castles of the nobles and depended on them for protection. As occupations and trades developed they led to the forming of occupational organizations called *guilds.* Guilds were a combination of labor union, trade organization, religious fraternity, and fraternal lodge.

The Church had its own hierarchy: monks, nuns, friars, priests, bishops, and so on. Although members of these groups were not allowed to marry they were not completely separate from the rest of the society. Some religious orders were limited to people of noble birth. Katherine George and Charles George[18] reported that 78 percent of all the saints in the Roman Catholic calendar had what we could call upper-class origins.

Although the feudal system hit its peak in Europe about eight hundred years ago and in Russia the serfs were freed only one hundred years ago, estate systems are something more than ancient history in Latin America.[19] In many Latin American countries the *hacienda* system still flourishes. A hacienda is a family-owned, large-scale agricultural operation. At the heart is the home of the owning family. Inside the walls are the manager, the foreman, and blacksmiths, leatherworkers, carpenters, and other specialists. The permanent labor force lives inside or near the hacienda. In principle, they're paid wages but usually these are food or goods. In some places, like Peru, villages are so short of land that either the village as a whole or individuals enter into a tenancy arrangement with the landowners. In return for enough land to cultivate to provide for bare subsistence, tenants owe the landholder a certain number of days of work for no money or for very little money. It's something we'd probably recognize as "sharecropping," and it's about as hard for a tenant to get out from under as it is for a sharecropper.

In the 1950s a group of anthropologists from Cornell University studied the Vicos hacienda from an interesting perspective. They bought the hacienda and essentially *owned* the peasants because the previous owners had held almost total control over the peasants.[20] Over the course of several years, they taught the peasants modern agricultural techniques and left them a land-owning, self-governing community. But within Peru the project caused a good deal of controversy. Peasants on other haciendas liked the idea of independence but the landowners are not particularly anxious to do what the Cornell anthropologists did. Apparently there is also a good deal of resentment on the part of many of their neighbors, who feel that the Vicosinos are now the most difficult and disagreeable Indians in Peru because they're no longer subservient and don't "know their place."

Class

Caste, slave, and estate systems are characteristic of agriculturally based, unindustrialized societies. Birth determines nearly all aspects of life: the kind of work one does, whom he marries, where he is buried. The kind of legal and religious constraints on what one can do for a living that exist in caste, slave, and estate systems don't exist in class systems. In industrial *class* societies what one does for a living influences all of the other aspects of his life. A person's labor and what he is paid for it are important aspects of life in contemporary industrial societies.

Karl Marx and Nineteenth-century England

Karl Marx, observing England in the 1800s, the nation in which industrialization was most advanced, formulated a theory of social class and history that today still dominates thinking about social stratification. Most of his ideas have been misinterpreted, reformulated, or refined. Nonetheless, Marx's ideas have served as a guide to what things about stratification are worth studying.

History for Marx was the story of the conflict between social classes. Social classes were the major actors in history. Social change occurred as classes clashed over who would control the *means of production* (tools, plants, factories) and its rewards.

If the study of social stratification is, as Max Weber suggested, the study of how *property, power,* and *prestige* are distributed, for Marx *property* was the guts of stratification. Power and prestige were simply by-products of *property,* from which everything else about the society flowed and to which everything else about the society sooner or later made an adjustment.

In the Marxian view, everything revolved about the production of goods and services and particularly who owned or controlled the means of production. At one time man lived off the land, no one owned the land, and supposedly no one exploited anyone else. With the invention of the idea of private property came exploitation and conflict. Masters exploited slaves, the nobility exploited the peasants, capitalists exploited workers. Sometime in the future, Marx

Not only children worked in the mines but women, often stripped to the waist, drawing coal carts through narrow tunnels like beasts of burden, as shown in another reform tract. "It is worse when you are in a family way," said one miner. The outcry rose so high that Parliament passed drastic laws removing all women from the mines and prohibiting boys from going underground before the age of 10. The Factory Act of 1833 has thrown forty thousand children out of work, providing state education for them until the age of 9.

believed, a society would be created in which the *workers* would run the society and no one would be exploited.

What Marx meant by *exploitation* was simply that the workers did all of the work and the "exploiters" took the profits and paid the workers barely enough to survive. The rich lived off the sweat of the poor laborers.

Marx's view of history was that in each time period there was a conflict between those currently exploiting the workers and those who had a more *efficient* system for exploiting the workers: slavery wasn't as efficient as feudalism; feudalism wasn't as efficient as capitalism. At the time he wrote Marx couldn't imagine a more efficient industrial system than capitalism for exploiting the workers. He thought that eventually the workers would rebel against *anybody's* exploiting them and would take over the means of production for themselves and abolish private property. The means of production would then be used to give everyone the fair return for his labor ("From each according to his capacity, to each according to his needs").

Marx based his model of class on first-hand observation of England in the nineteenth century. It was a society in which millions of peasants had been forced off their farms and into the city by changes in agriculture and by increases in population. From the country they came to the cities, to the factories to work for wages. They came to work under miserable conditions. The factories sometimes paid such low wages that workers starved at their machines. Small children worked fifteen-hour days, seven days a week. There were no safety precautions. Farm animals had better living conditions. Factory owners prospered while workers suffered.

The first volume of Marx's famous study, *Capital* (1867), was written some forty years after the passage of the first parliamentary acts intended to improve working conditions in factories. It wasn't easy to find evidence that there had been or were likely to be any changes. *Capital* contains hundreds of items like this one:

The manufacture of lucifer matches dates from 1833, from the discovery of the method of applying phosphorus to the match itself. Since 1845 this manufacture has rapidly developed in England, and has extended especially amongst the thickly populated parts of London as well as in Manchester, Birmingham, Liverpool, Bristol, Norwich, Newcastle and Glasgow. With it has spread a form of lockjaw, which a Vienna physician in 1845 discovered to be a disease peculiar to lucifer-matchmakers. Half the workers are children under thirteen, and young persons under eighteen. The manufacture is on account of its unhealthiness and unpleasantness in such bad odour that only the most miserable part of the laboring class, half-starved widows and so forth, deliver up their children to it, "the ragged, half-starved, untaught children."

Of the witnesses that Commissioner White examined (1863), 270 were under 18, 50 under ten, ten only eight, and five only six years old. A range of the working day from 12 to 14 to 15 hours, night-labour, irregular meal times, meals for the most part taken in the very workrooms that are pestilent with phosphorus. Dante would have found the worst horrors of his inferno surpassed in this manufacture.[21]

As Marx saw it there were two *historically important classes* of people, those who controlled the means of production (the *bourgeoisie*) and those who had nothing but their bodies and their labor (the *proletariat*).[22] The owners of the factories and the workers were, then, the two basic classes. Marx was, of course, aware that there were other occupations—small-business owners, white-collar workers, professionals, technical workers—but there were not as many of these people then as there are now, and Marx took for granted that these groups would sooner or later move up in the world and become capitalist factory owners or move down and end up as workers or the social scum even lower than workers that he called the *lumpenproletariat.*

Marx, as we've noted, saw the past *and* the future as a clash between *classes.* As he saw it, the classes had opposed interests. Those who owned the factories had an interest in maximizing profits and in paying the workers as little as they could get away with. In this era before the formation of unions, the owners could get away with a great deal. If the workers didn't like their miserable salaries, they could quit and find long lines of unemployed people waiting for their jobs. The workers, on the other hand, had an interest in taking their share of the profits made by the sweat of their brows; but though the workers resented being exploited, the owners had the power. They controlled the power of the state and used it to block any effective expression of discontent by the worker.

In Marx's view, the workers and the owners were *classes* by definition: they had opposed interests. Marx argued that whether or not the workers were objectively *conscious* of their class membership, they were still a class. Class was important for Marx because he saw the economic factors involved in class as the key to understanding that the rest of the society—power, culture, forms of family life, the educational system, and so on—reinforced and supported the differences that were initially generated by differences in *property.*

It was inevitable, in Marx's view, that the workers would become aware of their situation and act collectively to overthrow capitalism, *if* they did not allow themselves to feel hopeless, or to be duped into believing that they had a chance of moving up in the system, or to be misled by religious promises of a rich life in heaven. These were big *ifs*. Nevertheless, it was inevitable in the *long* run that the workers would become organized to fight their oppressors and to carry out their historic role in creating a new society. Marx didn't assume that they would do this easily or without some guidance from those intellectuals who knew the score. He observed that the workers were frequently unaware of their situation, that they were victims of what he called a *false consciousness,* in which they acted as though they didn't *have* to overthrow capitalism to achieve their due. However, he assumed that sooner or later the owners would drive the workers into such a wretched state that they'd have to realize the system must be overthrown. Then they would be objectively conscious of themselves as a class.

According to Marx, class conflict always exists. Sometimes the struggle is an *unconscious* struggle between workers and capitalists for shares in the productive output at a time when the workers' class consciousness isn't well developed, but it can also be a *conscious,* deliberate struggle between the classes when the workers become aware of their historic role, act collectively to improve their situation, and ultimately take over ownership of the instruments of production.

Class in America

Marx assumed, as we've said, that the revolution wasn't going to come until the workers gained the proper "consciousness" of their position and identified themselves as the working *class.* Studies of Americans do not indicate a strong consciousness of class. If we ask Americans questions about what social class they belong to we don't get a very enthusiastic response to the whole idea of class. If we push and insist on an answer we find that *which* answer we get depends very heavily on *how* we phrase the choices. For example, if we ask people whether they belong to (1) the middle class, (2) the lower class, (3) the working class, or (4) the upper class, as did Richard Centers in 1948,[23] we find roughly 3 percent say upper class, 43 percent middle class, 51 percent working class, and 1 percent lower class. If the suggested responses are changed we find, as Charles Tucker[24] did in 1966, 1 percent upper class, 16 percent upper middle, 41 percent middle, 9 percent lower middle, 31 percent working class, and 1 percent lower class (the percentage for working class drops 20 percent). If we ask if people are middle class *or* working class, as did the Survey Research Center[25] in 1964, we find roughly what Centers found: 43 percent middle class, 53 percent working class. All we can say for certain from the figures cited is that almost no one considers himself upper class or lower class, that most of us see ourselves when questioned as part of either the working or the middle class. Centers found that class self-identifications don't match "objective" class positions. It appears that the people who see themselves as being in the working or the middle class don't necessarily have the kinds of occupations we'd identify this way. Many professionals, businessmen, and white-collar workers identify themselves as "working class," and many unskilled manual workers identify themselves as "middle class." Centers was one of the first people to study class consciousness through public opinion polls and to try to relate it to attitudes toward a large number of public issues. His assumption was that people would vote and hold various attitudes according to the classes they *thought* they were a part of rather than according to the class they "objectively" belonged to. This idea is derived, of course, from Marx's ideas of class consciousness—true consciousness and false consciousness. Centers found that there is evidence of a relationship between the class one identifies oneself with and liberalism-conservatism on public issues.

Centers' theory used Marx's vocabulary but used the words somewhat differently than Marx did. According to Marx, you remember, the classes are "objective" facts. In Centers' theory classes are solely "subjective." In other words, a class exists only if there are people who claim membership in it. Most sociologists would reject the idea that a class is *nothing more than* a group of people who believe they are a class. They would point to numerous studies that indicate "objective" standards like occupation and income are much better predictors of attitudes and beliefs than self-identification.

There are many things in Marx's theory that contemporary sociologists reject, but one of the ideas they have retained is the idea that one's position in the economic system (occupation and income) is a key determinant of many other things. As you are certainly aware, contemporary sociologists talk about more than Marx's two classes, workers and owners. Although they don't always agree on how *many* classes (and which ones) there are, there is not much disagreement on the idea that different occupational groups have greater or less access to property, power, and prestige.

Marx was not much of a prophet, at least not as far as the United States was concerned, when he predicted that the lot of the working class would become increasingly miserable and wretched and that his revolution would become inevitable. Historical studies by Lewis Corey[26] and James Burnham question Marx's notion of the increasing misery of the factory worker. Examining the 1940 census, Corey found that the economic and occupational position of the working class had in fact improved rather than deteriorated.

As Table 9–1 illustrates, the percentage of industrial workers in America began to decline after 1920. In 1920, 66 percent of the sample were proletarians (factory workers) as opposed to 55 percent in 1940. While the size of the proletariat declined, the size of the middle class, especially the salaried white collar group Corey calls "the new middle class," grew by leaps and bounds. The 1970 census indicates a continuance of this trend, with an increase of white-collar workers from 37.5 percent of the population in 1950 to 48.3 percent in 1972.

Table 9-1. Class Divisions in the United States: 1870–1940 (in thousands)[a]

	1940	1930	1920	1910	1870
I. *Farmers*	5,265	6,012	6,387	6,132	3,100
1. Owners	3,227	3,463	3,954	3,864	2,325
2. Tenants	2,038	2,549	2,433	2,268	775
II. *Working class*	29,518	25,813	22,665	19,730	6,035
1. Industrial	16,124	16,198	15,118	12,982	3,225
a. Manufacturers	9,250[b]	9,150	9,450	7,425	1,812
b. Mining	824	887	982	862	179
c. Transportation	2,950[b]	2,961	2,386	2,204	465
d. Construction	3,100	3,200	2,300	2,490	768
2. Farm laborers	2,312	2,606	2,217	2,658	1,500[b]
3. Other workers	11,082	7,456	5,329	4,089	1,310
III. *Middle class*	16,633	14,884	11,682	8,870	2,289
1. Old-enterprisers	3,863	3,751	3,350	3,261	1,532[b]
a. Business	3,382	3,304	2,943	2,896	1,304
b. Professional	481	446	406	336	128
2. New salaried	12,769	11,580	8,332	5,609	756
a. Technical managerial	2,062	1,966	1,527	999	129
b. Professional	2,660	2,413	1,581	1,179	204
c. Clerical	3,889	3,345	2,719	1,402	68
d. Salespeople	3,347	3,003	1,877	1,595	282
e. Public service	439	418	290	208	48
IV. *Upper bourgeoisie*	240	300	200	—	—

[a] *Note:* The numbers are all persons "gainfully occupied" or the "labor force" (new Census terminology) minus unpaid family farm workers. "Labor force" and "gainfully occupied" are not strictly comparable; the 1940 numbers are "labor force" and would be slightly higher if the older concept had been used.
Under "Manufacturers" are included some workers not working in factories. "Transportation" includes workers in the communication industries. "Farm laborers" include only hired wageworkers. The "salaried" total includes "unspecified" salaried employees and telephone and telegraph operators. "Salespeople" includes clerks in stores. "Public service" includes federal, state, and local officials, police personnel, and probation officers; it excludes doorkeepers, laborers, and other wageworkers and does not include the much larger total in government service.
[b] Partly estimated.
Source: L. Corey, "The Middle Class," *The Antioch Review* (1945), 2.

James Burnham describes this trend as a "managerial revolution." Rather than seeing a movement from capitalism to socialism, Burnham points to the rise of a new ruling class: the managerial class, those who "are actually managing, on its technical side, the actual process of production, no matter what the legal and financial form—individual, corporate, governmental—of the process."[27] J. K. Galbraith called the managerial class "the technostructure of society."[28] The argument presented by Corey, Burnham, and Galbraith, put simply, appears to refute Marx's notion of the *immiseration* (increasing misery) inherent in capitalism. More people than ever are "middle class."

There are critics of this view. Although not accepting Marx's view of history, they charge that the income of the richest 20 percent of American families has been more than all the income earned by the bottom 80 percent. According to the Cambridge Institute, each of the families in the top 5 percent in America earn $24,000 or more a year.[29]

Table 9-2. Employed Persons, by Major Occupation Group: 1950–72[a]

Occupation Group	1950	1955	1960	1965	1969	1970	1971	1972
TOTAL	59,648	62,997	66,681	72,179	77,902	78,627	79,120	80,627
White-collar workers	22,372	24,585	28,726	32,104	26,845	37,997	28,252	38,892
Percent of total	37.5	39.0	43.1	44.5	47.3	48.3	48.3	48.2

[a] In thousands of persons fourteen years old and over through 1965; sixteen years and over thereafter. Prior to 1960, Alaska and Hawaii excluded. Annual averages except as indicated. From 1965 to 1972, not strictly comparable with previous years. See *Historical Statistics, Colonial Times to 1957,* Series D 72, 572, for related but not comparable data.

The census of 1970, as Table 9–3 shows, finds 60 percent of the American public earning less than $9,600 a year. The average income was a thousand dollars higher. As these figures indicate, the working class has not become impoverished; however, it is also apparent that the economic cleavage between the "rich" and "other people" has not diminished. For example, the top 20 percent of Americans own 77 percent of the personal wealth. The other 80 percent are left with 23 percent of the wealth.

As Marx used the term *class,* it refers to relationships to the means of production, and the basic distinction is between those who own the factories and those who "own" only their labor. For Marx these were the only important things about stratification. Power and prestige *follow* from property and wealth (money can buy power and prestige) but are only of secondary interest.

Table 9-3. Percentage of Total U.S. Income by Income Group

Number and Percentage of Households[a] by 1972 Household Income (Households as of March 1973)		*Percentage Share of Aggregate Household Income in 1967 and 1972, Received by Each Fifth of Households, Ranked by Income*		
Household Income	Household Percentage	Income Rank[b]	1972	1967
Total	100.0	Percent	100.0	100.0
Under $1,000	2.2	Lowest fifth	4.2	4.5
$1,000 to $1,999	5.3	Second fifth	10.5	10.5
$2,000 to $2,999	6.2	Third fifth	16.8	17.6
$3,000 to $3,999	5.7	Fourth fifth	24.6	24.7
$4,000 to $4,999	5.5	Highest fifth	43.9	42.7
$5,000 to $5,999	5.4	Top 5 percent	17.0	16.1
$6,000 to $6,999	5.2			
$7,000 to $7,999	5.5			
$8,000 to $9,999	10.5			
$10,000 to $11,999	10.3			
$12,000 to $14,999	12.7			
$15,000 to $24,999	19.3			
$25,000 and over	6.2			

[a] A household is two or more people living in the same dwelling unit and related to each other by blood, marriage, or adoption. A single person unrelated to the other occupants in the dwelling or living alone is a household by himself.

[b] Ranking is based on size of money income before taxes.

Source: U.S. Department of Commerce, *Current Population Reports: Consumer Income* Series P-60, No. 89 (Washington, D.C.: U.S. Government Printing Office, July 1973).

Max Weber and Multidimensional Ranking

Contemporary sociological and man-on-the-street thinking about stratification combines some of Marx's ideas with some of those of the German sociologist Max Weber. For Weber, the man who introduced the notion of "value free" assessments of sociological phenomena, there was *more* to stratification than just economic position. Weber suggested that Marx was correct in assuming that class, defined in terms of economic position, was important, but he felt that Marx overemphasized economic position. Weber thought that power and prestige were also important and *separate* aspects of stratification and that to assume that studying *only* economic class can lead to an understanding of contemporary stratification is a mistake. Weber suggested that we think of three separate bases for hierarchies: property differences generate *classes;* power differences lead to political *parties;* and prestige differences generate *status groups.* Let's look at these separately.

Class

Class, according to Weber, is a function of economic power. All people with similar *economic interests* and with similar *economic power* belong to the same class. Economic power is, in the simplest terms, the power to buy things directly, such as medical care, schooling, and property. But in addition, economic power is measured by a person's ability to dispose of goods and services in exchange for income, his ability to gratify his material wants, and his ability to pay for the education that will give him a better economic position. Weber refers to these kinds of things as *life chances.*

Weber did not believe that those who had similar life chances automatically or inevitably formed a community, as Marx had suggested. Nor did he believe that antagonism between classes was inevitable. For example, plantation owners in the American South and poor whites could and did coexist more or less peacefully. Nor did he believe that if class struggles did occur they would have to be revolutionary or would lead to major changes in the economic system; they could be nonrevolutionary and directed toward the redistribution of wealth and other privileges. In other words, Weber was more pessimistic than Marx about the likelihood of the proletariat's triumphing over the bourgeoisie. Having a common position in the marketplace just wasn't enough to create the necessary consensus, consciousness, and organization for such a social movement. He argued that Marx was off base in assuming that economic forces would automatically be translated into social forces.

Status, Honor, and Life Styles

A *status* group is a group of people who have the same style of life and receive about the same amount of "status honor" (or prestige) from other people. People in a given status group tend to have similar amounts of formal education, to teach their children the same values, to pick up the same manners and tastes, and to see themselves as having enough in common to think of one another as members of a group (A "belongs" and B does not). Weber suggested that although a sense of common identity might or might not occur for *class,* it *does* occur for *status.* According to Weber, whatever it is that originally gives people high status (money and occupational accomplishment, perhaps), those who have high status tend to develop life styles that continue to support their status, and they do so with an eye to keeping others out. For example, although perhaps originally people are honored because they've made a lot of money, they deemphasize this in explaining their status. They argue that the high status is due to family background, manners, education, and the like—things that are harder to gain or lose than money. Weber suggested that those who have high status develop ways of talking, dressing, appreciating food, drink, art, and music that take years to develop so that they can exclude others who lack these "skills" from competing for high prestige.

Weber noted that although there's often a very close relationship between class and status, equally often the two don't match at all. "With some over-simplification," Weber wrote, "one might thus say that classes are stratified according to their relations to the production and acquisition of goods; whereas status groups are stratified according to the principles of their *consumption* of goods as represented by special styles of life."[30] People who have piles of recently earned money may be social outcasts among people who have *less* money but are the community's social elite. Similarly, this social elite may respect people who've got the proper tastes and life styles but who have less money or no money—impoverished aristocrats, for example, who in everyday language we might say have a lot of "class."

It's been suggested that the middle classes in France supported the Revolution of 1789 not because they wanted economic rights (which they already had) but because they wanted the monarchy and the aristocrats to accord them high status and political power.

It's been indicated, too, that many people who voted against McGovern in the 1972 presidential election voted against their own economic (class) interests because they fiercely resented the challenge to their life styles by McGovern supporters, particularly the challenges to their concepts of patriotism, propriety, and morality.

Status and Power

As Weber saw it, power in modern industrial societies flowed not only from ownership of the means of production but also from bureaucratic positions. (Power is, according to Weber, *the chance of a man or a group to realize their will even against the opposition of others.*) His logic runs roughly like this: as

Position in the stratification system has an impact on every aspect of life.

society becomes more complex, large bureaucracies develop to run it. The dominant bureaucracy is the state, with its monopoly on arms and administration, and all institutions, including economic ones, are brought into a close, dependent relationship with it. These other institutions become more and more highly bureaucratized, and at the same time the centralized state gains more and more control over them. Consequently, the key power resources become rigidly hierarchical large-scale bureaucracies, such as trade unions, religious groups, political parties, large corporations, and the like. What these groups have in common is that they want *power* and can mobilize support from many members to obtain that power. What ties the members together may be common economic interests or status-related concerns or simply a desire for power.

As we've said, Weber argued that there are three kinds of hierarchies in contemporary stratification systems, one of economic class, one of status, and one of power. There are tendencies for people who are high in one hierarchy to attempt to become high in the others: millionaires run for political office, high government employees later join industry, industrialists get appointed to political posts, celebrities and artists join political campaigns or lend their names to franchise operations, and so on. Nonetheless, according to Weber these are three separate hierarchies, and economics is not the sole and prime mover, as the cruder Marxist analyses would have it.

Marx had argued that capitalism leads to certain kinds of exploitation and special privileges. When the private ownership of the means of production was abolished, then privilege would also be abolished. Weber argued that power lies in bureaucracies and that whether these are capitalist or socialist bureaucracies doesn't make any difference in the distribution of power and status.

Milovan Djilas, a Yugoslavian statesman, spent much time in prison for his arguments that in the Soviet Union and other Communist nations the state had not "withered away." Instead, a *new* class had emerged. This new body was based on the government bureaucracy, constituted of managers and professionals.[31] At the close of World War II, executives, engineers, and professionals earned 2.3 times as much as factory workers. In 1966, this percentage dropped; however, the "new class" continues to enjoy preferential treatment. Their children are more often admitted to the university and to Communist Party membership. For example, during the academic year of 1966–67, only 2.6 percent of the students at Rostov State University came from collective farms; 50.4 percent of the students had parents who were in the "new class."[32] Overall, the style of life of the "red executive" is far superior to that of the manual worker. This social experiment, which *eliminated private ownership,* replaced stratification based on property with a stratification system based on status and power.

Status in Yankee City

As we've noted, Americans are very reluctant to talk about "social class" or to admit to its existence, at least in the sort of terms Marx might use. (Of course, Marx would simply argue that class is significant regardless of whether or not we find it pleasant to discuss.) Americans *are* willing to talk about prestige or status and to acknowledge that some people have better "reputations" in the community, that some neighborhoods are "better" than others, that some sources of income are more "respectable" than others.

In the early 1930s W. Lloyd Warner took advantage of our willingness to discuss such things in instituting in a New England city his classic "Yankee City" series of studies, which launched the empirical study of stratification in American sociology.[33]

Warner asked community members to rank the community's families in terms of whatever categories were already *in use by the community* and to rate the reputations of different families. Warner's intention was to describe the *community's* status system rather than imposing *his own* system on the community. The result of his questioning was his "finding" that Yankee City had a six-"class" system. Note that what he called "classes" are what Weber called "status groups" rather than classes. In Warner's view, a social class is a group of people who are willing to associate with each other on a more or less equal basis. They do *not* associate closely with the members of higher or lower classes, in the first case because they don't want to be snubbed or exploited and in the second because they don't want to be "contaminated." (They'd never say this out loud, of course; they'd be more likely to say, "We have nothing in common.") Warner found that "Yankee City" had an *upper* upper class and a *lower* upper class, an *upper* middle class and a *lower* middle class, an *upper* lower class and a *lower* lower class.

Warner described his six groups as essentially hereditary groups, differing in wealth and income, education, occupation, style of life, speech patterns, and kinship arrangements.

Warner described the six classes this way:

1. The *upper upper class* is aristocratic by birth and possesses inherited wealth. The families are at least third-generation Americans. Their style of life involves stress upon family reputation, marriage within the class, social responsibility, and observance of etiquette and gracious living. Polo matches, large black tie dinners, and debutante balls are all a part of this style of life. An important thing to note is that upper upper rank is independent of wealth. In Warner's scheme, lower positions may in fact have *more* objective wealth but lack the social honor of the upper upper class.

2. The *lower upper class* is made up of the *nouveau riche* (new rich). This subclass consists of the newly arrived but not accepted families. These people try to copy the life style of the upper upper class but lack the social graces to bring it off. They have a strange mix of gracious living and "middle-class" success striving. In recent years, affluent executives, physicians, and lawyers have been the mainstays of this group.

3. The *upper middle class* is composed of those engaged in a career that will lead to success. Professionals, "junior executives," and striving businessmen people this category. Generally, they have gone to the better universities and do appreciate gracious living. However, they haven't yet accumulated enough wealth to be included in the lower upper category.

These three "units" Warner presented as having realized the American Dream of success. They are a notch above the "common man." The level of the *common man,* as Warner used this term, is the level where people are attempting to "make it."

4. The *lower middle class* is the world of the "average man." This group includes highly paid blue-collar workers and most white-collar workers and small businessmen, some 35 percent of the population. This group is characterized by a stress upon being *respectable* and upon *striving for success.* Being respectable means adhering to societal norms, living in the right neighborhood, and dressing correctly. This is the unit with the greatest social conformity.

5. The *upper lower class* consists of "honest and ordinary workers." These are blue-collar factory workers and a legion of semiskilled workers ranging from sales clerks to delivery men. Nearly 40 percent of the American labor force is in this group. The style of life is *hedonistic* or directed at living well from day to day. They are the major users of credit. Immediate gratification comes before striving for success.

In a more recent work Herbert Gans further divided the "upper lower class" into two more groups. Studying upper-lower-class people in Boston, Gans found "routine seekers" and "action seekers." [34] The routine seekers are people we might call creatures of habit. They watch the same television shows every week, eat the same meals on certain evenings—chicken every Sunday—and rarely break away from these routines. Notice that they are very much like the lower middle class. For the action seeker, on the other hand, "the goal is action, an opportunity for thrills, and for the chance to face and overcome a challenge. It may be sought in a crap game, a fight, a sexual interlude, a drinking bout, a gambling session, or in a fast and furious exchange of wise-cracks and insults."[35] This is the group that misuses credit and is oriented to the "eat, drink, and be merry" philosophy.

6. The *lower lower class* is made up of unskilled workers and nonworking people. These are the seasonal workers, the day laborers, and people on welfare. They are about 15 percent of the population. This group has generally been ignored, by Warner as well as others, as being outside of the American Dream Machine.

It is important to remember that Warner's class groups are not tied to income. Rather, their style of life and their values greatly determine where people are placed on the Warner scale.

Richard P. Coleman[36] presents an interesting example of the differences in life styles even when *income is the same.* Consider three families earning about $10,800 a year, yet each belonging to a different social class.

The upper-middle-class family would just be starting out. A young executive, professor, engineer, lawyer—all would spend a large portion of their income on the symbols of achievement: a good neighborhood, stereo equipment, expensive pieces of furniture. One item is bought at a time.

The lower-middle-class family is headed by a plumber, a salesman, an owner of a small store, who is probably buying his own home, but in a less prestigious neighborhood. They are more security-oriented; for example, they put their money into a savings account.

The upper-lower-class family, headed by, say, a truck driver or an automobile factory worker, may pay little attention to housing, instead spending most of their income on flashy cars, large color television sets, and other entertainments, such as campers and motor boats.

In the sphere of fashion and automobile models, style of life is again important. The upper-middle-class wife buys her clothes at specialty shops that are considered avante garde or "smart." Her appearance will be a main concern as it is thought to be an aid to her husband's quest for success.

The lower-middle-class wife may find chain stores more to her liking because she prefers to spend more on home decoration. She may make her own clothes but not because of economic want.

The upper-lower-class wife is more likely to be primarily concerned with flashy clothes and appliances. Her one or two attention-getting outfits are generally saved for such special occasions as going out on Saturday night.

These life-style differences are also found in automobile model preferences. The upper-middle-class will buy either the less expensive models of high-priced cars like Buicks, Oldsmobiles, or even Mercedes-Benzes or else Chevys, Fords, or Volkswagens. Lower-middle-class men tend to purchase the higher-priced models of the so-called low-priced three, like Bel Aires or Fairlanes or a series of imports from Japan and Germany.

Upper-lower-class males are less predictable, either buying a "sensibly" priced model of one of the low-priced three or going into debt for an expensive car that would seem to be beyond their price range. However, by playing down clothing and housing they may in fact be able, on credit, to buy a sportscar or even a Cadillac.

Warner's studies were studies of small communities, communities in which a small group of knowledgeable people could describe for a researcher the social standing of almost everyone in town. What do you do if you want to study a big city or the whole nation? Warner suggested that his reputational method could be converted into one that didn't require having acquaintances rate everyone in town. Very briefly, he and his associates tried to figure out the "objective" things, such as income and education, that would predict the reputations of families in the communities they studied. They found that there were certain factors that could be used to predict quite well who was in what reputational category. Occupation, source of income (that is, inheritance, fees and profits, salary, wages, public relief), house quality, and neighborhood were the best predictors. He suggested that these measures could be used even in large cities or for the nation as a whole.[37]

It is important to remember that Warner's method of description was based on what people *thought.* If the townsfolk said, "Mr. Jones is of high status," then Mr. Jones, as far as Warner was concerned, had a high social standing. "Objective" standards of class position have very little to do with reputation. Objective methods look instead at how much money one makes or one's occupation. The difference between these two methods is clearly shown when we look at the gangster of the 1930s. Objectively he made a great deal of money; however, when we ask about his reputation, he comes out way on the bottom of the social ladder.

Although for various reasons Warner's index has not been used very much in recent years, other indices have been developed that also give their main weight to occupational prestige level and some other factors—sometimes education, sometimes income, sometimes both. Kahl and Davis[38] compared nineteen indices of class position and found that the two indicators underlying all others were *occupational position* and quality of house and residential area, but particularly occupation.

Occupation was for Marx at the heart of "class." For Weberian analysts of "prestige" it turns out that occupation is again the best single predictor. Although sociologists continually warn each other that *class* and *status* are not identical,[39] for all practical purposes occupations and all that "occupation" implies about income, education, and so on are at the heart of placement in both the class and the status systems. Remember that sociologists have started with "class" as their independent variable and found it to be correlated with just about every dependent variable they can concoct, though, of course, they still disagree over what accounts for the relationships.

In 1947 C. C. North and Paul Hatt[40] designed a study of occupations, asking a cross-section of Americans to rank the prestige of each. Not surprisingly, professionals ranked highest and laborers ranked lowest. Table 9–4 comes from a study done in 1963. There is virtually no difference between these rankings and those done sixteen years earlier. Robert Hodges, Paul Siegel, and Peter Rossi[41] argued that there hadn't been much change in occupational rankings from smaller studies done back in 1925. Alex Inkeles and Peter Rossi[42] found that whether we study the United States or other industrialized nations such as Great Britain, New Zealand, Japan, Germany, or the Soviet Union, the rankings come out essentially the same way. *By and large* the most prestigious jobs pay the most. Obviously, this isn't always the case. It's often been suggested that in America one can start out as a street sweeper and become a college professor—if he's willing to take the drop in salary.) Do you see any pattern to the list of occupational ratings in Table 9–4 (pages 256–257) that would account for the higher income and prestige of some and the low prestige and income of others?

Why Stratification?

Kingsley Davis and Wilbert Moore[43] have offered a "functional" explanation of stratification that may help account for what's in Table 9–4. They are attempting to show that stratification is necessary and makes a vital contribution to the survival and continuation of society, that stratification is a "functional necessity." In 1945 Davis and Moore, in a classic article, suggested that all societies have tasks that they must accomplish in order to survive. Therefore, society must instill in its members the desire to occupy those social positions most important for the maintenance of society. Individual motivation is the key to the *society's* survival. The most effective way to create motivation is through the use of rewards. Rewards and their distribution become part of the social order and thus give rise to social ranking. If a carrot is provided for those who do socially important tasks, it's believed that people will strive to do them. This is the foundation of the American Dream.

Rewards in American society, according to Davis and Moore, reflect Max Weber's three-dimensional notions of ranking. People are *economically* rewarded with luxury. *A style of life* of entertainment and of gracious living are made possible. *Social honor* is bestowed upon important individuals. Rewards are, therefore, built into the position. Implicit in the Davis and Moore argument is the notion that social inequality is necessary for a society to survive. "Social inequality," they observed, "is thus an unconsciously evolved device by which societies insure that the most important positions are conscientiously filled by the most qualified persons. Hence, every society, no matter how simple or complex, must differentiate persons in terms of both prestige and esteem, and must therefore possess a certain amount of institutionalized inequality."

The highest rewards, then, must go to those with the most complicated and important jobs. Doctors, who spend years in training and can save lives, are to be afforded high honor, life styles, and income. Persons with easier, unskilled tasks receive much less.

Once again, however, other sociologists do not interpret events in the same way. Melvin Tumin[44] and others look at the same chart, but they don't see any functional necessity for such prestige and income. Davis and Moore's analysis stood for some eight years prior to Tumin's analysis of *functional inequality*. Tumin disagreed on seven basic points.

Tumin suggested that inequality was neither necessarily good nor functional for society. In fact, he reasoned that inequality is merely a description of what "is" rather than what "has to be." The singling out of certain tasks as important is valuative and not objective. Anyone with a good style of life is going to be able to concoct plausible reasons for why he's worth the money, but these reasons are not necessarily evidence for his value. Many highly paid, prestigious occupations are not necessary for the survival of society. For example, the members of the recently demised Internal Subversion Control Commission were paid $28,500 annually. The body, however, had not met for ten years. There are many other examples of well-paid jobs that are not functionally important or that require years of training but are not well paid. If we are to judge a job's importance to society by its salary, what do we make of the fact that the presidents of companies like General Motors or ITT make much more than the President of the United States?

Tumin also questioned the need for great economic rewards for long periods of training. College life, he said, is pleasant. Certainly people don't earn much money during the apprenticeship period, but the style of life is rewarding.

Important jobs are also enjoyable. People become lawyers, doctors, or college professors not solely for the economic rewards. Nor would people cease entering these professions if the external rewards were decreased.

The "scarcity of personnel" argument used to justify inequality he also considered dubious. Tumin contended that society *does not know* the number of talented people it has. Indeed, many people with potential have been excluded from many well-rewarded positions. Women have been discouraged from becoming brain surgeons. Blacks were not welcome in executive suites until recent years. Consequently, inequality is not just a matter of mere scarcity of personnel, according to Tumin.

Finally, the debate between Tumin and Davis-Moore boiled down to the classic difference of "ought to be" versus "is." Davis-Moore described what existed. Tumin suggested that stratification is not necessary to society.

The original subjects in the North-Hatt study were asked, "When you say certain jobs have 'excellent standing,' what do you think is the one main thing about such jobs that gives this standing?" The answers appear in Table

Table 9-4. Occupational Ranks and Prestige Scores

Source: R. W., Hodges, P. M. Siegel, and P. H. Rossi, "Occupational Prestige in the United States, 1925–1963," *American Journal of Sociology,* **70:** (1974), 286–302. Reprinted with permission of the author and the publisher. Copyright 1964, University of Chicago Press.

	Rank	Occupation	Prestige Score
	1	U.S. Supreme Court Justice	94
	2	Physician	93
Tied	3.5	Nuclear physicist	92
	3.5	Scientist	92
Tied	5.5	Government scientist	91
	5.5	State governor	91
Tied	8	Cabinet member in the federal government	90
	8	College professor	90
	8	United States Representative in Congress	90
Tied	11	Chemist	89
	11	Lawyer	89
	11	Diplomat in U.S. foreign service	89
Tied	14	Dentist	88
	14	Architect	88
	14	County judge	88
Tied	17.5	Psychologist	87
	17.5	Minister	87
	17.5	Member of the board of directors of a large corporation	87
Tied	21.5	Priest	86
	21.5	Head of a department in a state government	86
	21.5	Civil engineer	86
	21.5	Airline pilot	86
Tied	24.5	Banker	85
	24.5	Biologist	85
	26	Sociologist	83
Tied	27.5	Instructor in public schools	82
	27.5	Captain in regular army	82
Tied	29.5	Public school teacher	81
	29.5	Accountant for a large business	81
Tied	31.5	Owner of a factory that employs about 100 people	80
	31.5	Building contractor	80
Tied	34.5	Artist who paints pictures exhibited in galleries	78
	34.5	Musician in symphony orchestra	78
	34.5	Author of novels	78
	34.5	Economist	78
	37	Official of an international labor union	77
Tied	39	Railroad engineer	76
	39	Electrician	76
	39	County agricultural agent	76
Tied	41.5	Owner-operator of a printing shop	75
	41.5	Trained machinist	75
Tied	44	Farm owner and operator	74
	44	Undertaker	74
	44	Welfare worker for city government	74
	46	Newspaper columnist	73
	47	Policeman	72

Rank		Occupation	Prestige Score
	48	Reporter on a daily newspaper	71
Tied	49.5	Radio announcer	70
Tied	49.5	Bookkeeper	70
Tied	51.5	Tenant farmer (one who owns livestock and machinery and manages the farm)	69
Tied	51.5	Insurance agent	69
	53	Carpenter	68
Tied	54.5	Manager of a small store in a city	67
Tied	54.5	A local official of a labor union	67
Tied	57	Mail carrier	66
Tied	57	Railroad conductor	66
Tied	57	Traveling salesman for a wholesale concern	66
	59	Plumber	65
	60	Automobile repairman	64
Tied	62.5	Playground director	63
Tied	62.5	Barber	63
Tied	62.5	Machine operator in a factory	63
	61.5	Owner-operator of a lunch stand	63
Tied	65.5	Corporal in regular army	62
Tied	65.5	Garage mechanic	62
	67	Truck driver	59
	68	Fisherman who owns his own boat	58
Tied	70	Clerk in a store	56
Tied	70	Milk route man	56
Tied	70	Streetcar motorman	56
Tied	72.5	Lumberjack	55
Tied	72.5	Restaurant cook	55
	74	Singer in a nightclub	54
	75	Filling station attendant	52
Tied	77.5	Dockworker	50
Tied	77.5	Railroad section hand	50
Tied	77.5	Night watchman	50
Tied	77.5	Coal miner	50
Tied	80.5	Restaurant waiter	49
Tied	80.5	Taxi driver	49
Tied	83	Farmhand	48
Tied	83	Janitor	48
Tied	83	Bartender	48
	85	Clothes presser in a laundry	45
	86	Soda fountain clerk	44
	87	Sharecropper (one who owns no livestock or equipment and does not manage farm)	42
	88	Garbage collector	39
	89	Street sweeper	36
	90	Shoeshiner	34

Table 9–5. Comparison of Viewpoints on Stratification of Davis-Moore and Tumin

Davis-Moore Points

1. Some occupations are more important than others and require special skills and training.
2. Only a certain number of people have the skills necessary to perform these important tasks.
3. Learning the skills necessary to perform important tasks requires many years of training during which sacrifices are made.
4. To attract people into these complicated, but important, positions higher rewards must be offered.
5. These rewards consist of social honor, wealth, and a style of life that is attached to a social position.
6. Different rewards for different tasks lead to inequality and social ranking.
7. Social inequality is both *positive* and *functional* and exists in every society.

Tumin Points

1. The importance of a task is not objective; rather it depends upon social values.
2. It is impossible to identify all of the talented people in a society. Many persons are excluded from competing for prestigious positions.
3. The sacrifices of those in high-status positions are not as great as the rewards they receive.
4. Other motivations, such as "joy in work," also induce people to occupy these positions.
5. Stratification tends to perpetuate itself. People in advantageous positions continue in them.
6. Inequalities create a climate of hostility, suspicion, and conflict in society.
7. Society gives its greatest rewards for conformity and "playing the game," whereas the greatest contributions to society are made by nonconformists.

9–6. They would seem to give more support to Davis and Moore than to Tumin. Actually, we needn't insist that one side or the other has the only answer, especially in the most exaggerated forms of both arguments; there's merit to both sides. Davis and Moore appear to be right in arguing that if we want people to take on jobs that have a lot of responsibility and require a lot of training, somehow we'll have to reward then for doing so. Tumin appears to be right in arguing that the difference in rewards between the most important jobs and the least important jobs (as judged by the community) do not have

Table 9–6. North-Hatt Study: Attributes of Jobs with Excellent Standing"

Attribute	Percent
The job pays well.	18%
It serves humanity; it is an essential job.	16
Preparation requires much education, hard work, and money.	14
The job carries social prestige.	14
It requires high moral standards, honesty, responsibility.	9
It requires intelligence and ability.	9
It provides security, steady work.	5
The job has a good future; the field is not overcrowded.	3
The job is pleasant, safe, and easy.	2
It affords maximum chance for initiative and freedom.	0[a]
Miscellaneous answers; don't know; no answer.	10
	100%

[a] Less than .05%.

to be as great as they are to get people to take the more important ones. Prestige, power, and autonomy *are* rewards after all.

How Many Classes?

Marx argued that there are two (dominant historical) classes, those who own the means of production and those who do not. For his purposes, both intellectual and political, and for his time and place, perhaps this was sufficient. For sociologists this is just too simple a distinction. In examining contemporary industrial societies, particularly the United States, which has no hereditary ruling class, we find that Marx's classification does not seem to fit, although no other classification is a *natural* one either. Shall we base our classification on income and say that there are three classes: an upper class, a middle class, and lower class? What's the dividing line between middle and upper—$25,000 a year, or $50,000, or $100,000? Between middle and lower—$3,000, or $6,000, or $4,500? In certain respects any of those dividing lines will be equally useful in making predictions about people. In other respects any of those dividing lines ignores differences in life styles among people with the same income levels and makes predictions impossible. We won't go into the technicalities of constructing a social class scale here, but let's point out two things about the way sociologists describe and study "social class." First, the different classifications—whether they are as simple as "blue collar" versus "white collar," "rich" versus "poor," "college" versus "noncollege," or as complex as the indices that combine occupational prestige and education and income to define "upper-uppers" through "lower-lowers" in five or six or thirteen steps—*are all arbitrary*. They're *convenient* classifications that the researcher makes according to what his study involves, such as TV watching, taste, divorce rates, favorite perfume or Scotch, suicide rates, and so on. No one method of classification is really the "true" and "only" way of defining "class."

Second, it doesn't seem to matter whether we use one measure or another. By and large, *however* we measure "class," the findings come out pretty much the same way.[45] The lower classes, the middle classes, and the upper classes seem to live in different worlds, tend to have different beliefs, values, and attitudes.[46]

Power: The Third Dimension

When the creators of the Declaration of Independence and the U.S. Constitution set up shop, they did not believe they had any business trying to eliminate social and economic inequality. They did feel that political inequality (at least among white male property owners) was to be guarded against.

However much contemporary Americans accept the idea of economic and social inequality, we would like to believe that we have or can have a government "by the people and for the people." The government is the legal possessor of a good deal of power. We would like to believe this power is used for our benefit and that the government is responsive to our wishes.

The suggestions by Floyd Hunter and C. Wright Mills[47] in the 1950s that a "power elite" runs the country generated a good deal of controversy and a good deal of research. But as William Kornhauser[48] noted, whatever the differences of opinion between those who believe that *one* small, cohesive elite dominates America and those who believe instead that *several* counterbalancing elites *share* the power, both schools of thought are agreed that wherever power lies, it is hardly in the hands of *"the people."* The issue for students of power in American society is how many and what *groups* have power. They agree that unorganized individuals have little power.

Floyd Hunter's book *Community Power Structure,* which stimulated most of the studies of "power structures," revealed that "Regional City" (Atlanta, Georgia) was ruled by a small, cohesive, conspiratorial elite of businessmen, most of whom were not in public office.[49] This group, *the community power structure,* devised the major policies of the city, frequently during informal meetings at lunch. The business leaders of the community, Hunter found, exercised more power than the elected officials (who merely put the business leaders' plans into operation). Hunter had in essence found a ruling-class elite that was independent of the electorate. The voters, of course, had no control over the business leaders of Regional City.

A report on the way business leaders in Dayton, Ohio went about instituting scattered-site open housing is a mild illustration of the sort of thing Hunter found in Atlanta:

From his office high above this mid-America city, the elderly gentleman gazes out on the metropolitan landscape as he considers whether to answer. After a few moments, he smiles knowingly at the visitor and declares, "well, sooner or later, yes."

This simple reply from Frank Anger tells quite a lot about Dayton. It says the city, "sooner or later," will become the first in the nation to successfully scatter subsidized rental housing throughout its surrounding suburbs. And it tells why: because the business elite that holds the reins of power here believes in the idea.

Mr. Anger, retired chief executive officer of Winters National Bank and Trust Co., has been a member of that elite for a long time and knows its inner workings intimately. So, when he says "yes" he means he expects current opposition to subsidized housing among the southern suburbs to crumble in time under pressure from the business community.

No one is more aware of the essentiality of that community to the dispersal plan's success than the planning team that developed it—Dale F. Bertsch, director of the Miami Valley Regional Planning Commission, and his side-kick, Ann Shafor. "Without the support of the business community and the newspapers," Mr. Bertsch declares, "we'd have published a technical dissertation that would not have been carried out in action."

In this city, governed by a city manager and council, there is no strong political force. So, when action is required, it is the newspapers and the business elites that call the turn. The two work in tandem. Jim Fain, editor of *The Daily,* one of the two newspapers here, and a leading advocate of dispersal, is this year's chairman of the Area Progress Council, a select group of business leaders created in the early 1960s to give form to its management of community affairs.

The 30-or-so leaders meet on the first Saturday of each month at National Cash Register Co.'s quest facility, a farm in suburban Kettering. Though the group cherishes a "low profile," some of its deliberations are known. Late in 1968, after the 1966–67 uprisings in West Dayton's black slums, the APC assigned priority status to low- and moderate-income housing, among other concerns. The riots imparted a sense of "urgency" to the discussions, remembers Mr. Fain. . . .

(1) Most of the city's black population—about one-third of Dayton's total population of 243,000 is black—was crowded into the west side slum. Those blacks escaping the inner city were moving west and north into suburbia, largely into Jefferson Township, with neighboring Madison Township as the next likely escape route.

(2) Most of the area's subsidized housing was within the city limits, mainly in black neighborhoods. In 1969, all but 158 of the existing 3,137 subsidized rental units were within Dayton's borders. Further subsidized construction within the city would only have compounded the concentration of the poor and the black, and denied them access to jobs in suburbia.

(3) Subsidized housing sponsors seeking entry to suburbia were being rebuffed, setting up a confrontation situation. If the sponsors won any victories at all, they surely would come, because of the economics of the land and housing, in the working-class communities to the north and west of Dayton, threatening inundation and continued racial and economic concentration. The more affluent southern suburbs seemed solid and safe, as did the outlying rural counties.

Enter Dale Bertsch, Ann Shafor, and the Miami Valley Regional Planning Commission, or MVRPC, created in 1964 as the agency responsible for coordinating the expenditure of federal dollars in the area, which covers five member counties and 30 member municipalities. The Bertsch-Shafor team took seriously the federal mandate to study housing needs in the region. In 1968–69, at the request of mayors of close-in suburbs threatened by black expansion, MVRPC turned to housing:

Conclusion: The region was short some 14,000 low- and moderate-income units. The only way to convince suburbia to open its doors to such construction was a "fair share" plan of assigned quotas to limit the influx of housing in the north and west while opening up the south and east. "What the numbers do is show a community's quota in relation to others," explains Mr. Bertsch, "and thereby relieve the anxiety of suburbanites that they will be inundated."

The concept of accelerating production of subsidized housing and scattering it throughout the central city and the five-county region was cleared, informally, with the Area Progress Council ("Everything must be plugged into them," says Mr. Bertsch). . . .

The skirmishing is conducted in full public view, before citizens groups, by votes of local governing councils, and, in some cases, in the courts. Behind the trenches, however, hovers the "low profile" of the business elite, not always easy to discern but very definitely there.

Oakwood, a southern suburb that is home to a number of the elite, is a case in point. MVRPC chose this affluent community to become the first to join the plan, but angry residents overwhelmingly disapproved of the idea. When it came time for the city council to vote, however, it unanimously pledged participation, and set the course for other suburban jurisdictions.

"We had to make sure the first domino fell right, not wrong," remembers Mr. Bertsch. Does this mean the elite told Oakwood officials how to vote? Some office-holders do require "philosophical discussions," Mr. Fain concedes, but arm-twisting is not the elite's preferred style. Nor is it usually necessary, for when the elite reaches a consensus, it knows how to communicate.

Early in the game when APC assigned priority status to housing, George Sheer held a series of breakfasts with area leaders to inquire about the problem. The Chamber of Commerce, an arm of the elite, pledged $50,000 from a golf tournament as seed money for subsidized housing. The Junior League, consisting mostly of wives and daughters of APC members, also put up seed money and supported dispersal: "We decided to get into controversial issues and chose housing," explains past president Jean Mahoney, whose husband is president of the company that publishes both Dayton newspapers and an APC member as well. . . .

"Most people now know that the sainted fathers of the community are for integrated housing," says Mr. Fain today. "And so the dominoes continue to fall right." [50]

Hunter's study was criticized by many, who argued that he depended too much on anecdotes and gossip about who had power. Political scientist Robert Dahl,[51] in *Who Governs?,* argued that it would be more useful to study actual political decisions in a community, to find out who won when there were disagreements over these specific issues, and to find out what role different groups played in the outcome.

Whereas Hunter's study of Atlanta showed one single group involved in the important decisions, Dahl's study of New Haven showed that who has the power *depended on the issue.* No group won all the time, nor was there any one group that cared about all of the issues. (The three issues he focused on were urban planning and development, public school policy, and political nominations.) Dahl suggested that in New Haven, at least, a "polyarchy" existed rather than the "oligarchy" Hunter found. (An *oligarchy* is a single ruling group; a *polyarchy* is made up of a number of competing groups that influence governmental decisions.)

As Dahl saw New Haven, it was a *pluralist* system, by which he meant that the competing groups (composing the polyarchy) had roughly equal amounts of power and roughly equal opportunities to get community decisions to come out in their favor.

A pluralist system is more "democratic" than an elitist system in that more groups get a chance to have their say in any community decision-making. What Dahl found was closer to the sort of model of politics that the civics textbooks present: each citizen *through his groups*—political, professional, or trade groups, unions, and so on—has an equal say in community affairs.

The debate between "pluralists" and "elitists" frequently took the form of arguing from single case studies to the nation: "If city *X* is pluralist (elitist), *all* cities must be pluralist (elitist)." Obviously, one shouldn't argue from one case to all cities, but there was and still is a good deal of research that takes this form. There has also been a good deal of suspicion that what one finds depends more on his research methods than on the actual situation in the city he studies. Reputational studies (studies that ask people who they believe runs the city or who has a reputation for having power) seem to find more community elites than do studies that examine actual decisions and issues in a given city. Apparently there is no single *true* answer to the question of who runs our cities and communities.

Whether there is one single group (almost always business leaders) or several groups (business leaders plus political leaders, union leaders, and various organizational leaders) seems to depend on a number of variables. John Walton[52] suggests that up to now these four variables have been found to be the most important:

1. Communities economically dominated by organizations that have *absentee owners* tend to be *more pluralistic* than those whose economy is dominated by *locally owned* businesses.
2. Communities with *adequate economic resources* (a prosperous business community and low rates of poverty and unemployment) tend to be *more pluralistic* than those that have *inadequate economic resources* (underdevelopment, with high rates of poverty and unemployment).
3. *Satellite cities* (suburbs or towns dominated by a nearby city) tend to be *more pluralistic* than *independent cities* (central cities in metropolitan areas, and independent manufacturing, commercial, or agricultural centers).
4. Communities that have *two or more political parties* that regularly compete for public office tend to be *more pluralistic* than those that are *one-party communities.*

The Power Elite

Many sociologists have argued that the power structure in *single cities* doesn't really matter much. In other words, power at the *national* level is what really counts.

Probably the most controversial book ever published about power at the national level was C. Wright Mills's *The Power Elite* (1956). He suggested that America was run by a small group of men who formulated nearly all of the nation's policy but who, like the Regional City businessmen, were not accountable (or known) to the public.

Mills portrayed America as moving away from the period of the small town-meeting and the small competing interest groups ushered in by the American Revolution. In the 1890s, one group, the industrialists, grabbed the most power in America. However, the economic crisis of the 1930s and the rise of the New Deal cut down on the direct political influence of the wealthy and powerful. Millionaires and titans of industry were no longer held in high public regard. World War II restored corporate powers and also gave rise to the Cold War strategy. In the planning process, the military became an essential element. Mills suggested that there existed a power elite consisting of "those who occupy the command posts." Three groups constituted these positions: the military leaders, the corporation directors, and the government planners and executives. This power elite formulated all *important* public policy. They did so with little regard for others. Unlike Hunter in his report from Regional City, Mills did not see any conspiracy. Rather, he proposed a "coincidence of interests" among the admirals and generals and the corporate and public executives. They had much in common in their schooling, religious beliefs, and backgrounds. This common ground created a psychological and social similarity that allowed ease of communication. They drank and ate together and formulated policy. *Below* the power elite existed two other levels of power.

Congressmen, interest groups, and others, according to Mills, were the "middle levels of power." They did not formulate policy; they only passed judgment upon it. Indeed, Mills described the middle levels of power as merely "rubber stamps" of the decisions of the power elite.

Directly under the middle level lay the "masses." The masses were presented as essentially powerless and swayed by the elite's ability to manipulate the popular culture media. The people did not have access to television or newspapers except as viewers or readers.

Mills would probably have considered the following newspaper article *partial* evidence for his views, but he would have considered this only the "tip of the iceberg" (most of the iceberg, of course, being under water and out of sight):

> Hundreds of generals, high-level civil servants, commissioners and Congressmen each year switch from government jobs to closely related careers in private industry.
>
> Some of them live in two worlds, moving easily back and forth between government and industry—a pool of skilled professionals who alternate between sensitive political posts and high-salaried positions in business.
>
> Only last week, for example, Clark MacGregor, who served as President Nixon's campaign director, was named a vice-president in the Washington office of the United Aircraft Corporation, a major defense contractor.
>
> Occasionally, influential job switchers are caught up in a swirl of controversy, as the ethics of their dual existence is questioned.
>
> But generally there is little sense of outrage at their behavior, and, indeed, few proven cases of outright impropriety—perhaps because influence peddling is accepted as part of an old American tradition that says: "I can get it for you wholesale."

The moral question continues to be raised, however, each time these officials trade their military hats, spartan government offices, and modest salaries for plush, carpeted suites and quantum jumps in pay. Are they simply fostering a smoother relationship between business and government, as some suggest?

Or are they taking unfair advantage of a system that allows them to misuse their expertise and former contacts on behalf of a private corporate interest?

Ralph Nader, the consumer advocate, scoffs at the practice as "deferred bribes" and suggests that too often there is a cozy relationship between regulators and regulatees, between buyers and vendors.

Stewart L. Udall, a former Secretary of the Interior, adds that the abuses fostered by such mobility make it "incestuous and corrupting."

Most of the government officials who switch, however, Republicans and Democrats alike, defend their action as both legally and morally proper and deny that they are capitalizing on their former government connections.

Indeed, many of them question whether the government could operate effectively without such an infusion of talent from private industry.

"The government needs businessmen, and business needs the people who leave the government," said Robert N. Anthony, Assistant Secretary of Defense from 1965 to 1968. Professor Anthony returned to Harvard University's Graduate School of Business Administration after leaving the Defense Department. . . .

Is it morally proper for the former Commissioner of a Federal regulatory agency to reappear before his fellow Commissioners as a highly paid lobbyist on the other side of the table?

What are the ethical connotations of former Administration aids, who are now representing corporate interests, still holding broad powers within the party in office, and maintaining close links with the White House?

There are myriad examples of high-level job switches, some of them controversial, and others little publicized. . . .

So vast is the movement of government officials to closely allied fields that such shifts must be considered typical rather than atypical. Indeed, some government officials estimate that as many as 200,000 Federal employees at all levels leave their jobs each year.[53]

The interchangeability of these people seems to lend some support to Mills's argument about the "coincidence of interests" of a segment of American society. Other events, like the rise of the "super law firms" and of course the Watergate scandal, where a handful of men attempted to bend the power of the government for their own individual interests, also seem to ratify Mills's view of American power.[54] David Riesman dissented from the view that a power elite existed, however.

Veto Groups

David Riesman's characterization of American power relations in *The Lonely Crowd* was presented as an alternative to the idea of a power elite.[55] Riesman argued that American society has changed from one based on strong individual aggressiveness to a more socially oriented one. The *inner-directed* captain of industry who fought his way to success has been replaced by the "go along to get along" *other-directed* organization man. This product of the 1950s is always attuned to the cues of correct behavior from his environment. Riesman believed that the power of industrialists had faded. They had been replaced by a series of *veto groups,* who engaged in politics to protect and enhance their own interests. "The old-time captain of industry . . . was also the captain of politics . . . . none of them could get very far in the Alice in Wonderland croquet game of the veto groups."

Veto groups organize to block the actions of those who would threaten them. Conservationists oppose energy lobbies in the back rooms of Congress. Through

Table 9–7. Two Portraits of the American Power Structure

Power Structure	*Mills*	*Riesman*
Levels	a. Unified power elite b. Diversified and balanced plurality of interest groups c. Mass of unorganized people who have no power over elite	a. No dominant power elite b. Diversified and balanced plurality of interest groups c. Mass of unorganized people who have some power over interest groups
Changes	a. Increasing concentration of power	a. Increasing dispersion of power
Operation	a. One group who determine all major policies b. Manipulation of people at the bottom by group at the top	a. People holding positions that determine policy shift with the issue b. Monopolistic competition among organized groups
Bases	a. Coincidence of interests among major institutions (economic, military, governmental) b. Social similarities and psychological affinities among those who direct major institutions	a. Diversity of interests among major organized groups b. Sense of weakness and dependence among those in higher as well as lower status
Consequences	a. Enhancement of interests of corporations, armed forces, and executive branch of government b. Decline of politics as public debate c. Decline of responsibility and accountable power—loss of democracy	a. No one group or class favored significantly over others b. Decline of politics as duty and self-interest c. Decline of effective leadership

Source: Reprinted with permission of the Macmillan Company from "'Power Elite' or 'Veto Groups,'" by William Kornhauser, in *Class, Status, and Power* by Reinhard Bendix and Seymour Martin Lipset. Copyright 1966 by the Free Press, Division of the Macmillan Company. p. 215.

the use of the mass media they attempt to sway public opinion. Each veto group pursues its own interests through the *legislative process.*

Riesman contended that no one group has total control. Veto groups win a few, lose a few. They have diverse interests that coalesce on certain issues. Riesman attributed this trend to the decline of the economically, as well as morally, driven individualists of the past. No longer is a man driven by an ultimate goal; rather he is motivated by a spirit of getting along with others. In the sphere of power, this spirit calls for *sharing* rather than *domination.*

Who is right—the elitist writers who claim that unseen forces govern or the advocates of pluralism who see competing groups wielding power? The answer depends partly on one's ideology and one's research methods. Kornhauser suggested that both Mills and Riesman were biased, in opposite directions:

> Mills' major premise seems to be that all decisions are taken by and for special interests; there is no action oriented toward the general interests of the whole community. Furthermore, Mills seems to argue that because only a very few people occupy key decision-making positions, they are free to decide on whatever best suits their particular interests. But the degree of autonomy of decision-makers cannot be inferred from the number of decision-makers, nor from the scope of their decisions. It also is determined by the character of decision-making, especially the dependence of decision-makers on certain kinds of procedure and support. Just as Mills is presenting a distorted image of power in America when he fails to consider the pressures on those in high positions, so Riesman presents a biased picture by not giving sufficient attention to power differentials among the various groups in society. When Riesman implies that if power is dispersed, then it must be relatively equal among groups and interests, with no points of concentration, he is making an unwarranted inference.[56]

Perhaps the most reasonable thing we can say is that the distribution of power at the national level is now a more complicated matter than the Mills-Riesman debate allows for. Whatever future research turns up, for the moment our response to both schools of thought is the Scotch verdict of "not proven."

Mobility

In a "class" system there are no legal barriers to mobility, to moving up or down from the position one's father had. In a perfectly "open" system, the opportunities for mobility would be equal: the son of the president of General Motors would be as likely to end up making his living as a migrant worker as the son of a migrant worker to end up president of General Motors. To put it another way, in a *perfectly open* system, the occupational status of one's parents would have *absolutely no effect* on one's own occupational status. In a perfectly closed system, the status of one's parents would be the *only* factor to determine one's own status.

There has never been either a *perfectly* open system or a *perfectly* closed one. All societies are somewhere in between both extremes.

Societies vary in the amount of *social mobility* possible. The concept of *social mobility* was introduced by the Harvard sociologist Pitirim A. Sorokin.[57] Social mobility is the passage of individuals from one social rank to another. The movement can be *horizontal* or *vertical.*

Horizontal mobility is the shifting of an individual from one social group to another at the *same level.* Moving from one major-league baseball team to another or from one minor-league team to another is horizontal mobility. A professor transferring from a highly respected university like Yale to another highly respected university like Harvard is another example.

Vertical mobility involves a move from one social group to another at a *different level,* when a person goes up or down on the stratification ladder. A player moves up from the minor leagues to play for the New York Yankees or the Detroit Tigers. A professor moves from Jock Strap University to Berkeley or Harvard. Both instances are examples of *upward vertical mobility.*

On the other hand, leaving the majors for the minors, say the Tigers for the Toledo Mud Hens or leaving Harvard for a job at Jock Strap University is an instance of *downward vertical mobility.*

The American Dream stresses *upward vertical mobility.* The sociological question, then, becomes, "Is it a myth or a fact?"

When a teacher tells his fifth-graders that each one of them has a chance to become President of the United States, is a black, brown, or yellow girl making a mistake in offering to sell a white boy *her* chance to be President for a quarter?

Most sociological studies indicate that social mobility is more than ever very much a part of American life. S. M. Lipset, in a 1972 review of research on mobility, suggested, "The pattern of opportunity in American society clearly indicates that there has been no decline in social mobility; in fact, in some respects American society is *less* rigid in terms of social advancement than it was in the past."[58]

For example, *Scientific American* reported in 1964 that only 10.5 percent of leading big business executives were from wealthy families, as opposed to 45.6 percent in 1900. In 1964, 23.3 percent of successful business executives had economically "poor" backgrounds.[59]

The most thorough study we have is Peter M. Blau and Otis Dudley Duncan's 1962 survey of 20,700 American men.[60] According to this study, the major route to upward mobility is education. The child of a small farmer or laborer who goes to college, particularly if he receives graduate training, is likely to occupy a much higher social ranking than his parents. The size of one's family also influences upward mobility. People from smaller families are more upwardly mobile than those from larger families. Place of residence equally affects mobility, with urban dwellers enjoying a higher social mobility rate than rural residents.

There are several other factors that predict mobility. Father's education, father's occupational level, one's own education, and the kind of job he takes for his first job are particularly important. We have developed mathematical formulas that tell us how much weight to give to each of these factors if we want to predict someone's occupational status. Unfortunately, these formulas apply only to whites. When we match blacks and whites on these predictors of occupational status (that is, hold these factors *constant*), we find that somehow we don't predict very well for blacks. In fact, when we hold occupational status, education, IQ, family background, and so on constant, we find that there is *still* a difference between blacks and whites of roughly $1,400.[61] In other words, discrimination leads to our having *two* stratification systems. Reinhold Bendix and S. M. Lipset's study of mobility published in 1959 reported: "Today there are two working classes in America, a white working class and a Negro, Mexican, and a Puerto Rican one. A real social and economic cleavage is created by widespread discrimination against these minority groups.[62] Peter Blau and Otis Duncan, writing in 1967, found similar conditions. Duncan, Featherman, and Duncan indicated pretty much the same thing in 1972.[63]

Table 9–8. Transition Percentages, Father's Occupation to 1962 (Condensed Classification), by Race, for Civilian Men 25–64 Years Old, March 1962

	1962 Occupation[a]						Total	
Race and Father's Occupation[a]	*Higher White Collar (1)*	*Lower White Collar (2)*	*Higher Manual (3)*	*Lower Manual (4)*	*Farm (5)*	*NA (7)*	*Percent*	*Number (000)*
Negro								
Higher white collar (1)	10.4	9.7	19.4	53.0	0.0	7.5	100.0	134
Lower white collar (2)	14.5	9.1	0.0	69.1	0.0	7.3	100.0	55
Higher manual (3)	8.8	6.8	11.2	64.1	2.8	6.4	100.0	251
Lower manual (4)	8.0	7.0	11.5	63.2	1.8	8.4	100.0	973
Farm (5)	3.1	3.0	6.4	59.8	16.2	11.6	100.0	1,389
NA (6)	2.4	6.5	11.1	65.9	3.1	11.1	100.0	712
Total, percent	5.2	5.4	9.5	62.2	7.7	10.0	100.0	–
Total, number (000)	182	190	334	2,184	272	352	–	3,514
Non-Negro								
Higher white collar (1)	54.3	15.3	11.5	11.9	1.3	5.6	100.0	5,836
Lower white collar (2)	45.1	18.3	13.5	14.6	1.5	7.1	100.0	2,652
Higher manual (3)	28.1	11.8	27.9	24.0	1.0	7.3	100.0	6,512
Lower manual (4)	21.3	11.5	22.5	36.0	1.7	6.9	100.0	8,798
Farm (5)	16.5	7.0	19.8	28.8	20.4	7.5	100.0	9,991
NA (6)	26.0	10.3	21.0	32.5	3.9	6.4	100.0	2,666
Total, percent	28.6	11.3	20.2	26.2	6.8	6.9	100.0	–
Total, number (000)	10,414	4,130	7,359	9,560	2,475	2,517	–	36,455

[a](1) Professional, technical, and kindred workers; managers, officials, and proprietors, except farm; (2) sales workers; clerical and kindred workers; (3) craftsmen, foremen, and kindred workers; (4) operatives and kindred workers; service workers; laborers, except farm; (5) farmers and farm managers; farm laborers and foremen; (6) father's occupation not reported; (7) respondent not in experienced civilian labor force.

Source: O. D. Duncan, D. L. Featherman, and B. Duncan, *Socioeconomic Background and Achievement* (New York: Seminar Press, 1972), Table 4–2, p. 56.

Table 9–9. Mobility into Elite (Upper-White-Collar) Occupations[a]

	Percentage of All Men in Elite	Manual Class into Elite	Middle Class into Elite
Denmark	3.30%	1.07%	4.58%
France	8.53	3.52	12.50
Japan	11.74	6.95	15.12
USA	11.60	9.91	20.90
W. Germany	4.58	1.46	8.28

[a]Note: Rates of mobility have to be considered in terms of the elite occupational slots *available,* i.e., in terms of the percentage of all men in the elite.

Source: Peter Blau and Otis Duncan, *The American Occupational Structure* (New York: John Wiley & Sons, Inc., 1967), Table 12.1, p. 43.

Table 9–8, for example, indicates that white men typically tend to move up to higher status jobs if they start from lowly origins. If they start out at higher levels they tend to remain at higher levels. Blacks, regardless of origin, tend to end up at lower level manual jobs.

This is not to say that education is useless for minority group members who seek mobility—quite the opposite. But even if they do all the things whites do in order to be mobile, it's going to make a good deal less difference as long as we continue to let *ascribed* characteristics like race interfere with what, for whites, is a system based more or less on achievement.

Recent census figures indicate that the gaps between black and white income *are* diminishing very rapidly at the middle-class level.[64] The 1970 census indicated that for the first time in America's history there were more middle-class than lower-class blacks. For those who were poor, on the other hand, unemployment and income figures, particularly for families without a male head, indicated that things were not improving.

How does American mobility compare to that of other nations? By and large, quite well. The data we have available for comparing mobility across nations is quite crude; basically it makes possible studies only of movement from blue-collar occupations to white-collar occupations (and vice versa). If we examine the data in Table 9–9, we find that the United States is at least as "open" as any other nation. This openness is found when people try to reach "elite positions" such as well-paying professional, managerial, or technical jobs. The United States is *not* as open as most of us would like to believe.[65] People still cannot find the jobs they want. People cannot always work or live where they want to. Nonetheless, the data suggest that the "is" may be slowly moving closer to the "ought to be" of an open social system.

Summary

Social stratification is the ranking of social positions on a scale of high to low. Stratification may be measured in the areas of economics, prestige, and political power. In each area there are those on the "bottom" and those on the "top." There exist the wealthy and the poor, the powerful and the powerless, those we look up to and others we are totally unimpressed with. These are the highs and lows of social stratification.

In societies with *ascribed* status, people are born and die in the same position.

Table 9–10. Sex, Marriage, and Life Style[a]

	Highbrow	*Upper Middlebrow*	*Lower Middlebrow*	*Lowbrow*
How Girl Meets Boy	He was an usher at her best friend's wedding.	At college, in the psychology lab.	In the office, by the water cooler.	On the block.
The Proposal	In his room during the Harvard-Princeton game.	In the back seat of a Volkswagen.	After three drinks in an apartment he borrowed.	In her room one night when Mom and Dad were at the movies.
The Wedding	In her living room, by a federal judge.	College chapel (nondenominational).	City Hall.	Neighborhood church.
The Honeymoon	Mediterranean.	Bahamas.	Any Hilton Hotel.	Disneyland.
Marriage Manual	*Kama Sutra.*	*Sexual Efficiency in Marriage,* Volumes I and II.	Van de Velde.	None.
Sex Novels She Reads	Jane Austen.	*Lady Chatterley's Lover.*	*Myra Breckinridge* and any novel by Harold Robbins.	*Valley of the Dolls.*
Sleeping Arrangements	Double bed.	King-size bed or twin beds with one headboard.	Twin beds with matching night tables.	Double bed.
Sleeping Attire	He: nothing. She: nothing.	He: red turtleneck nightshirt. She: gown with matching peignoir.	He: pajamas. She: pajamas.	He: underwear. She: nightgown.
Background Music	Ravi Shankar or Beatles.	Wagner.	Sound track of *Dr. Zhivago.*	Jackie Gleason and Silver Strings.
Turn-Ons	Pot.	Champagne and oysters.	Manhattans & whiskey sours.	Beer.
The Schedule	Spontaneously, on an average of 2.5 weekly (that means 2 times one week and 3 times another).	Twice a week and when the kids go to the Sunday matinee.	Twice a week and when the kids go to the Sunday school.	Twice on Saturday night.

Number of Children	1 each by previous marriage or as many as God provides.	2.4.	3.	As many as God provides.
Anniversary Celebrations	A weekend in Dublin.	He gives her a new dishwasher. She gives him a power lawn mower.	Corsage and dinner out.	Whitman Sampler and dinner at Howard Johnson's.
Quarrels	"I don't care what your analyst says."	"I don't care if he is your brother."	"What do you think I'm made of?"	"Drop dead!"
If the Marriage Needs Help	He consults her analyst. She consults his.	They go (a) to marriage counselor; (b) to the minister.	He: to his successful brother. She: to her best friend.	He: to the bartender. She: to her mother.
The Affair	"But I assumed you knew."	"It was basically a problem in communication."	"It was bigger than both of us."	"Some things no woman should have to put up with."
Sex Education	"Ask Doctor Grauber, dear, when you see him tomorrow."	"Well, you see, Daddy has something called a . . . etc." And "Daddy and Mommy love each other very much."	"Well, you see, Daddy puts the seed in Mommy's tummy, etc., etc."	"We got you at the hospital."
Vacations	Europe in May. She takes the children to the Cape. He commutes.	Europe in July. Family camping in Yosemite.	He hunts or fishes. She visits her mother with the children.	They visit Brother Charlie in Des Moines.
Financial Arrangements	Separate trust funds.	Joint checking account.	She budgets.	He gets weekly allowance.
Who Raises the Children	English nanny, boarding school, and Dr. Grauber.	Mommy and Daddy, Cub Scouts, and Dr. Freud.	Mom and Dad, the Little League, and Dr. Spock.	Mom, the gang, Ann Landers, and good luck!

[a] *Note:* What Simon and Gagnon are describing is not the only kind of sex life or life style of each social class but rather one *type* of life style within each class.

Source: From William Simon and John Gagnon, "How Fashionable Is Your Sex Life?" *McCalls* **94** (October 1969), 58–59. Reprinted with permission of the authors and *McCalls*.

Emphasis on *achieved* status permits people to move from one rank to another. In the United States we have a system of achieved stratification, although some groups find it much more difficult, if not impossible, to climb the ladder of success. Minorities and people born into conditions of poverty are examples of those who find the ladder harder to climb. Sociological studies generally suggest that the ladder is not impossible to climb; however, there are at least two opinions on this subject. The data seem to support the optimists, but not by much.

Notes

1. S. Kuznets, "Quantitative Aspects of the Economic Growth of Nations," *Economic Development and Cultural Change,* **11** (1965). For some recent data covering a wider range of nations, see Irving B. Kravis, "A World of Unequal Incomes." *Annals of the American Academy of Political and Social Science* (September 1973), 61–80.

2. Not all sociologists use the term *slave system* or think of slavery as a form of stratification. It is used in C. S. Heller, ed., *Structured Social Inequality: A Reader in Comparative Social Stratification* (New York: Macmillan Publishing Co., Inc., 1969).

3. E. R. Leach, "Caste, Class and Slavery: The Taxonomic Problem," in E. O. Lauman, P. M. Siegel, and R. W. Hodge, eds., *The Logic of Social Hierarchies* (Chicago: Markham Publishing Co., 1970), pp. 83–94; M. Bloch, "Feudalism as a Type of Society," pp. 100–106 in the same book; and A. A. Sio, "Interpretations of Slavery: The Slave Status in the Americas," in C. S. Heller, op. cit., pp. 63–73.

4. Cited in C. S. Heller, op. cit., p. 51.

5. G. D. Berreman, "Caste in India and the United States," *American Journal of Sociology,* **64** (1960), 120–127.

6. C. C. Taylor, D. Ensminger, H. W. Johnson, and J. Joyce, *India's Roots of Democracy* (London: Longmans, 1965), pp. 48–50.

7. An interesting illustration of this is the case of the Shanans, who claimed that they were actually entitled to be classified as part of the Nadar caste and entitled to a higher rank. Over a period of some seventy years through many court battles they earned the legal right to this higher position. See L. I. Rudolph, "The Modernity of Tradition: The Democratic Incarnation of Caste in India," *American Political Science Review,* **59** (1965), 975–989.

8. "2500 Untouchables Shed Hinduism and Embrace Buddism in Delhi Rite," *New York Times* (March 12, 1972), p. 2.

9. The *New York Times* reported the case of a man whose official classification (by the government's Race Classification Board) was "colored," but his daughter was classified as Bantu. This meant that they *could not live in the same house by law.* The law does permit exceptions for domestic servants, so the man is planning to employ his daughter as his housekeeper. *New York Times* (June 10, 1973), Section 4, p. 6.

10. D. Mechanic, "Apartheid Medicine," *Society,* (March–April 1973), 36–44.

11. G. Myrdal, *An American Dilemma* (New York: Harper and Row, Publishers, 1944), p. 669.

12. R. Mack, *Race, Class and Power,* 2nd Ed. (New York: American Book Company, 1968), p. 342.

13. See A. Rose, "Race and Ethnic Relations," in R. K. Merton and R. A. Nisbet, eds., *Contemporary Social Problems,* 2nd Ed. (New York: Harcourt Brace Jovanovich, Inc., 1966), pp. 443–445. It should be noted that civil rights legislation and litigation in the 1960s knocked down the *legal* barriers to equality; however, there still exists considerable support for these notions and practices.

14. C. Vann Woodward, *The Strange Career of Jim Crow,* Rev Ed. (New York: Oxford University Press, 1957), p. 83.

15. See R. Blauner, "Internal Colonialism and Ghetto Revolt," *Social Problems,* **16** (1969), 393–408. Also A. J. Reiss, Jr., and H. E. Aldrich, "Absentee Ownership and Management in the Black Ghetto: Social and Economic Consequences," *Social Problems,* **18** (1971), 319–338; and H. E. Aldrich, "Employment Opportunities for Blacks in the Black Ghetto: The Role of White-Owned Businesses," *American Journal of Sociology,* **78** (1973), 1402–1425.

16. K. B. Clark, *Youth in the Ghetto* (New York: Haryou Associates, 1964), quoted in Blauner, op. cit., p. 397.

17. Those who feel the ethnic and class models are *more* useful overall than the colony model argue that using a given model also implies certain strategies for *solving* ghetto problems. The critics feel that the strategies suggested by the colony model (such as transferring white-owned businesses in the ghetto to blacks) will not be as effective or economically viable as *other* strategies for solving ghetto problems. For details see W. K. Tabb, "Race Relations Models and Social Change," *Social Problems,* **18** (1971), 431–443; and N. Glazer, "Blacks and Ethnic Groups: The Difference, and the Political Difference It Makes," *Social Problems,* **18** (1971), 444–461.

18. K. George and C. H. George, "Roman Catholic Sainthood and Social Status," in R. Bendix and S. M. Lipset, eds., *Class, Status and Power: Social Stratification in Comparative Perspective,* 2nd Ed. (New York: The Free Press, 1966), pp. 394–401.

19. The discussion that follows is based on R. L. Beals and H. Hoijer, *An Introduction to Anthropology,* 4th Ed. (New York: Macmillan Publishing Co., Inc., 1971), pp. 297–300, 613–614.

20. Ibid.

21. K. Marx, *Capital: A Critical Analysis of Capitalist Production* (New York: International Publishers, 1947), p. 230.

22. See K. Marx, *Selected Writings in Sociology and Social Philosophy,* trans. T. B. Bottomore and M. Rubel, eds. (New York: McGraw-Hill Book Company, 1964); and N. Bukharin, *Historical Materialism: A System of Sociology* (Ann Arbor: University of Michigan Press, 1969).

23. R. Centers, "The American Class Structure: A Psychological Analysis," in H. Proshansky and B. Seidenberg, eds., *Basic Studies in Social Psychology* (New York: Holt, Rinehart, & Winston, Inc., 1965), pp. 334–335.

24. C. W. Tucker, "On Working-Class Identification," *American Sociological Review,* **31** (1966), 855–856; and C. W. Tucker, "A Comparative Analysis of Subjective Social Class: 1945–1963," *Social Forces,* **46** (1968), 508–514.

25. E. M. Schreiber and G. T. Nygreen, "Subjective Social Class in America: 1945–1968," *Social Forces,* **48** (1970), 348–356.

26. L. Corey, "The Middle Class," in R. Bendix and S. M. Lipset, eds., *Class, Status, and Power: A Reader in Social Stratification* (New York: The Free Press, 1953), pp. 371–380.

27. J. Burnham, *The Managerial Revolution* (Bloomington: Indiana University Press, 1962), p. 80.

28. J. K. Galbraith, *The New Industrial State* (Boston: Houghton Mifflin Company, 1967).

29. T. Wicker, "The Rich Get Richer, Etc.," *New York Times* (June 29, 1973), p. 39; and "Myths Destroyed by Simple Fable," (UPI) Bowling Green, Ohio *Daily Sentinel Tribune* (March 5, 1974), p. 8. Also see F. Lundberg, *The Rich and the Super Rich* (New York: Lyle Stuart, 1968); and G. Kolko, *Wealth and Power in America: An Analysis of Social Class and Income Distribution* (New York: Praeger Publishers, Inc., 1962).

30. M. Weber, *Essays in Sociology* (Baltimore: Penguin Books, 1963).

31. See T. B. Bottomore, *Elites and Society* (Baltimore: Penguin Books, 1964); and G. Parry, *Political Elites* (New York: Praeger Publishers, Inc., 1969); M. Djilas, *"The New Class": An Analysis of the Communist System* (New York: Praeger Publishers, Inc., 1957); and A. Inkeles, "Social Stratification and Mobility in the Soviet Union: 1940–1950," *American Sociological Review,* **15** (1950), 465–479.

32. See A. Simirenko, "From Vertical to Horizontal Inequality: The Case of the Soviet Union," *Social Problems,* **20** (1972), 150–161.

33. W. L. Warner and P. S. Lunt, *The Social Life of a Modern Community* (New Haven, Conn.: Yale University Press, 1941); and W. L. Warner, *The Status System of a Modern Community* (New Haven, Conn.: Yale University Press, 1942).

34. H. J. Gans, *The Urban Villagers: Groups and Class in the Life of Italian-Americans* (New York: The Free Press, 1962).
35. Ibid., p. 29.
36. R. P. Coleman, "The Significance of Social Stratification in Selling," in P. Bliss, ed., *Marketing and the Behavioral Sciences* (Boston: Allyn & Bacon, Inc., 1963), pp. 156–171.
37. W. L. Warner, M. Meeker, and K. Eels, *Social Class in America* (Chicago: Science Research Associates, Inc., 1949).
38. J. A. Kahl and J. A. Davis, "A Comparison of Indexes of Socio-Economic Status," *American Sociological Review,* **20** (1955), 317–325.
39. See, for example, L. Reissman, *Class in American Society* (New York: The Free Press, 1959), pp. 160ff.
40. National Opinion Research Center, "Jobs and Occupations: A Popular Evaluation," *Opinion News,* **9** (September 1, 1947), 3–13.
41. R. W. Hodge, P. M. Siegel, and P. H. Rossi, "Occupational Prestige in the United States, 1925–1963," *American Journal of Sociology,* **70** (1964), 286–302.
42. A. Inkeles and P. H. Rossi, "National Comparisons of Occupational Prestige," *American Journal of Sociology,* **61** (1956), 329–339.
43. K. Davis and W. Moore, "Some Principles of Stratification," *American Sociological Review,* **10** (1945), 242–249.
44. M. Tumin, "Some Principles of Stratification: A Critical Analysis," *American Sociological Review,* **18** (1953), 387–393.
45. There are circumstances under which the particular measure used does make a good deal of difference. See for example, R. W. Hodge, "Social Integration, Psychological Well-Being, and Their Socioeconomic Correlates." *Sociological Inquiry,* **40** (1970), 182–206.
46. M. Rokeach and S. Parker provide an interesting illustration in "Values as Social Indicators of Poverty and Race Relations in America," *Annals of the American Academy of Political and Social Science,* **388** (1970), 97–111.
47. F. Hunter, *Top Leadership, U.S.A.* (Chapel Hill: University of North Carolina Press, 1969); and C. W. Mills, *The Power Elite* (New York: Oxford University Press, 1956).
48. W. Kornhauser, "'Power Elite' or 'Veto Groups,'" in R. Bendix and S. M. Lipset, eds. *Class, Status, and Power,* 2nd Ed. (New York: The Free Press, 1966). 210–218.
49. F. Hunter, *Community Power Structure: A Study of Decision Makers* (Chapel Hill: University of North Carolina Press, 1953).
50. M. W. Karmin, "How Dayton's Elite Opened Its Suburbs," *Wall Street Journal* (May 11, 1972).
51. R. Dahl, *Who Governs? Democracy and Power in an American City* (New Haven, Conn.: Yale University Press, 1963).
52. J. Walton, "Differential Patterns of Community Power Structure: An Explanation Based on Interdependence," in J. Walton and D. E. Carns, ed ., *Cities in Change: Studies on the Urban Condition* (Boston: Allyn & Bacon, Inc., 1973), pp. 502–517.
53. M. C. Jensen, "Musical Chairs in Business and Industry," *New York Times* (November 12, 1972), Section 3, p. 1.
54. See C. Bernstein and B. Woodward, *All the President's Men,* (New York: Simon & Shuster, Inc., 1974).
55. D. Riesman, "The Images of Power," in *The Lonely Crowd* (New York: Doubleday Anchor Edition, 1953), pp. 239–271.
56. W. Kornhauser, "'Power Elite' or 'Veto Groups'?" in Bendix and Lipset, op. cit., p. 216.
57. P. A. Sorokin, *Social Mobility* (New York: Harper & Row, Publishers, 1927).
58. S. M. Lipset, "Social Mobility and Equal Opportunity," *The Public Interest,* (Fall 1972), 90.
59. *The Big Business Executive, 1964: A Study of His Social and Educational Background* (New York: Scientific American Publishers, n.d.).

60. P. M. Blau and O. D. Duncan, *The American Occupational Structure* (New York: John Wiley & Sons, Inc., 1967).

61. O. D. Duncan, "Inheritance of Poverty or Inheritance of Race," in D. Moynihan, ed., *On Understanding Poverty* (New York: Basic Books, 1968), pp. 85–110. In a study of Mexican-Americans in Austin, Texas, using the same formulas, Williams et al. found a $320 discrepancy between Anglo- and Mexican-American incomes, which they attribute to income discrimination. See J. A. Williams, Jr., P. G. Besson, and D. R. Johnson, "Some Factors Associated with Income Among Mexican Americans," *Social Science Quarterly.* **54** (1973), 710–715.

62. S. M. Lipset and R. Bendix, *Social Mobility in Industrial Society* (Berkeley: University of California Press, 1959).

63. O. D. Duncan, D. L. Featherman, and B. Duncan, *Socioeconomic Background and Achievement* (New York: Seminar Press, 1972).

64. As Ben Wattenberg and Richard Scammon note in a controversial article, "Black Progress and Liberal Rhetoric," in *Commentary* (April 1973), 35–44. Also see "Letters to the Editor," *Commentary* (August 1973), pp. 4–22.

65. Not all portraits of social opportunity in America are quite as rosy. The slogan "poverty amid affluence" is one frequently heard. See H. M. Wachtel, "Capitalism and Poverty in America: Paradox or Contradiction?" *Monthly Review* (1972), 51–64; and G. Goodman, Jr., "Black Youth's Quest for Job Security: A Study in Despair," *New York Times* (June 18, 1973), p. 33.

Intergroup Relations

TEN

THE ABILITY to use symbols gives humans the ability to develop complex, sophisticated societies. The ability to use symbols makes it possible for us to create subtle distinctions between our own groups and other groups on the basis of quite trivial differences in such things as "race, creed, and national origin." And also to use these distinctions to justify behavior toward these "others" that would disgrace the most vicious animals.

Although in this century there has been a great deal of concern about *racial* conflicts, since the earliest days of recorded history *religion* and *nationality* have served as equally powerful bases for defining others as nonhuman and therefore deserving of no more consideration than would be given a cockroach.

Defining others as nonhuman, regardless of the basis, makes possible behavior like this:

VILLAVICENCIO, Colombia, July 9, 1972—Out of the llanos, the vast prairies that stretch across Colombia and Venezuela from the Andes to the Orinoco, lawlessness still reigns as it did in the old American West. Swashbuckling cowboys and primitive Indians compete for life and over notions of right with the fast gun and the flashing machete.

Evidence that untamed life on the prairies has changed little since the time of the conquistadores was provided in a courtroom here last week when a half-dozen cowboys charged with murder freely told in horrifying detail how they had lured 16 Indians to their ranch with the promise of a feast and massacred them for fun.

"If I had known that killing Indians was a crime, I would not have wasted all that time walking just so they could lock me up," said 22-year-old Marcelino Jimenez, who hiked for five days to a police outpost after learning the authorities were looking for him.

"From childhood, I have been told that everyone kills Indians," said another defendant, who added: "All I did was kill the little Indian girl and finish off two who were more dead than alive anyway."

And Luis Enrique Morin, 33 years old, the range boss who planned the massacre, asserted: "For me, Indians are animals, like deer or iguanas, except that deer don't damage our crops or kill our pigs. Since way back, Indian-hunting has been common practice in these parts."[1]

You don't have to go to Colombia to find such cases, of course. If we were to go back through American history, we could come up with equally horrifying illustrations in regard to Indians. Consider this story:

Macleod reports the experiences of a white settler in California who was participating in a massacre of Indians in the vicinity of his home. After all the adults had been killed, he came upon a group of children who were huddled together in fear. As he looked at their eyes, he could not help but notice how cute they were, and he was unable to get himself to shoot them with his .56-caliber rifle—because it tore them up so bad. He had to do it with his .38-caliber revolver.[2]

Unfortunately, we could fill volumes with such cases, and there is not a society, past or present, for which we couldn't find evidence of equally abominable behavior. There seems to be something about *group life* that makes such behavior "natural." Little children don't "naturally" exhibit hostility toward those who are racially or culturally different, but socialized humans *do.* In other words, we are suggesting that intolerance of those who are different is not "instinctive" but rather that it seems to be a product of learning and social experience.

As we look at the contemporary world we see many societies. Almost none of our contemporary societies is homogeneous in terms of race, religion, or culture. Each society has at least one minority that differs from the majority in one or more of these respects.

"Majority" and "Minority"

Sociologists have a peculiar way of using the terms *majority* and *minority.* Nonsociologists (quite properly) think of these terms as referring to the relative sizes of groups. Sociologists generally use the terms to indicate the relative *power* of groups rather than their relative *size.*

A minority group, for sociologists, is a group that has less power than a majority group, The Bantus (blacks) in South Africa and Rhodesia are considered minorities in this sense despite the fact that they outnumber the whites. In the same sense many women in the United States have come to think of women as a minority despite the fact that women slightly outnumber men. Since when are women a minority group? Remember that those who think of women as a minority are not using sheer numbers but *privilege* and *power* as their criteria for deciding who is or is not a minority.[3] It is not a new insight to suggest that there are similarities between certain groups generally considered minorities (particularly blacks and women). In the mid-1940s Gunnar Myrdal,[4] in an appendix to his classic study of blacks in America, pointed to a number of similarities between blacks and women:

1. Both groups have high social visibility because of physical appearance or dress.
2. Both were originally forms of property, controlled by an absolute patriarch.
3. Women and blacks were at one time unable to vote—the Fifteenth Amendment (permitting blacks to vote) came half a century before the Nineteenth (permitting women to vote).
4. Both have been believed to have an inferior mental endowment, and limited educational opportunities have been provided for them.
5. Each was assigned a "place" in the social system and as long as they stayed

in this subordinate status, they were approved; attempts to alter this scheme were disapproved.

6. Neither group, historically, had legal rights over property or guardianship of children.

7. Myths were created about the "contented woman" who did not want the vote or other civil rights and equal opportunities, just as myths were created about the "contented black."

8. It has been hard for either to attain important public office.

9. Certain low-prestige, low-salary jobs were allotted for women and for blacks.

10. It was thought "unnatural" for white men to work under black supervisors or males to be supervised by women.

Goodwin Watson and David Johnson[5] added some more parallels to Myrdal's list, including these:

11. In both cases it has been argued that God made them different and it is His (Her?) will that there should not be real equality.

12. Both blacks and women are appreciated—even loved—in their nurturant role. The dominant group enjoys being nursed, fed, clothed, and cared for by these servants.

13. Women and blacks are said to be more emotional than rational.

14. Both groups, in studying history, find that white males fill most of the heroic roles. "Less than 1 percent of the statues erected to great historic figures in America honor either women or blacks. A typical school child's list of the important names in history will seldom include any woman or black. This probably limits aspiration for many children."

15. Both groups are said to be inclined toward superstition, magic, and traditional religion.

16. It has been considered proper to pay both groups less than is paid white males. Women and blacks are said not to have such heavy responsibilities.

17. It is convenient to ignore or deny any real problem in the relationships between blacks and whites, males and females, and to argue that everything could be worked out harmoniously if "agitators" would keep out.

18. "There is a mystique behind the rational discussion of sex and race discrimination. The myths of Pandora and of Eve attribute to women the source of evil in life. The term 'Black' applied to Arts and Magic also denotes evil and may be extended to race."

Of course, the parallels between women and blacks can be overdrawn. It is not clear, for example, to what extent the women's movement can or should use as strategies and tactics for women's liberation those that are appropriate for a black liberation movement. Nevertheless, the parallels between these minorities are striking despite the fact that the relative sizes of the two minorities differ (blacks being about 12 percent of the U.S. population and women being roughly 51 percent).

Nationalism and Minorities

Minorities get to be minorities in a variety of ways. Some are migrants to another country (voluntary or otherwise). Others are a majority in their own country until some other nation makes their country into a colony. Still others find that as a result of war or other diplomatic activity, national borders have been drawn in such a way as suddenly to make them a minority in a newly formed country. These are the most frequent ways in which minorities have been formed in recent centuries.

It isn't impossible in principle for two different groups to coexist peacefully in the same area, each doing its own thing, but it is unusual for this to happen. The usual procedure is for one group to observe the differences between its culture and the other group's; then, when and if there is *competition* for scarce resources (land, jobs, and so on) and a *power* difference between both groups, the more powerful group takes advantage of the opportunity and subordinates the less powerful group. (If the groups are not in competition and/or have roughly equal power, they're more likely to work out some kind of more or less peaceful accommodation.[6]

Problems of majority and minority relations are not exactly a recent phenomenon. The Old Testament of the Bible, it's been said, could serve as a text on intergroup relations in all their variety. Nevertheless, with the rise of nationalism, of world trade, and of increased secularization over the course of the last few hundred years, the problems of minorities have developed new dimensions and new significance for problems of world and national order.[7]

Following the Renaissance, the concept of nationalism led European rulers to centralize power in opposition to the claims of the papacy for universal dominance and in opposition to the extreme decentralization of power of feudalism. Nationalism also led these nations to develop various national institutions that were modeled after those of the majority. Attempts were made to require minorities to bring their own customs into line with those of the majority. These demands for national unity occurred at the same time that many minorities, like the Poles, Croats and Serbs, were becoming more self-conscious and resistant to the idea of being absorbed into large nations. The Central and Eastern European peoples had been dominated by one empire or another for centuries and had also developed their own nationalisms, which encouraged them to break away from the rising nations.

As European nationalism led to imperialism and the conquest of non-Europeans, new kinds of minority problems were created. The problems of dealing with "external" minorities with a fantastic diversity of cultures, races, and religions in the colonies were added to the problems of dealing with "internal" minorities within the mother country. For example, as G. E. Simpson and J. M. Yinger observed, "England had scarcely worked out a peaceful *modus vivendi* with Scotland and Wales and was still fighting bitterly with Ireland when she was faced with the problems of policy dealing with American Indians, Asiatic Indians, Arabs, Africans, Malayans and a host of other peoples."[8]

Policies Toward Minorities

How have dominant groups (majorities) traditionally handled internal and external minorities? Simpson and Yinger describe several varieties of policies.[9]

1. Assimilation.
   a. Forced.
   b. Permitted.
2. Pluralism.
3. Population transfer.
   a. Peaceful transfer.
   b. Forced migration.
4. Continued subjugation.
5. Extermination.

Let's look at these one at a time.

Assimilation

One way to "solve" the problem of what to do with minorities is to eliminate the minority *as a minority,* to *assimilate* them.

A dominant group may attempt to *force* assimilation by refusing to permit a minority the right to practice its own religion, speak its own language, or follow its own customs. The Russian czars, for example, went through periods of "Russification," during which they offered minorities that insisted on preserving their own separate identities the alternatives of rigid segregation, expulsion, or extermination. The Nazis demanded assimilation, but also claimed that certain groups were "unassimilable" and adopted the policies of forced population transfers and extermination. The assumption behind these policies of forced assimilation is that members of different nationalities with different languages and customs can't possibly live side by side in the same state and that it is therefore legitimate to suppress the language and culture of the weaker nationality for the greater glory of the nation.

A peaceful, *permitted* assimilation policy in principle permits minorities to absorb the dominant patterns at their own speed, in their own way. In the United States we have assumed, by and large, that this is a one-way process. Minorities have been expected to surrender their distinctive characteristics and become "Americanized." It's been assumed that the content and nature of what was "American" in language, culture, and institutional patterns had been developed by the early nineteenth century and that new immigrants could or should contribute little. On the other hand, we have also at one time or another been skeptical about the likelihood that each of our racial and ethnic minorities could ever be assimilated.

Assimilation has a number of dimensions. Milton Gordon[10] distinguishes among four types of assimilation: (1) the minority's picking up the "proper" behavior and cultural traits (cultural assimilation or "acculturation") through (2) identification exclusively with the host society (identificational assimilation); (3) intermarriage (marital assimilation); and (4) structural assimilation. Structural assimilation occurs when the minority participates on a *large scale* (not as select token individuals) in the cliques, clubs, and institutions of the host society. There obviously is an order to these. One can behave like and identify with the majority and even intermarry without really being accepted as an intimate and a social equal by the majority. Structural assimilation implies complete acceptance of a minority as equals.

The descendants of Northern European immigrants (e.g., English, Germans, Scandinavians, Irish) of the nineteenth and twentieth centuries are the furthest along the road to structural assimilation. The Eastern Europeans (Italians, Poles, Jews) are less far along, and the racial minorities (Chinese, Japanese, blacks, Chicanos, Filipinos, Indians) are furthest away from structural assimilation. Surrendering one's own language, identity, and customs requires no activity on the part of the majority, nor, on the other hand, does it guarantee complete acceptance by the majority. Structural assimilation requires the cooperation of the dominant group.

Pluralism

Pluralism is the peaceful coexistence of two or more groups. Some minorities are not interested in being assimilated and losing their separate identities. Some majorities are willing to permit a good deal of cultural variability as long as they see this variability as compatible with national unity and security.

Swiss Pluralism

Perhaps the most outstanding example of a successfully pluralist nation is Switzerland,[11] where German, French, Italian, and Romansh Swiss have retained their cultural and language differences and are tied together by common political and economic interests. Switzerland has an unusual history. It developed as a voluntary federation of separate communities long before the emergence of the nation-state of Europe. Most other nation-states, as we've observed, had been pulled together by absolute monarchs, who imposed centralized administration on culturally heterogeneous territories. During the nineteenth and twentieth centuries power was taken by the people to free themselves from despotism and replace it with self-rule. The sovereignty of the people was believed to require a continuation of the idea of culturally and ethnically homogenizing all the people in a given state. Of course this idea gave rise to great resistance on the part of those who did not care to be homogenized.

Switzerland's political history ran counter to the trend toward unification and centralization because the Swiss Confederation, an alliance of small autonomous communities, had defeated various rulers (including the German emperor) by 1499 and had managed to cut themselves free of the Holy Roman Empire in 1648. In other words, Switzerland was never really a traditional nation-state; it had been an alliance of autonomous communities for several hundred years before modern concepts of the nation-state came into existence. By the time the modern Swiss state was established in 1848, its German, French, and Italian communities had had a long history of self-government and autonomy, and the nation had accepted the idea that each language was equal to the others before language became an ideological symbol of nationhood elsewhere.

Switzerland is held together, according to Kurt B. Mayer, by an interesting balance of economic, political, and cultural differences. These divide the nation in such complex ways that they *neutralize* each other. For example, two thirds of the German-speaking Swiss are Protestants and one third are Roman Catholics. The French-speaking Swiss are roughly half Protestant and half Roman Catholic. The Romansh-speakers are roughly two-thirds Protestant and one-third Roman Catholic. The Italian-speaking Swiss are the only more or less religiously homogeneous group: 94 percent are Catholics. Religion divides the groups one way, and language cuts across religion to tie the same groups together. The political units (cantons), which are roughly the size of U.S. counties, cut across the language and religious groups and have an enormous amount of political autonomy, so that often one's loyalty to a political unit outweighs his loyalty to coreligionists or fellow language speakers, and he is more likely to identify himself as a resident of a particular canton than to say, "I am Swiss."

The industrialized and nonindustrialized areas are not homogeneous either and are scattered across regions and religions. Urban-rural and industrial-nonindustrial divisions also cut across language and religion. These cross-cutting structural differences make it easier for the Swiss to carry out their commitments to a multicultural nation in which the right to separate languages and cultural traditions is honored and encouraged.

Pluralism in Yugoslavia and the United States

Yugoslavia is a nation-state made up of a number of distinct nationality groups that have their own languages, religions, and histories.[12] Putting together a single state in Yugoslavia created problems roughly the same as those that would be created in putting together a single state out of, say, Italy, Germany, France, Sweden, and Egypt. Each group in Yugoslavia retains memories of historical grievances and experiences and a concern about the preservation of its language and its distinctive culture, as well as jealous concern about its fair share of the economy. By means of a delicate balancing act the government of Yugoslavia has kept these various distinctive nations from seceding from Yugoslavia. Although the Yugoslavs have not completely solved their majority-minority problems, particularly economic inequalities, we include Yugoslavia in our discussion because in most respects its approach to majority-minority relations is the polar opposite of our system in the United States and because the differences among its people, unlike Switzerland's, do *not* cut across and neutralize one another.

The Socialist Federal Republic of Yugoslavia is made up of five major nationalities—Serbs, Croats, Slovenes, Macedonians, and Montenegrins—and nine other distinguishable ethnic minorities.[13] The state is divided into six republics and two autonomous provinces. Five of the republics have populations composed primarily of *one* of the major nationalities. That is, the different nationalities are not dispersed geographically as they are in the United States. From largest to smallest the republics are Serbia, Croatia, Slovenia, Macedonia, and Montenegro. The Montenegrins are culturally Serb, but unlike the other Serbs, were never part of the Turkish Empire. The sixth republic, Bosnia-Herzegovina, has a mixture of Serbs, Croats, and Muslims (most of whom are culturally Slavic; their ancestors were converted to Islam under the Ottoman Turks). Then there are the ethnic minorities, which have a majority in none of the republics. These ethnic minorities, sometimes called "national minorities," make up about one eighth of the population. The nine largest minorities are the Albanians, the Hungarians, the Rumanians, the Slovaks, the Czechs, the Ruthenians, the Italians, and the Turks. Most of the ethnic minorities are culturally related to the populations of surrounding nations.

The Socialist Republic of Serbia is the largest subdivision in Yugoslavia, containing three quarters of Yugoslavia's minority populations. It is further subdivided into the autonomous provinces of Voivodina and Kossovo. Voivodina is the most ethnically mixed area in Yugoslavia, containing mainly Hungarian, Slovak, Czech, Rumanian, Bulgarian, Serb, and Croat populations. All live physically close to each other and all maintain their national identities. Kossovo contains mainly Albanians and Serbs, with a small Turkish minority.

Historically religion has played an important role in dividing the peoples of Yugoslavia. For many centuries the northern republics of Yugoslavia—Croatia and Slovenia—were part of the Austro-Hungarian Empire. They are Catholic, come from a feudal tradition, use Latin as a *lingua franca* (common language for communication), and use the Roman alphabet. They have a political tradition, as a continuation of the Holy Roman Empire, based on Roman and Canon Law.

The Serbs are part of a Byzantine tradition. They are Orthodox in religion, use the Cyrillic alphabet in writing, and have their own language.

The Muslims are the third largest religious grouping and are essentially members of three ethnic strains. The Muslims of Bosnia-Herzegovina are largely Slavs who converted to Islam. The Muslims of Kossovo are Albanians who converted to Islam. The Turks who are scattered over all those areas of Yugoslavia that the Ottoman Empire ruled remain Muslim.

Although Yugoslavia is a socialist nation, economic decision-making is not centralized but is in the hands of worker-run plantwide, industrywide, and regional councils. The workers decide what to do with the profits: whether to invest them and where to invest them (they can also allot the profits to themselves in salaries). Over recent years, this system of economic control has produced a strain in ethnic relations because the prosperous northern industrial areas have not chosen to invest very much in developing the agricultural southern areas. As a result, there are substantial income differences between the industrial north and the agricultural south, and members of the northern nationality groups are more prosperous than the members of the southern nationality groups.

The Yugoslav government has a somewhat different response to the maintenance of cultural differences than does the United States. Our traditional philosophy has been that if we could eliminate the barriers to the full assimilation of *individuals* into the larger society, the *groups* to which the individuals belong would automatically profit as well and that it would be wrong to acknowledge officially or accept any idea of "group rights." The Yugoslav philosophy has been that the best way to advance *individual* interests is to guarantee *group rights* to political representation and to guarantee cultural autonomy to each group. The Yugoslav system guarantees each group a certain number of government positions, based on their population proportions, and guarantees each group the right to schooling in its own language. Yugoslavia guarantees any group that can round up as few as fifteen children in a given area a teacher who will teach in their own language.

Our American pattern has been an insistence on "Americanizing" children and on the use of English in schools regardless of the child's native language. The unfortunate educational consequence has been that many children have found themselves assigned to classes for the mentally retarded because they cannot handle an English-language exam as well as they could have handled one in, say, Spanish.[14] Another consequence has been the alienation of children of various minority groups from the school system. These children have found their peculiar educational needs and cultural preferences ignored, scorned, or condemned by a system that insisted on only one definition of "American," a definition that excluded them.

Yugoslavia and the United States, despite their different approaches to the idea of officially supported cultural pluralism, have similar problems in dealing with groups that have a long history of deprivation and disadvantage. In Yugoslavia the Albanians have traditionally been a rural, illiterate group, with a religion and culture distinct from that of the other groups. Instituting Albanian-language schools and an Albanian quota for civil service posts has not substantially changed their status as a group or their inability as individuals to function effectively within the urban, industrial areas of Yugoslavia.

In the United States the less industrial southern and southwestern states are areas in which black, Indian, and Spanish-speaking groups have found themselves in a position of disadvantage. Where improvements have come about

WHITE MEN ONLY
COLORED ONLY

in the status of deprived groups in the United States it has been to a large extent because the federal government has insisted that individual constitutional rights take priority over local discriminatory patterns and has used its power to support such efforts. The Yugoslav government, on the other hand, decentralized its power by distributing greater power to local and regional units to make possible the cultural, political, and economic autonomy of their respective ethnic groups.

Our *centralization* of the power of the federal government in the United States to overcome discrimination by local groups has been criticized as being destructive of cultural pluralism. Yugoslavian *decentralization* of power in the name of cultural pluralism has been attacked as a device for perpetuating economic inequalities between ethnically distinct regions. In the early days before this decentralization, the central government had the power to decide where economic investments were to be made and it chose to develop the northern areas at the expense of the southern ones. Now the developed regions have the power to choose where to invest and they *also* refuse to invest in the south. The southerners have hinted that the government's claim not to have the power to tell the regions what to do is a convenient cop-out for neglect of the south.

The Croats in the north are industrialized, but they claim that they would be *more* industrialized if the Serb-dominated central government would encourage more investment in Croatia and permit them to keep their foreign exchange earnings within their republic. They also resent the fact that somehow the federal capital of Belgrade (Serbia) has come to overshadow Zagreb (Croatia) as Yugoslavia's first city, although Zagreb is an older city and economic conditions in the two cities were not initially (after World War II) very different. The Croats feel that the Serbs have a disproportionate share of positions in the armed forces and the security services. They also feel that the proposed joint Serbo-Croat language contains more Serbian words than Croatian words. This fight over language may seem trivial to you, but the complaints about this new language started a controversy, fueled by some other issues involving Croat culture, that almost required calling out the army to put down student protests in 1971.

Obviously the United States and Yugoslavia have taken different approaches to the question of ethnic pluralism. The Yugoslavs are attempting to eliminate minority disadvantages through constitutional *group* guarantees that ensure cultural survival and the proportionate representation of ethnic groups in governmental bodies. The United States has attempted to create a situation in which the constitutional rights of the *individual* are guaranteed and people are judged only on their individual merits.

In recent years in the United States, however, efforts have been made through "affirmative action" programs to guarantee the proportional representation of minority groups in the various areas of public life. It has been argued by some that the recognition of "group rights" is essential to the cultural autonomy and political and economic equality of minorities.

Hunt and Walker point out that a price must be paid for justice in intergroup relations, whether the starting point is the group or the individual: "If the emphasis is on group parity, individual freedom is necessarily curtailed and many social classifications must be made on the basis of ethnicity rather than on individual qualities. If the emphasis is on individual rights, cultural groups may decay or disappear even though individuals associated historically with such groups advance in socioeconomic status."[15] The following report illustrates the difficulties of moving from one system to the other as well as indicating that a political system based on group rights is not guaranteed any more political tranquility than a system which officially denies group rights:

BEIRUT, Lebanon, February 23, 1974— . . . Some top-level civil service posts were shifted from Christians to Moslems this week, creating an emotional controversy that has shaken the delicate political balance in Lebanon.

Camille Chamoun, the former President who is leader of the National Liberal party, charged that the loss of posts traditionally held by Maronites, the largest Christian sect in the country, was tantamount to "liquidating" the community. . . .

The civil service shake-up, which had long been under discussion, is hailed by some Lebanese as the most significant reform since the country gained independence from a French mandate during World War II.

Since independence, political and top appointive posts have been distributed proportionally, according to the long-outdated 1932 census, among Maronites and other Christians, Sunni Moslems, Shiite Moslems, Druses and minorities including Armenians. The president is always a Maronite, the premier a Sunni Moslem and the speaker of Parliament a Shiite Moslem.

The purpose of the civil service reform, according to its proponents, was to break the restraints of sectarian appointments and foster a modern, efficient administration.

"We adopted the principle of the nonsectarian aspect of a civil post," Premier Takieddin Solh said after the shake-up on Monday. "From this day forward, all posts belong to all communities."

The 1932 census showed that Christians in Lebanon outnumbered non-Christians by six to five. Power has been allotted accordingly since then, although Moslems, with a higher birth rate, now believe that they are in the majority.

The ratio of distribution of top civil service posts under the reform appears unchanged. But the Maronite leaders are upset by the loss of key positions they have held since independence. Among them are the posts of chairman of the civil service board, director general of education and director general of the Ministry of Interior.

Sunni Moslems were appointed to the civil service board and education posts, and a Shiite was given the Ministry of Interior. The important post of director general of the Foreign Ministry also is expected to go to a Moslem.

There have been warnings by Mr. Chamoun and others that the controversy might develop into a crisis with unpredictable consequences.[16]

In certain respects it is reasonable to argue that cultural pluralism is still a reality in the United States, despite our official indifference to the support or strengthening of such pluralism. The grandchildren of European immigrants have not been completely homogenized. Marriages *by and large* take place within religious groupings: Catholics tend to wed Catholics, Protestants other Protestants, and Jews other Jews. Personal relationships tend to be limited largely to people of the same class, religion, and ethnic background.[17] Furthermore, as you can see in Tables 10–1, 10–2, and 10–3, political and social attitudes do seem to follow certain ethnic lines, with most other groups being more liberal than white Anglo-Saxon Protestants. Can we assume that these differences will disappear in another generation or two? We can only speculate. No one knows "for sure." The model of ethnic assimilation proposed by A. M. Greeley, which we discussed in Chapter 4, implies a certain inevitable, irreversible sequence that may or may not be accurate.

Table 10–1. Racial Attitudes Among College Graduates of Different Religious and Ethnic Backgrounds (June 1961 graduates, surveyed in 1968)

"White racism is the cause of Negro riots in the city."[a]	*Proportion Agreeing*
Blacks	84%
German Jews	54
Catholic Irish	51
Polish Jews	43
Catholic Poles	43
Protestant Scandinavians	37
Catholic Italians	35
Catholic Germans	34
Protestant English	30
Protestant Irish	28
Protestant Germans	28

[a]This was one of the conclusions of the Kerner Report (*Report of the National Advisory Commission on Civil Disorders,* [Washington, D.C.: U.S. Government Printing Office, 1968]).

Source: A. M. Greeley, *Why Can't They Be Like Us?* (New York: E. P. Dutton & Co., Inc., 1971), p. 74.

Population Transfer

One policy occasionally adopted by majorities is the transfer of minorities from one geographical area to another. Minorities may accept population transfer as a way of minimizing tensions by physical separation from hostile majority group members. Population transfer can be a peaceful process brought about by genuine concern for the rights and desires of individual minority group members. More often, however, population transfer has been part of a discriminatory policy, a way of "solving" the problem by driving minority group members out of an area—sometimes out of one part of the nation and sometimes completely out of the country.

Transfers can be *direct* or *indirect.* In a *direct* transfer the government specifically requires and forces the minority to leave. An *indirect* transfer results from extralegal pressure. Simpson and Yinger observed that

> Many nations and cities drove out Jews in the late medieval period; the United States drove the Indians out of area after area; the British kept the Irish beyond the Pale; the Soviet Union deported millions of her citizens, members of religious and national minorities, during World War II; and Nazi Germany followed a relentless policy, aimed at a homogeneous nation, by forcibly transferring large numbers of persons of many minorities. The *indirect* policy is to make life so unbearable for members of the minority that they "choose" to migrate. Thus

Table 10–2. Attitudes of American White Ethnic Groups Toward the Vietnam War, 1967[a]

Group	*Doves (Percentage)*	*Doves Number*
Jewish	48%	(47)
Western European Catholic	29%	(149)
Southern European Catholic	26%	(60)
Western European Protestant	17%	(499)
Native American	15%	(104)
Eastern European Catholic	7%	(42)

[a]This study of attitudes *precedes* the large-scale protests.

Source: A. M. Greeley, "Political Attitudes Among American White Ethnics," *Public Opinion Quarterly,* **36** (1972), p. 215.

Table 10–3. Attitudes on Selected Political Issues

Source: Gallup Polls, Cited in A. M. Greeley, "Political Attitudes Among American White Ethnics," *Public Opinion Quarterly,* **36:** (1972), p. 215.

	Northern White Blue-Collar Workers				
	Protestant		Catholic		National Average
	Percentage	*Number*	*Percentage*	*Number*	
In favor of 18-year-old vote					
1968	61%	217	65%	150	66%
1969	62	221	64	129	61
In favor of basing welfare on cost of living	79	191	79	130	77
In favor of guaranteed annual wage	29	228	47	134	32
Would vote for a black president	72	193	78	142	67
Integration moving too fast	57	280	42	127	48
Deeply concerned about pollution	50	258	55	110	51

czarist Russia drove out millions of Jews. This was also part of Germany's policy.[18]

As another example of direct transfer, during World War II the United States confined more than 110,000 West Coast Japanese in "relocation camps." The grounds for doing this were that because we were at war with Japan we could not count on the undivided loyalty of these Japanese-Americans. (We did, though, take for granted the loyalty of Italian-Americans and German-Americans, as well as that of Japanese living in Hawaii.)[19]

Population transfer may occasionally be effective as a way of minimizing certain tensions, but there is a price to be paid in human rights and the price seems to come largely out of the hides of the minority.

The Biharis of Bangladesh illustrate one instance of what can happen to a transferred group:

DACCA, Bangladesh, March 9, 1973—Bewildered and terrified the Biharis of Bangladesh are huddled in tents at packed camps around cities and ports. They are dispossessed.

"We have nothing, we are nothing," said a 20-year-old student, Mokhtar Hussain, pounding his fist on a table in the camp at Mohammedpur, north of Dacca. "We sit idle. Who wants us? No one. No one."

Fifteen months after the independence of Bangladesh, the Bihari minority remains in bitter isolation in muddy camps where food is scarce, sanitation is minimal and small pox and cholera are constant threats. The camps, with their thousands of widows and infants, are ghettos of despair.

In recent weeks, Sheik Mujibur Rahman, the Prime Minister of Bangladesh, has made clear that he wants to evict most of the Biharis, the non-Bengali Moslem minority, numbering 600,000 to 900,000.

"I cannot allow foreigners to live in my land for so long," he said.

Because Pakistan, a Moslem state, is reluctant to take the Biharis, they are bereft. Their plight is compounded by the hatred of the Bengalis, who say that the Biharis collaborated with the Pakistani Army in 1971 during the violent nine-month occupation aimed at crushing the Bengali autonomy movement.

Relief workers compare the predicament of the Biharis to that of the Uganda Asians and the Palestinian Arabs: no country is prepared to welcome them. What makes their plight even more acute, however, is their lack of political influence abroad or of allies.

"Every minute, every second there is fear," murmured Ashfaque Hamid, a 46-year-old former postmaster, walking in the Mohammedpur camp along a swarming lane covered with garbage and flies. "We are worse than beggars. A beggar has freedom. We cannot leave the camp. We cannot even beg."

The roots of the anger toward the Biharis were planted decades before the Bangladesh war. Following the partition of British India in 1947, hundreds of thousands of Moslems from the Indian state of Bihar fled to nearby East Bengal, which became the eastern wing of Pakistan. During this violent period of partition—in which nearly one million people were killed in communal violence—a total of eight million Moslems moved from India into Pakistan, while a similar number of Hindus and Sikhs fled to India, which is predominantly Hindu.

For the Pakistani authorities, the Biharis were useful in much the same way as the Asians in Uganda had served the British: as middle-level civil servants, technicians, clerks, railwaymen, foremen. The Biharis were discouraged from assimilating into the Bengali community. And, perhaps most important of all for the Government of Pakistan, the Bihari community served as an ally when the Bengalis grew restive against the domination by the Government, which was in West Pakistan.

During the Pakistani Army's crackdown, in which thousands of Bengalis were killed, the Biharis were among President Agha Mohammad Yahya Khan's active supporters. In the following months, however, Bengali retaliation left thousands of Biharis murdered. One of the worst massacres took place in March, 1972, at the port of Khulna, where Bengalis set fire to the homes of the Biharis and killed about 1,000 of them, some with knives and machete-like blades.

After Bangladesh achieved independence, most West Pakistani civilians and soldiers were evacuated and placed in camps in India. But the Biharis were left behind. Many expected a mass slaughter, but this failed to take place. Homes and shops were looted and there were murders and rapes. But mass killing was averted because first Indian Army guards were placed around Bihari camps and later Sheik Mujib barred action against the Biharis.

Now the Biharis are in camps, receiving food and medicinal help from the International Committee of the Red Cross. Some Red Cross officials admit that milk and food supplies are running low and that illness and disease are rampant. There have been some cases of smallpox and cholera.

What makes the plight of the Biharis now even more precarious is that as the International Red Cross operation nears an end, food distribution is being handed over to the Bangladesh Red Cross, a largely political organization tied to the ruling Awami League. The league itself has been the target of numerous allegations involving corruption and the disappearance of relief supplies.

Recently, Shiek Mujib said a Government poll indicated that 260,000 Biharis wanted to go to Pakistan, while 150,000 opted to stay in Bangladesh, and could do so. (The figures are far below the actual number of Biharis in Bangladesh).

Sheik Mujib has urged the United Nations to help in the exchange of the 260,000 Biharis for the 400,000 Bengalis in West Pakistan who want to settle in Bangladesh. Pakistan's hesitance about taking the Biharis is said to be based on economic and political reasons, including the fact that the group would form a sizeable political minority bloc.

"We cannot stay in Bangladesh, it can never be our home," M. H. Khan, a 58-year-old stationmaster, said over a cup of sweet, milky tea in a camp office. "This land is not for us. It can never be for us. But what should we do now? I ask you, what should we do?"[20]

Continued Subjugation

The policies we have discussed have been intended either to incorporate the minorities into a society or to drive them out. Often, however, the dominant group does not want to do either: they want to keep the minority groups around but in their subservient and exploitable "place." Simpson and Yinger describe this policy simply as *continued subjugation.*

Extermination

Conflict between groups can be so severe that one group comes to believe that only the physical destruction of the other will do. The United States destroyed two thirds of the Indians before we changed our policies. The British completely wiped out the small Tasmanian population—put bounties on their heads and used them for dog food. The Boers of South Africa likewise hunted down the Hottentots like animals. Germany between 1933 and 1945 murdered six million Jews.

These responses to minorities—assimilate them, permit pluralism, relocate them, continue to subjugate them, exterminate them—seem to cover the alternatives open to a majority group. These policies are not mutually exclusive, however. At various times and places a given group may use several or all of them, sometimes as conscious, long-range plans and sometimes as spur-of-the-moment responses to specific situations.

It ought to be noted that these majority policies are only a *part* of the story, as minorities may cooperate with or resist these policies. Accurate predictions about and complete explanations of the course of group relations obviously have to consider both sides of the majority-minority relationship. Sociology has not yet developed sophisticated theories that can handle *all* of the relevant, complex factors at once. Nonetheless, sociology's contribution to the understanding of intergroup relations has been significant.

Traditional Ideas: True, False, and "It Depends"

Sociology's contribution to the understanding of intergroup relations lies not only in documenting and trying to analyze instances of good and not-so-good group relations. Sociologists have also demonstrated that many traditional explanations of the causes and cures of intergroup problems are not accurate and that others are only *partially* accurate although there is a good deal of truth in them. For example, sociologists have observed that the idea that humans automatically and inevitably dislike people who have different customs or are of different races is not particularly accurate or useful.

Although in everyday life we freely classify people into "races" on the basis of "white," "black", "yellow," or "red" skin, defining race scientifically is not as simple as that. If we were to take into account blood types, gene pools, skin textures, or hair textures, for example, rather than simply skin color tones, we could classify people into thirty-four "races"[21] (or more). The point is that race is not a "natural" category but is an *arbitrary* classification that as citizens or scientists we choose to use but could also choose *not* to use or choose to use differently. Even without sophisticated genetic tests, we could classify a person with one "black" grandparent as "white" (as is done in countries like Brazil) or as "black" (as was historically the case in the United States). Given that race is an *arbitrary* category, any assertion that there is something "natural" about rejecting people of other "races" is senseless. Race is basically a *social* category rather than a clear-cut biological category, and race relations have to be understood in terms of *social* causes and effects rather than "natural" ones.

The point that "race" is an arbitrary way of classifying people is made tragically clear in this story:

JOHANNESBURG, South Africa, October 11, 1967 (AP)—Sandra Laing is a girl whom no schools want.

Her parents won an 18-month-long struggle to have her officially declared white, only to discover they can't find a school that wants her.

Parents in Sheepmoor, a tiny town in eastern Transvaal province, have threatened to remove their children from the local white primary school if 11-year-old Sandra is sent there as directed by the education department.

South African schools are strictly segregated along racial lines. Trouble occurs in borderline cases where a child is of dark appearance, as Sandra Laing is.

Sandra was going to boarding school in the country town of Piet Retief 18 months ago. Parents of other pupils objected to her presence, children taunted her, and eventually she was sent home by the school authorities.

Subsequently she was declared colored—that is, mulatto—by a government-appointed board, even though her parents are white. Then a change in the law provided that descent and not appearance is to be the deciding factor in borderline cases. She was reclassified white.

Sandra's storekeeper father, Abraham Laing, decided not to send her back to the same boarding school because of the scorn he felt she would meet.

He approached a number of convents, but they turned him down. Some said they had no vacancies. Others said that the Afrikaan-speaking girl would find the English-speaking situation in the convents difficult.

Then the education department notified Mr. Laing he must apply for Sandra to be admitted to the Sheepmoor school, the nearest their home.

Principal L. Dreyer said: "This is a terrible situation. I have my instructions from the education department to admit Sandra Laing. My hands are tied.

"However, I have reason to believe that, if this happens, most of the parents of the 53 other children at the school will remove their children."

Mrs. E. Van Tender, mother of two pupils at the school and a member of the school committee, commented: "The day Sandra Laing sets feet in the school, my children will be taken home. And they will stay home."

Abraham Laing doesn't know what to do about his daughter.[22]

Here are more illustrations of the arbitrary character of racial distinctions.

Take for example Germany's Nazis, who were so anxious to eliminate "inferior races" and strengthen the "Aryan race": big, blond, blue-eyed types. (Their leader in this insane enterprise, Herr Hitler, was a little, brown-haired, brown-eyed man.) Their Japanese allies were declared "honorary Aryans" and their Italian allies a subdivision of the Aryan race.

The white South Africans are quite race-conscious, as we all know. As the result of a favorable trade treaty with Japan, their Japanese citizens (about sixty people) have been classified "white," even though they look—at least to the "untrained" eye—like the Chinese, who are not "white."

At one time in Louisiana, in the days when blacks and whites were legally required to go to separate schools, Italians were required to go to school with the blacks.

The Japanese have within their midst a hereditary low-caste group sometimes called the Burakumin, sometimes the Eta.[23] They have been subject to fierce prejudice, rejection, and discrimination very similar to that experienced by America's blacks, although they are of the same race (by any definition of *race*) as the dominant Japanese. (The Japanese have always denied this.)

The Mexicans, who represent an amazing amalgam of white, Indian, and black, have a great tolerance and respect for a variety of skin colors—but their color blindness does not seem to extend to Chinese.

The French are less prejudiced against blacks than against Algerian Arabs, who have recently entered France to take on the dirty jobs of French industry, though the Arabs are physically more similar to the French than are the blacks.

Of course, race *can* be used to define a minority, but so can religion, language, and nationality. The Flemish and the Walloons in Belgium fight each other no less fiercely than the Protestants and the Catholics of northern Ireland, despite the fact that both the Flemish and the Walloons are Roman Catholics. Their clash is over language.[24]

Any observable difference, then, cultural, religious, racial, or even regional (see Table 10–4), can be the initial source of a distinction between "us" and "them," *if a group chooses to make distinctions.* But hostility and discrimination

Table 10–4. Recurring North-South Stereotypes[a]

Northerners see themselves as:	Southerners see themselves as:
1. Of strong character	1. Eloquent
2. Powerful militarily	2. Artistic
3. Economically vigorous	3. Socially refined
4. Good organizers	4. Patient
5. Industrious, hard-working	5. Clever, intelligent
6. Reliable	6. Obliging
7. Manly	7. Graceful
8. Serious	8. Amiable
9. Thrifty	9. Generous
Southerners see northerners as:	**Northerners see southerners as:**
1. Powerful economically	1. Economically weak
2. Powerful militarily	2. Militarily weak
3. Hard-working, energetic	3. Lazy
4. Physically strong	4. Weak
5. Slow and heavy	5. Quick and fast
6. Rough and dirty	6. Amiable and oily
7. Egocentric	7. Unreliable
8. Stingy	8. Wasteful
9. Pessimistic	9. Optimistic
10. Hardhearted	10. Lighthearted
11. Serious	11. Crafty
12. Stupid	12. Clever
13. Fanatic	13. Spineless

[a]Levine and Campbell cite studies by U. R. Ehrenfels on north-south stereotypes in twenty nations north of the equator. (In Brazil, south of the equator, the stereotypes are reversed and southerners have a "northerly" reputation.)

Source: Robert A. Levine and Donald T. Campbell, *Ethnocentrism: Theories of Conflict, Ethnic Attitudes and Group Behavior* (New York: John Wiley & Sons, Inc., 1972), p. 162.

often continue even when the actual initial differences are no longer visible (as was the case in the 1930s with the German Jews, who were culturally completely German and who had to be forced to wear armbands so the Nazis could identify them). As we observed earlier, these various differences are likely to have social significance *only* when there is competition for something scarce, like power, prestige, or property (see Chapter Nine, "Social Stratification," for a discussion of these stratification variables).

To some extent, *ethnic* and racial stratification* overlaps the general stratification system in all sorts of interesting ways. For example, when a majority group distinguishes itself from a minority group, it is likely that the minority will also ultimately be distinguishable from the majority on all of the stratification variables. Indians, blacks, and Chicanos are not only physically identifiable by skin color, for example, but they also tend to be at the bottom of the pile when it comes to prestige, property, and power. As we observed in Chapter

*A group is an ethnic group if its members share *cultural* characteristics, a racial group if its members share *biological* characteristics.

Nine, these ascribed characteristics also have significant effects on one's likelihood of gaining larger amounts of these benefits.

Although, as we have indicated, "visibility" is as much in the mind of the observers as it is in what they actually see, once we choose to set up certain physical differences as a way of classifying people into and out of social categories, it's hard to turn off those distinctions. The most significant difference between Indians, blacks, and Chicanos and the European immigrants is that whereas the Europeans can lose their distinctive characteristics—accents, customs, names, noses, if necessary—and move toward the heart of the economy, Indians, blacks, and Chicanos cannot. Their "visibility" compounds their problems of mobility in a way that the other minorities have never experienced.

This is *not* to say that the European immigrants have not had very serious handicaps to overcome.[25] Nor is it clear that they have it "made" even now. For example, a recent study of Poles, Italians, Latins, and blacks in Chicago's largest corporations (many of which are among the nation's leading corporations) indicates that in terms of population proportions, not only blacks and Latins but also Poles and Italians are underrepresented as top executives and as members of boards of directors, as indicated in Table 10–5.[26] (The figure for Italians is somewhat inflated by the fact that there's one man who is on the boards of nine companies. Without him the Italian figure would be 1.3 rather than 1.9.)

Predjudice and Discrimination: Chicken and Egg

You may have observed that we have had little to say about "prejudice" so far, although we have mentioned discrimination. There is a reason for that. Sociologists have only a *secondary* interest in prejudice as a phenomenon. They assume that one can discriminate without being prejudiced: ("My other customers won't like it if I serve you," "My other workers will quit if I hire you," and so on). They conversely assume that if discrimination is made difficult by fair-employment legislation, community norms, and so on, those who are prejudiced will tend to keep their prejudices to themselves and will not act on them.

There is more to the sociologist's emphasis on discrimination (behavior) rather than prejudice (feelings and attitudes). By and large sociologists reject the idea that prejudice causes discrimination. To the extent that the two are connected, they suspect that discrimination causes prejudice, or that discrimination causes prejudice which causes more discrimination. The starting point, for sociologists, is *not* prejudice. As Simpson and Yinger put it, we must not mistake the "fruits of discrimination" for the "roots of discrimination." Discrimination, in other words, causes differences between groups, differences that later may be held against the victimized group.

Table 10-5. Proportional Representation of Selected Ethnic Groups in the Chicago Metropolitan Area Population and on the Boards of Directors and Among the Officers of the 106 Largest Chicago Area Corporations[a]

		Directors		Officers	
	Percentage of Area Population	*Number*	*Percentage*	*Number*	*Percentage*
Poles	6.9	4	0.3	10	0.7
Italians	4.8	26	1.9	39	2.9
Latins	4.4	1	0.1	2	0.1
Blacks	17.6	5	0.4	1	0.1
All Other	66.3	1,305	97.3	1,303	96.2
TOTAL	100.0	1,341	100.0	1,355	100.0

[a] The "Area Population" refers to the Chicago metropolitan area: the six counties of Cook, Kane, Will, DuPage, Lake, and McHenry, whose population in 1970 was 6,979,000.

The percentages of area population were prepared by Michael E. Schiltz, director of Loyola University's Graduate Program in Urban Studies. For Poles, Italians, and Latins, the estimates include first, second, and third generations, based on U.S. Bureau of Census data.

The black population is based on 1970 data from the U.S. Census Bureau.

For the purposes of this study, the honorary board members were not included, nor were officers of less than vice-presidential rank, such as assistant vice-presidents, assistant secretaries, or assistant treasurers. Where a firm was controlled by a holding company, only the directors and the officers of the holding company were counted. An officer who was also a member of the board of directors of the same firm was counted twice, once as a director and again as an officer.

Source: Russell Barta, "The Representation of Poles, Italians, Latins and Blacks in the Executive Suites of Chicago's Largest Corporations" (Chicago: Institute of Urban Life for the National Center for Urban Ethnic Affairs, 1974).

The starting point is discrimination, and the first problem is to eliminate discrimination, not prejudice—although we assume that if discrimination is eliminated, prejudice will eventually fall by the wayside.

Personal Contact

One observation sometimes made in the attempt to account for tension between groups is that when people do not personally know members of other groups, it is easy to stereotype them as being "all alike." Although there's some truth to this, for a variety of reasons putting people in personal contact with each other does not always have the effect of reducing prejudice and stereotyping.

First, even though one experiences a pleasant relationship with a member of the other group, he may argue, "But he is different. All the others match my stereotype."

Second, even when experience with members of the other group produces some change in attitude, the change is often limited to a particular context and is not applied to other situations. Although a person now accepts a member of the other group as a coworker, or a fellow soldier, he still may not want to accept the other as a neighbor or a leisure-time companion.

Third, although a person may find that he does get along well with members of the other group, his commitment to his own group ("My group, right or wrong") may put him on the opposite side of the political fence on major issues and force him to choose solidarity with fellow group members over personal friendship:

BELFAST (AP), August 24, 1969—Just after dark on the wildest of the wild nights the doorbell tinkled in a Roman Catholic greengrocer's shop in the Crumlin Road. "Tommy, come in," said the woman behind the counter, recognizing her Protestant neighbor and good customer of long standing.

The man ignored the greeting. "I lost my home on Agnes St. tonight," he announced bitterly. "You have five minutes to get out before you're burned out."

"Sure, I had nothing to do with that," cried the woman, bursting into tears.

"I can't help that," the man said. "None of us can help anything any more." And he disappeared in the crimson glow of the crossroads where already a double-deck municipal bus, symbol of Protestant political power, was a burned skeleton and just behind it a public house, the symbol of Roman Catholic riotousness and rebellion, was leaping into flames.[27]

Yehuda Amir finds that contact between members of different groups sometimes reduces prejudice and sometimes strengthens prejudice.[28] Contact appears to *reduce* prejudice

a) when there is equal status contact between the members of the various ethnic groups, b) when the contact is between members of a majority group and *higher* status members of a minority group, c) when an "authority" and/or the social climate are in favor of and promote the intergroup contact, d) when the contact is of an intimate rather than a casual nature, e) when the ethnic intergroup contact is pleasant or rewarding, f) when the members of *both* groups in the particular contact situation interact in functionally important activities or develop common goals or superordinate goals that are higher ranking in importance than the individual goals of *each* of the groups.[29]

On the other hand, contact may *strengthen* prejudice

a) when the contact situation produces competition between the groups, b) when the contact is unpleasant, involuntary, tension-laden; c) when the prestige or the status of one group is lowered as a result of the contact situation, d) when members of a group or the group as a whole are in a state of frustration (i.e., inadequate personality structure, recent defeat or failure, economic depression, etc.)—here contact with another group may lead to the establishment of an ethnic "scapegoat," e) when the groups in contact have moral or ethnic standards which are objectionable to each other, f) in the case of contact between a majority and a minority group, when the members of the minority group are of a lower status or are lower in any relevant characteristic than the members of the majority group.[30]

Two classic studies demonstrate that prejudice and discrimination are only imperfectly connected. A study by J. D. Lohman and D. C. Reitzes[31] describes, for example, a group of industrial workers who supported and applauded their racially integrated union but lived in a segregated neighborhood that they vigorously defended against "invasion" by their nonwhite fellow union members. Minard,[32] studying miners in West Virginia, observed that most of the white miners (about 60 percent) worked with black miners as equals in the mines but outside the mine lived in a segregated world and treated them as inferiors. Twenty percent were friendly with black miners both outside and inside the mine. For the majority, it was the "situation" that determined their behavior:

> The boundary line between the two communities is usually the mine's mouth. Management assists the miners in recognizing their entrance into the outside community with its distinctions in status by providing separate baths and locker rooms. The color line, that is, becomes immediately visible as soon as the miners' eyes accustomed to the inner darkness of the mine have accommodated themselves to the light of the outside world. . . .
>
> The white miner adjusts to these conflicting influences by adoption of a dual role. Within the mine he assumes a role toward his fellow workers posited upon acceptance of practical equality of status. Outside his role as member of the white community involves an elevation of status in which he becomes a member of a superior caste group.[33]

Some final observations about the imperfect relationship between prejudice and discrimination come from a study by Albert I. Hermalin and Reynolds Farley.[34] They observed that we are in a period of controversy over the "right" of children to attend "neighborhood schools" balanced against the right of black children to go to unsegregated schools, with the busing of children a way of integrating schools that is unattractive to parents of both races. Obviously we could have both desegregated *and* neighborhood schools if *neighborhoods* were integrated. If we ask whites how they feel about having black neighbors who have the same income and educational level as they themselves, we find that more than 80 percent say that would be okay with them. Seventy-five percent of whites nationwide favor integrated schools. In Detroit in 1972, 70 percent of whites disagreed with the idea that white and black children should go to *separate* schools, but 90 percent of suburban and city whites are against busing.

In terms of public statements about prejudice, then, the majority of suburban whites say that they don't object to having black neighbors of *equal income and education,* that they don't believe in separate schools, but that they don't believe in busing children to integrate schools.

Hermalin and Farley studied twenty-nine urbanized areas, including thirty-nine central cities and their surrounding suburbs across the nation but giving special attention to Detroit. They found, as you will have guessed, that blacks are heavily concentrated in the central cities and that whites are heavily concentrated in the suburbs. In Detroit in 1970, for example, 70 percent of white households and 11 percent of black households were in the suburban ring around the city. What Hermalin and Farley were primarily looking for were ways of estimating the proportions of blacks who would be living in the suburbs *if, in fact,* income and value of housing were the *only* factors determining residence. To do this they examined income data for whites and blacks both in and out of the suburbs, as well as the value of the homes owned or rented by members of each group.

Using income as a method of predicting who ought to be living where, they found that "If Detroit area black families were represented in the suburbs to the same extent as white with comparable incomes, 67 percent rather than the observed 12 percent of black families would have suburban residences."[35] The result would be the same if housing value rather than income were to be used as the criterion. Although black incomes rose during the decade between 1960 and 1970, almost no change occurred in the proportion of blacks at *any* income level living in the suburban ring. To put it another way, blacks whose income increases move to more expensive houses *in black areas* rather than to the suburbs.

The survey results indicate that *in principle* prosperous suburban whites "prefer" prosperous blacks as neighbors to poor whites, but they end up with poor whites as neighbors more often than with prosperous blacks. Black families with incomes between $15,000 and $25,000 are *under*represented in the suburbs, whereas white families with incomes between $5,000 and $7,000 a year are *over*represented. Proportionately, there are more poor whites than prosperous blacks in the suburbs of the twenty-nine urbanized areas. Apparently a low-income white family can obtain a suburban home or apartment more readily than a high income black family.

If we take the statements of suburban whites at face value as indications that they are not prejudiced toward prosperous blacks, how do we account for the fact that blacks can't seem to move into the suburbs? Obviously blacks' inability to afford suburban housing is not a useful explanation, nor is prejudice by suburban residents strong enough *by itself* to explain the absence of blacks from suburbia. In the first case even prosperous blacks can't break out of central cities, and in the second case white suburbanites seem not to object to having prosperous blacks as neighbors.

Judge Roth of Detroit, who in 1972 ordered school busing across city lines because there were not enough whites within the city lines to integrate the schools, observed that the magic word is *discrimination:*

> The city of Detroit is a community generally divided by racial lines. Residential segregation within the city and throughout the larger metropolitan areas is substantial, pervasive, and of long standing. Black citizens are located in separate and distinct areas within the city and are not generally to be found in the suburbs. While the racially unrestricted choice of black persons and economic factors may have played some part in the development of this pattern of residential segregation, it is, in the main, the result of past and present practices and

customs of racial discrimination, both public and private, which have and do restrict the housing opportunities of black people.

Governmental action and inaction at all levels: federal, state, and local, have combined with those of private organizations, such as loaning institutions, real estate associations, and brokerage firms, to establish and maintain the patterns of residential segregation throughout the Detroit metropolitan area.[36]

The Hermalin and Farley study ends on several hopeful notes. They observed that, contrary to popular opinion:

Increasing the proportion of blacks in white areas of the city or in the suburban ring does not require locating low income or subsidized housing in the suburbs, nor must residential integration await the further upgrading of black income. Policy makers should be made aware that this change does not require massive expenditures of federal, state, or local money. Further steps to equalize the economic status of blacks and whites or to provide better housing to all low income people are indeed desirable on other grounds, but these steps need not delay the increased amount of residential integration already possible.[37]

They further observed that although there are still informal real estate practices, mortgage lending arrangements, and other factors that block blacks from obtaining housing for which they are economically qualified, we have finally removed explicit federal and state practices that in the past hindered residential integration (such as some Federal Housing Administration lending practices that existed into the 1960s).

Their article ends with the point it began with, that busing is not the only way to integrate schools: "The economic potential exists to largely achieve both integrated schools and neighborhood schools through greater residential integration."[38] Moreover, they suggest that the educational effects of school integration achieved through residential integration rather than busing may "promote a contact among blacks and whites of approximate socioeconomic equality that may better accomplish both educational goals and racial harmony."[39]

Their argument sounds perfectly sensible, but what is sensible and what actually occurs in intergroup relations are often two different things, as can be seen in the fact that the date on their hopeful article was October 1973. In February of 1974 the Supreme Court heard arguments by suburban schools protesting busing and complaining that eventually 300,000 pupils would have to be bussed if the metropolitan desegregation plan approved by lower federal courts (to combine white suburban schools and black city schools) was to be carried out. Those favoring the plan argued that only a metropolitan district could counter the consequences of state education and housing policies that had confined black students to the central city. As observed earlier, we could have both desegregated schools *and* neighborhood schools if neighborhoods were integrated. In July of 1974 the Supreme Court rejected the busing plan.[40]

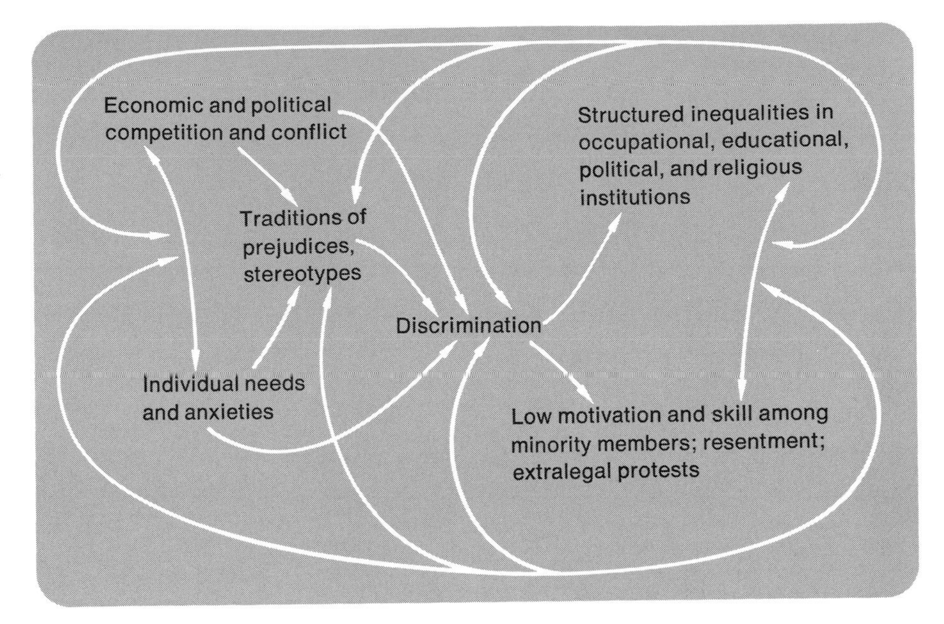

Figure 10–1. The Discrimination Cycle. (*Source:* In slightly modified form from G. E. Simpson and J. M. Yinger, *Racial and Cultural Minorities: An Analysis of Prejudice and Discrimination,* 4th Ed. [New York: Harper and Row, Publishers, 1972], p. 157).

Well, What Do You Expect?

Sociologists have found that minority status is related to all sorts of behavior. Minority group members tend to differ from the majority in income, crime rates, mortality rates, success at school, divorce rates, life styles, and so on. Figure 10–1 indicates schematically some of the complex relationships in the various aspects of intergroup behavior. As you can see, all kinds of "vicious cycles" result from minority status and the perpetuation of minority status. The precise details of how minority status leads to discrimination, how discrimination leads to prejudice, how prejudice leads to more discrimination, and how discrimination leads to various kinds of behavior are not always clear. Although the *details* are not always clear, we do have some pretty good ideas about how some of these variables are connected.

Let's examine a little piece of the puzzle, education. One of the most significant areas in which minorities and majorities differ is in success at school. Success at school is a key to other variables, like the kinds of jobs one becomes able to compete for, and one's job has further implications for many other aspects of his life.

We have a great deal of evidence that family background is a very good predictor of success at school. Poor children and minority children (the categories overlap, but they are not identical) tend not to do well at school.[41] Part of this lack of success seems to be attributable to differences in motivation, preparation, and encouragement from the home, with middle-class children having certain advantages, advantages that seem to make it possible for them to do well *even in inferior schools.* For children who are not middle-class, the quality of their schools makes a great deal of difference.

As the famous Coleman Report (a study of all third, sixth, ninth, and twelfth graders in four thousand schools across the United States) observes, minority students and poor students *do not* tend to go to schools that are equal to those of majority students to begin with. R. A. Dentler, summarizing this report, observed:

> The basic findings of the Coleman Report are these: In the metropolitan North Negro and Puerto Rican pupils, as compared to white pupils, attend schools in older, larger, and more crowded buildings. They have access to fewer laboratories and library books, auditoriums and gymnasiums. Their elementary teachers show a slightly lower score on a short vocabulary test. Even their cafeterias and athletic playing fields are in shorter supply. . . . The Coleman data are comprehensive enough and the findings distinct enough to release us from endless cycling on questions of equality of public educational services. Facilities, staffs, and services are distributed unequally. Without exception, on the factors catalogued, the pattern of the inequality uniformly reinforces handicaps brought to the school by the low-income, minority-group learner.[42]

Coleman observed:

> The average white student's achievement is less affected by the strengths or weaknesses of his school's facilities, curricula, and teachers than is the average minority pupil's. To put it another way, the achievement of minority pupils depends more on the schools they attend than does the achievement of majority pupils. . . . The conclusion can then be drawn that improving the school of a minority pupil will increase his achievement more than will improving the school of a white child increase his. Similarly, the average minority pupil's achievement will suffer more in a school of low quality than will the average white pupil's. In short, whites . . . are less affected one way or the other by the quality of their schools than are minority pupils. This indicates that it is for the most disadvantaged children that improvement in school quality will make the most difference in achievement.[43]

A number of obvious factors play a part in the difference in success of middle-class and non-middle-class children. Many of these factors can be altered by the spending of more money for tutoring, equipment, books, and other resources. (In 1974 Ralph Tyler concluded that programs that are successful at helping "disadvantaged children" tend to cost between $600 and $900 a year per pupil more than the "standard" programs that are effective for pupils who are not "disadvantaged.")[44]

Over the last few years we have discovered that certain factors affecting minority performance in school have nothing to do with the availability of money or equipment. We can briefly summarize them this way: many teachers *expect* poor performances and *therefore* they *get* poor performances. That sounds too easy. Would *expecting* success really *produce* success? *Yes!* The classic study in this area of "teacher expectancies" was done by Robert Rosenthal and Lenore Jacobson.[45] They gave a battery of tests to all the children from kindergarten to fifth grade in a predominantly lower-class school in San Francisco. They announced to the teachers that certain children were, according to the tests, going to show a sharp "spurt" in intellectual performance over the course of the coming school year. Twenty percent of the students were described as "spurters." How did Rosenthal and Jacobson know these children would show such improvement? They didn't. The names were picked at random, but of course the teachers didn't know that.

Not only did the children selected as "spurters" do well in class, the next year they even showed measurable gains in IQ. Teachers also described these children at the end of the year as more appealing, better adjusted, more affectionate, and less in need of social approval than the children who had not been singled out as "spurters." Remember that the only actual original difference between the two groups was in the label applied by the researchers.

There were some children who showed intellectual gains over the course of the year despite the fact that they had *not* been described as spurters, and some of these children had already been designated by the school as belonging in low-ability groups. When these "control" children showed intellectual growth (especially those who had been placed in low-ability groups), they were rated *un*favorably by their teachers. The least favorable ratings by teachers went to those children in the control group who had gained *most* intellectually. The teachers, then, described in very favorable terms those who were expected to spurt and in very unfavorable terms those who showed intellectual growth when they had *not* been expected to.

Rosenthal and Jacobson show only that by telling teachers that randomly selected children would do well in school they could *improve* the children's school performance. They didn't collect any information on the way these expectations got transmitted by the teachers to the children or on the different work methods the teachers used with those they expected success from and with those they did not expect success from.

Let's look at some other studies for clues to these things. W. Victor Beez[46] took 60 five- and six-year-olds who had been signed up for summer Head Start programs and randomly assigned them to "low-ability" and "high-ability" groups, ignoring their actual IQs, which ranged from 55 to 127 on the Peabody Picture Vocabulary Test. The "teachers" in his experiment were summer graduate students in education and had an average of four years' teaching experience. He concocted biographies for the children and gave each "teacher" a folder that described the child he was to tutor as either a "deprived" child with low ability and a low *average* IQ or a highly motivated child with high ability and a normal IQ. Each teacher was asked to teach a certain set of tasks to one of the children and was given either the folder describing the "high-ability" child or the one describing the "low-ability" child. (The same description was used for each high- or low-ability child, except that Beez put in the child's real name and age.)

After the teacher read the false report, the child was brought into the room and the teacher was asked to teach the child to identify a series of symbols or words printed on individual cards ("STOP," "GO," "WALK," "BOYS," "GIRLS," "DANGER," and so on). He was given ten minutes in which to teach the child to identify as many symbols as possible. Beez observed the amount of time spent on each card, the number of signs covered, the number of times the teacher went over each card, and so on. After this task and another task (doing puzzles), the "teacher" was asked to fill out a questionnaire about the child he had been assigned to teach.

Beez found that the teachers of the "high-ability" children tried to teach more symbols (an average of 10.3 words) than the teachers of the "low-ability" children (an average of 5.66 words). Eighty-seven percent of the teachers expecting better performance tried to cover eight or more symbols; only 13 percent of the teachers expecting poor performance tried to cover as many as eight symbols. How many symbols did the children learn? The average for the "high-ability" group was 5.9 symbols and for the "low ability" group 3.1 symbols (77 percent of the "high-ability" pupils learned five or more symbols; 13 percent of the "low-ability" pupils learned five or more symbols).

Beez observed that there were differences in the teachers' evaluations of a variety of characteristics of the children, in the amount of time spent on each symbol, and on some other variables that we won't go into. He commented:

> Some anecdotal material is of interest. One child in the "high ability" group whose actual IQ was 71 (measured *after* the experiment) was taught 14 signs and learned 7; another child in the "low ability" group with a tested IQ of 127 was taught only 5 signs and learned 3.
>
> After the total experiment was over, the author reported to the groups of [subjects] on the actual intent of the experiment. While the "high ability" teachers were rather pleased, the "low-ability" teachers seemed more inclined to argue ("but my child *really* was retarded"). Two teachers, in fact, believed that the report had given the IQ as falling within the retarded range.
>
> Mismatches between the report and the events of the teaching situation occurred, but did not seem to affect [subject] expectations. One child did not speak, though the report described him as "frequently initiating conversation." [The subject] nevertheless rated the report as "most helpful." In another case, a boy was misidentified as a girl in the report; S found the report "most helpful" and proceeded with "high ability" expectations.[47]

Pamela C. Rubovitz and Martin L. Maehr[48] have provided us with more fascinating experimental evidence of different responses to children described as "gifted" or "not gifted," half of whom were white and half black.

The "teachers" were white female undergraduates enrolled in a teacher-training course; the pupils were seventh- and eighth-graders. Each "teacher" was given a class made up of four randomly selected children. Altogether 264 children were involved.

Each class had one black child described as "gifted," one black child described as "nongifted," one "gifted" white child, and one "nongifted" white child. The teachers were led to believe that the "gifted" children had IQs between 130 and 135 and the "nongifted" had IQs between 98 and 102. Of course, the labels and the IQs were assigned randomly. An observer then watched what happened over the course of the next forty minutes. The observer was tallying instances of several kinds of behavior.

Here are some of the findings. More *attention* was given to the white students overall than to the blacks. That's a crude measure. What kind of attention was given? Fewer statements were requested of blacks than of whites. More statements by blacks than by whites were ignored. Black students were praised less and criticized more than whites. The most striking differences were between the "gifted" whites and the "gifted" blacks. It was the "gifted" black who was given the *least* attention, received the *least* praise, and was *most* criticized. In all of these he was followed by the "nongifted" black and then by the "nongifted" white. The "gifted" white received the most attention, was called on more, and was praised more (but received a bit more criticism) than the "non-gifted" white.

Overall, then, the "gifted" students were given a *positive* response if they were white, a *negative* response if they were black. Rubovitz and Maehr also observed that in informal interviews with the teachers after the "class," the "gifted" white student "was chosen most frequently as the most liked student, the brightest student, and the certain leader of the class."[49]

Remember that these were children who were randomly given these labels (actually they all had average tested intelligence), and remember that we are talking about the responses of sixty-six different "teachers" handling sixty-six "classes" made up of four different students each time. We are not talking about the responses of a few unique "teachers" to any particular group of four students but about a systematic pattern of biased responses by *most* of these "teachers." Attention, praise, encouragement, and criticism, then, are some of the means by which *teacher expectations* get translated into *student performance.*

We've given you a brief look at some studies in which teachers were led to believe that certain children would perform well or perform normally. You can't ethically tell teachers in an experiment that children will perform *badly,* but teachers may get the idea by themselves. Take, for example, W. Burleigh Seaver's[50] study, in which he examined the grades of first-graders who had an older brother or sister who had preceded them through the same school and done well or badly. He was interested in finding out what effect having an older brother or sister with a certain reputation would have on the first-grader's grades. He found that the first-graders tended to get good grades if the brother or sister had been a good student and low grades if big brother or sister had not been a good student. Then he examined the grades given the younger child by teachers who had also had the older child in their classes ("expectancy group") and those who had had *only* the younger child in class ("control group"). He found that if the older child had done well, so did the younger one—but the expectancy teachers gave the younger ones *better* grades than the control teachers gave them. Likewise, if the older child had not been a good pupil, the younger child also got low grades, but they were *lower* in the expectancy group than in the control classes.

We have focused on younger children, who might be considered more easily affected by teacher responses than, say, adolescents. Walter E. Schaffer, Carol Olexa, and Kenneth Polk[51] demonstrated that placing high school students in college preparatory tracks or general tracks affected grades, commitments to school and dropout rates, delinquent behavior, self-esteem, and several other student characteristics. They demonstrated that these various differences *resulted* from placement in the two different tracks rather than being *causes* of placement in the two tracks.

First comes the label "college material" or "not college material," *then* comes the behavior that convinces teachers and schools that they were correct in expecting good things of the first group and not very good things of the second. As Schafer, Olexa, and Polk put it, the "forecasters" are not only *forecasting* the weather, they are *producing* it.

Let's move away from public schools and youngsters and move on to an interesting study by Albert S. King[52] of adults in three job-training programs. These were adults whose educational backgrounds were weak. They were "hard-core" unemployed people who were just entering the job-training programs. The programs trained people for three kinds of jobs: the women were learning to be pressers; the men were learning to be welders or mechanics. They were all given a test that was described to their supervisors as a "specially developed aptitude test for the disadvantaged." The supervisors had no knowledge about the past behavior of the trainees, but they were given the results of this fake test and asked not to discuss them with anyone. The supervisors were told that all the trainees had performed satisfactorily and would show progress in their training but that one group (actually selected at random) had "exceptionally high aptitude" and could be expected to show exceptional gains from the training they were about to undergo. There we have the control group and the experimental group, respectively.

What difference did these false predictions make? The supervisors' ratings of the special group at the end of the programs (four months for pressers, five months for welders, nine months for mechanics) were higher than their ratings of the control subjects. The experimental trainees were rated as "being more knowledgeable about jobs, producing better volume of neat and accurate work, showing greater ability to learn new duties, having more initiative, giving better cooperation, exerting more logic in job tasks, and generally showing the best performance."[53] There is more. The trainees were asked near the end of the program to rank the other trainees in three areas: whom they would most like to work with, whom they would most like to be with, and whom they judged as having shown the best overall performance. Their fellow trainees, who of course knew nothing about the false expectations planted with the supervisors, rated the experimental group much more favorably on all three measures than they rated fellow members of the control group. Objectively, the experimental group actually did end up learning faster and having fewer absences or dropouts from the program than those arbitrarily assigned to the control group.

King did another little experiment with some of the trainees to learn something about the way supervisors transmitted their expectations to the trainees. He showed each welding trainee two *almost* identical photographs of his supervisor. The difference between the two photos was in the eyes; one photo was modified to make the pupil size of the supervisor's eyes much larger than the other. Some trainees from both experimental and control groups were then asked two questions: "Do you see any differences in these pictures of your supervisor?" and "Whether you see any difference or not, can you select the photo that shows how you usually see the supervisor looking at you?"

None of the trainees noticed that the two photos were different and most picked a photo for the second question without specifying their reason. All five experimental trainees picked the photo with the *enlarged* pupils. Five of the seven control trainees picked the *other* photo. Why did all those in the experimental group pick the photo with the larger pupil size?

> One highly persuasive psychological explanation is that large pupil-size serves to convery more favorable attitudes and expectations. The basic principle is quite simple. With respect to pupil-size, there is a continuum of responses that range from large dilation for favorable attitudes to extreme contraction or "pinpoints of hate" for unfavorable feelings toward another person. Clearly, the eye contact in face-to-face relations is likely to serve as an unintentional, but nevertheless remarkable, indicator of the attitude, interest, and expectations supervisors hold for subordinates. Most likely, expectations are communicated without any awareness by either supervisor or subordinate. Although trainees were not aware of the subtleties involved, these, as well as other complex and unnoticed cues operating in interpersonal relations with supervisor, may have come to shape their own attitudes, motivations, and job performance.[54]

Expectancies didn't produce an effect only through these highly subtle psychological means. King suggested that the supervisors probably gave closer attention and some preferential treatment to the trainees who'd been selected as "special." It was not at all clear to King how the supervisors' expectations influenced those peer ratings, but somehow the others did pick up the supervisors' expectations. Such is the "Power of Positive Expectations"!

Summary

A majority, defined in terms of power and privilege rather than size, may respond to minorities by policies of assimilation, pluralism, relocation, subjugation, or extermination. Assimilation may cost the minority its cultural distinctiveness without guaranteeing complete acceptance. Pluralism may guarantee group rights at the cost of some individual freedoms without guaranteeing political stability or equal treatment. Discrimination interests sociologists more than prejudice does and may create vicious circles that produce continued discrimination. The expectation of inferior school performance from minorities and the poor are a major cause of inferior performance by minorities and the poor.

Notes

1. "Colombia Trial Bares Life (Everyone Kills Indians) on Plains," *New York Times* (July 9, 1972), p. 9. Nineteen seventy-two was also the year in which in the African nation of Burundi the politically dominant Tutsis (15 percent of the population, in the wake of an unsuccessful coup d'etat by the Hutu tribe (85 percent of the population), slaughtered some eighty thousand Hutu. In 1973 more massacres of the Hutu took place. See "Witnesses Tell of Horror in New Burundi Slaughter," *New York Times* (June 17, 1973), p. 1.

2. T. Shibutani and K. M. Kwan, *Ethnic Stratification* (New York: Macmillan Publishing Co., Inc., 1965), p. 8. The reference is to W. C. MacLeod, *The American Indian Frontier* (New York: Alfred A. Knopf, Inc., 1928), p. 487.

3. Louis Wirth provided this definition of a minority, which you will observe says nothing about size: "a group of people who, because of their physical or cultural characteristics, are singled out from the others in the society in which they live for differential and unequal treatment and who therefore regard themselves as objects of collective discrimination." L. Wirth, "The Problem of Minority Groups," in R. Linton, ed. *The Science of Man in the World Crisis* (New York: Columbia University Press, 1945), p. 347. A recent book has argued that by this standard there are a number of groups that are not usually considered monorities that do fit such a definition. The articles in E. Sagarin, ed., *The Other Minorities* (Waltham, Mass.: Ginn and Company, 1971), discuss from this perspective: women, homosexuals, adolescents, the aged, the crippled, the dwarf, the mentally retarded, lepers, ex-convicts, police, the "radical right," and intellectuals.

4. G. Myrdal, *An American Dilemma: The Negro Problem and Modern Democracy* (New York: Harper and Row, Publishers, 1944). See also Helen M. Hacker, "Women as a Minority Group," *Social Forces,* **30** (1951), 60–69.

5. G. Watson and D. Johnson, *Social Psychology: Issues and Insights,* 2nd Ed. (Philadelphia: J. B. Lippincott Co., 1972), pp. 345–346.

6. This set of observations is based on D. L. Noel, "A Theory of the Origin of Ethnic Stratification" *Social Problems,* **16** (1968), 157–172; and E. A. T. Barth and D. L. Noel, "Conceptual Frameworks for the Analysis of Race Relations: An Evaluation," *Social Forces,* **50** (1972), 333–348. They suggest that three variables that determine the outcome of initial contacts between different groups are ethnocentrism, competition, and power. For examples of different groups which co-existed peacefully in mutually satisfying exchange relationships, see Lindgren's discussion of the Tungus and Cossacks of Northwest Manchuria and M. W. Smith's discussion of the relationship between the Puyallup Indians of Washington and the early white settlers. E. J. Lindgren, "An Example of Culture Contact Without Conflict: Reindeer Tungus and Cossacks of Northwest Manchuria," *American Anthropologist,* **40** (1938), 605–621; M. W. Smith, "The Puyallup of Washington," in R. Linton (ed.), *Acculturation in Seven American Indian Tribes.* (New York: Appleton-Century, 1940), pp. 3–36.

7. This section of the chapter draws heavily on G. E. Simpson and J. M. Yinger, *Racial and Cultural Minorities: An Analysis of Prejudice and Discrimination,* 4th Ed. (New York: Harper and Row, Publishers, 1972), Chapter 1.

8. Ibid., p. 16.

9. Ibid., pp. 17ff.

10. M. Gordon, *Assimilation in American Life* (New York: Oxford University Press, 1964).

11. The discussion of Switzerland is based on Kurt B. Mayer, "The Jura Problem: Ethnic

Conflict in Switzerland," *Social Research,* **35** (1968), 707–741. The Jura are a French-speaking group in Switzerland's Berne canton (predominately German), and for a variety of reasons they lack the "cross-cutting cleavages" that tie the other groups to Switzerland. There have been attempts by separatists to get the region to secede from Berne and become a separate canton. See also K. B. Mayer, "Cultural Pluralism and Linguistic Equilibrium," *American Sociological Review,* **16** (1971), 157–163.

12. The section on Yugoslavia draws heavily on Chester L. Hunt and Lewis Walker, *Ethnic Dynamics: Patterns of Intergroup Relations in Various Societies* (Homewood, Ill.: Dorsey Press, 1974), pp. 363–398.

13. These approximate population figures for 1961 are drawn from Hunt and Walker, op. cit., p. 367: Serbs, 8 million; Croats, 4 million; Slovenes, 1.5 million; Macedonians, 1 million; Montenegrins, 500,000; Moslems (ethnic), 1 million; Yugoslavs, 300,000; Albanians, 1 million; Hungarians, 500,000; Turks, 200,000; Slovaks, 90,000; Bulgarians, 60,000; Rumanians, 60,000; Ruthenians, 38,000; Italians, 25,000; Czechs, 30,000; Gypsies, Vlachs, and others, 140,000.

14. See, for example, "Tests That Destroy," *Newsweek* (September 20, 1971), p. 97.

15. Hunt and Walker, op. cit., p. 397. For a good overview of the way a number of different nations handle the questions of religious, cultural, and linguistic "group rights" in education, see Vernon Van Dyke, "Equality Discrimination in Education: A Comparative and International Analysis," *International Studies Quarterly,* **17** (1973), 375–404; and V. Van Dyke, "Human Rights Without Discrimination," *American Political Science Review,* **67** (1973), 1267–1274.

16. Raymond H. Anderson, "Religious Balance in Lebanon Upset" *New York Times* (February 23, 1974), p. 6.

17. See A. M. Greeley, *Why Can't They Be Like Us?: America's White Ethnic Groups* (New York: American Jewish Committee, 1969); or the expanded version of the book (New York: E. P. Dutton & Co., Inc., 1971). See also A. M. Greeley, "Political Attitudes Among American White Ethnics," *Public Opinion Quarterly,* **36** (1972), 213–220.

18. Simpson and Yinger, op. cit., p. 22.

19. For a recent discussion of the relocation see S. Frank Miyamoto, "The Forced Evacuation of the Japanese Minority During World War II," *Journal of Social Issues,* **29** (1973), 11–31. This issue of the journal is devoted to studies of Asian-Americans.

20. Bernard Weintraub, "Biharis of Bangladesh Subsist in Ghettos of Despair," *New York Times* (March 15, 1973), p. 2. An article by Weintraub a year later indicated almost no change in the status of the Biharis: "Victims of History, Stranded Biharis in Bangladesh Slide Toward Tragedy," *New York Times* (February 5, 1974), p. 10.

21. Simpson and Yinger, op. cit., Chapter 2, provide a good summary and discussion of different ways to define "race."

22. "South African Girl Left in Limbo Over Education," *Toledo Blade* (October 11, 1967), p. 56.

23. See John Donohue, "An Eta Community in Japan: The Social Persistence of Outcast Groups," *American Anthropologist,* **59** (1957), 1000–1017; and R. P. Dore and K. Aoyagi, "The Buraku Minority in Urban Japan," in A. M. Rose and C. B. Rose, eds., *Minority Problems* (New York: Harper and Row, Publishers, 1965), pp. 88–92. See also "Ainu Power," *Newsweek* (December, 3, 1973), p. 54. The Ainu are a Caucasian tribe in Northern Japan whose history and plight parallel in many respects those of American Indians.

24. Hunt and Walker, op. cit., include interesting discussions of the French-Arab, Flemish-Walloon, and Irish Protestant-Catholic clashes, as well as a discussion of the Mexicans and Chinese.

25. Oscar Handlin's *The Uprooted,* 2nd Ed., enlarged (New York: Atlantic Monthly Press, 1973), provides a very readable history of the problems of European immigrants to the United States.

26. Russell Barta, "The Representation of Poles, Italians, Latins and Blacks in the Executive Suites of Chicago's Largest Corporations" (Chicago: Institute of Urban Life, 1974). We feel compelled to point out that in a strict logical sense the results of such a head count cannot be considered to *prove* discrimination, although, of course, they raise some interesting questions.

27. Cited in Hunt and Walker, op. cit., p. 36.

28. Yehuda Amir, "Contact Hypothesis in Ethnic Relations," *Psychological Bulletin,* **71** (1969), 319–342. See also W. S. Ford, "Interracial Public Housing in a Border City: Another Look at the Contact Hypothesis," *American Journal of Sociology,* **78** (1973), 1426–1447.

29. Amir, op. cit., p. 338.

30. Ibid.

31. J. D. Lohman and D. C. Reitzes, "Note on Race Relations in Mass Society," *American Journal of Sociology,* **58** (1952), 240–246.

32. R. D. Minard, "Race Relationships in the Pocahontas Coal Field," *Journal of Social Issues,* **8** (1952), 29–44.

33. Ibid., p. 30.

34. Albert I. Hermalin and Reynolds Farley, "The Potential for Residential Integration in Cities and Suburbs: Implications for the Busing Controversy," *American Sociological Review,* **38** (1973), 595–610. For an exploration of the complex relationships between attitudes toward busing and attitudes toward integration and a number of other issues, see J. Kelley, "The Politics of School Busing," *Public Opinion Quarterly,* **38** (1974), 23–39.

35. Hermalin and Farley, op. cit., p. 602.

36. Cited in Hermalin and Farley, p. 609.

37. Ibid.

38. Ibid.

39. Ibid.

40. "Government Urges High Court to Bar Detroit-Area School Plan," *New York Times* (February 28, 1974), p. 38. Also see "High Court Ruling Blocks City-Suburb School Links to Achieve Integration" *New York Times* (July 26, 1974), p. 1.

41. A recent, massive, twenty-two-nation study of educational achievement shows that home background is no less significant elsewhere. See Fred M. Hechinger, "Pupil Performance: Home Is a Crucial Factor," *New York Times* (May 27, 1973), Section 4, p. 9; and G. and F. Hechinger, "Are Schools Better in Other Countries?," *American Education,* **10** (1974), 6–8. See also the whole issue of *Acta Sociologica,* **16:**4 (1973).

42. R. A. Dentler, "Equality of Educational Opportunity: A Special Review, " *The Urban Review,* **1** (1966), 27–28.

43. J. S. Coleman, *Equality of Educational Opportunity* (Washington, D.C.: U.S. Department of Health, Education, and Welfare, 1966), p. 21. See also F. Mosteller and D. Moynihan (eds.), *On Equality of Educational Opportunity: Papers Deriving from the Harvard University Faculty Seminar on the Coleman Report* (New York: Random House, Inc., 1972).

44. R. W. Tyler, "The Federal Role in Education," *The Public Interest,* **34** (1974), 164–187.

45. Robert Rosenthal and Lenore Jacobson, *Pygmalion in the Classroom: Teacher Expectancy and Pupil's Intellectual Development* (New York: Holt, Rinehart & Winston, Inc., 1968). Rosenthal provides a brief review of the findings of 242 studies in this area in "The Pygmalion Effect Lives," *Psychology Today,* (September 1973), 56–63.

46. W. Victor Beez, "Influence of Biased Psychological Reports on Teacher Behavior and Pupil Performance," in M. B. Miles and W. W. Charters, Jr., eds., *Learning in Social Settings* (Boston: Allyn & Bacon, Inc., 1970), pp. 328–334.

47. Ibid., pp. 333–334.

48. Pamela C. Rubovitz and Martin L. Maehr, "Pygmalion Black and White," *Journal of Personality and Social Psychology,* **25** (1973), 210–218.

49. Ibid., p. 217.

50. W. Burleigh Seaver, "Effects of Naturally Induced Teacher Expectancies," *Journal of Personality and Social Psychology,* **28** (1973), 333–342.

51. Walter E. Schafer, Carol Olexa, and Kenneth Polk, "Programmed for Social Class: Tracking in High School," *Transaction,* (October 1970), 39ff.

52. Albert S. King, "Self-fulfilling Prophecies in Training the Hard Core: Supervisors Expecta-

tions and the Underprivileged Workers' Performance," *Social Science Quarterly,* **52** (1971), 369–378.

53. Ibid., p. 373.

54. Ibid., pp. 376–377. For a recent discussion of pupil size as a psychological measure see M. P. Janisse and W. S. Peavler, "Pupillary Response Today: Emotion in the Eye," *Psychology Today,* (February 1974), 60–63.

ELEVEN

Deviance

How Do You Define Deviance?

RECENTLY one sociologist asked 180 people to tell him which acts and persons they considered "deviant." Among the more than 250 replies were these predictable responses: homosexuals, prostitutes, drug addicts, radicals, and criminals.

But the responses also included these:

> liars, career women, Democrats, reckless drivers, atheists, Christians, suburbanites, the retired, young folks, card players, bearded men, artists, pacifists, priests, prudes, hippies, straights, girls who wear makeup, the President, conservatives, integrationists, executives, divorcees, perverts, motorcycle gangs, smart-alec students, know-it-all professors, modern people, and Americans.[1]

If someone asked you to look at this list and then to define *deviance* you'd probably end up tearing out your hair and mumbling to yourself. In time, you're likely to say, "The only thing these people have in common is that something they do annoys someone else." You'd be right. That's all they *do* have in common. This suggests that if we are to study "what makes people deviant" the answers are more likely to be found if we look at *other* people than if we look at the alleged deviant.

There's little value in trying to answer broad questions like, "Why are people deviant?" or "What do deviants have in common that will help us explain deviance?" On the other hand, there may be some value in asking questions like, "What kinds of things are likely to *happen* to people who are considered deviant by others?" Although the "causes" of different kinds of "deviance" may not be the same or even similar, we do, in fact, have reason to believe that the *responses* to "deviance" have a number of similarities. Before we explore these responses, let's look at the list again.

There seem to be three major criteria used by the respondents for including people in the list. Sociologists interested in deviance use these same three standards in deciding which kinds of behavior to include in their theories about deviance. Some of the behavior we can call instances of *concrete deviance,* some of them are instances of *behavioral deviance,* and some of them are instances of *valuative deviance.*

Concrete deviance is any characteristic that is statistically unusual or different or untypical behavior. The circus midget, the seven-foot-tall basketball player, the spinster, the bachelor, the genius, the mentally retarded person, the left-handed person, the person with tattoos all over his body, the person who is badly physically scarred or who is missing an arm or a leg are all deviants by this definition.

For some sociologists and most laymen this is an unsatisfying way of defining *deviance.* They would object on these grounds: first, statistically unusual behavior is not necessarily considered *immoral* behavior by others, and we should really focus on behavior that has some relevance to the society's judgments of morality. Second, even where statistically unusual behavior does have some moral dimension, we ought to classify such behavior as deviant only if the society has laws or other rules forbidding such behavior. Third, most of the behavior that we could define as deviant by using statistical criteria is irrelevant. Such behavior does not threaten the society and harms no one, including the "deviant," and we therefore ought to exclude it from our definitions of deviance. A final criticism, which would probably be raised more often by laymen than by sociologists, is that morality cannot be understood or defined by head counts. If we let "deviant" and "nondeviant" be decided by counts of *how many* people do something, we may find that the people we, as moralists, would like to call "deviants" are in the *majority* and that those who are "righteous" by our moral standards are, in terms of statistics, "deviants." For example, if our personal moral system says that bigots or adulterers are "deviant" and the statistics indicate that they're in the majority, we balk at the idea of calling the nonbigots and nonadulterers "deviants." Sociologists find it easier, and often valuable, to consider the statistical approach a useful and valid way of defining deviance. This is particularly true when the sociologist's interest is in the study of *reactions* to people defined as deviant by those around them, rather than in the semantic and moral problems of defining *deviance.*[2]

Behavioral deviance is behavior that is thought by the community to be harmful to the society, or to particular individuals within the society, and therefore too costly to permit. This is behavior that we are likely to think of as "criminal." We pass laws against it. These are the kinds of behavior to which many sociologists and nonsociologists feel we ought to limit our attentions and definitions of deviance.

What kinds of behavior are deviant by a behavioral definition? Rape, murder, kidnapping, armed robbery, incest, assassination of the President, treason. These are some of the kinds of behavior that most people feel threaten the social order and are too costly to society to permit. Behavioral deviance, then, is behavior that a majority of members of the society believe violates the dominant values of the society. There are some who would include under this type of definition any behavior that is thought by the society to be a threat to the survival of the society, *regardless* of whether, in fact, it is a threat to the society's survival.

As the early French sociologist Émile Durkheim observed:

> There are many acts which have been and still are regarded as criminal ("deviant") without in themselves being harmful to society. What social danger is there in touching a tabooed object, an impure animal or man, in letting the sacred fire die down, in eating certain meats, in failure to make the traditional sacrifice over the grave of parents, in not exactly pronouncing the ritual formula, in not celebrating holidays, etc.[3]

There are some sociologists who argue that if we know something about the values of a society or about what things threaten the society's values and survival we *know* which kinds of behavior are "deviant" or contrary to these values. This is so *regardless* of whether the community has any rules about such behavior or perceives it as threatening.

For example, we may be interested in understanding why police sometimes beat up demonstrators because we see this as a violation of the society's valued constitutional guarantees of free speech. It may be the case that the general public does *not* see the police's actions as "deviant." Nonetheless, many sociologists consider the beating up of demonstrators by police to be "deviant" behavior, that is, a violation of the society's values as well as a violation of formal rules about how police should handle crowds. On the other hand, the general public may consider marihuana smokers to be deviants and a threat to the survival of the society, whereas the sociologist may point to the much greater cost to society of alcoholism and therefore focus more sociological attention on alcoholics than on marihuana smokers.

Sociologists who use a behavioral definition of deviance generally prefer to define deviance in terms of whether or not the majority of the community believes the behavior in question to be a threat to the society's well-being or survival. They have been accused by supporters of the third approach (the valuative approach) of being guilty of two important errors. The first error, as the critics see it, is the assumption that certain behavior is *intrinsically* deviant, that is, that there's something about the behavior itself that makes it deviant or not deviant. A second criticism is that those who use the behavioral definition of deviance may be assuming that there's more agreement on values by people in the society than is, in fact, the case.

The third approach, the *valuative* approach to defining deviance, prefers to focus on the processes by which one group manages to get its own ideas of morality and deviance imposed on a society and its legal codes. This may occur despite the fact that many other people and groups within the society *don't* consider the behavior to be wrong. In other words, by this sort of definition deviant behavior is *any* behavior that an interested group can persuade or force the society to consider officially deviant. The most obvious instance of this sort of definition of deviance is the case of Prohibition in the United States: a well-organized minority managed to get their own moral views on alcohol embodied in the law. Those who take the valuative approach to defining deviance tend to believe that there is *no* behavior that is intrinsically deviant and no behavior that is always and everywhere considered deviant. They see "deviance" as a *label* that we impose on behavior we disapprove of, a property of our *definition of the behavior rather than of the behavior itself.* In other words, this approach assumes that it is more sensible to say that behavior is *deviant only because it is forbidden rather than that behavior is forbidden only because it is deviant.* This is the sort of statement that takes a while to sink in. It's something like saying, "Chickens are what eggs use to reproduce themselves."

In recent years the valuative or "labeling" approach to deviance has been particularly popular with those sociologists who are interested in political conflicts. In a political conflict, one group attempts to label its opponents as deviants or criminals, whereas the opponents see themselves as protesters, as victims, as anything *but* deviants.

The *concrete* approach has received relatively little attention from sociologists.[4] Most research and theory have focused on behavior that has "moral" and legal implications.

The *behavioral* approach has been most useful for understanding "deviant" behavior about which there is a good deal of agreement throughout the society *and* on which the legal system permits little discretion. For example, child molesting, rape, armed robbery, and murder are acts that we find almost unanimous disapproval of. Police and judges are not permitted much discretion in whether to arrest or prosecute someone who has been caught doing these things.

The *valuative* approach has been more useful for the study of behavior about which there is no consensus on whether it should be made a legal issue. For example, gambling, homosexuality, abortion, drug abuse, alcohol abuse, and mental illness are behaviors not universally condemned as sinful or immoral. There is disagreement not only about whether they are wrong but about whether, if they are wrong, they should be legal matters. But there is also room for great discretion on the part of police and the courts as to whether and how to process through the legal machinery people who "deviate" in these ways. In other words, a policeman who spots a murder has no choice but to arrest the murderer. But a policeman spotting a delinquent, a drunk, a marihuana smoker, or a person who behaves strangely may arrest him, or he may let him go with a warning, or a boot in the rear, depending on the person's attitude. Community pressures, personal bias, and many other factors determine that one person will go to jail for an act, whereas another person will escape all blame for committing the same "deviant" act.

In many respects the disagreements between those who prefer the behavioral and the valuative approaches reflect what we have been referring to as the "order" and "conflict" schools, respectively, within sociology. As we indicated earlier, neither school has a monopoly on "truth" and we can learn something from both approaches.

Some Sociological Questions

Sociologists do not claim to have all the answers to questions about deviance. In fact, they are not always certain they know what the appropriate questions are. They have, on the other hand, done sufficient research to realize that many of the questions and answers that have *traditionally* been offered to account for deviance are inappropriate. As we indicated earlier, the range of behavior that societies consider deviant is so large that simple questions like "Why are people deviant?" can't be answered, at least not with a single, sensible answer. Rather, we have come to ask narrower questions like: Why does one society consider immoral a behavior that another society ignores or admires? Why does one society have a good deal of a certain behavior (which they consider deviant) whereas another society that *also* considers such behavior deviant seems to have very little? For example, there are more homicides in New York or Detroit in any given year than in all of England. Given that a society has a high or a low incidence of a particular type of crime or deviant behavior, which *groups* (by age, sex, class, race, nationality) within the society seem to be the major contributors? Why? If the whole society does not agree on what behavior is deviant, how does one group manage to get its own definition of deviance imposed on the legal system? As you can see, such questions make no reference to the character or motives of the deviants. The questions also include the lawmaker *as well as* the law breaker.

In other words, the *independent variables* for sociologists interested in deviance are the characteristics of societies and the groups within those societies. The *dependent variables* are *types* of deviant behavior and *rates* of deviant behavior. The personal characteristics of deviants are generally considered to be either irrelevant or to be links *between* the independent and the dependent variables and therefore of only secondary interest to sociologists.

Biological Deviance: The Mark of Cain

One ancient and tenacious explanation of deviant behavior assumes that there is some type or form of biological difference between those who are deviant and those who are not. We can find theological roots for this approach in the Bible. The descendants of Cain, the biblical figure who murdered his brother, allegedly carry "the mark" and are "born" criminals. Their criminal behavior appears as naturally and automatically as does the development of a caterpillar into a butterfly. In other words, certain biological characteristics, or defects, supposedly lead to antisocial behavior.

An Italian psychiatrist named Cesare Lombroso did the most to further the idea of "born criminals" during the nineteenth century.[5] Using the evolutionary theory of Charles Darwin, Lombroso argued that individuals with certain physical characteristics similar to those of primitive man are naturally prone to antisocial behavior. He claimed that "born criminals" could be found through identifiable malformations of their skeletons, especially their skulls. According to Lombroso, a brain size that is either above or below average, big ears, excessively long arms, a projecting or receding jaw, and high cheekbones are all signs of criminal tendencies because they are evolutionary throwbacks to an earlier kind of human species. Epilepsy and red hair are also indicators of the "born criminal."

Some years later, the English physician Charles B. Goring applied Lombroso's classification system to three thousand convicts. He found that although the physical characteristics Lombroso had described *did* appear frequently in the prison population, these and other symptoms were *equally common* in the public at large. This finding discredited the Lombrosian school.

The biological approach reappeared in the 1920s with the works of Henry Goddard, who maintained that criminality is a result of general hereditary physical and intellectual degeneracy. He particularly felt that "feeble-mindedness" is inherited and responsible for producing long family lines of social misfits. This approach was discredited too by those who found that "feeble-mindedness" and low intelligence did not distinguish between prison inmates and the general public any more than the Lombrosian list of physical traits had.

In the 1950s, psychologist William H. Sheldon reintroduced the biological interpretation of deviance. He suggested a connection between deviant behavior and *body type.* He reported three basic *somatotypes* or body types: the *endomorph,* the *mesomorph,* and the *ectomorph.* An *endomorph* is a stout, round, soft person of medium height. A *mesomorph* is a lean, agile person possessing above-average strength in his arms, chest, and limbs. An *ectomorph* is skinny with a delicate body, sharp features, and fine hair. Sheldon believed each physical type was linked to a particular personality type. He reported that juvenile delinquents in a very small sample (sixteen people) were endowed with the qualities of a *mesomorph.*[6] The small sample interested scholars but hardly convinced them.

Sheldon and Eleanor Glueck, using the somatotype classification system, discovered that 60.1 percent[7] of a sample of five hundred delinquent boys were athletic or mesomorphic. Their nondelinquent sample contained more excessively fat and overly thin and sickly youngsters. The Gluecks reasoned that the mesomorph, who relies on his strength to solve a problem as quickly as possible, is likely to become deviant, whereas the ectomorph is more intellectual and cautious. The endomorph, being large and lazy, will tend to ignore problems.

In subsequent studies, the Gluecks further refined the body-type classification. The *mesomorph* was described as an impulsive individual with much physical, emotional, and nervous energy. The *endomorph* was described as more restrained, inhibited, and disturbed. They also added a *balanced physique type,* who combines the positive features of both and thus is a more sociable individual.[8] The addition of psychological characteristics to body structure engaged the sympathies of some social scientists, especially criminologists, but still has not convinced most sociologists. Sociologists are more willing to accept the argument that physical characteristics may be related to deviance through the social consequences of stereotyping or through the direct relationship between body type and the abilities demanded of different kinds of deviance rather than through any direct biological cause-effect relationship with deviance.

Consider the possibility that it's quite hard to be a ninety-six-pound mugger or a three-hundred-pound second-story man. If you were choosing someone to join a fighting gang, which of the two physical types would you be likely to choose?

As illustrations of the relationship between stereotyping and deviance, consider these two observations. T. Shibutani reports that among the Ashanti of West Africa, children are named after the day of the week on which they're born. Wednesdays are thought to have a tendency to be delinquents, and regularly the tribe finds that in fact people born on Wednesday are disproportionately guilty of violent crimes, confirming the tribe's expectations.[9] Could it be that the society treats Wednesday's children differently? In a recent experiment, researchers showed college students photographs of children who were either physically attractive or physically unattractive. Then the researchers described certain alleged behavior of the children in the photos, behavior like throwing rocks at injured dogs or throwing a snowball with a sharp piece of ice in it at another child and causing a deep and bleeding cut. The fictitious behavior was the same, but the children to whom it was attributed were sometimes the attractive ones and sometimes the unattractive ones. The subjects' responses changed dramatically, depending on which children were allegedly guilty. The misbehavior of an attractive child was described as less serious and as giving little indication of the child's "real" nature. The same behavior allegedly performed by the unattractive child was considered more serious and a sign of the child's true, rotten character. This experiment suggests that children who have certain physical characteristics may be treated differently and forced into the role of "deviant" more often than those who have other characteristics. And any relationship between physical characteristics and deviance is more likely to be a result of responses to the reactions of observers than a direct connection between physical characteristics and deviance.[10] However, the study indicates how hard it is to shake stereotypes that assume that there are biological differences between deviants and nondeviants.[11]

Another form of biological explanation of deviance that has received a good deal of attention in recent years suggests that there are certain differences in chromosomes that lead certain men to become violent criminals. The belief that there's a chromosomal cause of wrongdoing was revived in the British medical journal *Lancet.* Dr. Saul Weiner reported that there are "supermales" who have an extra male chromosome. Ordinarily, the cells of a male contain 46 chromosomes among which are one X chromosome and one Y chromosome (XY). The cells of a female have 46 chromosomes among which are two X chromosomes (XX). The Y chromosome determines whether a person will be a male or a female. Although most of us have forty-six chromosomes, in a small percentage of cases men were found to have forty-seven chromosomes, thus making them *XYY supermales.* Dr. Weiner argued that these supermales are prone to "antisocial or criminal behavior." A number of studies were conducted in prisons to see if the XYY imbalance was prevalent among male inmates. In most cases about 2 percent of the prison population was found to possess the XYY chromosome,[12] which was estimated to be at "four to five times the presumed general population rate."[13] This moved geneticists and lawyers to assume that the XYY chromosome *causes* deviant behavior and that therefore those who have it cannot be held legally responsible for their behavior. This conclusion is by no means clear-cut, as the 1970 *Report on the XYY Chromosomal Abnormality* reports:

Many XYY individuals display no such abnormalities. Indeed, it is not yet known whether these persons have a higher frequency of such abnormalities. Moreover, the widespread publicity notwithstanding, individuals with the XYY anomaly have

Table 11-1. Crime Victimization in Thirteen Selected Cities

	Crime Rate per 1,000 Residents 12 and Over				Household Victimization per 1,000 Households			Commercial Victimization per 1,000 Business Establishments		
	Crimes of Violence	*Rape and Attempted Rape*	*Robbery*	*Assault*	*Burglary*	*Household Larceny*	*Auto Theft*	*Burglary*	*Robbery*	*Ratio of Unreported Crime to Reported Crime*
Detroit	68	3	32	33	174	106	49	615	179	**2.7 to 1**
Denver	67	3	17	46	158	168	44	443	54	**2.9 to 1**
[a]Philadelphia	63	1	28	34	109	87	42	390	116	**5.1 to 1**
Portland, Ore.	59	3	17	40	151	149	34	355	39	**2.6 to 1**
Baltimore	57	1	26	28	116	100	35	578	135	**2.2 to 1**
[a]Chicago	56	3	26	27	118	77	36	317	77	**2.8 to 1**
Cleveland	54	2	24	28	124	80	76	367	77	**2.4 to 1**
[a]Los Angeles	53	2	16	35	148	131	42	311	47	**2.9 to 1**
Atlanta	48	2	16	30	161	102	29	741	157	**2.3 to 1**
Dallas	43	2	10	31	147	147	24	355	48	**2.6 to 1**
Newark	42	1	29	12	123	44	37	631	98	**1.4 to 1**
St. Louis	42	1	16	25	125	81	47	531	94	**1.5 to 1**
[a]New York	38	1	24	11	68	33	26	328	103	**2.1 to 1**

[a]Information for five largest cities covers 1972. Information for eight others is based on surveys carried out in July–October 1972 covering previous 12 months.

Source: National Crime Panel Surveys. Law Enforcement Assistance Administration. Justice Department. Released April 15, 1974.

not been found to be more aggressive than matched offenders with normal chromosome constitutions. In this respect, it appears that premature and incautious speculations may have led to XYY persons being falsely stigmatized as unusually aggressive and violent.[14]

Sociologists continue to be skeptical of biological explanations for several reasons. The specific studies of Lombroso, Sheldon, the Gluecks, and Weiner were based on data collected within a prison population, and they assume that the characteristics studied must be *the* factors that put their possessors into prison. The researchers assumed, in other words, that the only significant differences between the prisoners and the general population were these biological characteristics. The evidence would be more convincing if the researchers had in fact *demonstrated* instead of *assumed* that the general public does not tend to possess these characteristics.

More significantly, there is reason to believe that those people who are convicted for criminal behavior are merely a random sample of those who violate criminal laws, that only a small percentage of those who have broken the law are convicted. In fact, most crimes are not even reported, as Table 11-1 indicates.

Finally, the idea that there are "born criminals" poses problems when we recognize that different societies consider different kinds of behavior deviant or criminal. We might conceivably find that biological characteristic X is related to a certain behavior that is considered deviant in society A but is not seen as deviant in society B. We would then be saying that characteristic X is typical of criminals in society A and of good citizens in society B. Absurd!

Of course we might argue that there is some biological characteristic that makes people violate *whatever* rules a society has, so that *regardless* of what behavior a society considers appropriate, possessors of that characteristic will violate the rules. Obviously this would mean either that "the genes" know what the law is or that the members of the legislature are genetics experts who deliberately enact laws so that "born criminals" will violate them. That doesn't sound very reasonable either.[15] Even more absurd!

Psychological Characteristics of Deviants

As noted earlier, sociologists tend to be skeptical of psychological approaches to understanding deviance. The major reason is that psychological explanations have not been useful for understanding *rates* of deviance. In other words, even if we should discover a psychological characteristic that accounts for armed robbery or rape, we would be hard pressed to understand why one society or one region of a society or one group within a society traditionally has a high rate of armed robbery or rape and another has very little armed robbery or rape. Nor would we be able to account for increases or decreases in armed robbery or rape over a period of months or years. We'd be hard pressed on the one hand to understand why some societies or regions or groups seem to have a monopoly of people with psychological characteristic X and others have very few such people. In the second case we'd have to try to account for why the people who have the characteristic weren't doing their thing last year or last spring or why they've suddenly come out of the woodwork.

A good case can probably be made for the relationship between certain personality characteristics and the likelihood of being involved in certain types of deviance, but as indicated earlier, this information is useful *only* if the psychological information is coordinated with information about the social factors, which for sociologists are the primary variables. Note that in suggesting the possibility that there may be certain personality characteristics that may be related to certain types of deviance, we are *not* suggesting that these are necessarily pathological. We are not suggesting that to be deviant one must be "mentally ill." We're referring to personality characteristics that are within the range of behavior that can be considered "normal."

Social Factors and Deviance

The 1920 census revealed that pastoral America had become a nation of city dwellers. Most Americans now lived in cities. Sociologists, especially those at the University of Chicago, came to see the city as a form of laboratory in which to study human behavior. They wanted to see how man would adjust to living in the everyday hustle and bustle of city life. The city came to be seen as a learning experience for its new dwellers, who were uprooted from the farms and small towns of the South, the Midwest, and Eastern Europe.[16] It was in the melting pot of the big city that some of the earliest sociological explanations of deviant behavior and crime were born. These discussions concentrated upon the ways that different values and social positions predisposed people to become deviants. The two most important explanatory concepts that emerged during the 1930s were Thorsten Sellin's *culture conflict* and Edwin H. Sutherland's *differential association theory.*

Culture Conflict and Differential Association

Thorsten Sellin suggested that all groups possess rules of conduct, or "conduct norms."[17] Different groups have different "conduct norms" and different values. The city is the meeting place of different norms and the unsettled state of the city is due to the migration there of people from different backgrounds. Behavior that is proper back home is not proper in the city, and the result is "culture conflicts." Sellin wrote: "Culture conflicts are sometimes regarded as by-products of a cultural growth process—the growth of civilization—sometimes as the result of migration of conduct norms from one culture complex or area to another."[18] As immigrants from many countries poured into cities such as New York and Chicago they brought with them varying conduct norms and cultural values. They had different religious beliefs, different concepts of right and wrong, and different courtship processes. Culture conflict occurred when the immigrants' conduct norms were in direct opposition to American legal codes. During Prohibition, for example, Polish and Italian Catholic immigrants saw nothing sinful in the consumption of alcohol. Their cultural values did not prohibit them from using or serving others the illegal beverage. Another example, provided by Sellin, is the Sicilian custom of vendettas on behalf of family honor. A Sicilian father in New Jersey murdered the seducer of his daughter. He was surprised when he was arrested and tried because he "had done the right thing." In this manner cultural conflicts lead to what we consider illegal or criminal behavior.

Sociologists like Donald Cressey have expanded the culture conflict argument to include *normative conflict,* which is a struggle over legal codes and what should be the law of the land. Here we find various groups, organized around age, sex, nationality, race, religion, or class, all attempting to "resolve" their codes of conduct in the legislative and judicial process; but as Cressey suggests, "'resolution' does not mean that the ensuing law norms are subscribed to uniformly or universally."[19]

As Sellin was working out his explanation of deviance, Edwin Sutherland was developing what has come to be called *differential association theory* (DAT), which simply means that people fall in with bad companions and become deviants. This common-sense notion, voiced frequently by unhappy parents who dislike their children's friends, is the basis of Sutherland's theory. Put formally, DAT has eight basic elements.

1. *Criminal behavior is learned.* People learn to become criminals just as they learn to become rock musicians, baseball players, or college professors. Crime is not biological but social. People learn to deal dope on the street, not in a maternity ward.[20]

2. *Criminal behavior is learned from other people through communication.* People acquire knowledge by talking to and watching other people.

3. *Important learning occurs within small intimate groups.* People value the opinions of their friends and relatives. These opinions and attitudes are accepted more easily than those that come from impersonal sources. For example, people generally reflect the religious and political values held by their parents, friends, and neighbors.

4. *When criminal behavior is learned, the learning includes:* (a) *the techniques of committing the crime; and* (b) *the specific rationalizations, excuses, and attitudes of the criminal.* How does one "hot-wire" a car or buy "dope" on the street? The average person does not have this information. Somebody has to teach him. What are the excuses given the authorities when one is caught? Criminals learn from other criminals how to approach the judge and what to tell probation officers and social workers. All of this is *learned.*

5. *People learn different values in society.* Not all people have the same attitudes about the law or obeying it. The average American is generally a law-abiding citizen. However, even he may feel a few laws are worthless or unjust. Many college students feel the marihuana laws are stupid and violate them regularly. Other people in society may believe *most* laws are unfair and see little wrong in violating them. People who live in "cultures of poverty" may see little wrong in "ripping off the Man." During the urban riots of the 1960s, one looter exclaimed, "It dawned on me at the height of the hysteria, as I was passing a certain store, that I have been paying on my present television set for more than five years. And [therefore] that store owed me five televisions. So I got three and I believe they owe me two." Another looter said, "Listen, man, this is the only time in my life I've got a chance to get these things."[21]

6. *People whose contacts are primarily with criminals will learn to be criminals.* This is the *essence* of *differential association.* When a person grows up in a neighborhood or in a family that stresses criminal patterns, he will most likely learn to be a criminal. In 1933 Clifford Shaw reported:

> Every boy has some ideal he looks up to and admires. His ideal may be Babe Ruth, Jack Dempsey, or Al Capone. When I was twelve, we moved into a neighborhood with a lot of gangsters. They were all swell dressers and had big cars and carried "gats." Us kids saw these swell guys and mingled with them in the cigar store on the corner. Jack Gurney was the one in the mob that I had a fancy to. . . . He was a sweller dresser and had lots of dough. . . . I liked to be near him and felt stuck up over the other guys because he came to my home to see my sis.[22]

Some forty years later, an inner-city youth may well feel the same way looking up to Wilt Chamberlain, Muhammad Ali, or the local street-gang leader, pimp, or dope dealer with the "big hog" Continental or Cadillac.

7. *Differential associations may vary in frequency, duration, importance, and intensity.* Group identification changes during an individual's lifetime. The friends of childhood and the old neighborhood are often left behind. The ghetto child who wishes to become a doctor can, if the desire is strong enough and he overcomes the handicaps of his childhood and finds associations that support this ambition. However, DAT indicates that in a crime culture chances are good that the youth will grow up to be a deviant.

8. *Deviant behavior is the expression of the general needs and values of the society.* Thieves steal in order to obtain money. Most people go to work five days a week to secure the same thing. If you want a Ferrari, you can either steal it off the streets or buy the same car from the dealer. The goals of thieves and straight citizens are the same, but their means of obtaining these goals differ.

Sutherland's DAT has been useful in the study of crimes fostered by groups like street gangs or the Mafia. It has also been useful in the study of the various subcultures found in the nation's cities and of ghettos, barrios, and enclaves of poor southern whites who have migrated into the core areas of large northern cities like Detroit and Chicago. DAT does not, however, help us in understanding other forms of crime and deviance, such as embezzling, child molesting, or alcoholism. DAT is a very important sociological theory in that it has generated a number of studies and interpretations of deviant behavior, primarily Robert K. Merton's explanation of deviance.[23]

Social Adaptation and Anomie

Merton combined Sutherland's notion of general needs and values with Émile Durkheim's ideas on social integration (see Chapter Two, "Origins of Sociology"). Merton noted that each society must provide people with the avenues to reach socially approved goals if people are to conform to its rules. A society must furnish people *opportunities* to succeed as well as ideas about what "success" entails. Social integration occurs when needs and opportunities are in balance. However, Merton observed that not all people are accorded the means or given the chance to achieve socially approved goals of success, health, happiness, and wealth. This lack of opportunity creates an *anomic* or *normless* situation, in which people disagree on the rules, or refuse to accept the official rules, or evade the rules. These different approaches to means and goals he called *adaptations.*

Conformity can be described as the total acceptance of societal goals *and* the means of achieving them. Working hard, going to school, buying a house, and saving money to buy the car you want are all instances of conformity.

Innovation is the acceptance of the cultural goals but *not* the means. You may want to pass the examination in this course. You can do it by studying the material and passing the examination, or you may try to cheat or even bribe the instructor. This is what Merton called *innovation,* as is white- or blue-collar crime, doping athletes to win football games, or organized crime. Much of the crime committed by the disadvantaged may be classified as innovative attempts to achieve goals when the society fails to provide access

Table 11–2.

	Culture Goals	*Institutionalized Means*
I. Conformity	+[a]	+
II. Innovation	+	–[b]
III. Ritualism	–	+
IV. Retreatism	–	–
V. Rebellion[c]	±	±

[a] + = present
[b] – = not present
[c] This fifth alternative is clearly different from the others. It involves efforts to *change* the existing structure rather than to perform *within* the structure and introduces additional problems with which we are not at the moment concerned.

to the accepted means to these goals. Consider the person who makes $3,000 a year and is consistently reminded on his television set to go and "buy, buy, buy" a new car. Without the means to earn enough money to buy one, he just may steal one.

Ritualism is emphasizing the means and ignoring the goals. A ritualist, according to Merton, is totally involved with the rules and has little concern with the outcome. He forgets what the goals are and concentrates on the means. Bureaucrats in college registration offices, or any other large organization, may be examples of this type of person. This type of person, although overzealous, is not necessarily considered deviant unless he carries his adherence to the rules to the point of psychotic mania.

Retreatism is a rejection of *both* the means *and* the goals of society. In the jargon of the 1960s, it means dropping out. Drug addicts, alcoholics, hobos, people in communes, and counterculture people are all retreatists.

Rebellion is a rejection of the existing order along with the advocating of *another* form of social organization. For example, people in the United States who maintain that communism, fascism, or socialism is better than our existing system are rebels. They want to tear down the old and build anew.

Only *three* of these categories are illustrations of what is usually considered deviance: innovation, retreatism, and rebellion. Each involves dissent from the existing order of means and ends. Culture conflict, DAT, and Merton's notion of anomie all emphasize competing values and the individual's ability to reach certain basic goals in society. Deviance and criminality, for these theorists, involve questions of *values* and *opportunities.*

Albert Cohen further refined the ideas of Sellin, Cressey, and Sutherland when he suggested that delinquent gangs are comprised of youngsters "denied status in the respectable society because they cannot meet the criteria of the respectable status system. The delinquent subculture deals with these problems by providing criteria of status which these children *can* meet."[24] Cohen contended that all of us in the United States are exposed to the American Dream. Like all Americans the "street corner boy" accepts the middle-class standards of success and status, but he does not have the means to achieve these goals. Where does the working-class youth find status? In the gang. The gang is composed of other youngsters who find themselves incapable of succeeding in middle-class institutions like the school. In the gang they can strive for success using non-middle-class tools like violence and theft. Cohen took Merton's ideas on opportunity differences and wedded them to Sutherland's idea of social groups teaching and encouraging deviant behavior. And Cohen added an interesting twist. He suggested that frustration and anxiety about failure in school leads lower-class boys to develop a subculture centered around doing the *opposite* of what middle-class values demand. If middle-class values suggest rationality (for example, forgoing immediate gratification) and control of aggression, the delinquent subculture stresses nonutilitarian behavior (like stealing things that you can't use and can't sell), malicious and negative behavior, and generally doing for kicks and immediate gratification all the things that middle-class values oppose. Cohen suggested that such behavior is a *reaction* to the fact that deep down, the boys he is describing really *accept* the middle-class values; and because they do, and won't admit this to themselves, they must go overboard to convince themselves that they really *don't* care about being unable to succeed in the middle-class world. Note that Cohen's theory draws on Merton's *general* theory of deviance to discuss *one particular kind* of deviance, that of lower-class delinquent gangs.

Richard A. Cloward and Lloyd E. Ohlin[25] also elaborated on Merton's value-opportunity theory to account for lower-class delinquency. They too suggested that there is agreement on the value of financial and material success throughout the society but that opportunity to achieve material success through employment and other legitimate channels is not equally available to all. In response, criminal subcultures develop alternate routes to success. Cloward and Ohlin do *not* agree with Cohen's idea that lower-class delinquents turn middle-class values upside down for the sake of finding ways to attain *status.* They have argued instead that delinquents want to get *wealth* by illegitimate means and are not interested in middle-class status. But, they pointed out, opportunities to be successful as a criminal *may not be easily available either.* They suggested that there are three distinct types of subcultures that may or may not exist in one's neighborhood and that may offer illegal opportunities: an *organized criminal* subculture, a *fighting* subculture, and a *retreatist* subculture. Where there is organized crime and a neighborhood criminal tradition, youngsters may become junior criminals, hoping to move up to the adult criminal level. There are in some areas, for example, adults who may be able to teach young people criminal skills and who are looking for promising, talented young criminals.

The second kind of subculture exists in neighborhoods lacking an adult criminal subculture, where delinquents may turn to gang fighting and gaining success as warriors. Other potential delinquents join up with these existing gangs.

The third subculture is made up of losers in both the legitimate *and* the nonlegitimate (criminal) worlds. They haven't the opportunities for success of the middle class, but they're not tough enough to succeed as fighters and they can't find profitable criminal opportunities either. These losers retreat from the world into the world of drugs and form a third subculture.

G. M. Sykes and David Matza[26] also studied delinquent boys but they disagreed with Cohen and Cloward and Ohlin. Sykes and Matza suggested that rather than rejecting middle-class values, delinquents learn to *neutralize* these values and to justify their particular behavior as "legitimate" exceptions to otherwise valid rules. In other words, Sykes and Matza suggested that delinquents do accept the moral validity of the society's rules but that they learn ways to disclaim the moral implications of their own behavior and to avoid feelings of guilt. Sykes and Matza suggested at least five techniques of neutralization:

1. *Denial of responsibility.* Denial of responsibility involves the explanation that the deviant act was "an accident." "I didn't know the gun was loaded," explains the robber after being apprehended for shooting a store owner.

2. *Denial of injury.* Denial of injury is a disclaimer of evil *intent.* Vandalism may be pictured as mischief. Auto theft becomes the mere "borrowing of the car." "It's nothing really," explains the deviant.

3. *Denial of the victim.* In denial of the victim the injury is seen as a form of rightful punishment. Attacks upon homosexuals, minority groups who "get out of place," or political protesters are justified as moral retaliation. "We're only stealing from the rich" is another such dodge. Denial of the victim allows one to say, "They had it coming." This reverses the roles of the deviant and the victim, and sometimes outsiders may agree. For example, when the Hell's Angels attacked antiwar demonstrators, many "solid citizens" applauded the bike club.

4. *The condemnation of the condemners.* The condemnation of the condemners, or rejection of the rejectors, is saying that the rule enforcers are no better than the rule violators. "The police are corrupt," or stupid and worse; "Teachers show favoritism." These are examples of the discrediting of established authority symbols.

5. *The appeal to higher loyalties.* The appeal to higher loyalties is offered for behavior performed to "help a buddy." The classic illustration of this is the private eye, the hero of the novel and the television series, who breaks every legal statute in the books to save a friend. Political terrorists while robbing, kidnapping, and engaging in other unlawful activities similarly appeal to a "higher good."

All five of these justifications are *neutralization* devices. By using them, Sykes and Matza contended, the deviant appears to be in accord with dominant social values, at least in his own eyes.

J. Milton Yinger added a further dimension to the discussion of deviants and social values and norms.[27] Yinger suggested that applying the notion of *subculture* to deviant groups may be misleading because the term implies an acceptance of many dominant values. Subcultures based on religion, language, diet, or moral values are *not* necessarily in conflict with dominant social values; whereas delinquent gangs, as described by Cohen and Cloward and Ohlin, do by their actions intentionally clash with the overall culture. Consequently, Yinger thought, deviants should be described as members not of subcultures but of contracultures whose conduct norms are in direct opposition to the total society. "In a contraculture," wrote Yinger, "the conflict element is central; many of the values, indeed, are specifically contradictions of the values of the dominant culture."[28] In recent years, this definition has been applied to groups

	Violent Personal Criminal Behavior	Occasional Property Criminal Behavior	Public Order Criminal Behavior	Conventional Criminal Behavior	Political Criminal Behavior
Illustrations	Homicide, rape, assault.	Forgery, shoplifting, vandalism, auto theft.	Prostitution, homosexuality, drunkenness, drug use, loan sharking.	Larceny, burglary, robbery.	Civil disorder, conspiracy, dra dodging, police brutality, wa crimes.
Criminal Career of the Offender	Crime is not part of the offender's career. He usually does not conceive of self as criminal.	Little or no criminal self-conception. The offender does not identify with crime. He is able to rationalize his behavior.	Most offenders do not regard their behavior as criminal. They do not have a clearly defined criminal career. Ambiguity in self-concept produced in continued contact with legal agents.	Offenders begin their careers early in life, often in gang associations. Crimes committed for economic gain. Vacillation in self-conception. Partial commitment to a criminal subculture.	Political offenders do not usually conceive of themselves as criminals and do not ide tify with crime. They are defined as criminal because they are perceived as threa ing the status quo (as in crime against government), they are criminal when they violate the laws that regulat the government itself (crime by government).
Group Support of Criminal Behavior	Little or no group support. Offenses committed for personal reasons. Some support in subculturalnorms.	Little group support. Generally individual offenses. Associations tend to be recreational.	Offenses such as prostitution, homosexual behavior, and drug use grow out of, and are supported by, rather clearly defined subcultures. Considerable association with other offenders.	Behavior supported by group norms. Early associations with other offenders in slum areas. Status achieved in groups. Some persons continue primary associations with other offenders, whereas others pursue different careers.	Support is received by particu lar groups or by segments society. They identify or ass ciate with persons who sha similar values. Behavior is r inforced by specific norms.
Societal Reaction and Legal Processing	Strong social reaction. Harsh punishments. Long imprisonment.	Social reaction is not severe when the offender does not have a previous record. Leniency in legal processing, probation.	Strong reaction by some segments of society, weak reaction by others. Only a small portion of the offenses result in arrest. Sentences are strong for some offenses, such as the possession of narcotic drugs.	A series of arrests and convictions. Institutionalization and rehabilitation of the offender. Agency programs that preserve the status quo without changing social conditions.	Official reactions tend to be s vere in the case of crimes against government. Consid erable harassment may be perienced and heavy sentences may be imposed. Public acceptance of politic offenses depends on the ex tent to which the policies a actions of the government accepted. Reactions to gov ernmental crime depend on the consciousness of the p lic regarding activities of th government.

Table 11–3. Typology of Criminal Behavior Systems.

Source: Based on M. B. Clinard and R. Quinney, *Criminal Behavior Systems: A Typology,* 2nd Ed. (New York: Holt, Rinehart & Winston, Inc., 1973), pp. 18–20.

Occupational Criminal Behavior	*Corporate Criminal Behavior*	*Organized Criminal Behavior*	*Professional Criminal Behavior*
alpractice, bilking Medicare, fee splitting, misappropriating client funds, looting estates, "ambulance chasing," black marketeering, pilfering and embezzling, tax fraud, phony repairs.	Restraint of trade, false advertising, manufacture of unsafe food, price fixing, pollution.	Control of gambling, prostitution and drug traffic, racketeering and protection, corruption of public officials.	Confidence games, pickpocketing, forgery, counterfeiting, burglary, extortion.
ittle or no criminal self-conception. Occasional violation of the law, accompanied by appropriate rationalizations. Violation tends to be a part of one's work. Offenders accept the conventional values in the society.	The violating corporate official and his corporation have high social status in society. Offenses are an integral part of corporate business operations. Violations are rationalized as being basic to business enterprise.	Crime is pursued as a livelihood. There is a progression in crime and an increasing isolation from the larger society. A criminal self-conception develops.	A highly developed criminal career. Professional offenders engage in specialized offenses, all of which are directed toward economic gain. They enjoy high status in the world of crime. They are committed to other professional criminals.
ome occupations, or groups within occupations, tolerate or even support offenses. The offender is integrated into social groups and societal norms.	Crime by corporations and corporate officials receives support from similar, even competing, businesses and officials. Lawbreaking is a normative pattern within many corporations. Corporate crime involves a great amount of organization among the participants.	Support for organized criminal behavior is achieved through an organizational structure, a code of conduct, prescribed methods of operation, and a system of protection. The offender is integrated into organized crime.	Professional offenders associate primarily with other offenders. Behavior is prescribed by the norms of professional criminals. The extent of organization among professional criminals varies with the kind of offense.
eactions have traditionally been mild and indifferent. Official penalties have been lenient, often restricted to the sanctions administered by the professional association. Public reaction is becoming less tolerant.	Strong legal actions have not usually been taken against corporations or their officials. Legal actions have been in the form of warnings and injunctions, rather than in terms of criminal penalties. Public reactions and legal actions, however, are increasing in respect to corporate crime.	Considerable public toleration of organized crime. Offenses are not usually visible to the public. Immunity of offenders, as provided by effective organization, prevents detection and arrest. Convictions are usually for minor offenses.	Considerable public toleration because of the low visibility of professional crime. Offenders are able to escape conviction by "fixing" cases.

in society whose life style and political attitudes are in conflict with dominant values. Hippies and street people were all described as members of *The* Counterculture.[29] Culture conflict theory, normative conflict theory, differential association theory, anomie theory, and the other theories discussed here emphasize the differences between certain subgroups in the society and the larger society. Although the theories disagree in many details, they agree that deviance within these subgroups is behavior that conforms to, and is encouraged by, one set of group norms and violates the norms of the larger society. This kind of deviance from the larger society's norms, in other words, is conformity to some other group's norms.

Although these theories of deviance could, in principle, be applied to many types of deviant behavior, in practice they have been most useful in accounting for lower-class drug abuse, street gangs, and organized crime.

There are other types of deviant behavior for which these theories have been less useful—shoplifting, check forging, child molesting, and "white-collar crime," for examples.

As has been suggested, there seems to be no way that a single, master theory will be developed in the near future that will persuasively account for *all* of the things we call deviant.

In recent years there have been several attempts to develop *typologies* of deviant behavior and to compile for each *type* the combinations of factors specific to that particular type of behavior. In other words, the typologies assume that armed robbers, rapists, political terrorists, and check forgers have different kinds of characteristics and require different theoretical explanations.[30] Table 11-3 gives one recent typology. Note that no one set of variables accounts for all of the types of behavior, but note too that certain variables play a role in all, sometimes a minor role and sometimes a major role. The table gives an idea of the kinds of social factors that help to produce and support different types of deviance. The table is also a useful summary of sociological research on these various kinds of behavior.

Labeling: What's in a Name?

The conventional approach to deviance that we have been using so far implies that the only interesting and important questions are about what causes people to do things that the society considers deviant and that a variety of agencies (police, courts, and so on) are empowered to stop people from doing.

Those sociologists who have been identified with the school of thought called the *labeling approach*[31] have argued that the most significant questions are about how certain behavior comes to be given the label *deviant* and what the consequences are for a person or group who have been declared deviant. The initial reasons for such behavior are of much less interest to the labeling theorists than the consequences of having been labeled a deviant.

Let's start with an example:

Two groups of men look hostilely at one another. Each group draws close together and whispers. Slowly they start approaching each other, stopping for a brief moment before racing toward each other yelling, "Get 'em." They knock each other to the ground. What is happening? We could be talking about a gang fight or the opening seconds of the Super Bowl. Whether or not something "deviant" has occurred depends on the situation. American values denounce as useless and dangerous violence in the form of street fighting, but we applaud violence in a boxing ring or in the football stadium on Sunday afternoons when the titans of pro football meet in combat. Placing a bet with a bookie is illegal, but it is quite lawful to place a bet at a race track or at New York City's Off Track Betting offices or in a Nevada casino. Deviance, therefore, is not a property of the act itself, but resides in the social definition of the behavior. To put it another way, behavior is "deviant" because someone has convinced lawmakers to declare it deviant.

I may observe your behavior and say, "That's crazy," "That's perverted," or "That's sinful," or announce that "President X is a fascist and President Y is a communist." Although I may say these things, unless I get some support from others they are just so much name-calling. It is said that "Sticks and stones may break my bones, but names can never harm me." When the name-calling gains a certain measure of social support, sticks, stones, and jail cells may follow name-calling and "mere" name-calling becomes a serious business.

How does "one man's opinion" get translated into a socially supported norm? How does it get legal support? Labeling theorists point to small groups of people we can call rule creators. These are people who help *create* and *enforce* laws. Rule creators are unhappy about something; some evil disturbs them. They believe that if society is to survive, the evil must be suppressed. The rule creators start a crusade against the evil. They petition lawmakers to do something about the evil. They may (or may not) have a selfish motive for getting certain behavior declared illegal.

The term *evil* obviously can be applied to many kinds of behavior, and may involve objections to something as trivial as kissing in public or as serious as the death penalty or abortion. In the 1950s many citizens' groups tried to have Elvis Presley banned from public radio and television. In the 1960s many groups supported subjecting skyjackers to the death penalty.[32] In the late 1960s the record industry beseeched Congress to supply greater protection for their products. Record albums were being illegally reproduced by two groups of people: counterculture youth, who disapproved of copyrights on ideological grounds, and organized counterfeiters, who saw profits to be made in reproducing albums without paying royalties or incurring production expenses.[33] The record companies approached Congress asking for help in fighting off the young people, whom they considered *political* deviants and who were allegedly putting the companies out of business. But they made little mention of the *criminal* counterfeiters, who actually represented a larger financial threat than did the young people. The legislation that was passed contributed to the profit margins of the record companies; it is not known whether the legislation actually contributed to the political purification of the nation.

Rule creators face problems in convincing legislators to pass rules on their behalf, but getting someone to enforce these rules is also a problem. Record company executives, for example, complain that police and district attorneys' offices are not enforcing the antipiracy laws.[34]

Rule *enforcers* may have different interests than rule *creators.* Rule enforcers are those people and agencies—ranging from the local patrolman to federal agencies, from local courts to the Supreme Court—whose official purpose is to enforce laws.

To do their respective jobs properly, enforcers, particularly police, must have public support. However, not all *laws* enjoy public support. Law enforcers frequently feel that to enforce such laws costs them respect. Marihuana smoking, although against the law, is a widespread practice with millions of people. Should the police devote all their time to capturing pot smokers, ignoring crimes of violence like mugging and burglary? In many cases police turn their backs on various acts we can call *victimless crimes.* In victimless crimes the deviant provides a service that is illegal to willing customers. Prostitution, bookmaking, drug possession, and cockfighting are all victimless crimes.[35] The customer, in other words, has no desire to lodge a complaint. He doesn't see himself as a "victim."

Cockfighting, which pits two roosters against one another in a fight to the death, is illegal in most states. But a large number of people support and attend these illegal contests. They do not consider themselves criminals and do not see cockfighting as immoral or as an act of cruelty to animals. *Grit and Steel,* a magazine devoted to cockfighting, argued, "The sport just involves making the rooster better at what they do naturally, which is fight another cock to death as soon as they see it." Another supporter wrote, "As a chicken he is brought up with the tenderest care and attention; as a young cock he is kept in luxury and freedom, monarch of all he surveys. . . . He is given the joy of battle, and if he dies, what more could a brave heart ask?"[36] Rule enforcers find victimless crimes tricky because the enforcers may in fact lose public support by overzealous action. Overresponse to political protests on college campuses found police officers being called "pigs" and worse by the middle-class white students normally considered to be supporters of law and order. Police are still not welcome on many campuses. The so-called police riots at the 1968 Democratic National Convention in Chicago found officers being severely criticized by politicians and the news media. The enforcement of marihuana laws is also unpopular among many people, generating similar results.

Rule enforcers are separated from rule creators by the enforcers' occupational values. The importance police place on their status in the community frequently affects their enforcement of the law. In a study of a small Illinois police department, William Westley reported that violence was most frequently used against the public for "disrespect for the police."[37] One interesting example of selective law enforcement against individuals "guilty" of "disrespect for the police" involved the Black Panther Party.[38]

The Black Panther Party was founded in 1966 in Oakland, California. The group's relations with the police bordered on open warfare. Several police officers were shot and killed by Black Panthers. Members of the movement also were gunned down. It was this group that popularized the term *pig* as applied to police officers. The Panthers had nothing but contempt for the police, who returned the compliment.

Members of the Black Panther Party in Los Angeles complained for months of police harassment. They charged that they received so many traffic citations that they feared losing their drivers' licenses. The reason for this flood of citations, they claimed, was the "Black Panther" sticker displayed on the rear bumper of their cars. The police denied this, saying Black Panthers were "irresponsible citizens."

Frances Heussenstamm recruited a group of university students for an experiment. Each had exemplary driving records and no moving violations for a period of a year. In addition, each student promised to drive as carefully as possible during the experiment. The cars they drove were inspected to remove all defective equipment. Then, bright day-glo orange-and-black bumper stickers reading "Black Panther Party" were attached to their vehicles.

A defense fund of $500 was established to pay for any fines the students might incur. The results came in quickly. The participants received thirty-three citations in seventeen days, and the fine fund was exhausted. The encounters with police, according to Heussenstamm, ranged "from affable and 'standard polite' to surly, accompanied by search of the vehicle. Five were thoroughly gone over and their drivers were shaken down. One white girl, a striking blonde and a member of a leading campus sorority, was questioned at length about her reasons for supporting the 'criminal activity' of the Black Panther Party."[39] These actions by the police did little to combat actual crime; rather they represented an attempt to suppress a movement fond of calling them "fascist pigs." This illustration shows that rule enforcers occasionally interpret their role in a way that has less to do with actual legal statutes than with how law officers feel about certain "deviant" groups in society.

Occupational status problems also affect relations *between* various groups of law enforcers. The quest for greater public respect in some cases hinders police cooperation. Many local police agencies greatly resent the FBI. Federal agents are seen as "glory hunters" and "headline grabbers."[40] In New York City the regular police department is at odds with the Housing Authority police. This quote from the *New York Times* indicates how concern about status and respect can influence law enforcement:

> Only the day before Detectives Rufflin and Stubbs were shot, several Housing Authority colleagues working with them on a homicide investigation were ejected from a stake-out by city detectives, one of whom reportedly told them: "If you

wanted to be real cops, you should have joined the New York Police Department." . . .

Last summer . . . a housing patrolman chasing a suspect was stopped by a city policeman who refused to let him leave the project. The suspect escaped.

Brooklyn housing detectives in a Brownsville project, after closing out two homicides, were barred from investigating a third by city detectives of the 13th homicide squad who had arrived at the scene before them.[41]

The situation had become so serious at one point that members of each enforcement agency were threatening members of the other with arrest. The only loser in this affair, according to the *New York Times,* was the citizen.

Both excessive, selective rule enforcement and departmental rivalry go against the desires of the rule creators who get laws enacted. Control agencies such as the police frequently change the intentions of the laws. They either do not enforce those laws they see as mere public nuisances or strictly enforce laws against those they personally see as real threats to themselves or the society.

Types of Deviant Labels

A major concern of the labeling theorists has been what happens to a person to whom the label *deviant* has been applied. Although it is relatively easy to see a theoretical distinction between deviant *behavior* and deviant *people,* in practice those who perform deviant behavior come to be thought of as deviant people. Why make the distinction? Most of us take the way a person behaves to be a sign of a character trait, something deep inside and unlikely to change. We assume that a person's *present* behavior indicates something about his *past* behavior and his *future* behavior. We assume that deviants are a breed apart, that the world is made up of deviants (who always were and always will be deviant) and nondeviants (who never were and never will be), and, of course, we wish there were some physical sign that would help us tell them apart (see the section in this chapter on "Biological Deviance").

The labeling theorists suggest that this approach is inaccurate and may *create* permanent deviants of people who would not have continued certain behavior had they not been caught and labeled *deviant.*

Edwin Lemert, in his classic *Social Pathology,* makes a distinction between *situational* or *primary* deviance and *secondary* deviance, which results from the *consequences* of primary deviance.[42]

The important point is that people may respond to stress, to impulse, to drink, to group pressures—to temporary situations—and do things they ordinarily would never do and would never dream of doing again. They may do these things and still consider themselves good, law-abiding citizens.

Primary deviance is *situational.* It is a spur-of-the-moment event. The smoking of one joint at a friend's party does not make the individual a deviant in the eyes of society, and, more important, it does not make *him* feel he is a "deviant." Homosexuality in prisons, sexual promiscuity during wartime or at a convention, or participation in a riot are all forms of situational, primary deviance. When a child steals a candy bar or a record for the first time, he is a primary deviant.

Secondary deviance is deviance that results from reactions to *primary* deviance. In other words, one may commit an illegal act and not be considered a deviant by others or by himself. If others should decide to declare him officially deviant—fire him, arrest him, hospitalize him— he comes to be considered a deviant by others and by himself. Then he may find himself more or less compelled to continue his deviance and may cut himself off from opportunities to "go straight."

Consider, for example, the ex-convict who finds that he cannot get a job because of his record. Consider the girl who at first accepts presents for sexual favors and discovers after a while that others do not treat her as a friendly amateur but as a professional. Then she finds herself agreeing that in fact she is a prostitute, and because she can't escape the label, she devotes herself to her profession.

In other words, the labeling theorists argue that becoming a deviant involves what Robert K. Merton called "the self-fulfilling prophecy": *first* a person is labeled by others as deviant and *then* in fact lives up to this label, frequently because he has no other options left. The theorists argue that those people who do the same things but do *not* get hit with the label can and do quit the behavior, whereas those who get caught also get cut off from the social support that would enable them to quit. Subcultures made up of fellow outcasts make up the social world of the now-committed deviant and encourage and assist him to justify and continue his deviance.

The labeling theorists, then, are relatively unconcerned about why one initially performs deviant behavior. They are concerned instead with the factors that make it possible for some to escape a label and that make it impossible for others. Finally, they seek the consequences for those to whom the label is successfully applied.

A recent study illustrates the difficulty of convincing others who apply the label that one's behavior no longer deserves that label.

A Case of Labeling

Psychiatrist D. L. Rosenhan and eight "normal" friends had themselves committed to twelve different mental hospitals.[43] They told the admissions offices of each hospital that they heard voices. Except for lying about their real identities they told the straight truth to every question asked them. Once admitted as patients, they declared that they no longer heard voices and felt well enough to leave. Although all behaved as normally as they knew how to behave, it took them an average of nineteen days to convince the hospitals to release them. The object of their experiment was to find out whether or not psychiatric hospitals could identify "sane" people. Each left the hospital with a diagnosis saying that his symptoms were "in remission" (which means the hospitals would not declare him sane but would, at best, admit that his symptoms were no longer showing).

It became obvious to the pseudo-patients that everything they said and did "proved" they were not sane to their keepers (about one third of their fellow patients spotted them as frauds, as newspaper reporters or professors who were checking up on the hospital):

As far as I can determine, diagnoses were in no way affected by the relative health of the circumstances of a pseudo-patient's life. Rather, the reverse occurred: the perception of his circumstances was shaped entirely by the diagnosis. A clear example of such translation is found in the case of a pseudo-patient who had had a close relationship with his mother but was rather remote from his father during his early childhood. During adolescence and beyond, however, his father became a close friend, while his relationship with his mother cooled. His present relationship with his wife was characteristically close and warm. Apart from occasional angry exchanges, friction was minimal. The children had rarely been spanked. Surely there is nothing especially pathological about such a history. Indeed, many readers may see a similar pattern in their own experiences, with no markedly deleterious consequences. Observe, however, how such a history was translated in the psychopathological context, this from the case summary prepared after the patient was discharged.

"This white 39-year-old male . . . manifests a long history of considerable ambivalence in close relationships, which begins in early childhood. A warm relationship with his mother cools during his adolescence. A distant relationship to his father is described as becoming very intense. Affective stability is absent. His attempts to control emotionality with his wife and children are punctuated by angry outbursts and, in the case of the children, spankings. And while he says that he has several good friends, one senses considerable ambivalence embedded in those relationships also."[44]

After completing this experiment, Rosenhan told others about his experiences. Staff members of a certain hospital doubted that such errors could occur at *their* hospital, so Rosenhan told them that he would send one or more phonies to their hospital during the following three months and defied the staff to spot them. Staff members rated all incoming patients for the next three months on a little 10-point rating scale, a score of 1 or 2 indicating high confidence that the patient being admitted was one of Rosenhan's fakers:

Judgments were obtained on 193 patients who were admitted for psychiatric treatment. All staff who had had sustained contact with or primary responsibility for the patient—attendants, nurses, psychiatrists, physicians, and psychologists—were asked to make judgments. Forty-one patients were alleged, with high confidence, to be pseudo-patients by at least one member of the staff. Twenty-three were considered suspect by at least one psychiatrist. Nineteen were suspected by one psychiatrist and one other staff member. Actually, no genuine psuedo-patient (at least from my group) presented himself during this period.[45]

The labeling theorists have been sensitive to the fact that for many types of deviant, being caught and labeled publicly as deviants is the beginning of a lifelong deviant career and that, had they never been caught, the first offense might have been the last. In attempting to make this basic point, the labeling theorists have not necessarily persuaded sociologists that labeling can account for *all* types of deviance. (As Table 11-3 indicates, labeling plays a larger role in producing and continuing certain types of behavior than others.) However, the labeling theorists have made sociologists aware that there is an enormous amount of *chance* involved in whether or not one's behavior becomes known to law enforcers. They are also aware that these law enforcers, the police and the courts, have an enormous amount of discretion as to how to deal with alleged deviants and that the cure (the application of the label) may be worse than the illness (the initial act) for both the "deviant" and the society.

Aberrants Versus Nonconformists

Aside from psychiatric labels, like *schizophrenic* and *neurotic,* and legal labels, like *felon* and *petty offender,* there is another set of labels used to describe deviants and their relationship to the rules of the society.

Robert Merton points out that deviants may be *aberrant* or they may be *nonconformist.*[46] For those of you with a religious turn of mind, the distinction is roughly that between the heretic and the sinner, the former *challenging* the rules, the latter simply *ignoring* them.

The *nonconformist* defies society through his deviance. He *publicly* announces his dissent. The homosexual who joins the gay liberation movement, for example, insists that he is not a pervert or a sick person but that he is proposing a legitimate, "alternative life style."

The nonconformist *challenges* the correctness of existing norms and values. Sit-ins against racial discrimination and the Vietnam war were forms of this kind of deviance. The nonconformist attempts to change the existing norms. He desires to make his, or his group's, "ought to be" the society's "is." Society's response may be favorable to his seemingly selfless pursuit of good. Usually we can at least respect the nonconformist's sincerity if not his ideas.

Finally, the nonconformist usually makes *high moral claims.* He is fighting for peace, equality, justice, and for all that is good.

Merton's description of the political deviant suggests that society may often

deal less harshly with him than with the aberrant criminal. However, numerous studies by sociologists indicate that a fine, thin line exists between the two. Some political nonconformity *can* be labeled as criminal.[47] Police in many instances react to "protesters" as "criminals." Civil rights marchers, antiwar protesters, and gay liberationists have frequently been arrested for *criminal* behavior. Whether the nonconformist or the criminal label is accepted as the accurate one is largely determined by the nature of the nonconformity and the cause of the "deviant behavior." For example, the American public was very sympathetic to the nonconformist behavior of southern blacks when they marched to the local courthouse seeking the right to vote. The public disapproved of the use of dogs, gas, and billy clubs against the black marchers. Other groups who have used the same tactics and have been similarly attacked by the authorities have received little support because "they were breaking the law." The violent confrontation between the Chicago police and the antiwar demonstrators during the week of the 1968 Democratic National Convention found millions of television viewers applauding as the protesters were clubbed to the streets.[48] The point is that the nonconformist attempts to gain public support—or at least tolerance—for his cause by trying to get others to label him a protester. Those who oppose the nonconformist try to make the label *criminal* stick.

The *aberrant* deviant *shuns public attention.* He works in the dead of night. He attempts to hide his deviance, whereas the nonconformist flaunts his. The burglar and the rapist use darkness to conceal their identity.

The aberrant does not deny the legitimacy of the laws he violates. He may justify his deeds, but he does not argue that rape, murder, or robbery are good deeds.

The aberrant attempts to *escape the law* rather than change it. When caught, he pleads not guilty or points to "extenuating circumstances" ("I did it *because*" of insanity, poverty, or some other reason).

The aberrant makes *no claim to moral values.* The aberrant does not steal from the wealthy "to give to the poor." Instead he, like master thief Willie Sutton, robs banks "because that's where the money is." He has nothing to contribute or to restore. He is interested in personal gain. The embezzler, the car thief, the mugger cannot claim his actions are for the common good. Indeed, society treats murderers who claim "God told me to do it" as insane. The defense of the infamous Manson Family, that they engaged in mass murder to escape "Helter Skelter" or an "impending race war," did not persuade a jury of their innocence.

Summary of the Labeling Perspective

Deviance is a label applied to certain kinds of behavior; it is not a property of that behavior. Rule creators are those who urge society's rule makers and rule enforcers to declare certain behavior deviant. Labels are applied to people as well as their behavior, and we have reason to believe that these labels may contribute to the continuation of the behavior that the labelers want to eliminate. Sociologists make distinctions among several types of deviance and several types of labels. Primary versus secondary deviance and aberrance versus nonconformity, are two sets of distinctions they have found particularly useful.

The Reality and the Mythology of Deviance

Deviant behavior is surrounded by a great deal of myth and misinformation. Labeling theorists sometimes appear to be suggesting that there would be *no* deviance if we simply abolished all laws and labels and therefore made illegal behavior disappear by the simple act of declaring *everything* legal. Nonetheless, there are certain kinds of behavior that in the eyes of most citizens are unquestionably *deviant* and unquestionably *terrifying,* whatever word games sociologists seem to be playing. Murder, assault, and narcotic addiction are three such behaviors, and they are also behaviors about which a good deal of misinformation exists. Studies have repeatedly found a paradox: the further

Deviance is a label applied to certain behaviors.

away people are from such behavior, the more immediate and frightening it seems to be.

Violence and Victims

Residents of suburbs are more frightened of being mugged on their quiet, tree-lined streets than are inner-city residents, though street crime is much more likely in urban areas.

One survey conducted by the *New York Times* in Webster, Iowa showed the major concern to be "crime in the streets" and "hoodlums." The hoodlums, according to the townspeople, seemed to be urban blacks and student demonstrators. After further probing, the *Times* reporter found that the culprits really were local kids "drinking beer and driving fast."

Sociologist Tony Poveda found a similar state of affairs in a northern California town. He suggested that the notorious hood bedeviling the community was a local teenager.[49] Official figures support Poveda's conclusions. Of the 6 million serious crimes (or 2,907 per 100,000 persons) committed in 1971, most occurred in urban areas.[50] A third of these crimes took place in cities with 250,000 or more people. Only five percent took place in rural areas. Especially

Crime Index Offenses	Total U.S.	Area: Cities over 250,000	Suburban	Rural
TOTAL	2906.7	5413.5	2410.8	1032.3
Violent	392.7	1047.5	205.7	133.4
Property	2514.0	4366.0	2205.1	898.9
Murder	8.5	19.2	4.2	6.9
Forcible rape	20.3	43.6	14.4	11.1
Robbery	187.1	633.4	69.7	14.9
Aggravated assault	176.8	351.4	177.4	100.5
Burglary	1148.3	2026.1	974.5	484.9
Larceny $50 and over	909.2	1240.8	924.4	344.4
Auto theft	456.5	1099.1	306.3	69.6

Table 11-4. Crime Rate by Area, 1971 (rate per 100,000 inhabitants)

victimized were persons with incomes of $6,000 or less, particularly blacks. The rates of black male offenses against other black males were eight times higher than crimes committed by whites against whites. These figures challenge the popular myth of "the ghetto dwellers, the black, and the poor stalking and striking out against the middle-class and the prosperous."[51]

Until the 1972 Supreme Court ruling against capital punishment, murder was the crime for which most felons were sentenced to death. Cold-blooded murder is *the* crime, as countless detective stories and television dramas aptly demonstrate. The image of the murderer is a sinister one. The killer in a Sherlock Holmes or Charlie Chan story acts upon motives of greed, lust, or vengeance. He is the stranger in the night, the unsuspected butler, or the hired killer striking the victim without a moment's warning. Polls indicate more citizens fear violence from this unknown source than any other crime.

According to statistics for 1965, being killed by willful homicide was as likely as death by drowning or fire and only half as likely as death by suicide or any accident not caused by a car. There is an 80 percent greater chance you'll be killed by a car than by a murderer. Nor does murder usually happen on the streets of America's cities or suburbs. Strangers in the night are *not* the major culprits.

Murder is an affair between friends, lovers, and relatives. Using a sample of 456 murders committed from 1957 to 1960 in the United Kingdom, T. P. Morris and Louis Blom-Cooper found that 53 percent of those involved were related and 18 percent were friends and acquaintances. A total of 81 percent were on relatively close terms.[52] Marvin E. Wolfgang in a study of Philadelphia homicides reported that two thirds of 188 murders were committed by relatives, friends, and people known to the victim. Indeed, most murders occur in the victim's own home, thus suggesting that the fear of strangers is misplaced.

The *bedroom* is the most dangerous room in the house. According to Wolfgang, "It provides the setting for almost a fifth of all homicides, more than any other place except the highway."[53] Women were most frequently killed in the bedroom (35 percent of female victims as opposed to 14 percent of male victims).

The next most popular room is the *kitchen.* Women killed most of their victims, generally males, in the kitchen with butcher knives. Twenty-nine percent of the murders committed by women occurred in the kitchen during the cooking of a meal. Again, these statistics really question the general public image of the professional killer or the drug-crazed hoodlum as the greatest threat to life.

The United States has a relatively high homicide rate compared to most European countries but a lower rate than most Latin American and African countries. Our rate per 100,000 population is 6.0, Australia's is 1.5, Canada's is 1.3. For England and Wales it's 0.7.[54] Contrary to the beliefs of many, our criminal homicide rate is apparently lower than it was in the 1930s[55] (although it may be that better medical technology prevents many assaults with deadly weapons from ending as homicides). The figures on differences in homicide rates indicate that there are cultural (and subcultural) differences in the frequency of crimes of violence: there is a variation in the attitude that violence is a legitimate way to resolve disputes.

Marvin Wolfgang and Franco Ferracuti[56] suggested that there are *subcultures of violence,* varying in size and strength by region, class, and group, which exaggerate the *society's* attitudes and acceptance of violence. In such subcultures, people learn that violence is acceptable, is not a cause for feeling guilt, and is likely to be used by the other guy if you don't use it first. Such subcultures are particularly likely to be found in the slums of large cities:

In a 1955 study of 489 homicide cases in Houston, Texas, for example, over 87 percent of them occurred in four areas, not far apart, located in certain slum areas near the center of the city. For the most part, other areas within the city had no criminal homicides at all. Nearly all the homicides occurred in areas populated chiefly by blacks and Spanish-Americans. In more than 70 percent of the cases the victim and the murderer lived less than 2 miles apart, and in 32.8 percent of the cases they lived in the same house or on the same block. The conflicts that gave rise to the disputes were chiefly between members of the same social group, and in 87 percent of the cases the murderer and his victim had known each other before. Some indication of the relationship between criminal homicides and the pattern of life in certain areas of the city is suggested by the fact that 65 percent of all criminal homicides in Philadelphia occur during weekends, particularly on Saturday night.

In Cleveland two-thirds of the homicides studied in the late 1950s took place in 12 percent of the city, primarily in black areas with slum conditions. In Delhi, India approximately two-thirds of all murders between 1962 and 1964 occurred in poor or lower middle-class areas. Similarly, criminal homicides and other crimes of violence in London were found to be concentrated in slum areas where violence is used to settle domestic disputes and neighborhood quarrels.[57]

Narcotics

What occupational group has the highest drug addiction rates? No, not rock musicians. Physicians![58] People believe a lot of things about drugs that are simply not true. David Musto's fascinating history of narcotics control[59] cites a number of strange ideas Americans have about narcotics. In some respects the history of narcotics control in the United States is really a history of racial and ethnic relations and of the fantasies and myths about these relations.

A 1910 federal survey asserted that cocaine "is often the direct incentive to the crime of rape by Negroes of the South and other sections of the country." Southern sheriffs believed that cocaine made blacks better pistol marksmen and that it made them impervious to .32-caliber bullets. Many police departments switched to .38s. The principal users of opium were Chinese immigrants. The federal report also noted that "one of the most unfortunate phases of the habit of smoking opium in this country is the large number of women who have become involved and were living as common law wives or cohabiting with Chinese in the China-towns of our various cities."

Marihuana came to be considered a threat relatively late in the 1930s by the Federal Bureau of Narcotics. But San Franciscans started worrying after World War I, frightened by "a large influx of Hindoos . . . demanding cannabis indica" and initiating "the whites into their habit." During the Depression the Southwest demanded and got marihuana legislation, apparently having been offended by a deadly combination of bad habits of Mexicans, that is, smoking marihuana and *competing for scarce jobs.*

The subject of the nature of narcotic addiction and the character of the addict is fraught with mythology and misinformation. W. B. Eldridge examined many of the common beliefs and suggested some more plausible alternative statements:[60]

1. *Narcotics ravage the human body.* A common image of the narcotics user is an emaciated, physically depleted individual shuffling down a big city street. One police publication provided this example: "To be a confirmed drug addict is to be one of the walking dead. . . . The teeth have rotted out; the appetite is lost and the stomach and intestines don't function properly. The gall bladder becomes inflamed; eyes and skin turn a bilious yellow."[61] However, most physicians unfamiliar with drug addiction find it difficult to detect the addict. Charles Winick observed, "There are few pathognomic physical characteristics by which the opiate addict can be recognized as such. . . . It is difficult to recognize a marijuana smoker, although he sometimes has a characteristic facial flush."[62] Indeed, most symptoms of addiction can be found only through chemical tests *and* during withdrawal.

2. *Narcotics destroy morality.* It is generally believed that the use of drugs causes moral deterioration, that it makes people lose track of right and wrong. David Jenkins presented a valid illustration:

I lost my self-control because the devil is in dope. . . . At first my wife did not want me to get into drugs, because I stayed away from her and the baby too long. . . . As they were alone nights the devil caused her to join me and become addicted to dope. I did not trust her and she did not trust me. Both of us judged one another. I thought I was doing what she was doing. I would beat her day after day. She would try to beat me at the game.

. . . After we were separated, this led me to more arrests. I was accused of violating the state narcotics laws for forging names on prescriptions. My car would be pulled over often. I barely escaped by throwing the grass out into the wind and let it blow away. The speed of the car caused the grass to scatter into the wind so the cops could not gather up enough for evidence.[63]

The idea of moral decline of the addict, however, is most often applied to white middle-class youth who "drop out." Yet a preponderance of drug use occurs in the lowest strata of American society among those with "little to lose." It takes place in subcultures not allowed to be a part of the "moral fiber of society."

3. *Narcotic addicts are a sexual menace.* The press in recent years has delighted in presenting pictures or orgiastic dope parties. The drug user freqently has been termed a rapist with uncontrollable passion. In the case of opiate addiction, this is a false picture as the drug depresses the user's sexual appetite. The evidence regarding the use of marihuana and LSD is not as clear. Segments of the underground press claim that "sex is better" with these drugs because the partners are more relaxed. A student claims, "I use pot as a social crutch. I want to join in. When I'm floating and lighter-headed, I can make it easier with chicks."[64] This euphoric state, however, is a far cry from the Dope-Crazed Sex Menace envisioned by many citizens. Indeed, it can be argued that the sexual mores in countercultures that use marihuana and LSD are merely more open and liberal than are those of the general public.

4. *Narcotic addicts are criminals.* Because narcotic usage is illegal, all drug users are by definition criminals. Arrest statistics indicate that many addicts engage in other forms of criminal activity to support their drug habits. On the other hand, sociologists question greatly the thesis that drug usage causes criminal behavior beyond the usage itself. Richard H. Blum suggested:

Whether or not heroin use influences later criminality is not clear. Since, *prior* to the initial heroin experience itself, the user is *already* likely to be a delinquent associating with other delinquents, heroin cannot be assumed to "cause" his crime. . . . It must be noted that there is no evidence showing that heroin users steal more or more successfully than their delinquent peers *not using* heroin.[65]

Eldridge pointed to the educational and income status of the groups from which addicts are drawn, saying, "Addiction is always a cost clearly beyond the earning power of most of them."[66] What is being suggested here is that many affluent drug users may not be associated with street crime. For example, rock and jazz musicians who earn substantial salaries can afford to sustain a habit. Physicians also can pay for their drugs. Most middle-class marihuana users do not resort to theft or any other criminal activity.

5. *Addiction is contagious.* Turning the corner and coming down *your* block: the neighborhood dope pusher. The pusher is seen as standing outside of elementary schools giving narcotics, like candy, to unsuspecting school children. Penalties for selling narcotics are quite high. Politicians frequently advocate severe sentences. In 1973 Governor Nelson Rockefeller of New York called for, and got, a mandatory life sentence for pushers without possibility of parole. President Nixon, in a crime bill, would have had dealers similarly confined after a second conviction.[67] The arguments for these sentences are based on the belief that a *deliberate* effort is made by users to recruit new users. In fact, this is not the case. Most users are introduced to drugs by other users who are friends. It is usually quite casual, *not* planned. As Eldridge noted, "It is true that addiction is spread by addicts—that's what makes it a highly dangerous contagion—but the spread is usually a casual one. Often an addict shows great reluctance in 'breaking in' a neophyte."[68] The drug contagion thesis is a difficult one to prove because it is greatly colored by what is called an *addictive* or harmful substance.

Alcohol, according to the 1973 National Commission on Marihuana and Drug Abuse, is by far the most used and abused drug in America. It is clearly the most popular depressant with teen-agers and adults. With adolescents the most popular intoxicants aside from beer are cheap, sweet wines. Ironically, the use of alcohol by adolescents is not deemed a major contagious social problem. Norm Southerby of the Los Angeles County Alcohol Safety Action Program told *Newsweek* of a nineteen-year-old girl's switch from marihuana to alcohol. "She'd get so drunk that she would be throwing up in the morning," he said, "yet her parents were happy." A Levittown school superintendent added, "I get parents in here to talk about an incident involving their kid drinking, and the first thing they say is 'Thank God it's not drugs.'"[69]

There is little doubt that the indiscriminate use of *any* drug is harmful to the individual. An excessive use of an illegal drug by a significant portion of any population does have an impact on society. The understanding of this influence and its treatment as a social problem can be accomplished only through familiarity with the actual facts of the phenomenon rather than the myths that surround it. Many who do research on marihuana smoking have been concerned with the misinformation surrounding this popular drug. Schaflander suggested:

> The most ominous development in drug usage evaluation and control is the deep credibility gap that exists between narcotic and police officials and high school and college students. Adult authorities and parents compound this gap when

Table 11-5. The Mind Benders at a Glance

Official Name of Drug or Chemical	*Slang Name(s)*	*Usual Single Adult Dose*	*Duration of Action (Hours)*	*Method of Taking*	*Legitimate Medical Uses (Present and Projected)*	*Potential for Psychological Dependence*[a]	*Potential for Tolerance Leading to Increased Dosage*
Alcohol Whisky, Gin, Beer, Wine	Booze Hooch Suds	1½ oz. gin or whisky, 12 oz. beer	2–4	Swallowing liquid	Rare. Sometimes used as a sedative (for tension).	High	Yes
Caffeine Coffee, Tea, Coca-Cola No-Doz, APC	Java	1–2 cups 1 bottle 5 mg.	2–4	Swallowing liquid	Mild stimulant. Treatment of some forms of coma.	Moderate	Yes
Nicotine (and Coal Tar) Cigarettes, Cigars	Fags, nails	1–2 cigarettes	1–2	Smoking (inhalation)	None (used as an insecticide).	High	Yes
Sedatives Alcohol—see above Barbiturates Amytal Nembutal	Downers Barbs Blue devils Yellow jackets, dolls	50–100 mg.	4	Swallowing pills or capsules	Treatment of insomnia and tension. Induction of anesthesia.	High	Yes
Seconal Phenobarbital Doriden (Glutethimide) Chloral Hydrate Miltown, Equanil (Meprobamate)	Red devils Phennies Goofers	500 mg. 500 mg. 400 mg.					

[a]The term *habituation* has sometimes been used to refer to psychological dependence and the term *addiction* to refer to the combination of tolerance and an abstinence (withdrawal) syndrome.

[b]Drug abuse (dependency) properly means (excessive, often compulsive) use of a drug to an extent that it damages an individual's health or social or vocational adjustment or is otherwise specifically harmful to society.

[c]Always to be considered in evaluating the effects of these drugs is the amount consumed, purity, frequency, time interval since ingestion, food in the stomach, combinations with other drugs, and most importantly, the personality or character of the individual taking it and the setting or context in which it is taken. The determinations made in this chart are based upon the evidence with human use of these drugs rather than upon isolated artificial experimental situations, animal research, or political (propagandistic) statements.

[d]Only scattered, inadequate health, educational, or rehabilitation programs (usually prison hospitals) exist for narcotic addicts and alcoholics (usually outpatient clinics) with nothing for the others except sometimes prison.

[f]CNS = central nervous system.

Source: Human Behavior, (January/February, 1972), 64–65.

ʾotential for ʾhysical Ɔepend-ence	Overall Potential for Abuse and Toxicity[b]	Reasons Drug Is Sought by Users (Drug Effects and Social Factors)	Usual Short-term effects Psychological, Pharmacological, Social)[c]	Usual Long-term Effects (Psychological, Pharmacological, Social)	Form of Legal Regulation and Control[d]
Yes	High	To relax. To escape from tensions, problems, and inhibitions. To get "high" (euphoria). Seeking manhood or rebelling (particularly those under 21). Social custom and conformity. Massive advertising and promotion. Ready availability.	CNS[f] depressant. Relaxation (sedation). Euphoria. Drowsiness. Impaired judgment, reaction time, coordination, and emotional control. Frequent aggressive behavior and driving accidents.	Diversion of energy and money from more creative and productive pursuits. Habituation. Possible obesity with chronic excessive use. Irreversible damage to brain and liver. Addiction with severe withdrawal illness (DT's) with heavy use. Many deaths.	Available and advertised without limitation in many forms with only minimal regulation by age (21 or 18), hours of sale, location, taxation, ban on bootlegging and driving laws. Some "black market" for those under age and those evading taxes. Minimal penalties.
No	Very Minimal	For a "pick-up" or stimulation. "Taking a break." Social custom and low cost. Advertising. Ready availability.	CNS stimulant. Increased alertness. Reduction of fatigue.	Sometimes insomnia, restlessness, or gastric irritation. Habituation.	Available and advertised without limit with no regulation for children or adults.
No	High	For a "pick-up" or stimulation. "Taking a break." Social custom. Advertising. Ready availability.	CNS stimulant. Relaxation (or distraction) from the process of smoking.	Lung (and other) cancer, heart and blood vessel disease, cough, etc. Higher infant mortality. Many deaths. Habituation. Diversion of energy and money, Air pollution. Fire.	Available and advertised without limit with only minimal regulation by age, taxation, and labeling of packages.
Yes	High	To relax or sleep. To get "high" (euphoria). Widely prescribed by physicians, both for specific and nonspecific complaints. General climate encouraging taking pills for everything.	CNS depressants. Sleep induction. Relaxation (sedation). Sometimes euphoria. Drowsiness. Impaired judgment, reaction time, coordination and emotional control. Relief of anxiety-tension. Muscle relaxation.	Irritability, weight loss, addiction with severe withdrawal illness (like DT's). Diversion of energy and money. Habituation, addiction.	Available in large amounts by ordinary medical prescription, which can be repeatedly refilled or can be obtained from more than one physician. Widely advertised and "detailed" to M.D.'s and pharmacists. Other manufacture, sale, or possession prohibited under federal drug abuse and similar state (dangerous) drug laws. Moderate penalties. Widespread illicit traffic.

Table 11-5. (Continued)

Official Name of Drug or Chemical	Slang Name(s)	Usual Single Adult Dose	Duration of Action (Hours)	Method of Taking	Legitimate Medical Uses (Present and Projected)	Potential for Psychological Dependence[a]	Potential for Tolerance Leading to Increased Dosage
Stimulants	Uppers					High	Yes
Caffeine—see above							
Nicotine—see above							
Amphetamines	Pep pills, wake-ups	2.5–5.0 mg.	4	Swallowing pills, capsules or injecting in vein	Treatment of obesity, narcolepsy, fatigue, depression.		
Benzedrine	Bennies, cartwheels						
Methedrine	Crystal, speed, meth						
Dexedrine	Dexies or Xmas trees						
Preludin	(spansules)						
Cocaine	Coke, snow	Variable		Sniffing or injecting	Anesthesia of the eye and throat.		
Tranquilizers							
Librium (Chlordiazepoxide)		5–10 mg.	4–6	Swallowing pills or capsules	Treatment of anxiety, tension, alcoholism, neurosis, psychosis, psychosomatic disorders, and vomiting.	Minimal	No
Phenothiazines							
Thorazine		10–25 mg.					
Compazine		10 mg.					
Stelazine		2 mg.					
Reserpine (Rauwolfia)		1 mg.					
Marihuana or Cannabis Sativa[e]	Pot, grass, tea, weed, stuff, hash, joint, reefers	Variable—1 cigarette or pipe, or 1 drink or cake (India)	4	Smoking (inhalation) Swallowing	Treatment of depression, tension, loss of appetite, and high blood pressure.	Moderate	No
Narcotics (Opiates, Analgesics)							
Opium	Op	10–12 "pipes" (Asia)	4	Smoking (inhalation)	Treatment of severe pain, diarrhea, and cough.	High	Yes
Heroin	Horse, H, smack, shit, junk	Variable—bag or payer with 5–10 percent heroin		Injecting in muscle or vein			
Morphine		15 mg.					
Codeine		30 mg.					
Percodan		1 tablet					
Demerol		50–100 mg.					
Methadone	Dolly						
Cough Syrups (Cheracol, Hycodan, Romilar, etc.)		2–4 oz. (for suphoria)		Swallowing			

[e] Hashish or charas is a more concentrated form of the active ingredient THC (Tetrahydrocannabinol) and is consumed in smaller doses analagous to vodka-beer ratios.

Potential for Physical Dependence	Overall Potential for Abuse and Toxicity[b]	Reasons Drug Is Sought by Users (Drug Effects and Social Factors)	Usual Short-term effects Psychological, Pharmacological, Social)[c]	Usual Long-term Effects (Psychological, Pharmacological, Social)	Form of Legal Regulation and Control[d]
No	High				
		For stimulation and relief of fatigue. To get "high" (euphoria). General climate encouraging taking pills for everything.	CNS stimulants. Increased alertness, reduction of fatigue, loss of appetite, insomnia, often euphoria.	Restlessness, irritability, weight loss, toxic psychosis (mainly paranoid). Diversion of energy and money. Habituation. Extreme irritability, toxic psychosis.	Amphetamines, same as sedatives above. Cocaine, same as narcotics below.
No	Minimal	Medical (including psychiatric) treatment of anxiety or tension states, alcoholism, psychoses, and other disorders.	Selective CNS depressants. Relaxation, relief of anxiety-tension. Suppression of hallucinations or delusions, improved functioning.	Sometimes drowsiness, dryness of mouth, blurring of vision, skin rash, tremor. Occasionally jaundice, agranulocytosis, or death.	Same as sedatives above, except not usually included under the special federal or state drug laws. Negligible illicit traffic.
No	Minimal to moderate	To get "high" (euphoria). As an escape. To relax. To socialize. To conform to various subcultures that sanction its use. For rebellion. Attraction of behavior labeled as deviant. Availability.	Relaxation, euphoria, increased appetite, some alteration of time perception, possible impairment of judgment and coordination. Mixed CNS depressant-stimulant.	Usually none. Possible diversion of energy and money. Habituation. Occasional acute panic reactions.	Unavailable (although permissable) for ordinary medical prescription. Possession sale, and cultivation prohibited by state and federal narcotic or marijuana laws. Special penalties. Widespread illicit traffic.
Yes	High	To get "high" (euphoria). As an escape. To avoid withdrawal symptoms. As a substitute for aggressive and sexual drives that cause anxiety. To conform to various subcultures that sanction use. For rebellion.	CNS depressants. Sedation, euphoria, relief of pain, impaired intellectual functioning and coordination.	Constipation, loss of appetite and weight, temporary Impotency or sterility. Habituation, addiction with unpleasant and painful withdrawal illness.	Available (except heroin) by special (narcotics) medical prescriptions. Some available by ordinary prescription or over the counter. Other manufacture, sale, or possession prohibited under state and federal narcotics laws. Severe penalties. Extensive illicit traffic.

Table 11-5. (Continued)

Official Name of Drug or Chemical	Slang Name(s)	Usual Single Adult Dose	Duration of Action (Hours)	Method of Taking	Legitimate Medical Uses (Present and Projected)	Potential for Psychological Dependence[a]	Potential for Tolerance Leading to Increased Dosage
LSD	Acid, sugar cubes, trip	150 micrograms	10–12	Swallowing liquid capsule, pill (or sugar cube)	Experimental study of mind and brain function. Enhancement of creativity and problem solving. Treatment of alcoholism, mental illness, and the dying person (chemical warfare).	Minimal	Yes (rare)
Psilocybin	Mushrooms	25 mg.	6–8				
STP		5 mg.		Smoking			
DMT				Chewing plant			
Mescaline (Peyote)	Cactus	350 mg.	12–14				
Antidepressants							
Ritalin		10 mg.	4–6	Swallowing pills or capsules	Treatment of moderate to severe depression.	Minimal	No
Dibenzapines (Tofranil, Elavil)		25 mg., 10 mg.					
MAO Inhibitors (Nardill, Parnate)		15 mg., 10 mg.					
Miscellaneous							
Glue, Gasoline, and Solvents		Variable		Inhalation	None, except antihistamines used for allergy and amyl nitrate for fainting.	Minimal to moderate	Not known
Amyl Nitrite							
Antihistaminics		1–2 ampules					
Nutmeg		25–50 mg.					
Nonprescription "Sedatives" (Compoz)		Variable		Swallowing			
Catnip							
Nitrous Oxide							

they lump all drugs together, under one umbrella, and condemn them as *equally* dangerous.[70]

Sociologists, by digging beyond the mythology of deviance, can at least suggest which avenues of action may not be fruitful. For example, drives against marihuana smokers will have little if any effect upon sex crimes. The brighter lighting of suburban streets will not reduce most violent crime. Nor will the jailing of a handful of narcotic traffickers stop new people from experimenting, much to their peril, with dangerous drugs. Knowing that these avenues are dead ends can help society find a solution to the problem with some dispatch. The knowledge that most homicides happen between friends and frequently in the home has many implications for criminal justice. Can the threat of punishment stop crimes of passion? Should more gun controls be imposed? Will better street lighting really stop violent homicides? Indeed, there are some problems that are beyond the powers of lawmakers and law enforcers to solve. Crime control can be effective only when much of the mythology surrounding it has been stripped away.

ɔtential for hysical epend-ence	Overall Potential for Abuse and Toxicity[b]	Reasons Drug Is Sought by Users (Drug Effects and Social Factors)	Usual Short-term effects Psychological, Pharmacological, Social)[c]	Usual Long-term Effects (Psychological, Pharmacological, Social)	Form of Legal Regulation and Control[d]
No	Moderate	Curiosity created by recent widespread publicity. Seeking for meaning and consciousness expansion. Rebellion. Attraction of behavior recently labeled as deviant. Availability.	Production of visual imagery, increased sensory awareness, anxiety, nausea, impaired coordination; sometimes consciousness expansion.	Usually none. Sometimes precipitates or intensifies an already existing psychosis; more commonly can produce a panic reaction.	Available only to a few medical researchers (or to members of the Native American Church). Other manufacture, sale, or possession prohibited by state dangerous drug or federal drug abuse laws. Moderate penalties. Extensive illicit traffic.
No	Minimal	Medical (including psychiatric) treatment of depression.	Relief of depression (elevation of mood), stimulation.	Basically the same as tranquilizers above.	Same as tranquilizers above.
No	Moderate to high	Curiosity. To get "high" (euphoria). Thrill seeking. Ready availability.	When used for mind alteration generally produces a "high" (euphoria) with impaired coordination and judgment.	Variable—some of the substances can seriously damage the liver or kidney and some produce hallucinations.	Generally easily available. Some require prescriptions. In several states glue banned for those under 21.

Summary

Behavior, from a sociological perspective, does not naturally fall into the categories "deviant" and "nondeviant." What is or is not deviant always depends on a judgment made by a given society and/or by groups within that society. What is harmful (or is *thought* to be harmful) to one society or to the interests of certain groups within the society may not be harmful (or be *thought* harmful) to other groups or to other societies.

For a complete understanding of deviance, we must look not only at the person who *violates* rules but also at those who *make* the rules and at those who *enforce* the rules.

Notes

1. J. L. Simmons, *Deviants* (Berkeley, Calif.: Glendessary Press, 1969), p. 3.
2. For example, Newcomb and his associates observed that the kinds of unconventional ideas and behavior that are disapproved of at most colleges are highly *approved* at Bennington College. Students who have *conventional* political and religious views receive the isolation, scorn, social pressure, and ridicule from their unconventional peers that those peers would be experiencing at most other schools. See T. M. Newcomb, R. Flacks, and D. P. Warwick, "Group Norms and

Creative Individualism: A Case Study," in M. M. Miles and W. W. Charters, eds., *Learning in Social Settings* (Boston: Allyn & Bacon, Inc., 1970), pp. 524–555.

3. E. Durkheim, *The Division of Labor in Society,* trans. George Simpson (New York: The Free Press, 1947), p. 72.

4. Two fascinating books that make clear the similarities between the treatment of "moral" deviants like prostitutes, ex-convicts, homosexuals, and drug addicts and "physical" deviants like deaf people, retardates, blind people, dwarfs, and physically handicapped people are E. Goffman, *Stigma* (Englewood Cliffs, N.J.: Prentice-Hall, Inc., 1963), and E. Sagarin, *Odd Man In* (Chicago: Quadrangle Books, 1969).

5. Our discussion of "born criminals" is based on Richard D. Knudten, *Crime in a Complex Society* (Homewood, Ill.: Dorsey Press, 1970), and on D. C. Gibbons, *Society, Crime and Criminal Careers,* 2nd Ed. (Englewood Cliffs, N.J.: Prentice-Hall, Inc., 1973).

6. W. H. Sheldon, *Varieties of Delinquent Youth* (New York: Harper and Row, Publishers, 1949).

7. See Sheldon and E. Glueck, *Unraveling Juvenile Delinquency* (Cambridge, Mass.: Harvard University Press, 1951).

8. S. and E. Glueck, *Physique and Delinquency* (New York: Harper and Row, Publishers, 1956).

9. T. Shibutani, *Society and Personality: An Interactionist Approach to Social Psychology* (Englewood Cliffs, N.J.: Prentice-Hall, Inc., 1961), p. 265.

10. K. K. Dion, "Physical Attractiveness and Evaluation of Childrens' Transgressions," *Journal of Personality and Social Psychology,* **24** (1972), 207–213.

11. In a recent study, students looking at a sample of a dozen photographs were quite confident in selecting those who were "guilty" of murder, robbery, and treason and less sure about who was "innocent." For homosexuality, subjects were more sure about who was "innocent" than about who was "guilty." Of course, actually none of the people in the photos were guilty of anything, but they fit the stereotypes the students held. D. J. Shoemaker, D. R. South and J. Lowe, "Facial Stereotypes of Deviants and Judgments of Guilt or Innocence," *Social Forces,* **51** (1973), 427–439.

12. See D. R. Owen, "The 47 XYY Male: A Review." *Psychological Bulletin,* **78** (1972), 209–233.

13. Ibid., p. 213.

14. Quoted in N. N. Kittrie, "Will the XYY Syndrome Abolish Guilt?" *Federal Probation,* **35** (1971), 31.

15. These two points were drawn from E. Rubington and M. S. Weinberg, eds., *The Study of Social Problems: Five Perspectives* (New York: Oxford University Press, 1971), p. 198.

16. See C. W. Mills, "The Professional Ideology of Social Pathologists," *American Journal of Sociology,* **49** (1943), 165–181.

17. See D. R. Cressey, "Culture Conflict, Differential Association, and Normative Conflict," in M. Wolfgang, ed., *Crime and Culture: Essays in Honor of Thorsten Sellin* (New York: John Wiley & Sons, Inc., 1968), 43–54.

18. T. Sellin, *Culture Conflict and Crime* (New York: Social Science Research Council, 1938), p. 58.

19. Cressey, op. cit., p. 53.

20. See E. H. Sutherland and D. R. Cressey, *Principles of Criminology* (Philadelphia: J. B. Lippincott Co., 1972). For example, a recent study shows that amount of parental control is a much more significant predictor of delinquency than attitudes toward deviant behavior or access to delinquent friends and neighbors. See G. F. Jensen, "Parents, Peers, and Delinquent Action: A Test of the Differential Association Perspective," *American Journal of Sociology,* **78** (1972), 562–575.

21. Quoted in R. Fogelson, *Violence as Protest: A Study of Riots and Ghettos,* (Garden City, N.Y.: Doubleday & Company, Inc., 1971), pp. 86, 91. Also see C. H. McCaghy, J. K. Skipper, Jr., and M. Lefton, eds., *In Their Own Behalf* (New York: Appleton-Century-Crofts, 2nd Ed., 1974.

22. Quoted in R. A. Cloward and L. Ohlin, *Delinquency and Opportunity: A Theory of Delinquent Gangs* (New York: The Free Press, 1960), p. 162.

23. R. K. Merton, "Social Structure and Anomie," *American Sociological Review,* **3** (1938), 672–682.

24. A. K. Cohen, *Delinquent Boys: The Culture of the Gang* (New York: The Free Press, 1955), p. 121.

25. Cloward and Ohlin, op cit., p. 162.

26. G. M. Sykes and D. Matza, "Techniques of Neutralization: A Theory of Delinquency," *American Sociological Review,* **22** (1957), 664–670.

27. J. M. Yinger, "Contraculture and Subculture," *American Sociological Review,* **25** (1960), 625–635.

28. Ibid., p. 630.

29. T. Roszak, *The Making of the Counterculture: Reflections on the Technocratic Society and Its Youthful Opposition* (Garden City, N.Y.: Doubleday & Company, Inc., 1969). Also see J. Douglas, *Youth in Turmoil* (Chevy Chase, Md.: National Institute of Mental Health, 1970).

30. See, for example, D. Gibbons, op cit., and M. Clinard and R. Quinney. *Criminal Behavior Systems,* 2nd Ed., (New York: Holt, Rinehart & Winston, Inc., 1973).

31. E. M. Lemert, H. S. Becker, A. Cicourel, K. Erikson, E. Goffman, J. Kitsuse, and T. Scheff are the most prominent labeling theorists. For a recent assessment of the approach, see N. J. Davis, "Labeling Theory in Deviance Research: A Critique and Reconsideration," *Sociological Quarterly,* **13** (1972), 447–474.

32. The mayor of a small up-state New York village recently proposed and got support for a law prohibiting X-rated films from being shown in his community. The Associated Press reported that the ban would not "have any immediate affect on this town, however. *Lewiston has no movie theater," in "X-Rated Film Ban Wanted Anyway," Toledo Blade* (March 14, 1973), p. 5. See also L. A. Zurcher, Jr., et al., "The Anti-Pornography Campaign: A Symbolic Crusade," *Social Problems,* **19** (1971), 217–237.

33. See C. H. McCaghy and R. S. Denisoff, "The Criminalization of Record Piracy: Analysis of an Economic and Political Conflict," in R. S. Denisoff and C. H. McCaghy, eds., *Deviance, Conflict and Criminality* (Chicago: Rand McNally & Co., 1973), pp. 297–309.

34. Ibid.

35. E. M. Schur, *Crimes Without Victims* (Englewood Cliffs, N.J.: Prentice-Hall, Inc., 1965).

36. Quoted from C. H. McCaghy and A. G. Neal, "Justifications for Illegal Sport: The Case of Cockfighters," *Journal of Popular Culture* (in press).

37. W. A. Westley, "Violence and the Police," *American Journal of Sociology,* **59** (1953), 34–41. Also see C. A. Hartjen, "Police-Citizen Encounters: Social Order in Interpersonal Interaction," *Criminology,* **10** (1972), 61–84; and P. Chevigny, *Police Power: Police Abuses in New York City* (New York: Random House, Inc., 1969).

38. F. K. Heussenstamm, "Bumper Stickers and the Cops," *Transaction,* **8** (1971), 32–33.

39. Ibid., p. 33.

40. Anonymous, "Inside the Cop Shop," unpublished paper in the files of R. S. Denisoff.

41. C. S. Wren, "Rivalry in Blue: Housing Police vs. City Police," *New York Times* (February 15, 1973), p. 77.

42. E. Lemert, *Social Pathology* (New York: McGraw-Hill Book Company, 1951). Also see on the "self-fulfilling prophecy" R. K. Merton, *Social Theory and Social Structure,* revised and expanded edition (New York: The Free Press, 1968).

43. D. L. Rosenhan, "On Being Sane in Insane Places," *Science,* **179** (1973), 250–258.

44. Ibid., p. 253.

45. Ibid., p. 252.

46. R. K. Merton, "Social Problems and Sociological Theory," in R. K. Merton and R. Nisbet, eds., *Contemporary Social Problems* (New York: Harcourt Brace Jovanovich, Inc., 1971), pp. 830–831.

47. See I. L. Horowitz and M. Leiberson, "Social Deviance and Political Marginality," *Social Problems,* **15** (1968), 280–296; R. Ross and G. L. Staines, "The Politics of Analyzing Social Problems," *Social Problems,* **20** (1972), 18–40; and J. Geschwender, "Civil Rights Protest and Riots: A Disappearing Distinction," *Social Science Quarterly,* **49** (1968), 474–484.

48. See *Rights in Conflict: The Walker Report to the National Commission on the Causes and Prevention of Violence* (New York: E. P. Dutton & Co., Inc., 1968).

49. See T. G. Poveda, "The Fear of Crime in a Small City," *Crime and Delinquency,* **18** (1972), 147–153.

50. See J. F. Coates, "Urban Violence: The Pattern of Disorder." *Annals of the American Academy of Political and Social Science,* **405** (1973), 25–40.

51. Ibid., p. 30. A recent study of homicide in New York City indicates that blacks are eight times more likely to be murdered than whites and that 82 percent of the murders were cases of a person of one race murdering someone of the *same* race. "Black Murder Victims in the City Outnumber White Victims 8 to 1," *New York Times* (August 5, 1973), p. 1.

52. T. P. Morris and L. Blom-Copper, *A Calendar of Murder* (London: M. Joseph, 1964).

53. M. E. Wolfgang, "Who Kills Whom?" in Various Authors *Change: Readings in Society and Human Behavior* (Del Mar, Calif.: CRM Books, 1971), p. 259.

54. Cited in Clinard and Quinney, op cit., p. 27.

55. Ibid.

56. M. E. Wolfgang and F. Ferracuti, *The Subculture of Violence: Toward an Integrated Theory in Criminology* (London: Tavistock Publications, Social Science Paperbacks, 1967).

57. Clinard and Quinney, op. cit., pp. 36–37.

58. C. Winick, "Physician Narcotic Addicts," *Social Problems,* **7** (1959), 240–254.

59. D. F. Musto, *The American Disease: Origins of Narcotic Control* (New Haven, Conn.: Yale University Press, 1973).

60. Discussion based on W. B. Eldridge, *Narcotics and the Law,* Rev. Ed. (Chicago: University of Chicago Press, 1967), pp. 13–34. A word of *caution* here is important. Eldridge *excluded* the drug cocaine from his study because of its lack of popularity in the United States in 1967. He acknowledges that cocaine may produce some of the effects he discusses. Cocaine in the 1970s has become quite popular with some users.

61. Ibid.

62. Ibid.

63. D. Jenkins, "The Devil Dealt Dope in Denver." *TVD* (March–April 1973), n.p.

64. Quoted in G. M. Schaflander, *Passion, Pot and Politics* (Boston: Little, Brown and Company, 1971), p. 51.

65. R. H. Blum. "Drugs, Behavior and Crime," in J. H. McGrath and F. R. Ścarpitti, eds., *Youth and Drugs: Perspectives on a Social Problem* (Glenview, Ill.: Scott, Foresman and Company, 1970), p. 167.

66. Ibid., pp. 18–19.

67. T. Wicker, "Playing to the Fear of Crime," *New York Times* (March 13, 1973), 37.

68. Eldridge, op cit.

69. Quoted in "The Latest Teen Drug: Alcohol," *Newsweek* (March 5, 1973), p. 68.

70. Schaflander, op cit. In 1969 President Nixon called marihuana and LSD use a "serious national threat." Others have looked at the same phenomenon and claimed that drug use in America is merely a movement toward new directions and forms of consciousness. See C. A. Reich, *The Greening of America* (New York: Random House, Inc., 1970). See also K. Westues, *Society's Shadow: Studies in the Sociology of Countercultures* (Toronto: McGraw-Hill-Ryerson, Ltd., 1972).

TWELVE
Demography

General Definition

DEMOGRAPHY is the science that deals with the study of human populations.* A brief formal definition would describe demography as *the science whose goal is the description of the number, type, and geographic arrangement of the people living in a specified area and the description and analysis of the causes and effects of changes in this cluster of people.* A more complete definition, however, would spell out the specific variables that are the major focus of population study. To begin with, the *demographer* (one whose vocation is the study of human populations) is concerned with acquiring statistical information about three particular properties of a population: (1) the number of people in the aggregate (*population size*); (2) the kinds of people making up the aggregate (*population composition*); and (3) the spatial arrangement of the aggregate within its area of habitation (*population distribution*). These three aspects of a population—size, composition, and distribution—are the *major demographic variables,* and they represent the fundamental subject matter of the science of demography. Thus, we can formulate an initial definition of demography as *the science that is concerned with the observation, measurement, and description of the size, composition, and distribution of the population in any specified area of human habitation.*

The interests of the demographer extend well beyond the mere description of specific facts about a population at one point in time (*population status*). Demographers are also interested in trying to find out whether these three major demographic variables are changing and what is the direction, speed and extent of any changes that might be occurring (*population dynamics*). For example, if the unit for study is a large metropolitan complex, the demographer would be interested in such questions as: (1) Is the size of the population going up, remaining relatively stable, or going down? (2) If the population is increasing or decreasing, how rapidly is this change taking place? (3) Is the population becoming younger or older? (4) What is the trend with respect to the proportion of people residing in the inner city as opposed to the proportion living in the suburban fringe areas? (5) How are the ethnic composition and the economic status of the inner-city population changing relative to those of the suburban population? These and similar questions are what the demographer seeks to answer in studying the population of any given area.

The demographer is also interested in the ways in which changes are occurring. When he observes, for example, that a population is increasing in size or that the pattern of its distribution in space is changing, he is interested in knowing what factors are operating to produce these changes. Demographically speaking, there are only three ways in which any population can change: (1) people can be born into it (*fertility*); (2) people can leave it by dying (*mortality*); and (3) people can move into or out of the area of habitation (*migration*). These three variables—fertility, mortality, and migration—are known as the *basic demographic processes,* and it is through these processes that changes in popu-

*This chapter was written especially for this book by Edward R. Stockwell.

lation size, composition, and distribution take place. The demographer observes, for example, that the size of the population in a given area is increasing. He is interested in whether this increase is due to an excess of births over deaths, to a greater number of people moving into than out of the area, or to some combination of these two processes. Also, if he sees that the population is becoming younger, he is interested in knowing if this is because there has been an increase in the number of births or because larger numbers of young people have moved into the area (or older people have moved out). Finally, if he

notes that the spatial arrangement of the population within the area is shifting, the demographer seeks to determine whether this is because people are moving into or out of different regions within the area or if it is because of significant differences among the various parts of the area with respect to levels of fertility and mortality.

Demography may now be defined more completely as the science that is concerned with ascertaining (1) the size, composition, and distribution of the population in any given area of human habitation; (2) the changes that have occurred or are occurring in these three major demographic variables; and (3) the processes—or the trends with regard to fertility, mortality, and migration—that are the cause of these changes.

In its narrowest sense, demography is a science concerned largely with the statistical measurement and description of population phenomena. In the broader sense, however, demography also involves the *explanation* and *analysis* of observed population facts. In this respect, it is convenient to distinguish between the narrow realm of pure or *formal demography* and the broader area of general population study or *social demography*. In general, the term *formal demography* is reserved for the purely mathematical aspects of population study and is used primarily to refer to the statistical description of the demographic variables and processes *and* the interrelations among them. *Social demography,* on the other hand, is largely *interpretive* and is concerned with enhancing our knowledge and understanding of the underlying *determinants* and *consequences* of observed population phenomena.

Formal demography concerns itself solely with population facts and the cause-effect relations among them. *Social* demography is interested in the effects of nondemographic factors on demographic variables and vice versa. Formal demography entails such things as the computation of birth, death, and migration rates and the statistical description of how these processes, and changes in these processes over time, both affect and are affected by the major demographic variables of population size, composition, and distribution. The formal demographer tries to answer questions like these: What are the current trends in the levels of fertility and mortality? What influences will these trends have (or have they had) on the rate of population growth? What are the characteristics of the people moving into or out of an area? How is this pattern of migration affecting the composition of the population in that area? What differences are there among various parts of an area in the balance between births and deaths (or in the balance between migration in and out)? To what extent are such differences bringing about a redistribution of the population within the area? Answering such questions requires the statistical manipulation of population data, and such statistical analysis is the core of formal demography.

The demographer is not solely interested in statistical description. He is not interested, for example, in noting merely that a sudden rise in the birth rate has caused an increase of such-and-such magnitude in the population in an area or that migration out of an area has resulted in a decline in numbers in that area. Rather, he is also interested in the various underlying social, psychological, and economic forces that have influenced such changes; and he is interested in the possible implications of such changes for the established order of the society. For example, if fertility should increase while mortality remains fairly stable, as it did in the United States during the late 1940s, the demographer is not only interested in how much fertility has risen or in how much the population has increased as a result. He is also interested in what forces in the larger society prompted births to increase in the first place. Have new attitudes and values emerged about the "ideal" number of children or desirable family size? Have there been any changes in marriage customs or in the structure of the family that could explain the increase in births (such as younger age at marriage or a decline in the importance of economic self-sufficiency as a prerequisite to marriage and childbearing)? Or has the general economic and political climate altered in such a way as to create an atmosphere conducive to a higher level of fertility?

As well as asking the reasons for the increase in births, the demographer is also interested in the consequences for society of the fertility increase and the resulting population growth. What are its implications for the adequacy of the available school facilities? Will the increased number of consumers have any effect on the rate of saving and investment and thereby on the rate of economic growth? What effect will the growing number and proportion of young people in the population have on juvenile delinquency, the demand for housing and recreation areas, styles of dress, tastes in entertainment, and the general attitudes and values of the society as a whole?

In short, given a specific population fact or trend, the demographer is not content with a mere quantitative analysis of this fact or trend and how it came into being. Although such "What?" and "How?" analyses form an integral part of all demographic research, they do not lead to a complete knowledge and understanding of the population fact or trend in question. To gain a fully adequate knowledge and understanding of a specific population phenomenon, the demographer pushes a step further and asks "Why?" and "What does it mean?"

One convenient way to clarify further the distinction between formal demography and social demography is to describe them in terms of the role that demographic and nondemographic factors play as either *independent* (causal) or *dependent* (effect) variables.[1] In formal demographic studies some population facts are used to explain other population facts. That is, the independent and dependent variables are both strictly demographic facts (as when trends in birth and/or death rates are used to explain changes in the age structure of a population, or, conversely, when changing age composition is used to explain changes in levels of fertility or mortality). In broader social demographic analyses, however, various nondemographic factors play a major role as either independent or dependent variables. On the one hand, there are studies in which nondemographic factors are used as *independent* variables to explain some demographic fact (e.g., religion is used to explain differences in birth rates, or income is used to explain differences in mortality). On the other hand, there are studies in which nondemographic factors are the *dependent* variables to be explained by means of certain demographic facts (e.g., voting behavior is explained in terms of age composition, or a decline in the birth rate is explained in terms of a changing economic environment). In both types of social demographic studies the key factor is that nondemographic phenomena play a major role as either independent variables (causes or determinants of population trends) or dependent variables (effects or consequences of population trends).

In the very broadest sense, then, the science of demography may be defined as having four basic objectives. They are

1. To observe, measure and describe the size, composition, and distribution of the population in any given area of habitation.
2. To observe, measure, and describe the changes that maybe take place in the size, composition, and/or distribution of the population over time.
3. To observe, measure, and describe the processes (the levels of fertility, mortality, and migration) through which such changes are effected.
4. To explain the underlying determinants and the consequences of the observed trends and changes.

The first three of these objectives involve the measurement and description of the demographic variables and the interrelations among them, and they constitute the core of pure or formal demography. The fourth objective constitutes the subject matter of the more general social demography. It is at this point, where the underlying determinants and the consequences of population trends and changes are sought, that the demographer leaves the narrow confines of his own specialty and enters the broad area of interdisciplinary study.

Demography and Other Disciplines

When the demographer moves beyond the realm of simple observation and description, when he seeks to interpret and explain his data in nondemographic terms, he turns to a variety of theoretical sciences for help. He turns to *geography* for aid in explaining the spatial distribution of population over the world's land surface; to *medicine* and *public health* for help in analyzing mortality trends and differentials and in explaining the changing importance of specific causes of death; and to *economics* for an understanding of the effects of population change on such things as the size and the productive capacity of the labor force, the adequacy of available resources, and the implications population changes have for the rate of economic development. The demographer looks to *biology* for knowledge and understanding of the workings of the human reproductive system; to *political science* for help in understanding the effects of population change on the balance of world power and on trends in international relations; and to *sociology* and *anthropology* to help him understand and analyze the intricate relationships between demographic phenomena and the sociocultural environment. In short, the study of population calls upon a wide variety of scientific disciplines, all of which aid the demographer in broadening his knowledge and gaining a better understanding of the causes and implications of changes in human populations.

Although demography is truly an interdisciplinary science, and although the demographer calls on scholars in a wide variety of fields for help in explaining and interpreting his data, it must be emphasized that the main causes of population trends are *social* and that demography is essentially and basically a social science. The demographic processes take place within the man-made environment of human society, and they are both influenced by and exert an influence on this environment. The extent to which the cultural milieu of this man-made environment can influence population phenomena can easily be seen if we consider the reproductive capacity of the human female. During her reproductive span (roughly between the ages of fifteen and fifty) the average woman is biologically capable of bearing from fifteen to twenty or more children; yet very few women ever realize this potential. A whole complex of social factors prevents a woman from doing so and helps to keep human fertility on a level far below that which it is biologically capable of attaining. Among these factors, to name only a few, are laws governing the age of consent at marriage; social attitudes concerning the age at which a person should marry (very few marriages actually take place immediately upon attainment of the legal age of consent); legal obligations to feed and clothe children; the economic handicap of a large family; and moral obligations to provide one's children with more than the minimal requirements for survival (such as providing a college education if possible).

It is likewise easy to demonstrate the influence of population phenomena on the society. On the most fundamental level population *size* determines the mechanisms of social control of a society: whereas normative sanctions may be sufficient to maintain order in small, face-to-face groupings, growth in numbers necessitates a shift to more formalized rules and laws. In our society today, changes in population size affect our needs with regard to schools and recreation areas, housing, transportation facilities, public and professional services, and welfare programs, to name just a few.

The *composition* of a population is closely related to many other differences that characterize various segments of the population. Furthermore, the specific needs of a given population are determined to a great extent by the composition of its members (as well as their number). For example, the educational composition of a population will determine not only the technical skills and the productive capacity of the labor force but will also influence such things as levels of fertility, consumption habits, and tastes in entertainment. Also, the age composition of a population will have an influence on the burden of economic dependency, problems of aging, the adequacy of the available school facilities, and the general outlook or philosophy of life of the population.

Finally, the influence of population *distribution* on society can be seen in such things as the increasing concentration of the population in large urban clusters, leading to a greater freedom for the individual, the decline of local community solidarity, the emergence of a more blasé outlook on life, and the development of a more liberal philosophy concerning man's relation to other men. This urbanization trend has also led to the emergence of a wide range of problems—housing shortages, the growth of slums and ethnic ghettos, daily traffic jams, air and water pollution, overcrowded schools, and shortages of public health and welfare personnel. More recently, the growing popularity of suburban living—encouraged by the emergence of the automobile and the development of a large, interconnected system of highways—has created a need for the expansion of local services, such as education, offered by the rapidly growing suburban communities. The suburbanization trend has also been influential in generating vast urban renewal programs in many of our larger cities in an attempt to make them more attractive places in which to live and thereby, it is hoped, slow down the exodus to "suburbia."

Some Basic Concepts and Measures

Mortality

Mortality is most commonly measured by the *death rate* and *average life expectancy. Death rate* means the *crude death rate,* which is defined as the number of deaths occurring in a given population during a calendar year per 1,000 people in the population. To illustrate, there were an estimated 1,921,000 deaths in the United States during 1970.[2] The average number of people living in the country during the year (that is, the mid-point population, or the population as of July 1, 1970) was estimated at 204,879,000. The crude death rate is computed as $1{,}921{,}000 \div 204{,}879{,}000 \times 1{,}000 = 9.41$. This means that in 1970, there were slightly more than 9 deaths for every 1,000 people in the United States. Compared with an overall world death-rate of approximately 15 per 1,000 population, this clearly shows that the United States had a relatively low death rate.

Average life expectancy means the number of years lived, on the average, by each member of a given population. Looked at from a slightly different perspective, average life expectancy may be regarded as a crude measure of the *average age at death prevailing in a given population.* The relatively low death rate in the United States is also revealed by an average life expectancy in 1970 of about seventy years, compared with less than thirty-five years in many countries of the world.

The generally low death rate in the United States today does not characterize all segments of the population to the same extent. In 1970, for example, the average life expectancy of the white population in this country was six years longer than that of the nonwhite group, and within both of these broad racial classes females outlived males by a significant number of years (see Table 12–1).

Table 12–1. Average Life Expectancy for the United States, 1970

Classification	*Life Expectancy (Years)*
All classes	70.9
White	71.7
Male	68.0
Female	75.6
All other	65.3
Male	61.3
Female	69.4

Source: Vital Statistics of the United States: 1970, Vol. 2, Section 5, *Life Tables* (Washington, D.C., 1973).

Considering the differences between the sexes in life expectancy, the tendency in the past was to explain it in terms of the more strenuous role that men play in the life of society or in terms of such things as occupational hazards, military deaths in wartime, and the greater tensions among men because of familial responsibilities and the greater pressures that our society places on them to achieve. But there is ample evidence that differences in the life experiences of the two sexes cannot account completely for the higher mortality of men. Because the male death rate is higher in infancy as well as in old age and because more males than females are stillborn, the discrepancy must stem, at least in part, from some unidentified biological difference. The existence of such a biological difference is further suggested by the fact that the female advantage has been increasing during a period when women have gradually been assuming a role and a status in industry and business much more similar to those of men. (Between 1940 and 1970, for example, the proportion of adult women who were members of the labor force in the United States rose from 25 percent to 41 percent.) At least one study, under carefully controlled conditions, has provided strong evidence that biological factors are much more important than sociocultural pressures and strains in accounting for the male-female mortality differential. Francis C. Madigan compared the mortality rates of male and female members of Catholic teaching orders. He observed that the life styles of these two groups are more similar than those of men and women generally are. If sociocultural factors are responsible for mortality differences, he argued, the mortality differences between the brothers and the sisters should be *less* than they are in the general population. He found that in these more or less culturally comparable groups the mortality differences were *greater* than for the population as a whole, suggesting that biological factors are more important than sociocultural ones in causing different death rates by sex.[3] Thus, contrary to popular mythology, the female may not be the weaker sex after all. At least this seems to be the case as far as the death rate is concerned.

With respect to the white-nonwhite differential in life expectancy, the underlying causes must be sought among the social and especially the economic differences between whites and nonwhites. In the United States in 1970, for example, the median family income of the white population was $9,961, or more than 60 percent higher than the median income of $6,067 recorded for the black family. (For the nation as a whole, blacks comprise nearly 90 percent of the nonwhite population.) Associated with this pronounced economic differential are the quality of diet, medical care, and so on. Although this white-nonwhite mortality differential has been getting smaller, a substantial number of Americans continue to suffer from higher levels of mortality than the general population as a direct result of their occupying an economically inferior position. The principal conclusion of a recent important investigation of differential mortality in the United States was that socioeconomic status, whether measured by family income, by educational level, or by occupational class, is a major determinant of mortality levels in the world's wealthiest nation.[4] Moreover, there is no doubt that a further reduction of the national death rate can be achieved through a narrowing of currently existing socioeconomic mortality differentials—especially through a lowering of the excessively high death rates characterizing the most disadvantaged nonwhite segments of our population.

Infant Mortality

A specialized death rate that is commonly used to measure the health and welfare of a population is the *infant mortality rate,* defined as the number of deaths under one year of age per 1,000 live births occurring during a calendar year. It measures the probability that a newborn baby will survive the hazards of infancy and live to celebrate his first birthday.

The infant mortality rate in the United States has declined considerably during the present century, from a level of about 100 to less than 20 deaths per 1,000 live births today. Moreover, even the high rate of 100 during the early 1900s was considerably below the levels that had prevailed throughout the early years of the nation's history. We can more fully appreciate the remarkable progress that has been made in reducing the loss of life during infancy if we realize that in colonial America roughly 1 out of every 6 babies failed to survive until its first birthday. By 1915 this rate had been reduced to 1 in 10, and by 1970 only about 1 infant in 50 died during the first year of life.

In spite of our remarkable achievement, several other countries have even lower infant mortality rates. In 1973, for example, at least a dozen countries had infant mortality rates below the level of 19 noted for the United States, with the lowest rates (12–14 per 1,000 live births) being found in Iceland and the Scandinavian countries.[5] The explanation for the higher infant death rate in this country lies in the earlier noted group differences within our population, especially the excessive mortality levels characterizing the economically disadvantaged groups (for example, in 1972 the nonwhite infant mortality rate exceeded that of the white population by nearly 80 percent).[6]

Although infant mortality rates of 25 or less are found in most of the modern, industrialized nations of the world today, some countries, notably the underdeveloped countries of Asia and Africa and Latin America, have an infant mortality rate that is still as high as or even higher than the rate at the beginning of the twentieth century in this country. Such differences in infant mortality reflect not only differences in health standards among populations but also, perhaps more importantly, differences in socioeconomic status. Current statistics bear out the assertion that the infant mortality rate is the most sensitive index we possess of the levels of social and economic well-being of various population groups.

Fertility

The second basic demographic process is fertility. Like mortality, fertility is basically biological, but unlike death it is *not inevitable.* On the contrary, whether a couple has a baby is frequently a matter of their own choice. Thus the explanation of changes in fertility must be sought in human attitudes and desires regarding the bearing of children.

The level of fertility in any population is most commonly measured by the *crude birth rate.* This rate is computed the way the crude death rate is: it is the number of live births occurring per 1,000 people in a given population during a calendar year. To illustrate, there were an estimated 3,718,000 live births in the United States during the twelve months from January 1 to December 31, 1970. As already noted, the average number of people living in the country during that year was 204,879,000; hence, the crude birth rate can be computed as $3{,}718{,}000 \div 204{,}879{,}000 \times 1{,}000 = 18.2$. This means that in 1970 there were roughly 18 births for every 1,000 people in the United States. More recently it has been estimated by the National Center for Health Statistics that the American birth rate has fallen to about 15 per 1,000. This is the lowest level ever attained in this country, and it has led some to suggest that the United States may be on the threshold of achieving a stationary population.

The highest fertility levels in the world today are found in the economically underdeveloped countries of Asia, Africa, and Latin America, where it is not uncommon to find birth rates on the order of 45 or even 50 per 1,000. At the other extreme, many of the low-fertility countries of Europe and Oceania (Australia and New Zealand) have crude birth rates as low as 14 or 15 per 1,000.

As is the case with mortality, levels of fertility are not the same for all segments of the American population. A major difference between the two, however, is that the differentials in fertility are largely "voluntary." That is, they are the results of differences in attitudes and preferences rather than in levels of economic well-being.

In the United States today the major fertility differentials are associated with religion and socioeconomic status (particularly with the education of the wife). As the data in Table 12–2 clearly indicate, Catholic women expect to have more children than Protestant women, and in both groups the largest families are expected by women in the lowest educational category. This socioeconomic differential is much less pronounced among Catholics, and Catholic women with four or more years of education beyond grade school have recently been identified as an especially high fertility group in the United States (on a level with the lowest educated Protestant women).

As we said before, variations in fertility levels reflect differences in attitudes and preferences. These differences are translated into actuality through birth control. That is, as is also apparent in Table 12–2, those groups that expect

Table 12-2. Expected Fertility and Birth Control Attitudes and Practices for Protestant and Catholic Women, by Education of Wife, 1965

Source: Norman B. Ryder and Charles F. Westoff, *Reproduction in the United States, 1955* (Princeton, N.J.: Princeton University Press, 1971), Tables IV-21, V-1, V-3, and V-11.

	Number of Children Expected		Percentage Favoring Birth Control		Percentage Who Have Used Some Method of Birth Control	
Education	*Protestant*	*Catholic*	*Protestant*	*Catholic*	*Protestant*	*Catholic*
Total	3.0	3.9	92	70	87	78
College	2.7	3.8	97	67	90	81
High School (4 years)	2.8	3.8	93	73	88	82
High School (1–3 years)	3.4	3.8	89	72	86	75
Grade School	3.9	4.7	79	52	72	55

to have the smallest number of children are the same groups that exhibit both the strongest approval and the greatest use of birth control.

Migration

The third basic demographic process is migration, or the movement of people from one geographic area of residence to another. There are two types of migration: *group* migration (such as tribal wanderings in preindustrial times) and *individual* or family migration (such as the worldwide cityward movement away from declining rural areas). Migratory moves can also be classified in terms of their underlying causes. People move from one area to another either because some set of forces or circumstances drives them out of the old habitat (*push* factors) or because a different set of circumstances attracts them to a new area (*pull* factors). More often than not, both push and pull factors are found in some degree, with the magnitude and location of the two complementary forces determining the volume and direction of migratory streams. For example, in explaining the causes of the "great Atlantic crossing," which witnessed the movement of some 20 million persons from Europe to the United States during the nineteenth century, one can cite a number of significant push factors in the various sending countries. Among them would be political and religious persecution, economic instability, and rural overpopulation as major advances in agricultural technology reduced the size of the farm labor force more rapidly than the excess could be absorbed into still-infant industries. Balanced against these push factors were the strong pull forces exerted by the United States: political and religious freedom, rapid economic expansion, the availability of large tracts of underdeveloped lands, and a surplus of relatively high-paying jobs in developing industries.

Another way of looking at migration is to consider whether it is *voluntary* or *involuntary*. Much of the group migration that occurred in the ancient world was involuntary in the sense that the exhaustion of the environment's food-producing capacity necessitated a move to a new habitat. In contrast to the push associated with involuntary migration, voluntary migration is more often the result of some positive pull toward a new and hopefully better home. Although there are exceptions, dramatically illustrated by the presence even today of large numbers of refugees from war (in Southeast Asia, for example), most migration in the world today tends to be both individual and voluntary and is largely motivated by positive pull factors.

Still another way of classifying migration is in terms of whether it occurs between different countries (*international migration*) or within the confines of a single country (*internal migration*). Most migration in the world today is internal migration the *internal, voluntary* movement of *individuals* who are *pulled* to areas of greater opportunity. The international-internal division is generally regarded as the major classification of migration. For one thing, it provides a ready scheme for discussing those movements that alter the distribution of world population as opposed to more localized movements that have only a slight impact on the world population situation—but that can have profound significance for the local areas involved.

Migration and Population Distribution

Of the three demographic processes (birth, death, and migration), by far the most significant from a sociological point of view is human migration. One reason is that migration often brings diverse groups into contact with one another and creates problems of *assimilation* (the process in which the beliefs, customs, and behavior patterns of one group are merged with those of another, generally larger, group). These problems of assimilation are reflected in such things as the existence of ethnic ghettos, marginal men (people caught between the conflicting values of two cultures), and higher incidences of deviant behavior among migration groups. Although not all the world's ills result from a loss or breakdown of primary associations, the necessity of abandoning familiar surroundings for a new and perhaps strange environment often leads to personal and social disorganization; so it is not surprising to find that migrants are often characterized by higher rates of delinquency, adult crime, mental illness, prostitution, divorce, and other social ills.

On the more positive side, migration has historically served to bring people from diverse cultures (with different customs, knowledge, skills, and technology) into contact with one another. Although the consequences have occasionally been adverse (as in the destruction that accompanied the Mongol invasions of Europe), this intermingling has generally exerted a positive influence on the growth and development of human civilization. Thus human migration may be regarded as a major mechanism of social and cultural diffusion.

Migration has also played a key role in helping mankind maintain a more or less even balance between the distribution of numbers and resources. In the preindustrial world the number of people that could be supported in a given area was determined largely by the food-producing capacity of that area. If the population increased beyond the numbers that could be supported, it became necessary for some people to migrate to a new area: the alternative was for the surplus to be killed off in some fashion (such as war, disease, or starvation). In more modern times, the role of migration in maintaining a balance between numbers and resources is illustrated by the rural-to-urban movement of the population. As improved agricultural techniques reduce employment opportunities in rural areas, surplus farm workers move to the cities, where the growth of nonagricultural industries creates jobs to absorb them.

From a purely demographic viewpoint, migration is significant because it is the major process through which man has spread out from his points of origin and become distributed throughout the world and because it is the major mechanism underlying changes that have taken and are still taking place in the pattern of human settlement.

The Rural-to-Urban Movement

The most pervasive trend with regard to migration and population redistribution has been (and continues to be) the ever-increasing concentration of the population in urban areas. In the United States, this rural-to-urban shift is revealed: (1) by an increase in the number and size of urban places, and (2) by an increase in the number and proportion of the population living in urban places. According to the first American population census in 1790, there were only twenty-four urban places in the entire United States, and these twenty-four places contained only 5 percent of the total national population. Since that time, however, the growth of the nation has been characterized by a continuous increase in the number of urban places and by a continuous shift in the distribution of the population away from rural areas to the emerging cities (see Table 12–3). At the end of the Civil War decade (1870), the number of urban places had risen sharply to 663, and approximately one fourth of the national population was living in urban areas. In 1920 the urban population exceeded the rural population for the first time, and by 1970 nearly three fourths of the American people were living in one of 7,062 urban places.

Another indication of the pronounced urbanization that has characterized the historical development of the United States is the change that has occurred in the size of urban places. At the beginning of the present century there were only 442 urban places with populations in excess of 10,000, and only 78 had as many as 50,000 inhabitants. In 1970, however, there were 2,301 places in the nation with 10,000 or more inhabitants, and there were 396 places whose population exceeded 50,000. Thus, as the basic economic trend of the past two centuries of American history has been the transformation from an agrarian to an industrial society, the basic demographic trend has been a redistribution of the population from the declining rural farm areas to the growing urban industrial centers.

Year	Number of Urban Places	Percentage of Population in Urban Places	Number of Urban Places with Population Over 10,000	50,000
1790	24	5.1%	5	—
1800	33	6.1	6	1
1810	46	7.3	11	2
1820	61	7.2	13	3
1830	90	8.8	23	4
1840	131	10.8	37	5
1850	236	15.3	62	10
1860	392	19.8	93	16
1870	663	25.7	168	25
1880	939	28.2	233	35
1890	1,348	35.1	354	58
1900	1,740	39.6	442	78
1910	2,266	45.6	598	110
1920	2,725	51.2	754	145
1930	3,179	56.1	984	192
1940	3,485	56.5	1,079	200
1950	4,077	59.6	1,354	238
New Definition				
1950	4,764	64.0	1,265	233
1960	6,041	69.9	1,899	333
1970	7,062	73.5	2,301	396

Table 12–3. Urbanization Trends in the United States, 1790–1970.

Source: U.S. Bureau of the Census, *Census of Population: 1970, Number of Inhabitants,* Final Report PC(1)-A1, *United States Summary* (Washington, D.C., 1971), Table 7.

The Suburbanization Trend

Suburbanization has not meant an end to the long-term shift of the population away from rural areas, but it has served to modify significantly the pattern of population distribution within the built-up sections of the country. The nature of this shift is clearly revealed by the data in Table 12–4. In 1950, when roughly six out of every ten Americans was living in what the Bureau of the Census has called *standard metropolitan statistical areas* (SMSAs),[7] slightly more than half of the metropolitan residents (57 percent) were living in the large central cities. The number of residents in the SMSAs has continued to increase, but the more significant trend has been a pronounced decline in the proportion of the SMSA population living in the central cities. By 1970, the SMSAs contained nearly 70 percent of the total American population, but within these areas the proportion residing in the large central cities had fallen to only 46 percent. During the most recent decade between censuses (1960–70), the SMSA central-city population increased by only 6 percent, whereas the metropolitan population living outside these central cities increased by 27 percent. This "flight to the suburbs" has been so great that a number of central

Table 12-4. City/Fringe Distribution of the Metropolitan Population of the United States, 1950–70

Residence Class	*1950*	*1960*	*1970*
Total population	151,325,798	179,323,175	203,211,926
SMSA population	94,579,008	119,594,754	139,418,811
In central cities	53,695,948	59,947,129	63,796,943
Outside central cities	40,883,060	59,647,625	75,621,868
Percentage of total population living in SMSAs	62.5	66.7	68.6
Percentage of SMSA population living in central cities	56.8	50.1	45.8

Source: U.S. Bureau of the Census, *Census of Population: 1970, Number of Inhabitants,* Final Report PC(1)-A1, *United States Summary* (Washington, D.C., 1971), Table 34.

cities have actually experienced a decline in population size. To be specific, of the 308 SMSA central cities identified in the 1970 census, 119 (39 percent) had lost population during the preceding decade. The population in 26 central cities declined 10 percent or more, and population losses exceeded 15 percent in 11 central cities (see Table 12–5).[8]

One other point has to be stressed in this section: *suburbanization has been primarily a middle-class white phenomenon.* To illustrate, between 1960 and 1970 the number of whites residing in SMSA central cities declined by nearly 607,000, or by slightly more than 1 percent. In sharp contrast the number of nonwhites (black and other races) living in metropolitan centers increased by nearly 4 million or by 36 percent. The nature of this phenomenon is such that in 1970 41 percent of the nation's white SMSA residents were living in central cities, whereas nearly twice as high a percentage (76 percent) of the nonwhite SMSA residents lived in central cities. Nonwhites comprised roughly one quarter (23 percent) of the nation's SMSA central-city population in 1970, but only 6 percent of the suburban population was nonwhite.[9]

Table 12-5. Population Loss in Eleven Central Cities, 1960–70

City	*Percentage of Loss*
Augusta, Ga.	−15.2%
Binghamton, N.Y.	−15.6
Wilmington, Del.	−16.1
Youngstown, Ohio	−16.1
Charleston, W.Va.	−16.7
St. Louis, Mo.	−17.0
East Chicago, Ind.	−18.5
Harlingen, Tex.	−18.7
Atlantic City, N.J.	−19.6
Savannah, Ga.	−20.7
Johnstown, Pa.	−21.3

Source: U.S. Bureau of the Census; *Metropolitan Area Statistics* (Washington, D.C., 1971).

The consequence of these differential patterns of growth has been to promote greater racial disparity between urban centers and their surrounding suburbs. Moreover, given the decidedly lower socioeconomic status of the nonwhite population as a whole (for example, in 1970 the median income for white families was $9,961 as contrasted to only $6,308 for nonwhite families), this trend has also widened the gap between city and suburb with regard to per capita wealth. Many of the larger cities in the nation are in very real danger of becoming centers of ethnic poverty, and it has been suggested that "this growing difference in racial composition between the central cities and their rings, combined as it is with differences in education and housing, is one of the major social problems facing the United States today."[10] As long as this disparity persists, as long as the most economically deprived minority groups in our society are forced to crowd together in the least desirable areas of our cities, there is little hope that these problems will be solved. On the contrary, the evidence indicates that the population trends that have in part caused the present urban crisis are continuing, and it is highly probable that the many problems of the emerging "slum cities" (housing blight, crime, unemployment, and so on) could become much worse during the 1970s than they were during the 1960s.

Population Structure

For the demographer, one of the most fundamental features of any population is its structure, or the distribution of its members according to *age* and *sex.* Almost any aspect of human behavior—from subjective attitudes and physiological capabilities to objective characteristics such as income, labor force participation, occupation, or group membership—may be expected to vary with age and sex. In addition, the specific needs of a given society, both now and in the future, will in large part be determined by the age-sex structure of its population. For example, women differ from men in the kinds of jobs they hold, the length of time they remain in the labor force, the income they earn, their consumption patterns, and their attitudes toward various social and economic issues. A population with a high proportion of young members may be expected to differ in its productive capacities from one that has a high proportion of older members. The adequacy of such facilities as housing, schools, and convalescent hospitals depends, respectively, on the number of young people who are marrying and starting families, the number of children at the school and preschool ages, and the number of older people.

Because women have a lower death rate than men and because women can bear children only at specific ages, the levels of fertility and mortality and the rate of natural increase (the excess of births and deaths) in any population are directly related to its age and sex composition. Finally, the number of elderly people in a society has important implications for such considerations as jobs for older workers, medical and health benefits, and pensions for the aged.

Age

The statistics presented in Table 12–6 highlight the major trends in the age and sex composition of the population of the United States since the beginning of the century.[11] Considering *age* first, the simplest tool for describing a population's age composition is the *median age* (the point at which the population divides in half, half of the cases falling below this value and half of the cases exceeding it). According to the medians presented in the first column of Table 12–6, the major trend prior to 1950 was for the population to become older. Between 1900 and 1950, the median age in the United States increased from 22.9 to 30.2, or by 7.3 years (nearly one and one-half years per decade). Partly because of the reduction of foreign immigration after the federal adoption of restrictive legislation, but mostly as a result of the cumulative effects of the

Table 12-6. Selected Age and Sex Characteristics of the Population of the United States, 1900–1970

Source: U.S. Bureau of the Census, *1970 Census of Population,* Final Report PC(1)-B1, *General Population Characteristics: United States Summary* (Washington, D.C., 1972).

		Percent of Population			
Year	*Median Age*	*Under 15 Years*	*15 to 65 Years*	*65 Years and over*	*Males per 100 Females*
1900	22.9	34.4	61.5	4.1	104.4
1910	24.1	32.1	63.6	4.3	106.0
1920	25.3	31.8	63.5	4.7	104.0
1930	26.4	29.4	65.2	5.4	102.5
1940	29.0	25.1	68.1	6.8	100.7
1950	30.2	26.9	65.0	8.1	98.6
1960	29.5	31.1	59.7	9.2	97.0
1970	28.1	28.4	61.8	9.8	94.8

historical decline in fertility, the rise in the median age was most pronounced after 1920. The marked increase of 2.6 years between 1930 and 1940 reflects the particularly low birth rate of the Depression decade, and the substantially smaller increase between 1940 and 1950 reflects the initial impact of the postwar fertility revival.

The trend since 1950 has been for the population to become younger. In 1960, the median age of 29.5 was .7 years lower than it had been ten years previously, and the 1970 median (28.1 years) was 1.4 years below that of 1960. This reversal of a trend that had been in evidence for several decades can only be explained by reference to the cessation of the long-time fertility decline during World War II and a subsequent rise in the birth rate and its continuation at fairly high levels throughout the 1950's. This reversal of the downward trend in the birth rate, which has been called the "baby boom," was only temporary. Since 1957 the birth rate in this country has undergone a precipitous decline and is today at one of its lowest levels in our history. More significantly, the absolute number of births per year has been declining since 1961. Should the present low level of fertility persist into the 1970s, it would soon lead to another major reversal in the trend of the median age, and the population would once again become an aging one. As of 1970, however, the reduced number of births since 1961 had not been sufficient to offset the pronounced impact of the postwar baby boom on the overall age of the American population.

Although the median age is useful in providing a general indication of the age composition of a population, it is of limited value in more detailed analyses. The procedure commonly used for greater precision is to examine the proportion of the population falling into particular age groups. Three broad age groups may be assumed to correspond roughly to the three major stages of the life cycle: *youth* (under fifteen years); *adulthood* (fifteen to sixty-four years); and *old age* (sixty-five years and over). Prior to the 1940–50 decade, there was a consistent decline in the proportion of the population under fifteen years of age. At the beginning of the present century slightly more than one out of every three persons in the United States fell into this age group, but by

1940, after several decades of declining birth rates, this ratio had fallen to one in four. Since 1940, however, the erratic pattern of fertility has resulted in two reversals of this trend. First, the postwar baby boom led to an increase in the proportion of youth, especially during the 1950s, and by 1960 the number of persons under fifteen years of age was once again roughly one out of three. Second, the sharp declines in fertility during the most recent decade have brought about another decline in this proportion—to 28.4 percent in 1970.

For the adult ages, the effect of the fluctuating fertility rate of the present century was the reverse of its effect on the relative size of the youth group. As the proportion of youth fell during the years of declining fertility, the proportion of the population fifteen to sixty-four years of age increased, from 62 percent in 1900 to 68 percent in 1940. Between 1940 and 1960, as a consequence of the postwar baby boom, the percentage of the population falling into the adult ages declined to a level below that existing at the beginning of the century. However, the fertility decline of the 1960s has led to the emergence of a new upward trend, and at the time of the 1970 Census, approximately 62 percent of the American population was between the ages of fifteen and sixty-four years.

The major difference between the 1970 population and the population at the beginning of the century is in the size of the elderly group. Between 1900 and 1970 the proportion of the population sixty-five years of age and over more than doubled, and the absolute number of older people increased from slightly more than 3 million to more than 20 million.

With the exception of the temporary interruption caused by the postwar baby boom, then, the trend has clearly been for the American population to become older. The major social issues of the late 1950s and 1960s were largely youth related (for example, overcrowded schools, rising juvenile delinquency, the emergence of a middle-class drug culture, political activism on college campuses). However, because of the basic demographic trend of our society we face a continuing need for efficient programs to deal with such problems as medical and health care for the aged, social welfare benefits, jobs for older workers, and their postretirement activities and interests.

Sex

With regard to the sex composition of the population, the most significant conclusion to be drawn from the statistics in Table 12–6 is that the United States is more and more becoming a female-dominated society. The sex composition of the population is commonly measured by the *sex ratio,* or the number of males per 100 females. Reflecting the heavy volume of immigration (especially male immigration) during the late nineteenth and early twentieth centuries, the sex ratio of the United States was on the rise until 1910: at that time there were 106 males for every 100 females in the population. Since then the sex ratio has declined consistently, and by 1970 there were only 94.8 males for every 100 females in the United States.

A number of factors have combined to bring about this reduction in the sex ratio. Part of the decline can be attributed to the losses incurred in two world wars and the stationing of armed forces overseas. But the major factors have been reductions in both foreign immigration and mortality. On the one hand, the decline in immigration during recent decades has been accompanied by a shift in the composition of the new arrivals: what was once a largely male-dominated stream is now a small trickle with a slight female majority. On the other hand, the marked declines in mortality during the present century have been more pronounced for women than for men, thus reducing the relative number of males in the population. Should the present trend in the composition of immigrant groups and the sex mortality differentials continue, there is little prospect for any increase in the sex ratio in the future. On the contrary, it appears that women will continue to outnumber men in the years ahead and, in all likelihood, will do so to an even greater degree than now.

Because of migration trends, the sex ratio varies markedly among the various sections of the country. The general rural-to-urban migration trend, for example, has involved more females than males, with the result that in 1970 the sex ratio in small rural areas was 101, whereas in the urban areas the sex ratio was 92. The differential distribution of men and women is of interest because a particularly pronounced imbalance between the sexes may be associated with other social problems. *Prostitution,* for example, often flourishes where there is a heavy preponderance of males (as in the frontier towns and the mining camps of the Old West). On the other hand, a preponderance of females is often accompanied by a higher rate of *illegitimacy* (as in many of our larger cities today). In either case, imbalance between the sexes can pose a challenge to traditional patterns of family living.

The sex ratio also bears an interesting relationship to age, and in the United States today there is at least one problem relating to age variations in sex composition. For some unknown biological reason, more boys are born than girls. Thus there is a preponderance of males in the population at the younger ages. From the very first moment of life, however, death takes a greater toll among males than females. Thus the initially high sex ratio is gradually decreased by mortality as the older ages are approached. To illustrate, in 1970 the sex ratio of persons under five years of age in the United States was approximately 104. At the younger adult ages (roughly fifteen to twenty-four) the two sexes were fairly evenly balanced, but thereafter there was an ever-increasing preponderance of females in the population: the sex ratio was 95 at ages thirty-five to thirty-nine; by ages sixty-five to sixty-nine it had fallen to about 81; and among persons eighty-five and older there were only 56 males for every 100 females in the United States.

A major implication of this situation relates to the care of older persons. In an earlier era when the American family was more multifunctional than it is today, the care of the elderly was not a matter for public concern. As the role of the family has become more centered around reproduction and child rearing, however, its earlier broad functions in education, protection, welfare, and so on have been transferred to outside agencies in the community. One corollary of this development has been an increase in welfare programs and legislation for the elderly. Given the pronounced sex imbalance at the older ages, it is clear that contemporary problems of caring for the elderly are primarily problems of caring for *elderly women*—a significant fact to bear in mind in planning for nursing homes, housing projects, medical care programs, and recreational facilities.

Population Pyramids

The most common device for the quick examination of the age-sex composition of a population is the population pyramid. This is a graphic device that permits a demographer to tell at a glance what the age-sex distribution is. It also tells him a great deal about past demographic trends in the population and what their consequences are likely to be. To illustrate, Figure 12-1 is an age-sex pyramid of the American population in 1970. A glance at this pyramid clearly reveals such things as (1) the very low fertility of the 1930s (for example, note the smaller numbers at ages thirty-five to fourty-four); (2) the rising

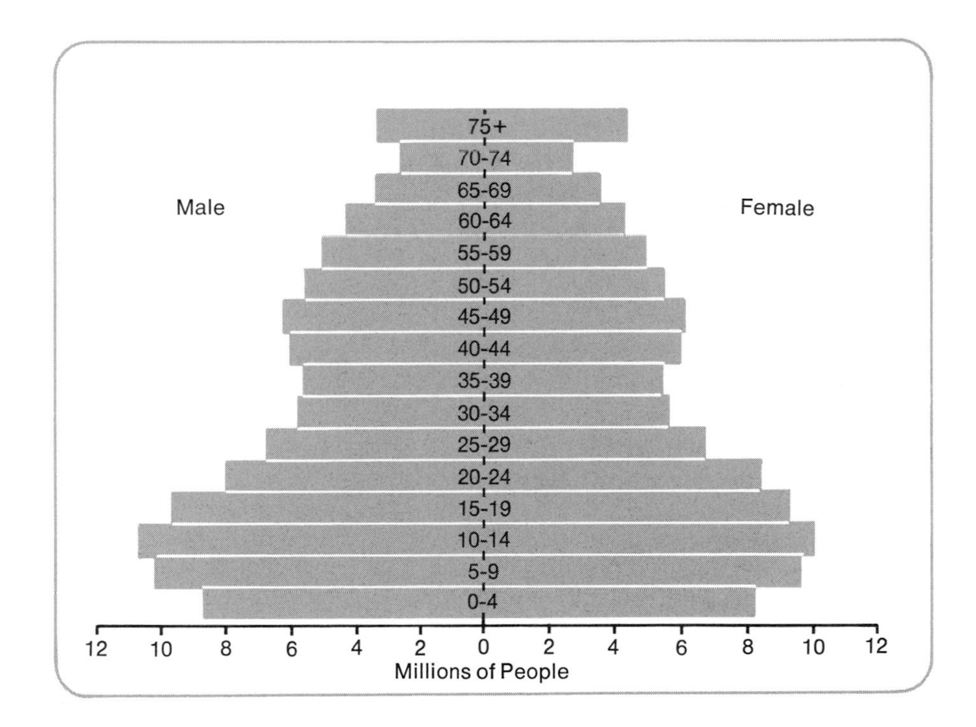

Figure 12-1. Age-sex pyramid of the United States, 1970.

fertility of the 1945–60 years (for example, note the increasing numbers from ages twenty-five to twenty-nine, down to ages ten to fourteen); and (3) the revival of the long-term fertility decline during the 1960s (as indicated by the smaller numbers at ages five to nine and especially at ages zero to four years). A glance at this pyramid also tells us such things as (1) that recent pressures on elementary school facilities are being eased considerably; (2) that those businesses that cater to young families can look forward to a booming market during the 1970s as the products of the baby boom marry and form families; (3) that the nation is going to have to create a much larger number of jobs each year to accommodate the larger number of labor force entrants; and (4) that, looking way ahead, the economy in the late 1980s and 1990s will have to adjust again to a smaller labor force.

The World Population Crisis

Since the end of World War II the extremely rapid and unprecedented population growth in many of the non-Western countries of Asia, Africa, and Latin America has generated a surge of interest in the study of human populations. This concern over numerical growth is not unique and in fact can be traced back to a number of scholars in classical antiquity. In the modern era, however, concern over population growth dates from the late eighteenth century and is commonly associated with the name of Thomas Robert Malthus.

In a relatively short essay that has had a profound impact on economic thought and theory right down to the present, Malthus made two salient observations: (1) man cannot live without food and (2) the human sex drive is very powerful—so powerful, in fact, that man is constantly in danger of increasing his numbers at a faster rate than he is able to increase his food supply. In Malthus' words, "the power of population is infinitely greater than the power in the earth to produce subsistence for man. Population, when unchecked, increases in a geometrical ratio. Subsistence increases only in an arithmetic ratio. A slight acquaintance with numbers will show the immensity of the first power in comparison with the second." In order to keep population within the limits set by man's ability to produce food, Malthus believed that some check on population growth would always be necessary. He recognized two such checks: *positive checks* (by which he meant such things as war, famine, and disease), which hold population size down by keeping death rates high, and *preventive checks* (by which he meant moral restraint, or the postponement of marriage and abstinence within marriage), which control population size by keeping birth rates down. But because he regarded the human sex drive as so powerful that man would be unlikely to exercise moral restraint, Malthus foresaw a world in which war, disease, and periodic famine would always be necessary to curb man's tendency to increase beyond the maximum number that could be supported by the available means of subsistence.

Needless to say, the Malthusian "principle of population" was not received with open arms when it first appeared in print in 1798. The late eighteenth century was a period of widespread optimism concerning man's future, and philosophers and social critics were coming more and more to believe that man was perfectible and capable of creating a better world. In this atmosphere the virtually unmitigated pessimism of "Parson Malthus" was decidedly unwelcome, and it generated a literary controversy that carried over into the field of economics and lasted well into the nineteenth century. During the late nineteenth century, however, declining mortality and the resulting rapid rates of population growth were accompanied by tremendous social and economic advances that contributed to substantial increases in the level of living in the European community. In light of these developments there seemed little basis for bothering with the silly notions of an eccentric English clergyman, and the world appeared more or less to forget Malthus. But developments during the years since World War II have reawakened concern over the old Malthusian hypothesis that the human race is doomed to a miserable existence because of the ever-present tendency for population to outstrip the food supply.

World Population Growth Trends

For a full appreciation of the Malthusian revival in the post-World War II era, it is necessary to know a little bit about the history of the world population growth. According to estimates prepared under the auspices of the United Nations there were approximately 2.5 billion people living on earth at the midpoint of the twentieth century. By 1970 the inhabitants of this planet numbered over 3.6 billion. This is a far cry from the 500 million or so people who were living on earth in 1650, at the beginning of the modern era, and it represents roughly a sevenfold increase in numbers since that time (see Table 12–7).

Table 12–7. Size and Growth of World Population Since 1650.

Source: United Nations, *The Determinants and Consequences of Population Trends* (ST/SOA/A-17) (New York, 1953) p. 11; and United Nations, *1971 Demographic Yearbook* (New York, 1972) p. 111.

Year	*Population in Millions*	*Average Annual Rate of Increase (Percent) Between Dates*
1650	545	—
1750	728	0.3
1800	906	0.5
1850	1,171	0.6
1900	1,608	0.7
1920	1,810	0.6
1930	2,013	1.1
1940	2,246	1.1
1950	2,486	1.1
1960	2,982	2.0
1970	3,632	2.2

The magnitude of the increase in population in the modern era can be more readily appreciated by a compression of the time dimensions. If the length of time that man has existed on earth is compressed into a single day, then this modern era represents less than one minute; yet this briefest period of human existence has witnessed the greatest increase in numbers. It took hundreds of thousands of years for the population of the world to reach its half-billion level at the beginning of the modern era. It took less than two hundred years for the next half billion to be added, and less than fifty years for the next half billion after that. At the present rate of growth, however, it will take only seven years for the world's population to increase by another half-billion people! Considered somewhat differently, the population of this planet doubled between 1650 and 1850, a period of two hundred years. It doubled again between 1850 and 1930, a period of eighty years. And if it keeps going at its present rate, the third doubling of world population in the modern era will take place in less than thirty-five years. As a consequence of these developments, such terms as the *population bomb* and the *population explosion* have become part of our everyday vocabulary, and Malthusian concerns over population growth have been revived in recent years.

The Demographic Transition

A better understanding of the causes and the nature of the world population growth rate is provided by the concept of *demographic transition.* Demographically speaking, world population growth is determined by only two factors: fertility and mortality. Population grows to the extent that the number of people born each year exceed the number who die. Thus the first step in attempting to explain the unprecedented growth of modern times is to ascertain the relative importance of these two variables. Throughout the thousands of centuries that preceded the modern era, the brutally harsh conditions of life made human survival an extremely touch-and-go affair. Although the population data before the modern era are very scanty for all parts of the world, the evidence that can be gleaned from various anthropological and archaeological sources indicates that the death rate of primitive man was very high. A newborn infant had only a fifty-fifty chance of surviving to adulthood, and the average length of life could not have been much more than twenty to twenty-five years. In the face of such high death rates, a high fertility level was necessary for the survival of the species, and birth rates often approached their biological maximum. As human culture developed over the ages, however, the chances of survival improved. The first great advancement came with the neolithic cultural achievements of agriculture and the domestication of animals, roughly six to eight thousand years ago. With a more stable food supply, the base was laid for a larger population. But widespread disease resulting from the extremely unsanitary conditions of life continued to keep death rates high, and although population began to increase, it grew so slowly and gradually as to appear almost stationary by modern standards.

It was not until the advent of the Industrial Revolution—the latest stage in man's cultural development—that the first real burst of population growth came. The Industrial Revolution brought with it the emergence and advancement of modern science, and as a result the mortality pattern of a million years was broken. The discovery of vaccination for smallpox by Edward Jenner in 1796 was the first in a long line of discoveries and inventions destined to improve the chances of survival substantially, particularly among infants and young children. This and other applications of the scientific method to biology and medicine—with continued improvements in agricultural technology, the development of better means of transportation and communication, and all the social, economic, and psychological changes that accompanied the emergence of an urban industrial civilization—combined to set in motion forces that dramatically lowered death rates and substantially increased human reproductive efficiency.

Although death rates began to fall fairly rapidly, the birth rate was not at first affected by these developments, and fertility remained at high levels for several generations. This widening spread between levels of fertility and mortality (which meant that an increasingly larger proportion of those born survived through adulthood) is commonly referred to as the *demographic gap,* and it was the creation of this gap that produced the mushrooming of population growth in the modern era.

Eventually, as social and cultural values shifted from an emphasis on the group to an emphasis on the welfare and development of the individual, and as continued technological progress provided the means for controlling fertility, the birth rate began to slow down to match the earlier decline in the death rate. A new demographic balance between low birth and death rates was achieved, and the rate of population growth—at least in the industrial nations of the Western world—slowed down considerably. This shift from the old balance of high birth and death rates, through a period of sustained growth as a declining death rate created an imbalance between fertility and mortality, to a new balance of low birth and death rates, is called the *demographic transition.* The completion of this transition marks the end of rapid population growth.

The Problem Today

The problem of increasing numbers we face today derives from the fact that less than half of the world's population has completed this transition. The majority of people in the world today have just entered the initial phase of rapid population growth; in the years ahead, the numbers contributed by these people will considerably dwarf any previous growth the world has ever known.

Two facts stand out to reinforce the expectation of explosive growth in the years ahead. In the first place, the base population today is much larger than it was when the Western nations began their transition, and even a moderate rate of growth will, when applied to a larger population base, yield substantial numerical increases. In the second place, because the underdeveloped countries can make immediate use of modern techniques for postponing death, a mortality decline today can occur much more rapidly than it did in the past.

It is this second fact that explains the unprecedented growth rates that have emerged in the non-Western world in recent times. Whereas the decline of the death rate in Europe took place gradually over several generations, the ability to make immediate use of modern techniques for postponing death (techniques that took years to develop and perfect) means that the decline of mortality in the underdeveloped areas of the world today has taken place much more rapidly than it did in the demographic history of the highly developed countries.

Fertility, on the other hand, is generally much slower to respond to the efforts at reduction associated with modernization. On the contrary, there is some evidence to suggest that the initial response of fertility to modernization may be a slight *increase* in the birth rate (because of such things as a decline in involuntary sterility and spontaneous abortions as diet and general health conditions improve). The very rapid and substantial mortality decline in conjunction with a high, perhaps slightly increasing birth rate has meant that the demographic gap has not only opened more rapidly than it did in the past, but it is also much wider than it has ever been, resulting in unprecedented rates of population growth in many of the world's underdeveloped countries during recent years. In the demographic history of Europe, the decline in the death rate was so gradual that the decline in fertility had begun before the death rate reached its lowest levels. This in turn meant that the rate of natural increase seldom exceeded 1.5 percent a year. Today, however, the rapid and substantial mortality declines in the underdeveloped countries have frequently resulted in growth rates of 3.0 to 3.5 percent a year (or rates that would lead to a doubling of the population in about twenty years)! So far fertility has not declined in these areas, and until it does they will continue to be characterized by the rapid rates of population growth that so frequently act as a major obstacle to economic development.

The contrast between the "old" demographic transition and the new growth pattern in much of the underdeveloped world since the end of World War II is revealed dramatically in Table 12–8, which compares birth and death rate trends in Sweden and Ceylon. In Sweden it took well over a hundred years for the crude death rate to decline from an annual level of 25 to 10 per 1,000, and, most significantly, the gradualness of the mortality decline meant that by the time the death rate had reached a level of 15 to 17 per 1,000, the birth rate had also begun to decline so that at no time during its transition did Sweden's annual rate of natural increase exceed 15 per 1,000 (or 1.5 percent per year). In Ceylon, however, the death rate fell from about 25 to below 10

Dates	Sweden			Ceylon		
	Crude Rates of			Crude Rates of		
	Birth	Death	Natural Increase	Birth	Death	Natural Increase
1818–1822	34.2	24.9	9.3	—	—	—
1828–1832	32.5	25.8	6.7	—	—	—
1838–1842	30.5	21.7	8.8	—	—	—
1848–1852	31.5	20.6	10.9	—	—	—
1858–1862	34.1	19.9	14.2	—	—	—
1868–1872	29.0	19.3	9.7	—	—	—
1878–1882	29.6	17.6	12.0	—	—	—
1888–1892	27.9	16.8	11.1	—	—	—
1898–1902	26.8	16.2	10.6	38.4	28.2	10.2
1908–1912	24.7	14.1	10.6	37.8	31.1	6.7
1918–1922	21.0	14.2	6.8	38.4	31.6	6.8
1928–1932	15.2	12.0	3.2	38.7	24.0	14.7
1938–1942	15.7	11.1	4.6	36.2	20.1	16.1
1948–1952	18.2	10.2	8.0	39.7	14.6	25.1
1960	13.7	10.0	3.7	36.6	8.6	28.0
1970	13.7	9.9	3.8	29.4	7.5	21.9

Table 12–8. Comparative Vital Rate Trends for Sweden and Ceylon

Source: Historical data from Warren S. Thompson, *Population Problems,* 4th Ed. (New York: McGraw-Hill Book Company, 1953), pp. 162 and 236. Data for 1960 and 1970 were obtained, respectively, from the 1966 and 1971 *Demographic Yearbook* of the United Nations.

per 1,000 in less than thirty years, reaching this low level far in advance of any downward trend in fertility. Consequently, the crude rate of natural increase was between 15 and 30 per year until the most recent period, when a slight fall in the crude birth rate has led to an annual growth rate of just over 2 percent.

The case of Ceylon illustrates the situation that exists throughout much of the world today: rapidly increasing rates of population growth as substantial mortality declines since the end of World War II have created a truly unprecedented demographic gap between birth and death rates. Furthermore, given the economic and cultural influences on fertility in these countries, it is unrealistic to look for any substantial decline in the birth rate in the immediate future.

The unlikelihood of any immediate fertility decline, coupled with the more drastic mortality reductions possible today, assures us of continued rapid world population growth. In no country of the Western world was the fertility decline sharp enough to close the demographic gap in less than a hundred years. Although it may not take this long for the non-Western world to bring its fertility under control and complete its transition, it is certainly not going to take place overnight. As long as the gap between fertility and mortality persists among most of the world's people—and it is likely to persist for some time to come—we cannot expect any respite from the problems of rapid population growth in the world today.

American Population Problems

Placing major attention on the current world population crisis, although justifiable, should not lead us to neglect our own population problems in this country. In considering whether or not a given area is "underpopulated" or "overpopulated," we should not judge solely on the absolute number of people living in the area but upon the balance between numbers and resources *in relation to existing technology.* With these considerations in mind, it may seem somewhat paradoxical to think of the United States as having a "problem" insofar as the size and growth of the population is concerned. After all, the nation as a whole is the wealthiest in the world, technological progress has been and continues to be rapid, and despite occasional shortages our people are living at a level of material comfort and well-being never before experienced by man—and not now experienced by anyone else. Nevertheless, although the overall population picture in the United States may indeed appear rosy in contrast with the depressing situation faced throughout much of the rest of the world, it could be very dangerous to our national welfare if we let complacency or naïve optimism obscure the potential crises facing the nation.

Population and Resources

Although the people of the United States have the fullest bellies in the world and need not live with chronic food shortages and the constant threat of famine, the growing need to export large quantities of grain to less fortunate nations during the late 1960s and into the 1970s means that we are no longer bothered by the huge surpluses that resulted from our once-perennial problem of overproduction. We still have (and will continue to have for a long time to come) an abundance of food of every kind, but any American consumer is well aware that in recent years a shift from surplus to relative scarcity has caused sizable increases in domestic food prices and a corresponding rise in the cost of living.

What's more, food is not the only necessary resource, and the United States has long consumed much more than its "fair share" of the world's raw materials. At the turn of the century the United States was producing substantially more nonfood raw materials than it was consuming, but since the end of World War II we have been consuming more than we have produced. Today, we must import a substantial portion of the raw materials that we use in our industries, and we import a large fraction of the oil that is the energy base of our society. Although no difficulties were encountered during the 1950s and 1960s, the early years of the 1970s have been marked by growing domestic shortages in a number of items (most notably fuel oil) and a corresponding tightening up on exports by our traditional foreign suppliers.

To sum up, the demand for both food and nonfood resources increases steadily as the population grows. Although the United States is certainly not on the verge of becoming one of the hungry nations of the world and although the raw materials situation is not likely to become critical for some time to

Population problems are determined by the relationship between population size, available resources, and the level of technology.

come, recent years have clearly been characterized by a steadily increasing pressure of numbers on resources. In many cases, domestic production has not been able to keep up with increasing demands for resources, and costs have risen sharply as we have had to rely more and more heavily on foreign imports.

The Quality of American Life

Although we cannot afford to close our eyes to the severe hunger and poverty in many parts of the underdeveloped world, the United States clearly does not face a similar crisis in the foreseeable future as a result of population growth. Rather than threatening life itself, population growth in the United States has its greatest impact on the quality of life. As Lincoln and Alice Day noted, the most significant consequence of excessive population growth in the more affluent nations such as ours is that it acts to depress many of the personal freedoms and pleasures we have come to take for granted. Thus, they said, a continued population increase in the United States could well mean that we shall be unable to enjoy many of the aesthetic rewards that should go along with the increasing affluence of our society.[12]

One of the most obvious problems that comes to mind here relates to *space,* particularly space for recreation. Although a walk along the littered shore of a public beach on Monday morning after a hot summer weekend may cause the cynic to wonder just how much we really appreciate the beauty of our natural resources, the fact is that Americans have long been lovers of the "great outdoors." Our appreciation of natural beauty and of the need to preserve it is attested to by the vast amounts of public land set aside for parks and other recreational purposes. The problem today is that the amount of available land is finite; yet the continued growth of population (not to mention the trend toward shorter working hours and increased leisure time) is constantly increasing the need for parks, beaches, picnic grounds, and camping areas, not to mention just plain wilderness. In the areas outside larger American cities, once-empty meadows and rolling green hills have been bulldozed away to make room for Levittown-type residential areas and blacktop parking lots for sprawling suburban shopping centers.

Although the efforts of some farsighted individuals and groups have helped to ensure that some open spaces still exist, they are woefully inadequate to the aesthetic and psychological needs of the population—and they are becoming more inadequate as numbers continue to increase. Everywhere today Americans are leaving overcrowded cities to spend their vacations at similarly overcrowded beaches, at overcrowded picnic areas, at overcrowded lake and mountain resorts, and at overcrowded camping areas (if they are lucky enough to get in). Rapid population growth during the postwar years has greatly increased the need for readily available space and recreational facilities; at the same time, the finite nature of land resources makes these needs even more

One of the most obvious problems that comes to mind relates to space—particularly space for recreation.

difficult to fill. The problem will not recede if population growth, with its attendant increase in density, continues during the coming decades.

Accompanying the increased demand for space and all the other features of "good living" has been an *increase in costs.* What most Americans today regard as necessary to meet the minimum standards for the "good life"—garbage collection, air and water purification, traffic control, police and fire protection, schools, libraries, hospitals, roads, and the myriad other public-supported social services—today cost more and more merely to maintain, let alone improve. Moreover, when we consider such things as the increasing pollution of many of our major waterways, the problem of maintenance gives way to the problem of re-creating what has already been lost. Fresh air is already a thing of the past for many American cities that today are surrounded by or enveloped in a haze of polluted air. Roadways are already overtaxed by an ever-increasing number of automobiles and motorists. Housing needs have increased faster than the supply, with the result that building costs have soared. Public health and welfare agencies have too few workers and inadequate budgets to cope efficiently with the rising problems of our burgeoning urban centers. The shortage of physicians and other trained professionals (nurses, physical therapists, social workers, and so forth) is daily becoming more acute. The sad truth of the matter is that in many areas—not only in recreation, but also in more vital areas such as health, education, and welfare—the quality of American life already shows signs of deterioration. Continued increases in the size of the population will make it increasingly necessary to spend more and more on every conceivable kind of public service, and as maintenance costs rise, it will become less and less possible to achieve further progress in raising the standard of living. As a result, unfortunately, we may very easily see a pronounced speeding up of the already visible deterioration in the quality of American life.

Some Observations on Other Costs of Population Growth

Another area in which the quality of American life is threatened is individual freedom and privacy. Americans have long cherished their privacy—as witness the western pioneer who decided it was time to move when the smoke from his neighbor's fire became visible. And our love of the basic democratic freedoms (freedom of speech, thought, assembly, travel, and so on) is well attested to by the wars we have fought (in other countries as well as our own) to protect them. But today we stand in real danger of losing this cherished freedom and privacy.

On the one hand, we live in a world where international stability is seriously threatened by the ever-present danger of an "explosion" among the seething masses in the world's underdeveloped areas. On the other hand, within our own country we are faced with the steady growth of formal organization and bureaucracy with its emphasis on conformity and its deemphasis on the individual and individuality.

The first threat to us, the implications of the present population crisis for the stability of the world, is sufficiently serious to merit further attention. To begin with, the sad truth of the matter is that population growth today is most rapid where it is least needed: in the economically underdeveloped nations where poverty and human suffering is most widespread. More often than not this rapid growth of population means that any increases in national income must be used to maintain a larger number of people at the old low level of living instead of contributing to a higher level of living for a smaller number. That is, the "revolution of rising expectations" is one in which the rising expectations are largely unmet. Instead of rising levels of social and economic well-being we see rising levels of frustration that often boil over into violent confrontations. In other words, international crises in the years ahead will probably not be between modern industrial states but will involve underdeveloped countries in one way or another, and a major *contributing* cause of these crises is likely to be overpopulation. Thus, the struggling nations must be offered all the help possible, not only economic aid but also help in lowering their birth rates and thereby their rate of population growth. Success or failure in their struggle to achieve a higher level of living may well hinge on their ability to control their rate of population growth; and it will clearly be to the advantage of Western nations to do everything in their power to facilitate the modernization of the underdeveloped countries.

The second threat to individual freedom in the United States (the threat from within) is less dramatic—and consequently all the more insidious—than the threat posed by the international situation. This threat arises from the simple fact that societal life necessarily becomes more complex as increasing numbers create the need for more organization. More organization means, in effect, the further enhancement of group or societal values rather than individual values. As numbers increase, so does the need for police and fire protection, educational facilities, sanitation control, health and welfare programs, and so on. In smaller societies such services, when needed, can generally be handled on an individual level. As the population grows, however, the task of providing such services becomes too large to be carried out on an individual basis, and collective action becomes more and more necessary. And as groups created for collective action increase in importance, the freedom of the individual declines proportionately.

The impact of population growth on the greater control of the individual (and the consequent loss of individual freedom) can be seen in a number of ways. The more numbers increase, the greater the need for formalized laws to regulate more and more aspects of human behavior. Our behavior is already controlled in many ways: traffic speed laws, stop signs, and stoplights; requirements for a license to marry, to drive a car, to hunt, to fish, and so on. Such seemingly incidental control measures could become considerably more widespread if the population grows much larger. Many communities throughout the nation, for example, have suddenly found themselves faced with numerous problems resulting from haphazard land development, and they have recently established planning and zoning commissions as well as created legislation (building codes, zoning restrictions) in an effort to achieve more orderly development. The controls adopted could become even more stringent if the population continues to increase—even, as some have suggested, to limiting what has traditionally been the "right" to bear children. Perhaps we could indeed see a day when it is just as common to apply for a license (and be tested for suitability!) to become a parent as it is to become a motor vehicle operator.

Increasing control over the individual also results from the need for greater centralization. As numbers continue to swell, and in particular as density continues to increase, the autonomy that many local communities now cherish will have to be sacrificed to the dictates of regional needs. In the urban sprawl of the northeastern metropolitan belt, for example, where localities run into and overlap each other in what is fast becoming a virtually uninterrupted chain along the entire length of the Atlantic Coast, the idea that one community can exist and function independently of its neighbors begins to sound ridiculous. Given this situation, the existence of autonomous communities acting independently of one another is virtually impossible, and it is readily apparent that there is need for some sort of new governmental unit with powers over a wider geographical area.

Still another indication of the deleterious impact of population growth on individual freedom is the widening gulf between the individual and the various groups controlling his destiny. Such groups are not limited to those governmental bodies that "run" the country; they also include the "managing elite" of labor unions, educational institutions, religious bodies, and corporations. When Andrew Jackson was President, any American could call at the White House and expect to be received cordially, but the idea of a President today trying to welcome every complainant or well-wisher is horrendous to contemplate. Similarly, a generation ago it was not infrequent for college professors to entertain their classes at home, but today's student is likely to wait in line for long periods of time just to obtain his grade from a graduate assistant. Both of these illustrations reflect the impact of simple increases in sheer numbers. This gap between the individual and the members of the formal organizations with which he is associated does not necessarily damage the organizations concerned. But it does mean that the individual has less influence on decisions concerning his welfare.

It should now be clear that with a large and increasing population the individual is not only more and more constrained to follow the dictates of the group, but he also has less and less of a say in determining those dictates. Population growth is admittedly not the only cause of the deemphasis of the individual in the modern era, but it is a major element in that coalition of forces that has transformed society from one in which individual values are paramount to one in which the group dominates.

As long as population continues to grow we can anticipate increasing control over individual actions, principally through the expansion of government programs and activities. But even though greater control is inevitable, the magnitude and strictness of the control is still an open question: just how stringent this control will be depends on how soon the population of the United States becomes stable. The more people there are when the population becomes stabilized (as eventually it must, given the finite qualities of the earth), the greater will be the control exercised over individual activities. Thus it would be to our advantage to adopt and adhere to a positive population policy that seeks to curtail numerical growth in order to maintain the quality of life we now have and also to permit a greater sharing of the good things of society. The fact that population growth is recognized as a potential problem is clearly evidenced by the appointment in 1969 of a Presidential Commission on Population Growth and the American Future. After several months of study and testimony from a great many experts in a variety of related fields, a report was issued that rejected the traditional American growth ethic *and* that contained a large number of specific recommendations for facilitating population control and for enhancing the overall quality of American life.[13] Unfortunately, as is too often true of such commission reports, because of the casual rejection of its contents by the highest officials in the land, the implementation of the programs it recommended is likely to be significantly impeded. The fact remains, however, that population stabilization must come soon in the United States if we are to maintain (let alone extend) many of the traditional high qualities of our "American way of life." Greater control may be inevitable, but the smaller the ultimate population the less stringent (and therefore less painful) the controls will be.

Notes

1. Kenneth C. W. Kammeyer, *An Introduction to Population* (San Francisco: Chandler Publishing Co., 1971), pp. 1–4.
2. National Center for Health Statistics, *Monthly Vital Statistics Reports,* **22:**8 (November 14, 1973).
3. Francis C. Madigan, "Are Sex Mortality Differentials Biologically Caused?" *Millbank Memorial Fund Quarterly* (April 1957), 202–223.
4. Evelyn M. Kitagawa and Philip M. Hauser, *Differential Mortality in the United States: A Study in Socioeconomic Epidemiology* (Cambridge, Mass.: Harvard University Press, 1973).
5. Data from 1973 World Population Data Sheet—Population Reference Bureau, Inc.
6. National Center for Health Statistics, *Monthly Vital Statistics Reports,* **21:**13 (June 27, 1973).
7. Standard metropolitan statistical areas are large urban agglomerations that generally include a central city or cities of fifty thousand or more, the county or counties in which the central city is located, and adjacent counties that are sufficiently integrated with the socioeconomic life of the central city to qualify as part of its area of influence. For a more explicit discussion of the SMSA concept and the criteria used to establish the SMSA's, see U.S. Bureau of the Budget, *Standard Metropolitan Statistical Areas* (Washington, D.C., 1961); and U.S. Bureau of the Census, *U.S. Census of Population: 1960,* Final Report PC (3)-1D, *Standard Metropolitan Statistical Areas* (Washington, D.C., 1963).
8. U.S. Bureau of the Census, *Metropolitan Area Statistics* (Washington, D.C., November 1971).
9. Ibid.
10. Warren S. Thompson and David T. Lewis, *Population Problems,* 5th Ed. (New York: McGraw-Hill Book Company, 1965), p. 162.
11. For a more detailed discussion of this topic see Edward G. Stockwell, "The Changing Age Composition of the American Population," *Social Biology,* (March, 1972), 1–8.
12. Lincoln H. Day and Alice T. Day, *Too Many Americans* (New York: Dell Publishing Co., 1964).
13. *Population and the American Future: The Report of the Commission on Population and the American Future* (Washington, D.C.: U.S. Government Printing Office, 1972).

Collective Behavior

A General Definition

SOCIOLOGISTS are generally concerned with routine and recurrent patterns of social life. When sociologists talk about collective behavior they usually mean the bizarre, unusual, unique, and one-shot events that occur only on a sporadic, haphazard basis.[1] Collective behavior includes a grab bag of topics such as panics, riots, disasters, fads, crazes, and other unique events.

Collective behavior is the action of a *collectivity* (unorganized group), in which traditional social controls or constraints appear to break down. A collectivity, according to R. E. Park and E. W. Burgess, has no tradition: "It has no point of reference in its own past to which its members can refer for guidance. It has therefore neither symbols, ceremonies, rites, nor ritual; it poses no obligations and creates no loyalties."[2] A collectivity seems to take on a form of its own. Crowds, mobs, and even some audiences do not appear to be guided by the signposts of culture. They appear free of normal social controls. Nineteenth-century French sociologist Gustav LeBon said, "A crowd is not merely impulsive and mobile. Like a savage, it is not prepared to admit that anything can come between its desire and the realization of its desire."[3]

A collectivity is said to provide a certain emotional freedom absent in other groups. The collectivity does not have rules for choosing members. The members of the collectivity are there by *circumstance.* The group seems to have an identity and a direction independent of the individual member.[4]

R. H. Turner and L. M. Killian have suggested that the goals of a collectivity become clear only long after it has ceased to exist. They wrote, "The collectivity is oriented toward an object of attention and arrives at some shared objective, but these are not defined in advance, and there are no formal procedures for reaching decisions."[5] Collective behavior can be described as lacking normal controls or role expectations, and a collectivity often seems to be without direction or constraint.

Early students of collective behavior like Gustav LeBon and psychoanalyst Sigmund Freud used as their model the French Revolution. They presented the collectivity as a *milling mob* of people overtaken by a *group mind* or herd instinct. The mob appeared to be free of normal controls when it stormed the Bastille and roamed the streets of Paris in search of fleeing French nobles. Members of the mob were presented as faceless people carried away by a *social contagion.* "Social contagion," according to Herbert Blumer, is "an intense form of milling and collective excitement: in it the development of rapport and unreflective responsiveness of individuals to one another becomes pronounced. . . . it attracts and infects individuals, many of whom originally are detached and indifferent spectators and bystanders."[6] The spread of this contagion leads to the creation of a panic, a crowd, a mob, or a mania.

Ladd Wheeler suggests a distinction between *social facilitation* and *behavioral contagion.*[7] *Social facilitation* occurs when, under the influence of others, people perform behaviors which fit their values and about which they have no reservations. For example, the plea for the sharing of facilities by the assembled throngs at the Woodstock Festival fit the flower-child philosophy of many of the participants.

Behavioral contagion involves a breakdown of social constraints. Under the influence of others, people perform behaviors about which they *do* have reservations or mixed feelings. When the individual observes that actions previously forbidden are being engaged in, he may well participate. Returning to the Woodstock Festival, many young people for the first time smoked marihuana or took LSD in imitation of others. The lack of police enforcement, however, provided the conditions that allowed for this experimentation. People who *always wanted* to smoke marihuana now felt freer to do so. A similar statement may be made about the looter in the urban riot who loads up his car with cases of whisky and expensive appliances. The creation of the riot situation allows the looter to "rip off the Man" without fear of punishment or other constraints. Wheeler's description of contagion goes beyond LeBon's in that he specified a *willingness* on the part of the individual to be swept up into seemingly mindless activity.

In collective behavior, a central concept is that of *anonymity.* In a crowd or mob the individual is faceless. He believes himself invisible and thus free from social control. The teen-ager first popping pills at Woodstock cannot be identified by parents or neighbors. Collectivities provide a shield of anonymity for the individual, allowing him to do without fear of punishment things he always wanted to do. One can smoke dope at rock festivals, shout obscenities at football games, or shriek wildly at an idol's concert. But how many people would puff on a joint at the annual family Christmas party or call a 290-pound tackle a "son of a bitch" to his face? Very few.

In his classic paper on collective behavior, Herbert Blumer listed three different types of collectivities: the *crowd,* the *mass,* and the *public.*

Types of Collective Behavior

Crowds

A *crowd* is a chance collection of individuals.[8] A collectivity becomes a crowd when it develops *rapport.* This rapport develops when a common attitude emerges or a number of people are attracted by the same object.[9] This means that a crowd is a group of people drawn together by a common attraction. The focus of attention may be provocative, interesting, or passive. An irritating event may create tension or a feeling of uneasiness that develops into some kind of reaction. If someone shouts "Fire!" in a crowded place, the emotional excitement triggered can result in some form of action. The stimulus must continue to act as a focus of attention as well as the heightener of a common *mood.* This reinforcement of a prevailing mood transforms the collectivity into a crowd with a common purpose and gives the unit a personality and a purpose that it previously did not have.

The nature of a crowd depends upon a number of factors. First, what is its focus of attention? A fire-and-brimstone revival preacher or a strutting rock-and-roll idol will generate quite a different response than a white-bearded

NORTHWESTERN

Santa Claus soliciting for the Salvation Army during the Christmas season.

Crowd formation and response also hinge upon the social situation. A white policeman giving a black woman a ticket may elicit a different reaction on the streets of Harlem or Watts than in a white suburb.

Finally, the nature of the crowd focus or center of attention will suggest the form of response. For example, the sight of what is believed to be police brutality may trigger the cry "Off the pig," or the sight of Elvis Presley may cause girls to scream. A crowd gathered in the park watching a folksinger may merely applaud and wander away. These conditions then suggest what form the crowd will take.

Herbert Blumer listed four types of crowds: *casual, conventional* (audience), *acting* (mob), and *expressive.*

The *casual* crowd consists of a group of people whose attention is momentarily directed at one common object. Witnesses of an accident and "sidewalk superintendents" at a construction site make up a casual crowd.

Thirty-eight New York citizens looking out their windows constituted a casual crowd one spring night in 1964 as Kitty Genovese walked to her apartment in Kew Gardens. She was attacked by a man with a knife. She screamed for help. Nothing happened. A voice yelled, "Leave her alone." The attacker momentarily retreated. The victim tried to reach her home. The attacker returned. The neighbors viewed in silence and did nothing. The man left and returned, finally killing the young woman. Thirty-eight people later told police they had witnessed the assault. They were a casual crowd attracted by one event.[10]

A *conventional* crowd appears at sports contests, races, concerts, plays, or any other regularly scheduled event. The fifty thousand fans who storm into Baltimore's Memorial Stadium to see the Colts are a conventional crowd, as are those who quietly attend a Sunday service at St. Patrick's Cathedral.

The *mob* is an *active crowd* that comes together for a common purpose, such as giving rise to a rebellion or lynching a victim. It is a group born from "aroused impulse."[11] Once the goal of the mob is accomplished it has no further reason to exist.

Hadley Cantril presented an example of a lynch mob:

On July 18, 1930, a seven-year-old white girl, the daughter of a tobacco farmer, came home crying because Oliver Moore, a Negro house boy, had hurt her while playing a game with her and her younger sister in the barn. Because of the condition of the girl's clothes, the parents concluded that the Negro's game had been attempted rape. Moore ran away while the farmer and his wife were consulting. The county sheriff with a posse of excited citizens and a brace of bloodhounds set out in search of the Negro. The searches were fruitless, but Moore was at last apprehended by a single white man on August 16. A preliminary trial was held on August 19. The father and the girls told their story. The Negro was not allowed to say anything and no lawyers volunteered their services to defend Moore, who was then lodged in the county jail to await appearance in the superior court. Since no unusual excitement had accompanied the preliminary trial, both the sheriff and the judge felt the prisoner would be quite safe in the local jail.

About one o'clock the next morning, however, a deputy sheriff in charge of the jail opened the door when he heard a knock. A number of people were outside. Some of them were masked. The sheriff was quickly covered by guns, the keys to the jail were found by a mob member, the Negro taken out and tied in one of about twenty cars waiting outside. The whole abduction was efficiently handled and the orders of the mob leader quietly carried out. The mob was obviously well organized. Some time later the county sheriff was notified. He organized a posse to pursue the mob but did not know which way to go. About dawn the Negro's body was found hanging to a tree "riddled with bullet and buckshot." The lynching was staged as near as possible to the barn where the alleged "crime" had occurred.[12]

Once the lynching had occurred, the mob dissolved into the night.

The *expressive* crowd is similar to the mob, but it lacks a goal or purpose. The fundamental characteristic of this type of crowd is "an excitement expressed in physical movement merely as a form of release."[13] Old-time evangelistic camp meetings and contemporary rock festivals are examples of expressive crowds. "It's not just the music that's important," said one veteran festival goer, "sitting in the car for five hours waiting to get into the Poconos may have been a physical drag, but it was a social high; after four hours of smoking dope, rapping with other people and just hanging out in general, it almost didn't matter whether we got to hear the music or not."[14]

Rock critic Paul Williams said of Woodstock, "It felt like a living organism, being inside, being a cell, music and bloodstream, energy-food overflowing through us."[15] The festivals were "happenings," a witnessing of group pleasure. The purpose of the festival, for participants, was the festival itself.

Masses

A *mass* is a *diffuse* collectivity that is larger than a crowd: "The mass is represented by people who participate in mass behavior, such as those who are excited by some national event."[16] The mass is diffuse, detached, and anonymous. It is an audience. A migration of people from one country to another can also be considered as a mass—in this case, a mass migration.

A mass is *heterogeneous.* Its members come from all walks of life. A mass includes people of varying class, race, age, sex, and so on. Anyone can be a member of a mass. All they need do is direct their attention to the object of mass behavior such as a televised event or the first lunar landing or the Super Bowl. Immigrants become part of a mass by deciding to leave their homeland.

The mass is *anonymous.* Because of its size, the members of a mass do not know one another. People watching the same television show need not be socially related in any way. This is, in fact, the third property of a mass.

The members of a mass are *detached* from one another. People watch the Super Bowl in bars, homes, motels, and hotels all over the country.

A mass is highly unstructured and lacks any unity. It is generally passive and not goal-directed.

The notion of a mass has been criticized by some sociologists who feel that it is too general and vague. Daniel Bell objected, "They may be silent, separate, detached, and anonymous while watching the movie, but afterward they talk about it with friends and exchange opinions and judgments. . . . Would one say that several hundred or a thousand individuals home alone at night, but all reading the same book, constitute a 'mass'?"[17] Herbert Gans agreed with Bell that in the area of entertainment the term *mass* is not correct. Rather, an audience consists of many *taste subcultures* or *taste cultures* that are bound together by variables such as age and education.[18] In recent years sociologists have increasingly reduced the mass or audience into *demographic units.* Demographic units are units that can be identified on the basis of some common objective measure, such as income, education, or age.

Publics

A public is a dissimilar group of people who are interested in a common issue but who do not necessarily have a common opinion about it.[19] A public is simply a *following* for an issue, a person, or an art form. Elvis Presley has a *public,* so do popular music, stocks, baseball scores, and foreign policy. However, publics are in a constant state of flux. "As issues vary," writes Herbert Blumer, "so do the corresponding publics."[20] Consider the popular music public.

The popular music public is a collectivity that buys some $2-billion worth of the forty-three hundred albums and fifty-three hundred singles released each year. However, it would be a vast mistake to assume that this public is comprised of thirteen-year-old girls with transistor radios growing out of their ears. Instead, the pop music public ranges from six-year-olds to housewives in their late forties. Certainly, a housewife will feel quite differently than her ten-year-old daughter about the momentary "rave" idol. In popular music, taste publics can be identified on the basis of race, sex, and, most importantly, age (see Chapter Fourteen, "Popular Culture"). Age determines how a person experiences popular music and in what manner. A nine-year-old "in love" with a "bubble-gum" idol like David Cassidy or Donny Osmond quickly changes her tastes as real dates enter her life. Then popular music becomes a background noise for doing homework, dating, and dancing. The relationship of the fan to the pop music star is changed. He is a temporary Saturday-night idol. The rest of the time everyday dating predominates. Upon graduation from high school, people marry, find work, or go off to college or the university. Again, taste changes occur. College students generally have slightly different preferences than their noncollegiate counterparts. Students favor folk music and jazz.

Table 13–1. Music Preferences by Age[a]

Bubble-gummers (9 to 12)	Teen idols—Donny Osmond David Cassidy Bobby Sherman Monkees (Davy Jones) Beatles Fabian (Frankie Avalon) Ricky Nelson Elvis Presley
Teeny-boppers (13 to 18)	Top Forty—*"Punk" Rock* Alice Cooper Grand Funk Railroad Black Sabbath James Gang Three Dog Night Grass Roots Black Oak Arkansas
College Students (18 and over)	Albums—*Folk-Art-Rock* Simon and Garfunkel James Taylor Bob Dylan Carly Simon Moody Blues Others

[a]These categories are not always mutually exclusive, as certain songs have transcended age and education classifications.
Source: R. S. Denisoff, *Solid Gold: The Pop Record Industry* (New Brunswick, N.J.: TransAction Books, 1975).

After the education and courtship years are over most people discontinue their interest in music. Housewives, for example, may use radio as as daytime companion, preferring lush, loud arrangements that do not require a great deal of attention.

All of these people are a part of the popular music public, however different their tastes may be.

Expressions of Collective Behavior

Public Opinion

Sociologists define *public opinion* as "that which is communicated to decision-makers as a consequence of the functioning of a public."[21] Public opinion always concerns an issue: How does the public feel about the president, taxes, or sexual practices? In a democracy public opinion is quite important, as it indicates "the will of the people." However, the will of the people is far from unanimous.

Consider the reaction to the Watergate scandal. In July of 1973, after months of television and print media coverage, people were asked if they thought President Nixon was involved in the wrongdoing. Table 13–2 gives a breakdown of responses to the question: "Here are four statements concerning President

Table 13-2.

Source: "Poll Shows 71% Feel Nixon Knew" *New York Times,* July 8, 1973, p. 8.

Which of These Statements Comes Closest to Your Own Point of View?"

	June 1–4 Percentage	*June 22–25 Percentage*
Nixon planned the Watergate bugging from the beginning	8	8
Nixon did not plan the bugging but knew about it before it took place	28	27
Nixon found out about the bugging after it occurred but tried to cover it up	31	36
Nixon had no knowledge of the bugging and spoke up as soon as he learned about it	19	17
No opinion/not heard or read about Watergate	14	12

"Should President Nixon Be Compelled to Leave Office?"

	Yes Pct.	*No Pct*	*No opinion Pct.*
Nationwide	18	71	11
Nixon planned bugging	60	29	11
Not planned but knew in advance	28	61	11
Found out and tried to cover up	12	81	7
No knowledge of the bugging	3	94	3

Nixon's connection with the Watergate affair. Will you please tell me which one comes closest to your own point of view?" The table shows that not only was there a considerable difference of opinion but not all of the people were aware of even the most publicized events.

G. R. Funkhauser, in an analysis of news magazines in the 1960's, found that certain issues repeatedly appeared in print.[22] (A similar analysis appears in Table 13-3.) Funkhauser suggests that the public tends to consider important

Table 13-3. Amount of Coverage Given by National News Magazines to Various Issues During the 1960's, and Rank Scores of the Issues as "Most Important Problem Facing America" During That Period

Issues	*Number of Articles*	*Coverage Rank*	*Importance Rank*
Vietnam war	861	1	1
Race relations (and urban riots)	687	2	2
Campus unrest	267	3	4
Inflation	234	4	5
Television and mass media	218	5	12[a]
Crime	203	6	3
Drugs	173	7	9
Environment and pollution	109	8	6
Smoking	99	9	12[a]
Poverty	74	10	7
Sex (declining morality)	62	11	8
Womens rights	47	12	12[a]
Science and society	37	13	12[a]
Population	36	14	12[a]

[a] These items were never ranked as "the most important problem" by Gallup Poll respondents, so are ranked equally below the items that were.

Source: The Gallup Opinion Index, Nos. 1–67, 1965–1970.

the issues that the media emphasize, but the public and the media may or may not agree on how to resolve these issues.

Issues not stressed in the media have little effect on public opinion. Even some headline-provoking issues escape many people. During the American involvement in Indochina, a sample of Las Vegas citizens were found to be ignorant of what countries were located in that region.

Many diverse opinions are to be found on a particular subject as to cause, effect, and, most importantly, *cure.*[23] The Harris poll, for example, posed the question: "If it appeared that the Communists were going to take over the government of Laos, would you favor sending in American troops to keep the communists from taking over, continuing to send in military advisers as we are now, or staying out of Laos altogether?"[24] There were five possible replies: "Send troops," "Send advisers," "Stay out," "Not sure," "No opinion." In the case of the Vietnam war, replies over the course of seven years shifted from "Send troops" and "No opinion" to "Stay out" and "Get out." The *cure* over time changed.

Nelson Foote and Clyde Hart suggested two steps in the formation of public opinion: a *program phase* and the *appraisal phase.* In the program phase the seeming cure for a social problem is favored by the public. The passage of a law, a presidential edict, a Supreme Court decision appears to be the solution. In the *appraisal* phase some disillusion with the apparent solution occurs. People complain that the program was "too little, too late" or "not enough" or even "overkill."[25]

Public opinion, according to Hadley Cantril, has three distinct characteristics: *intensity, stability,* and *depth.*[26] The *intensity* of public opinion depends on how strongly people feel about certain issues. People have deep feelings about questions such as homosexuality, capital punishment, or the legalization of marihuana and other drugs.

The *stability* of public opinion involves both *intensity* and *duration of time.* For example, public opinion on anti-Communism in America since World War II has been very stable, a pillar of public policy. Belief in the "free enterprise system" is also very stable.

The *depth* of public opinion depends on the psychological motivations of people and how easily these motivations can be changed. The issues on which people feel very deeply are the so-called gut issues and sacred cows of politics and public rhetoric. Why, we can ask, are people opposed to a black or a woman President of the United States or to legal marriages for homosexuals? It is in this area of public taboos and prejudices that the depth of public opinion is to be found.

Rumors

One form of public opinion is rumor. Rumors are the product of people trying to create order from disorder. They take facts and merge them with fears, fantasies, and prejudices. A rumor is improvised news or, more precisely, a communication form "through which men caught together in an ambiguous situation attempt to construct a meaningful interpretation of it by pooling their intellectual resources."[27] A rumor is an explanation that people devise when the available information seems inadequate. Rumors arise when people feel the need to make sense out of a chaotic situation, generally in a time of uncertainty. One of many examples would be the climate in the city of Chicago prior to the 1968 Democratic National Convention. Rumors were everywhere about an invasion of revolutionaries and hippies. The Walker Commission, which investigated what happened in Chicago, reported:

> There were reports of proposals to dynamite natural gas lines; to dump hallucinating drugs into the city's water system; to print forged credentials so that demonstrators could slip into the convention hall; to stage a mass stall-in of old jalopies on the expressways and thereby disrupt traffic; to take over gas stations, flood sewers with gasoline, then burn the city; to fornicate in the parks and on Lake Michigan's beaches; to release greased pigs throughout Chicago, at the Federal Building and at the Amphitheater; to slash tires along the city's freeways and tie up traffic in all directions; to scatter razor sharp three-inch nails along the city's freeways; to place underground agents in hotels, restaurants, and kitchens where food was prepared for delegates, and drug food and drink; to paint cars like independent taxicabs and forceably take delegates to Wisconsin or some other place far from the convention; to engage Yippie girls as "hookers" to attract delegates and dose their drinks with LSD; to bombard the Amphitheater with mortars from several miles away; to jam communications lines from mobile units; to disrupt the operations of airport control towers, hotel elevators, and railways switching yards; to gather 230 "hyper-potent" hippie males into a special battalion to seduce the wives, daughters and girl friends of convention delegates; to assemble 100,000 people to burn draft cards with the fires spelling out: "Beat Army"; to turn on fire hydrants, set off false alarms and police alarms, and string wire between trees in Grand Park and Lincoln Park to trip up three-wheeled vehicles of the Chicago police; to dress Yippies like Viet Cong and walk the streets shaking hands or passing out rice; to infiltrate the right wing with short-haired Yippies and at the right moment exclaim: "You know, these Yippies have something to say!"; to have ten thousand nude bodies floating on Lake Michigan—the list could go on.[28]

The so-called Chicago police riot that followed was partially generated by these rumors. Many other riots have also been kindled by rumors. For example, the 1917 East St. Louis race riot began when a Negro accidentally wounded a white store-owner. In a matter of minutes people were saying the shooting was intentional and that a white woman was *insulted* during the shooting. Minutes later the story was that the "victims" of the shooting were *two* white girls. During the Watts riot of 1965 rumors ran wild in both the black and the white sections of Los Angeles.[29]

Another example of a rumor was the "great sex movie scandal." *TV Guide* reported:

An uncommonly arresting report appeared early this year in the *Paxton Herald,* a paper published at Harrisburg, Pa. It said:

"CBS has announced that they will begin showing X-rated movies on the late show. If there is no protest, they will be shown later all hours of the day. We will have homosexuality, incest, child molestation and nudity almost daily."

The same startling piece of news, with changes of phrasing here and there, has appeared during the past 17 months in literally hundreds of general and religious newspapers, magazines, newsletters and other publications from Coast to Coast. The wholly predictable result has been a thunderous chorus of public indignation against CBS.

As of late June this year, the hapless network had received the unprecedented and staggering total of 429,820 letters protesting the "forthcoming series" of X-movies—and the letters, now tapering off, have been pouring in at a rate of some 5,000 a week.

Not only have nearly half a million people expressed their anger individually, but at least two legislative bodies have adopted formal and solemn resolutions condemning CBS for its sinister plans. The Rockland County (N.Y.) Legislature voted in March this year to "go on record strongly objecting to the showing of X-rated or R-rated movies on television"; the South Carolina General Assembly voted to express its "complete displeasure with [CBS's] intended inclusion within its projected program format of X-rated movies."

That should teach CBS to mind its manners in our living rooms!

There is only one thing wrong with this great public chastisement: it isn't necessary. The fact is that CBS has never broadcast an X-rated movie, has no such movies in its inventory, denies that it plans to buy any and has certainly never "announced" such plans. The entire public outcry is based on a falsehood.

Any rumor so widespread and presistent must have powerful forces behind it. *TV GUIDE* set out to find what those forces are. How did the rumor start? By whom, for what reasons?

Network president Robert D. Wood, a hearty, balding man, grins sadly and shakes his head when asked about the rumor's source. "It's like a virus epidemic," he says. "We can't trace it back to one individual. All we can do is try to contain it. We've replied to every one of those 429,000 letters. I've even taped a statement for our affiliate stations to broadcast, and some of them have shown it six or seven times. But the rumor is bigger than we are. It won't quit."[30]

What actually had occurred was that an innocent wire-service report had announced that CBS had purchased 247 movies to replace a late-night talk show. *One* of the films was an X-rated film that was edited into "acceptable form." A conservative organization, Christian Crusade, circulated this story to its members. The result was a massive campaign totally based upon misinformation:

Thus the seed was planted. Other religious, fraternal and political groups learned of Hargis' [the CC leader's] letter and took up the cry. As the story passed from hand to hand, it grew. Before the end of that February, the storytellers had added the intriguing detail that CBS was using "The Damned" as a kind of test, to see whether the U.S. public would swallow more sex-rated films in the future. The knights of Columbus, a Catholic fraternal order, wrote to the Federal Communications Commission: "If the movie escapes hostile public reaction, the network probably will dispense more X- and R-rated films. . . ." In later word-of-mouth versions of the story, the word "probably" was dropped.

"The Damned," when it appeared on TV on the night of Feb. 28, 1972, was not an X movie—either officially or by common viewer judgment. It was so free of potentially offensive material, in fact, that one reviewer thought it should have been retitled "The Darned." "But once a movie is branded X," says network president Wood, "that brand stays in people's minds no matter what you do." CBS had hoped the hullabaloo would die out after the film was shown. Instead, it got worse.[31]

Even under less dramatic conditions rumors are also quite prevalent. Troop movements and promotions in the military are a constant source of speculation in the enlisted men's quarters.[32] In the popular record industry, where fashions and trends come and go, rumors constitute an important part of the daily operations. There are rumors of groups breaking up, coming together, pending divorces, and management changes. In fact, artists and publicists frequently use the rumor mill as a vehicle to influence people. One artist, mildly unhappy with his record company, tried to improve matters by starting a rumor that he was thinking of changing labels. His record company acted on the rumor as if it were a reality—and dropped his contract. Rumors arise in uncertain situations. The more the uncertainty, the more the improvised-news potential.

The improvisation of rumors, according to Gordon Allport and L. Postman, goes through three levels of change.[33] In *leveling* one eliminates some of the facts from the story. *Sharpening* is the reorganization of the available information without regard for truth. For example, many people reorganized a number of unrelated events to "prove" there was a conspiracy to kill President Kennedy. In *assimilation* the story is woven around a theme favorable to the teller. One member of the radical right explained the murder of Kennedy as being ordered by the Kremlin because the President was becoming too independent of its orders. Some people on the political left felt that Lee Harvey Oswald was really a member of the John Birch Society or a CIA agent disguised as a Marxist. The Warren Commission, which thoroughly studied the tragic event, discounted both of these rumors.

In keeping with Allport and Postman, some sociologists discuss the "snowballing"effect of rumors. One "fact" is built upon another.[34] President Kennedy was shot at 12:30 (CST). For an hour prior to the official announcement of his death, rumors circulated. Each was based upon the sniper shooting. Some claimed the shooting was engineered by Vice President Johnson. Others claimed the Vice President had also collapsed from either a heart attack or a gunshot wound. Each rumor was built upon the original shooting. This is the so-called *snowball effect.*

On October 14, 1969, an Ohio Wesleyan University student wrote a phony story allegedly proving that Beatle Paul McCartney was dead. A Detroit disc jockey on WKNR repeated the story. The rumor of McCartney's death spread over two continents. Beatles fans found various clues on the group's records to "prove" the accuracy of the hoax. *Rolling Stone* reported:

> Evidently it got its start when somebody first noticed that there's a voice saying "Turn me on, dead man," on "Revolution No. 9" when played backwards.
>
> This called for some "research" into earlier and later Beatles. On *Sgt. Pepper* it was noted that there is a hand over Paul's head on the cover (a Greek or American Indian sign of death), and on the back cover his back is turned. The guitar on the grave on the cover is lefthanded, just like you-know-who.
>
> On *Magical Mystery Tour* on the inside there's another hand over Paul's head. He's wearing a black carnation, though the others wear red ones. At the end of "I Am a Walrus" somebody says, "I buried Paul." The walrus on the cover is the only personage there in black, and, as everybody knows, "the walrus is Paul" (source: "Glass Onion," *The Beatles*).
>
> On *Abbey Road,* Paul is out of step with the other three on the cover, and are his eyes closed or not? The rumor says they are and that this is his funeral procession. Fred LaBour, writing in the *Michigan Daily,* University of Michigan paper, says John looks like an "anthropomorphic God, followed by Ringo the undertaker, followed by Paul the resurrected, barefoot with a cigaret in his right hand (the original was left-handed), followed by George, the grave digger." He points out that they are leaving a cemetery.[35]

McCartney, of course, was alive and well. However, the rumors of his death snowballed, building one wild interpretation upon another.

There is some controversy over whether rumors are necessarily always false or distorted. H. Taylor Buckner argues that whether they are or are not depends on several factors.[36] He suggests that there are three kinds of mental sets with which an individual can approach a rumor and that these determine whether he will pass the rumor to others and whether it will be passed accurately. These sets are influenced by characteristics of the individual as well as by the nature of the rumor and by the situation.

The individual may be able to take a *critical set* and use his critical ability to judge the truth or falsity of rumors. He may take an *uncritical set* if he is unable to use his critical ability to test a rumor's truth. Or he may take a *transmission set* and transmit the rumor without caring whether it is true or false.

A critical set is easier to apply in certain situations than others. The situation may be such that a rumor can be quelled by the mere checking of fact. For example, when Paul McCartney was rumored to have died, one could easily have called a local news source to verify the truth of the story. The stability of the situation allowed for this action. But imagine that a rumor occurs when there is no way of proving it true or false. What if someone ran in and cried, "The British have started World War III," and there were no news media available. What to do?

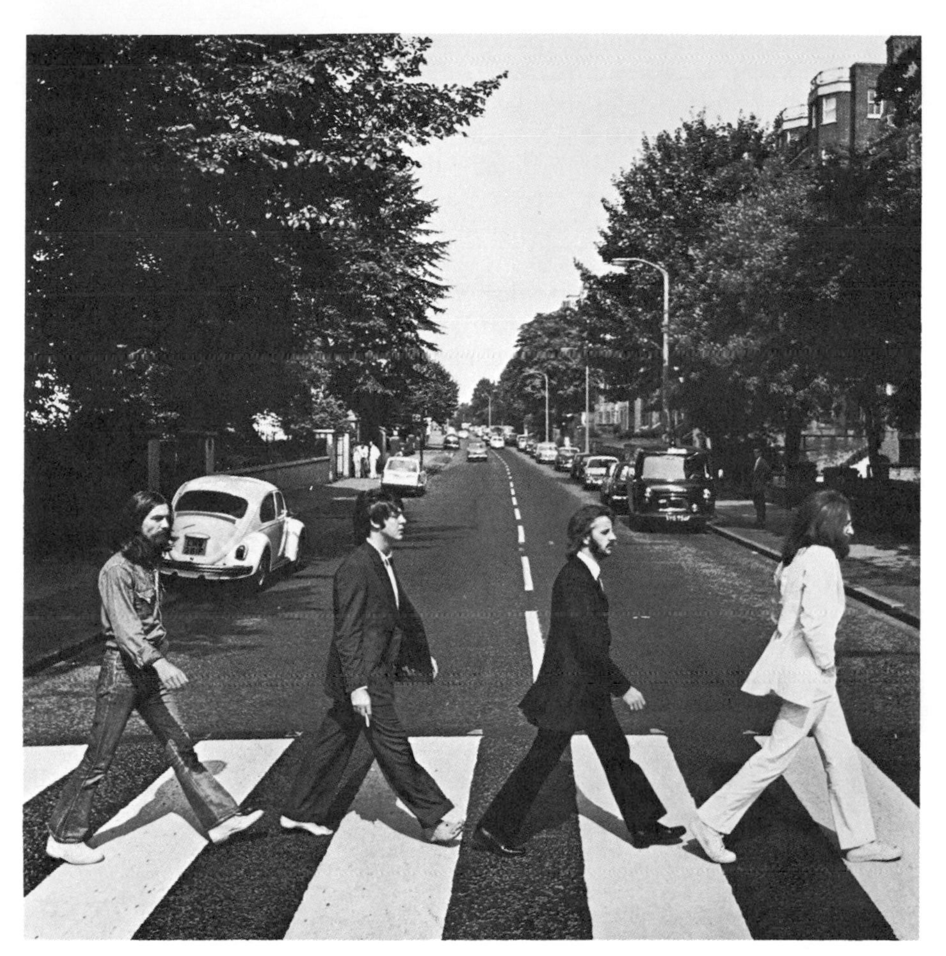

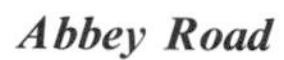
Abbey Road

The critical ability of the individual is also important. On the Halloween night of 1938, Orson Welles broadcast a radio play of H. G. Wells's book *The War of the Worlds.* This play was about an invasion from Mars. A million Americans were panic-stricken. Their critical abilities were not put to the test. The frightened did not think to switch stations. Surely, the Columbia Broadcasting System would not be the *only* network carrying an event of such monstrous proportions. They could also have telephoned their local newspapers.[37] Individual critical ability, then, as well as the situation, affects the spread of a rumor. A critic may well kill off a rumor or merely transmit those portions that are seemingly plausible.

Some situations do not allow for critical judgment. A telephoned warning, "A tornado is coming," or "The valley dam has given away," requires prompt action. An imposed news blackout can also create an environment in which verification is impossible.

A psychological or intellectual bias may also muddy one's critical judgment.

Some rumors are about things people want to happen. The premature coming of summer vacation, the end of a war, or a tax cut have all been rumors that people gladly accepted. Some people with strong beliefs use these to interpret events. Some religious cults have predicted the second coming of Christ and the end of the world. When the date of the second coming came and went, they were unshaken in their beliefs. For example, Leon Festinger and his associates studied a group that believed the world was coming to an end on December 21. College students in the group quit studying, gave away all of their textbooks, and waited for the day of the Great Flood. Nothing happened. Yet some believers clinged to their beliefs. One believer explained that the nonevent was merely a test of his beliefs:

Fred seemed more at ease with the world. His face was more relaxed. He kept saying he was glad the disaster hadn't happened because he was glad to be alive. He said that this term he is doing well in his studies; last term he didn't do well at all because he didn't study at all. He says his faith has not changed, but he sees no need to go to meetings. He thinks now that the flood was never intended to occur; that is, space people just told us that there would be a disaster as a test for us, a test of our faith to see if we could stand up under crisis.[38]

In situations like these, Buckner maintained, people tend to fit rumors in with their framework of ideas, attitudes, and prejudices. The rumor is passed on *uncritically.*

The *transmission set* is like the child's game "Pass-it-on." One person tells something to another, he tells another, and so on down a chain of people. In the process changes may occur in the message.[39] It is important to remember, however, that not all instances of "Pass-it-on" actually distort the message. The number of people in the game and the nature of the message seem to influence the end result.[40]

The spread of a rumor, according to Buckner, is also dependent on the types of groups that transmit the information. Tightly knit groups that interact regularly with one another, as in the military, in a prison, or in the record industry, are apt to be more critical and to verify information about troop dispersements, cell assignments, or recording contracts.

Loose or diffuse groups that are spread out are more likely to accept rumors uncritically. Also, in a diffuse group the individual hears the rumor only once, with little opportunity to inquire into its truth. According to Buckner, the acceptance of a rumor *can* transform a diffuse group into a close-knit group. In the 1971 Chicago race riot, stories of the number of deaths united people with the common interest of "getting even."

Buckner's theory is based on the assumption that certain individual orientations and structural conditions must be present for rumor to catch on. Individual fantasy is not enough. The mere cry of "The Martians are coming" by itself would not be sufficient. However, in 1938 when Orson Welles did his

War of the Worlds broadcast, the social setting made a panic possible. As Cantril suggested:

During August, September, and part of October, 1938, millions of Americans were listening to their radios regularly, to the latest stories of a developing international crisis. Probably never before in the history of broadcasting had so many people in this country been glued to their sets. Stations at all hours were willing to interrupt pre-arranged programs for the latest news broadcast.[41]

When Welles used this same technique of *seemingly* interrupting a music broadcast to announce the Martian invasion many people thought it was the real thing.

Panics

Nearly all sociological definitions of panics have three elements: "fear, flight, and limited access to escape routes."[42] Kurt Lang and Gladys Lang observed, "Each person's concern is with his own safety and personal security, whether the danger is physical, psychological, social, or financial."[43] The classic examples of panic behavior are taken from crowded areas, such as theaters, night clubs, or sports arenas, when some unexpected threat to the spectators occurs. The Iroquois Theater Fire of 1903 is widely presented as the model of panic behavior:

Somebody had of course yelled "Fire!"—there is almost always a fool of that species in an audience; and there are always hundreds of people who go crazy the moment they hear the word. . . .

The horror in the auditorium was beyond all description. There were thirty exits, but few of them were marked by lights; some had heavy portieres over the doors, and some of the doors were locked or fastened with levers which no one knew how to work.

It was said that some of the exit doors . . . were either rusted or frozen. They were finally burst open, but precious moments had been lost—moments which meant death for many behind those doors. The fire-escape ladders could not accommodate the crowd, and many fell or jumped to their death on the pavement below. Some were not killed only because they landed on the cushion of bodies of those who had gone before.

But it was inside the house that the greatest loss of life occurred, especially on the stairways leading down from the second balcony. Here most of the dead were trampled or smothered, though many jumped or fell over the balustrade to the floor of the foyer. In places on the stairways, particularly where a turn caused a jam, bodies were piled seven or eight feet deep. . . . An occasional living person was found in the heaps, but most of these were terribly injured. The heel prints on the dead faces mutely testified to the cruel fact that human animals stricken by terror are as mad and ruthless as stampeding cattle. Many bodies had the clothes torn from them, and some had the flesh trodden from their bones.[44]

From this example it should not be inferred that every retreat to apparent safety is a panic. As Russell Dynes, codirector of the Ohio State University Disaster Center, has indicated, "Often what gets interpreted as panic is only people acting in a very rational manner. If you're in a fire in a theater, it makes good sense to try to get out as quickly as you can."[45] The panic behavior is displayed when people, in time of stress caused by some emergency, flee toward some object of peril.[46] Mixed into the very logical action to get away from danger is the irrational emotional response of ignoring other routes that may be available. For example, people crowd into the few nearest doorways, creating a bottleneck. Many people have died by jumping from windows in tall buildings when a fire was in progress. Had they waited for the firemen, they might have been saved. The individual feeling himself trapped runs to the nearest exit without regard for anyone around him. "Every man for himself" seems to be a common characteristic of panic behavior. In these situations a feeling of powerlessness and individuality occurs. It is man against the blaze, earthquake, tornado. The natural response is flight.

Panic behavior, according to most sociologists and psychologists, can be broken down into six elements.[47] It begins with a *crisis,* such as a natural disaster or a revolution. The individual's everyday world and his normal expectations are disrupted. Generally this disruption is a *threat* to personal safety. The reaction to the threat is *intense fear.* The individual attempts to remove himself from the situation. The *situational factors* are the conditions and the environment the individual must deal with to free himself from the cause of his distress. The exits in a burning building, a storm center, a lifeboat all may be considered situational factors. *Behavior contagion* causes the breakdown of group cooperation and is characterized by milling and excitement.[48] It is at this point that the last stage of panic occurs: *a breakdown in mutual cooperation.* It is every man for himself. Here normal constraints fail and irrational behavior results. The results can be catastrophic or disastrous.

Disasters and Collective Behavior

Types of Disasters

The most common form of crisis discussed by students of collective behavior is the *disaster.* The disaster, according to Allen Barton, is a *collective stress situation* created from either *within* or *without* the social system. As in a *panic* or *riot* situation, the normal everyday workings of social life are temporarily disrupted.[49] Disasters can be either man-made or natural.

The most common example of man-made disaster is military warfare. The dropping of the atomic bomb in Japan in the closing days of World War II is but one illustration of the havoc caused by human tools of destruction.

Natural disasters include earthquakes, tornadoes, floods, hurricanes, blights, plagues, and all of the other terrible events caused by Mother Nature.

L. J. Carr has identified four types of natural disasters based on severity and length of time.[50]

The *instantaneous total disaster* is one that strikes unexpectedly and is over before anyone can react. The impact is complete. The falling of the atomic bomb on Hiroshima, the bursting of the dam that poured millions of tons of water upon the Italian village of Langarone, or the 1973 earthquake in Managua, Nicaragua are all illustrations of this type of disaster. A resident of Managua said:

I was asleep when, suddenly, the roof of my house fell on top of me. I awoke to see the moon and the stars shining where the roof had been. I was badly scratched, but luckily, I wasn't really injured. I got out of bed and ran to the front door. It was locked and I couldn't find the key. I called for help to a passerby and, with him pushing from the outside and me pulling from the inside, we forced the door. When I got outside, I heard my neighbor calling for help. His wife and child were pinned under a heavy pillar. We raised the pillar and got them free.

I sat outside of what was left of my house until dawn, hoping to get back inside to save some personal belongings. But it was too dangerous; the rest of the house seemed ready to collapse. Half a block away, I could hear women screaming, praying to God to stop the quakes. All around me I could see smoke from burning buildings. And I saw dead people lying on the street, including a little girl who was half-decapitated.[51]

The *instantaneous-focalized disaster* occurs when a segment of a community is totally destroyed while the remainder is left untouched. A coal mine cave-in or the destruction of a local school are but two examples of this type of disaster. One of the most dramatic events of this type took place in 1964 in the community of Aberfan, Wales:

The women of Wales' gaunt villages grow up with an ear for a special sound: the piercing siren's cry that proclaims disaster for their men in the coal pits deep below the ground. But last week, the pits contrived an even uglier form of tragedy for the tiny mining town of Aberfan. In a sudden, sodden avalanche of coal slag that crushed fifteen houses and a school, the women and children of Aberfan became the victims.

For days, heavy rains had drenched Aberfan's "slag tip," one of the stygian black mountains of underground rubble that loom high above Welch mining towns like spiritless cathedrals of the industrial age. Early last Friday morning, loosened by the downpour, half the hill split off into a 2 million-ton torrent of coal, rock and mud that cascaded half a mile down the valley toward Aberfan.

At Pantglas Junior School, the children had just arrived, said morning prayers, and were about to start a class. "We heard a noise," recalled 10-year-old Dilys Powell, "and the whole room seemed to be flying around. Desks were falling over and the children screamed. The children were lying all over the place. The teacher was on the floor. His leg was caught but he managed to free himself and smashed the door window with a stone. He got some of the children out and told them to go home."

Desperate Effort: Some did escape, but an estimated 220 people, the vast majority children aged 7 to 11, were trapped in the buried school and houses nearby. Desperate mothers rushed to the scene and, joined by more than 1,000 miners, began a massive rescue effort in the weltering mire. With both bulldozers and bleeding fingers, they tore at the wet debris, except when calls of "silence!" halted the work so that rescuers could listen for a possible cry of life.[52]

The *progressive-diffuse disaster* is one that lasts for a prolonged period of time, such as a flood or a forest fire. Homes are gradually threatened; people are dislocated. No immediate remedy is in sight. In May of 1973, the Missouri and Mississippi rivers overflowed their tributaries, submerging some 11 million acres in eight states. Within a week some thirty thousand people had been removed from their homes, twenty-one people had died, and some $200 million worth of damage had been done.[53] As the damage toll kept rising, Clarence Viceroy, chief hydrologist for the National Weather Service's River Forecast Center, told *Newsweek,* "I keep giving the forecast and all I can say is 'continued rise.' The volume is coming and there's nothing anyone can do about it except the good Lord—and He's lettin' it come."[54]

The *progressive-focalized disaster* is one of limited duration and is confined to shipwrecks or a crippled airliner. The standard example, of course, is the sinking of the *S.S. Titanic.* In 1912 the luxury liner *Titanic* sailed from England with twenty-two hundred passengers and crew. The liner struck an iceberg and gradually sank. In a matter of hours, fifteen hundred people perished either from the original impact—insufficient lifeboats were provided—or in the water.[55] The nature of the disaster greatly effects the emotional responses to be found among its victims.

The two kinds of *instantaneous* disaster generally occur without warning and take a tremendous toll. Students of disaster are not in total agreement on the value of forewarning; however, some studies have shown that "complete warning of an impending disaster may be actually harmful."[56] C. E. Fitz and E. S. Marks found that deaths and injuries were *higher* for groups that had some forewarning than for those communities with either no warning or a great deal of warning. Of course, those with a good deal of time to prepare for a flood or a tornado remained safer that those with little warning. But surprisingly those with *no* awareness of the impending disaster *did better* that those with a brief forewarning. In a disaster situation a little knowledge is a dangerous thing. Limited information may cause people to behave irrationally or to panic.

On the other hand, the two types of *progressive* disaster do allow for some preparation. Men fight floods with sandbags. A sinking ship may provide time to flee to life boats if they are available or send out an SOS message. Other resources may be mobilized to save life and limb. The possibility of panic under these conditions is relatively diminished. Therefore, emotional disturbance is somewhat controlled.

Emotional disturbance is usually caused by two conditions. The separation from loved ones and friends is one cause. The other cause of emotional disturbance is the traumatic effect of seeing a large number of dead and mangled bodies.

Separation from one's family and friends causes worry and concern. Fathers and mothers worry about the well-being of their children. Frightened children seek out their parents. This dislocation only heightens the disruption of the disaster itself. In all types of disasters, separation is possible. The chances, of course, are greatest under *instantaneous* conditions. Children and parents may be apart because of work and school schedules. Consequently, the time of day the disaster occurs becomes important. A tornado that strikes in the evening, when the family are home from the day's activities is not as apt to provoke anxiety about the safety of loved ones. Conversely, should a tornado occur during the morning hours, the chances of separation are greater.

The *focal* disaster also often occurs when the family is apart. Many tragedies have happened when children were in school, as in Aberfan, Wales, or fathers were trapped in gas-filled coal mines. The emotional anxiety in this case, however, is less than in the instantaneous disaster, as the observers are not threatened by the same danger.

Concerning the reaction to visible casualities, C. E. Fritz and E. S. Marks reported: "For most of the disasters studied, the number of respondents who had some direct experience of the dead was small. There is evidence, however, that such experiences were profoundly disturbing and that disturbance increased with the degree of exposure."[57] The presence of the dead both underlines the danger of the situation and poses new threats. *Newsweek,* reporting on an earthquake, observed: "The stench of decomposing corpses made breathing almost unbearable and, with rising fears of epidemic, perfunctory burials in common graves became the rule."[58] The *instantaneous* total disaster usually has more apparent casualities, although the caved-in coal mine or the crushed schoolhouse can be shielded from the general community or at least be put temporarily out of mind.

The sight and odor of death underline for those trapped in the disaster area the magnitude and danger of their situation. There is often the problem of *survival* in the aftermath of a disaster. The danger of famine or plague is great after an earthquake or flood. The *instantaneous total* disaster is the most likely to breed this problem. In both *progressive* and *focal* disasters, the threat to survival may not be as great. Help may be available from those not caught in the disaster areas.

Air crashes and shipwrecks can on occasion pose a threat to survival as dire as that of a tornado, earthquake, or flood. Survival in isolated areas, in life boats, or in a hot, steaming jungle can be extremely hazardous. Under these stress conditions very extreme actions may take place.

On October 13, 1972, a Uruguayan Air Force plane crashed, killing twenty-nine persons. Sixteen survivors were trapped for sixty-nine days in mountain temperatures as low as nine degrees below zero. After being rescued, they revealed how they managed to stay alive. They were forced to resort to cannibalism, as had the trapped Donner Party in 1864. *Newsweek* reported:

> Reluctantly and painfully, the survivors themselves confirmed the story. Canessa, a medical student, had convinced them that they all faced certain death if they rejected the only conceivable source of protein. "It was like a heart transplant," explained one survivor, observing that it was acceptable to take the heart of a dead person to keep another alive. And in Rome, a prominent Catholic theologian defended the eating of human corpses when it is necessary for survival. "From a theological and ethical point of view," wrote the Reverend Gino Concetti in the Vatican newspaper L'Observatore Romano, "the action cannot be branded as cannibalism."
>
> "It was done, and so be it," one of the survivors, 19-year-old Antonio Vizinting, told *Newsweek's* John Sherman. "I don't think I have anything to regret and I don't think it was something evil. I think we used something without movement, without life, something completely material, with which 16 human beings can continue to live, perhaps aid their fellow men, and know what paths God has prepared for them. . . .
>
> "I don't think I'll suffer a trauma or anything of the sort. I'll remember this with a great deal of affection and love toward all those beings or persons who died, because thanks to them I am alive at this moment. . . . The subject must be approached as something elevated, as a sort of communion. We were entering into communion with a human body. Instead of doing it with the body of Christ, we were doing it with the body of a comrade in order to prevail."
>
> Vizinting, a law student, wondered whether the actions of the survivors would be viewed with sympathy back home in Uruguay. "It must be remembered that we're not cannibals or brutal about this," he says. "That would hurt me, if people were to think that, if the press were to say we acted like animals. We were completely conscious of what we were doing, in full possession of our faculties. We never lost our rationality to environment." Vizinting paused thoughtfully, then said: "We never turned into animals devouring another being or grabbed a piece of leg. We always did it with respect in little bits."[59]

In "less" desperate situations, in which at least the hope of rescue and aid are present, similar feelings may be expressed. A Managuan victim said, "We turn into animals when we get so hungry."[60] However, the possibility of rescue and aid can find victims engaging in extra survival activities. For example, looting is a prevalent activity following any disaster. In Managua, scavengers were sighted stealing appliances and other valuable items *rather than food.* Profiteers also are frequently found in these disasters. In one Lake Erie flood, dump truck operators, who once asked permission to dump a load of dirt and rock off local boat docks, began to charge $25 a load, and there were reports that land speculators were using emergency loans from the Small Business Administration to buy up threatened property at bargain rates.

In light of these *new* threats many residents choose to remain in the danger area rather than flee. Those who remain or return attempt to rebuild their lives.

Responses to Disasters

Turner and Killian suggest that *five* general categories of people can be identified in disaster situations.[61]

During the crisis atmosphere of a disaster some people demand immediate action. "Do something," they exclaim. But, they have no clear-cut plan of action. These people are called the *committed.* Rue Bucher described the committed as those people who base their demand on the facts that they have decided are important in the situation. These facts frequently are incorrect.[62]

The *concerned* person has the same amount of interest as the *committed* person. But he does not feel the urge to do something for the sake of doing something. He may feel it appropriate to leave action to the legitimate authorities. He just goes along with group sentiment on what is to be done.

The difference between the *committed* and the *concerned* is partially determined by how people see the cause and the responsibility for the disaster. The concerned response is usual when blame is laid at the feet of government as has been the case when levees, dikes, and dams have collapsed. In the Aberfan, Wales incident the victims were very hostile to both the mining company and the British authorities. Interpretation greatly colors which classification the disaster victim chooses.

Turner and Killian call the third classification the *do-gooder,* who enjoys group participation regardless of the course of events. "They get certain gratifications out of participating in the collectivity itself."[63]

The next group of people are the *spectators.* The spectator is the thrill seeker who is drawn to disaster by his curiosity. He stands back and watches the effects of the disaster. The aid efforts, the misery, the television cameras all provide a magnet for disaster spectators.

The *exploiter* is the person who capitalizes on or makes personal gain from human tragedy. The looter is an obvious example. Bankers and businessmen and contractors can charge inordinate prices to rebuild a devastated community. Some politicians visit the stricken area more in search of votes than facts.

These five categories are found in varying degrees in any disaster.

The ability of these five groups to act in any disaster situation greatly depends upon the mood that prevails at the time of the mishap. This mood will greatly influence the response of the people directly affected. For example, a community already besieged by other problems inflicted from outside may well blame external forces for their problems. A community plagued with factional disputes may also be unwilling to pull together even in time of crisis. Mood, therefore, can be very important.

Disasters fall, according to Rue Bucher, into two types.[64] One kind of disaster is totally *unexpected.* The disaster should not have occurred according to the everyday rules of the game. Why does a train derail? An airliner crash? A mine cave in? These things should not happen, but they do.

On the other hand, many disasters are quite *predictable.* Californians live in the fear of earthquakes. People on the Florida coast know hurricanes pass through their state. In the inner regions of the United States tornadoes are always a threat. Residents along the banks of many rivers know a flood is always a possibility. The expectations of disaster victims are very important as both their immediate and their long-range response depends on their expectations.

Fixing the blame for a disaster is important to people. An act of God is painful but imponderable. Nothing could have prevented it. When a disaster can be attributed to man, the reactions are different. A positive reaction may be "They did all they could." There is another, more bitter form of reaction when the disaster is believed to have been caused by man's negligence or lack of concern. A fire starts because someone has not done his job. A building collapses because of faulty construction due to political graft. A plane crashes because of government economic cutbacks. A dam gives way because of improper safety standards. Under these conditions the cause of the disaster produces hatred and action against those believed responsible. In such situations the community is quickly united in a common hatred of the villain of the disaster.[65] Mine owners, airline executives, politicians, and public safety officials have frequently found themselves as the accused in many disaster situations. However, the return to normality may be slowed because of legal and political conflict. For example, after the floods in 1972, much of the rebuilding of the Wilkes-Barre area in Pennsylvania was hampered because of local opposition and antagonism to federal efforts in the area. Many residents felt the U.S. Army Corp of Engineers was responsible for the original flooding of the region because of a faulty dam. Similar reactions have been described in rebuilding efforts after earthquakes and after the inner-city riots of the 1960's.

Riots and Collective Behavior

Sociologists have always been fascinated by abnormal happenings like revolution, bizarre behavior, and riots. All of these disrupt the everyday workings of the world in which we live. They bring into question many of the things we take for granted. Gary Marx underlines this fact by defining a *riot* as "relatively spontaneous group violence contrary to traditional *norms.*"[66] A riot is a unique event, an extreme manifestation of disorder. The rules and values of society do not appear to apply. That is, it is totally *anomic:* riots are without rules. In studying civil disorders sociologists are concerned with two aspects of collective behavior: the phases of riots and the direction of riots.

Phases of Riots

Ralph Conant suggests that all riots go through four stages: the *precipitating incident,* the *confrontation,* the *Roman holiday,* and the *seige.*[67]

The *precipitating incident* is any act or event that comes to be seen as evidence of social injustice against a group. The precipitating event inflames a community and becomes the justification for a riot. A precipitating event usually occurs in a public place; an outrage committed out of public view and mind has little impact. Stanley Lieberson and Charles Silverman,[68] in studying race riots over a fifty-year span, identified the precipitating events shown in Table 13-4.

In the *confrontation,* the participants in the riot are incited to action, perhaps by people in the crowd who vocalize the injustice of the precipitating event, like an arrest, a rumored "outrage," and so on. A confrontation frequently occurs when carloads of police arrive and attempt to "clear the area" by dispersing the crowd who have witnessed the precipitating event. Most reports dealing with the 1965 Watts riots indicate that the sidewalk confrontation between police and bystanders inflamed the crowd. Further police tactics only made the situation worse. An observer recalled, "About every three minutes a foray of police automobiles rushed into the center of Imperial and Avalon with sirens screaming and with red lights flashing (which incidentally called everybody else in the community out on the street)."[69] The inability of the police to control the rioting only allowed it to spread, and indeed police roadblocks both drew attention to the situation and inflamed more of the residents.

The *Roman holiday* occurs when the police have temporarily lost control of the situation. In this phase crowds and gangs roam the streets, looting at will and engaging in sporadic clashes with the police. During this phase attempts may be made to organize the crowd into workable political units. This is the twilight zone of the riot. The streets become a war of each against all.

The last phase is the *siege.* The siege is open warfare between the rioters

Table 13-4. Causes of Racial Riots, 1913–63

Cause	*Number of Riots*
Rape, murder, attack, or holdup of white women by Negro men	10
Killing, arrest, interference, assault, or search of Negro men by white policemen	15
Interracial murder or shooting	11
Interracial fight	16
Civil liberties, public facilities, segregation, political events, and housing	14
Negro strikebreaking, upgrading, or other job-based conflicts	5
Desecration of an American flag by Negroes	1
No information available	4
TOTAL	76

Source: S. Lieberman and A. Silverman, "Precipitants and Conditions of Race Riots," *American Sociological Review,* **30:** (1965), 887–898.

and the civil authorities. At this point police are augmented by the National Guard or other military forces. Looters have usually withdrawn with their booty, leaving the rooftops to snipers and the streets to semimilitary political action. This phase is critical for the civil authorities, as they must win in order to prevent the riot from becoming a revolution or a civil war. In France, for example, riots did in fact escalate into the French Revolution. In the United States riots have been contained and quelled in time.

Direction of Riots

These four phases of riots contain within them the two types of riots most frequently identified in the sociological literature. Richard LaPiere introduced two directional forms that riots are apt to take. One type is the *uncoordinated* and the other the *coordinated.*[70]

The *uncoordinated* riot is without direction or purpose (such as social protest). It takes on the air of unsystematic destruction. The rioters are like a mindless herd or a tornado raging in the streets. The crowd, as Sigmund Freud and Gustav LeBon indicated, has a mind of its own, and the individual loses his inhibitions and gives himself over to the impulses of the mob. Although most sociologists reject the "herd" notion of riots, there is evidence that some activities of riot participants, like looting and pilfering, do fit this classification. For example, the mob that ruled the streets of Boston during the three-day 1919 riots was motivated by no real social issue.

A more popular concept is what LaPiere termed the *coordinated riot. A coordinated riot is one with direction and goals.* The storming of the Bastille, a lynching, the burning of a ghetto, all appear to have a sense of purpose.

The coordinated riot is not a mindless, senseless outburst. It is caused by what are real conditions for the rioters, and the violence is directed toward these conditions. Allen Grimshaw observed, "Social violence is assault upon an individual or his property solely or primarily because of membership in a social category."[71] Lynchings, race riots, and political riots all fit into this category.

A. I. Waskow described a racial attack by one group on another as a *pogrom.*[72] A classic example of a *pogrom* was the New York draft riots of 1863, in which rampaging whites killed hundreds of Negroes. The whites were objecting to the Civil War: "Why be drafted, perhaps killed, to free Negroes while northern blacks stay at home?"

A *race riot,* on the other hand, is not one-sided. Both sides use violence, with casualties occurring on both sides. As Waskow suggested, the famous 1919 Chicago riot was an "ideal" example. On a hot July night, a false rumor spread through the inner city that a Negro had been drowned by a white. The police, the story went, had done nothing. As the rumor circulated, some blacks attacked some whites. The extent of these attacks was grossly exaggerated. As a result, gangs of white youth prowled the Chicago streets in search of blacks, and a race riot went into full swing. Twenty-three blacks and fifteen whites were killed in the thirteen-day riot.

A pogrom and a race riot are both purposeful and directed. They have goals. Consequently, it is important to remember that riots are usually not just mindless mobs roaming the streets, indiscriminately striking out at the first thing that moves.

The degree of purpose and direction in rioting is difficult to assess. Gustav LeBon wrote, "Crowds, doubtless, are always unconscious."[73] As we have said, most sociologists no longer accept this mindless, herdlike portrait of crowds and rioters. Instead, a rationality has been accorded collective violence. Robert M. Fogelson, for one, wrote, "The 1960's riots were *articulate protests* against genuine grievances in the black ghettos."[74] However, only the direction of the crowd in riot can be seen; the individual motivations can only be guessed at. Why do people riot? George Rude indicated, "The crowd may riot because it is hungry or fears to be so, because it has some deep social grievance, because it seeks an immediate reform to the millenium, or because it wants to destroy an enemy or acclaim a 'hero'; but it is seldom for any single one of these reasons alone."[75] Consider the following example. During the 1965 Watts riot, a woman was passing an appliance store that had sold her a television five years before. She still owed money for the set. "That store owes me five televisions," she said, "so I got three and they owe me two."[76] This woman became a looter and a rioter. But what was her motivation? Greed, protest, or the opportunity of the moment or all three?

Explanations of Riots

The first popular explanation of rioting is called the *riffraff theory,* which sees riots as caused by small bands of rowdies and hoodlums. This theory has three related elements. First, a small percentage of the population is presented as participating in the riot. In the urban riots of the 1960's reportedly only 2 percent of the community was supposedly engaged in the disorders. The rioters are presented as not being representative in the community. They are "school dropouts, young punks, common hoodlums, and drunken kids and outside agitators."[77] Second, outside agitators, usually political radicals, are seen as leading ragtag mobs for their own seditious purposes. Third, this theory asserts that 98 to 99 percent of the black population was against the use of violence and supported the civil government.

These three elements of the riffraff theory are quite popular with journalists and politicians. However, data gathered by David O. Sears and Jefferey Paige contradicted much of this theory. They reported that 10 to 20 percent of the ghetto community were involved in the riots, that the rioters were representative of the community, and that a large portion of the black community sympathized with, if they did not support, the rioters. Thirty-four percent of the blacks in Los Angeles believed that the riots helped their cause.[78] Sears and T. M. Thomlinson found that 38 percent of the residents viewed riots as revolts or revolutions; 64 percent approved the targets of the rioters; and 62 percent saw the disorders as black protests.[79]

The refutation of the riffraff theory, which comfortably blamed riots upon social deviants, caused sociologists to look for a more convenient and compatible explanation. Fogelson presented riots as fundamentally purposive and directional. In his view, riots are caused by exploitive social conditions. James A. Geschwender and others have reached similar conclusions. These conclusions basically repeat Fogelson's statement that "riots were protests because they were attempts to call the attention of white society to the blacks' widespread dissatisfaction with racial subordination and segregation."[80]

Studies of the precipitating events that spark riots seem to support La Piere's coordinated theory of riots. Lieberson and Silverman observe that social conditions create an atmosphere in which a dramatic event, like murder, assault, or police brutality, will spark a riot.[81]

Leonard Berkowitz added to this the frustration-aggression thesis. Blacks, for example, are frustrated by discriminatory treatment and other adverse social conditions. The resulting aggression, in the form of collective violence or rioting, is thus the outgrowth of social conditions.[82] Berkowitz felt that rising expectations create a riot potential. As aspirations rise, any blockage can create gross disappointment, which will trigger a riot.

What, we may ask, are the social conditions that give birth to race riots? Economics, housing conditions, the size of the city, and the personality traits of ghetto dwellers have all been picked as causal variables at one time or another. Recent studies seem to indicate that no one factor or even one series of factors is adequate to explain racial riots. Sheryl Moinat and her associates examined *eighty* variables allegedly associated with black ghetto riots and concluded, "A new theory of riot participation is needed. The typical rioter profile and the riffraff theory of riot participation are seen as myth. A third view of riot participation, the 'sociological' rioter theory, is incomplete."[83] Another sociologist, Clark McPhail, observed, "Civil disorders are complex and differentiated phenomena. Attempts to account for their occurrence and individual participation therein have failed to acknowledge this complexity, theoretically and operationally."[84] Certainly social conditions are important; however, only in the most general sense can sociologists observe that "X seems to give birth to riots." Understanding the social causes of riots is a very complicated business.

Riots are not always highminded political exercises motivated solely by the squalor of slums or by economic deprivations. Some individual greed and criminal activity have been part and parcel of some riots. Richard A. Berk and Howard E. Aldrich found that in riot areas the attractiveness of merchandise has a great deal to do with looting. Riot participants find appliance, clothing, and liquor stores more attractive than plumbing shops. They reported, "Stores carrying more expensive merchandise appear to be more popular targets. If one assumes that the price of merchandise affects its desirability, the attractive merchandise motivation gains credibility. This strongly implies that vandals could be acting in part for personal gain, though the reader should not automatically assume it. Possibly more expensive items like television sets are perceived as important symbols of white society, or possibly an effective retaliation against merchants by theft of valuable merchandise."[85]

Gary Marx added another aspect by recalling LaPiere's notion of the uncoordinated riot. Marx suggested that some riots may in fact be free of social protest or issues. Rather, they may well have motives beyond the protest theory.[86]

Riots are the ultimate form of collective behavior, and they bring into play many of the concepts we have already discussed. Rumors run rampant during riots. Panic reigns in the streets. Emotional contagion sweeps over participants.

Summary

Collective behavior results from some breakdown or disorganization of social life. It takes numerous forms. Man-made events such as war, riots, and crazes are included in the concept of collective behavior. Group reactions to natural phenomena such as plagues, tornados, floods, earthquakes also come under this heading. Collective behavior, then, is any unusual activity generally not anticipated in everyday social life. Sociologists study collective behavior in hopes of finding common patterns running through the seemingly irrational, inconsistent behavior of certain types of aggregations of people.

Notes

1. J. B. Perry, Jr., and M. D. Pugh, *Collective Response to Social Stress* (in progress). This is a more or less accurate description of the approach traditionally taken to the study of collective behavior. Weller and Quarantelli argue that the differences between everyday, "institutionalized" behavior and "collective behavior" have been greatly exaggerated and call for more studies of the social aspects of collective behavior and less emphasis on characteristics of individual participants. See J. M. Weller and E. L. Quarantelli, "Neglected Characteristics of Collective Behavior," *American Journal of Sociology,* **79** (1973), pp. 665–685. See also C. Couch, "Collective Behavior: An Examination of Some Stereotypes," *Social Problems,* **15** (1968), pp. 310–322.

2. R. E. Park and E. W. Burgess, *Introduction to the Science of Sociology* (Chicago: University of Chicago Press, 1921), p. 790.

3. G. Lebon, *The Crowd: A Study of the Popular Mind* (New York: The Viking Press, Inc., 1960), p. 38.

4. O. E. Klapp, *Currents of Unrest: An Introduction to Collective Behavior* (New York: Holt, Rinehart & Winston, Inc., 1972), pp. 19–35.

5. R. H. Turner and L. M. Killian, *Collective Behavior,* 2nd Ed. (Englewood Cliffs, N.J.: Prentice-Hall, Inc., 1972), p. 5.

6. H. Blumer, "Collective Behavior," in A. M. Lee, ed., *Principles of Sociology,* 3rd Ed. (New York: Barnes & Noble, Inc., 1969), p. 77.

7. L. Wheeler, "Toward a Theory of Behavioral Contagion," *Psychological Review,* **73** (1966), pp. 179–192.

8. Park and Burgess, op. cit., p. 893.

9. This discussion is based upon Klapp, op cit., pp. 49–65; Blumer, op cit.; and K. Lang and G. E. Lang, *Collective Dynamics* (New York: Thomas Y. Crowell Company, 1961), pp. 118–121.

10. A. M. Rosenthal, *Thirty-Eight Witnesses* (New York: McGraw-Hill Book Company, 1964). For an opposite reaction, see R. A. McFadden, "3 Residents Seize 2 Men in Mugging," *New York Times* (June 17, 1973), 31.

11. Blumer, op. cit., p. 83.

12. H. Cantril, *The Psychology of Social Movements* (New York: John Wiley & Sons, Inc., 1963), pp. 94–95.

13. Blumer, op. cit., p. 83.

14. Quoted in D. Heckman, "Rock Festivals on Upbeat Again," *New York Times* (August 11, 1972), p. 12.

15. P. Williams, "Getting Together," Atlantic Records press release. For a discussion, see R. A. Peterson, "The Unnatural History of Rock Festivals: An Instance of Media Facilitation." *Popular Music and Society,* **2** (1973), pp. 97–123.

16. Blumer, op. cit., p. 86.

17. D. Bell, *The End of Ideology,* Rev. Ed. (New York: The Free Press, 1962), p. 26.

18. H. Gans, "Popular Culture in America: Social Problem in a Mass Society or Social Asset in a Pluralistic Society?" in H. Becker, ed., *Social Problems: A Modern Approach* (New York: John Wiley & Sons, Inc., 1966), pp. 550–569.

19. Turner and Killian, op. cit., pp. 179–180.

20. Blumer, op. cit., p. 89.

21. Turner and Killian, op. cit., p. 180.

22. G. R. Funkhauser, "The Issues of the Sixties: An Exploratory Study in the Dynamics of Public Opinion," *Public Opinion Quarterly,* **27** (Spring 1973), pp. 62–75.

23. W. C. Crain, "Young Activists' Conceptions of an Ideal Society: Ideological Dimensions and Developmental Considerations." *Youth and Society,* **4** (December 1972). pp. 203–235.

24. Quoted in H. Erskine, "The Polls: Pacifism and the Generation Gap," *Public Opinion Quarterly,* **36** (1973), p. 264.

25. N. Foote and C. Hart, "Public Opinion and Collective Behavior," in M. Sherif and M. O. Wilson, eds., *Group Relations at the Crossroads* (New York: Harper and Row, Publishers, 1952), pp. 308–331.

26. H. Cantril, "Public Opinion in Flux," *Annals,* **220** (1942), pp. 136–150.

27. T. Shibutani, *Improvised News: A Sociological Study of Rumor* (Indianapolis: The Bobbs-Merrill Co., Inc., 1966), p. 17.

28. D. Walker, *Rights in Conflict: The Violent Confrontation of Demonstrators and Police in the Parks and Streets of Chicago During the Week of the Democratic National Convention of 1968* (Washington, D.C.: U.S. Government Printing Office, 1968) pp. 85–86.

29. A. Oberschall, "The Los Angeles Riot of August, 1965," *Social Problems,* **15** (Winter 1968), pp. 322–341.

30. M. Gunther, "The Great Sex Movie Scandal That Never Was," *TV Guide* (July 28, 1973), p. 7.

31. Ibid., p. 8.

32. T. Caplow, "Rumors in War," *Social Forces,* **25** (1946–47), pp. 298–302.

33. G. Allport and L. Postman, *The Psychology of Rumor* (New York: Henry Holt & Co., Inc., 1947).

34. W. A. Peterson and N. P. Gist, "Rumor and Public Opinion," *American Journal of Sociology,* **57** (1951), pp. 159–167. Also see Caplow, op. cit., p. 302.

35. "One and One and One Is Three?" *Rolling Stone,* **46** (November 15, 1969), p. 6. Also see K. G. Sheinkopf and M. R. Weintz, "The Beatles are Dead! Long Live the Beatles," *Popular Music and Society,* **2** (1973), pp. 321–326.

36. H. T. Buckner, "A Theory of Rumor Transmission," *Public Opinion Quarterly,* **29** (1965), pp. 54–70.
37. H. Cantril, *The Invasion from Mars: A Study in the Psychology of Panic* (Princeton, N.J.: Princeton University Press, 1940).
38. L. Festinger, H. Riecken, and S. Schachter, *When Prophecy Fails* (Minneapolis: University of Minnesota Press, 1959), p. 220; and J. Lofland, *The Doomsday Cult* (Englewood Cliffs, N.J.: Prentice-Hall, Inc., 1966).
39. S. Anthony, "Anxiety and Rumor," *Journal of Social Psychology,* **89** (1973), pp. 91–98.
40. T. Higham, "The Experimental Study of the Transmission of Rumor," *British Journal of Psychology,* **42** (1951), pp. 42–55.
41. Cantril, *Invasion,* op. cit., p. 159.
42. D. P. Schultz, *Panic Behavior: Discussion and Readings* (New York: Random House, Inc., 1964), p. 8.
43. Lang and Lang, op. cit., p. 83.
44. E. Foy and A. F. Harlow, *Clowning Through Life* (New York: E. P. Dutton & Co., Inc., 1928), pp. 104–113.
45. T. Walton, "Disasters Are OSU Center's Reason for Existence," *Toledo Blade* (March 4, 1973), p. 6.
46. E. L. Quarantelli, "The Nature and Conditions of Panic," *American Journal of Sociology,* **60** (1954), pp. 267–275.
47. Schultz, op. cit., p. 54.
48. A. Mintz, "Non-Adaptive Group Behavior," *Journal of Abnormal and Social Psychology,* **46** (1951), pp. 150–159.
49. A. H. Barton, *Communities in Disaster: A Sociological Analysis of Collective Stress Situations* (Garden City, N.Y.: Anchor Books, 1970).
50. L. J. Carr, "Disaster and the Sequence-Pattern Concept of Social Change," *American Journal of Sociology,* **38** (1932–1933), pp. 209–210).
51. "The Managua Earthquake: How a City Died," *Newsweek* (January 8, 1973), pp. 28–29.
52. "Never One Like This," *Newsweek* (October 31, 1964), p. 54. For a follow-up see T. Coleman. "Aberfan Disaster: 'Happiness Ended Last October,'" *Saturday Evening Post* (October 21, 1967), pp. 91–95.
53. "Ol' Man River Just Keeps Rising," *Newsweek* (May 7, 1973), p. 38.
54. "Floods: 'Sandbags and Sympathy,'" *Newsweek* (April 30, 1973), p. 27.
55. See W. Lord, *A Night To Remember* (New York: Holt, Rinehart & Winston, Inc., 1955).
56. C. E. Fritz and E. S. Marks, "The NORC Studies of Human Behavior in Disaster," *Journal of Social Issues,* **10** (1954), pp. 26–41. Compare "The Tornado Trackers," *Newsweek* (April 16, 1973), p. 55.
57. Ibid.
58. "Chile: Deliverance," *Newsweek* (January 8, 1973), p. 27. Also see Piers Paul Read, *Alive: The Story of the Andes Survivors* (New York: J. B. Lippincott Co., 1974).
59. "The Managua Earthquake," op. cit., p. 28.
60. Ibid.
61. Turner and Killian, op. cit., p. 27–29.
62. R. Bucher, "Blame and Hostility in Disaster," *American Journal of Sociology,* **62** (1957), pp. 468–475.
63. Turner and Killian, op. cit., p. 28.
64. Bucher, op. cit.
65. See L. Coser, *The Functions of Social Conflict* (New York: The Free Press, 1957).
66. G. T. Marx, "Issueless Riots," in J. F. Short, Jr., and M. E. Wolfgang, eds., *Collective Violence* (Chicago: Aldine Publishing Company, 1972). pp. 47–59.
67. R. W. Conant, "The Phases of a Riot," in R. H. Turner and L. M. Killian, eds., *Collective Behavior,* 2nd Ed. (Englewood Cliffs, N.J.: Prentice-Hall, Inc., 1972), pp. 108–110.

68. S. Lieberson and A. Silverman, "Precipitants and Conditions of Race Riots," *American Sociological Review,* **30** (1965), pp. 887–898.

69. J. A. Buggs, "Report from Los Angeles," in R. R. Evans, ed., *Readings in Collective Behavior* (Chicago: Rand McNally & Co., 1969), p. 495.

70. R. T. LaPiere, *Collective Behavior* (New York: McGraw-Hill Book Company, 1938), pp. 529–542.

71. A. D. Grimshaw, "Interpreting Collective Violence: An Argument for the Importance of Social Structure," in Short and Wolfgang, op. cit., pp. 36–46.

72. A. I. Waskow, *From Race Riot to Sit-In* (Garden City, N.Y.: Doubleday Anchor Books. 1966), p. 9.

73. LeBon, op. cit., p. 7.

74. R. M. Fogelson, *Violence as Protest: A Study of Riots and Ghettos* (Garden City, N.Y.: Doubleday & Company, Inc., 1971), p. 22.

75. G. Rude, *The Crowd in History, 1730–1848* (New York: Oxford University Press, 1964), p. 217.

76. Fogelson, op. cit., p. 91.

77. "FBI Riot Report—Reds Not to Blame," *San Francisco Chronicle* (September 27, 1964), p. 1.

78. R. M. Fogelson and R. B. Hill, *Who Riots: A Study of Participation in the 1967 Riots* (New York: Bureau of Applied Social Research, Columbia University, 1968), p. 242.

79. D. O. Sears and T. M. Thomlinson, "Riot Ideology in Los Angeles: A Study of Negro Attitudes," *Social Science Quarterly,* **49** (1968), pp. 485–503.

80. Fogelson, op cit., p. 22. See especially J. A. Geschwender, ed., *The Black Revolt: The Civil Rights Movement, Ghetto Uprisings, and Separatism* (Englewood Cliffs, N.J.: Prentice-Hall, Inc., 1971).

81. S. Lieberson and A. Silverman, op. cit., pp. 887–898.

82. L. Berkowitz, "The Study of Urban Violence: Some Implications of Laboratory Studies of Frustration and Aggression," *American Behavioral Scientist,* **11** (1968), pp. 14–17.

83. S. Moinat, W. Raine, S. Burbeck, and K. Davison, "Black Ghetto Residents as Rioters," *Journal of Social Issues,* **28** (1972), p. 60.

84. C. McPhail, "Civil Disorder Participation: A Critical Examination of Recent Research," *American Sociological Review,* **36** (1971), p. 1070.

85. R. A. Berk and H. E. Aldrich, "Patterns of Vandalism During Civil Disorders as an Indicator of Selection of Targets," *American Sociological Review,* **37** (1972), p. 541.

86. Marx, op. cit., pp. 48–59.

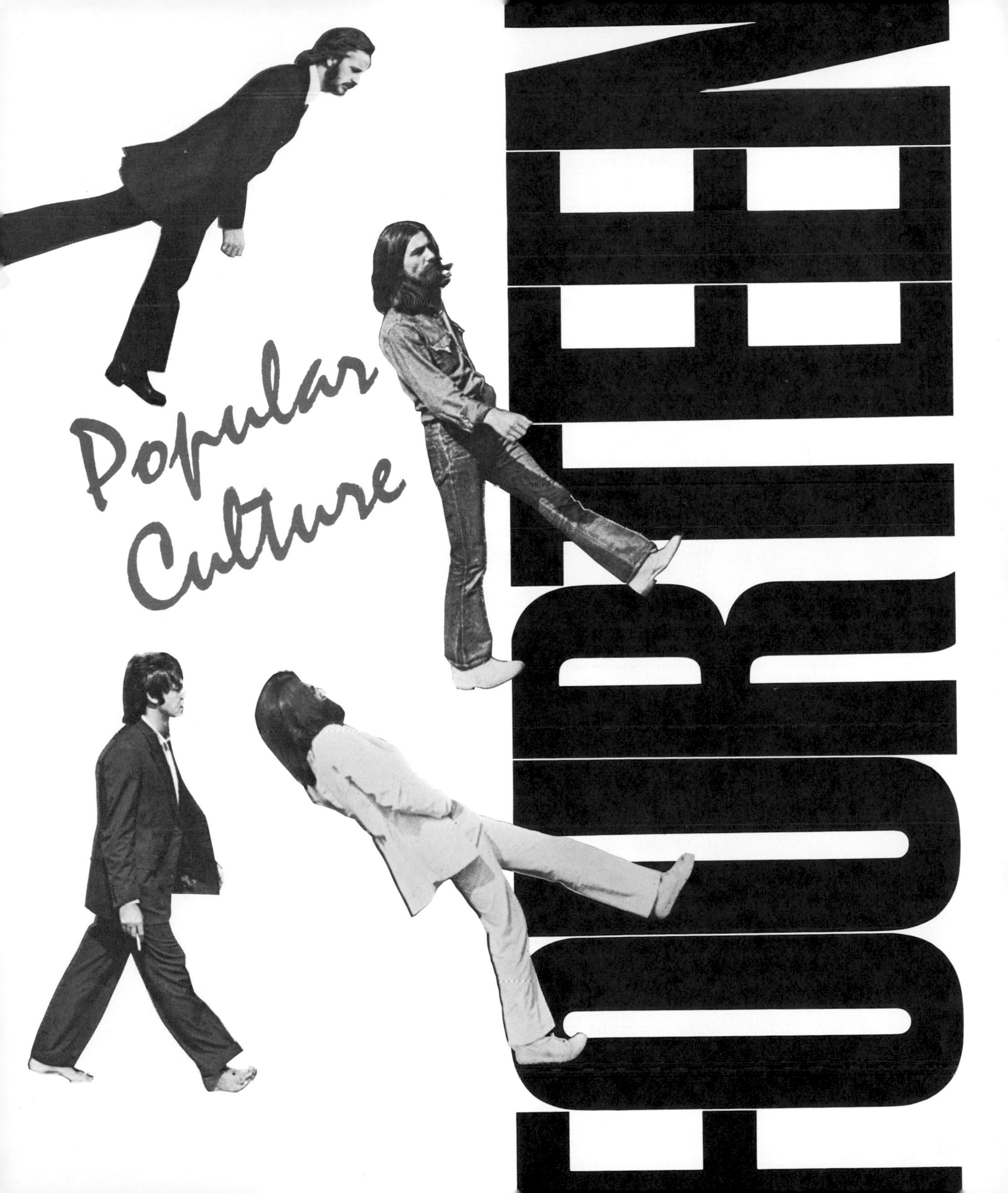
FOURTEEN
Popular Culture

What Is Popular Culture?

"POPULAR CULTURE," philosopher George Santayana once said, "is really what people do when they are not working." Popular culture activities make up the largest portion of what people do when they're free from trying to earn their daily bread. The average man, woman, and child spend six hours daily in front of a television set. Adolescents and young adults spend around four hours a day listening to the radio or to phonograph records. Americans spend $45 million a year at the movies. The amount of time alone that people spend on popular culture indicates that it is quite an important aspect of American life.

The average American voluntarily devotes his time to popular culture, whereas his enthusiasm for and commitment to work, politics, religion, and other activities may be pretty slight. Most people go to work, for example, only because they have to, but they support pop culture because of choice and in some cases habit. They may choose to watch television, see a movie, listen to the radio or a stereo set, or read a novel. On weekends, they may travel to fairs, festivals, or concerts or attend an athletic event.

By studying popular culture sociologists can begin to look at social behavior apart from the business of human housekeeping. As we have seen, economics, politics, and many other activities are directed at the maintenance of social life. These are things that need to be done. Food must be purchased, the rent must be paid, and some kind of regulation of all of these activities is necessary. But once these needs have been satisfied, people can "relax" and seemingly "do what they want to." This voluntary aspect is what makes popular culture important to the sociologist.

Popular culture is the entertainment subdivision of culture (see Chapter Four, "Culture"). People frequently confuse the two terms. *Popular culture consists of the typical ways in which people spend their time when not working.*[1] *This includes all forms of entertainment in sound, sight, and the printed word.* Some forms of leisure are not included in this category. Taking a nap on Saturday afternoon, for example, does not fall under the definition of popular culture. Sitting around listening to records, watching television, reading a book all *are* part of popular culture. Popular culture generally embraces all levels of society and is considered "folk," "popular," or the "pastimes of the masses."[2] Another way of saying this is that popular culture is entertainment not supported by the intellectual, economic, or political elite of any society. It is not "high brow" or "fine art." Instead, popular culture is all the entertainment that is left after one subtracts fine painting, opera, and the other forms of entertainment available to only a handful of wealthy and highly educated people.

The lack of coercion in popular culture makes it an interesting topic for sociologists, not only because it is a laboratory of what people do in their free time but also because it appears to lack any long-standing pattern. Remember, sociologists are dedicated to finding patterns in social living. They attempt to find order in chaos. In popular culture the consistent lack of uniformity is itself a pattern. Change, both expected and unexpected, is the rule rather than the exception in popular culture.

The major characteristic of popular culture, then, is its *lack of uniformity.* Popular culture is entertainment that people support in any particular moment. There is *no* consistent style or form that makes up popular culture.

Popular films in the 1930s stressed musicals; in the 1950s westerns such as *Shane* and *High Noon* were the top hits. In the 1960s movies like *Easy Rider* and *M*A*S*H* received the most attention; black detectives and Ku Fung experts took over in the early 1970s.

In popular music there is *no one* musical style that *is* popular music. Even when swing artists Glenn Miller, Benny Goodman, and Frank Sinatra were the most popular musicians, other styles managed to sneak onto the hit parade and the best-seller lists. Similarly, during the height of the popularity of the Beatles and the Rolling Stones, artists with totally different styles were also on the *Billboard* "Hot One Hundred," a list of the most played 45s.

Popular music is *many* things for *many* people. For a younger sister it is usually a "teen-scream" idol whom she will outgrow. For many blacks, popular music is "soul." For college students it may be the latest jazz-rock band or a guitar-picking writer of songs like Bob Dylan, James Taylor, or Cat Stevens.

Popular culture is immediate. It has no tradition. It can be an overnight sensation or a lasting style that ebbs and flows over several decades. The hula hoop enjoyed its place in the popular-culture sun for several months, whereas swing and rock music held on for more than twenty years.

Popular culture does not require pretraining or preparation. People do not take a class in Television 1A or Introduction to Rock in order to appreciate "Mannix," Lucille Ball, the Beatles, or the Rolling Stones. Unlike "classical" music, painting, or movies, no training in appreciation is needed. Popular culture is generally free of all the background we associate with "high culture." Unlike opera or first-night openings on Broadway, you don't have to get dressed up to enjoy pop culture.

Popular culture exists because it has audiences *large enough to support it.* This audience may lend its support for a long or a short time. A song may be a hit for ten weeks and then become a "golden oldie." A book may be a best seller and a topic of conversation for three months and then disappear. A movie can be a smash for a year as it makes its way from the big cities to the country drive-ins. Popular culture events come in four basic forms: *crazes, fads, fashions,* and *trends.* These forms are distinguished by the amount of time they remain in the public eye. These terms are useful, as they allow us to distinguish overnight sensations from trends that may have real consequences for the state of popular culture and, indeed, the entire society. For example, the fact that a record of popcorn cooking becomes a hit has little meaning. The lasting popularity of Bob Dylan because of the content of his songs may have much greater social impact.

A *craze* is an event that is unexpected or bizarre. It is of fleeting interest. It appears overnight and vanishes almost as quickly; it usually lasts a few weeks to several months. The hula hoop, "streaking" (running in the nude), and swallowing gold fish are all examples of crazes. Crazes can have lasting conse-

Popular culture consists of the typical ways in which people spend their time when not working.

quences, as illustrated by the Florida land boom of the 1920s or the famous Holland tulip mania, during which the Dutch temporarily considered tulip bulbs as valuable as gold.

A *fad* is a passing phenomenon that involves a *large number* of people or at least a sizable proportion of some subcultural group. Fads last longer than crazes, remaining in vogue months and even years. Fads usually affect only a portion of the people. Fads in clothing styles, children's toys, and popular music appear regularly. The fleeting prominence of calypso music in the 1950s. the Davy Crockett coonskin cap, and the maxiskirt were all fads. They didn't last more than a few years and were supported only by easily identifiable groups in society. Fads are generally identified with young people and the popular culture media they support.

Fashions have many of the same characteristics as fads. Unlike fads, *fashions are a part of a continuous process.* Ralph Turner and Lewis Killian observed,

"Each style follows the preceding and replaces it with a continuity in the style changes themselves."[3] Popular music is a series of fashions. Rock-a-billy, black street-corner a cappella quartets, folksongs, the Liverpool sound of the early Beatles, folk rock, and acid rock represented changing fashions in music. Similar fashions are evident each new television season with westerns, situation comedies, or detective dramas dominating the format of a particular year. Fashions are familiar in the clothing and the automobile industries.

Fads and fashions occur in what we call *trends.* A trend is a long-term process that does not change quickly. One trend is the love theme in film, television, and recording. The love story is a continuing theme set in different situations and locations. Musical styles, movie formats, and book topics are also subject to trends. Rock-and-roll, which all but dominated the sphere of popular music from the mid-1950s to the present, is a trend.

Popular culture is made up of crazes, fads, fashions, and trends. Stages are determined by the public's fancy. They last as long as television viewers or record buyers support the craze, fad, fashion, or trend. *Time is an important element in popular culture.* Another is economic support.

Vox Populi: Let the People Speak

"It is the audience that finally determines what will be seen on stage; if playgoers desire trash, it will be supplied; if they want excellence, the theater will respond."[4] Don Everly of the singing duo said, "You can't shove something down someone's throat, because you believe it. . . . [The] audience is where you find what's good . . . somehow they know." Kenny Rogers of the First Edition agreed, "Rock bands reflect a great deal in kids. . . . The groups do what the kids want to hear. Like it or not."[5] People do *ultimately* determine what will be popular; however, the decisions about what they get to choose from are made by the various popular-culture *industries. Popular culture industries* are the corporations and businesses that serve popular culture tastes. They are the movie companies, the record producers, the book publishers, the play backers, and the many others that put money into the entertainment media. They determine what fare the audience will have to choose from. However, they rarely can predict *exactly* which record, show, or book will be a popular success. The measurement of popularity differs from one industry to another.

What constitutes popularity in the television industry and in other media is very different. Many television shows with a less than .20 Nielson rating have been canceled for "lack of audience support." A rating this size frequently means that over *10 million* people had been watching the show. The late-night Dick Cavett Show was cut back despite the program's 5 million viewers. Other entertainment media can only look with envy at the size of television audiences.

The record industry gives a gold record for every million dollars a single or tape or album earns. A "single," costing less than a dollar, must find more than a million customers. An album must attract 502,000 buyers. Tapes need fewer buyers because of their high cost. Just to break even, an album must sell at least 15,000 copies. The book publishing industry considers any book selling more than 10,000 copies a success. A Broadway play that returns an investment of $100,000 or can lure 20,000 customers is a success. The leap from television to the book publishing industry or the commercial stage shows that popularity is based upon profit. Success in each part of the popular culture industry is calculated by the *potential audience* and the *amount of product* released. Contrast the gigantic television industry with book publishing.

The size of the television audience in the United States is larger than the audience of any other medium. Indeed, more people own television sets than have indoor bathrooms, according to the 1970 census. Ninety-six percent of American homes have a television set. As a result, the potential audience is very large. The first moon walk reportedly attracted over 80 million viewers. The pro-football Super Bowl annually finds over 60 million Americans in front of their sets. A top-rated show commands the attention of some 40 million people.[6] Most studies of viewing habits indicate that nearly all Americans, regardless of social class and education, watch *some* television.[7]

Four television networks (the National Broadcasting Company, the Columbia Broadcasting System, the American Broadcasting Company, and the Public Broadcasting System), through 832 commercial and 167 educational stations, compete for the attention of this large reservoir of viewers. They do this with approximately eighteen hours of material each day. The most important time period is the "prime-time" period between 7:30 and 11:00 P.M. The audience is largest at this time; therefore, a program must have high ratings if it is to be renewed or to continue on the air.

Book publishers produce around twenty-eight thousand new books each year. Twenty-two thousand of these are new titles. Each title must compete for an estimated 11 percent of the nation's book-buying population. "A national survey found that book reading 'yesterday' was reported by only 5.8 percent of college educated respondents and by only 0.9 percent of those with less than a high school education."[8] The audience for books is limited and the competition is very stiff. Rarely do books do as well as Dr. Spock's baby care guides, *The Joy of Cooking, The Exorcist,* or the James Bond or Mike Hammer spy and private-eye thrillers.

Most popular culture media fall between these two extremes in audience and product size. Movies and magazines lean toward the television industry, whereas the record business is similar to book publishing.

The production of a television series, a Broadway play, a motion picture, or a slick magazine involves considerable cost. The investment behind one record or one book is much less than that required for a TV series, a Broadway show, or a movie, thus allowing greater diversity and volume. Many record and book companies, for example, operate on the "buckshot" principle that 70 to 90 percent of the albums or books they produce will fail. However, the

Table 14–1. Differences in Media Use Patterns According to Income and Race

Source: Bradley S. Greenberg and Brenda Dervin, *Communication Among the Poor* (East Lansing: Michigan State University Press, 1967–68),

	General Population	*Poor Whites (150)*	*Poor Blacks (131)*
TV time "yesterday"			
None	40.8%	22.7%	25.2%
Under 4 hours	41.7	25.3	19.8
4 hours or more	17.1	52.0	55.0
Radio time "yesterday"			
None	29.1	40.0	36.7
Under 2 hours	39.2	32.7	25.9
2 hours or more	31.6	26.0	35.9
Read newspaper daily	77.2	69.4	58.8
Read a magazine "yesterday"	52.9	38.3	38.2
Attended movie within past month	29.6	12.0	16.0
Do not own phonograph	13.6	29.3	16.0
Phonograph listening "yesterday"			
None	62.6	24.7	13.0
Under 1 hour	9.2	33.3	48.1
1 hour or more	14.0	12.7	22.9
Medium preferred for world news			
Television	34.9	65.3	65.6
Radio	25.7	12.0	19.8
Newspaper	31.5	18.0	10.7
People	4.4	4.7	3.1
Medium preferred for local news			
Television	20.4	32.7	26.7
Radio	31.0	34.0	32.1
Newspaper	40.3	25.3	18.3
People	6.8	6.7	21.4

successes are expected to pay for all of the failures. "Less than 10 percent of the records make a profit," according to *Business Week,* "but the onslaught of new titles is necessary."[9]

Popular culture lacks the stability of the so-called "high culture" or traditional art forms. Beethoven, Bach, Shakespeare, Van Gogh, and Rembrandt can survive for centuries, whereas most popular artists enjoy public acclaim for less than five years. The fleeting nature of popular culture and the "quality" of the people who support it have generated considerable debate about the merits of it. The debate, which very much involves sociology, centers on four main issues: (1) massification and pluralism; (2) cultural definitions of pop culture; (3) the effect of pop culture on society; and (4) the creation of popular culture.[10]

Massification and Pluralism

Prior to the Industrial Revolution art was created for the exclusive pleasure of the educated nobility. The invention of the Gutenberg press and other technological developments made possible the mass production of novels, songs, and plays. Art was then created to appeal to the uneducated folk. The motivation was strictly profit. Until then it had been created for religious and political purposes in support of the status quo. The elite considered the common people the "masses." The artistic taste of the masses was called *mass culture. Mass culture was the culture of the people.* This definition, according to the elite, implied four objectionable properties:

1. Mass culture is undesirable because it is produced by businessmen only for profit. Mass culture has no intrinsic merit, as the masses are *not capable of artistic judgment.*

2. Mass culture *takes from the more traditional forms of art and debases them.* For example, the relatives of composer Richard Strauss refused to allow the record of "Also Sprach Zarathustra" by jazz artist Deodato to be released in Europe because of "the treatment of the music."[11] Critics also feared that talented artists would be lured away to the more commercial media of popular culture rather than "pursuing their art."

3. The consumption of mass culture is *harmful to its audience.* This argument has been applied to nearly every form of popular art. Violence on television and in comic books has been used to explain juvenile delinquency. Popular music has been accused of corrupting the morals of the youth by a long list of social critics, beginning with the Greek philosopher Plato. Others have charged that mass culture merely "narcoticizes" its audience: it lulls people into a sense of unreality.

4. The wide distribution of popular culture *encourages standardization and possibly a totalitarian form of government.* A passive audience becomes responsive to the techniques of mass persuasion used by those bent on dictatorship. This argument was especially popular during and after World War II, when scholars looked very critically at the Nazis' use of the mass media for propaganda purposes. T. S. Adorno, a political refugee from Germany, wrote: "Standardization of song hits keeps the customers in line by doing their listening for them, as it were. Pseudo-individualization, for its part, keeps them in line by making them forget that what they listen to is already listened to for them, or 'predigested.'"[12]

The massification argument can be boiled down into one sentence: *Mass culture is a standardized and homogenized form of art without any value that may in fact have harmful effects on a society.* In this context television becomes "a vast wasteland," popular music "background noise," movies "smut," and popular novels "trash."

Sociologists have attempted to discover through research if this was in fact the case. Have radio, television, pop music, film, and novels created a passive, unthinking "mass" open to any possible suggestion?

Numerous sociologists have taken issue with the massification thesis, countering with the *pluralist* view that popular culture is in fact diverse and reflects many different tastes and preferences.[13] Two of the more persuasive arguments have been presented by Harold Wilensky and Herbert J. Gans.

Harold Wilensky found that social *uniformity* and cultural homogenization do take place. But there is a simultaneous growth in diversity.[14] Popular culture may be uniform, as on commercial television. Nonetheless, people with different educational, age, and racial backgrounds go *beyond* the available mass media. The rise of black-oriented films, "progressive" FM radio, "underground media," and even the Public Broadcasting System are all examples of diverse groups going outside of uniform entertainment and changing the character of popular culture.

Herbert Gans expanded the pluralistic argument. Popular culture, he contended, is a salad of *taste cultures* that together make up "the national taste culture: the total array of art, entertainment, leisure, and related consumer products, available in the society."[15] Each taste culture possesses users, consumers, and audiences, which Gans calls *taste publics* (groups of people with common interests). *Taste publics are people with common tastes who make similar choices about what is good or bad in popular culture.* These decisions are related to certain identifiable social traits, including ethnicity, religion, region, and most important age, education, and social class.[16] For example, youth are very much a taste public, supporting specific trends and fashions in music, film, clothing, and literature. American blacks exhibit other tastes in music, film, and other popular culture media. Geographical differences, especially in music, are quite pronounced. Evidence of this is country and western music, whose strength resided in rural areas for decades, or polkas, which are very popular in Minnesota, Wisconsin, and sections of the Dakotas. A film like *Billy Jack* was a success in the Midwest but did very poorly in big cities. Education is a good predictor of individuals' tastes in areas other than television viewing.

Popular music is a taste culture. It has singers, writers, producers, publicity and promotion people, and a bevy of executives who create the record you buy. Within this taste culture are different publics (groups of people with common interests) who evaluate and buy songs, records, and tapes of popular music. These publics include disc jockeys, record critics, high school and college students, housewives, and the occasional over-thirty male. Disc jockeys look at popular music as a means to attract more listeners to their programs. Record critics look for aesthetic quality as well as music that will provide them with a good article. Junior high school girls have fantasy affairs with pop idols like Elvis Presley, the Monkees, Donny Osmond, or Tony DeFranco. Older students use popular music as an important part of the courtship rite ("You can dance to it."[17]). On the basis of these predispositions people gather together in taste publics and select those songs, films, and books they like. If enough taste publics come together, then a fad, fashion, or trend may be established. Remember, taste publics are always changing. Studies of taste publics do show that there is diversity in many taste cultures.[18] However, it is important to bear in mind that formulas like the Top Forty formats and television quiz shows and soap operas still are dominant segments of popular culture.

Cultural Definitions of Popular Culture

Artistic and aesthetic preferences, like deviance, rest in the "eyes and ears of the beholder." Originally, when a handful of aristocrats and churchmen defined aesthetic quality, *what they enjoyed became good.* Folk art did not concern them. Their disdain and fear of popular democracy changed this attitude of indifference to open scorn, hence the mass-mob description of "people's culture." Dwight MacDonald and others have divided taste preferences into three forms of *art: highcult, midcult,* and *masscult.*[19]

Highcult is the art discussed "in textbooks." It includes the "great books," "the classics" in music, Greek tragedies, and all of the artistic preferences handed down through the ages. *Highcult is art that has survived the test of time.*

Midcult is an art form that *passes* as high culture. Art critic Dwight MacDonald wrote, "It is rather a corruption of high culture which has enormous advantage over masscult . . . [because] it is able to pass itself off as the real thing." He presents an example: "Midcult is the Revised Standard Version of the Bible, put out several years ago under the aegis of the Yale Divinity School, that *destroys* our greatest monument of English prose, the King James Version, in order to make the text 'clear and meaningful to people today,' which is like taking apart Westminster Abbey to make Disneyland out of the fragments."[20] *Midcult is basically a vulgarization of high culture.*

Masscult is the "low brow junk" churned out by the mass media.[21] It is indiscriminate and a homogenized form of unsuccessful art: "It is non-art. It is even anti-art."[22] Into this category MacDonald and others have lumped much of popular music, Norman Rockwell paintings, Andy Warhol posters, romance magazines, soap operas, and most material broadcast on television. *Masscult,* for MacDonald, *has no merit but the mere pursuit of profit.*

Dwight MacDonald's categories, although prejudiced against popular culture, do suggest that many different groups like different artistic forms. This supports Gans's idea regarding the existence of taste publics which can be identified on the basis of class and education. The higher the class position and amount of education the more likely the individual is to be attuned to "highcult." Similarly, the middle and lower strata of society are likely to enjoy "midcult" or "masscult." However, the rather rigid designations do not always work. What is masscult or popular culture one day may become highcult the next.

"Different folks have different artistic strokes."

William Shakespeare's dramas at the old Globe Theater were written for a masscult audience. As every English course quickly tells you, today Shakespeare is very much "highcult." This changeover need not take centuries. Consider the case of the once-superpopular rock band the Beatles.

The Beatles upon their arrival in the United States were branded as being totally without artistic merit, except by their teen-age fans, most of whom were thirteen- to fifteen-year-old girls.[23] College students carried picket signs reading "Bach Not Beatles." The Beatles were "masscult." As their audience changed and became increasingly older and better educated, the status of the Liverpool quartet was altered. In 1969, several college professors proclaimed the Beatles carriers of high culture. Geoffrey Marshall requested that the group be treated by record companies like any *serious* classical quartet: all of the information found on symphonic LPs should be included on Beatles' LP covers. He wrote,

"It may be a booby's pursuit, taking the Beatles seriously, but there are growing numbers doing so and they could use more accurate information."[24] Brandeis art historian Carl Belz elevated the British band to the status of fine art or high culture. He concluded his book *The Story of Rock* with a chapter devoted to "Rock and Fine Art." He contended, "The Beatles' transformation of consciousness in content has a clear parallel in the history of fine art."[25] The Beatles became the new high culture. Prestigious New York Philharmonic conductor Leonard Bernstein told a television audience the Beatles' music was so "exciting and vital, and may I say, significant, that it claims the attention of every thinking person." The Beatles in five years jumped from purveyors of masscult to distributors of highcult. A change in their music did take place, *but more important, a diversification of their audience occurred to include people of high social status.* The experience of the Beatles is not unique.

Silent movies, folksong, jazz, and other popular art forms have risen in "quality" as their audiences changed. Jazz was the "sound of the 'red light district'" and folksong was "hillbilly," until highly educated people discovered these music forms. Consequently, the sociologists' concern with the cultural definitions of popular art has nothing to do with aesthetic quality but rather with the taste publics that support them. That is, sociologists are interested in understanding why certain groups have certain tastes in popular culture. They should not make artistic judgments about what is "good" or "not good."

Effect of Pop Culture on Society

One of the central issues in popular culture is what effect it has on society. Plato believed popular music and poetry corrupted youth. Fifty-seven percent of police chiefs surveyed in a government study of pornography said reading obscene books plays an important part in causing juvenile delinquency. Comic books, movies, television programs, and songs have all been accused of creating some socially undesirable outcome. Discussions among laymen and sociologists of the impact of popular culture generally center on four interpretations: *selective perception, social groups, group influence,* and *changing norms.*[26]

1. *Selective perception* means that different people respond to different messages. No longer are people described as a mass or a herd of sheep open to any suggestion. Rather we borrow from the "scientific approach" and argue that people with X trait may be influenced by Y message. Critics claim there are many X-trait people around and too many Y-type messages available. The mentally deficient are believed to be more sold by advertising pitches than those of average intelligence. Many psychoanalysts feel that people with sexually arrested development may be more open to pornographic material than those who've had a "normal" childhood. A classic example of certain people being open to a message is the Halloween scare of 1938.

On October 30, 1938, Orson Welles broadcast H. G. Wells's *The War of the*

Worlds. This radio play told the story of the landing of a fleet of Martian spaceships on a New Jersey farm field. Despite an opening statement announcing that this was a dramatization, many people mistook the broadcast for the real thing. Some ran frightened into the streets, others grabbed shotguns. The radio network's switchboards lit up. Estimates of those who panicked range from 3 to 8 million. The press asked, "How could people panic without checking into the accuracy of the broadcast?"

Hadley Cantril and his associates found that people with seven traits were more apt to be uncritical in accepting the story of the men from Mars than those without these seven traits: phobias, insecurity, high degree of worry, lack of self-confidence, fatalism, high religiosity, and frequent church attendance.[27]

2. The *social groups* or *categories* approach suggests that certain social groups are more open to media messages. Here the individual is not as important as the group to which he belongs. People are linked to groups defined by age, sex, marital status, educational level, geographical location, and so on. Young single males are allegedly most aroused by erotic material. Young people are allegedly corrupted by rock and roll. Black people are allegedly most likely to be swayed by agitators on television. All of these statements make the assumption that specific groups of people are influenced in specific ways by popular culture.

3. *Group influence* is believed to affect how a person reacts to messages from popular culture. This approach goes a step further than just group membership. For example, various studies of political campaigns indicate that people accept the political opinions of those people around them, such as family, friends, neighbors, and co-workers. The media only tend to *reinforce* the attitudes generated by informal contacts.[28] Election campaigns, it has been repeatedly found, do not change people's minds except in 5 percent of the independent electorate. This 5 percent, of course, can be very important in a close race. Nonetheless, the influence of television on elections seems to be limited to belief reinforcement. The famous Kennedy-Nixon debates of 1960 found Democrats claiming that their candidate won, whereas Republicans overwhelmingly chose Mr. Nixon as the winner.[29] During the 1948 campaign, Truman supporters interpreted his political positions to be *in accord with theirs* even when this was not the case. Supporters of a controversial labor-management bill, the Taft-Hartley Act, which Truman *opposed* publicly every chance he got, told interviewers that the President *favored* the legislation.

The use of political protest songs appears to be most effective in reinforcing the beliefs of the committed rather than attracting outsiders. For example, 95 percent of the civil rights songs stressed the "*we* shall overcome" motif as opposed to appeals for outside support.[30] This is basically preaching to the converted or those already in agreement.

4. The *changing norms* interpretation is the most difficult to define, as it does not look at the individual or his social group. The media are seen as presenting a false picture that people accept as true. People then react to this false

information as if it were correct. Consequently, writes Melvin DeFleur, "conduct is indirectly shaped by exposure to communications."[31] Because of this feeling, cries of "news management" by politicians, from mayors to presidents, emerge. Figures like former Vice President Spiro Agnew have charged the press, television, radio, and the "Eastern Liberal Establishment" with influencing cultural norms by slanting the news. Similar arguments are made in relation to motion pictures, pop music, books, and other media, indicating that popular culture is incorrectly redefining social standards.[32] These complaints are typical:

"The general low moral standards displayed on T.V., movie theaters, fashions. People don't seem to give a darn."

"I feel that books nowadays—the popular books—there isn't very much that is private in either books or movies. They talk about things that are private. It is the stamp of approval of society to accept any sexual behavior that I am against. I think that a story can be told without people going naked. Pornography is shown in magazines in even the neighborhood drug stores."[33]

People in many instances believe that the media create a "moral tone." Radical students watching TV and reading the newspapers in the 1960s believed that other students supported them when in fact they did not. Charles Korte reported, "There was a significant tendency for students to overestimate the degree to which other students endorsed the radical position."[34] Robert K. Merton called this response "group soliloquy." He meant that people have a tendency to talk only with those who agree with them. As a result they conclude that the entire population agrees with their particular views. Bigots talk and drink with other bigots and then believe that everybody hates "them."[35]

These four interpretations of the impact of popular culture on society are the most current in public opinion and also appear to some degree in sociological journals. Studies of the actual effects of popular culture upon political and moral attitudes are frequently controversial and inconclusive. Three of the most volatile areas of controversy have been popular music lyrics, pornography, and violence on television.

Pop Music: You Know Something's Happening . . .

"Give me the making of the songs of a nation, and I care not who makes its laws," exclaimed English politician Andrew Fletcher. He was not the first nor the last to voice the sentiment that "music can soothe the savage beast" or awake the sleeping giant.[36]

The argument that a song could be a social and political weapon has been advocated many times. Woody Guthrie inscribed "This Machine Kills Fascists" on his guitar. Nikolai Lenin said music should arouse people, hit them on the head. The political right wing in America has portrayed popular music as a force that brainwashes youth and "destroys America as we know it." The

Federal Communications Commission has also taken issue with popular music lyrics, cautioning broadcasters not to air songs with "drug messages." The reason for this order was ostensibly that pop songs were encouraging listeners to "tune in, turn on, and drop out."

People expressing these views generally look at the lyrics rather than studying the people who listen to them. It is assumed that if a song protests or advocates "turning on," the people who hear the lyrics must be affected.

Studies of popular music audiences have shown that "drug lyrics" and "protest songs" are not dangerous. John Robinson and Paul Hirsch, in a study of Michigan high school students, reported that a majority of the students were not able to interpret correctly the lyrics of the songs they heard broadcast. No more than 27 percent of the respondents could correctly interpret the themes of four popular songs.[37]

Similar results were obtained from questionnaires administered to community college and university students. Only 14 percent of those university students having heard "Eve of Destruction" totally understood its message. Forty-four percent got it partially right.[38]

Only John Robinson has reported any relationship between popular music and political or cultural deviance. Three years after reporting *no* relationship, he discovered a "definite link between the appreciation of antiestablishment music and drug use, particularly marihuana."[39] He found that only 25 percent of those having only one favorite protest song smoked marihuana, whereas 80 percent of those having two or three favorite antiestablishment songs did. This connection does *not* establish that the songs caused the marihuana usage. All it says is that people who are pot smokers seem to like antiestablishment songs. Despite popular belief, there is very little sociological evidence either that music has a great impact upon cultural values or that it influences the young in any way.

Pornography: The Forbidden Fruit

Pornography is believed to be responsible for a multitude of social ills. Promiscuity, criminal behavior, and homosexuality have all been attributed to erotic books and films. One critic told Congress, "Eroticism frees the imaginations not only of children but of the child that is in the hearts of all men, leading them to go much further than they would go on their own. Inflamed fantasy leads to inflamed action."[40] Social psychologist Ernest van den Haag declared, "Pornography deindividualizes and dehumanizes sexual acts; by eliminating all the content it reduces people simply to bearers of impersonal sensations of pleasure and pain. This dehumanization eliminates the empathy that restrains us ultimately from sadism and nonconsensual acts."[41] Another critic charged, "A notable increase in homosexual offenses can be traced to the availability of magazines devoted to these perversities."[42]

A review of the studies pertaining to cause-and-effect relationships has not substantiated most of these charges. Photographs, books, and films showing

Table 14–2. Presumed Consequences of Exposure to Erotica

Sexual	Nonsexual
Criminal or Generally Regarded as Harmful	
1. Sexually aggressive acts of a criminal nature	17. Homicide
2. Unlawful sexual practices	18. Suicide
3. Nonconsensual sex acts	19. Delinquency
4. Incest	20. Criminal acts
5. Sexually perverse behavior	21. Indecent personal habits
6. Adultery	22. Unhealthy habits
7. Illegal sexual activities	23. Unhealthy thoughts
8. Socially disapproved sexual behavior	24. Rejection of reality
9. Sexual practices harmful to self	25. Ennui
10. Deadly serious pursuit of sexual satisfaction	26. Submission to authoritarianism
11. Dehumanized sexual acts	
12. Preoccupation (obsession) with sex	
13. Change of direction of sexual development from natural pathway	
14. Blocking of psychosexual maturation	
15. Misinformation about sex	
16. Moral breakdown	
Neutral	
27. Sex attitudes	
28. Sex values	
29. Sex information	
30. Sex habits	
Beneficial/Helpful	
31. Drains off illegitimate sexual desires	
32. Provides outlet for otherwise frustrated sexual drives	
33. Releases strong sexual urges without harming others	
34. Pleasure	
35. Provides discharge of "antisocial" sexual appetites	
36. Assists consummation of legitimate sexual union	

Source: The Report of the Commission on Obscenity and Pornography, New York: Bantam Books, 1970. p. 175.

erotic acts do produce a sexual response from a considerable proportion of the adult population. The affect is greatly influenced by the sex of the respondent. Females and married couples are much less receptive to pornography than are young single males. Also, the social circumstances have a good deal to do with the type of response researchers find. Overexposure to stimuli finds subjects less interested. Romantic themes in films have more effect upon female viewers, whereas males prefer "skin flicks." In light of this evidence, two sociologists on the President's Commission on Obscenity and Pornography concluded:

There is no substantial evidence that exposure of juveniles is necessarily harmful. . . . We make special note of the fact that convicted sex offenders have had *less* exposure and juveniles adjudged delinquent no more exposure to erotica than persons not so convicted or adjudged. Moreover, there is no significant association between what society has declared as criminal or delinquent, in general, and exposure to erotic stimuli.[43]

Other members of the commission were not willing to go this far, indicating that as long as society deemed pornography a problem it would remain one. As with lyrics, the causal relationship between X and Y is difficult to establish.

Gunsmoke: Television And Violence

Following a wave of political assassinations and urban riots, Americans began to search for the roots of these violent acts. What was it in America, we asked, that gave rise to the murder of a President, a Senator, and a civil rights leader and to countless riots and political confrontations? Television came to be seen as an all-powerful force as opposed to the printed word or radio. Television, the all-pervasive presence, became the culprit in the minds of many people. All of the killing portrayed in gangster, detective, and western plots, not to mention Saturday morning cartoons, was considered a factor in glorifying the use of force.

Television attracted large audiences and *showed* violence. The conclusion was drawn that there was a *relationship* between television violence and criminal aggression in everyday life. Some deviant adult behavior has been attributed to television. On December 13, 1966, NBC presented "The Doomsday Flight." The drama focused upon a bomb planted in a transcontinental airliner. The villain was a deranged man who repeatedly called the airline with information about the bomb. What followed was a series of bomb threats to the airlines. Within twenty-four hours of the broadcast five threats had been received. During the next week eight threats were made to TWA, Eastern, American, Pan-American, and Northwest. These calls equaled the number of threats received in the previous month. The network was asked not to repeat the film for reasons of air safety. Several years later, several actual attempts were made after the showing of a drama depicting an extortion plot, again with a bomb in an airliner. Again, television was blamed.

Psychologists in a number of studies have reported that children do mimic adult behavior. Children have been believed to be the group most susceptible to the televising of violence. Psychologist Fredric Wertham suggested, "My definite opinion is that continuous exposure of children's minds to scenes of crime and brutality has had a deeper effect on them [children] than is generally realized. . . . television has become a school for violence."[44] A *Ladies Home Journal* correspondent announced that between the ages of five and fourteen, children watch "the violent destruction of 13,000 human beings on television."[45] Furthermore, television was presented as a baby sitter that occupied the life of the average child for two to three hours a day, during which time it provided the young viewer with information (and misinformation) about social reality.[46] Numerous examples have appeared in the media.

In Britain, a twelve-year-old boy hanged himself while imitating his television hero, Batman. Television network executives issued a warning to millions of viewers against using some of the masked crusader's tactics in play activities. "We regret that the death of Charles Lee should be attributed to his viewing of Batman," they said. "Young viewers are cautioned that they should make no attempt to imitate Batman's activities." Furthermore, before each episode young viewers were reminded that "Batman does not in fact fly and that all of his exploits are accomplished by means of his secret equipment."[47]

In 1972, the Surgeon General's Scientific Advisory Committee on Television and Social Behavior found, "First, violence depicted on television can immediately or shortly thereafter induce mimicking or copying by children. Second, under certain circumstances television can instigate an increase in aggressive acts."[48] On the basis of forty-three independently conducted studies, the Committee further advised, "The accumulated evidence, however, *does not warrant the conclusion that televised violence has a uniformly adverse effect* nor the conclusion that it has an adverse effect on the majority of children. It cannot even be said that the majority of children in various studies we have reviewed showed an increase in aggressive behavior in response to the violent fare to which they have been exposed."[49] Like most studies of the effect of television, the Surgeon General's report was interpreted by many as inconclusive.[50] The evidence does appear to support the idea of reinforcement of previously held beliefs and *selective perception* arguments. Television does support values the individual already holds. Individuals watching the Chicago police beating protest marchers in 1968 saw either heroism or brutality on the basis of their *preexisting* beliefs. Susceptibility to televised violence is also attributed to some psychological maladjustment independent of the program.[51]

Adverse effects of popular culture upon social values and individual behavior are at this time unproven. Protest songs, pornography, television violence—all deemed culprits—have not been proved to be culprits. One reason may well be that popular culture is essentially entertainment and is perceived as such by participants.

Summary

Sociologists study popular culture in order to understand the way in which people spend their leisure time. They also learn a good deal about the concerns and interests of various age, sex, race, economic, and cultural groups. Furthermore, popular culture allows the social scientist to look at the ways the media interact with their audiences as well as the components that determine what will be a "hit" or a "miss."

Notes

1. Definition suggested by Tom Kando, "Popular Culture and Its Sociology: Two Controversies," *Journal of Popular Culture* (in press).

2. R. B. Browne, "Notes Toward a Definition of Popular Culture," in R. B. Browne and R. J. Ambrosetti, eds., *Popular Culture and Curricula,* Rev. Ed. (Bowling Green, Ohio: Bowling Green University Popular Press, 1972), p. 11. In studies of popular culture prior to the 1960s it was frequently called *mass culture,* which implied that the subject being studied was inferior to "higher" art forms such as painting, the "great books," or the classics by Brahms, Bach, and Beethoven. The best example of this approach is found in B. Rosenberg and D. M. White, eds., *Mass Culture: The Popular Arts in America* (New York: The Free Press, 1957).

3. R. Turner and L. Killian, *Collective Behavior,* 2nd Ed. (Englewood Cliffs, N.J.: Prentice-Hall, Inc., 1972), p. 215. Some sociologists have treated fads and fashions as being similar events. See R. Meyersohn and E. Katz, "Notes on a Natural History of Fads," *American Journal of Sociology,* **62** (1957), 594–601; and N. J. Smelser, *Theory of Collective Behavior* (New York: The Free Press, 1963).

4. T. G. Moore, *The Economics of the American Theater* (Durham, N.C.: Duke University Press, 1968), p. 79.

5. R. S. Denisoff, *Solid Gold: The Pop Record Industry* (New Brunswick, N.J.: TransAction Books, 1975). p. 5.

6. Figures from J. Lyle, "Contemporary Functions of the Mass Media," in R. K. Baker and S. J. Ball, eds., *Mass Media and Violence,* Vol. 11 (Washington, D.C.: U.S. Government Printing Office, 1969), pp. 187–216.

7. See H. L. Wilensky, "Mass Society and Mass Culture: Interdependence or Independence?" *American Sociological Review,* **29** (1962), 173–197.

8. Lyle, op. cit., p. 196.

9. "He Makes Music Pay at CBS," *Business Week* (October 7, 1967), 115.

10. See L. Lowenthal, *Literature, Popular Culture and Society* (Englewood Cliffs, N.J.: Prentice-Hall, Inc., 1961), pp. xviii–cciii; and R. S. Denisoff and R. A. Peterson, eds., *The Sounds of Social Change* (Chicago: Rand McNally & Co., 1972), pp. 1–12.

11. "Thus Sprach Strausses," *Billboard* (April 14, 1972), 1, 47.

12. T. W. Adorno, "On Popular Music," *Studies in Philosophy and Social Science,* **1** (1941), 25.

13. See D. McQuail, *Towards a Sociology of Mass Communications* (London: Collier-Macmillan, Ltd., 1969), pp. 18–35; and M. L. DeFleur, *Theories of Mass Communication,* 2nd Ed. (New York: David McKay Co., Inc., 1970).

14. Wilensky, op. cit., pp. 173–197.

15. See H. J. Gans, "Popular Culture in America: Social Problem in a Mass Society or Social Asset in a Pluralist Society?" in H. S. Becker, ed., *Social Problems: A Modern Approach* (New York: John Wiley & Sons, Inc., 1966), p. 551.

16. Ibid., p. 582. Also see A. Toffler, *The Culture Consumers: Art and Affluence in America* (Baltimore: Penguin Books, 1965).

17. See J. Hopkins, *The Rock Story* (New York: Pocket Books, 1970).

18. R. S. Denisoff and M. H. Levine, "Youth and Popular Music: A Test of the Taste Culture Hypothesis," *Youth and Society,* **4** (1972), 237–255.

19. Definitions are paraphrases of categories provided by D. MacDonald, *Against the American Grain* (New York: Random House, Inc., 1962).

20. Ibid., p. 38.

21. Toffler, op. cit., p. 234.

22. MacDonald, op. cit., p. 4.

23. See D. Dempsey, "Why the Girls Scream, Weep, Flip," *New York Times Magazine* (February 23, 1964), p. 15.

24. G. Marshall, "Taking the Beatles Seriously: Problems of Text," *Journal of Popular Culture,* **3** (1969), 33.

25. C. Belz, *The Story of Rock* (New York: Oxford University Press, 1969).

26. M. L. DeFleur, op. cit., pp. 118–139.

27. H. Cantril, *The Invasion from Mars* (Princeton, N.J.: Princeton University Press, 1940).

28. P. F. Lazarsfeld, B. Berelson, and H. Gaudet, *The People's Choice* (New York: Duell, Sloan and Pearce, 1944). Also see B. Berelson, P. F. Lazarsfeld, and W. McPhee, *Voting: A Study of Opinion Formation in a Presidential Campaign* (Chicago: University of Chicago Press, 1954).

29. See "The Great Debate of 1960," in D. Krech, R. Crutchfield, and E. Bullachey, eds., *Individual in Society* (New York: McGraw-Hill Book Company, 1962), p. 235.

30. R. S. Denisoff, "Protest Movements: Class Consciousness and the Propaganda Song," *Sociological Quarterly,* **9** (1968), 228–247.

31. DeFleur, op. cit., p. 130.

32. J. H. Pennybacker and W. W. Braden, eds., *Broadcasting and the Public Interest* (New York: Random House, Inc., 1969).

33. *The Report of the Commission on Obscenity and Pornography* (New York: Bantam Books, 1970), p. 189. The quotes are from a public opinion poll of attitudes toward erotic materials.

34. C. Korte, "Pluralistic Ignorance About Student Radicalism," *Sociometry,* **35** (1972), 576–587.

35. P. I. Rose, *They and We* (New York: Random House, Inc., 1964), pp. 80–81.

36. For a discussion, see R. S. Denisoff, "The Evolution of the Protest Song," in Denisoff and Peterson, op. cit., pp. 15–25.

37. J. P. Robinson and P. Hirsch, "It's The Sound That Does It," *Psychology Today,* **3** (1969), 42–45.

38. R. S. Denisoff and M. H. Levine, "The Popular Protest Song: The Case of 'Eve of Destruction,'" *Public Opinion Quarterly,* **35** (1971), 117–122.

39. "The Counterculture Beat," *Human Behavior* **2** (1973), p. 15.

40. Quoted in *Report . . . Pornography,* op. cit., pp. 175–176. Also see J. Money and R. Athanasiou, "Pornography: Review and Bibliographic Annotations," *American Journal of Obstetrics and Gynecology,* **115** (1973), 130–146.

41. E. van den Haag, "Is Pornography a Cause of Crime?" *Encounter,* (1967), 53.

42. Quoted in *Report . . . Pornography,* op. cit., p. 176.

43. O. N. Larsen and M. E. Wolfgang, "A Minority Statement," in *Report . . . Pornography,* op. cit., p. 447.

44. F. Wertham, "School for Violence," *New York Times* (July 5, 1964), p. 8.

45. E. Merriam, "We're Teaching Our Children That Violence Is Fun," *Ladies Home Journal* (October 1964), 44.

46. See P. Mussen and E. Rutherford, "Effects of Aggressive Cartoons on Children's Aggressive Play," *Journal of Abnormal and Social Psychology,* **62** (1961), 461–464. Also see W. R. Catton, Jr., "Mass Media as Producers of Effects: An Overview of Research Trends," in R. K. Baker and S. J. Ball, eds., *Mass Media and Violence* (Washington, D.C.: U.S. Government Printing Office, 1969), pp. 247–259; and L. Bogart, "Warning: The Surgeon General Has Determined That TV Violence Is Moderately Dangerous to Your Child's Mental Health," *Public Opinion Quarterly,* **36** (1972–1973), 491–521.

47. Quoted in Baker and Ball, op. cit., p. 271.

48. J. Gould, "TV Violence Held Unharmful to Youth," *New York Times* (January 11, 1972). p. 63.

49. Ibid.

50. See E. Efron, "A Million-Dollar Misunderstanding," *TV Guide* (November 11, 1972), pp. 8–13.

51. See O. N. Larsen, ed., *Violence and the Mass Media* (New York: Harper and Row, Publishers, 1968).

FIFTEEN
Social Movements
FIFTEEN

Types of Social Movements

CARRYING picket signs, marchers sing:

> One man's hands can't break a prison down,
> Two men's hands can't break a prison down,
> But if two and two and fifty make a million
> We'll see that day come 'round. . . .
> We'll see that day come 'round. . . .*

In this protest song is found the essence of a social movement. *A social movement is simply a group of people joining together in order to change something in the society they dislike.* The important words here are *group, change,* and *dislike.* How *big* must a protest group be in order to qualify as a movement? What sort of change are they concerned about? What about society upsets them? Under what conditions will they be successful in producing the changes they're after. These are some of the questions sociologists ask when they look at social movements.

Folksinger Arlo Guthrie in his antidraft song "Alice's Restaurant" described what would happen if people began going to their military induction centers and singing his song: "Like if one person does it and walks out, they may think he's sick and they won't take him. If two people do it they might think they're both fagots and won't take either of them. If three people do it, they might think it was an organization. Can you imagine *fifty* people a day walking in, singing a bar of 'Alice's Restaurant' and walkin' out? They might think it's a *movement.*"[1] When a group reaches a certain size it is considered a movement. Unfortunately there is no set number that tells us "X is a social movement." Some movements have had several thousand adherents, whereas others have numbered in the millions. As Arlo Guthrie's song indicates, a movement is usually defined as such by public opinion.

The public's awareness of a movement is *issue-oriented.* The news media tell us that some group is trying to correct or change something in society. Maybe it's the tax structure, or environmental pollution, or the Pentagon's defense budget.

How the movement approaches change also influences the public's definition of it. There are two basic definitions or labels placed on a movement: *legitimate* and *nonlegitimate.*

A legitimate movement is one that accepts most of the rules and regulations of society. It appears to be working within and for national values and traditions. It claims to be working to improve existing social institutions. Movements concerned with the pollution of the environment or with the full participation of *all* people in industry or with high food prices are not in themselves questioning basic American values. They are only attempting to improve or preserve them. When the public accepts this definition of a movement, it is then *legitimate.*

*Fall River Music Inc.

A *nonlegitimate* social movement is one that questions the widely held values of a society. It attempts to replace the old values with new ones (remember Merton's notion of nonconformity in Chapter Eleven?). This type of movement violates people's sense of order. People call its members "all kooks, nuts, perverts," and so on.

Nonlegitimate movements can be radical or just reform-minded. Nonlegitimacy is a tag placed on them by society. For example, many people consider the movement of American Indians to seek a better position in American society nonlegitimate. A similar reaction is applied to women, blacks, and other groups petitioning for social change. Therefore, a reform movement is or is not nonlegitimate depending on how people respond to it.

A *radical* movement is always nonlegitimate. It has three distinguishing characteristics, all of which are determined by its belief in the creation of a new order.[2] First, the movement accepts *only* its own vision of the world as being correct. All other viewpoints and opinions are treated as false. No tolerance exists for other views. Second, the movement works outside of the usual political means. It rejects existing means, such as elections and lobbying, as useless. Third, it finds other means, some illegal like violence and intimidation, to achieve its goals. The ends are felt to justify any means. These views are based upon the belief that the movement's vision of society is better than anyone else's.

A radical movement's unique or special vision of society is called an *ideology*. An ideology is a special kind of belief system about the way things are and ought to be. An ideology is a model. A political ideology is a model of how government should be, whereas a social ideology is a model that points to a different way of life in the future. Communism is an ideology because it presents a blueprint for a new organization of society in which each will receive "according to his needs." Other models of society, such as anarchism, fascism, and so on, are all ideologies that define for members what is and ought to be.

It is important to remember that a radical movement's ideology is not shared by most people in the society. This fact alone further separates it from the mainstream of public opinion. As Egon Bittner suggested, the ideological movement attempts to impose upon a disorderly world "a unified and internally consistent interpretation of the meaning of the world."[3] In a sense radical movements become aliens in their own world.

Sociologists have identified four types of movements: *reformist, regressive, revolutionary,* and *expressive.*

The *reformist* movement is addressed to *one* social problem. Reformers wish to correct only a single "injustice" in the social system. The movement tries to repair the old tire, not to buy a new one or, indeed, a new car. Civil rights advocates, environmentalists, antiabortionists, tax reformers, suffragettes, prohibitionists, and those working for the legalization of marihuana all fall into this group. Reformers do not wish to remake America, only one part of it.

They are not radical. Therefore, reformists work within the system. Because of these limited aims, a reform movement stands the greatest chance of success. Movements such as organized labor, the Anti-Saloon League, and the women's right-to-vote have all accomplished their legislative goals in past years. These groups were basically nonideological, lacking any grand model of what social order ought to be. They merely wanted something fixed.

Regressive movements are those that attempt to move back the clock to another period in history. They try to do this by stopping trends toward change, all the while trying to project their view of the past into the present. Right-wing and fascist movements, for example, are characterized by a longing for the days of past glory. The Ku Klux Klan and the National States Rights Party glorify their visions of the pre-Civil War South. Traditional rural values are presented as the ideal. The Nazi movement in Germany romanticized Germany's history, pointing with pride to past heroes, glories, and wars. The Third Reich of Hitler was to be a return to the glory days of Prussian history.

The ideology of the regressive movement is concerned with individual feats of daring, morality, and strength pitted against the corrupting influences of society. Society and its institutions are the "bad guys." The government, the Supreme Court, and the Department of Health, Education, and Welfare become the villains as they erase the "good old days." The radical right's fear of fluoridation of water is one example. Members of the Minutemen and the John Birch Society were thoroughly convinced that the addition of fluorine to public drinking water was part of a Communist plot to subvert the hearts and minds of the American people. The fact of the matter, however, was that the fluoride was put in the water supply to strengthen children's teeth against cavities. Robert Welch, the president of the John Birch Society, charged in the late 1950's that then-President Dwight Eisenhower, a conservative Republican, was an "agent of the Communist Conspiracy." Only those with a similar view of the world agreed.

Popular music has not escaped the radical right's attention. David Noebel of the Christian Crusade charged the Beatles with brainwashing American teen-agers. Noebel wrote, "Cybernetic warfare is the ultimate weapon and we can't afford one nerve-jammed child. Throw your Beatles and rock and roll records in the city dump. We have been unashamed of being labelled a Christian nation, let's make sure four mop-headed anti-Christ beatniks don't destroy our children's emotional and mental stability and ultimately destroy our nation."[4] Noebel's solution was to return to the "faith of our fathers." The revolt against changing times is a basic characteristic of a regressive movement. Because of this reliance on and glorification of tradition, of the simple values and virtues of the past, regressive movements enjoy a minor chance of success, although the chances are far less than for reformist movements.

Revolutionary movements are those concerned with achieving *total* social change. The movement imposes its ideological blueprint upon a society, usually through a violent takeover. The have-nots replace the haves. The "outs" become the "ins." The slave becomes the master. The French Revolution of 1789, the Bolshevik rise in Russia, and Castro's coming to power in Cuba are all historical instances of successful revolutionary movements.

The ideology of revolutionary movements focuses on the basic goodness of man. It assumes a higher standard for the world. The revolutionary movement believes man capable of living in some better social order that can be achieved only by the destruction of the existing order. This is an absolute view of the world, with "good guys" and "bad guys" being clearly identified. In Communist ideology the "capitalists" are the villains and the "workers" the heroes. With this total interpretation of the world, revolutionaries are very much nonlegitimate. Most people oppose the radical's model of society. "You can't march without a permit," exclaims the university president or the police chief. Revolutionaries reply, "We aren't going to play your fascist pig game." The result is an impasse, where the revolutionaries' only hope, as dim as it may be, is violence. They have no other choice. "Change," wrote Chairman Mao Tse-tung, "comes from a barrel of a gun." "Violence is the midwife of history," according to Karl Marx. Revolutionary movements, with their total commitment to their ends, generally find terrorism and violence the only tools available to them.

It is important to remember that a revolutionary movement must be identified as such on the basis of both *ideology* and *tactics*. A movement that advocates total social change but does nothing to accomplish this aim, besides talk or write about it, is the fourth type: the expressive movement.

The *expressive* movement is simply a group of individuals engaged in verbally and symbolically objecting to some condition. They merely demonstrate their displeasure and do little actually to bring about change. Vigils against an injustice or the burning of bras or flags in order to publicize a cause are all examples of an expressive movement. At the 1968 Miss America Pageant, a group of women's liberationists led by Robin Morgan urged that all good women toss bras, girdles, curlers, false eyelashes, wigs, and issues of *Cosmopolitan, Ladies Home Journal,* and *Family Circle* into trash cans.[5] The actual event did little to change the status of women in America, even though the women's discontent was carried by all of the news media. Numerous other organizations are of the expressive type. The several organizations formed to bring home American prisoners of war from jails in Hanoi were basically expressive. They were powerless to influence the North Vietnamese government, but through the selling of copper bracelets, marches and mailings, they kept other Americans from forgetting the flyers held captive during the Indochina conflict.

To summarize, social movements can be judged only on three fundamental levels: (1) their stated goals; (2) their tactics, that is, how they attempt to achieve their aims; and (3) the relationship of their movement to the society in which it exists. This relationship is determined by and determines the perceived legitimacy or nonlegitimacy of any movement.

For the sociologist, social movements are important for many reasons. Social movements are believed to rise and fall in response to some malfunction or strain in society. Consequently, we ask why did X movement appear at a particular historical period? The second question is even more complex: Why is it that only a tiny percentage of people ever participate in social movements? Many social problems affect all of us! Sociologists have a series of answers to these complicated questions.

Most sociological studies begin by presenting the social movement as a result of some problem situation, social strain, alienation, or other malfunction or unpleasantness that the individual or the society is experiencing. A key point is that something in the society gave rise to the movement or motivated the participant to join. For example, laid-off workers joined the Unemployed Councils during the Great Depression. Some blacks affiliated with the National Association for the Advancement of Colored People because of racial segregation. Women became part of the National Organization for Women to combat unfair hiring practices. Homosexuals joined the gay liberation movement to combat discrimination. All of these statements have in them the idea that a given problem causes the rise of a given movement. In fact, a problem can give rise to a dozen or more movements with many different solutions. The Great Depression of the 1930's and the Vietnam war caused the appearance of many groups, both on the far right and on the far left, with different programs and policies for solving the same social ill. Therefore, societal conditions give rise to social movements.

Another approach, although very similar, stresses the reasons people *join* movements. Personality traits, frustration, and personal crises have all been used by sociologists to explain the participation of particular individuals in movements. "Authoritarian personalities," "true believers," and those experiencing real or imagined "problem situations" have all been described as prime candidates for membership in social movements. Even entire classes have been described as experiencing "status anxieties" or "status frustrations" that cause their championing of social causes and movements.

The first explanation is *historical,* and the second emphasizes the *psychological* characteristics of the membership in movements. *The two are not the same.* The reason a movement emerges to do battle with established social practices and institutions may be quite different from why certain people join the movement. The social movement's declared purpose is to bring about some form of change in society. Many people join hoping to help the movement get what it wants. But some people join for reasons that have little to do with the aims of the movement.

A number of social movements have become fraternal organizations to which members belong for the social activities sponsored by the group, like dances, parties, picnics, and sing-alongs. The Ku Klux Klan for many years served as a form of social club, like the American Legion or the Lions Club, in many a small southern city. The most radical thing they did in some communities was to put on a white hood twice a year. During the 1920's, the American

Communist Party in New York provided entertainment and safety for newly arrived Eastern European immigrants who had little if any interest in the "coming revolution." Several decades later, the Communist Party and some of its front groups—groups unofficially linked to the movement—sponsored some of the finest folk music concerts in New York City. People came because of the music, not the politics. One former Communist wrote, "For the most part they were the kind of people I wanted to have for friends, I didn't concern myself with their politics. . . . They sang songs, ones that I'd never heard before, folk songs, political agitational songs, but all songs seemed to reflect my emotions."[6]

In several large cities the gay liberation movement stresses the group's social affairs rather than politics. In several chapters the social secretary appears to have more prestige and power than the president, who is more concerned with ideological and political affairs.[7] Senior citizens have also found comfort in groups such as the Townsend Movement and the Women's Christian Temperance Union. In the 1960's, some students joined the Students for a Democratic Society or the Progressive Labor Party because participation allowed them to meet interesting members of the opposite sex. When asked why he joined one group rather than another, one student told a reporter, "They have better pot and chicks than others do." For this student, political involvement meant having a good time. If this helped the cause, fine; but the social change was not his major concern or motivation. This is an important distinction, as it allows the sociologist to separate individual characteristics from the frequently very *rational* goals of a movement.

The Rise and Fall of Social Movements

All social movements have a history. They have typical careers and life spans.[8] Nearly all studies point to the conditions that give rise and momentum to movements that are directed at some kind of change. These analyses also look for the social conditions that influence the success or failure of a movement. These steps or necessary conditions involve a *social problem,* an *awareness of the problem,* the *proposal of solutions to the problem,* the *mobilization of supporters and maintenance of the movement, the attempt to remedy* the perceived social ill, and the *demise of the movement.*

The Social Problem

Every society experiences an imbalance between people's aspirations and their ability to satisfy them. Scarcity is a fact of life. You may wish to have the finest stereo equipment or the most expensive automobile, but as long as the money is not available the desire remains just that, a wish. The stereo-store owner doesn't take this wish terribly seriously when it's balanced against the cold reality: your lack of money. This is your personal problem, which you, *not* he or society, must deal with. Only if you steal these goods does the problem become social.

Other disparities are structural. Social groups may be disadvantaged because of the way in which the society is organized. The disadvantaged position of a group or a race or a sex may be accepted as merely the "way things are." There are *no* societies on record that did not have some inequalities, injustices, or some kind of rankings of the rich and the poor, the powerful and the subservient. People born into these societies tend to take these *social strains* or contradictions as a matter of course.

Strains are *rarely* attributed to the society. Originally people may see them as simply the "way things are." Or they may see something wrong with their inability to cope with the situation. It is a "personal problem." Consider the emergence of the women's liberation movement. The United States has always been a male-dominated society. Until the passage of the Nineteenth Amendment, men enjoyed political as well as economic supremacy. Having the right to vote did not change women's economic status. This did not change even as women increasingly entered the labor force during and after World War II. Job and pay discrimination remained very much a part of American business and industry.

In the 1950's women comprised more than a third of the labor force, but they were worse off than they had been some fifteen years earlier. Dean Knudsen reported that women's status in the last twenty-five years as measured by income, education, and occupation has declined relative to that of males.[9] Other studies have indicated that as industrialization increases the position of women seems to decline further.[10] Marlene Dixon wrote, "Rather than moving equally into all sectors of the occupational structure, they were being forced into the low-paying, service, clerical, and semi-skilled categories."[11] During the 1950's, most women accepted their station without public protest. Attempts to organize them into unions failed because many believed their jobs were only temporary until "they did not have to work."[12] Only professional women lodged complaints about this inequality between males and themselves in America's institutions. At the time the home was generally believed the ideal place for women by both sexes.[13]

In 1961 John F. Kennedy established the President's Commission on the Status of Women to be chaired by Eleanor Roosevelt, the wife of a former President. This commission was not terribly important except as a body for bringing into public awareness the problem as it was perceived by an ever-growing number of women with university and working backgrounds.

The growing incomes of many Americans following World War II made it possible for increasing numbers of women to attend college or the university. Girls went to find careers *or* husbands with promising futures as doctors, lawyers, and engineers. Upon graduating they found housework dull and tedious. Still they defined their problem as just a "personal trouble" or as some inadequacy in themselves, a personal inability "to cope with" the kids and keeping house. Women, as author Betty Friedan suggested, felt individual guilt over what was essentially a social problem: "If we still had ambitions, ideas about ourselves as people in our own right—well, we were simply freaks, neurotics, and we confessed our sin or neurosis to priest or psychoanalyst, and tried hard to adjust."[14] The feeling continued to be one of *individual* guilt. Friedan continued, "We didn't admit to each other if we felt there should be more in life than peanut butter sandwiches with the kids . . . even if we did feel guilty about the tattle-tale gray."[15] Women, until 1963, by and large treated the problem of inequality as a personal one that they had to adjust to. Only the change in definition from a personal trouble to a social problem gives rise to a social movement.

Awareness of the Problem

Something must happen to change the individual's identification of a problem as a "personal trouble" to its identification as a "public issue." Only when this takes place does the problem become one of societal concern. People begin to redefine a problem as a public issue when *others* also complain about the same thing. Betty Friedan's book *The Feminine Mystique*, published in 1963, moved women to question the status quo and reject their feelings of guilt. Readers began to accept the idea that the homemaker role is not natural. Friedan recalled, "I began to get letters from other women who *now* saw through the feminine mystique, who wanted to stop doing their children's homework and start doing their own. . . . society had to change, somehow, for women to make it as people."[16] *The Feminine Mystique* told readers that women no longer had to become merely housewives or secretaries, that *other possibilities* were open to them. This, however, was more easily recognized than accomplished.

Why did this happen in 1963 and not ten years sooner or even later? Why the attitude change? The sociologist must look at the "time of an idea." Herbert Blumer called this "cultural drift." That is, "gradual and pervasive changes in the values of people . . . cultural drifts stand for a general shifting in the ideas of people, particularly along the line of the conceptions which people have of themselves, and of their rights and privileges."[17] In 1963 the civil rights movement was a dominant public concern. This was the decade of liberation. Women, as Marlene Dixon indicated, were "swept up by their ferment along with blacks, Latins, American Indians, and poor whites."[18] Throughout the nation's campuses the theme of equal rights was being advocated: "All men and women are created equal." This argument had originally been used to include blacks under the safeguards of the legal system. It could also be applied to women. Women, too, were discriminated against. The goal of social equality was further highlighted in the minds of women when, in 1965, the Kennedy

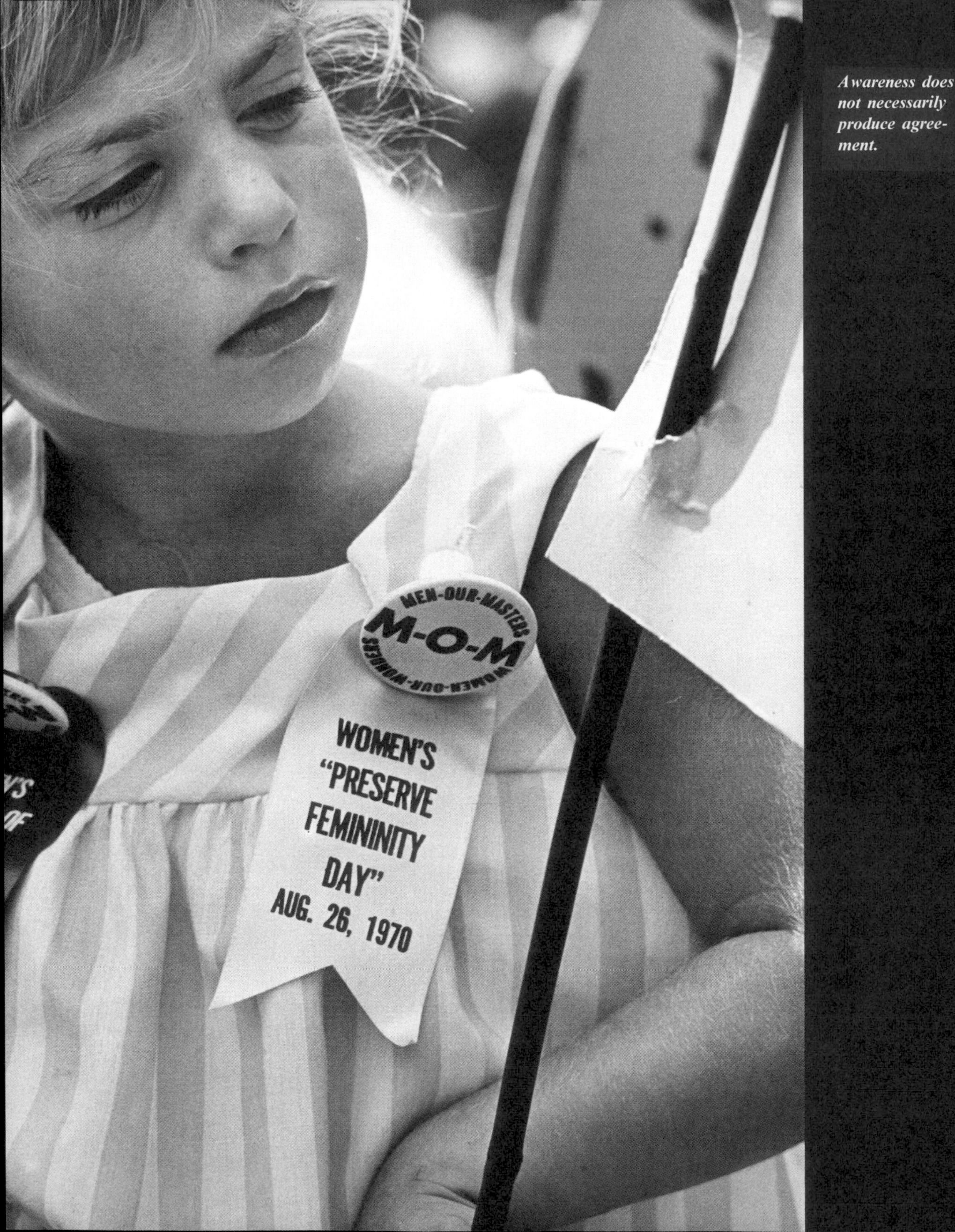

Awareness does not necessarily produce agreement.

AUGUST 26

Commission on the Status of Women finally reported that wages and hiring practices were, in fact, unfair. Women became more involved in the liberation fight of the 1960's when Congress voted Title VII of the 1964 Civil Rights Act, banning discrimination in employment. Women were included in the bill by a strange twist of fate. Southern Congressman Howard Smith (D-Va.), who opposed the bill, included women both as a joke and as the means to defeat the legislation to protect black people. But neither the Commission Report nor Title VII accomplished for women what they wanted. If they desired equal participation, only one avenue remained open to them: proposing their own solutions and finding a vehicle through which they could accomplish their goals.

Proposal of Solutions to the Problem

It is here that we must make an important addition to our definition of a social movement. A social movement can be *one* organization with an ideology, a mimeograph machine, officers, pamphlets, leaflets, members, posters, and songs. At the organizational level we can look at the American Communist Party, the John Birch Society, the American Nazi Party, the Socialist Workers Party, or the Black Panthers. All of these are movements with a *specific organization.* These are the easiest to study, as we can deal with all of the concrete parts of an organization. But as Rudolf Heberle indicated, "Movements *as such* are not organized groups."[19] We can also speak of the Communist movement, the radical right, the black power movement, the gay liberation movement, or the women's liberation movement. *None* of these *are actual organizations;* they are a collection of groups and supporters who have loosely similar goals but disagree on tactics or propose different solutions to the problem. The international Communist movement included a large number of organizations in the United States, ranging from the Communist Party through the Socialist Workers Party, the Progressive Labor Party, and dozens of other smaller organizations.

The women's liberation movement is also fragmented. The women's liberation movement includes in its ranks the middle-class professional National Organization for Women (NOW), Human Rights for Women, and the Women's Equity Action League, as well as smaller groups with such picturesque names as Society for the Cutting Up of Men (SCUM), Women's International Terrorist Conspiracy from Hell (WITCH), Red Stockings, and Bread and Roses. Each group, although "working for women's rights," also defines its goals in different ways. When we speak about the women's liberation movement, we are talking about all of these groups. In the case of women's rights, it is possible to be more precise, again, on the basis of legitimacy and the degree of social change desired. Jo Freeman observed, "The women's liberation movement manifests itself in an almost infinite variety of groups, styles, and organizations. Yet, this diversity has sprung from only two distinct origins whose numerous offspring remain clustered largely around two sources. The two branches are often called 'reform' and 'radical,' or 'women's rights' and 'women's liberation.'"[20] For the outsider, the differences between the groups make little difference. "They're all women's libbers," we may say. This is not true.

NOW was formed in 1966 by Betty Friedan as a vehicle through which discrimination against women could be eliminated. NOW is essentially a reformist movement with moderate goals. The membership is fundamentally middle class and the bulk of its supporters are professional women. NOW is not a revolutionary movement. Friedan explained, "I never did see it in terms of class or race: women, as an oppressed class, fighting to overthrow or take power away from men as a class, the oppressors. I knew the movement had to include men as equal members, though women would have to take the lead in the first stage."[21] Therefore, Friedan and the original founders of NOW were willing to accept *full participation* in the *existing order.* Men would be equal partners, not the enemy.

The more radical segments of the women's liberation movement see NOW as too conservative. Instead, groups like SCUM recommend a "hate men philosophy."[22] Still other groups and writers suggest that males are a dominant oppressive class that must be toppled in the best revolutionary tradition. One interpretation places women in the same position as Marx's oppressed classes: "There is a material basis for women's status: we are not merely discriminated against, we are exploited. At present, our unpaid labor in the home is necessary if the entire system is to function."[23] The Red Stockings have taken this exploitation argument and said, "Women are an oppressed class. Our oppression is total, affecting every facet of our lives. We are exploited as sex objects, breeders, domestic servants, and cheap labor. We are considered inferior beings whose only purpose is to enhance men's lives."[24] WITCH defines the family and its structure as being akin to the capitalist economic system. These definitions of the situation place the spokespersons in a posture of no compromise with the enemy: the status quo. Thus they go outside of the system in an attempt to achieve their goals. These goals have ranged from the mere advocacy of different forms of media, such as the creation of the new women's magazine *Ms.,* to the abolition of the nuclear family, to the strictly lesbian sexual relationship. The type of program an organization advocates will greatly affect the organization's ability to recruit new members and ultimately its chances for success.

Mobilization and Maintenance of the Movement

For a social movement to succeed it must *survive.* As elementary as that may appear, survival for a movement is no easy task, especially for one suggesting changes that most people in the society oppose. The lifeblood of a movement comes from the people who come and join, and more importantly, *stay.* Consequently, movements must "win the hearts and minds" of people, as well as maintain the commitment of the members. This is quite easy to do *if* the proposed change is a reformist one and the requirements for membership are minor. Reformers are not considered a menace to society. Police do not harass them. Employers do not fire them. Friends do not disavow them.

Zero Population Growth (ZPG) is an example of such a movement. It rarely takes positions that are liable to offend large numbers of people. The participation requirements are small, consisting mainly of the payment of annual dues. ZPG may occasionally have a meeting of a local chapter. However, it rarely makes stringent demands on the membership. NOW and the National Association for the Advancement of Colored People (NAACP), although more active than ZPG—for example, they organize marches and other demonstrations—again do little to disrupt the everyday lives of their members.

In the area of mobilization and maintenance the radical movement, either regressive or revolutionary, has a definite handicap. People are generally reluctant to risk friends, jobs, and peace of mind to enter the uncertain world of radical politics. Even if social ostracism is minor, the time and energy commitments expected by radical movements may deter many from staying in such a group.

Radical movements generally expect a vast commitment of time and energy to the organization. Being a member of the Communist Party in the 1930's involved total dedication. Party members were sent out to collect subscriptions on weekends for the movement's various publications, like the *Daily Worker.* Week nights were spent in discussion groups and meetings. Saturday night was occupied by a benefit dance or song fest for the migrant workers or for some other cause the party was backing at the time. Collections to support various "struggles" and to free arrested officials were a weekly if not a daily occurrence. More recently, the Weathermen, the John Birch Society, and other organizations have kept their members equally busy. A great deal of dedication is necessary to continue participation. The dropout rate in radical social movements is very great. Most people have better things to do than stuff envelopes or pass out leaflets, *unless* they fervently believe in the cause.

Many social movements attempt to present their case to the public without offending potential members. A reform movement that is contained in one organization can generally dictate its public image. For example, ZPG, which rarely takes positions that will offend the general public, can stress the positive aspect of their program for population control as a matter of organization policy. Similarly, the NAACP in the early 1960's underlined its belief in "equal rights" rather than total integration. Martin Luther King, when leading the Southern Christian Leadership Conference, repeatedly told white audiences, "I want to be your brother, not your brother-in-law."

NOW, with three hundred chapters and twenty thousand members, has also attempted to highlight its desire to work within the system and has not urged "radical programs." However, NOW is not the only organization in the women's liberation movement, and the public is apt not to distinguish among all of the participating organizations. One of the key issues is the subject of lesbianism. Citing the clinical Masters and Johnson study of human sexuality, several liberationists have argued that female sexual pleasure is greater *without* a male partner and that homosexual relations are ideal. Within the women's liberation movement this notion created a heated controversy. The argument did not center on the subject of lesbianism but rather on *public reaction* to it. Journalist and movement leader Gloria Steinem said, "There are people who worry about it one way or another but they tend to worry about it as a public relations problem, that it will scare women away."[25]

Betty Friedan, the founder of NOW, wrote in the *New York Times,* "The disrupters of the women's movement were the ones continually trying to push lesbianism or hatred of men, even though many weren't lesbians themselves and didn't act privately as if they hated men."[26] Many members of NOW said to lesbians, "Do your own thing, but stay in the movement's closet because you hurt the group's image and turn off middle American women."[27] The lesbianism issue, according to some NOW spokeswomen, has hurt the movement. They point to the decline in participation in the organization's annual protest march. In 1970 marchers numbered ten thousand. In 1972 only four thousand people took to the streets for women's rights. The more radical members of the women's liberation movement discount these tactical arguments, suggesting that Friedan was "severely myopic, a lesbian-phobe, a dyke-baiter, a woman who has sold out, a disgrace to any movement, a reformist in the middle of a revolution, a conjurer of phantoms . . . also the Joe McCarthy of the women's movement."[28]

Debates of this kind are commonplace in the ranks of social movements and underline the dilemma of reaching the public and at the same time maintaining the loyalty of the membership. This is no simple task, as the interests and opinions of the membership frequently are at odds with those outside the movement. For example, a Communist speaker telling a group of students that a better life for them is possible only if they tear down the corporations of America will not usually make many converts. Many in the audience are planning careers in the very organizations the speaker is attacking. Only supporters who are not planning careers in industry will nod in agreement and condemn the "false consciousness" of their fellow students. Although a right-wing speaker may stir his supporters to cheers by claiming that CBS News, the Beatles, or Joan Baez are part of the international Communist conspiracy, nonbelievers may think him a bit crazy. So it is with the women's liberation movement and the lesbian issue. Women totally committed to a program of women's rights may see little wrong with this sexual preference, but they must consider the reactions of those outside of the movement. This consideration requires compromising the "is" with the "ought to be." The success of a movement hinges upon its ability to avoid a split over the "art of the possible" versus "absolute victory." Historically, most nonreformist movements have chosen absolute victory and have been reduced to small bands waiting for the glorious day when they are proved correct. In the United States only those movements with limited goals and a willingness to compromise have succeeded. Hundreds if not thousands of movements have failed.[29]

The primary task of a social movement is to exist long enough for a sufficient number of people to come around to their way of looking at the world. In the meantime, the movement remains an alien in its own country. Consequently, a great deal of energy is devoted to maintaining the movement, sometimes at the expense of mobilizing outsiders. Some movements have attempted to do both. Gabriel Almond, in analyzing the U.S. Communist Party publication *Daily Worker*'s editorial page, found such phraseology as "defending," "safeguarding," and "protecting" the American workers. Furthermore, the paper pictured the movement as "hard-pressed," "hounded," "bullied," "slandered," "insulted," and "denied a livelihood." The public image these statements were designed to create was of a Communist Party that was merely defending the worker, all the while being attacked by insensitive capitalists and government. This material was for public consumption.

Almond found in journals published for the membership a slightly different use of terms. For the membership the Communist Party was "waging struggles," "launching campaigns," "taking the offensive," "striking," "seizing strategic bases." Organizationally, the internal publications used terminology such as "building," "constructing," "forging ahead," "gaining momentum," "going all out," and "reaches and surpasses its goals." In contrast to the public posture of being an underdog, the internal slogans were "selfless," "enthusiastic," "persistent," "resolute," "relentless," "solid," and "unwavering."[30] Even the protest songs of social movements underline *public appeal* and *group solidarity*. Songs published in Communist Party songbooks and those popular among the membership during the 1930's and 1940's attempted to use the word *we* as much as possible, thus cementing the movement's solidarity. Some songs attempted both to recruit new members and to promote internal cohesion. The party's anthem, the "Internationale," rang out:

> Arise, ye prisoners of starvation
> Arise, ye wretched of the earth
> For justice thunders condemnation
> A better world's in birth.
>
> Tis the final conflict
> Let each stand in his place
> The International Soviet
> Shall be the human race

A song reportedly sung on Chicago picket lines during the 1930's emphasized group solidarity:

Lenin is our leader, we shall not be moved.
Lenin is our leader, we shall not be moved.
Just like a tree that's standing by the water
We shall not be moved.

Another song, "The Youthful Guardsmen," attempted both to gain new members and to maintain group solidarity:

Young comrades, come and join us
Our struggle will endure
'Till ev'ry enemy is down
And victory is sure.
In struggle and in valiant fight
We're marching to the workers might.

Nearly all songs used by social movements for political purposes have similar lyrics. The word *we* is all-important. "We Shall Not Be Moved," "We Shall Overcome," and "Hold the Fort, We Are Coming" are but a few examples. In periods when a social movement is cut off from recruiting, its songs reflect this change. During the time of Senator Joseph McCarthy's search for Communists in high places, members of the party were being brought to court and summoned before congressional committees because of their political beliefs. Songs in the movement then reflected the movement's isolation and quest for survival. One of the most popular songs in the Communist underground during the early 1950's aptly summarized what a radical movement must do:

Hold the line, hold the line
As we held the line at Peekskill*
We will hold it everywhere,
Hold the line, hold the line
We will hold the line forever
Till there's freedom everywhere.

"Wasn't That a Time" was addressed to the "terrible times" of the McCarthy era. Again, the dedication of followers was asked with no mention of outsiders:

Our faith cries out THEY SHALL NOT PASS!
We cry NO PASARAN!
We pledge our lives, our honor, all
To free this prisoned land.

*In September, 1949 an outdoor concert was given by the black opera singer Paul Robeson, who had a long history of supporting left-wing causes. American Legionnaires in the small community of Peekskill, New York attempted to stop the concert by attacking people in the audience. Those under attack fought back, thus allowing the concert to go on. Some segments of the American left considered this a great moral victory over the radical right.[31]

A movement in such a defensive position is generally doomed to failure.

Many historians and political scientists have come to view radical movements as the generators of ideas that the Democrats and Republicans eventually incorporate into their party platforms. Sidney Lens observed:

> It is impossible to chronicle the story of the United States without noting the radical's contribution to it. Never has the radical achieved anything approximating total victory—not even in the Revolution—but he has usually been able to modify restrictive institutions. Though his ultimate dream of the ideal society has not reached fruition, he sowed unnumerable reforms which the reformer later reaped. In these victories lay both his fulfillment and his frustration.[32]

Certainly free public schools, Social Security, the welfare program, the abolition of slavery, free speech, and a shorter work week are all attributable to some radical movement in American history. However, the originators of the ideas rarely lived to see them become part of the established society.

Demise of the Social Movement

Social movements disappear because of a number of factors. These can be divided into *external* factors, or those coming from outside the movement, and *internal* factors, which originate within the movement.

External Factors

The external factors that can bring about the demise of a social movement are *cooptation, discreditation,* and *repression.*

Cooptation. Cooptation is the process of winning a truce by bringing the opposition's leadership or platform into the governing seat of power. This can be accomplished in two ways. First, the government can invite the movement's leader to become part of the ruling body. The opposition leader then becomes a part of the establishment. This technique is frequently used in grammar schools when a troublemaker is made the class monitor. He is then the teacher's aide rather than his opponent. As Bertrand Russell once quipped, "British radicals are made members of the House of Lords, never to be heard from again." A movement leader, once he is in a favored position in the status quo, has little reason to make waves. This was one of the rationales used to urge the admission of Communist China into the United Nations. As William Gamson suggested, "A hostile China is viewed as a greater threat outside the United Nations than inside. Once inside . . . China would acquire interests which would make it a partner in maintaining the stability of the international system. It lacks such interests as an 'outlaw' with relatively little stake in maintaining peace and cooperative relations with other countries."[33]

The second type of cooptation is *protest absorption.* In this case those in power take over the ideology or program advocated by the movement. President Franklin D. Roosevelt during the Great Depression successful coopted many programs from the American left. Social Security was taken from the Townsend movement. Several other programs were lifted from Norman Thomas's Socialist Party of America.

In recent years Presidents have similarly attempted to incorporate ideas from social movements. Lyndon Johnson embraced a good portion of the civil rights program advocated by the NAACP. He even ended his speech to Congress calling for greater protection of black people with the phrase "We shall overcome." Richard Nixon used an identical approach to the ecology movement, espousing the cleaning up of the environment. The absorption of a program by those in power leaves the movement with little else to do but yell, "We've been robbed." They have, and there is nothing left for them to do. "The story of the decline of the Socialist Party since 1933 is, according to historian David Shannon, "for the most part the story of the political success of the New Deal."[34] Reform movements are the most likely candidates for cooptation as their demands are usually reasonable and capable of being absorbed into the existing system. Regressive and revolutionary movements, seeing those in power as evil incarnate, are rarely coopted. Their vision of victory is total, not partial. Instead, the regressive and the revolutionary movement are most likely to be either discredited or repressed.

Discreditation. Discreditation is the process of labeling an individual or movement as operating on false premises and not "in the public interest." Movements are usually discredited by respected social institutions. When Congress, the press, or other credible sources state, "X movement is not in the public interest," many people accept this judgment. After all, the movement is already somewhat suspect. A reform movement, being fundamentally "inside the system," is difficult to discredit unless the labelers can make it seem to be radical and extremist in character. This process is called *public degradation.* Public degradation involves the ridicule of the movement and its leadership. The movement is made to appear either politically or socially deviant. If the moral integrity of the leadership or its members is questioned, the entire movement can be dealt a harmful blow. Critics of the National Women's Organization, for example, have attempted to suggest that the entire movement is a plot by a handful of lesbians to impose their sexual preferences upon American society. This view is false; however, it is a classic example of an attempt at public degradation.

Many movements have fallen because of false charges. Marcus Garvey's Universal Negro Improvement Association, a back-to-Africa movement, was discredited by the press and the government. Garvey, in the early 1920's, attempted to create the Black Star Line, which was to be a fleet of ships that would transport blacks to Africa. Through editorial agitation and complaints from several members of the organization, Garvey was charged with mail fraud and deceptive practices for selling stock in the shipping line. Garvey denied any wrongdoing, replying, "Enemies of the Negro race and enemies of my movement with the race have been plotting for some time to besmirch my character in order to hold me up to public ridicule and to cause me to lose favor among my people."[35] Regardless of his guilt or innocence, Garvey's trial and conviction effectively crippled the entire movement.

The Townsend movement of the 1930's experienced a similar fate. Francis Townsend developed a plan that was designed to guarantee a monthly pension for all people over the age of sixty. This program was the forerunner of Social Security. During the Depression, when millions of people were out of work and savings were rapidly being depleted, the plan appealed to millions of elderly Americans as well as to many young people. In 1935 Townsend became a political force to be reckoned with, constituting a "clear and present danger" to both major political parties. Historian Arthur Schlesinger, Jr., reported the reaction to the movement: "Democrats and Republicans in Congress might be able to cooperate on little else, but they could at least take steps to eliminate the common nuisance. In the Spring of 1936 they decided to close ranks in order to smash Townsend once and for all. The chosen mechanism was a congressional investigation."[36] Townsend was publicly accused of embezzling funds from the movement's treasury. Feeling the hearing against him was rigged, Townsend refused to testify. He was cited for contempt and found guilty. His thirty-day jail sentence was commuted by President Roosevelt, who was attempting to court Townsend's political supporters. The movement's newspaper, *The Weekly,* charged the entire investigation was a plot backed by the arch-conservative Liberty League, supported by many millionaires. Townsend became somewhat of a martyr in the eyes of his followers, but public support began to wane. The passage of the Social Security Act completely finished the Townsend movement as a viable political movement. Many other leaders of movements have experienced similar disclosures about their economic or moral misdeeds. Some of the charges, of course, have been true. Making police records public or documenting that X leader is unfaithful to his wife, or a heavy drinker, or a sexual deviant frequently has the political effect of labeling the movement as being without merit as "they all must be a bunch of kooks, perverts, or worse."

The most common form of political degradation is to label a movement as radical when it is in fact quite moderate. For example, during the 1920's and 1930's, many legitimate reform movements were tarred with the charge of being a "Communist front." As a result the public thought these movements much more extreme than they really were. The Gastonia textile strike of 1929 is a classic example. A band of southern textile workers organized by the National Textile Workers Union went on a prolonged strike because of poor working conditions and even poorer pay. The employers appealed to both the public and the strikers with statements such as:

Our Religion, Our Morals, Our Common Decency, Our Government, and the very Foundations of Modern Civilization, all that we are now and all that we plan for our children IS IN DANGER. Communism will destroy the efforts of Christians of 2,000 years. Do we want it? Will we have it? No!! It must go from the Southerland.[37]

An advertisement in a local paper read, "RED RUSSIANISM LIFTS ITS GORY HANDS RIGHT HERE IN GASTONIA."[38] The student movement of the 1960's was also charged with Communist aims. Some even accused the students of being members of the international Communist conspiracy. On May 13, 1960, a group of people, mainly students, demonstrated in San Francisco against the House Un-American Activities Committee (now the House Internal Security Committee). They were a collection of civil libertarians, students, and a few political progressives who objected to the committee's tactics. The response to the protest and demonstration, which ended in a bloody confrontation with police, was one of discreditation. J. Edgar Hoover, the Director of the Federal Bureau of Investigation, charged:

The Communists demonstrated in San Francisco just how powerful a weapon Communist infiltration is. They revealed how it is possible for only a few Communist agitators, using mob psychology, to turn peaceful demonstrations into riots. Their success there must serve as a warning that their infiltration efforts aimed not only at the youth and student groups, but also at our labor unions, churches, professional groups, artists, newspapers, government, and the like, can create chaos and shatter our internal security.[39]

The "unwitting dupe" statement became especially popular in dealing with student demonstrations. During the free speech movement at the University of California (Berkeley), the *San Francisco Examiner* reported that "the majority of the demonstrators were not students and that up to forty percent of the hard-core leaders were adherents of the 'Mao-Red Chinese Communist Line.'" A few of the students were portrayed as having "direct organizational ties of radical, extremist, or even Communist nature" or as "dupes, unwilling or otherwise, of trained agitators."[40] The *Oakland Tribune's* October 1 edition included a photograph of a student sitting on a police car. Beside the coed are a pile of books. The title of the book on top included the word *Marxism.* The caption read, "A textbook on Marxism was among the crowd." Colin Miller discovered "the intention of equating the demonstration with Communism was clear. Actually, the book's full title is *Essentials of Marxism,* a paperback published by Bantam Books. It is a textbook for Social Studies 1A, a freshman course. Obviously, the word Marxism in the photograph had been retouched. Every other word on the cover was blurred."[41]

The Free Speech Movement, although discredited, did achieve its original goals of greater political activism on the Berkeley campus because its cause did appear just to many on the campus who considered the *Oakland Tribune* and the *San Francisco Examiner* to be biased. After all, free speech is guaranteed by the Constitution. Discreditation will not work when people feel the cause of the protestors and the movement is justified and in keeping with societal values.[42]

An attempt to discredit a movement must be judged on its appeal to the norms or standards of the community, the community's sense of injustice, and the degree of disorder in the movement's tactics. The folk wisdom of any community determines whether a group is seen as engaging in *protest* as opposed to disruptive deviance. To be considered as legitimate, a protest must meet five conditions:

1. To be considered legitimate, a movement must show signs of moral virtue and appear "deserving." The public must, in light of its folk wisdom, be able to say, "I can see their point." For example, Mexican-American farm workers in California, although called Communists by some, have appealed to folk wisdom by saying, "We want a union just like everybody else." Blacks attempting to vote in the rural South could make similar statements and evoke considerable sympathy from northern whites and their political representatives.

2. To be considered legitimate, a movement must be able to point to a continuing powerlessness that is recognized by most people. Folk wisdom dictates that a movement must be peopled by the "underprivileged" who obviously are "down and out." This group must *also* be primarily concerned with not gaining an *advantage* in society but only equality. "One man, one vote" and "collective bargaining" both strike the note of "All men are created equal." The civil rights movement in the South during the early 1960's benefited greatly from this approach. The women's liberation movement has been able to get equal opportunity in hiring and salaries, again because of the notion of fair play.

However, folk wisdom generally denies a movement that claims superiority. The claim that a race, sex, class, or occupational group that is disadvantaged should receive superior treatment can be the death blow to a movement. Public response may take the form of "I made it the hard way, why can't they," or "Nobody ever gave me a break." Public response to the political protests of the 1960's bears out this finding. Demonstrations by poor rural blacks received a much more favorable response than those by privileged, white, middle-class college students. For a movement to escape discredit it must establish "need."

3. To be considered legitimate, a movement must avoid intentional violation of the rules of the game. It must appear to be reasonable and not conspiratorial. "Even riots or naive expressions of rage," noted Ralph Turner, "released under the stimulus of rumor and crowd excitement are consistent with a folk-image of protest."[43] However, stealing, bombing, kidnapping, are not excusable. Those groups are quickly discredited who are seen as conspiring to impose their will on others. The late Martin Luther King and farm workers' leader Cesar Chavez have used the avoidance of violence with great success, underlining their right to dissent. Any escalation of tactics and the degree of violence is then placed at the feet of the authorities. Indeed, public indignation at police brutality frequently hinges upon the "plain folks" approach a movement takes.

4. To be considered legitimate, a movement must appear to be selfless. The movement must be free of self-aggrandizement, the taking of private funds, or the enjoyment of violence. The mere implication that movement members are using a "just cause" to line their own pockets or have a good time goes against the grain of folk wisdom. The yippies and other anti-Vietnam-war movements and leaders were condemned by many for just these abuses. As we have seen, when movement leaders seem to show a gain from the struggle, they find themselves in trouble with critics and, frequently, with insiders. The cry "opportunist" is a powerful one, as Francis Townsend, Marcus Garvey, and yippie leader Abbie Hoffman discovered.

5. To be considered legitimate, a movement must be moderate. The movement must accommodate certain basic values of the society. The American Indians who seized the Washington headquarters of the Bureau of Indian Affairs gained public understanding by controlling the amount of violence to individuals and damage to property that occurred. Excessive destruction that appears mindless and indiscriminate will certainly lead to discreditation. In the United States the unprovoked taking of human life has irreparably harmed those accused of the act. As Robert Murray suggested, "The word 'radical' in 1919 automatically carried with it the implication of dynamite. Stereotyped in the public mind was an everpresent picture of the 'Red' with wild eyes, bushy, unkept hair, and tattered clothes, holding a smoking bomb in his hands."[44] The linking of bombs to social movements of the left has greatly damaged most of them. The Weathermen's advocacy of violence and the several bombings attributed to them found their youth culture constituency rejecting them. The use of political violence in America is against the nation's folk wisdom. It is native folk wisdom that determines the legitimacy of a movement.

Once public opinion recognizes a social problem, the time of an idea may have come. When this happens, folk wisdom may change, allowing a previous "personal trouble" to become a public issue. Consequently, what was previously considered just a form of personal deviance may be transformed into a political statement. Riots in urban ghettos prior to 1965 were seen either as mindless examples of mob psychology or as the criminal activities of society's undesirables. The public's awareness of black deprivation and lack of civil rights found many people labeling riots and other crimes as acts of rebellion or revolution or uprising.

The acceptance of the movement's definition of the problem allows outsiders either to ignore or to forgive excesses. This tolerance is highly unstable, as public sympathy for the underdog is apt to shift, especially if the social cost begins to rise.

The price of disorder is uncertainty and instability. As we have seen, a certain amount of protest activity may be welcome in light of an obvious social inequality or a threat to the values of a society. The citizens will accept temporary social inconvenience if it is perceived as being in the context of the general good. For example, sacrifices during wartime are frequently supported by the feeling "My country, right or wrong" or "It's for the good of the country." So it is with movements.

Programs for improving the schools of the disadvantaged, although not popular with taxpayers, passed the Congress during the 1960s. However, as the social cost of "integration" increased with the introduction of busing, social disorder became greater. As a result the number of people who objected rose. In the 1970s the future of school integration through the use of busing is unpredictable. Social movements that *appear* to question and oppose the values and the folk wisdom of a society are quickly labeled as extremist and have little chance of success. In such a case a more common response to the movement is repression.

Repression. Repression is the process of attempting to eliminate a social movement physically. For example, a government may outlaw a movement. Revolutionary and regressive movements are especially open to repression, as they frequently operate at the edges of social acceptability or legality. Consequently, lawmakers may find it quite easy to label them as criminal and act accordingly. For example, a revolutionary movement, when advocating the use of violence, is inviting a response from those in power. The Industrial Workers of the World (IWW), the Green Corn Rebellion, and more recently, the Black Panther Party, the Weathermen, and the Minutemen were all repressed.

The process of repression includes the jailing of members and various other tactics designed to end the movement's ability to act. The plight of the IWW (also called the Wobblies) in the late 1910s is one illustration: "The Wobblies and other dissidents faced the constant threat of beatings, deportation, shooting, and lynching."[45] The reaction to the Socialist Party of Oklahoma in 1917 was identical: "The rebels were tried in federal court under the Espionage Act and found guilty. Most received suspended sentences upon promise to return to their farms, but five years later eight of the leaders were still serving long sentences in the federal penitentiary at Leavenworth, Kansas. . . . The Green Corn Rebellion killed the Socialist Party in Oklahoma."[46]

Repression is not always successful. The mere banning of a movement can drive it underground, as was the case with the American Communist Party during the 1950s. In many countries revolutionary movements operate underground and illegally. The Bolsheviks in czarist Russia, the Irish Republican Army (IRA), the Palestinian Liberation Front, and Al Fatah are all examples of clandestine movements operating against a government.

From their secret hideaways revolutionary movements can wage a war of political violence. One example is the movement Allul al Aswad, also called Black September.

Black September takes its name from the month in 1970 when Jordan's King Hussein tried to drive Al Fatah, a Palestinian commando group, from his land. During the repression thousands of Al Fatah members were killed and jailed. Others fled from Jordan. Led by Abu al Iyad, a number of disillusioned Al Fatah members formed Black September. Their chief political weapon was terrorism. On November 28, 1971 they gunned down Jordan's Prime Minister, Wasfi Tal. They hijacked airliners. In one episode that deeply shocked the world, they invaded the 1972 Munich Olympics, kidnapping the Israeli gymnastic team; eleven Israelis and five Septemberists were killed. Septemberists repeatedly appeared in various countries, all the while using political violence to force Israel to accept their demands. These tactics have come under severe attack. As one Arab leader told *Newsweek*, "I understand their feelings of rage; I have them, too, but blood for blood's sake is not what our cause is about and sometimes they seem to have forgotten that."[47] Similar statements have been made about the Mau Mau in Africa and the IRA in Northern Ireland. When a movement or its activities are declared illegal, the movement either dissolves or resorts to more militant and sometimes violent means to achieve its ends. This becomes a form of internal war, in which movements either succeed in fomenting a revolution or find their members being jailed.

INTERNAL FACTORS

Although external forces can and do effect a social movement's chances of success, these outside influences may not be necessary to trip up a social movement. Movements frequently are their own worst enemies. In facing a hostile world, movements must have a solid, cohesive, united front. In attempting to maintain such a posture, movements sometimes destroy themselves. In stressing uniformity or total agreement on leadership, ideology, and tactics, movements may be ripped apart, leaving in their wake disillusioned members and *splinter groups.*

This process is called *fragmentation.* It is the first internal problem of a social movement. Fragmentation happens when one movement gives birth to a number of smaller movements. Splinter groups are those that spin off from an existing movement. Martin Luther's Protestant movement was a group that splintered from the dominant Catholic Church. The history of the American Marxist movement is filled with examples of splinter groups spinning off from a parent movement. The Communist Party of the United States was the dominant Marxist movement after 1924, enjoying the support of the Soviet Union. However, after a series of battles over leadership, tactics, and approaches, the movement gave birth to many others, such as the American Trotskyists. The Trotskyists began with an organization of two thousand members and ended with nearly two hundred splinter groups supported by two thousand people. These various groups became known as "tendencies" or branches on the same ideological tree. A Trotskyist parodied this split in a song called the "Ultimate Sectarian":

> Bill Bailey belonged to every radical party that ever came to be.
> Till he finally decided to start his own party so he wouldn't disagree.
> He got himself an office with a sign outside the door with "Marxist League"
> in red letters. . . .

The theme of the song is that the Ultimate Sectarian was reduced to a one-man "movement."

One of the major criticisms of the American left historically has been its waste of time and energy on ideological debates and personality conflicts, all the while ignoring its avowed mission of mobilizing the workers into a revolutionary movement. In 1966, Progressive Labor (PL), a Marxist-Leninist-Maoist group, joined the Students for a Democratic Society (SDS). They attempted to take over the SDS. The fight over the leadership of SDS was a bitter one. The battle pitted the ideologically wise PL against the SDS's loosely organized mixed membership of reformers and radicals. As Harold Jacobs wrote, "By the Fall of 1968, SDS was racked by an inner-divisiveness which not only prevented important political work at the national level from getting done, but *soon sapped the entire organization of its validity*."[48] The debate shattered the SDS into hundreds of warring units. In time PL was ousted from the SDS. The result was two other organizations: the Weathermen, an anti-PL group, and the Revolutionary Youth Movement (RYM), which was also anti-PL. RYM was also divided into two units over the issue of violence. RYM II was a strong advocate of violence, and RYM I saw the working class as the agent of social change, not militant middle-class students. From the SDS, in a short span of three years, emerged small, impotent groups who spent as much time fighting one another as their avowed enemy, the American establishment.

Institutionalization is another internal problem with which a movement must cope. A social movement that survives for any length of time begins to develop a social bureaucracy, with leaders and followers and with rules, privileges, and all of the other trappings of a large institution. When this happens, the organization may become more concerned with maintaining itself as a unit than with the changes it is proposing.[49] What good is a movement without a cause? Or what is the value of a leader without followers? Howard Becker provided one answer: "The success of the crusade, therefore, leaves the crusader without a vocation. Such a man, at loose ends, may generalize his interest and discover something new to view with alarm. A new evil about which something ought to be done. He becomes a professional discoverer of wrongs to be righted, of situations requiring new rules."[50]

One illustration is the National Foundation for Infantile Paralysis. Once a vaccine was found by Jonas Salk to eliminate the crippling disease polio, the organization was without a cause. They rapidly changed their name to the National Foundation and turned their attention to other health problems.

Organizations such as the Townsend movement and the trade unions have redirected their energies into new areas. These changes have totally transformed the organizations. Indeed, some sociologists have pointed to social movements as an area in which new institutions are born.

On the other hand, institutions frequently linger on long after the need for their services has expired. The Women's Christian Temperance Union (WCTU) is an example. With the passage of the Eighteenth Amendment, the goals of the "drys" were accomplished. Prohibition, "the Grand Experiment," failed. The WCTU, however, still hangs on, hoping to reimpose its views on the evils of drinking.[51]

The number of social movements that succeed is quite small. In the United States nearly all of them have been reform oriented. Nonetheless, some of the unsuccessful linger on, waiting for that glorious day when their dreams will be realized.

Why People Protest

The question of why people protest is one filled with mystery. Some sociologists have simply looked to social conditions saying *X* strain produces *Y* social movement. As we have seen, this explanation does not really tell us much, for *X* strain may generate movements Y^1, Y^2, Y^3, and so on. The question, then, becomes why a given person or a group of people join and participate in a specific social movement. Most answers to this question have come from the social psychologists, who are concerned with human motivation. In the area of social movements, according to Joseph F. Zygmunt, "Motivational analysis has been aimed at identifying the psychological factors which render people susceptible to the appeals of movements and which motivate and sustain affiliation with them."[52] The key words here are *susceptible, appeals,* and *affiliation. Susceptibility* concerns the type of people most likely to join a social movement. *Appeal* involves the kinds of reasons that attract those people who are susceptible. *Affiliation* is the actual process of joining the social movement.

Susceptibility: Personality Types

Susceptibility concerns the type of person most likely to join a social movement. This person is usually identified as being a specific *personality type* or as experiencing a specific *personality problem.*

The use of personality types in psychology to explain social events is as old as the work of Cesare Lombroso, an early social scientist who believed that he could identify criminals by their physical or psychological characteristics. People interested in political protest have also used this technique.

Beginning with the rise of the Nazi movement in Germany, certain personality types have come to be seen as "movement joiners." Erich Fromm was most prominent in the birth of this approach. It was Fromm who coined the term *authoritarian character.* Fromm represented this character-type as "the personality structure which is the human basis of Fascism."[53] Fromm's argument that a specific personality type was responsible for the rise of right-wing or regressive movements was pursued by German political refugee Theodore Adorno and his associates. Adorno wished to find the "potentially fascistic individual, one whose personality structure is such as to render him particularly

susceptible to anti-democratic propaganda."[54] This personality type, according to Adorno, can be divided into six groups: the *stereotyper,* the *conventionalist,* the *authoritarian,* the *rebel-psychopath,* the *crank,* and the *manipulator.*

The *stereotyper* unquestioningly accepts as truth such prejudiced stereotypes as "All women's liberationists are ugly," "All Poles are stupid," or "All black people are lazy." The stereotyper is the Archie Bunker of the "All in the Family" television program. He knows that "certain types of people" all have specific defects. This type of personality will find appeal in a social movement that deals in the stereotypes he believes.

The *conventionalist* is the superconformist. This is the person who expects all of life to go a certain preordained way. The violation of rules greatly upsets him. It was believed by Adorno that this personality type would be especially open to a regressive movement such as Nazism that promised to restore traditional ways of doing things.

The *authoritarian* takes pleasure in the giving and taking of orders. The idea of sacrifice for a cause is important to his psychological makeup. He may become the movement functionary, who does all of the unpleasant tasks such as stuffing envelopes, running errands, or manning cold, wet picket lines. Without this personality type, social movements would be hard pressed to survive. For this individual, ideology or program is not as important as the actual discipline within the movement.

The *rebel-psychopath* rejects all authority as invalid. He rebels against laws, values, and norms. For him the movement is a tool through which to destroy the status quo. However, he rapidly discovers that a movement also has rules and dominant ideas. The rebel may well be the father of splinter groups and the "ultimate sectarian." Adorno and his associates described the rebel -psychopath as "a religious disobeyer of prevailing codes and standards whose main characteristic is that he cannot wait."[55]

The *crank* cannot accept reality. Instead, he attempts to create his own. In some cases the belief system of the social movement becomes his real world. The movement's "ought to be" becomes his "is." However, no reality totally satisfies him so he may drift from one movement to another.

The *manipulator* enjoys using people. In the social movement he gets the opportunity to use people in the name of the cause. For this personality type, the means becomes all-important rather than the ends. His whole aim is to keep the movement going so as to continue in his superior position.

All of these types were seen by Adorno as the backbone of social movements of the right. The leader, the follower, and the bureaucrat are all included in the Adorno categories. An equally inclusive, but more popular, personality type has been Eric Hoffer's "true believer."

Eric Hoffer identified an individual who was "frustrated," "disaffected," and "rejected." This person he called the "true believer," who is a "guiltridden hitchhiker who thumbs a ride on every cause from Christianity to Communism." For Hoffer's "true believer" it is not the ideas that are important but the participation. "When people are ripe for a mass movement," asserted Hoffer, "they are usually ripe for any effective movement, and not solely for one with a particular doctrine or program."[56] Hoffer provided eleven categories of people likely to become true believers: the poor, the misfits, the outcasts, minorities, adolescent youth, the ambitious, the vice-ridden or obsessive, the physically or mentally impotent, the selfish, the bored, and finally the sinners.[57] All of these people, Hoffer believed, could become true believers if they experienced frustration at either the individual or the societal level. An underlying theme of Hoffer's argument is that people who are already discontented or deviant are the backbone of social movements.

The Frustrated and Protest

Frustration, according to many social psychologists, is a prime reason for participation in movements. Sigmund Freud described society as a policeman that prevents many from satisfying their psychological drives. This constraint leads to frustration and aggression. Again with the rise of the German Nazi movement this explanation was popularized in regard to social movements. Allen L. Edwards told his readers, "The supporters of any social movement . . . tend to come from those groups which are already *frustrated* or *anticipate frustration* in some respect and which see in this particular movement a means of . . . obtaining relief for their anxiety."[58] Erich Fromm wrote, "The increasing social *frustration* led to a projection which became an important source for National Socialism: instead of being aware of the economic and social fate of the old middle class, its members consciously thought of their fate in terms of the nation. The national defeat and the Treaty of Versailles [the treaty that ended World War II] . . . became the symbols to which the actual frustration—the social one—was shifted."[59] N. R. Maier added, "German people experienced a long period of *frustration,*" therefore the emergence of the Third Reich.[60] Other studies have made similar claims. Joel Rinaldo, in *Psychoanalysis of the Reformer,* indicated that the desire to change society is motivated by "a frustrated sexual need producing hysteria [an excessive or uncontrollable fear or emotion] . . . in the individual."[61]

The social frustration argument has been applied not only to the individual but to classes and occupational groups. Here the frustration is found in status and prestige inconsistency rather than in the psyche of the individual. Richard Hofstadter, for one, described the "revolt against modernity," as exhibited by groups whose prestige is on the decline, like the Fundamentalists.[62] The Freudian notion has not been totally abandoned, although it has been modified.[63] John Lofland and Rodney Stark, in studying conversion to religious cults, suggested that frustration was an important factor.[64] Similar descriptions have been applied to black protesters, campus groups, and the American radical right.[65]

Alienation and Protest

Alienation has also been identified as a state that predisposes the individual to join a social movement (see Chapter Five). P. B. Horton and C. L. Hunt observed

> Alienation and anomie become widespread states of mind in a disorganized society. Their symptoms are insecurity, confusion, restlessness, and suggestibility. Once-honored rules no longer seem binding and once-cherished goals no longer attainable, while no other rules or goals seem worth the effort. Such a *confused and frustrated setting is ideal for the appearance of social movements.*[66]

Alienation has been used to characterize those in social movements. Irving Howe and Lewis Coser applied the concept to members of the U.S. Communist Party. Members of the Communist Party were outsiders in the social world.

Their ideology separated them from the common-sense world of Walt Disney movies, *Life* magazine, and pop music. The Party then was a home for them. William Kornhauser and Murray Levin have argued that alienated people are most likely to follow a leader with charismatic (magical) dynamic qualities into undemocratic forms of government.[67] The student protests of the 1960's also generated discussions of the alienation of students. Supporters of the Berkeley Free Speech Movement explained the reason for the demonstrations: "The nature of this deepest motivation is superficially summed up in the word alienation, the object of hostility and the cause of alienation is summed up in the symbol of the IBM card."[68] The cold, impersonal university was seen as creating alienation, which made students "not only distinct from the general culture, but in some discord with it."[69] Richard Flacks and others thought that alienated students were the core of the student protest movement.

Kenneth Keniston, on the other hand, argued that activists and protestors are not alienated but quite rationally attempting to correct abject social ills. He reported, "Alienated students are more likely to be disturbed. . . . they are less committed to academic values and intellectual achievement than are protesters. . . . Whereas the protesting student is likely to accept the basic political and social values of his parents, the alienated student almost always rejects his parents' values."[70] This issue has not been successfully resolved, as studies of many campuses have not showed alienation as either causing or preventing participation in movements. One researcher reported, "Alienation does not appear to explain the differences in activism."[71] Despite this inconclusiveness, alienation remains a concept popular in the study of social movements.

Appeal and Affiliation

"When a person is ready to become a radical," a former Communist said, "it is just an accident whether he becomes a Stalinist [a member of the CPUSA] or Trotskyist [a member of the Socialist Workers Party]. . . . The first people he has contact with, he joins."[72] Affiliation is a very inexact area of movement research. One of the most popular approaches to this subject is the need fulfillment argument developed by Hadley Cantril in his 1941 book *The Psychology of Social Movements.* Cantril said that people learn the various norms and values in a society differently. One person's sense of justice and well-being is different from that of another. What develops is a discrepancy in values between the person and society. Such discrepancies commonly fall into four categories: (1) individual achievement and goals; (2) individual values and social values; (3) individual need and satisfaction; and (4) individual values and societal tolerance. When these individual wants or values are at odds with the society's, the person is discontented. He will then either attempt to solve his real or imagined problem through a social movement or simply join the movement as a means of escaping the discrepancy. This type of person is most likely to join and stay in a movement because "the movement is a small world in itself commanding the total allegiance of its members and providing a totality of values and gratifications requiring renunciation of the larger world outside."[73] That is, social movements, whatever their purpose, provide satisfactions not available in the external world. Roger Brown indicated,

> "The satisfactions offered by the movement lie in several areas. It promises to satisfy material needs and provide security. It is simple enough to be understood and gives people a real goal in this confusing situation."[74]

Hans Toch attempted to refine Cantril's need fulfillment theory, arguing that each person is taught a set of values and practices.[75] He learns to expect simple and uncomplicated explanations of the world. The world in which we live is not simple. Man must adjust. Those who do not experience disillusionment become aware of a "problem situation" or "a personal or social deficit." These are the people who enter social movements after a precipitating event, such as being asked to join or being swept up in a confrontation with authorities. These people are *predisposed* to join a social movement designed to remedy their difficulties. In the next steps, according to Toch, the person feels that "change is concretely attainable," and then he feels "a desire to become involved in accomplishment of change." The individual at this point in the progression is open to external appeals made by existing social movements.

In *Young Radicals,* Kenneth Keniston agreed with Toch, suggesting that activists act out in fact the core values learned from their parents. The reality of society, urged Keniston, violated those values learned in the home. This is called "the confrontation with inequity."[76] At this point, potential protesters no longer see the problem as abstract. Rather, it becomes part of their reality and they react. It is here that radical interpretation occurs: the protester has now redefined the world in such a way that his views are in tune with a radical movement. At this juncture joining the movement is the logical thing to do.

Although we can make some statements about the kind of people who are active in a social movement, it is very difficult to specify what sort of person *will join* a given movement. We can make some generalizations based on historical data. However, each example we give can be countered with a contradictory one. Lewis Feuer suggested that young people historically have been engaged in revolutionary movements.[77] This is quite true, but they also were prominent in Nazi Youth and in Italian Fascist groups. We can also say that American farmers are most likely to support regressive movements. This seems correct until we discover that the liberal Progressive Party as well as the Socialists of the 1920's found many of their followers in the farm belt of America.

In discussing personality types we encounter an identical problem. Does a specific personality disorder or type place a person in a social movement? The answer is no. Authoritarian personalities may belong to the neighborhood church, community club, or golf club. They may be totally apolitical. What, then, will place them in the movement? Psychological interpretations alone do not give us the answer, but neither do statements such as *X* strain produces *Y* movement.

Social or personal problems that cause tensions in a person may make him dissatisfied with the existing order. This dissatisfaction does not by itself place him in the ranks of radicals or revolutionaries. Nor does the mere presence of feelings of dissatisfaction explain the purpose of a social movement, although the social movement may help to channel the resentment of the individual. However, dissatisfaction of the individual does not explain why a movement comes into existence in the first place. Marx, Lenin, Castro, Mao, and Hitler did not begin their social movements merely to help people with problem situations. However, sociologists should not ignore totally psychological reasons for participation in movements. The point is, neither approach provides us with a complete picture.

Summary

Social movements are collections of individuals organized together to bring about some kind of change. The type of change desired determines the movement's relationship to the society and, most importantly, its chances for success. The less change advocated, the greater the possibility of success.

Social movements go through various steps or stages toward either success or failure. Again, these steps are determined by the goals of the movement and the public's perceptions of them.

Certain types of people are found in social movements, but it is not possible to predict on the basis of personality traits whether a person will become a political activist.

Notes

1. Arlo Guthrie, "Alice's Restaurant," *Broadside* (*NYC*), **80** (1967), 18.
2. J. K. Gusfield, "Mass Society and Extremist Politics," *American Sociological Review,* **27** (1962), 19–30.
3. E. Bittner, "Radicalism and the Organization of Radical Movement," *American Sociological Review,* **28** (1963), 928–940.
4. D. A. Noebel, *Communism, Hypnotism and the Beatles: An Analysis of the Communist Use of Music* (Tulsa, Okla.: Christian Crusade Publications, 1965), p. 10.
5. *Time* (September 13, 1968), 36.
6. H. Matusow, *False Witness* (New York: Cameron and Kahn, 1955), p. 24.
7. B. Nangle, "The Gay Liberation Movement," unpublished paper, Bowling Green State University, 1973.
8. A number of writers have suggested the various stages and steps movements go through. Some of the most popular are found in N. J. Smelser, *Theory of Collective Behavior* (New York: The Free Press, 1968); C. W. King, *Social Movements in the United States* (New York: Random

House, Inc., 1956); and M. N. Zald and R. Ash, "Social Movement Organizations: Growth, Decay and Change," *Social Forces,* **44** (1966), 327–340.

9. D. D. Knudsen, "The Declining Status of Women: Popular Myths and the Failure of Functionalist Thought," *Social Forces,* **48** (1969), 183–192.

10. P. Smith, *Daughters of the Promised Land* (Boston: Little, Brown and Company, 1970).

11. M. Dixon, "Why Women's Liberation," in M. H. Garskof, ed., *Roles Women Play: Readings Toward Women's Liberation* (Belmont, Calif.: Wadsworth Publishing Co., Inc., 1971), pp. 166–167.

12. See C. W. Mills, *White Collar* (New York: Oxford University Press, 1951).

13. A. M. Rose, "The Adequacy of Women's Expectations for Adult Roles," *Social Forces,* **30** (1951), 69–77.

14. B. Friedan, "Up from the Kitchen Floor," *New York Times Magazine* (March 4, 1973), 8.

15. Ibid.

16. Ibid., p. 9.

17. H. Blumer, "Social Movements," in A. M. Lee, ed., *Principles of Sociology* (New York: Barnes & Noble, Inc., 1951), pp. 199–200.

18. Dixon, op. cit., p. 165.

19. R. Heberle, *Social Movements: An Introduction to Political Sociology* (New York: Appleton-Century-Crofts, 1952), p. 8.

20. J. Freeman, "Origins of Women's Movement," *American Journal of Sociology,* **78** (1973), 795.

21. Friedan, op. cit., p. 30.

22. E. Reed, *A Marxist Approach: Problems of Women's Liberation* (New York: Monthly Review Press, 1969), p. 21.

23. M. Benston, "The Political Economy of Women's Liberation," in Garskof, op cit., p. 202.

24. S. Brownmiller, "The New Feminism," *Current,* (1970), 38.

25. E. Nemy, "The Movement . . . Is Big Enough to Roll with All These Punches," *New York Times* (October 2, 1972), 46.

26. Friedan, op. cit., p. 29.

27. J. Johnston, "Feminists Score Friedan Article Assailing Movement Disrupters," *New York Times* (March 8, 1973), 40.

28. Ibid., p. 40.

29. See S. Lens, *Radicalism in America* (New York: Thomas Y. Crowell Company, 1966); and G. B. Rush and R. S. Denisoff, *Social and Political Movements* (New York: Appleton-Century-Crofts, 1971).

30. G. Almond, *The Appeals of Communism* (Princeton, N.J.: Princeton University Press, 1954), pp. 81–95.

31. See H. Fast, *Peekskill USA* (New York: Civil Rights Congress, 1951).

32. Lens, op. cit., p. 2.

33. W. A. Gamson, *Power and Discontent* (Homewood, Ill.: The Dorsey Press, 1968), p. 136.

34. D. A. Shannon, *The Socialist Party of America* (New York: Macmillan Publishing Co., Inc., 1955), p. 229.

35. Quoted in E. D. Cronon, *Black Moses: The Story of Marcus Garvey and the Universal Negro Improvement Association* (Madison: University of Wisconsin Press, 1955), p. 100.

36. A. M. Schlesinger, Jr., *The Politics of Upheaval* (Boston: Houghton Mifflin Company, 1960), p. 551.

37. L. Pope, *Millhands and Preachers: A Study of Gastonia* (New Haven, Conn.: Yale University Press, 1941), p. 253.

38. Ibid., p. 254.

39. Quoted in A. T. Anderson and B. P. Biggs, eds., *A Focus on Rebellion* (San Francisco: Chandler Publishing Co., 1962), p. 114.

40. Examples from C. Miller, "The Press and the Student Revolt," in M. V. Miller and S. Gilmore, eds., *Revolution at Berkeley* (New York: Dell Publishing Co., 1965), p. 323.

41. Ibid., p. 318.
42. R. H. Turner, "The Public Perception of Protest," *American Sociological Review*, **34** (1969), 818–819.
43. Ibid., p. 819.
44. R. K. Murray, *Red Scare: A Study in National Hysteria, 1919–1920* (Minneapolis: University of Minnesota Press, 1955), p. 69.
45. P. Renshaw, *The Wobblies: The Story of Syndicalism in the United States* (Garden City, N.Y.: Anchor Books, 1968), p. 187.
46. Shannon, op. cit., p. 108.
47. "Black September's Assassins," *Newsweek* (March 19, 1973), 45. Also see H. Eckstein, "On the Etiology of Internal War," *History and Theory*, (1965), 133–163; and H. L. Nieburg, *Political Violence: The Behavioral Process* (New York: St. Martin's Press, Inc., 1969).
48. H. Jacobs, ed., *Weathermen* (Berkeley, Calif.: Ramparts Press, 1970), p. 4.
49. See R. Michels, *Political Parties* (New York: The Free Press, 1949); C. W. Mills, *New Men of Power* (New York: Harcourt Brace Jovanovich, Inc., 1948); and S. M. Lipset, *Agrarian Socialism; The Cooperative Commonwealth Federation in Saskatchewan: A Study in Political Sociology* (Garden City, N.Y.: Doubleday & Company, Inc., 1968).
50. H. Becker, *The Outsider* (New York: The Free Press, 1963), p. 155.
51. See J. R. Gusfield, "Social Structure and Moral Reform: A Study of the Women's Christian Temperance Union," *American Journal of Sociology*, **61** (1955), 221–232.
52. J. F. Zygmunt, "Movements and Motives: Some Unresolved Issues in the Psychology of Social Movements," *Human Relations*, **25** (1971), 449.
53. E. Fromm, *Escape from Freedom* (New York: Farrar and Rinehart, 1941), p. 164.
54. T. Adorno et al., *The Authoritarian Personality* (New York: Harper and Row, Publishers, 1950), p. 1. This linking of authoritarianism with the radical right has been criticized especially by Edward Shils, "Authoritarianism: 'Right' and 'Left,'" in R. Christie and M. Jahoda, eds., *Studies in the Scope and Method of the "Authoritarian Personality"* (New York: The Free Press, 1954), pp. 24–49.
55. Ibid., p. 764.
56. E. Hoffer, *The True Believer* (New York: Mentor Books, 1951), p. 25.
57. L. Killian has objected to the broadness of the list, saying, "It may well be objected that this typology is so comprehensive that it excludes no one and thus renders the concept 'the true believer' meaningless." See "Social Movements," in R. E. L. Faris, ed., *Handbook of Modern Sociology* (Chicago: Rand McNally & Co., 1964), p. 444.
58. A. L. Edwards, "The Signs of Incipient Fascism," *Journal of Abnormal and Social Psychology*, **39** (1944), 310.
59. Fromm, op. cit., p. 216.
60. N. R. Maier, "The Role of Frustration in Social Movements," *Psychological Review*, **49** (1942), 591–592.
61. J. Rinaldo, *Psychoanalysis of the Reformer* (New York: Lee Publishing Co., 1921); and H. D. Lasswell, *Psychopathology and Politics* (Chicago: University of Chicago Press, 1930).
62. R. Hofstadter, *Anti-Intellectualism in American Life* (New York: McGraw-Hill Book Company, 1972), p. 494.
63. J. Mermar, "A Psychoanalyst Looks at the Nuclear Arms Race" (mimeographed paper), University of California at Los Angeles, 1962.
64. J. Lofland and R. Stark, "Becoming a World Saver: A Theory of Conversion to a Deviant Perspective," *American Sociological Review*, **30** (1965), 862–874.
65. I. S. Rohter, "The Rightists," *Transaction*, **4** (1967), 27–35. For a critique see Rush and Denisoff, op. cit., pp. 135–137.
66. P. B. Horton and C. L. Hunt, *Sociology*, 3rd Ed. (New York: McGraw-Hill Book Company, 1972), p. 494.
67. W. Kornhauser, *Politics of Mass Society* (New York: The Free Press, 1959); and Murray B. Levin, *The Alienated Voter: Politics in Boston* (New York: Holt, Rinehart & Winston, Inc., 1959), pp. 66–75.

68. R. Kaufman and M. Folson, "FSM: An Interpretive Essay," in *Free Speech Movement* (San Francisco: W. E. B. DuBois Clubs of America, 1965), p. 29.

69. R. Flacks, *Youth and Social Change* (Chicago: Markham Publishing Co., 1971), p. 43. Also see J. Gusfield, "Beyond Berkeley," in H. Becker, ed., *Campus Power Struggle* (New York: TransAction Books, 1970), pp. 15–26.

70. K. Keniston, "The Sources of Student Dissent," *The Journal of Social Issues,* **23** (1967), 149.

71. D. Kirby, "A Counter-Culture Explanation of Student Activism," *Social Problems,* **19** (1971), 214. Also see A. M. Lee, "An Obituary for 'Alienation,'" *Social Problems,* **20** (1972), 121–126.

72. Quoted in M. Grodzins, *The Loyal and the Disloyal* (Chicago: Chicago University Press, 1956), p. 145.

73. R. Turner and L. Killian, eds., *Collective Behavior* (Englewood Cliffs, N.J.: Prentice-Hall, Inc., 1957), p. 421.

74. R. W. Brown, "Mass Phenomena," in Gardner Lindzey, ed., *Handbook of Social Psychology,* Vol. 2 (Reading, Mass.: Addison-Wesley Publishing Co., Inc., 1954), p. 872.

75. H. Toch, *The Social Psychology of Social Movements* (Indianapolis: The Bobbs-Merrill Co., Inc., 1965).

76. K. Keniston, *Young Radicals: Notes on Committed Youth* (New York: Harcourt Brace Jovanovich, Inc., 1968).

77. L. Feuer, *The Conflict of Generations* (New York: Basic Books), 1969.

SIXTEEN

Social Change

What Is Social Change?

WESTERN MOVIES, at one time, always featured a posse of indignant townspeople racing up to a farmhouse and demanding, "Which way did the outlaws go?" ("They went that 'a 'way" or "They headed for the pass.") Although not chasing outlaws, sociologists have also been concerned with the question of where things are going. They pose the question: "Where are the trends taking us?" or "In which direction is society heading?" The degree and nature of social change was a central issue for early sociology (see Chapter Two). Unfortunately, there isn't anyone who can answer the question, "Which way are we going?" But sociologists spend a good deal of time trying to explain how changes in society take place.

Social change is the alteration or modification of social institutions and societies over some period of time. Implied in this definition are three fundamental parts: (1) the amount of a change; (2) the duration of a change; and (3) the nature of a change.[1]

One of the features of social change that interests sociologists is the *amount* or *magnitude of a change.* An election is quite different in magnitude from a revolution. A change in dating practices is quite different from the abolition of the family. Change, either *large* or *small, significant* or *minor,* is measured by the impact of a change upon society.

The *duration of a change* is the amount of time an alteration in society takes. *Gradual* versus *abrupt* change is the key to the question of time. A long-term change is quite different from something that happens overnight. The election of a Communist government that has the full consent of the governed is quite different from a violent revolutionary takeover that occurs in a matter of a few, sudden days. The change of a country from feudalism to industrialism takes much longer than a change brought about by a series of five- and seven-year plans for accelerated growth or a "great leap forward."

The *nature of a change* is closely linked to the first two conditions. The nature of a change is measured by the degree of disruption in the society. The *severity of a change* is central. What is the amount of *social cost incurred?* What price progress?

The answer to this last question allows us to identify two major approaches to social change: *evolutionary* and *revolutionary.* According to Francis R. Allen, the following distinctions can be made: "*Evolution* refers to alterations in society or culture that are *lawful, orderly,* and *gradual;* an unfolding of forces actually or potentially present is implied. *Revolution* connotes a sudden and far-reaching change from the usual social and/or cultural ongoing. The latter implies a major break in the *continuity of development,* which often is contrary to the official law."[2] The break in continuity is made through political violence. Recall that in Chapter Two we suggested that sociology was born because of the debate over the issue of political violence in nineteenth-century Europe. Conservatives like Louis de Bonald, Herbert Spencer, and Auguste Comte feared dramatic, disruptive change and favored long-term evolutionary alterations in society. Such changes were generally seen as independent of the actions of men.

Table 16–1. Patterns of Growth

	Evolutionary	*Revolutionary*
Scale	small	large
Time span	long	short
Nature	peaceful	violent

Revolutionaries and visionaries, who welcomed change, desired quick, decisive, large-scale modifications that would almost instantaneously create a higher form of society. In the revolutionary model, man was an important element of bringing about change. Karl Marx, M. A. Bakunin, and countless lesser-known figures championed this view.

Basic Assumptions

Social change is the movement of society from one form to another. The transition may be from the simple to the complex, from the primitive to the sophisticated. It is a change from farm to factory, from the biblical Garden of Eden to modern society. Social scientists have analyzed this transformation in great detail[3] (see Chapter 5).

Common to all of these schemes as a starting point is the model of a small, simple community in which individuals were governed by many forces beyond their control. The weather, the climate, and parentage all determined the life style of man in both the primitive and the feudal systems. People were born into communal positions and kept there by the belief systems of the tribal or feudal society. People did not question this way of life, as it appeared to be preordained and was supported by all.

The Industrial Revolution ended this pastoral way of life. People were jammed into the dirty factories and cities of Europe. Philosophers proclaimed, "God is dead." Technological and political events destroyed the guidelines of the past. People were set adrift. Life was impersonal. The relations between

Table 16–2. Stages of Social Change: Popular Concepts

	Primitive	*Feudal*	*Industrial*
Otto von Gierke		*Genossenschaft* (medieval)	*Herrschaft* (modern nation-state)
Lewis Henry Morgan	savagery	barbarism	civilization
Henry Maine		status	contract
Fustel de Covlanges		stable, closed	open society
Ferdinand Toënnies	Gemeinschaft	*Gemeinschaft*	*Gesellschaft*
Max Weber	traditional	traditional	rational
Émile Durkheim		mechanical	organic
Auguste Comte	theological	metaphysical	positive
Robert Redfield	folk	folk	urban
Howard Becker		sacred	secular
Karl Marx	primitive	feudal	capitalist-Communist
David Riesman	traditional	traditional	inner–other-directed

people were determined by economics. The cold "cash nexus" relationship, as Ferdinand Toënnies described it, predominated. In technological societies, people treated each other as mere economic objects. This was the evolutionary process as seen by students of social change.

The question became then, "What causes this change, and is it not possible to restructure the direction?" Numerous answers were given. These answers suggested the interplay of social conditions, innovation, and values. Change was characterized as being generated by some disharmony. Innovation and change were the result of "something" being wrong. The attempt to *correct* the disharmony brought about the change.

Regardless of their feelings on the subject of social change, few sociologists and philosophers questioned the notion that societies move from simple to complex, from small to large, or from worse to better.[4] Found in these directional statements were, as Robert Nisbet said, a number of essential premises:

1. Change is natural.
2. Change is immanent.
3. Change is continuous.
4. Change is necessary.
5. Change is uniform.[5]

Change Is Natural

Nearly all models of man and society recognize social change as natural. Theologians have seen history as moving toward the day of final judgment. Philosophers like Plato and Georg W. F. Hegel discussed the historical thrust toward an absolute "ought to be." Early sociologists like Comte and Marx described a succession of changes that occurred throughout history. As Nisbet suggested, "Past, present, and future could thus be given connection in a single, directional series."[6]

Change Is Immanent

Immanence means that the *cause of the change is in the unit that is changing.* The notion that change is generated by internal or *immanent* factors was introduced by P. A. Sorokin, who argued that the nature of a society predetermines the types of change it will go through.[7] A violent society will probably move in the direction of a military state. A society that leans toward the pleasure principle will move toward a more *sensate* and hedonistic style of life. For example, a society that stresses individualism will create a philosophy of "Do your own thing" and will evaluate marriages on the basis of individual happiness. Each social institution contains within itself the cause, need, and reason for its own change.

Change Is Continuous

Continuity refers to the steps a society passes through to reach a particular stage of development. Anthropologists talk about the rise of civilization through various stages: the Stone Age, the Iron Age, the Hellenic Age, the Dark Ages, and the Industrial Revolution. Comte introduced three stages of knowledge through which each society must pass: the religious, the metaphysical, and the scientific (or positive). Marx insisted that each society must pass through each of the stages of economic development before moving to the next stage. In fact, Marx discounted czarist Russia as being ripe for socialism *because* it was still in a feudal mode of production. First, he claimed, Russia must experience capitalism: "She will not succeed without having first transformed a good part of her peasants into proletarians; and after that, once taken to the bosom of the capitalist regime, she will experience its pitiless laws like other profane peoples."[8] A more contemporary set of stages was presented by economist W. W. Rostow, who described a six-step plan for the movement of a society from preindustrialism to a technological Valhalla.[9]

1. *The traditional society.* The traditional society is the basic primitive unit. The economic development is very simple. The society is organized for mere survival. It teeters on the brink of starvation. There is little progress, either because of the nearsightedness of the leadership or because of sheer lack of knowledge.

2. *The preconditioning for takeoff.* The time before the takeoff is a period filled with controversy. It is a time of discontent and tension. The direction of change is not clear, but the members of the society are unhappy. Discontent runs rampant throughout the land. New directions are sought. False starts are made. People confuse cosmetic actions of government with real change. In time these actions are doomed to failure. The social tension will provide a catalyst for movement to the next stage.

3. *The takeoff.* The takeoff is caused by some violent action that propels the society into a new form of economic organization. Planning is introduced. Goals become clear. Resources are mobilized to achieve these goals. New money is available. Funds from other nations become available to bring about the spurt of economic energy necessary for sustained growth. For example, British investors greatly helped finance the takeoff of the American economy in the post-Civil War period. Russia similarly aided the Castro regime in Cuba and Mao in China.

4. *The drive to maturity.* The drive to maturity is characterized by an increase in the rate of capital accumulated and also in individual per capita income. With the rise in salaries and profits, new inventions, goods, and services are made available. The economy moves from just being concerned with survival to a consumer- and pleasure-oriented economy. Concern with color television sets replaces worry about food and clothing.

5. *The age of high mass consumption.* We live in an age of high mass consumption. People buy a lot to maintain the corporations and institutions

that have emerged both to *create* and to *service needs.* This stage has been described by John K. Galbraith as "the affluent society."

6. *The search for quality.* At this point some discontent with the technological society may emerge. Vance Packard labeled the affluent society, the one in which we live, "the waste makers." Many social critics emerge to question the validity of mass consumption.

Dorothy L. Sayers observed, "A society in which consumption has to be artificially stimulated in order to keep production going is a society founded on trash and waste, and such a society is a house built upon sand."[10] This statement as well as others made in the 1960s and 1970s have brought into question the next property of social change.

Change Is Necessary

A cardinal principle of the nineteenth century was that change leads to a better life. Herbert Spencer called change the "beneficent necessity." None but the most reactionary conservatives questioned this notion. The methods of change did come under question, but the aim of progress was rarely if ever questioned. Comte, Durkheim, Marx, Bakunin—a strange mix—all applauded the value of science and its ability to secure a better world. They would have totally accepted the slogan "Better Things for Better Living Through Science." The belief that history was a movement toward improved social conditions was rarely doubted. Even today people continue to smoke and have large families in the belief that science will find a solution before some catastrophe such as cancer or "standing room only" occurs.

In the 1960s, as we have briefly indicated, many scholars began seriously to question the connections among change, progress, and a better world. Terms like *alienation* and *mass society* were used to describe modern technological societies. Some critics lauded the development of "Consciousness III" or the "counterculture," which stressed a return to more basic and primitive styles of life (see Chapter Four, "Culture," and Chapter Fifteen, "Social Movements"). Movements appeared to preserve the environment, to protect endangered species of animals, and to return to the soil on communal farms.[11] These events are relatively new, as most of the world since the mid-nineteenth-century has placed its fate in the hands of science.

Change Is Uniform

History repeats itself. Change was viewed by many early social theorists as a repetitive process. All nations went through the same stages, according to Comte and Marx. There existed, they thought, common uniform laws for the rise of civilization. David McClelland, in *The Achieving Society,* suggested that each advanced civilization goes through three repetitive stages: (1) the population is motivated toward achievement; (2) those who are the highest achievers reach positions of importance, and they grab all of the political power in the society; and (3) people living under this all-powerful elite become hedonist and retreat into their own groups or become group-oriented. McClelland thought this third stage existed in ancient Greece as well as in England in the days of William Shakespeare.

More recently the notion of *exceptionalism* has come to be accepted. This means that *different societies evolve and develop in different ways.* Not all capitalist nations relive the experiences of Great Britain or the United States. Communist nations are also quite dissimilar.[12] However, sociologists have attempted to find some uniform properties in the area of social change.

In sum, the two general processes of change are *evolution* and *revolution.* One is gradual and peaceful and involves a minimum of disruption. The other is quick and violent and frequently involves considerable inconvenience. Within each of these processes there are several dominant trends of change.

Social Dynamics: Evolution

The "Natural" Drive Toward Perfection

Social dynamics are the forces of social change that appear to operate on the basis of natural laws. These forces can either be tied to human action or operate independently of man. Some early sociologists like Auguste Comte presented social dynamics as a form of the "invisible hand of progress" guiding man to an Age of Positivism (Science). Comte believed there existed a *natural tendency* for mankind to move from an uncomfortable point of stress (disequilibrium) to a point of harmonious plenty (equilibrium). When things were amiss, solutions would be found. The key problem was an *increase in social interaction,* which simply meant the growth in the population while the supporting environment remained the same. As the number of people increased, the resources were taxed to the state of discomfort and hunger. At this point, men banded together into larger groups to solve the problem. The more people the better to cope with the social problem. For Auguste Comte, history was a series of stages of disharmony and harmony. In time, he reasoned, the largest possible unit of humanity would be formed, and it would be able to solve all of the problems of mankind. This would happen in the Age of Humanity. Comte, as his critics quickly pointed out, did not consider the influence of values. People, he felt, had little choice but to improve in the face of adversity. What is important in Comte's scheme is the stress upon the idea that *problems cause social change.* For him, necessity was the mother of invention.

Herbert Spencer presented a very similar scheme of things. Society, for Spencer, was an organism that grew and moved toward perfection. As it grew, an internal leadership developed. This leadership controlled its own population, at the same time warring with external enemies. This was the *military* form of social organization. Then the society began to increase and grow in complexity. This increase encouraged the growth of numerous groups or classes. Highly complex organizations moved the society toward internal considerations of self-maintenance and survival. Spencer's view of change was based on the principle of natural selection introduced by Charles Darwin. The fittest individuals and societies survived. The weak fell by the wayside. This was considered a part of "natural law."

Valuative Change

Karl Marx modified Comte's and Spencer's deterministic view of change. Marx, too, said that the force of history moves on to solve social disharmony. But, he said, an independent force—dialectical materialism (the historical push of economics)—must join hands with the values of a society in order to bring about change. Class consciousness created by economic conditions would bring about social change (see Chapter Nine). As we will see, *revolution* was a tool in Marx's overall *evolutionary* theory. Indeed, Marx welcomed Charles Darwin's *Origin of Species* as proof that his theory of change was correct. Darwin was the popularizer of the theory of evolution and natural selection.

William F. Ogburn further modified Marx's ideas by saying that economic innovations occur *before* changes in values. He was suggesting that scientific breakthroughs occur much more rapidly than people are willing to accept them. He introduced the term *cultural lag,* which means that two parts of a culture experience *different rates of change.*[13] One part, the material or technological, changes *before* the nonmaterial segment of society changes. An invention may be available long before it is accepted in the society. The nonmaterial aspect of culture must adjust to the material aspect in order to use an invention to its fullest capacity. There are countless examples of innovations' being ignored because of hostile public opinion. The typewriter, the automobile, and television were all available long before the public was ready to use these "newfangled inventions." Ogburn saw the position of women in a technological society as an example of cultural lag. With the advent of modern machinery, he suggested, their lack of physical strength was no longer an excuse to bar women from many jobs previously held by men. The only real barrier was how people felt about women in factories and plants.

This is equally true of social policy. Many social policies were ignored as "too radical" for decades prior to becoming law. Social Security, workmen's compensation, equal employment, Medicare, and many other programs were at one time considered unthinkable and unworkable. Although some sociologists are uneasy about the idea of separating material from nonmaterial culture, Ogburn does show an interesting form of evolutionary theory: society moves gradually in the direction of progress. Material culture usually changes at a faster rate than nonmaterial culture. Therefore, change takes time to occur. Inherent in this time lapse is cultural lag, which causes a conflict between the inventor and the rest of society. In time, the inventor is vindicated and his brainchild is accepted.[14] Society adapts to the change.

Ogburn's theory of cultural lag has *generally* proved correct; however, some examples do appear to contradict it. For example, the American public has accepted and demanded some inventions that have hardly been tested. The ready acceptance of many "wonder drugs," such as the birth control pill, forced pharmaceutical houses to hurry the products onto the market without testing them thoroughly for safety.

Whereas numerous other models of change also present values as being secondary in importance to population increases and technological inventions, other sociologists have laid great stress upon the "time of an idea." Émile Durkheim, although critical of Comte for the determinism in his model, saw society as beginning with certain values that all people hold in common. These agreed-upon values provide the glue for a *mechanical* form of solidarity or consensus. As population increases and resources become taxed, these values are brought into question. On the basis of its values, a society can make decisions about the direction of change it wishes to take. The direction is not automatic. Rather, Durkheim was concerned with the influence of values and ideas upon social change. For example, a Catholic country with a high regard for life will frown upon abortion, suicide, and birth control. Other choices must be found for population control. This type of society will then stress technological advances or even emigration. Then technological change will occur.

Other countries not accepting the Catholic doctrine banning artificial birth control devices may try these means prior to looking to technology. Values, therefore, permit change and determine its direction. However, Durkheim assumed that when the population pressure reaches a certain point, communication would increase and new ideas would give birth to a technological change. The rise of the technological society will find a form of *organic solidarity.* Under conditions of organic solidarity common values no longer hold the society together. Instead, it is held together by *mutual interdependence.* People need each other's technological skills in order to survive. The butcher needs the baker. Both of them will require the services of a physician and an undertaker. In the development of dissimilar occupational groups, many new values and norms will come forth. These values will make possible more future technological innovation.

Max Weber, in *The Protestant Ethic and the Spirit of Capitalism,* presented one of the best-known cases of values' facilitating social change.[15] Weber argued that capitalism was the direct result of the "inner-worldly asceticism" generated by the rise of Protestantism. That is, the religious doctrines of Martin Luther and John Calvin gave birth to capitalism. Luther and Calvin, according to Weber, redefined man's relationship to work.[16] In the religious writings of these two theologians were found the notion of *Beruf* ("duty to work" or "the calling"). This was the notion that it was man's duty to labor in the vineyard of the Lord. Religious purity was linked to work.

Calvin believed that the righteous were chosen beforehand by God. This is called the *doctrine of predestination.* Those with "the calling" were identifiable by their economic success through hard work. After all, "an evil tree cannot bring forth good fruit." Calvin believed further that those with "the calling" should not accumulate wealth and then spend it on slow horses and fast women. This would corrupt the flesh. Rather than spending their profit on worldly pleasures, men should *reinvest* it in work ventures. This "worldly asceticism" led to the doctrine of *deferred gratification,* that is, postponing immediate pleasure in favor of some future reward. Men should put off worldly pleasures for rewards in the afterlife.

These two principles of hard work and postponed gratification made up the *Protestant ethic,* which laid stress on (1) discipline and hard work, (2) the

accumulation of wealth, and (3) competition and self-reliance. These three values, in turn, made up the *spirit of capitalism.*

Weber's argument that the values found in Calvin and Luther had brought about the rise of capitalism was a very controversial idea. It refuted Marx's notion that religion was merely the *reflection* of the capitalist economic system. Religion, said Marx, obscured the economic realities. It was "the opiate of the masses." Marx argued that a technologically-caused change in economic relations had caused Christianity to accommodate to the new system of exchange.[17]

In his 1929 analysis of Gastonia, North Carolina, Liston Pope found that religious values and emphases changed there because of economic alterations in the community. The churches preached fundamental agricultural values. With the arrival of the textile factories, the churches adjusted to the current values of hard work and promptness. Pope reported, "Ministers and churches

Problems cause social change

played a significant part . . . in facilitating the industrial transformation of Gaston County. When the cotton mills began to rise, ministers and leading church men ventured boldly into the field of economics, lending the moral sanction and *active support of the churches to the new enterprise.*"[18]

Stephen M. Sales, in a study of an economically depressed city in the 1960s, reported that economic conditions did in fact influence religious values. He looked at the Seattle area, which was dependent almost entirely upon the aerospace industry. "As goes Boeing," said the residents, "so goes Seattle." Because of government cutbacks in the late 1960s, the unemployment rate was near 16 percent. Someone posted a sign: "Would the Last Person Leaving Seattle Please Turn Off the Lights." Sales found that under these conditions Fundamentalist churches stressing the afterlife enjoyed a conversion boom. The liberal churches experienced a decline in membership and attendance. This led Sales to conclude that "only certain churches become attractive in times of greatest stress and insecurity, while others appear to lose some of their appeal during these periods. Thus, it is apparently not religion as such that is the opiate of the people, but only some kinds of religion."[19] This finding supports the idea that economic well-being does have an impact upon the religious values people may hold. In Seattle, people experiencing the privations of an aerospace slump sought solace in the more traditional fire-and-brimstone churches as opposed to the liberal denominations.

Cultural Mentalities

P. A. Sorokin proposed the idea that all societies are held together by *common* patterns of thought and values. Each society, he felt, had a central theme that made life meaningful to the individual citizen. Americans stress individualism and privacy. Citizens of the USSR place considerable emphasis on the group or the collective. A person walks down the street whistling the latest pop tune. In the United States, we say, "He's doing his own thing." In Russia, it's *unculturna* ("uncultured") and others will tell the musical walker exactly that. Childbirth in American hospitals occurs in the privacy of the delivery room. Not so in the USSR. Soviet hospitals have common labor rooms where expectant mothers comfort one another. They, like American women, are delighted with their system of bringing babies into the world (see the section in Chapter Four on ethnocentrism). The central theme dividing the United States and the Soviet Union is the stresses placed on individualism and the collective, respectively. Sorokin called central themes "cultural mentalities." *Cultural mentalities are the manner in which a society interprets reality.* There are three cultural mentalities: the *ideational,* the *sensate,* and the *idealistic,* which is simply a mix of the first two.*

*Although the idealistic mentality combines both the ideational and the sensate, it is *never* a perfect balance; consequently Sorokin treats it as a mid-point between the two.

The ideational mentality is a spiritual interpretation of reality. The needs of man are believed to lie in high ideals. The perfection of man either on earth or in heaven is the central theme. The ideational minimizes the wants of the body and sensual pleasure. A statement like "Mortify the flesh, for your treasure lies in heaven" is illustrative of this mentality.

The ideational mentality is addressed to a definitive moral code in which "Truth" is clear and absolute. The Soviet Union is an ideational society, one that strives toward an absolute state of society: communism. The citizens are urged to work toward the future. Consumer goods are scarce. Sexual codes are puritanical. Nation-states like Sparta, and contemporarily China, have also emphasized the ideational, spiritual quality of society.

The sensate mentality focuses on physical pleasure. Sorokin observed, "Its needs and aims are mainly physical, and maximum satisfaction is sought of these needs."[20] The orientation is the here and now: "Eat, drink, and be merry." "From the senses come all trustworthiness," wrote German philosopher Friedrich Wilhelm Nietzsche, "all good conscience, all evidence of truth." "Heaven is a back scratch," stated anthropologist Ashley Montagu. The United States closely mirrors Sorokin's notion of the sensate cultural mentality. It is not striving toward some future goal. Its citizens enjoy and pursue many creature comforts. A large house, a swimming pool, fancy cars, color television sets, season tickets to pro football games are all valued. Sensual pleasure is stressed through group sensitivity-training sessions, sex therapy, and books like *The Sensuous Woman, The Sensuous Man,* and *The Sensuous Couple.*[21]

Reliance on relative values and fads is also part of the sensate mentality. The changing of musical styles, the rise and fall of various types of alcohol and narcotics are all part of this constant pleasure-seeking.

No society is *totally* wedded to either the ideational or the sensate. Alcoholism is a serious problem in the Soviet Union. Most Americans claim belief in high moral and religious values. Nonetheless, each society has a *dominant* cultural mentality.

Sorokin presented history as going through phases that parallel the three cultural mentalities. The Graeco-Roman culture was first held together by the *ideational* form, then moved toward the *idealistic,* and reached the *sensate.* The order is not always the same. Sorokin perceived the present state of Western civilization to be in an advanced *sensate* state, moving toward the *ideational.* In 1937, he presented what he believed to be the conditions of the downfall of the sensate cultural mentality:

1. The sensate culture, emphasizing pleasure, will lose track of normative values and right and wrong. Everything will become relative. Moral anarchy will prevail.

2. Man will "sink still deeper into the mulch of the sociocultural sewers."[22] Men will increasingly spend time and energy in physical gratification, like sex and the use of drugs and labor-saving devices.

3. The valuative system will begin to erode. One opinion will be as good as any other. Respect for authority will decline.

4. Respect for the rights of others will fade. "The contractual democracy, contractual capitalism, including private property, contractual free society of free men, will be swept away.[23]

5. The philosophy of "Might makes right" will take over. With values no longer enough to bind men together, force and governmental deception or fraud will become increasingly prevalent.

6. Freedom will become a myth and a minority will rule.

7. Governments, having seized power, will become more authoritarian and tyrannical.

8. Sensate values will continue to increase, leading to the breakdown of the family.

9. Losing all of the traditional institutions, society will cease to function effectively. People will be too concerned with pleasure.

10. Innovation will begin to wane. People will be less capable of coping with real problems.

11. The result will be moral and economic anarchy.

12. The sanctity of life and property will fade. Suicide, crime, and mental and social disease will rise.

13. The population will divide into two groups: supporters of the sensate and their antagonists, the ideationalists. (In this last condition lies the key to Sorokin's notion of social change.)

A society cannot ignore its *need to survive* for a protracted period of time. When "Eat, drink and be merry" becomes all-pervasive, the tasks of everyday living are ignored. As a result, conditions become so chaotic and people so desperate that an opposing idea appears that is directly opposite to the original. For example, the Christians appeared to protest the decadence of the Roman Empire. They preached an ascetic and stoical style of life. St. Paul decried the use of sex for pleasure, excessive drinking, and many other practices favored in the palaces of the Caesars. Today, Fundamentalist preachers exhort Americans to turn aside from their "drug, sex, booze"-oriented society.

What Sorokin suggested is that when any society goes to an ideological extreme ("the tendency toward dogmatism"), it ignores *other equally important* needs. When this happens the pendulum of history shifts the other way.

Sociologists, of course, do not know if Sorokin's predictions are correct; however, there is little doubt that some of his 1937 descriptions do fit some social trends of the 1960s and 1970s.

Common to all the theorists we've been discussing is the simple idea that population growth and the values and organization of society are closely interrelated. Even today, we can see Catholic countries stressing technological change to fight poverty while other nations like India and China are advocating birth control programs.

The role of values in social change is very difficult to analyze, and two primary approaches to this subject exist. The first presents values as being at the mercy of technological changes; the other presents values as a significant force in determining modifications in social life. In the first, technology rules; in the second, social values rule.

Social Dynamics: Revolution

Revolution is a term thrown about very loosely in everyday speech. We refer to the "rock revolution" and the "fashion revolution" or a "revolutionary design in automobiles." These phrases usually describe the quick rise of a particular style of music, clothing, or cars. In the area of social change, a revolution is *a fast-moving, "sweeping, fundamental change in political organization, social structure, economic property control, and the predominant myth of a social order that causes a major break in the continuity of development."*[24] More simply, revolution is *the violent overthrow of existing ways of doing things.* "Revolution," wrote Chalmers Johnson, "requires the use of violence by members of the system in order to cause the system to change."[25] Revolution intensifies the evolutionary pace of social change either by speeding it up or by reversing it in some other direction. Unlike evolution, revolution is disruptive and violent *and* is based on the *will of men.*

The term *revolution* was popularized by the "radical" astronomer Nicolaus Copernicus, who said the earth *revolved* around the sun, rather than being the center of the universe as was previously believed. Copernicus, it was said, *revolutionized* astronomy.[26]

Generally, the word *revolution* has a political meaning. Revolution, as Aristotle originally saw it, was a cry against injustice. He portrayed men as banding together in desperation to abolish evil. Karl Marx and Friedrich Engels concluded their famous plea for revolution, *The Communist Manifesto,* saying, "Ends can be attained only by the forcible overthrow of all existing social conditions. Let the ruling classes tremble at a Communist revolution. The proletarians *have nothing to lose but their chains.*"[27] Writer Albert Camus provided an excellent example of political revolution in his book *The Rebel.* Revolution occurs when the Slave becomes aware that he belongs to an unjust Master. The Slave feels indignation. He denies the Master's absolute freedom to control him. He shouts, "I rebel." He asserts his right to freedom. In revolution the Master is either killed or overthrown. The Slave then becomes Master. As in George Orwell's book *Animal Farm,* the pigs, having driven off the farmer, begin to walk on their hind feet and give orders to the chickens.[28]

When we think of political revolutions, pictures of mobs in the streets of Moscow or Paris come to mind, as in Sergei Eisenstein's film *Ten Days That Shook the World* and Charles Dickens's famous novel *A Tale of Two Cities.* However, a more objective way of looking at revolutions is to classify them by their scope and the magnitude of the succeeding change.

In *The Old Regime and the French Revolution,* Alexis de Tocqueville specified four types of revolutions: *political, social, religious,* and *total.*[29]

Political Revolution

The *political revolution* is one that produces a change in government or in the quality of an existing government. In a *private palace revolution,* one small group grabs power from another. The Borgia family of fifteenth-century Italy offers a classic case of the private palace revolution: various members of the family murdered (usually poisoned) government officials and clergy in order to gain and maintain political power. Shakespeare's famous character Macbeth was involved in similar evildoing.[30]

The *public palace revolution* is very similar to the private palace revolution. However, it is larger in scale and involves more people. It may include, for example, the movement of troops or the seizing of the local radio station. The classic case of the public palace revolution is the coup d'état.[31] In the typical coup, the military throws out of office another military leader or a duly elected civilian government. Examples of coups are legion in Latin America, Asia, the Middle East, and Africa. The fall of President Diem in South Vietnam and the displacement of President Allende in Chile are two examples.

The failure of one attempted coup had worldwide significance. On a warm, sunny July day in 1944, Colonel Klaus Philip Count von Stauffenberg arrived in Rastenburg.[32] He was a member of a military conspiracy, and he carried with him a bomb concealed in a briefcase. In a conference barrack he was to attend a meeting at 1 P.M. with dictator Adolph Hitler. Ten minutes prior to the meeting Stauffenberg triggered the explosive device and excused himself. The bomb was six feet from the Führer. An aide, Colonel Heinz Brandt, pushed the briefcase, containing the bomb, further away from Hitler. He did so merely so that he could see more clearly the maps of installations in France and Germany that were being discussed. The gesture cost him his life and was probably instrumental in saving the Führer's.

The conspirators awaited news of Hitler's death. At 9 P.M. they learned of an imminent broadcast by Hitler. At 1 A.M. Hitler announced, "I am unhurt and well, and secondly, you should know of a crime unparalleled in German history."[33] Retaliation was swift. Seven thousand people were arrested by the Gestapo (the secret police) and 4,980 persons were executed, including some of the cream of the German general staff. The coup had failed.

The coup is a public event involving many people, quite different from the Borgias' clandestine method of operation.

A foremost characteristic of either kind of palace revolution is that the instigators are already close to positions of power. Poisoning a duke or blowing up a political leader in a military bunker requires access.

Political revolution has been called *internal war.* Harry Eckstein defined internal war as "any resort to violence within a political order to change its constitution, rulers, or policies."[34] This form of revolution requires some popular participation, as in the guerrilla wars fought in South Vietnam, Indonesia, and Cuba. Internal war can also be a civil conflict, such as the

American Civil War or the British Civil War. Wars of national liberation in the emerging nations also qualify as political revolutions.[35]

Social Revolution

The *social revolution* is a drastic alteration of some aspect of society like the economic system or the ranking of social positions. The Industrial Revolution, which ushered in the change from a pastoral society to an urban, industrialized society, was a social revolution. The introduction of the wheel in Tibet and of the steel axe in the Yir Yoront tribe of Australian aborigines are but two examples of causes of social revolution.

The Yir Yoront possessed no knowledge of metals. Their way of life was from the Stone Age. They existed by fishing and hunting. A key tool was the stone axe. This axe was central to the tribe's economy. As with wealth in America, the ownership of a stone axe was the Yir Yoront mark of status. Only adult men owned this valued object. They knew the location of various types of wood, stones, and the other components essential for the creation of the axe.

The widespread introduction of the mass-produced steel axe by missionaries altered the relationships in the tribe. The mission gave steel axes to the younger men and even women and children. As Laurence Sharp explained, "All this led to a revolutionary confusion of sex, age, and kinship roles, with a major gain in independence and loss of subordination on the part of those able now to acquire steel axes when they had been unable to possess stone axes before."[36] The leadership was challenged. Age, sex, no longer determined status positions. Ceremonies surrounding the technology of the village lost favor. The value systems began to change. Insecurity became a part of tribal life. The steel axe was the weapon of social revolution in this aboriginal tribe.

Religious Revolution

The *religious revolution* is the discarding of one set of values regarding the nature of man for a different set of beliefs. The conversion of Western Europe to Christianity and the acceptance of Islam in the Mideast were major religious revolutions. The movement from the rural, religious society to the technologically sophisticated world of secularism is a more recent example. The changeover from former beliefs to Communism as a dominant state ideology in Russia, China, and Cuba also qualifies as religious revolution.

Total Revolution

The *total revolution* or "great national revolution" incorporates all of the other elements described by Tocqueville, political, social, religious, and cultural.

It involves the overthrow of all dominant social institutions. There have been very few total revolutions. The model of the total revolution is the French Revolution of 1789, which was an attempt to bring about "liberty, fraternity and equality" by eliminating many if not all of the vestiges of the past. The monarchy, the Catholic Church, and other institutions were swept away by the Reign of Terror and the guillotine. As Crane Brinton suggested, "The great French Revolution of the eighteenth century . . . still remains for most of us in the Western world a kind of pattern revolution."[37] The typical picture of a total revolution includes mobs in the streets, fiery speakers, the charge at the palace gates, the fall of the old regime, and finally the purge or reign of terror.[38]

The Bolshevik Revolution was characterized by a similar chain of events.[39] The fall of the provisional government because it was unable to conduct a war and a social revolution simultaneously; the storming of the Winter Palace; the execution of the royal family; the civil war; and finally the ascendancy of the Council of Workers or Soviets paralleled events in the French experience of a century before.

The rise of Fidel Castro in Cuba also fits this pattern. The Batista regime fell to the ragtag army of Fidel Castro in 1959. Supported by the peasants and portions of the Cuban working class, the guerrilla army took power. It used the tactics used by the Russian revolutionists and adapted them to the conditions in Cuba.[40]

Ironically, each of these total revolutions was followed by the rise of totalitarian regimes. *Totalitarian governments are governments that have total power and are not restrained by any law.* After a revolution, a totalitarian government is created ostensibly to be the "caretaker" until things have calmed down and a democratic government can be formed. Karl Marx called this "interim" form of government "the *dictatorship* of the proletariat," which would cleanse society of the corrupting practices of the past. Camus brilliantly summed up the role of the "caretaker" government: "A religion that executes its obsolete sovereign must now establish the power of its new sovereign; it closes the churches and this leads to an endeavor to build a temple."[41] Movements that have destroyed the old regime must now re-create respect for government if they are to rule. In their zeal to construct a new world they frequently repeat or even go beyond the excesses of the previous ruling elite. The French Directory improved on the excesses of the regime it replaced. The Council of the Soviets originally attempted to integrate their opposition into a New Economic Policy but later resorted to the infamous "purges" of the 1930s.[42] The regimes of Mao in China and Castro in Cuba have also purged, executed, and imprisoned numerous "political deviants."

This process has been termed the *Thermidor Effect.* The Thermidor Effect appears during the period in which a new government attempts to gain public acceptance by either forgiving or repressing its opponents. It is, as Crane Brinton called it, "a convalescence from the fever of revolution."[43] The convalescent period is one of the neutralization of the new government's opposition.

The neutralization of political opposition focuses on those who can in some way win over people to their point of view. The Nazis, for example, threw their German political opponents into jail, thus silencing any criticism. Stalin imprisoned his critics, executed them, or sent them to concentration camps.

Neutralization

According to Philip Selznick, besides political critics another group is open to attack during this period: those who may create obstacles for the new government in implementing its programs.[44] The Mao regime in China originally tried to win over the professionals and the businessmen by persuasion. The jailing of these essential people was impractical if the nation's economic institutions were to function. When the "Hundred Flowers" program proved a failure and intellectual criticism grew, political repression was finally used. In post-World War II Germany, the process was *reversed.* The Allies wished to bar all ex-Nazis from positions of political and economic power. The advent of the Cold War and the West's fear of the Soviet Union found the United States and her allies withdrawing from this stance and welcoming bureaucrats from the Third Reich back into industry and government.

There are four basic forms of neutralization.

The first is the destruction of the opposition through *infiltration* and *disruption,* such as the use of the *agent provocateur* who joins an organization to discredit it by performing outrageous acts in its name. There are numerous examples of this form of disruption, among them the Zimmerman telegram, "Tommy the Traveler," and the political espionage of the 1972 presidential election.

In the Zimmerman telegram of 1916, which was published in the American press, Germany offered Mexico a war alliance against the then-neutral United States. British intelligence, eager for America to enter World War I, was believed to be responsible for concocting this phony telegram.

During the student protests of the 1960s *agents provocateurs* were placed in the ranks of various student organizations. "Tommy the Traveler" was perhaps the most publicized of the police agents operating in protest activities. *Time* magazine reported:

> A year ago, a handsome, tense, slender youth known as "Tommy the Traveler" appeared at Hobart College in Geneva, N.Y., and began to preach revolution to anyone who would listen. He claimed to be an S.D.S. organizer, and his principal converts were two freshmen, would-be revolutionaries who were fascinated by his violent rhetoric. To them he taught the uses of the M1 carbine and demonstrated the construction of various types of fire bombs.
>
> Last month his efforts seemed to have come to fruition when two of the students were arrested for allegedly fire-bombing the campus ROTC office, located in a dormitory where 120 students were sleeping. The fire was put out without any injuries. That was fortunate because Tommy the Traveler, the zealous revolutionary, was in fact an undercover policeman.[45]

During the 1972 Florida Democratic primary campaign, thousands of residents received a letter, signed by presidential aspirant Edmund Muskie, accusing his opponents Senators Jackson and Humphrey of "immoral sexual conduct." The letter was an attempt to hurt Muskie, the front runner, who finished fourth in the primary. The letter proved to be spurious. It was written and sent by a Republican national campaign worker for the Committee to Re-elect the President.[46]

The second form of neutralization is *denial of access to the means of public communication,* or *censorship.* Government opposition without a public forum or any other means of communicating its displeasure with government is ineffective. The use of news blackouts and government review of television and radio broadcasts are quite common in Thermidor periods.

Even in the early days of the American Republic there was censorship. In 1789, the Alien and Sedition Acts were made law. Incorporated into one of these acts was the passage: "Any person writing, uttering, or publishing 'any false, scandalous and malicious writing or writings against the *government, the Congress, or the President shall be liable* to a fine up to $2,000 and imprisonment up to two years." The law was designed to silence the opposition press. Under Federalist President John Adams a number of newspaper publishers and printers were indicted and ten were actually convicted. One prominent scholar, Dr. Thomas Cooper, was sentenced to six months in prison.[47] In time, these acts were nullified as contrary to First Amendment guarantees of free speech and a free press.

The third form of neutralization is *informal veto,* or the balancing of the opposition with pro-government forces. Lenin used this technique in the Council of the Soviets shortly after the Bolshevik Revolution. Hitler used a similar strategy in his rise to power. This method, however, is temporary as it is the least effective.

The most effective and extreme type of neutralization is *terror.* The use or threat of physical violence, frequently without reason or warning, has been a devastating tool of social control. Not knowing when "a knock will come in the middle of the night" creates a chaotic state of uncertainty. Under these conditions it becomes almost impossible to organize and mount an opposition to the government.

Inherent in the period of the Thermidor Effect is the development of the legitimacy of the government and its ability to survive. A government that is able to convince the citizens that it recognizes their rights and that they will benefit from the new order has the most chance of succeeding. For example, the Bolsheviks were able to maintain control. On the other hand, Saint-Just, Robespierre, and their Jacobin confederates did not accomplish this feat and were swept away by the rise of Napoleon I.[48]

Revolution, like evolution, has numerous forms and degrees. It is, however, usually discontinuous and violent. By this we mean it comes quickly and is usually over in a short period of time. It is also violent as established rulers rarely will give up their power voluntarily. Seemingly revolutions are a rapid form of social change, but we have seen they can be a long time in coming.

The Causes of Revolution

One of the original concerns of sociologists was the roots of social and political revolution. What motivated the crowds of Paris to storm the Bastille? Many reasons were given; however, one central theme did emerge. Revolutions are the product of an *imbalance between individual needs and wants and social opportunities.* People have certain needs. When the social order does not provide for their needs or desires, then men revolt in desperation. This very basic statement is reflected in Karl Marx's "each according to his needs," James C. Davis's "expected need satisfaction," Ivo Feierabend's and Betty Nesvold's "present expectations of future gratifications," and Ted Robert Gurr's "value expectations."[49] What each man is saying is that people rebel when their needs are not being satisfied by the economy or the government. The equation is quite simple until we go about actually trying to put it to the test. At what point, we may ask, does the social imbalance become so strained that revolution is the only course of action?

Sociologists speak of *social strain* as contributing to revolutions. Social conditions are seen as providing the catalyst for violent political outbursts. Marx argued that the injustices of the capitalist system would create an army of the unemployed who would then rise up and destroy the cause of their misery. Others, although not accepting the "immiseration" or increasing misery hypothesis, have also pointed to the social system as a primary factor in social upheavals.[50] Even so, social conditions have not always been sufficient to explain revolutionary activity. Many so-called rich countries have witnessed political violence. For example, the Weathermen in the United States were a group of upper-middle-class young people who engaged in guerrilla warfare. Conversely, many countries mired in poverty have been relatively free of revolutionary activity. Social conditions alone do not provide us with the answer.

Other theorists have focused on the individual, usually starting with the Freudian premise of frustration-aggression. "The premise," wrote Ted Robert Gurr, "is essentially a generalization of the frustration-anger-aggression principle from the individual to the social level. All these empirical theories elaborate on essentially the same basic premise by specifying what kinds of social conditions and processes of change increase social discontent to the threshold of violent conflict."[51] Frustration is a relative concept, however.

One man's needs are another man's luxury. Deprivation, therefore, is relative. *Relative deprivation,* a concept introduced by Samuel Stouffer in *The American Soldier,* means that the frustration and the perception of social strain are experienced differently by different people. This concept may help to explain why revolutions have sometimes occurred in periods when social conditions appeared to be improving and not always in times of severe hunger, famine, and needless war. *Individual need* can be more than just the need of bread and butter. "Let them eat cake" aroused the French merchant class to dethrone and behead the speaker. In 1973, a very similar statement, "Let them eat fish," by the U.S. Secretary of Agriculture only generated a token food boycott by unhappy consumers. The sense of frustration is not a constant.

Perhaps the most fruitful approach to the revolutionary process is found in the notion of imbalance.

Imbalance is a highly relative term. It takes into account the perceptions of the situation of the people involved as well as the objective reality, combining the notions of deprivation and social strain. Even the most historically deterministic of writers on the subject usually pay some attention to the state of awareness of those who are rebelling. Recall Camus's description of the act of rebellion: the Slave must be conscious of injustice. Marx's concept of class consciousness includes the requirement that the proletariat "must be aware of its historical role." Some explanations of revolution, then, stress social imbalance.

One such approach to revolution is derived from functionalism. Functionalists, as previously discussed in Chapter Two, view society as an interrelated whole with many components, such as values, norms, institutions, needs, and traditions. Within such a system an imbalance between working parts can take place. Originally, the imbalance affects only a handful of people.[52] When the societal problem is not solved, the entire structure is thrown out of equilibrium, causing a social *dysfunction.* Dysfunctions range in severity and scope from slight to mortal. Dysfunctions are the result of pressures that disrupt people's everyday lives. These disruptive forces are the product of technological changes, political oppression, nationalism, and a myriad of other causes. What brings about revolution is the refusal of the ruling elite to solve the problem upsetting its citizens. Chalmers Johnson said, "Revolution is the preferred method of change when (a) the level of dysfunctions exceeds the capacities of traditional or accepted methods of problem solving; and when (b) the system's elite, in effect, opposes change."[53] In these circumstances all that is needed is a precipitating event or *accelerator* and the revolution is on. The functionalist approach is, simply put, the *"pressure cooker" explanation of revolution. Pressures become so great a revolution erupts.*

Karl Marx also attributed revolution to social conditions. The "increasing misery" of workers would finally drive them into revolution.[54]

Within Marx's theory of revolution is the independent force of *technology.* Technology is seen as being *constantly* on the move, but it does not operate for the benefit of all men. Rather, technology in societies with classes serves only the owners of the factories, the tools, and the goods. It does not satisfy the needs of the bottom or exploited class. Under capitalism, technology in the form of automated machines displaces workers, creating an "army of the unemployed." Automation requires fewer employees. An imbalance is created between the needs of workers to survive and the social opportunities to do so. As privately owned technology progresses, the disparities among the capitalists, the workers, and the army of the unemployed grow wider and wider. These disparities finally reach the point where the workers in the factories join with the unemployed and overthrow the ruling class, creating one social class: the proletariat. Under these conditions all of the benefits of the technology will go to all of the people, "each according to his needs."

Major objections to interpretations of revolution based solely on social conditions are their alleged impreciseness. Marx's predicted political upheaval did not occur in Western Europe. Functionalist models of change have suffered from the problem of being inexact in forecasting at what point the pressure cooker will blow up.[55]

James C. Davies, in his theory of revolution, presented an alternative to Marx's notion of increasing misery. Davies claimed that revolutions and outbursts of collective violence occur most frequently after a prolonged period of rising expectations and rising rewards *when* a sudden reversal takes place. When this happens "the gap between expectations and gratifications quickly widens and becomes intolerable. The *frustration* that develops, when it is intense and widespread in society, seeks outlets in violent action."[56] This sharp turnaround in opportunities is called a historical *J-curve* (see Figure 16–1). Other writers have presented revolutions as mere power battles pitting the "ins" against the political "outs."[57]

Harry Eckstein presented revolution as a struggle between "positive forces" desiring social change and "negative forces" working against it.[58] The positive forces include:

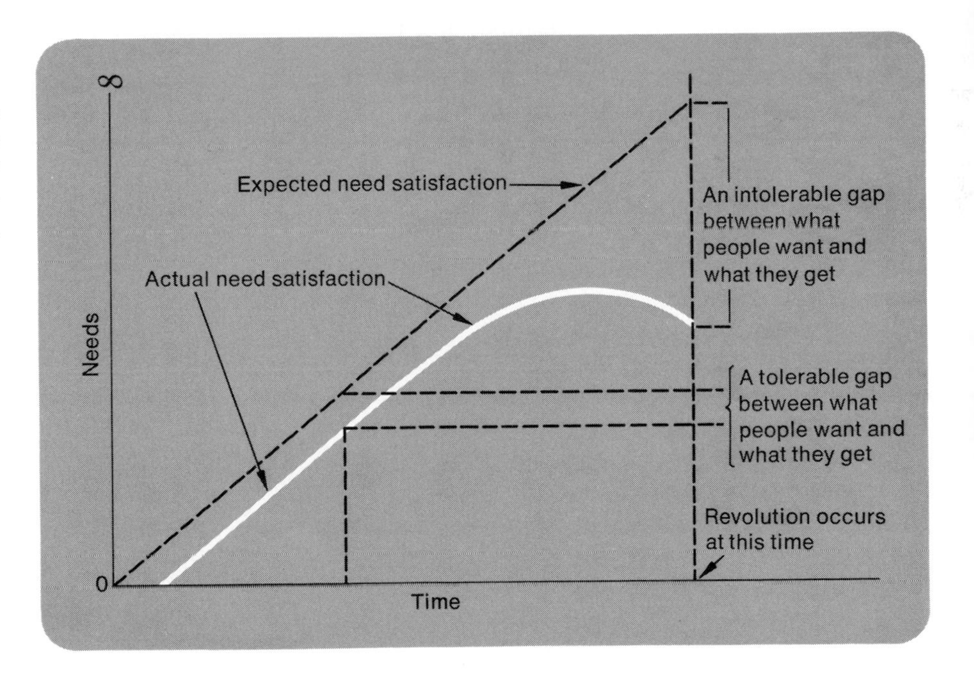

Figure 16–1. Need satisfaction and revolution (*Source:* James C. Davies, "Toward a Theory of Revolution," *American Sociological Review,* **6**:1 [Feb. 1962], 6.)

Inefficiency of the ruling elite. This may take the form of a lack of consensus or poor public performance.

Disorienting social processes, such as lack of confidence in the government. This is a public loss of face, as in a political scandal.

Subversion. This involves the formation of radical social movements and protest organizations.

For change to occur, those protesting social conditions must find some means to survive. This is difficult as other forces are at work to defeat them. The negative forces opposing those desiring change include:

Diversionary mechanisms. These are political moves either to cover up or to divert attention from areas of social discontent. Bread lines and circuses indicate the fall of empire.

Adjustive concessions. These are attempts by the government to correct perceived social ills.

Effective repression. This is the successful use of force to eliminate political opposition to the government.

Facilities. This is the physical plant that supports those in power, such as the army, the police, and other governmental agencies.

In Eckstein's scheme, revolution is the playing off of these two forces; as one weakens the other rises.

Ralf Dahrendorf presented conflict as combat between groups questing for power. Power is the prize in revolutionary activity. The rulers dominate other groups who are deprived of authority. This is a common feature of all political relationships. In Dahrendorf's model revolution is an *extreme* form of power struggle.

Interest groups called *associations* go through two phases to participate in political action. The first phase involves the basic interests of any group. For example, labor unions are interested in higher wages, more fringe benefits, better working conditions, and better retirement programs. Employers are interested in profits, lower wages, and longer working hours. These fundamental concerns are *latent interests.* These latent or inherent interests, according to Dahrendorf, are not always conscious ones. They do not become a central concern until they are threatened or in some manner strained. When this occurs, the second phase comes into play. An awareness of latent interests transforms them into *manifest interests.* Manifest interests become a goal that an association attempts to gain. When this goal is unattainable through normal channels, revolutionary activity may result. Dahrendorf wrote: "The violence of class conflict decreases if *absolute deprivation* of rewards and facilities on the part of a subjected class gives way to *relative deprivation.*"[59] Although not in accord with Davies's psychological interpretation, Dahrendorf repeated the deprivation or strain thesis of needs being in imbalance with social opportunities.

Nearly all theories of revolution stress the disparity between the needs of a nation's citizens and the opportunities afforded them to achieve these. Social imbalance, real or imagined, triggers political activity. When attempts to solve these inequities through conventional channels fail, then more extreme action may be taken. The actual act of revolution involves the opposition forces' ability to *confront* the government successfully. A government unable either to absorb or to destroy its opposition must fall, as it can no longer exercise authority or rule.

Barriers to Social Change

A great many of the studies on social change emphasize a movement forward, either by evolution or by revolution. But this discussion would not be complete without a brief look at opposing forces. There is resistance to change. Much of it has been thought to be merely an expression of ethnocentric ties to the past. For example, the Tibetan lamas opposed the introduction of the wheel in their mountain kingdom for nearly a thousand years. Resistance to change is not always based totally on stubbornness, stupidity, or ultraconservatism, however. As we have seen, the cost of revolution may be great. Revolutions are not merely romantic exercises. Much human misery and blood have been contributed in the name of social change. "Violence," wrote Karl Marx, "is the midwife of history." Mao echoed, "Change comes from the barrel of a gun." When conditions become so bad that people are willing to pay this cost, then revolutions take place.

The issue of cost also applies to the process of accelerated modernization. Until recently, many European nations, later joined by the United States, assumed that it was their duty to civilize the world. Through missionaries, armies, merchants, and finally colonial offices, "civilization" was carried to the four corners of the globe. It was called the "white man's burden" or "manifest destiny." As late as the 1960s, when President John F. Kennedy founded the Peace Corps, representatives of technological societies ventured out to help "less developed" peoples.

Some social observers and anthropologists have come to question the usefulness of disrupting cultural patterns for "more advanced" ways of doing things. Stuart Chase wrote the following advice to the residents of Tepoztlan, a small, rural Mexican village:

> You have in your possession something precious; something which the Western world has lost and flounders miserably trying to regain. Hold to it. Exert every ounce of your magnificent inertia to conserve your way of life. You must not move until you can be shown, by the most specific and concrete examples, that industrialization and the machine can provide a safer, happier, more rewarding existence. . . . The United States has nothing to offer you save its medical and agricultural science. Hold to your corncribs, to your economic security. Hold to your disregard of money, of pecuniary thrift, of clocks and watches, of hustle and bustle and busy emptiness. Hold to your damned wantlessness. Hold to your

handicrafts, and watch them jealously in the face of tourists and ignorant exporters. When they debase the work of your hands they debase you. . . . When you are sick, ask help from the school-teacher instead of the herb doctor. And if I were you, when and if the new highway comes looping over the mountains into your village street, I would buy all the boxes of extrasized carpet tacks I can afford.[60]

The resistance of so-called underdeveloped tribes and nations is not always caused totally by either ignorance or a clinging to the "old ways of doing things." These people may, in fact, be acting on the folk wisdom of their culture. This wisdom can be ethnocentric and can cause them to misread the intentions of those attempting to modernize their way of life, but it may lead them to the correct conclusion anyway. The American Indians of the nineteenth century correctly doubted the goodwill of the representatives of the Great White Father. In many parts of the globe even the best-intentioned of American foreign-aid programs have met with resistance. The symbol for the American aid program is a pair of hands clasped in friendship. This symbol is found on all tools, goods, foods, trucks, and tractors shipped overseas. The symbol was designed to signify the friendship and the desire to help of the American people. However, in parts of the world it has a different meaning. For some it is a symbol of slavery, one hand grabbing another. In Thailand, the symbol stands for the spirit world because the hands are not attached to a human body. In other parts of the world as well people have not understood the clasped hands as a symbol of American aid. Instead, some people have assumed the gifts came from the Soviet Union, the country the U.S. foreign-aid program was designed to contain.[61]

Another example comes from Rhodesia. European health officials mounted a campaign against a rising epidemic of tuberculosis. They designed a poster portraying a large crocodile, a mortal enemy of the natives, signifying the disease. The results were totally unexpected. Instead of seeing TB in the same light as the dreaded crocodile, the natives assumed that the feared animal caused tuberculosis. They did not seek medical help; instead they found yet another reason to fear the reptiles.[62]

Resistance to modernization is not totally unwarranted, as a series of philanthropic and well-intentioned programs have illustrated. Carol R. Ember and Melvin Ember have termed these efforts *pseudoimprovements,* which are "new techniques or processes which appear to help raise the quality of life among a group of people, but which in reality do not.[63] A classic illustration is provided by anthropologist George Foster.

Foster studied the Mexican village of Tzintzuntzan.[64] The small village was inhabited by Indians who were poor and basically suspicious of and resistant to change. They had few diversions from a dreary existence. The United Nations attempted to improve the life style of the natives. A community development program was started under the banner of CREFAL (Regional Center for the Development of Fundamental Education in Latin America).

The goals of the agency were to change the community's economic base by transforming it into a manufacturer of tourist goods like clothing, textiles, and furniture and to encourage chicken ranching.

The results of this modernization attempt were not what CREFAL or the villagers expected. CREFAL technicians convinced several local potters to change the traditional way of making pottery to conform to modern methods. A power-driven kerosene burner was installed. The brick kiln where the pots were made caught fire and blackened the pottery. The grate on the kiln broke and the pots fell to the ground and shattered. The potters rapidly found themselves in debt for the equivalent of two years' wages.

As another example from the same project, CREFAL established a cooperative of twenty-one youths who were taught to make woven-palm furniture. The experiment originally did quite well, even though the cost of each item was higher than that in neighboring villages. Most of the sales were to members of the development team and friends of the villagers. Once the modernization crew departed, sales took a nose dive. The cooperative shortly found itself 13,600 pesos in debt, and the National Cooperative Development Bank cut off their credit. The project, needless to say, was a failure.

Summary

Social change is a process whereby some modification occurs in society. This change can be large or small, gradual or rapid, violent or peaceful. Sociologists are concerned with how this process of change works. So far we have found that societies generally move from the simple to the complex and that technology is an important force in this alteration.

The speed of change is also an important question. Evolution is a slow process. When people desire rapid change because of dissatisfaction with societal conditions, they may resort to revolution. Revolutions are spawned by political, economic, and cultural conditions. However, we are not sure of the exact causes of revolution.

Social change is a continuous process very similar to a winding stream that makes its way to the mouth of a river. It is very difficult to chart its path. It speeds up in places and slows down in others. In some places the water is calm, in others raging. Social change is very much like that. Its rate is not constant. By studying this phenomenon over the years sociologists are beginning to chart the course of this historical river.

Notes

1. See R. P. Appelbaum, *Theories of Social Change* (Chicago: Markham Publishing Company, 1970), pp. 7–9.
2. R. F. Allen, *Socio-Cultural Dynamics: An Introduction to Social Change* (New York: Macmillan Publishing Co., Inc., 1971), pp. 52–53.
3. J. W. Burrow, *Evolution and Society: A Study in Victorian Social Theory* (London: Cambridge University Press, 1970), p. iii.

4. George G. Iggers, "The Idea of Progress: A Critical Reassessment," *American Historical Review,* **71** (1965), 1–17.

5. R. A. Nisbet, *Social Change and History: Aspects of the Western Theory of Development* (New York: Oxford University Press, 1969), pp. 166–168.

6. Ibid., p. 169.

7. P. A. Sorokin, *Social and Cultural Dynamics,* One-Vol. Ed. (Boston: Porter Sargent Publishing Company, 1957).

8. See Karl Marx, "Marx to the Editorial Board of the Otechestvenniye Zapiski," in L. Feuer, ed., *Marx and Engels: Basic Writings on Politics and Philosophy* (Garden City, N.Y.: Doubleday & Company, Inc., 1959), p. 440.

9. W. W. Rostow, *The Process of Economic Growth* (New York: W. W. Norton & Company, Inc., 1952) and *Politics and the Stages of Growth* (New York: Cambridge University Press, 1971). For one critique, see I. L. Fantl, "Rostow's Economic Stage Theory Revisited," *Journal of Business,* **4** (1966), 17–22.

10. Quoted in V. Packard, *The Waste Makers* (New York: David McKay Co., Inc., 1960), p. v. This stage has generated many discontents discussed in J. Ellul, *The Technological Society* (New York: Random House, Inc., 1957). Also see P. F. Drucker, *The Age of Discontinuity: Guidelines to Our Changing Society* (New York: Harper and Row, Publishers, 1968); and A. Toffler, *Future Shock* (New York: Random House, Inc., 1970).

11. See R. S. Denisoff and M. Pugh, "A Return to the Garden: The De-Evolutionary Theories of Roszak and Reich," in R. S. Denisoff, O. Callahan, and M. H. Levine, eds., *Contemporary Sociological Theory* (Itasca, Illinois: F. E. Peacock Publishing Co., 1974), pp. 426–430. Also see Phillip Nobile, ed., *The Consciousness III Controversy: Critics Look at the Greening of America* (New York: Pocket Books, 1971).

12. The Soviet Union at one time attempted to impose its model of development upon its smaller allies. After considerable debate, especially with Yugoslavia's flamboyant leader Marshall Tito, the USSR accepted the "exceptionalist" thesis. See Dan N. Jacobs, ed., *The New Communist Manifesto* (New York: Harper Torchbooks, 1962).

13. W. F. Ogburn, *On Culture and Social Change* (Chicago: University of Chicago Press, 1964).

14. Summary based on H. Hart, "Social Theory and Social Change," in L. Gross, ed., *Symposium on Sociological Theory* (New York: Harper and Row, Publishers, 1959), pp. 220–221.

15. M. Weber, *The Protestant Ethic and the Spirit of Capitalism* (New York: Charles Scribner's Sons, 1958).

16. This discussion is based upon R. Bendix, *Max Weber: An Intellectual Portrait* (Garden City, N.Y.: Anchor Books, 1960); Anthony Giddens, *Capitalism and Modern Social Theory* (London: Cambridge University Press, 1971); and H. H. Gerth and C. W. Mills, *Character and Social Structure: The Psychology of Social Institutions* (New York: Harcourt Brace Jovanovich, Inc., 1953), pp. 234–236, 360–363.

17. N. Birnbaum, "Conflicting Interpretations of the Rise of Capitalism," *British Journal of Sociology,* **4** (1953), 125–141.

18. L. Pope, *Millhands and Preachers* (New Haven, Conn.: Yale University Press, 1942), p. 162.

19. S. S. Sales, "Economic Threat as a Determinant of Conversion Rates in Authoritarian and Nonauthoritarian Churches," *Journal of Personality and Social Psychology,* **23** (1972), 427. Numerous students have pointed to the correlation between economic class and religious affiliation and belief. See N. D. Glenn and R. Hyland, "Religious Preference and Worldly Success: Some Evidence from National Surveys," *American Sociological Review,* **32** (1967), 73–85.

20. Sorokin, op cit., p. 27.

21. See "Rediscovering Your Body," *Harper's* (January, 1973), 3–10, 101–108.

22. Sorokin, op. cit., p. 699.

23. Ibid., pp. 699–700.

24. S. Neuman, "The International Civil War," *World Politics,* **1** (1949) 333–334.

25. C. Johnson, *Revolution and the Social System* (Stanford, Calif.: The Hoover Institution on War, Revolution and Peace, 1964), p. 16.

26. For the development of the term *revolution* see A. Hatto, "Revolution: An Enquiry into the Usefulness of an Historical Term," *Mind,* **58** (1969); and K. Griewank, "Emergence of the Concept of Revolution," in C. Paynton and R. Blackey, eds., *Why Revolution: Theories and Analyses* (Cambridge, Mass.: Schenkman Publishing Co., 1971), pp. 16–24.

27. K. Marx and F. Engels, *Manifesto of the Communist Party* (New York: International Publishers, 1948), p. 44.

28. A. Camus, *The Rebel: An Essay on Man in Revolt,* trans. A. Bower (New York: Alfred A. Knopf, Inc., 1956), pp. 13–22. Also see G. Orwell's delightful description of political revolutions, *Animal Farm* (New York: Harcourt, Brace, 1954).

29. See M. Richter, "Tocqueville's Contributions to the Theory of Revolution," in C. Friedrich, ed., *Revolution* (New York: Atherton Press, Inc., 1969), pp. 90–91.

30. See G. Petlee's "Revolution—Typology and Process," in Friedrich, op cit., pp. 15–18. Also see M. Mallett, *The Borgias: The Rise and Fall of a Renaissance Dynasty* (New York: Barnes & Noble, Inc., 1969).

31. See W. G. Andrews and U. Ra'anan, *The Politics of the Coup d'État* (New York: Van Nostrand Reinhold Company, 1969).

32. W. L. Shirer, *The Rise and Fall of the Third Reich* (New York: Simon & Schuster, Inc., 1960), p. 1069.

33. H. Eckstein, "On the Etiology of Internal Wars," in Paynton and Blackey, op cit., p. 124.

34. See T. R. Gurr, *Why Men Rebel* (Princeton, N.J.: Princeton Univeristy Press, 1970). See also H. L. Nieburg, *Political Violence: The Behavioral Process* (New York: St. Martin's Press, Inc., 1969).

35. This discussion is based on L. Sharp, "Steel Axes for Stone Age Australians," in E. H. Spicer, ed., *Human Problems in Technological Change* (New York: Russell Sage Foundation, 1952), p. 84.

36. Ibid.

37. C. Brinton, *The Anatomy of Revolution* (New York: Vintage Books, 1959), p. 3.

38. See G. Rude, *The Crowd in the French Revolution* (New York: Oxford University Press, 1959); and *The Crowd in History, 1730–1848* (New York: John Wiley & Sons, Inc., 1964).

39. See John Reed, *Ten Days That Shook the World* (New York: Vintage Books, 1960); and L. Trotsky, *The Russian Revolution: The Overthrow of Tsarism and the Triumph of the Soviets* (Garden City, N.Y.: Doubleday & Company, Inc., 1959).

40. For a sociological treatment, see M. Zeitlin, *Revolutionary Politics and the Cuban Working Class* (Princeton, N.J.: Princeton University Press, 1970); also see T. Fraper, *Castroism: Theory and Practice* (New York: Praeger Publishers, Inc., 1965). Also see R. DeBray, *Revolution in the Revolution: Armed Struggle and Political Struggle in Latin America* (New York: Grove Press, Inc., 1967).

41. Camus, op. cit., p. 121.

42. W. D. Connor, "The Manufacture of Deviance: The Case of the Soviet Purge, 1936–1938," *American Sociological Review,* **37** (1972), 403–413.

43. Brinton, op. cit., p. 215. Leon Trotsky used the same term to describe the loss of revolutionary ideals by those gaining power. See I. Deutscher, ed., *The Age of Permanent Revolution: A Trotsky Anthology* (New York: Dell Publishing Co., 1964).

44. See P. Selznick, *The Organizational Weapon: A Study of Bolshevik Strategy and Tactics* (New York: McGraw-Hill Book Company, 1952), pp. 229–230.

45. "Police: Tales of Three Cities," *Time* (June 22, 1970), 16.

46. M. Waldron, "Segretti Indicted in Mailing of Bogus Muskie Letter," *New York Times* (May 5, 1973), Section 1, p. 14.

47. M. Smelser, "George Washington and the Alien and Sedition Acts," *American Historical Review,* **59** (1954), 322–334.

48. R. Bendix, *Nation-Building and Citizenship* (New York: John Wiley & Sons, Inc., 1964).

49. Gurr, op. cit.

50. T. R. Gurr, "The Revolution: Social Change Nexus," *Comparative Politics,* **5** (1973), 359–392.

51. Ibid, pp. 364–365.

52. See R. Ross and S. L. Staines, "Politics of Analyzing Social Problems," *Social Problems,* **20** (1972), 18–40.

53. Ibid., p. 10. Chalmers Johnson has elaborated this argument in *Revolutionary Change* (Boston: Little, Brown and Company, 1966).

54. See K. Marx, *A Contribution to the Critique of Political Economy* (Chicago: Charles H. Kerr and Co., 1904), p. 104. See also R. C. Tucker, *The Marxian Revolutionary Idea* (New York: W. W. Norton & Company, Inc., 1969).

55. See L. Stone, "Theories of Revolution," *World Politics,* **18** (1966), 159–176.

56. J. C. Davies, "The J-Curve of Rising and Declining Satisfactions as a Cause of Some Great Revolutions and a Contained Rebellion," in H. D. Gratiaron and T. R. Gurr, eds., *Violence in America: Historical and Comparative Perspectives* (Washington, D.C.: U.S. Government Printing Office, 1969), pp. 671–709.

57. D. Snyder and C. Tilly, "Hardships and Collective Violence," *American Sociological Review,* **37** (1972), 520–532. See also J. Rule and C. Tilly, "1830 and the Un-Natural History of Revolution," *Journal of Social Issues,* **28:**1 (1972), 49–76.

58. Eckstein, op. cit., pp. 133–163.

59. Ralf Dahrendorf, *Class and Class Conflict in Industrial Society* (Stanford, Calif.: Stanford University Press, 1959), p. 239.

60. S. Chase, *Mexico: A Study of Two Americas* (New York: Macmillan Publishing Co., Inc., 1931), pp. 318–319.

61. Examples provided in C. R. Ember and M. Ember, *Anthropology* (New York: Appleton-Century-Crofts, 1973), p. 520.

62. G. M. Foster, *Applied Anthropology* (Boston: Little, Brown and Company, 1969), pp. 524–525.

63. Ibid., pp. 524–525.

64. G. M. Foster, *Tzintzuntzan: Mexican Peasants in a Changing World* (Boston: Little, Brown and Company, 1967).

Index